Less managing. More teaching. Greater learning.

INSTRUCTORS...

Would you like your **students** to show up for class **more prepared**? *(Let's face it, class is much more fun if everyone is engaged and prepared...)*

Want an **easy way to assign** homework online and track student **progress**? *(Less time grading means more time teaching...)*

Want an **instant view** of student or class performance relative to learning objectives? *(No more wondering if students understand...)*

Need to **collect data and generate reports** required for administration or accreditation? *(Say goodbye to manually tracking student learning outcomes...)*

Want to **record and post your lectures** for students to view online?

With McGraw-Hill's *Connect® Plus Operations Management*,

INSTRUCTORS GET:

- Simple **assignment management**, allowing you to spend more time teaching.
- **Auto-graded** assignments, quizzes, and tests.
- **Detailed Visual Reporting** where student and section results can be viewed and analyzed.
- Sophisticated **online testing** capability.
- A **filtering and reporting** function that allows you to easily select Excel-based homework problems, as well as assign and report on materials that are correlated to accreditation standards, learning outcomes, and Bloom's taxonomy.
- An easy-to-use **lecture capture** tool.
- The option to **upload course documents** for student access.

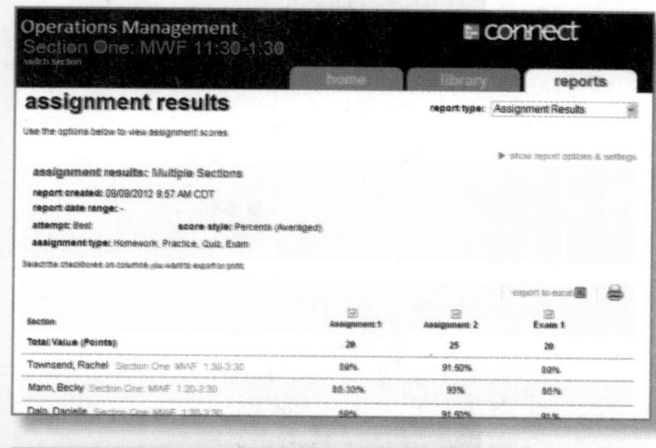

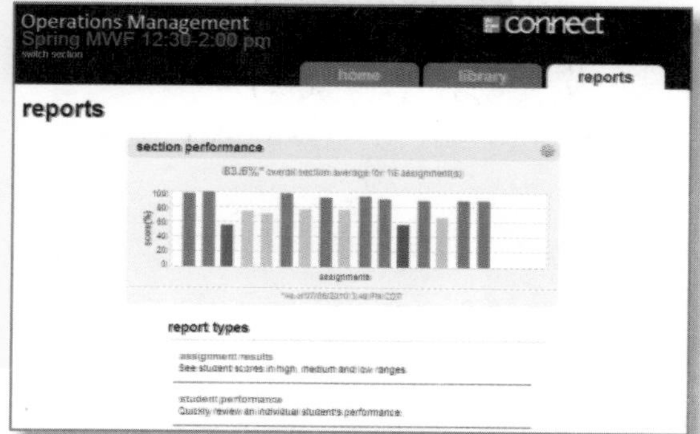

Want an online, **searchable version** of your textbook?

Wish your textbook could be **available online** while you're doing your assignments?

Connect® *Plus Operations Management* eBook

If you choose to use *Connect*® *Plus Operations Management*, you have an affordable and searchable online version of your book integrated with your other online tools.

Connect® *Plus Operations Management* eBook offers features like:

- Topic search
- Direct links from assignments
- Adjustable text size
- Jump to page number
- Print by section
- Highlight
- Take notes
- Access instructor highlights/notes

Want to get more **value** from your textbook purchase?

Think learning operations management should be a bit more **interesting**?

Check out the STUDENT RESOURCES section under the *Connect*® Library tab.

Here you'll find a wealth of resources designed to help you achieve your goals in the course. You'll find things like **quizzes, guided examples, narrated PowerPoints, and Internet activities** to help you study. Every student has different needs, so explore the STUDENT RESOURCES to find the materials best suited to you.

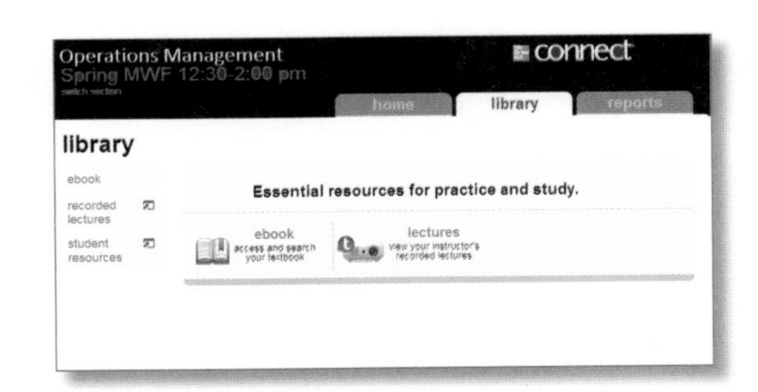

Managing Operations

Across the Supply Chain

Second Edition

Morgan Swink
Texas Christian University

Steven A. Melnyk
Michigan State University

M. Bixby Cooper
Michigan State University

Janet L. Hartley
Bowling Green State University

The McGraw-Hill Companies

MANAGING OPERATIONS ACROSS THE SUPPLY CHAIN, SECOND EDITION

Published by McGraw-Hill/Irwin, a business unit of The McGraw-Hill Companies, Inc., 1221 Avenue of the Americas, New York, NY, 10020.

Some ancillaries, including electronic and print components, may not be available to customers outside the United States.

This book is printed on acid-free paper.

1 2 3 4 5 6 7 8 9 0 RJE/RJE 1 0 9 8 7 6 5 4 3

ISBN 978-0-07-802403-0
MHID 0-07-802403-X

Senior vice president, products & markets: *Kurt L. Strand*
Vice president, General manager, products & markets: *Brent Gordon*
Vice president, Content production & technology services: *Kimberly Meriwether David*
Managing director: *Douglas Reiner*
Senior brand manager: *Thomas Hayward*
Executive director of development: *Ann Torbert*
Senior development editor: *Wanda J. Zeman*
Director of digital content: *Doug Ruby*
Senior Marketing Manager: *Heather A. Kazakoff*
Lead project manager: *Harvey Yep*
Senior buyer: *Michael R. McCormick*
Lead designer: *Matthew Baldwin*
Cover/interior designer: *Kay Lieberherr*
Cover image: © *Getty Images/Markus Brunner*
Senior content licensing specialist: *Jeremy Cheshareck*
Photo researcher: *Ira C. Roberts*
Lead media project manager: *Brian Nacik*
Typeface: *10/12 Times Roman*
Compositor: *Laserwords Private Limited*
Printer: *R. R. Donnelley*

Library of Congress Cataloging-in-Publication Data

Managing operations across the supply chain / Morgan Swink . . . [et al.].—2nd ed.
p. cm.—(The McGraw-Hill/Irwin series in operations and decision sciences)
Includes index.
ISBN-13: 978-0-07-802403-0 (alk. paper)
ISBN-10: 0-07-802403-X (alk. paper)
1. Business logistics. 2. Production management. 3. Industrial management.
I. Swink, Morgan, 1959–
HD38.5.M36175 2014
658.5—dc23

2012044031

The McGraw-Hill/Irwin Series Operations and Decision Sciences

Operations Management

Beckman and Rosenfield, **Operations, Strategy: Competing in the 21st Century,** *First Edition*

Benton, **Purchasing and Supply Chain Management,** *Second Edition*

Bowersox, Closs, Cooper, and Bowersox, **Supply Chain Logistics Management,** *Fourth Edition*

Brown and Hyer, **Managing Projects: A Team-Based Approach,** *First Edition*

Burt, Petcavage, and Pinkerton, **Supply Management,** *Eighth Edition*

Cachon and Terwiesch, **Matching Supply with Demand: An Introduction to Operations Management,** *Third Edition*

Cooper and Schindler, **Business Research Methods,** *Eleventh Edition*

Finch, **Interactive Models for Operations and Supply Chain Management,** *First Edition*

Fitzsimmons, Fitzsimmons, and Bordoloi, **Service Management: Operations, Strategy, Information Technology,** *Seventh Edition*

Gehrlein, **Operations Management Cases,** *First Edition*

Harrison and Samson, **Technology Management,** *First Edition*

Hayen, **SAP R/3 Enterprise Software: An Introduction,** *First Edition*

Hill, **Manufacturing Strategy: Text & Cases,** *Third Edition*

Hopp, **Supply Chain Science,** *First Edition*

Hopp and Spearman, **Factory Physics,** *Third Edition*

Jacobs, Berry, Whybark, and Vollmann, **Manufacturing Planning & Control for Supply Chain Management,** *Sixth Edition*

Jacobs and Chase, **Operations and Supply Management: The Core,** *Third Edition*

Jacobs and Chase, **Operations and Supply Management,** *Fourteenth Edition*

Jacobs and Whybark, **Why ERP?** *First Edition*

Larson and Gray, **Project Management: The Managerial Process,** *Fifth Edition*

Leenders, Johnson, and Flynn, **Purchasing and Supply Management,** *Fourteenth Edition*

Nahmias, **Production and Operations Analysis,** *Sixth Edition*

Olson, **Introduction to Information Systems Project Management,** *Second Edition*

Schroeder, Goldstein, Rungtusanatham, **Operations Management: Contemporary Concepts and Cases,** *Sixth Edition*

Seppanen, Kumar, and Chandra, **Process Analysis and Improvement,** *First Edition*

Simchi-Levi, Kaminsky, and Simchi-Levi, **Designing and Managing the Supply Chain: Concepts, Strategies, Case Studies,** *Third Edition*

Sterman, **Business Dynamics: Systems Thinking and Modeling for Complex World,** *First Edition*

Stevenson, **Operations Management,** *Eleventh Edition*

Swink, Melnyk, Cooper, and Hartley, **Managing Operations Across the Supply Chain,** *Second Edition*

Thomke, **Managing Product and Service Development: Text and Cases,** *First Edition*

Ulrich and Eppinger, **Product Design and Development,** *Fourth Edition*

Zipkin, **Foundations of Inventory Management,** *First Edition*

Quantitative Methods and Management Science

Hillier and Hillier, **Introduction to Management Science: A Modeling and Case Studies Approach with Spreadsheets,** *Fifth Edition*

Stevenson and Ozgur, **Introduction to Management Science with Spreadsheets,** *First Edition*

Dedication

To Jenni, Derek, Rachel, and Sarah, who make my life so full!
Morgan Swink

To my wife and children–Christine, Charles and Beth–for their support and patience.
To five great friends who have been "teachers" to me in my continual quest for more knowledge–Randall Schaefer, Joe Sandor, Ed Davis (Darden School, University of Virginia) Dave Frayer, and Nick Little (Michigan State University).
To these people, this book is dedicated.
Steven Melnyk

To my children who make my life complete.
Bix Cooper

To Glenn and Caleb, for their love and support.
Janet Hartley

About the Authors

Morgan Swink

is Professor, Eunice and James L. West Chair of Supply Chain Management, and Executive Director of the Supply and Value Chain Center at the Neeley School of Business, Texas Christian University. He holds a BS in Mechanical Engineering from Southern Methodist University, an MBA from the University of Dallas, and a PhD in Operations Management from Indiana University. Before becoming a professor, Dr. Swink worked for 10 years in a variety of manufacturing and product development positions at Texas Instruments Incorporated. He has co-authored three books and published over 50 articles in a variety of academic and managerial journals. Dr. Swink is formerly the Co-Editor in Chief for the *Journal of Operations Management.*

Steven A. Melnyk

is Professor of Operations Management at Michigan State University. Dr. Melnyk obtained his undergraduate degree from the University of Windsor and his doctorate from the Ivey School of Business, the University of Western Ontario. He has co-authored 15 books focusing on operations and the supply chain and has published 80 refereed articles in numerous international and national journals. He is Associate Editor for the *Journal of Business Logistics.* He also is a member of the editorial advisory board for the *Production and Inventory Management Journal,* the *Journal of Supply Chain Management,* and the *International Journal of Production Research.* Dr. Melnyk is co-editor (North America) for the *Journal of Humanitarian Logistics and Supply Chain Management.* Dr. Melynk has consulted with over 60 companies.

M. Bixby Cooper

is Associate Professor in the Department of Supply Chain Management at Michigan State University. He received his BS in Business Administration from the University of North Carolina, MBA from the University of Virginia, and PhD from the University of Alabama. Prior to joining Michigan State, he served on the faculty of Winthrop University and Louisiana State University. He is an active researcher and co-author of several books on distribution and logistics. Dr. Cooper has consulted with numerous organizations including Kellogg, Johnson and Johnson, Mead Johnson, Westinghouse, Novartis, Dayton Hudson (Target), Kerr-McGee, VF Industries, and Siemens.

Janet L. Hartley

is Professor and Director of the Supply Chain Management Institute of the Department of Management at Bowling Green State University. She received her BS in Chemical Engineering from the University of Missouri-Rolla, and the MBA and PhD degrees in Business Administration from the University of Cincinnati. Prior to graduate school, she developed new products and designed new manufacturing processes for the Clorox Company. She has published over 28 articles on supply management and supply chain management. She serves as an associate editor for the *Journal of Operations Management, Journal of Business Logistics,* and *Journal of Supply Chain Management.*

Preface

We continue to live in dynamic and exciting times. The recent 20 years have seen many changes that have affected nearly every aspect of business—including operations management. We have enhanced this second edition of our book to reflect key shifts in operations management, including transitions:

- ***From a focus on the internal system to a focus on the supply chain*** In today's highly competitive business environment, organizations must leverage the capabilities of their suppliers and customers. Operations managers must look beyond the "four walls" of the firm and take an integrated supply chain perspective of operations.
- ***From a local focus to a global focus*** As Thomas L. Friedman pointed out,[1] the world is indeed flat. Business solutions generated in Argentina are used to meet needs in the United States, and parts built by suppliers located in China are used to assemble cars in Canada. Commercial needs have overcome, to a large part, national borders, presenting new opportunities and challenges for operations managers.
- ***From an emphasis on tools and techniques to an emphasis on systems, people, and processes*** To be successful, operations managers must think more broadly than just the application of analytical tools and techniques. They must take a systems view to address important managerial issues such as designing processes, working with people, managing information flows, and building interorganizational relationships.
- ***From myopic pursuit of profit to a holistic pursuit of sustainability.*** Pressures on businesses have risen to the point that they can no longer ignore or give only lip-service to social and environmental issues. Operations managers have to balance the profit motive with the need to protect and even strengthen both people and the planet.

Managing Operations Across the Supply Chain provides a global, supply chain perspective of operations management for students in introductory courses in operations management and in supply chain management courses that do not require an operations management prerequisite. While the book is primarily written for undergraduates, it also can be used effectively in MBA courses. There are several features that help to differentiate this book in its view of operations management:

- ***Broader Treatment of Operations Management*** While many operations management textbooks have revised or added a chapter to address supply chain issues, we developed our book from the ground up to effectively integrate operations management and the supply chain. The primary focus of the book is operations management, but we provide a "supply chain" perspective. Operations management cuts across a firm's boundaries, bringing together its internal activities with the operations of customers, suppliers, and other partners around the world. We clarify the functional roles of operations, supply management, and logistics while examining the integrative processes that make up the supply chain. One unique aspect of the book is that we examine both the upstream (supply-side) and downstream (demand-side) aspects of the supply chain, including a discussion of marketing and customer relationships.
- ***Balanced Treatment*** The book balances the quantitative and qualitative coverage needed to equip operations and supply chain managers for the challenges and opportunities they face. It describes and applies analytical tools that operations managers use to support decision making. However, we also address the important managerial issues such as systems, people, and processes that are critical in a supply chain context.
- ***Use of Integrative Frameworks*** The various elements of operations management are introduced and developed using an operations strategy framework that brings together three critical elements: (1) the critical customer, (2) the value proposition, and (3) capabilities. Furthermore, the students are introduced to operations management in a structured way that begins with the "big" picture of operations strategy, proceeds to the foundations of operations management, integrating relationships, planning for integrated supply chain operations, and then ending with a discussion of how to manage the system looking to the future.
- ***Use of Three Integrating Themes*** Three key themes are highlighted throughout the book: global issues, relationships, and sustainability. Because most

[1]Thomas L. Friedman, *The World Is Flat: A Brief History of the Twenty-First Century* (New York: Farrar, Straus, and Giroux, 2006).

organizations have supply chains that reach beyond a single country, we examine global issues associated with operations and supply chain management. Organizations must collaborate with customers and suppliers to accomplish many operations activities. Thus, the book showcases how to build, maintain, and benefit from cross-functional and interorganizational relationships. To reduce costs and be competitive, organizations today must adapt sustainable business practices. We expect sustainability to increasingly become a key metric for operations and supply chain management performance. Accordingly, we have dedicated an entire chapter to sustainability, while also incorporating it throughout the book.

- ***Real, Integrated Examples*** The book brings operations and supply chain management to life through opening vignettes, Get Real highlights, and rich examples throughout the book. Companies such as Disney/Pixar®, HP, Boeing, IKEA, American Apparel, Starbucks, and Procter & Gamble, to name a few, are used to illustrate how to address real operations and supply chain challenges.

Managing Operations Across the Supply Chain offers a new, global, supply chain perspective of operations management—a treatment that embraces the foundations of operations management but includes new frameworks, concepts, and tools to address the demands of today and changing needs of the future. The book is organized into five major sections:

- **Part 1 Supply Chain: A Perspective for Operations Management** provides an overview of operations management as a field, and describes the strategic role operations has in business from the perspective of supply chain management.
- **Part 2 Foundations of Operations Management** discusses foundational process concepts and principles that govern all operational activities. This section examines concepts such as product/process innovation, quality, lean, and inventory fundamentals.
- **Part 3 Integrating Relationships Across the Supply Chain** deals with the primary functional relationships between internal operations management activities and other operational functions both inside and outside the firm. This section describes customer relationship management, supply management, and logistics management.
- **Part 4 Planning for Integrated Operations Across the Supply Chain** discusses planning approaches and technologies used at different levels of operations decision making. Key topics such as demand planning, forecasting, sales and operations planning, inventory management, and materials requirements planning are examined.
- **Part 5 Managing Change in Supply Chain Operations** discusses how operations managers use projects, change programs, and technologies to shape a sustainable future for operations and supply chain management.

Acknowledgments

We would like to express our appreciation to the people who have provided assistance in the development of this textbook. We express our sincere thanks to the following individuals for their thoughtful reviews and suggestions:

Rasoul Afifi, Northeastern Illinois University
Nazim Ahmed, Ball State University
John Aloysius, University of Arkansas
Gopesh Anand, University of Illinois
Ravi Behara, Florida Atlantic University
Michael Bendixen, Nova Southeastern
Ednilson Bernardes, Georgia Southern
Greg Bier, University of Missouri, Columbia
William Borders, Troy University, Ecampus
Sanjeev Bordoloi, University of Saint Thomas
Kimball Bullington, Middle Tennessee State University
Cenk Caliskan, Utah Valley University, Orem
Cem Canel, University of North Carolina, Wilmington
Thomas Choi, Arizona State University
Bruce Christensen, Weber State University
Petros Christofi, Duquesne University
Chen-Hua Chung, University of Kentucky
Robert Clark, Stony Brook University
Lori Cook, DePaul University
Dinesh Dave , Appalachian State University
Eddie Davila, Arizona State University
Scott Dellana, East Carolina University
Renato DeMatta, University of Iowa, Iowa City
Barbara Downey, University of Missouri
Kamvar Farahbod, California State University, Santa Barbara
Richard Franza, Kennesaw State University
Thomas Gattiker, Boise State University
David Gilliss, San Jose State University
Mike Godfrey, University of Wisconsin, Oshkosh
Mark Hanna, Loyola College (Maryland)
Michael D. Harper, University of Colorado, Denver
Steven Harrod, University of Dayton
Vishwanath Hegde, California State University, East Bay
Rhonda Hensley, North Carolina State University
Craig Hill, Georgia State University
Lisa Houts, California State University, Fresno
Ziaul Huq, University of Nebraska, Omaha
Tony Inman, Louisiana Tech University
Mark Ippolito, Indiana University
Doug Isanhart, University of Central Arkansas
Raj Jagannathan, University of Iowa
Vaidy Jayaraman, University of Miami
Rahul Kale, University of North Florida
Vijay Kannan, Utah State University
Matthew Keblis, University of Wyoming
Jim Keyes, University of Wisconsin, Stout
Alan S. Khade, California State University, Stanislaus
Michelle Lane, Bowling Green State University
Anita Lee-Post, University of Kentucky, Lexington
David Lewis, University of Massachusetts, Lowell
Dennis McCahon, Northeastern University
Laura M. Meade, Texas Christian University
Richard Morris, Georgia State University
Gisele Olney, University of Nebraska, Omaha
Joseph Ormsby, Stephen F. Austin State University
Ron Parker, Metropolitan State University
Fariborz Y. Partovi, Drexel University
Pat Penfield, Syracuse University
Felisa Preciado, Pennsylvania State University
Carrie Queenan, University of Notre Dame
K. V. Ramaswamy, Texas Southern University
Cesar Rego, University of Mississippi
Pedro Reyes, Baylor University
Germaine Saad, Georgia Southern University
Shane Schvaneveldt, Weber State University
Ruth Seiple, University of Cincinnati
Sridhar Seshadri, University of Texas, Austin
Avanti Sethi, University of Texas, Dallas
Lori Seward, University of Colorado
Kenneth A. Shaw, Oregon State University
John Sloan, Oregon State University
Marilyn Smith, Winthrop University
Jeremy Stafford, University of Northern Alabama
Drew Stapleton, University of Wisconsin, La Crosse
Larry Taub, University of North Carolina, Greensboro
Cecilia Temponi, Texas State University, San Marcos
Oya Turkel, Cleveland State University
Gustavo Vulcano, New York University
James Walters, Ball State University
Kevin Watson, Iowa State University
Elliott Weiss, University of Virginia
Cliff Welborn, Middle Tennessee State University
Theresa Wells, University of Wisconsin, Eau Claire
Larry White, Eastern Illinois University

Susan Williams, Northern Arizona University
Martha Wilson, California State University, Sacramento
Mustafa Yilmaz, Northeastern University
George Yorke, Texas Southern University

Other contributors included accuracy checker Laura M. Meade, Texas Christian University.

We want to thank the outstanding McGraw-Hill/Irwin production and marketing team who made this book possible—including Heather Kazakoff, marketing manager; Douglas Reiner, managing director; Harvey Yep, project manager; Michael McCormick, production supervisor; Brian Nacik, lead media project manager; Matthew Baldwin, designer; and Jeremy Chesshareck, photo research coordinator.

A special thanks to our outstanding editorial team. We greatly appreciate the support, encouragement, and patience shown by Wanda Zeman, our development editor. Thanks for keeping us on track! Our brand manager, Thomas Hayward, provided excellent guidance and leadership throughout the process. We truly appreciate it!

Morgan Swink
Steven A. Melnyk
M. Bixby Cooper
Janet L. Hartley

Walkthrough

The following section highlights the key features of the text and accompanying resources, which have been developed to help you learn, understand, and apply operations concepts.

CHAPTER ELEMENTS

Within each chapter, of the text, you will find the following elements. All of these have been developed to facilitate study and learning.

Chapter Opener

Each chapter begins with an outline of the chapter and a chapter vignette to help set the tone for the material that follows. Learning objectives provide a quick introduction to the material students will learn and should understand before moving to the next chapter.

Opening Vignette

Each chapter opens with an introduction to the important operations topics covered in the chapter. Students need to see the relevance of operations management in order to actively engage in learning the material.

1

Introduction to Managing Operations Across the Supply Chain

CHAPTER OUTLINE

LEARNING OBJECTIVES *After studying this chapter, you should be able to:*

LO1-1 Explain what operations management is and why it is important.
LO1-2 Describe the major decisions that operations managers typically make.
LO1-3 Explain the role of processes and "process thinking" in operations management.
LO1-4 Explain what the supply chain is and what it means to view operations management using a "supply chain perspective."
LO1-5 Identify the partners and functional groups that work together in operations management.
LO1-6 Define the planning activities associated with managing operations across the supply chain.

2

It Takes More than Cool Products to Make Apple Great

Apple often receives praise for its user-friendly and aesthetically pleasing product designs. But a less well-known contributor to Apple's success is its prowess in managing operations across its supply chain. This is the world of manufacturing, procurement, and logistics in which the chief executive officer, Tim Cook, excelled, earning him the trust of Steve Jobs. Apple has built a closed ecosystem where it exerts control over nearly every piece of the supply chain, from design to retail store. "Operations expertise is as big an asset for Apple as product innovation or marketing," says Mike Fawkes, the former supply-chain chief at Hewlett-Packard. "They've taken operational excellence to a level never seen before."

This operational edge is what enables Apple to handle massive product launches without having to maintain large, profit-sapping inventories. It's allowed a company often criticized for high prices to sell its iPad at a price that very few rivals can beat, while still earning a 25 percent margin on the device. Some of the basic elements of Apple's operational strategy include:

- Capitalize on volume. Because of its buying power, Apple gets big discounts on parts, manufacturing capacity, and air freight.
- Work closely with suppliers. Apple design guru Jony Ive and his engineers sometimes spend months living out of hotel rooms in order to be close to suppliers and manufacturers, helping to tweak the industrial processes and tools that translate prototypes into mass-produced devices.
- Focus on a few product lines, with little customization. Apple's unified strategy allows it to eliminate complexity and cost, while maximizing volume-based economies in its supply chain.
- Ensure supply availability and low prices. Apple makes big upfront payments to suppliers to lock in their capacity and to limit options for competitors.
- Keep a close eye on demand. By selling through its own retail stores, Apple can track demand by the store and by the hour; then it adjusts sales forecasts and production plans daily to respond quickly to demand changes.

Apple designs cool products. But its enormous profit margins—two to four times the profit margins of most other hardware companies—come in large part from its priority and focus on operations management.

Key Terms

Key terms are presented in bold and defined in the margin as they are introduced. A list of chapter key terms is also available at the end of the chapter.

Because most firms deliver products that involve both goods and services, operations managers recognize the importance of delivering a **total product experience**. This term refers to all of the outputs of an operation, both goods and services, that are combined to define a customer's complete consumption experience. The experience includes all aspects of purchasing, consuming, and disposing of the product.

total product experience All the goods and services that are combined to define a customer's complete consumption experience.

Prepare/Organize

A systematic approach to new material provides a learning framework. Every main topic in the chapter includes a Prepare section that asks a question designed to orient students to what will be covered in that section, followed by an Organize section that provides an outline of the material. Together they offer a framework and brief preview of the material that follows in the reading. These are also intended to be helpful as a quick reference and pointer to students as they review for quizzes or exams.

VIEWING OPERATIONS MANAGEMENT FROM A SUPPLY CHAIN MANAGEMENT PERSPECTIVE

We began this chapter by noting that operations managers must coordinate a system of activities both inside and outside their firm's boundaries. The network of organizations that contains this system of activities is often referred to as a *supply chain.* So how then is "supply chain management" different from "operations management"?

Supply chain management is the design and execution of relationships and flows that connect the parties and processes across a supply chain. Recall that our definition of *operations management* is the management of processes used to design, supply, produce, and deliver valuable goods and services to customers.

As you can see, there is a substantial degree of overlap between the two definitions. Operations management focuses on managing *processes* (design, supply, production, delivery); supply chain management focuses on managing *relationships* and *flows* (flows of information, materials, energy, money, and people). Think of supply chain management as a way of viewing operations management. You can also think of the supply chain as a network of organizations in which operations activities are conducted.

Prepare

What does it mean to view operations management from a supply chain perspective?

Organize

Viewing Operations Management from a Supply Chain Management Perspective
- Operations Management Partners Across the Supply Chain
- Cross-Functional Relationships in Operations Management
- The Changing Nature of Supply Chains
- Levels of Operational Planning Across the Supply Chain

Student Activity

Students are asked to do a personal activity that illustrates the concept being presented or covered, thereby helping them learn to apply the concepts and understand them more deeply.

student activity

Think of the last time you visited an amusement park (like Disney World). How many different goods and services did you consume as a part of your overall experience? How many of these products were "pure" goods and "pure" services? Which of these products was prepared before you ordered it, versus being prepared at the very time that you ordered it?

Numbered Examples

Numbered examples are integrated into chapters where analytic techniques are introduced. Students learn how to solve specific problems step-by-step and gain insight into general principles by seeing how they are applied.

EXAMPLE 3-1

A distribution center for an Internet bookseller can handle a peak demand of 200,000 orders in a single day, under ideal conditions. However, the facility was designed to handle up to 120,000 orders per day during normal operating conditions. Orders processed for the first two weeks of December averaged 150,000 per day. Calculate the utilization of the distribution center relative to both maximum capacity and effective capacity.

SOLUTION

Maximum capacity = 200,000 orders per day

Effective capacity = 120,000 orders per day

Actual orders = 150,000 orders per day

$$\text{Utilization of maximum capacity} = (150{,}000/200{,}000) \times 100\% = 75\%$$

$$\text{Utilization of effective capacity} = (150{,}000/120{,}000) \times 100\% = 125\%$$

This example illustrates that the Internet bookseller can accommodate high periods of demand by utilizing maximum capacity (e.g., by using overtime work) in the short run. However, if this high demand continued for more than a few weeks, it should consider increasing its effective capacity by expanding its distribution center and/or hiring more workers.

Figures and Photos

The text includes photographs and graphic illustrations to support student study and provide interest and motivation.

Amazon distribution center.

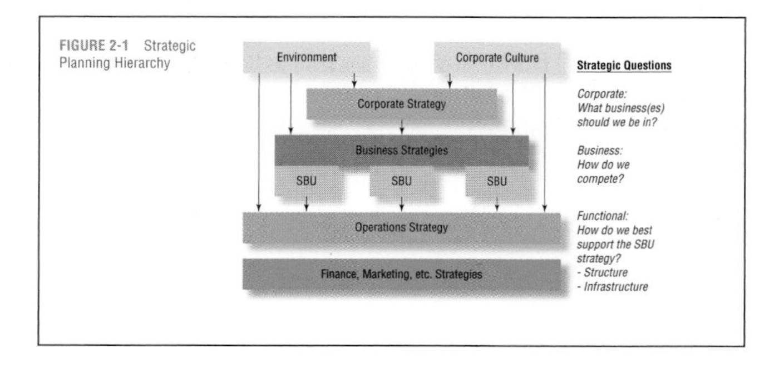

FIGURE 2-1 Strategic Planning Hierarchy

Get Real Boxes

Throughout the chapters, readings highlight important real-world applications. They provide examples of operations issues and offer a picture of the concepts in practice. These also provide a basis for classroom discussion and generate interest in the subject matter.

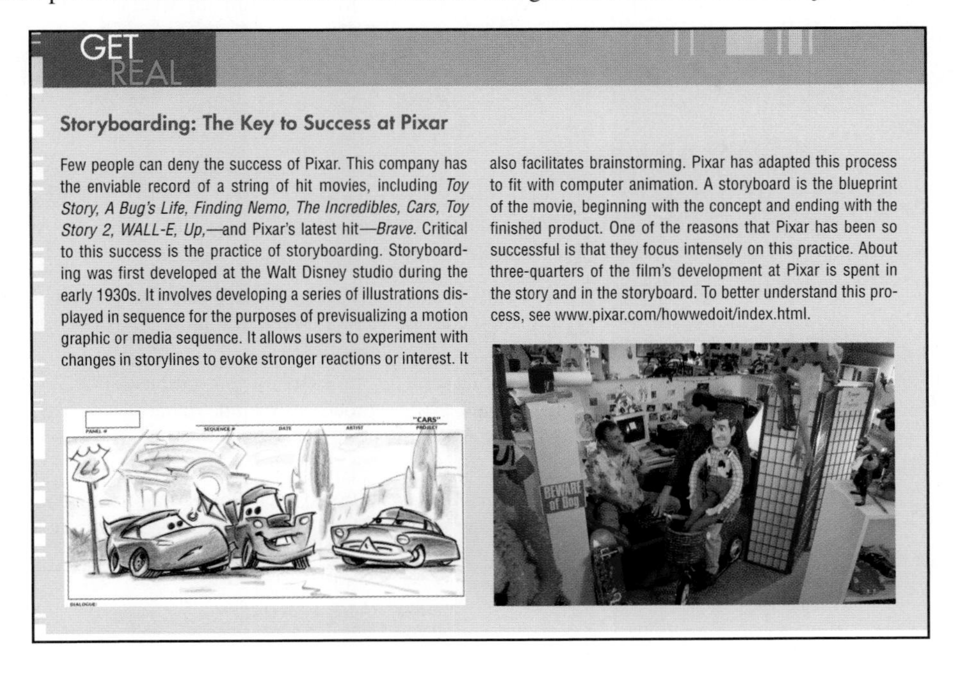
GET REAL

Storyboarding: The Key to Success at Pixar

Few people can deny the success of Pixar. This company has the enviable record of a string of hit movies, including *Toy Story, A Bug's Life, Finding Nemo, The Incredibles, Cars, Toy Story 2, WALL-E, Up,*—and Pixar's latest hit—*Brave*. Critical to this success is the practice of storyboarding. Storyboarding was first developed at the Walt Disney studio during the early 1930s. It involves developing a series of illustrations displayed in sequence for the purposes of previsualizing a motion graphic or media sequence. It allows users to experiment with changes in storylines to evoke stronger reactions or interest. It also facilitates brainstorming. Pixar has adapted this process to fit with computer animation. A storyboard is the blueprint of the movie, beginning with the concept and ending with the finished product. One of the reasons that Pixar has been so successful is that they focus intensely on this practice. About three-quarters of the film's development at Pixar is spent in the story and in the storyboard. To better understand this process, see www.pixar.com/howwedoit/index.html.

Logos

Logos are included throughout the text to point out relevant applications of relationships, sustainability, and global issues.

Since most organizations have supply chains that reach beyond a single country, we examine global issues associated with operations and supply chain management.

global

Organizations must collaborate with customers and suppliers to accomplish many operations activities. Thus, the book showcases how to build, maintain, and benefit from cross-functional and interorganizational relationships.

relationships

To reduce costs and be competitive, organizations today must adopt sustainable business practices. In fact, we expect sustainability to become a key metric for operations and supply chain management performance.

sustainability

END-OF-CHAPTER RESOURCES

For student study and review, the following items are provided at the end of each chapter:

Chapter Summary Chapters contain summaries that provide an overview of the material covered.

CHAPTER SUMMARY

Processes are the critical building blocks of operations across the supply chain. The importance of processes is emphasized in the following critical lessons:

1. Every business is defined by its various processes. These processes determine capabilities including what the organization can and cannot do regarding the types of product value delivered to customers.
2. A process is a collection of activities that uses resources to convert various inputs into outputs that customers value. Inputs used by processes include materials, energy, information, management, technology, and labor. Outputs consist of products, information, and experiences.
3. Processes are characterized by activities (i.e., operations, decisions, storage, transportation, delays, and inspections), flows (inputs and outputs), structures (organization schemes of activities), resources, and metrics.

Key Terms Key terms are highlighted in the text, and then repeated at the end of the chapter with page references.

KEY TERMS

bottlenecks 67
capacity 62
cycle time 69
Juran's Law 59
learning curve 66
Little's Law 68
serial/sequential structure 67
storage (inventory/store) 60

Discussion Questions Each chapter has a list of discussion questions. These are intended to serve as a student self-review or as class discussion starters.

DISCUSSION QUESTIONS

1. Describe the various operations within an amusement park that are most likely to become a bottleneck. How might an amusement park influence demand to better fit available capacity?
2. What are the primary resources that determine the capacity of each of the following?
   a. A grocery store.
   b. A hospital emergency room.
   c. A company that assembles appliances.
3. How can a university attain economies of scale? What impact might this have on quality and flexibility?
4. How would you define the maximum capacity for the front desk of a hotel? What is meant by the effective capacity? Define the difference in these two terms relative to

Solved Problems Solved problems are provided to illustrate problem solving and the main concepts in the chapter. These have been carefully prepared to enhance student understanding as well as to provide additional examples of problem solving.

SOLVED PROBLEM

Suppose you have been asked to determine the return on net worth for Great Northwest Canoe and Kayak, a small manufacturer of kayaks and canoes, located near Seattle, Washington. For this task, you have been given the following information:

Categories	Values
Sales	$32,000,000
Cost of goods sold	$20,000,000
Variable expenses	$ 4,000,000
Fixed expenses	$ 6,000,000
Inventory	$ 8,000,000

Problems Each chapter includes a set of problems for assignment. The problems are intended to be challenging but doable for students.

PROBLEMS

1. Given the following information:

Categories	Values
Sales	$48,000,000
Cost of goods sold	$24,000,000
Variable expenses	$ 8,000,000
Fixed expenses	$ 8,000,000
Inventory	$ 6,000,000
Accounts receivable	$ 3,000,000
Other current assets	$ 4,000,000
Fixed assets	$10,000,000

a. What is the net profit margin for this firm?
b. What is the asset turnover?
c. What is the return on assets?

Cases The text includes short cases for most chapters. The cases were selected to provide a broader, more integrated thinking opportunity for students without taking a full "case" approach.

CASE

Otis Toy Trains Explores the Supply Chain

Otis Toy Trains of Minneapolis, Minnesota, was a landmark company in the toy business. Since the 1900s, it had been responsible for building electrical and steam-driven toy trains. Since the 1950s, Otis trains had developed a major presence on children's television shows. Every person (especially boys) knew about Otis toy trains and nearly everyone wanted one. For many kids growing up in the 1960s to the 1980s, waking up on Christmas day and finding an Otis toy train set under the tree was a dream come true. However, the 1990s had not been good to Otis Toy Trains. The preferences of many children had changed. (a train model based on the train coaches that were used to transport the body of the recently assassinated President Lincoln from Washington, DC, to Springfield, IL, for final burial), the Zephyr (the famous streamlined train that ran between Chicago and Denver during the 1930s), and the Orange Blossom Special. Launched in limited numbers, this first series was an unqualified success. Subsequent launches were almost as successful. Over this time, the designers at Otis Toy Trains developed and refined the skill of identifying attractive train series and of designing products that were detailed, attractive, accurate, and highly

INSTRUCTOR RESOURCES

Online Learning Center (OLC) www.mhhe.com/swink2e

The Online Learning Center provides complete materials for study and review. At this book's Web site, instructors have access to teaching supports such as electronic files of the ancillary materials: Solutions Manual, Instructor's Manual, PowerPoint Lecture Slides, Digital Image Library, and Test Bank.

Instructor's Manual. Prepared by Laura Meade, Texas Christian University, this manual includes teaching notes, chapter overview, and an outline for each chapter.

Solutions Manual. Prepared by the authors, this manual contains solutions to all the end-of-chapter problems and cases.

Test Bank. Prepared by the authors, the Test Bank includes true/false, multiple-choice, and discussion questions/problems at varying levels of difficulty.

EZ Test Online. All test bank questions are available in EZ Test Online, a flexible electronic testing program. The answers to all questions are given, along with a rating of the level of difficulty, chapter learning objective met, Bloom's taxonomy question type, and the AACSB knowledge category.

PowerPoint Lecture Slides. The PowerPoint slides draw on the highlights of each chapter and provide an opportunity for the instructor to emphasize the key concepts in class discussions.

Digital Image Library. All the figures in the book are included for insertion in PowerPoint slides or for class discussion.

Operations Management Video Series

The operations management video series, free to text adopters, includes professionally developed videos showing students real applications of key manufacturing and service topics in real companies. Each segment includes on-site or plant footage, interviews with company managers, and focused presentations of OM applications in use to help the companies gain competitive advantage. Companies such as Zappos, FedEx, Subaru, Disney, BP, Chase Bank, DHL, Louisville Slugger, McDonald's, Noodles, and Honda are featured.

STUDENT RESOURCES

Online Learning Center (OLC) www.mhhe.com/swink2e

Students have access to study materials created specifically for the text.

- Quizzes—self-grading to assess knowledge of the material.
- PowerPoint Slides—give an overview of the chapter content.
- Excel Data Files—import into Excel for quick calculation and analysis.
- Study Outlines—provide a framework for taking notes.

CourseSmart (ISBM: 0077535049)

CourseSmart is a convenient way to find and buy eTextbooks. At CourseSmart you can save up to 60 percent off the cost of a print textbook, reduce your impact on the environment, and gain access to powerful Web tools for learning. CourseSmart has the largest selection of eTextbooks available anywhere, offering thousands of the most commonly adopted textbooks from a wide variety of higher education publishers. CourseSmart eTextbooks are available in one standard online reader with full text search, notes and highlighting, and e-mail tools for sharing notes between classmates. Visit www.CourseSmart.com for more information.

TECHNOLOGY

McGraw-Hill *Connect®* *Operations Management*

McGraw-Hill *Connect® Operations Management* is an online assignment and assessment solution that connects students with the tools and resources they'll need to achieve success through faster learning, higher retention, and more efficient studying. It provides instructors with tools to quickly pick content and assignments according to the topics they want to emphasize.

Online Assignments. *Connect Operations Management* helps students learn more efficiently by providing practice material and feedback when they are needed. *Connect* grades homework automatically and provides feedback on any questions that students may have missed.

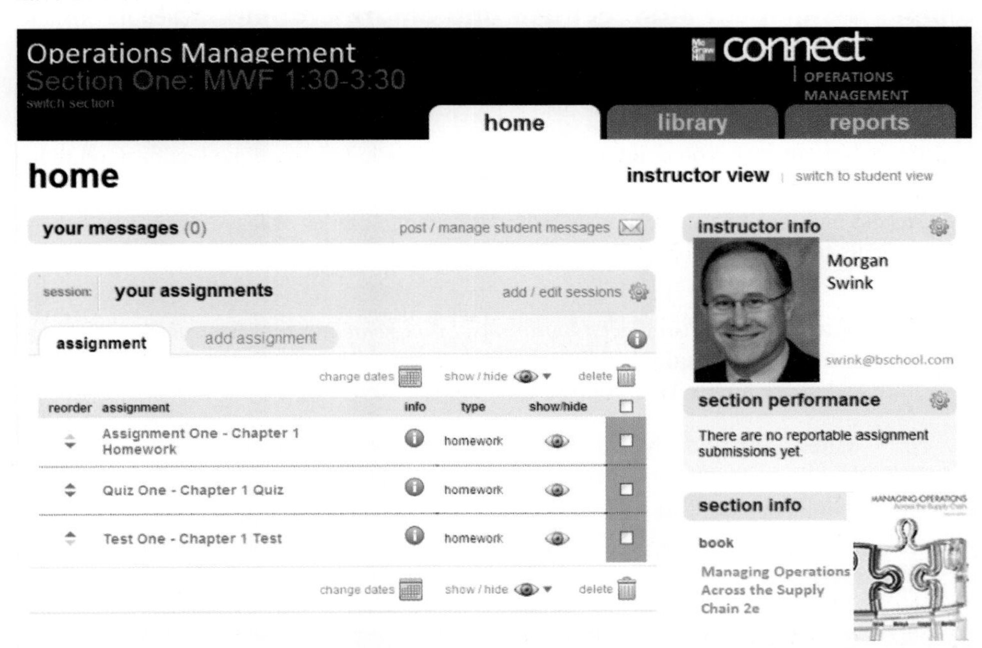

Integration of Excel Data Sets. A convenient feature is the inclusion of an Excel data file link in many problems using data files in their calculation. The link allows students to easily launch into Excel, work the problem, and return to *Connect* to key in the answer.

Student Resource Library. The *Connect Business Statistics* Student Library is the place for students to access additional resources. The Student Library provides quick access to recorded lectures, practice materials, eBooks, and more.

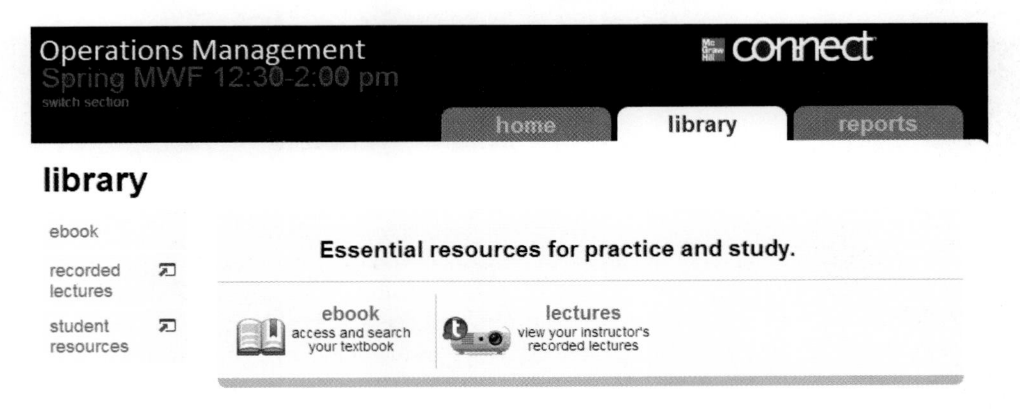

Guided Examples. These narrated video walkthroughs provide students with step-by-step guidelines for solving problems similar to those contained in the text. The student is given personalized instruction on how to solve a problem by applying the concepts presented in the chapter. The narrated voiceover shows the steps to take to work through an exercise. Students can go through each example multiple times if needed.

LearnSmart™

LearnSmart. LearnSmart adaptive self-study technology with *Connect Operations Management* helps students make the best use of their study time. LearnSmart provides a seamless combination of practice, assessment, and remediation for every concept in the textbook. LearnSmart's intelligent software adapts to students by supplying questions on a new concept when students are ready to learn it. With LearnSmart students will spend less time on topics they understand and instead focus on the topics they need to master.

Simple Assignment Management and Smart Grading. When it comes to studying, time is precious. *Connect Operations Management* helps students learn more efficiently by providing feedback and practice material when they need it, where they need it. When it comes to teaching, your time also is precious. The grading function enables you to:

- Have assignments scored automatically, giving students immediate feedback on their work and side-by-side comparisons with correct answers.
- Access and review each response; manually change grades or leave comments for students to review.

Student Reporting. *Connect Operations Management* keeps instructors informed about how each student, section, and class is performing, allowing for more productive use of lecture and office hours. The progress-tracking function enables you to:

- View scored work immediately (Add Assignment Results Screen) and track individual or group performance with assignment and grade reports.
- Access an instant view of student or class performance relative to learning objectives.
- Collect data and generate reports required by many accreditation organizations, such as AACSB.

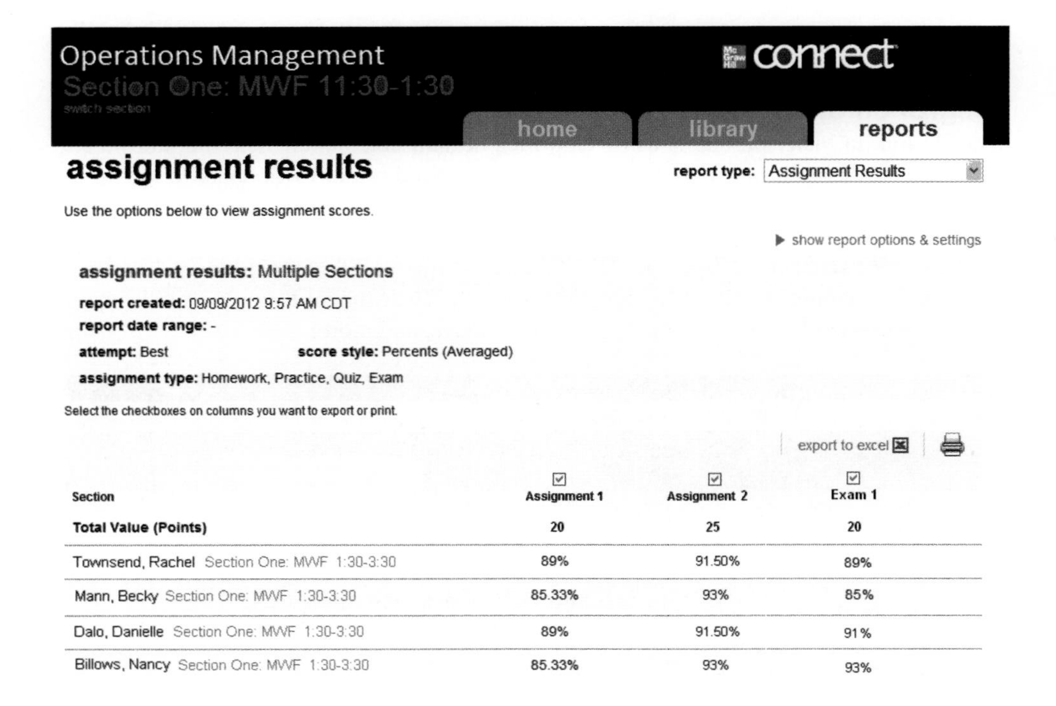

Section	Assignment 1	Assignment 2	Exam 1
Total Value (Points)	20	25	20
Townsend, Rachel Section One: MWF 1:30-3:30	89%	91.50%	89%
Mann, Becky Section One: MWF 1:30-3:30	85.33%	93%	85%
Dalo, Danielle Section One: MWF 1:30-3:30	89%	91.50%	91%
Billows, Nancy Section One: MWF 1:30-3:30	85.33%	93%	93%

Instructor Library. The *Connect Operations Management* Instructor Library is your repository for additional resources to improve student engagement in and out of class. You can select and use any asset that enhances your lecture. The *Connect Business Statistics* Instructor Library includes:

- eBook
- PowerPoint presentations
- Test Bank
- Instructor's Solutions Manual
- Digital Image Library

Connect® Plus Operations Management includes a seamless integration of an eBook and *Connect Operations Management* with rich functionality integrated into the product.

Integrated Media-Rich eBook. An integrated media-rich eBook allows students to access media in context with each chapter. Students can highlight, take notes, and access shared instructor highlights/notes to learn the course material.

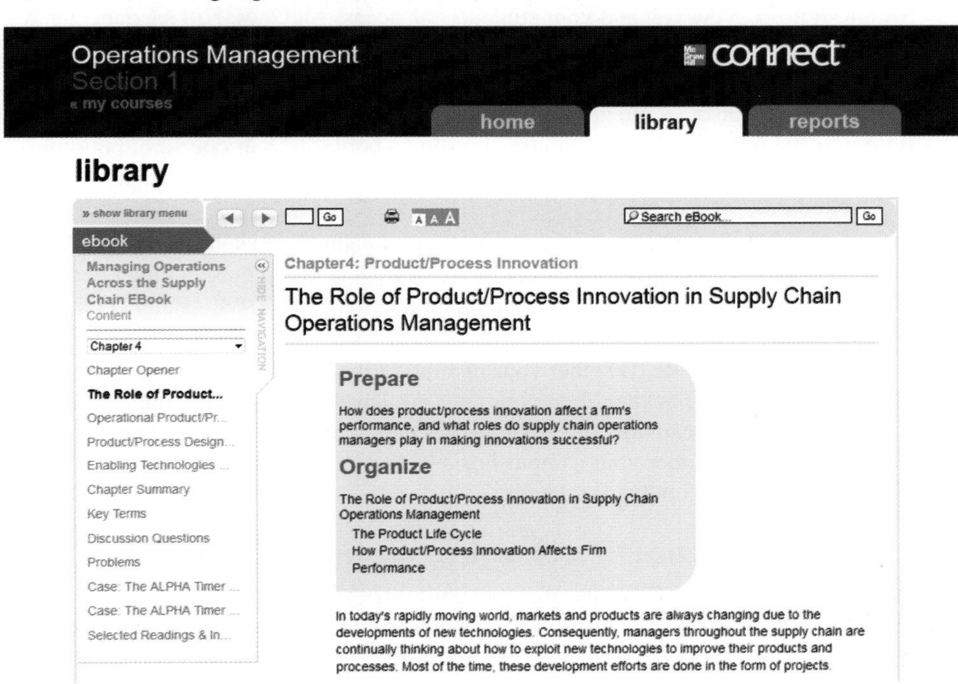

Dynamic Links. Dynamic links between the problems or questions you assign to your students and the location in the eBook where that problem or question is covered.

Powerful Search Function. A powerful search function to pinpoint and connect key concepts in a snap. This state-of-the-art, thoroughly tested system supports you in preparing students for the world that awaits. For more information about *Connect,* go to www.mcgrawhillconnect.com or contact your local McGraw-Hill sales representative.

Tegrity Campus: Lectures 24/7

Tegrity Campus is a service that makes class time available 24/7 by automatically capturing every lecture in a searchable format for students to review when they study and complete assignments. With a simple one-click start-and-stop process, you capture all computer screens and corresponding audio. Students can replay any part of any class with easy-to-use browser-based viewing on a PC or Mac.

Educators know that the more students can see, hear, and experience class resources, the better they learn. In fact, studies prove it. With *Tegrity Campus,* students quickly recall key moments by using *Tegrity Campus*'s unique search feature. This search helps students efficiently find what they need, when they need it, across an entire semester of class recordings. Help turn all your students' study time into learning moments immediately supported by your lecture. To learn more about *Tegrity,* watch a two-minute Flash demo at http://tegritycampus.mhhe.com.

Online Course Management

No matter what online course management system you use (WebCT, BlackBoard, or eCollege), we have a course content ePack available for your course. Our new ePacks are specifically designed to make it easy for students to navigate and access content online. For help, our online Digital Learning Consultants are ready to assist you with your online course needs. They provide training and will answer any questions you have throughout the life of your adoption. McGraw-Hill Higher Education and Blackboard have teamed up. What does this mean for you?

1. **Single sign-on.** Now you and your students can access McGraw-Hill's Connect and Create right from within your Blackboard course—all with one single sign-on.
2. **Deep integration of content and tools.** You get a single sign-on with Connect and Create, and you also get integration of McGraw-Hill content and content engines right into Blackboard. Whether you're choosing a book for your course or building Connect assignments, all the tools you need are right where you want them—inside of Blackboard.
3. **One gradebook.** Keeping several gradebooks and manually synchronizing grades into Blackboard is no longer necessary. When a student completes an integrated Connect assignment, the grade for that assignment automatically (and instantly) feeds your Blackboard grade center.
4. **A solution for everyone.** Whether your institution is already using Blackboard or you just want to try Blackboard on your own, we have a solution for you. McGraw-Hill and Blackboard can now offer you easy access to industry-leading technology and content, whether your campus hosts it, or we do. Be sure to ask your local McGraw-Hill representative for details.

Connect/LearnSmart Packaging Options:

Connect with LearnSmart 1 Semester Access Card: 0077535006
Connect Plus with LearnSmart 1 Semester Access Card: 0077535022

McGraw-Hill Customer Experience Contact Information

At McGraw-Hill, we understand that getting the most from new technology can be challenging. That's why our services don't stop after you purchase our products. You can e-mail our Product Specialists 24 hours a day to get product training online. Or you can search our knowledge bank of Frequently Asked Questions on our support Web site. For Customer Support, call **800-331-5094,** or visit www.mhhe.com/support. One of our Customer Experience Team members will be able to assist you in a timely fashion.

Chapter-by-Chapter Revisions for Second Edition

In this major revision to the book, we made many specific changes to the chapters; the larger changes are highlighted for each chapter below. Overall, we enhanced the discussion of sustainability issues throughout the book, including a new chapter focused on this topic (Chapter 16). We updated or replaced most of the opening vignettes and Get Real stories throughout the book. We added about 30 percent more practice problems, as well as more solved problems and examples. And we added at least one new case to almost every chapter.

Chapter 1: Introduction to Managing Operations Across the Supply Chain

- New opening vignette on Apple supply chain.
- Made stronger linkages of operations to other functions, economies, and business success.
- Incorporated deeper discussion of sustainability issues.

Chapter 2: Operations and Supply Chain Strategy

- New opening vignette on HBO and content.
- Greater integration of the business model.
- More extensive discussion of sustainability, including the triple bottom line.

Chapter 3 and 3S: Managing Processes and Capacity

- New opening vignette–Changes in the dry cleaning industry and the role of Tide.
- Updated the stories.
- More extensive discussion of metrics and performance measurement.
- Introduction of new material such as swim lanes into the process analysis section.
- Closer integration of capacity into the process discussion.

Chapter 4: Product/Process Innovation

- New opening vignette on the design and rollout of Coke "Freestyle" machines.
- Deeper explanations of product life cycle and innovation funnel.
- New **Get Real** describing Clorox and P&G codevelopment efforts.
- Added new case on QFD implementation.

Chapter 5: Manufacturing and Service Process Structures

- Moved capacity planning section to Chapter 3.
- Expanded the discussion of the use of technology in operations and the supply chain.
- Added a case to allow students to apply line balancing and service blueprinting.

Chapter 6: Managing Quality

- New **Get Real** box on food safety in the supply chain.
- Updated **Get Real** box comparing cost of quality in manufacturing and services.
- New section on industry interpretations of ISO 9000.
- New "Aqua-Fun" case emphasizing cost of quality.

Chapter 6 Supplement: Quality Improvement Tools

- Improved discussion of C_p and C_{pk}.
- Inclusion of p attribute control charts.
- Revised cause-and-effect analysis.

Chapter 7: Managing Inventories

- Formerly titled "Understanding Inventory Fundamentals," the material from the first edition's Chapter 14 (titled "Independent Demand Inventory Planning") has been incorporated into this chapter to provide comprehensive coverage in a single chapter.
- New opening vignette describing inventory management's impact at PolyOne Corp.
- Added discussion on causes of the bullwhip effect.
- Added new case requiring analysis of alternative safety stock policies.

Chapter 8: Lean Systems

- Expanded discussion of waste and the categories of waste.
- Expanded discussion of the various techniques (e.g., kanban scheduling).

- Expansion of the application of lean systems to include the service environment (i.e., lean services).
- Examples updated.

Chapter 9: Customer Service Management

- Title changed from "Customer Management."
- Expanded discussion of basic service to differentiate more clearly the differences in fill rate measurements.
- New **Get Real** stories describing Procter & Gamble's changes in measuring service performance and Tesco's "virtual store."
- Added new case to allow students to analyze customer service policies for different segments.

Chapter 10: Sourcing and Supply Management

- Increased the focus on sustainability.
- Updated the content to include contemporary topics such as low-cost country sourcing and nearshoring.
- Added an insourcing/outsourcing solved problem and additional homework problems.

Chapter 11: Logistics Management

- New opening vignette about Starbucks and its logistical challenges.
- Updated data on logistics cost.
- Revised table on freight modes and market share.
- Added discussion of transportation's impact on the environment, including a table showing greenhouse emissions by transportation mode.
- Replaced **Get Real** stories about True Value and Urban Outfitters with more up-to-date examples of Tuesday Morning and Dots.com.
- New case allowing students to analyze proposals from transportation carriers in terms of both cost and service.

Chapter 12: Demand Planning: Forecasting and Demand Management

- Reordered and clarified discussion of various forecasting methods.
- Incorporated material from Chapter 12 supplement directly into the chapter.

Chapter 13: Sales and Operations Planning

- New **Get Real** story (Whirlpool and Lowe's integrated planning process).
- Added content in comparing alternative production strategies, including ethical considerations and differences in make-to-stock vs. make-to-order.
- Added a case on aggregate planning in a professional law practice.

Old Chapter 14: Independent Demand Inventory Planning

- Merged material into Chapter 7.

Chapter 14 (was Chapter 15): Materials and Resource Requirements Planning

- Reorganized so that Master Production Scheduling (MPS) precedes Bill of Materials (BOM).
- Added a solved problem and problems.
- Added a case on ERP implementation.

Chapter 15 and 15S (was Chapter 16): Project Management

- Extended discussion of project execution, metrics, and termination.
- New case on planning a European tour.
- Enhanced discussion of probabilistic methods.

Chapter 16: Sustainable Operations Management—Preparing for the Future

- New chapter focused on the triune concerns of sustainability.
    - Business sustainability
    - Environmental sustainability
    - Social responsibility
- A more comprehensive discussion of environmental sustainability (what it involves, why it is emphasized now) and its implications for operations management.
- A broader discussion of social responsibility and how social pressures affect operations management decisions.
- A discussion of how change requires that business models must be continuously renewed.

Brief Contents

Part 5 MANAGING CHANGE IN SUPPLY CHAIN OPERATIONS 501

Contents

PART 1

SUPPLY CHAIN: A PERSPECTIVE FOR OPERATIONS MANAGEMENT

		relationships	sustainability	global
1	Introduction to Managing Operations Across the Supply Chain	X	X	X
2	Operations and Supply Chain Strategy	X	X	X

What is operations management? Have you ever stopped to consider all of the "nuts and bolts" of how organizations (business and not-for-profit) deliver goods and services to their customers? Think of all the details that must be managed to develop product concepts, to identify sources for raw materials, to decide how products will be made and delivered, and to establish how to serve customers. Operations management includes all of these types of decisions:

> Operations mangement is the management of processes used to design, supply, produce, and deliver valuable goods and services to customers.

In Part 1, *Supply Chain: A Perspective for Operations Management,* we define the scope of operations management as well as its strategic role. **Chapter 1** explains what operations management is and why it is important for all managers (accounting, marketing, finance, and other managers) to understand the basics of this management discipline. **Chapter 1** also introduces an important perspective, the *supply chain,* as a way to think about how to coordinate operational activities across different organizations. **Chapter 2** describes how strategic choices in operations management relate to an organization's overall objectives and to choices made in marketing, finance, and other functional areas. In addition, **Chapter 2** explains how to increase competitiveness through effective operations, and finally how to measure the effectiveness of operations activities.

1 Introduction to Managing Operations Across the Supply Chain

CHAPTER OUTLINE

LEARNING OBJECTIVES *After studying this chapter, you should be able to:*

LO1-1 Explain what operations management is and why it is important.

LO1-2 Describe the major decisions that operations managers typically make.

LO1-3 Explain the role of processes and "process thinking" in operations management.

LO1-4 Explain what the supply chain is and what it means to view operations management using a "supply chain perspective."

LO1-5 Identify the partners and functional groups that work together in operations management.

LO1-6 Define the planning activities associated with managing operations across the supply chain.

It Takes More than Cool Products to Make Apple Great

Apple often receives praise for its user-friendly and aesthetically pleasing product designs. But a less well-known contributor to Apple's success is its prowess in managing operations across its supply chain. This is the world of manufacturing, procurement, and logistics in which the chief executive officer, Tim Cook, excelled, earning him the trust of Steve Jobs. Apple has built a closed ecosystem where it exerts control over nearly every piece of the supply chain, from design to retail store. "Operations expertise is as big an asset for Apple as product innovation or marketing," says Mike Fawkes, the former supply-chain chief at Hewlett-Packard. "They've taken operational excellence to a level never seen before."

This operational edge is what enables Apple to handle massive product launches without having to maintain large, profit-sapping inventories. It's allowed a company often criticized for high prices to sell its iPad at a price that very few rivals can beat, while still earning a 25 percent margin on the device. Some of the basic elements of Apple's operational strategy include:

- Capitalize on volume. Because of its buying power, Apple gets big discounts on parts, manufacturing capacity, and air freight.
- Work closely with suppliers. Apple design guru Jony Ive and his engineers sometimes spend months living out of hotel rooms in order to be close to suppliers and manufacturers, helping to tweak the industrial processes and tools that translate prototypes into mass-produced devices.
- Focus on a few product lines, with little customization. Apple's unified strategy allows it to eliminate complexity and cost, while maximizing volume-based economies in its supply chain.
- Ensure supply availability and low prices. Apple makes big upfront payments to suppliers to lock in their capacity and to limit options for competitors.
- Keep a close eye on demand. By selling through its own retail stores, Apple can track demand by the store and by the hour; then it adjusts sales forecasts and production plans daily to respond quickly to demand changes.

Apple designs cool products. But its enormous profit margins—two to four times the profit margins of most other hardware companies—come in large part from its priority and focus on operations management.

This book, *Managing Operations Across the Supply Chain,* will help you to study "operations management" using a "supply chain" perspective. This perspective means that we will examine operational activities that take place *within firms* as well those *that cross firms' boundaries,* involving suppliers and customers of all types. This larger network of organizations makes up a firm's *supply chain.*

The Apple story illustrates the value of this broad perspective of operations management. The combination of excellence in both internal product design operations and external supply chain operations management makes Apple a dominant player in its industry. Operations management by definition spans a large number of activities that take place both inside and outside the business firm.

Prepare

What is operations management, and what is the supply chain?

Organize

A Broad Definition of Supply Chain Operations Management
- Important Decisions in Supply Chain Operations Management
- Differences in Goods and Services Operations
- Processes and Process Thinking

A BROAD DEFINITION OF SUPPLY CHAIN OPERATIONS MANAGEMENT

Operations management is the management of processes used to design, supply, produce, and deliver valuable goods and services to customers.

Operations management includes the planning and execution of tasks that may be long-term (yearly) or short-term (daily) in nature. Operations managers interact with managers in other business functions, both inside and outside the operations managers' own company. Operations management thus spans the boundaries of any single firm, bringing together the activities of internal operations (i.e., internal to a given company) with the operations of customers, suppliers, and other partners around the world. In the future, operations located around the globe will be even more tightly interconnected than they are today. The supply chain concept can be used to describe connections among business partners.

A **supply chain** is the global network of organizations and activities involved in (1) designing a set of goods and services and their related processes, (2) transforming inputs into goods and services, (3) consuming these goods and services, and (4) disposing of these goods and services.

operations management The management of processes used to design, supply, produce, and deliver valuable goods and services to customers.

supply chain The global network of organizations and activities involved in designing, transforming, consuming, and disposing of goods and services.

LO1-1 Explain what operations management is and why it is important.

Think about all the different organizations located in different companies that are involved in converting raw materials into a delivered finished product. Dozens of organizations are involved in producing and delivering even a simple product like bottled water. Together, supply chain organizations perform all the value-creating activities required to innovate, plan, source, make, deliver, and return or dispose of a given set of products and services.[1] Other terms sometimes substituted for *supply chain* include *demand chain, extended enterprise, supply network,* or *supply web.* All of these terms reflect the idea that a supply chain involves connections and relationships among organizations that play various roles for a given set of products.

Operations management activities located throughout a supply chain create and enhance the value of goods and services by increasing their economic value (e.g., lowering delivered cost), functional value (e.g., improving product quality or convenience), and psychosocial value (e.g., improving product aesthetics and desirability). The following statements help define and describe operations management:

- Operations management is mainly concerned with how resources will be developed and used to accomplish business goals.
- Operations management is about designing, executing, and improving business processes.
- Operations management deals with processes that transform inputs including materials, information, energy, money, and even people into goods and services.
- Within a supply chain context, operations management brings together four major sets of players: the firm, customers, suppliers, and stakeholders.

[1] Supply Chain Council, *Integrated Supply Chain Performance Measurement: A Multi-Industry Consortium Recommendation,* Supply Chain Council Report #5566, p. 1.

- To be effective, operations management must be consistent with the strategic goals of the firm.
- Operations management is dynamic because of changes in customers' demands, resources, competition, and technologies.

relationships

To work in this increasingly interconnected world, you will need to understand the foundational concepts, functional groups, and integrated activities involved in managing operations located across a supply chain. The Get Real box below describes why operations management is important to all of us.

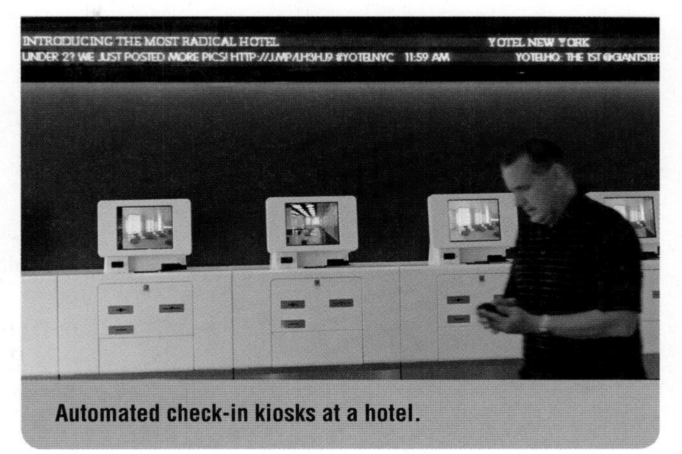

Automated check-in kiosks at a hotel.

Even if you do not pursue a career in operations management, it will be important for you to understand and appreciate the fundamental challenges associated with managing operations well. First, the decisions you make as a worker in marketing, finance, accounting, human resources, or other areas will have an impact on, and be impacted by, operations. For example, suppose that you work in a hotel where managers want to buy new kiosks that will allow guests to check themselves into the hotel. The effects of this decision extend beyond operational issues such as labor costs and efficiency. The decision will also have implications for the use of capital (a finance concern), the type of

GET REAL

Why You Need to Study Operations Management

Because it matters to people:

Operations management plays an important role in determining the quality of life for people around the world. New operational practices and technologies continue to radically improve the effectiveness of governments, not-for-profit institutions, and businesses in providing goods and services. Operations management also directly impacts sustainability issues including the environment, fair treatment of people, and safety. In doing so, operations management affects social systems and cultural norms, as well as the basic economic prosperity of people everywhere. Consider how your own life is affected. The speed with which organizations provide services to you determines the amount of leisure time you have. In an emergency, the speed and efficiency of a relief organization might even save your life. The cost and quality of products you consume affects your disposable income, your health, even your outlook on life. You can probably think of a good service experience that put a smile on your face, or a bad one that ruined your day! As an operations manager, you may someday have the opportunity and responsibility to positively affect your organization's success. In doing so, you may also be improving the quality of life of the firm's employees, its customers, and even society as a whole.

Because it matters to organizations:

Every product or service offering is a promise of some kind of benefit for someone. Organizations are successful only when they can consistently deliver upon the promises that they make. Operations management determines how well such promises are fulfilled. Research shows that operationally excellent organizations consistently outperform their rivals in financial and other terms. For example, a recent study[1] showed that companies possessing excellent supply chain operations outperformed their nearest competitors in the following ways:

- 50 percent higher net profit margins
- 20 percent lower sales, general & administration (SG&A) expenses
- 12 percent lower average inventories
- 30 percent less working capital expenses
- Twice the return on assets (ROA)
- Twice the return on equity (ROE)
- 44 percent higher economic value added
- Twice the returns on stock prices
- 2.4 times the risk-weighted stock returns
- 46 percent greater market-value-to-assets ratio

These differences in performance are truly stunning, and highlight the important contributions that operations management makes to the financial well-being of a firm.

[1]M. L. Swink, R. Golecha, and T. Richardson, "Does Becoming a Top Supply Chain Company Really Pay Off? An Analysis of Top SCM Companies and Their Rivals," *Supply Chain Management Review,* March 2010, pp. 14–21.

service provided to customers (a marketing concern), and the training of employees (a human resource management concern). Managers of various functions cannot work in isolation if they hope to make decisions that are good for the overall success of the firm. Second, all activities, including marketing, finance, accounting, and so on, have operational elements to them. For example, think about the operational processes required to run a sales office. Managers in all functions need to understand the principles of operations management in order to keep their functional processes running effectively and efficiently.

Important Decisions in Supply Chain Operations Management

LO1-2 Describe the major decisions that operations managers typically make.

Operations managers get involved in answering certain questions, namely:

What?

- What types of activities and what types of goods or services are to be delivered by the system?
- What product features do our intended customers care about?
- What activities and resources are needed, and how should they be developed, allocated, and controlled?

How?

- How is the good or service to be designed, made, and delivered?
- How much should our transformation process be able to deliver (and under what conditions)?
- How should we measure and assess performance?

When?

- When should products be made, activities be carried out, services be delivered, or capacities/facilities come on line?

Where and Who?

- Where should certain activities be done, and who should do them: suppliers, partners, or the firm?

relationships

Operations managers answer these questions by defining both the structural and infrastructural aspects of the operations management system. Structural decisions affect physical resources such as capacity, facilities, technology, and the supply chain network. Once made, decisions in these areas determine what the operations management system can and cannot do well. Altering these decisions often requires significant investments and lots of time—often years. Infrastructural decisions affect the workforce, production planning and control, process innovation, and organization. Decisions in these areas determine what is done, when it is done, and who does it. Decisions in all of these areas are interrelated, making operations management a complex and cross-functional activity.

Differences in Goods and Services Operations

Operational activities exist in order to produce tangible goods and intangible services. Books, cars, and televisions are all tangible goods. In contrast, services like health care, banking, and entertainment are largely experiential or informational. For example, at a hair salon, you *consume* the expertise and labor of the hair stylist as part of the experience of getting a haircut. The experiences and information you receive at school form a service called *education.* Table 1-1 summarizes some of the important differences between goods and services.

Some businesses are mostly about producing goods (e.g., production of gasoline), and some are mostly about delivering services (e.g., financial consulting). However, most businesses integrate a mix of goods-producing and service-producing operations activities.

TABLE 1-1 Characteristics of Goods and Services

Goods	Services
Tangible	Intangible
Can be inventoried	Cannot be inventoried
Little customer contact (consumption is often separate from production)	Extensive customer contact (simultaneous production and consumption)
Long lead times	Short lead times
Often capital-intensive	Often labor-intensive
Quality easily assessed	Quality more difficult to assess (more perceptual)
Material is transformed	Information or the customer is transformed

There are key structural differences in operational processes designed to provide mostly goods versus mostly services. Chapter 5 discusses these differences in depth, but we will highlight a few important ones here. First, goods can be produced in advance and stored in inventory until a customer buys or consumes them. Since services are intangible, they cannot be stored. The production and consumption of a service usually occur at the same time. While goods-manufacturing operations can use inventory to smooth out imbalances between production capacity and customer demand, a producer of services must maintain enough capacity to meet demand during peak periods; otherwise, it must postpone (backlog) the demand. For example, when you go into a restaurant during its busy time and the greeter asks you to wait in the lounge, you become part of a backlog of demand. Service operations managers often use reservation and appointment systems to help customers avoid long wait times.

In services, customers frequently can observe the operational processes directly. In fact, the customer may take part in producing and consuming the service at the same time (think of your roles as codesigner and quality inspector in getting a haircut). On the other hand, the production of goods may require little contact with the customer.

Finally, operations managers can easily establish measurable quality standards for tangible goods to evaluate whether they work adequately, how they appear, and so on. Quality control is more difficult for services, as it is not always easy to objectively measure a service product's attributes. Service operations managers often evaluate both methods of delivery and customer perceptions. For example, a quality control inspector for a movie theater might study how workers interact with customers as they sell tickets or food to customers. In addition, they may periodically survey customers to gauge their levels of satisfaction.

student activity

Think of the last time you visited an amusement park (like Disney World). How many different goods and services did you consume as a part of your overall experience? How many of these products were "pure" goods and "pure" services? Which of these products was prepared before you ordered it, versus being prepared at the very time that you ordered it?

In reality, there are very few pure goods and pure services. Most manufactured products also include services. When you buy a new car, for example, you may also buy financing, maintenance, and repair services. Many service products also include tangible items. A hospital, for example, provides medicines and bandages along with intangible diagnostic and treatment services.

Because most firms deliver products that involve both goods and services, operations managers recognize the importance of delivering a **total product experience**. This term refers to all of the outputs of an operation, both goods and services, that are combined to define a customer's complete consumption experience. The experience includes all aspects of purchasing, consuming, and disposing of the product.

total product experience All the goods and services that are combined to define a customer's complete consumption experience.

Processes and Process Thinking

process A system of activities that transforms inputs into valuable outputs.

LO1-3 Explain the role of processes and "process thinking" in operations management.

Operations management is a *process*-oriented discipline. What, then, is a **process**? It is a system of activities that *transforms* inputs into valuable outputs. Processes use resources (workers, machines, money, and knowledge) to transform inputs (such as materials, energy, money, people, and data) into outputs (goods and services). For example, one uses a grill (a resource) and heat (an input) to convert a raw hamburger patty (an input) into a cooked hamburger (an output).

Processes can also transform information, or even people (customers), from one condition into another. In decision making, for example, managers transform data into actionable information and decisions. Think about how you are "transformed" by going to a movie—this is a process in which you are both an input and an output! Other processes transform things by transporting them from one location to another, or by storing them (e.g., a warehouse stores finished goods). Finally, some activities check or inspect work to make sure that it meets standards for quality, quantity, or timeliness.

Every organization can be described as a bundle of processes that connect different organizational groups. For example, companies use *design processes* to develop new goods and services and *strategic planning processes* to determine how the firm should compete. They use *production processes* to plan and execute the supply, manufacture, and delivery of goods and services to customers. Finally, companies use *evaluation processes* to measure and report how well they are meeting their goals or using their resources.

It is valuable to think about operations as *sets of processes and subprocesses* with many interrelationships and linkages. Consider the operations of an airport. There are flight-scheduling processes, ticketing processes, facilities-management processes, security processes, vendor-management processes, and on and on. The structure governing how these processes work together determines the ability of the airport to serve its customers.

We all have experienced organizations with complex, bureaucratic processes that seem incapable of providing a desired service in a timely manner. The design of a process should reflect what customers want. If customers want quick response, for example, then the process should be designed to be fast and flexible. In this case operations managers must identify and eliminate unnecessary or redundant steps, reduce distances between steps or activities, and diminish the time needed to complete each step. This connection between the process design and customers' desires must be maintained. If customers' desires change, then processes may also have to change.

An airport operation contains dozens of interrelated processes.

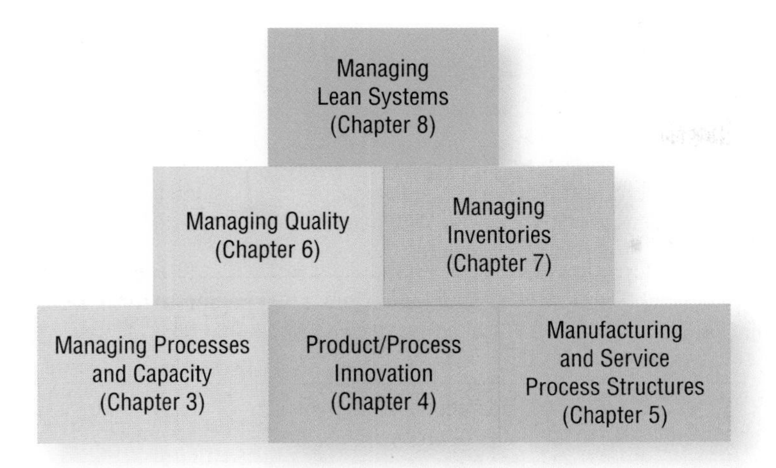

FIGURE 1-1
Foundational Concepts in Supply Chain Operations Management

Process thinking is so important that we have dedicated an entire section of this book to topics related to it. Figure 1-1 shows the conceptual building blocks of process thinking that are essential to the management of any operation. A separate chapter in this book addresses each building block. The bottom three blocks represent the foundational principles that describe how operational processes work, how product and process characteristics are intertwined, and how certain process structures are related to operational objectives. In order to make good decisions, operations managers need to understand the "physics" that govern processes, as well as understand how they relate to product design and development.

Building upon this foundational knowledge, operations managers can better understand how to make good decisions regarding product quality and the use of inventory (the second row of blocks in Figure 1-1). Product quality is a result of how people and technologies work together to execute processes. Inventory management can make processes more or less efficient, depending on whether the inventory is used wisely or unwisely.

lean operation An operation that produces maximum levels of efficiency and effectiveness using a minimal amount of resources.

The top block in Figure 1-1, "Managing Lean Systems," represents the application of all the aforementioned process-related concepts in ways that maximize the overall productivity of the operation. A **lean operation** produces maximum levels of efficiency and effectiveness using a minimal amount of resources.

OPERATIONS MANAGEMENT YESTERDAY AND TODAY: GROWTH OF THE SUPPLY CHAIN MANAGEMENT PERSPECTIVE

Prepare

Why has the supply chain perspective become important?

Organize

Operations Management Yesterday and Today: Growth of the Supply Chain Management Perspective
- Advances in Technology and Infrastructure
- Reduction in Governmental Barriers to Trade
- Focus on Core Capabilities
- Collaborative Networks

Many of the formal practices and concepts of operations management have their origins in the Industrial Revolution, which took place in the latter half of the 18th century. As an activity, however, operations management is much older. Signs of organized operations have been found in all ancient civilizations including Greece, Rome, and Egypt. Building the great pyramids was undoubtedly accomplished by means of organized operations, even if we don't know the exact nature of those operations.

Table 1-2 provides a brief history of operations management. Since the Industrial Revolution, modern operations management has evolved at different rates throughout the world. In America, the early 20th century witnessed a huge growth in demand and the rise of mass production. The latter half of the century was marked by standardization of operations practices and by fierce global competition. Today, continued globalization, the Internet, and numerous other technologies are radically transforming business operations.

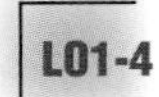
LO1-4 Explain what the supply chain is and what it means to view operations management using a "supply chain perspective."

The supply chain management perspective represents the latest technological shift in operations management. This now-dominant perspective is the result of certain forces in the marketplace, discussed below.

TABLE 1-2 A Brief History of Operations Management

Operations Era		Technological Advances	Operations Management Span of Focus
1800–1850	Technical Capitalists	Improved manufacturing technology; interchangeable parts; locating factories on waterways and in industrial centers; emerging transportation network	Internal production
1850–1890	Mass Production	Emergence of local factory; movement to urban areas; introduction of steam and electrical power; new machines; economies of scale	Internal production
1890–1920	Scientific Management	More systematic approaches to operations management; moving assembly line; beginnings of process thinking	Internal production
1920–1960	Demand Growth	Increased automation; introduction of computers and quantitative analysis	Internal production
1960–1980	Global Competition	Just-in-time systems; emergence of statistical process control; early outsourcing	Internal production
1980–2000	World-Class Manufacturing	Increased computerization and information systems; world-class practices and benchmarks; greater global sourcing and need for supply chain coordination	Production, design, supply
2000–Present	E-commerce	Internet; enhanced communications and transportation technologies; integrated management across functions, including goods and services operations	Global supply chain

Operations management existed even in ancient times.

Advances in Technology and Infrastructure

Advances in communications, computers, and transportation technologies have enabled extensive connectivity and the growth of supply chain partnerships. With easier information transactions, there is less of a need to include all operations at one location or within one organizational boundary. Constant information sharing between supply chain partners improves efficiencies in planning, in material movements, and in the transfer of funds.

At the same time, growing transportation technologies and infrastructures have made the shipping of goods and people faster, more reliable, and more economical than in decades past. Transportation infrastructure (airports, train tracks, shipping docks, and highways) continues to be built in developing countries. This growing infrastructure improves reliability of deliveries to remote places, thus opening opportunities to work with new suppliers and to serve new markets.

Reduction in Governmental Barriers to Trade

global

In recent years we have witnessed incredible changes in governments and social systems around the world. More and more nations have moved away from centrally controlled economies to pursue free market systems. Russia, India, and China represent a few important examples. These falling political barriers have opened up new opportunities to develop global supply chains. While these global supply chains can offer improved product costs and quality, they can also be more complex and risky. Today, operations managers must often manage long pipelines of inventories that cross multiple country borders.

Focus on Core Capabilities

With new technologies and global sources of supply, firms are now able to focus attention on their core capabilities—that is, things they do well. A **core capability** is a unique set of skills that confers competitive advantages to a firm, because rival firms cannot easily duplicate them.

core capability A unique set of skills that confers competitive advantages to a firm, because rival firms cannot easily duplicate them.

A focus on core capabilities leads a firm to concentrate on those few skills and areas of knowledge that make the firm distinct and competitive. The firm would then likely outsource other, noncore activities to suppliers who have advantages due to better skills or higher scale of operations. For example, Honda was one of the first companies to outsource many noncore activities such as component manufacturing, logistics, and other services. This allowed Honda to concentrate on design and assembly of motors and engines, its core capabilities.

The result of the core capabilities approach is supply chains in which each of the partnering organizations focuses on what it does best. The overall effect is to produce greater product value through higher quality and greater efficiencies. However, it also makes supply chain partners more interdependent.

relationships

Collaborative Networks

As firms become more reliant on their suppliers, the greatest improvements in product value are usually achieved through better coordination with these partners. However, when firms concentrate only on their immediate relationships, they address only a small portion of the total opportunity to improve the overall effectiveness of the system. For example, uncertainties in the availability of raw materials at a *supplier's* supplier can severely limit a firm's ability to deliver products to its customers. Problems like this are best avoided when partners across a supply chain network share their plans and capabilities, and work together to develop improvements. In addition, the creation of partnerships in integrated networks opens up opportunities to take advantage of complementary cost structures, the respective partners' technical expertise, market knowledge, and brand equities (reputations). By combining such assets, companies are able to make stronger product offerings together than they could individually.

supply chain management The design and execution of relationships and flows that connect the parties and processes across a supply chain.

VIEWING OPERATIONS MANAGEMENT FROM A SUPPLY CHAIN MANAGEMENT PERSPECTIVE

Prepare

What does it mean to view operations management from a supply chain perspective?

Organize

Viewing Operations Management from a Supply Chain Management Perspective

- Operations Management Partners Across the Supply Chain
- Cross-Functional Relationships in Operations Management
- The Changing Nature of Supply Chains
- Levels of Operational Planning Across the Supply Chain

We began this chapter by noting that operations managers must coordinate a system of activities both inside and outside their firm's boundaries. The network of organizations that contains this system of activities is often referred to as a *supply chain.* So how then is "supply chain management" different from "operations management"?

Supply chain management is the design and execution of relationships and flows that connect the parties and processes across a supply chain. Recall that our definition of *operations management* is the management of processes used to design, supply, produce, and deliver valuable goods and services to customers.

As you can see, there is a substantial degree of overlap between the two definitions. Operations management focuses on managing *processes* (design, supply, production, delivery); supply chain management focuses on managing *relationships* and *flows* (flows of information, materials, energy, money, and people). Think of supply chain management as a way of viewing operations management. You can also think of the supply chain as a network of organizations in which operations activities are conducted.

LO1-5 Identify the partners and functional groups that work together in operations management.

Operations Management Partners Across the Supply Chain

Operations managers interact with three important groups that are external to the firm: (1) customers, (2) suppliers, and (3) stakeholders. Figure 1-2 illustrates how operations management links internal operational processes with the operational processes of customers and suppliers. The figure also identifies some of the points of interaction between operational groups and other business functional groups within the firm.

Customers

customers Parties that use or consume the products of operations management processes.

Customers include anyone (individuals or organizations) that uses or consumes the products of operations management processes. The firm cannot structure an effective or efficient operations management function unless it has clearly identified its customers. Types of customers can include *internal* customers, *intermediate* customers, and *final* customers. For example, consider a car manufacturer. A company-owned distribution center might be considered an internal customer of the manufacturing group; a dealership is an intermediate customer; and people who buy the car and drive it off the dealer's lot are the final customers, or consumers.

While each of these customer groups is important, it is beneficial for operations managers to identify *critical customers.* Critical customers have the greatest impact on product designs, sales, and future growth opportunities. Often, but not always, the consumer is the critical customer. For example, you are the consumer of this book, yet another customer (your professor) has had greater impact on the product design, sales, and growth opportunities for this product.

Suppliers

suppliers Parties that provide inputs to operational processes.

relationships

Figure 1-2 identifies important types of **suppliers** in the supply chain. Suppliers provide inputs to operational processes. The horizontal dimension of Figure 1-2 illustrates the flow of materials, information, and money related to the sourcing, making, and delivery of products. The vertical dimension of Figure 1-2 depicts suppliers of technologies and support services. From a single firm's perspective, there are multiple types of suppliers:

- *Upstream product suppliers* typically provide raw materials, components, and services directly related to manufacturing or service production processes.
- *Downstream product suppliers* typically provide enhancements to finished goods such as assembly, packaging, storage, and transportation services.
- *Resource and technology suppliers* provide equipment, labor, product and process designs, and other resources needed to support a firm's processes.
- *Aftermarket suppliers* provide product service and support such as maintenance, repair, disposal, or recycling.

Not shown in Figure 1-2 are a host of other suppliers who make up a part of the total supply chain, including suppliers of indirect goods and services such as mail delivery, health care benefits, cleaning services, and so on. Since suppliers provide so many of a firm's needed resources, technologies, raw materials, and services, the total portfolio of a firm's suppliers affects its success to a great extent.

Stakeholders

stakeholders Groups of people who have a financial or other interest in the well-being of an operation.

In addition to customers and suppliers, other groups of people also have an interest in the well-being (financial and otherwise) of an operation. **Stakeholders** include employees and unions, the local community, social groups (such as animals' rights or environmental concerns), government, and financial investors.

Why differentiate between customers, suppliers, and stakeholders? Stakeholders' demands often differ from the demands of customers or suppliers. For example, customers

FIGURE 1-2 Partners and Operations Functional Activities in the Supply Chain

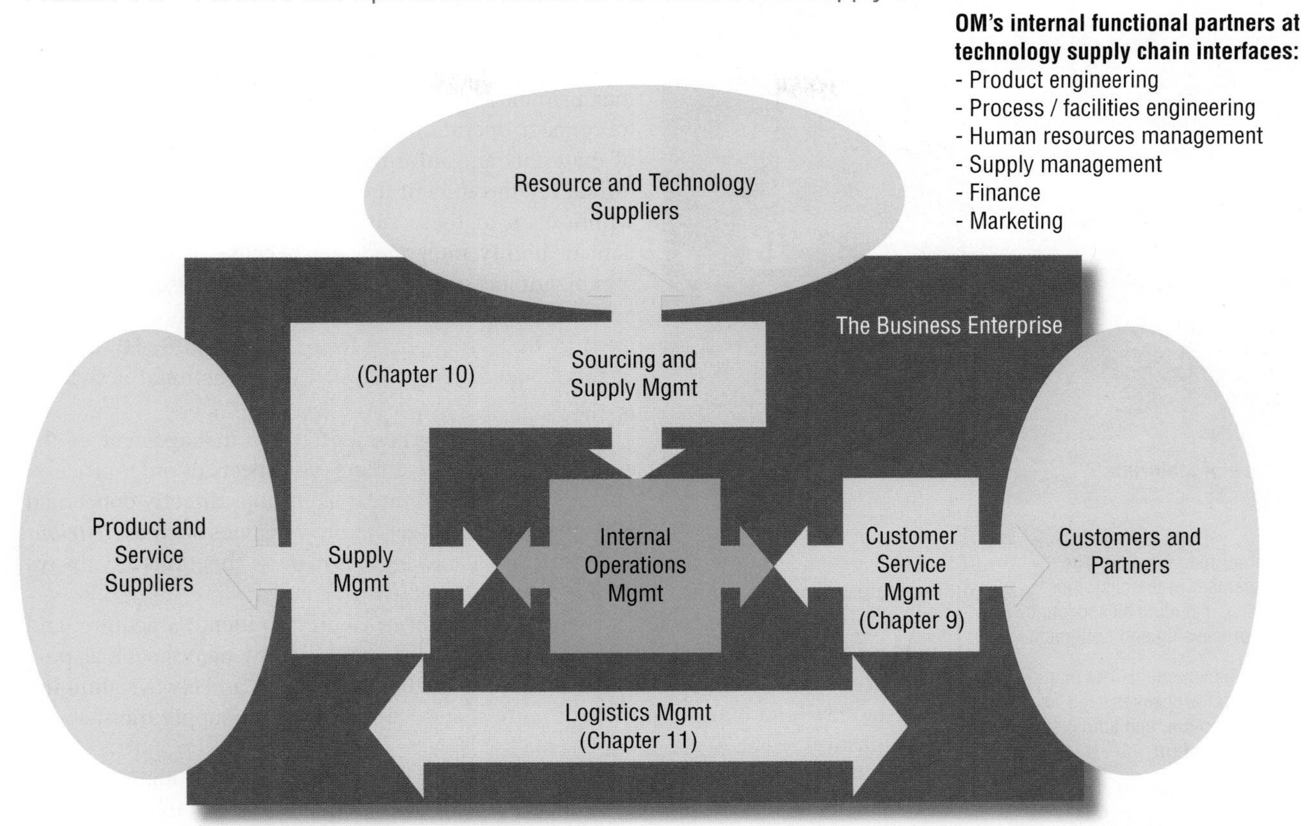

might care most about the price and quality of products, whereas some stakeholders might care most about environmental concerns. Like customers and suppliers, stakeholders can significantly affect how a firm operates.

Cross-Functional Relationships in Operations Management

We have already noted that operations managers must work closely with other functions in the firm. Managers making any operating decision should consider the decision's effects on other functions, including engineering, finance, marketing, human resources, and others. As shown in Figure 1-2, operations managers who work at the boundaries of the firm often work very closely with other functional groups. For example, an operations manager who works in supply management might work closely with finance managers to determine the most effective contract terms when purchasing equipment.

Some operations managers are primarily concerned with internal operations, such as manufacturing. These managers are always thinking about what operational capabilities are needed, and how to improve the cost, quality, and delivery of the products that the firm supplies to its customers. Other operations management groups work to integrate the internal operations of the firm with the external operations of supply chain partners. While Part 3 of this book specifically addresses these interfunctional relationships, we will provide a brief overview here.

Flow of materials

Functional Activities That Connect Operations Managers

As shown in Figure 1-2, customer management, supply management, and logistics management activities serve to connect operational managers as they manage flows of materials and information throughout their firm, and ultimately throughout the entire supply chain. Processes within each of these functional areas may be independent or highly integrated, yet because of the divisional organizational structure that most firms use, most business managers tend to think of operations management in these functional terms. Chapters 9, 10, and 11 in this book discuss each of these functional activities, respectively.

customer management The management of the customer interface, including all aspects of order processing and fulfillment.

supply management The management of processes used to identify, acquire, and administer inputs to the firm.

logistics management The management of the movement of materials and information within, into, and out of the firm.

Customer management is the management of the customer interface, including all aspects of order processing and fulfillment. Functional groups directly concerned with customer management have names such as *distribution, sales, order fulfillment,* and *customer service.* Managers in these functions are always thinking about ways to improve customer satisfaction in efficient ways.

Supply management is the management of processes used to identify, acquire, and administer inputs to the firm. Related functional groups are called by names such as *purchasing, sourcing,* and *procurement.* Managers in these functions are always thinking about insourcing and outsourcing opportunities, and ways to improve supply transactions and relationships.

Logistics management is the management of the movement of materials and information within, into, and out of the firm. Logistics functions go by names including *transportation/traffic management, warehousing, materials managers,* and so on. Managers in these functions are always thinking about ways to optimize these flows through better scheduling and the use of alternative transportation, storage, and information technologies.

An Example of Functional Relationships in a Supply Chain

Actual supply chains usually involve many processes including planning, sourcing, making, servicing, delivering, and so on. For example, consider the supply chain of a movie production company depicted in Figure 1-3. Boxes in the figure represent organizations or individuals; arrows represent flows of material, information, or people. To keep things simple, the figure shows only some of the major parties in the supply chain. You can probably easily think of other ones that are not included.

A movie production company's operations managers interact with many suppliers of goods and services that can be considered as either product-related or resource-related inputs. Accordingly, Figure 1-3 indicates stages of a product supply chain in the horizontal dimension, and stages of a resource/technology supply chain in the vertical dimension. Whether a supplier is a "product" supplier or a "resource" supplier is not always clear. Often, a single supplier may fit in both categories. For example, the director of a movie could be considered a resource in the sense that she brings creativity and knowledge to the moviemaking process. At the same time, her time and effort are consumed by the process of making the movie, and these could be considered to be product inputs. Usually, a product supplier provides an input that is fully consumed in the creation of a product or becomes part of the product (e.g., energy, raw materials, components). On the other hand, a resource or technology supplier provides an input that can be used again and again to create multiple products (e.g., information, product and process specifications, equipment, worker skills).

tier An upstream stage of supply.

In a supply chain, each upstream stage of supply is known as a **tier**. The tier number refers to how directly the supplier works with the firm. A *first-tier* supplier provides goods and services directly to the firm. For example, the stock film wholesaler is a first-tier supplier

FIGURE 1-3 Partial Supply Chain Network for a Movie Production Company

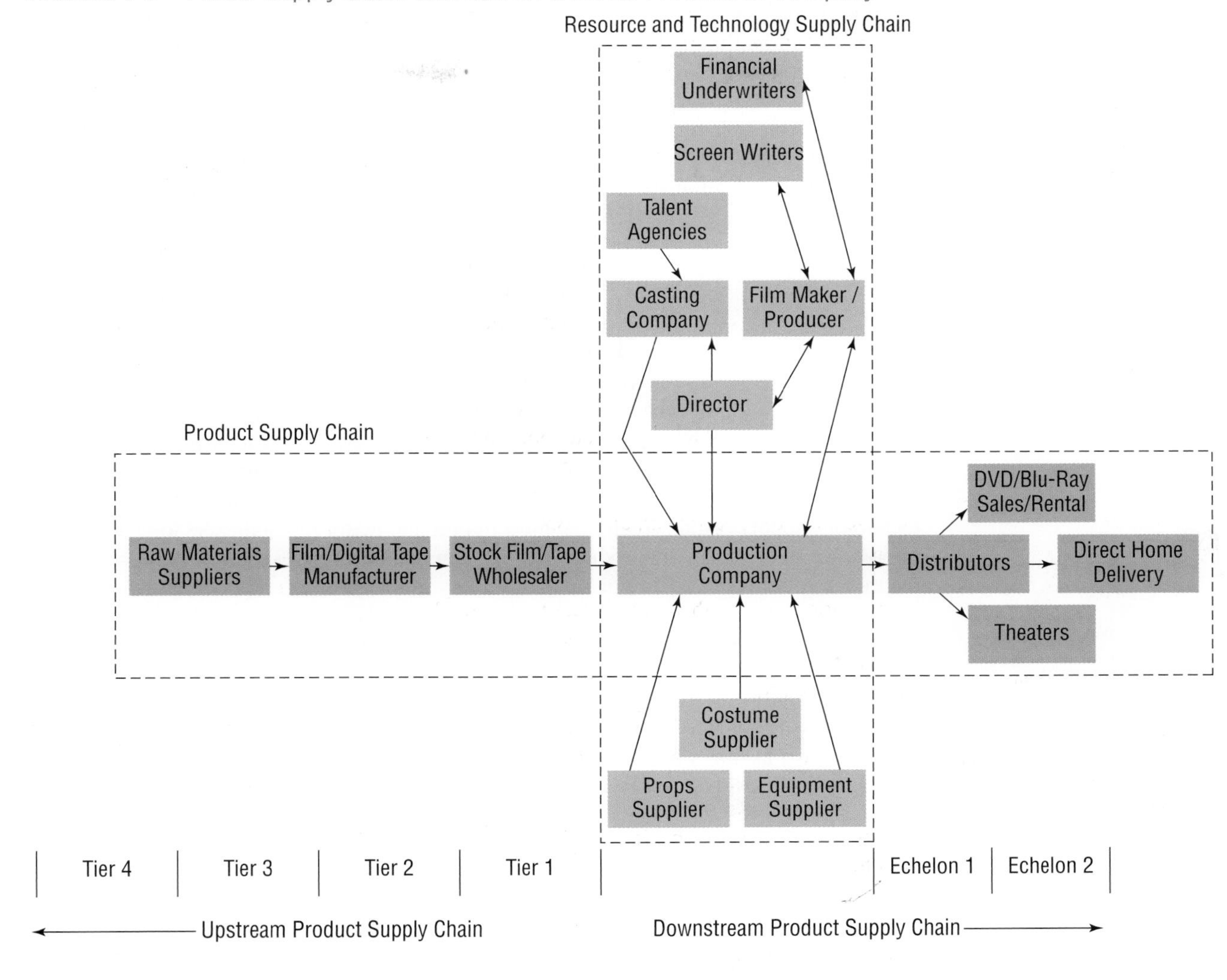

to the movie production company. A *second-tier* supplier provides inputs to the first-tier supplier, and so on. Each tier of the upstream supply chain could involve multiple suppliers for the same items or services. Also, a single supplier might provide inputs for multiple tiers of the supply chain. For example, the director in Figure 1-3 provides inputs to both the casting company and the movie production company.

student activity

Find a description of digital moviemaking technology on the Internet. Which of the stages and organizations depicted in Figure 1-3 are likely to be most affected by a shift to a completely digital process? How will the structure of the overall supply chain be changed?

Downstream stages of the supply chain are made up of layers of partners and customers commonly referred to as **echelons**. A single echelon might contain partners in locations all over the world. For example, there are usually many distributors for a given movie. These distributors can be thought of as suppliers of distribution services to the movie production company. The downstream supply chain can also be broken into different channels of distribution; theaters, direct/home delivery, and retail DVD/Blu-Ray sales are three channels shown in Figure 1-3.

echelon A downstream stage of supply or consumption.

Many different types of operations managers are needed in a movie production company. Supply managers help to identify and negotiate contracts with supply sources such as casting companies, directors, producers, equipment suppliers, film suppliers and so on. Internal production managers are needed to schedule all moviemaking activities such as casting, shooting, and editing. Sales and distribution managers identify and negotiate terms with worldwide distributors of the film. Other logistics managers work out the means for transporting actors and crew and storing film and equipment throughout the various locations involved in making the film.

Similar roles are filled by operations managers at all kinds of firms. The Get Real box on the next page provides some examples of operations management job descriptions for undergraduate and graduate students. Operations managers' responsibilities can be quite exciting, as they are absolutely integral to the success of any organization.

The Changing Nature of Supply Chains

Supply chains are complex. Ultimately, all firms in an industry are connected to one another through links of sourcing, making, servicing, and delivery for different products in various markets. Adding to the complexity is the fact that the structures of supply chains are constantly changing in order to accommodate changes in the business environment. New suppliers emerge and old ones die out. Regulations, laws, and societal pressures change. Markets and technologies evolve. Consider, for example, the technological changes that are sweeping through the moviemaking industry. One could argue that the resource-technology supply chain is really the most important one for moviemakers to manage. The importance of the upstream product supply chain, which provides the medium upon which the movie is delivered, is diminishing rapidly as digital movie production and distribution are rapidly replacing film-based media. In other businesses, where standardized products are produced many times over, the product supply chain plays a more prominent role in a company's strategy.

sustainability

Most of us are aware of the increasing concerns of societies and governments over environmental issues such as pollution, global warming, and hazardous wastes. Expectations are also rising for business firms to behave in more socially responsible ways regarding their labor practices, involvement in communities, and promotion of the general welfare. These increasing pressures act as tremendously important drivers of change in supply chains today. For example, some operations managers who formerly procured supplies from faraway sources are now sourcing them locally in order to reduce the carbon dioxide pollution created by transportation of goods over long distances. This is such an important topic that we have dedicated an entire chapter to it (Chapter 16: Sustainable Operations Management). Additionally, you will encounter numerous examples addressing these issues throughout the book.

LO1-6 Define the planning activities associated with managing operations across the supply chain.

Levels of Operational Planning Across the Supply Chain

To keep up with changes in supply chains and the business environment, the functional groups in operations management must periodically work together to plan out their actions. These plans include forecasts and decisions about what the demands on the system will be, what resources and inputs will be needed, how to deploy those resources, and how to process those inputs.

strategic planning A type of planning that addresses long-term decisions that define the operations objectives and capabilities for the firm and its partners.

tactical planning A type of planning that addresses intermediate-term decisions to target aggregate product demands and to establish how operational capacities will be used to meet them.

Figure 1-4 on page 18 shows the different levels and types of planning in operations management. Chapters in Parts 1 and 2 of this book address **strategic planning**, which includes high-level product and resource design decisions that define the overall operations objectives and capabilities for the firm and its partners. For example, strategic planning decisions would include what new products to develop, where to locate new plants, and what new technologies to buy. These types of decisions take a long time to implement, and the choices made put limits on the capacities and capabilities governing operational processes.

Chapters in Part 4 of this book address tactical and operational planning. These types of planning occur more frequently than strategic planning does. **Tactical planning** such as sales and operations planning seeks to identify and target customer demands for aggregate product families, and to establish the inventory and capacity plans needed to satisfy these

Jobs in Operations Management

The following job descriptions provide examples of typical responsibilities of operations managers located in internal operations, customer management, supply management, and logistics management functions.

Typical job titles: Customer Program Manager, Enterprise Integration Leader, Commodity Manager, Procurement Specialist, Senior Global Commodity Specialist, Strategic Sourcing Commodity Leader, Project Manager for Supply Chain Information Systems, Production Team Leader, Materials Planning Manager, Logistics Specialist.

Typical job responsibilities:

- Choosing and developing suppliers.
- Designing and implementing systems and processes for improving the customer interface, reducing transaction costs, reducing inventories, and improving service levels.
- Sourcing materials, components, technologies, and services.
- Monitoring and managing inventory at all steps of the supply chain.
- Managing logistics, warehouses, distribution inventories, and service parts.
- Managing internal operations or service functions.
- Managing quality and Six Sigma projects throughout the supply chain.
- Strategically analyzing the supply chain to increase revenues, improve service, reduce cost, and ultimately improve profit.

Excerpts from actual job descriptions:

At a computer manufacturer: As part of the Americas Services Logistics team, Supply Chain Consultants design, develop, and improve processes throughout the company's industry leading logistics network as well as manage projects across multinational teams for the Americas region. The Supply Chain Consultant works on developing new concepts and strategies for the company's third-party logistics providers (3PLs) that enable greater product availability at lower costs and greater customer satisfaction. In addition to partnering with 3PLs, Supply Chain Consultants work closely with the company's world-renowned Enterprise Command Center in order to provide 24/7 critical logistics support and crisis resolution to millions of customers throughout the Americas. The general qualifications of a Supply Chain Consultant include:

- Strong analytical skills.
- Advanced verbal and written communication skills.
- Able to generate new and innovative solutions to complex problems.
- Strong knowledge of supply chain and service logistics concepts and practices, third-party logistics provider management experience preferred.
- Advanced understanding of processes and process improvement, Six Sigma experience preferred.
- Able to effectively negotiate with internal and external partners.
- Strong project management experience.
- Proven leadership skills.
- Unwavering customer focus.
- Bachelor's degree in Operations, Logistics, Engineering or Supply Chain Management with 3–4 years experience.

At a health care products company: Our Development Program in Operations is a fast-paced set of rotations that can turn you into a well-rounded, results-driven leader who is ready to move into a decision-making supervisory position. By gaining first-hand experience in our distribution centers and corporate/regional offices, you'll learn the necessary skills to manage our streamlined distribution process and help drive operational results and customer satisfaction. Our distribution centers across the country will offer you hands-on experience to help you develop your skills in project management, business process improvement, and labor management. We encourage and coach all participants to achieve outstanding results by giving them challenging and rewarding responsibilities. The Development Program in Operations lasts twenty-four months and offers rotations that concentrate on warehouse operations, inventory management, transportation, corporate operations and purchasing.

At a paper products company: Our co-op and internships will offer you a chance to explore the breadth of opportunities available in the supply chain while working on real projects such as process improvements in flow planning for finished products, raw materials and finishing supplies, space utilization and optimization analysis, or warehouse operations systems analysis. You will be provided meaningful work experiences that contribute to the overall strategic business goals of the company. You'll be treated and respected as a valuable contributor and given your own responsibilities and accountabilities. Your intern experience will include performance evaluations that provide you with valuable professional feedback to gauge your strengths and measure areas of improvement.

At a not-for-profit organization: As director of donated goods operations you will help the organization provide people who have disabilities and other barriers to employment with opportunities to become independent, self-supporting

Continued

Continued

citizens through training, work experience, and employment in the community. Position duties include:

- Develop short- and long-range plans for the donated goods operation to achieve service goals, budgeted revenue, and maximized contributed margin.
- Expand donated goods operation to new markets, new product lines, develop new sites and creative sales techniques to expand community and business donation base.
- Establish and monitor performance criteria for donated goods operation to enhance donated goods operations through increased efficiencies.
- Develop and manage inventory control system, a total quality improvement system, and e-commerce activities to assure customer satisfaction at all levels.
- Make recommendations to the President/CEO regarding the need for capital equipment additions or replacements.
- Contribute positively to the Executive Management Team. Promote positive image of the organization both internally and externally.
- Participate in and uphold the values and processes devoted to continuous quality improvement in all organizational operations.

You can find more operations management career information at:

www.careersinsupplychain.org
www.ism.ws/careercenter

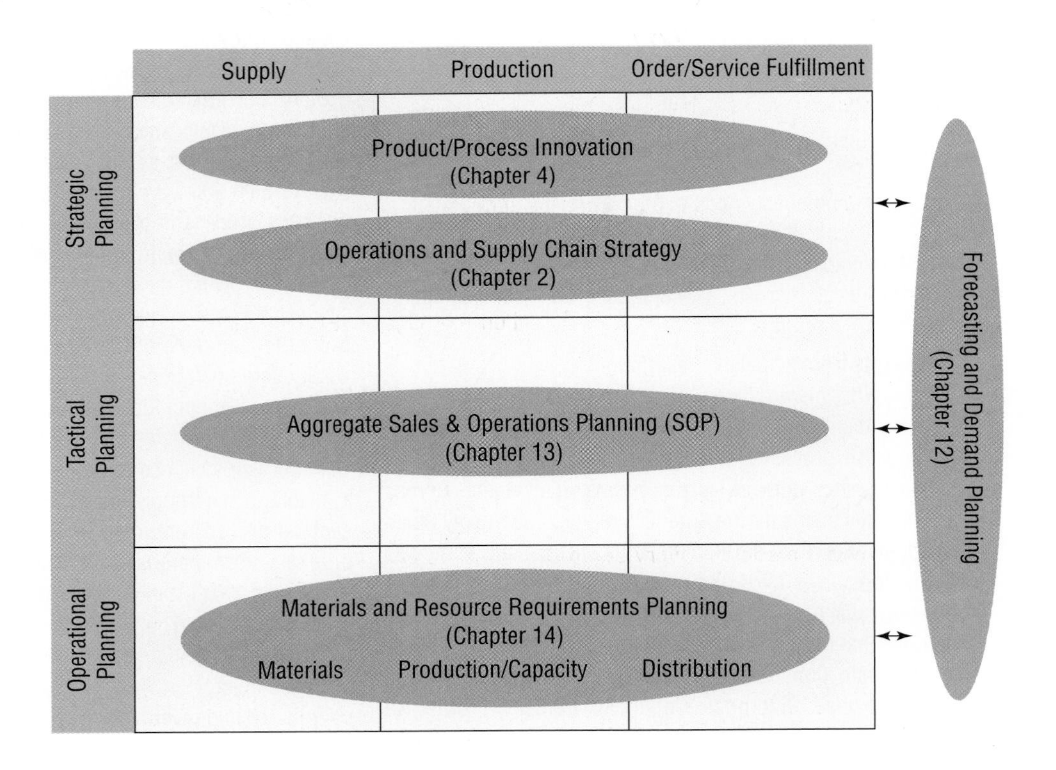

FIGURE 1-4 Operations Management: Planning Activities Across the Supply Chain

operational planning A type of planning that establishes short-term priorities and schedules to guide operational resource allocations.

overall demands. At the **operational planning** level, inventory and requirements planning activities address demands, materials, and capacities at the individual product level. Tactical planning usually spans months, whereas operational planning usually addresses weeks or days of activity. The chapters in Part 4 in this book also discuss planning approaches and technologies used in tactical and operational planning.

TABLE 1-3 A Content Map for This Book

Chapter	Relationships	Sustainability	Globalization
Part 1 Supply Chain: A Perspective for Operations Management			
1. Introduction to Managing Operations Across the Supply Chain	X	X	X
2. Operations and Supply Chain Strategy	X	X	X
Part 2 Foundations of Operations Management			
3. Managing Processes and Capacity	X	X	
4. Product/Process Innovation	X	X	X
5. Manufacturing and Service Process Structures	X	X	X
6. Managing Quality	X	X	X
7. Managing Inventories	X	X	X
8. Lean Systems	X		X
Part 3 Integrating Relationships Across the Supply Chain			
9. Customer Service Management	X		
10. Sourcing and Supply Management	X	X	X
11. Logistics Management	X	X	X
Part 4 Planning for Integrated Operations Across the Supply Chain			
12. Demand Planning: Forecasting and Demand Management	X		X
13. Sales and Operations Planning	X		X
14. Materials and Resource Requirements Planning	X		X
Part 5 Managing Change in Supply Chain Operations			
15. Project Management	X	X	X
16. Sustainable Operations Management-Preparing for the Future	X	X	X

HOW THIS BOOK IS STRUCTURED

Table 1-3 provides a content overview of this book, indicating the chapters in which critical operations management issues are addressed. Collectively, the five major parts of this book provide an introduction to the principles, programs, and practices of operations management:

- Part 1 provides an overview of operations management as a field, and describes its strategic role in a business from the perspective of supply chain management.
- Part 2 discusses foundational process-related concepts and principles that govern all operational processes.
- Part 3 deals with the primary functional relationships between internal operations management activities and other operational functions both inside and outside the firm.
- Part 4 discusses planning approaches and technologies used at different levels of operations decision making.

- Part 5 discusses how operations managers use projects, change programs, and technologies to shape the future of operations and supply chain management.

An overview and integration of the chapters contained in each part is provided at the beginning of each of the parts throughout this book.

CHAPTER SUMMARY

This chapter provides a broad overview and introduction to operations management. In discussing the scope and complexity of operations management, we have made the following points:

1. The goal of the modern firm is to develop and run an operations management system able to deliver superior product value to the firm's targeted consumers.
2. Operations management deals with the effective and efficient management of transformation processes. These processes include not only the making of products but also the design of products and related processes; sourcing of required materials and services; and delivery and management of relationships among customers, suppliers, and functions within the firm. As a system, operations management involves four major functional activities and their interactions: (1) customer relationships management, (2) internal operations (manufacturing and services) management, (3) supply management, and (4) logistics management.
3. The operations management system involves three major sets of partners outside the firm: (1) customers, (2) suppliers, and (3) stakeholders. Operations managers also work closely with other business functions within the firm.
4. The collective decisions made in areas of operations management determine the capabilities and success of the firm. In addition, the capabilities of a firm are heavily influenced by the capabilities of its suppliers.
5. For a number of reasons, the supply chain has grown to become a dominant way to look at operations management. Operations activities take place in various functional and geographic locations across a supply chain network. Whereas operations management is mainly about managing processes, supply chain management is mainly about managing flows and relationships.
6. Operations management is fundamentally dynamic; it is ever changing.

KEY TERMS

core capability 11
customer management 14
customers 12
echelon 15
lean operation 9
logistics management 14
operational planning 18
operations management 4
process 8
stakeholders 12
strategic planning 16
suppliers 12
supply chain 4
supply chain management 11
supply management 14
tactical planning 16
tier 14
total product experience 7

DISCUSSION QUESTIONS

1. Review *Fortune* magazine's "Most Admired" American companies for 1959, 1979, 1999, and the most current year. (The issue normally appears in August each year.) Which companies have remained on the top throughout this period? Which ones have disappeared? What do you think led to the survival or demise of these companies?
2. Select two products that you have recently purchased; one should be a service and the other a manufactured good. Think about the process that you used to make the decision to purchase each item. What product characteristics were most important to you? What operational activities determine these characteristics?
3. What are the primary operations management decisions in each of the following corporations?
   a. Marriott Hotels and Resorts.
   b. A private golf and tennis club.
   c. Ben & Jerry's.
   d. ExxonMobil Corporation.
4. Consider the following processes that you frequently encounter as a college student:
   a. Enrolling in classes.
   b. Taking a class.
   c. Buying a ticket for a play, concert, or basketball game.

   Describe each process and its inputs, activities, and outputs. What is being converted or transformed in each process? Who are the customers, suppliers, and stakeholders for each process?
5. Recall the last time you went to a fast-food restaurant such as McDonald's. Describe all of the goods and services that make up your *total product experience.*
6. The following firms have long been seen as having strong competitive advantages:
   a. IBM
   b. Coca-Cola
   c. Xerox
   d. Walmart

   Read about one of these companies. Also draw from your experience as a customer to identify that company's competitive advantage. Discuss how operations management relates to the company's competitive advantage.
7. Why should a firm consider the position of stakeholders when evaluating operational alternatives? Consider the role of government and its impact. (*Hint:* Consider working conditions and pollution.)
8. Most people have worked as "operations managers" at some time. Describe a job or experience that you had that involved the management of a process.

CASE

Business Textbook Supply Chain

Dave Eisenhart, senior editor for Mountain Publishing, Inc., looked out his window as he considered the operational implications of the changes he had just heard discussed in the company's annual strategic planning meeting. The future looked to be both exciting and scary. As an editor for Mountain's business textbook division, Dave had recently witnessed major changes in his primary market. First, the body of knowledge in business school curricula had exploded over the past decade. It was getting harder and harder to cover all the content that any professor might want in a single textbook, while keeping the size of the book manageable. Second, Dave had noted that more and more schools were moving to modular course structures, including many shorter courses, sometimes as short as a week long. Third, a growing number of students preferred to buy their books from sources other than traditional bookstores, such as Amazon.com and other online sources.

At the same time, new technologies were changing the way that textbook content could be produced and delivered. Print technologies were improving the speed and quality of printing, so that it was easy to envision a day when books could be printed one copy at a time, "on demand." Mountain and other companies had already started to offer custom published books for professors who wanted to combine chapters and cases from several different sources into a single readings packet for their students. While the quality of these "books" (packets) did not match that of traditional hardbound texts, many professors and students valued the flexibility associated with this option.

Finally, e-books were slowly making an entrance into the market. While the percentage of books purchased in electronic form was currently very small, the potential seemed to be very large, if and when a standardized reader technology ever became widely accepted in the marketplace.

Dave began to think about the operational activities dispersed across Mountain's supply chain for traditional textbooks. On the upstream (input) side, Mountain worked with authors (usually professors), text editors, graphic artists, commercial printers, and other suppliers to edit, design, and produce books. After typically large print runs (up to three years of forecasted demand) were produced, transportation suppliers delivered the books to Mountain's distribution centers located around the country. Orders from bookstores and online retailers were filled from these distribution centers. For traditional textbooks, each of these players in the supply chain played a fairly clear role in creating value through the goods and services they provided. However, as Dave considered the market and technological changes currently under way, the operational value that each of these players provided became less clear.

Questions

1. Draw a diagram that illustrates the textbook supply chain from the publisher's point of view.
2. Who are the various customers for textbooks? What do these customers want in terms of goods and services related to textbooks? From the publisher's point of view, who is the critical customer?
3. Who are the major players in the supply chain? What operational roles do they play in terms of creating value for the critical customers?
4. Given the anticipated changes in the market and in product and process technologies, how do you envision each supply chain player's role changing in the future?
5. What advice would you give to Dave Eisenhart regarding long-term operational changes the firm should consider?

SELECTED READINGS & INTERNET SITES

Association of Operations Management
www.apics.org

Council of Supply Chain Management Professionals
www.cscmp.org

Institute for Supply Management
www.ism.ws

Goldratt, E. M., and J. Cox. *The Goal: A Process of Ongoing Improvement.* Great Barrington, MA: North River Press, 2004.

Friedman, T. L. *The World Is Flat.* New York: Farrar, Straus and Giroux, 2006.

Journal of Operations Management. Amsterdam: Elsevier Science, B.V., 1980–current.

Manufacturing & Service Operations Management: M&SOM. Linthicum, MD: Institute for Operations Research and Management Sciences, 1999–current.

Production and Operations Management: An International Journal of the Production and Operations Management Society/POMS. Baltimore, MD: Production and Operations Management Society, 1992–current.

Swamidass, P. (ed). *Encyclopedia of Production and Manufacturing Management.* Norwell, MA: Kluwer Academic Publishing, 2000.

Womack, J. P.; D. T. Jones; and D. Roos. *The Machine That Changed the World.* New York: Rawson Associates, 1990.

2 Operations and Supply Chain Strategy

CHAPTER OUTLINE

LEARNING OBJECTIVES *After studying this chapter, you should be able to:*

LO2-1 Describe how operations strategy fits within a firm's overall strategic planning process.

LO2-2 Describe the need for "fit" between the critical customers, value propositions, and operations capabilities—the essential elements that define an operations strategy.

LO2-3 Describe customer-desired outcomes in terms of order winners, order qualifiers, and order losers.

LO2-4 Explain what product-related and process-related operational competitive priorities are, and how they are related to competitive advantage.

LO2-5 Explain how strategic performance can be assessed both operationally and financially by using the strategic profit model, the balanced scorecard, and the supply chain operational reference model.

Developing the Winning Formulae for Pay-TV: HBO Transforms Television—Again

global

In America, HBO (Home Box Office) is a premium subscription television network. Subscribers pay about $15 a month to access it. To keep its customers, HBO has continually transformed television. In the 1990s, HBO was the first cable channel to offer its subscribers access to current movies and special sporting events. As other networks began offering similar content, HBO needed a new value proposition. They recognized a key strategic difference between their network and the "free" stations (e.g., NBC, ABC, CBS, and CBC in Canada). Since free stations get their revenues from advertisers, they consider them to be their "critical" customers. Advertisers want content aimed at the widest possible "mass" markets. In contrast, HBO's critical customers (its subscribers) tend to be more sophisticated viewers who value more intelligent and interesting content. To deliver such content, HBO decided to build a supply chain for programs, rather than simply buying programs from outside studios. HBO hired writers; it produced its own scripts; it controlled how its shows were distributed on other channels and the Internet. Though initial attempts failed, HBO soon produced very successful series such as *Oz, The Sopranos, Sex in the City, The Wire, Band of Brothers* and, more recently *Boardwalk Empire* and *Game of Thrones.* In 2011, HBO received 104 Emmy nominations (television's Oscars)—more than any other network.

Today competition continues to change. Other cable stations (e.g., Showtime, AMC) are copying HBO's strategy (at a lower cost). Furthermore, net streaming—using the Internet to stream content directly to subscribers (a strategy pioneered by Netflix)—is attacking cable. HBO is responding by rolling out "HBO Go," an online video service that provides many shows and films directly to subscribers. HBO can do this because it owns the content. Thus, while HBO's early strategy developed its upstream supply chain, this latter strategy focuses on the downstream distribution chain. In both cases, HBO has gained competitive advantages by creating unique supply chain capabilities that enable it to offer value propositions desired by its critical customers.

operations strategy A set of *competitive priorities* coupled with supply chain structural and infrastructural design choices intended to create *capabilities* that support a set of *value propositions* targeted to address the needs of *critical customers.*

This chapter describes the decision processes and choices that make up an **operations strategy**, which is a set of *competitive priorities* coupled with supply chain structural and infrastructural design choices intended to create *capabilities* that support a set of *value propositions* targeted to address the needs of *critical customers.* Strategic decisions define the competitive objectives of an organization, establishing both the specific performance targets and the means by which the targets will be achieved.

To explain the process of strategic planning, this chapter will clarify the meanings of the terms *competitive priorities, capabilities, value propositions,* and *critical customers.* We begin by providing a brief overview of different levels of strategic planning in firms, and by describing how operations strategic choices create value. Then we describe a process of strategy development and deployment. The chapter concludes with a discussion of ways to communicate operations strategic choices and measure the performance of operational resources within the firm and across the supply chain.

Prepare

What are the different levels of strategic planning for businesses, and how are they interrelated?

Organize

Levels of Strategic Planning
- Corporate Strategic Planning
- Business Unit Strategic Planning
- Functional Strategic Planning

LEVELS OF STRATEGIC PLANNING

Within most firms, planning processes take place at several different levels. Internally, there is a hierarchy of strategic plans consisting of (1) corporate planning, (2) strategic business unit (SBU) planning, and (3) functional planning. These three levels should be closely linked (as shown in Figure 2-1) so that they are mutually consistent and supportive.

Strategic plans made at all levels need to take into account the business environment, including economic conditions, competitor actions, market opportunities, regulatory changes, and so on. A firm's culture also typically influences the objectives it sets and the decisions it makes in strategic planning. For example, one firm might be more aggressive or more risk averse than another firm.

In this section, we examine the objectives and interactions of strategic planning at the three levels. The remainder of the chapter focuses on operations strategy, one of the areas of functional strategy development.

Corporate Strategic Planning

LO2-1 Describe how operations strategy fits within a firm's overall strategic planning process.

Many firms are involved in more than one business. For example, General Electric operates more than 20 diverse businesses, from aircraft engines to financial services. Corporate strategic planning addresses the portfolio of businesses owned by a firm. Of the three

FIGURE 2-1 Strategic Planning Hierarchy

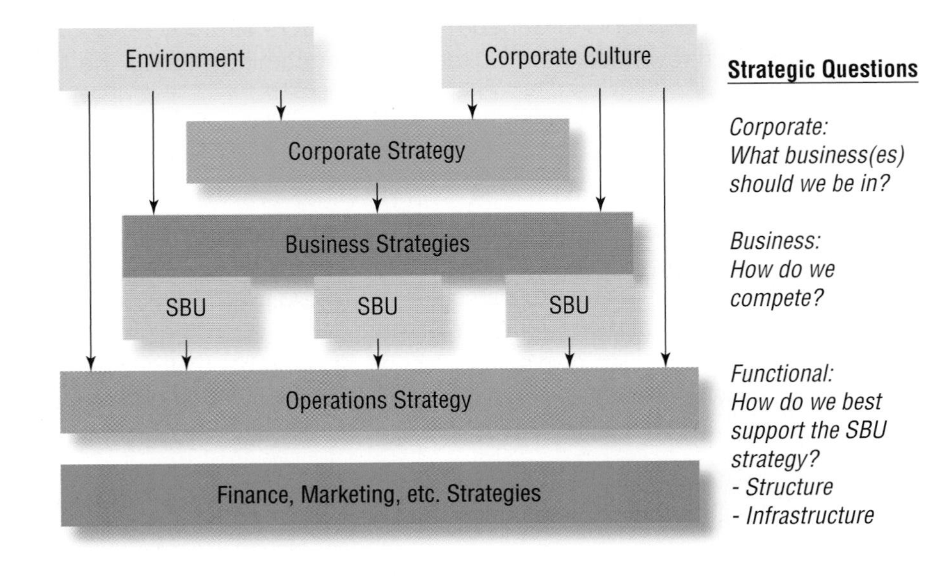

levels of strategic planning, corporate strategic planning is broadest in scope and the least constrained. Decisions made at this level limit the choices that can be made at lower strategic planning levels.

Essentially, a **corporate strategy** communicates the overall mission of the firm, and identifies the types of businesses that the firm wants to be in. For a large, multidivisional firm, key decisions in corporate strategy address what businesses to acquire and what businesses to divest. Corporate strategy typically covers a long time horizon, setting the overall values, direction, and goals of the firm as a whole. It also establishes how business performance will be measured and how risks will be managed.

corporate strategy Determines the overall mission of the firm and the types of businesses that the firm wants to be in.

Business Unit Strategic Planning

Because products and markets differ across business divisions, a separate management team (usually headed by a president or vice president) is usually needed to run each of these semi-independent organizations, or **strategic business units (SBUs)**. An SBU can be organized along product, market, or geographic dimensions.

strategic business unit (SBU) The semi-independent organizations used to manage different product and market segments.

Business unit strategy essentially deals with the question, "How should our business unit compete?" To answer this question managers make choices regarding what customers and market segments they will deem critical, what products to offer, and specifically how they will create advantages over the business unit's competitors. These choices collectively form the business model that the unit will pursue. There are numerous types of **business models**. For example, long ago Gillette developed the "razor and blades" business model—give away the razor but make your money on the replacement blades. Many businesses follow this same type of model (printers, industrial equipment). Dell successfully applied the "direct sales" business model in computers—sell computers directly to the end consumer. A "loyalty" business model rewards customers for continuing to deal with the firm. This model has been widely implemented in the airline industry (through the frequent flier program) and in the retail trade (e.g., as in Best Buy's "Reward Zone" program). Changes in technologies, competitors, and markets can at the same time destroy the viability of an existing business model while giving rise to new ones. Consider, for example, how customers' growing concerns over sustainability issues have opened up the possibility of new business models that offer organic and eco-friendly products. These kinds of changes make it important for operations and business strategy managers to continually evaluate their existing business models and possible business model innovations.

business unit strategy Determines how a strategic business unit will compete.

business model The combination of the choices determining the customers an SBU will target, the value propositions it will offer, and the supply chain/operations management capabilities it will employ.

sustainability

A business unit's strategy and business model are both shaped by the corporate strategy, by the specific requirements of the SBU's products and markets, and by the SBU's operating capabilities. One technique that managers use to assess these attributes is **SWOT** analysis (short for Strengths-Weaknesses-Opportunities-Threats). A SWOT analysis helps managers match strategies with strengths and opportunities while also reducing risks associated with weaknesses and threats. SWOT can be used in various ways—to kick off strategic thinking or as a serious detailed strategic assessment/planning tool. Questions often considered in a typical SWOT analysis are summarized in Table 2-1 on the next page.

SWOT A strategic planning technique to help firms identify opportunities where they can develop a sustainable competitive advantage and areas where the firm is significantly at risk.

Functional Strategic Planning

Every SBU consists of functional groups such as internal operations, marketing, accounting, engineering, supply management, logistics, and finance (to name a few). Each function has to generate a strategic plan—one that is coordinated with and supportive of the SBU plan. To that extent, the **functional strategy** must address certain critical questions:

functional strategy Determines how the function will support the overall business unit strategy.

- What specifically do we have to do to support the corporate and SBU strategies?
- What are the critical resources that we have to manage carefully if we are to achieve the corporate/SBU objectives?
- What metrics should we have in place to ensure we are making progress on these plans?

TABLE 2-1 SWOT Analysis—Example Questions

	Positive Factors	Negative Factors
Internal Factors	*Strengths* What advantages do we have? What do we do better than anyone else? What is our unique value proposition? What do our customers see as our strengths? What are our unique resources?	*Weaknesses* What could we improve? What should we avoid? What do our customers see as major weaknesses? What factors within our control prevent our ability to develop a competitive advantage? What limits our ability to pursue new strategies and opportunities?
External Factors	*Opportunities* What trends are we well positioned to take advantage of? What new technologies are we well positioned to take exploit? What new markets are opening up? What changes in social patterns and population profiles might provide opportunities for us?	*Threats* What obstacles do we face? What are competitors doing that could adversely affect us? Are there any changes in technology that could hurt us? What new governmental regulations or standards pose difficulties for us?

- What capabilities found in our function should be considered or recognized by the two higher stages of strategy?
- How should we coordinate our activities with those of the other functional areas within the firm to reduce friction and to enhance the ability of the firm/SBU to attain its overall objectives?

Of the three levels of strategic planning, the functional strategy is the most detailed, as well as the most constrained, as it must operate within a set of decisions made in the corporate and SBU strategic plans.

Prepare

How do managers develop an operations strategy?

Organize

DEVELOPING OPERATIONS STRATEGY: CREATING VALUE THROUGH STRATEGIC CHOICES

At the heart of operations strategy are choices made in three primary areas (see Figure 2-2):

- The *critical customer* is the customer or customer segment receiving priority because it is critical to the firm's current or future success.
- The *value proposition* is all of the tangible and intangible "benefits" that customers can expect to obtain by using the products offered by the firm.
- *Capabilities* are operational activities that the firm can perform well; these define the types of problems and solutions that operations can address proficiently.

Marketing managers often lead decision making regarding customers and products. However, decisions in all three areas listed above need to be jointly agreed upon by executives in marketing, operations, and financial functions of the firm, because the decisions are so interdependent. For example, the types of customers that are chosen determine the value propositions that are relevant, which in turn determine the types of capabilities that will

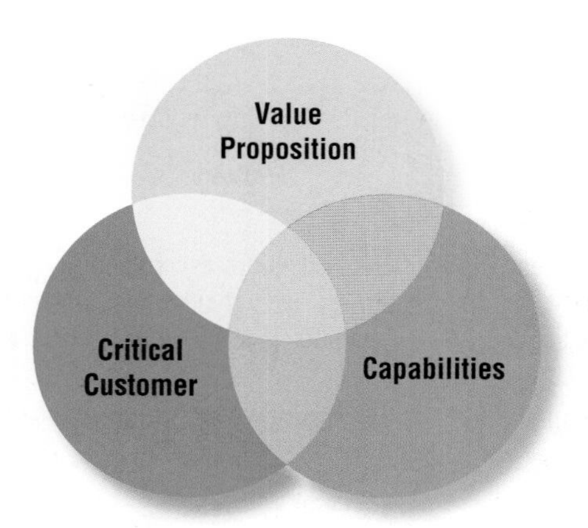

FIGURE 2-2 The Three Critical Elements of Operations Strategy

be required. As Figure 2-2 indicates, the objective of operations strategy development is to maximize the overlap among choices in these areas. The internal consistency of these choices is what ultimately creates value for the firm and for the marketplace.

To ensure that a high level of consistency is achieved, operations managers must develop a deep understanding of their critical customers. First, this means understanding what these customers value in products. Second, the critical features of the value proposition need to be communicated in terms that make sense to operations managers. Third, strategic initiatives must be launched. If the required operational capabilities do not exist, then they must be developed, or different customers and value propositions should be targeted. The following sections discuss these decisions in more detail.

LO2-2 Describe the need for "fit" between the critical customers, value propositions, and operations capabilities–the essential elements that define an operations strategy.

relationships

Critical Customers

The starting and ending point for effective and efficient supply chain operations is the customer. As defined in Chapter 1, **customers** are parties that use or consume the products of operations management processes. A customer is not necessarily the end user. For example, a store manager or purchasing agent who buys products for resale is a kind of customer (as noted in the Get Real box on the next page about Huffy Bikes). Almost all firms deal with multiple customers having varied desires and needs that change over time. Hence, each firm has to identify its **critical customers**.

customers Parties that use or consume the products of operations management processes.

Firms deem certain customers to be critical for a number of reasons. For example, a critical customer may be responsible for the largest current or future sales of the firm, or it may be the one with the highest prestige. In the automotive industry, Toyota is often such a customer because of its very high quality and performance standards; a supplier working with Toyota is often viewed as a top rated supplier.

critical customer A customer that the firm has targeted as being important to its future success.

Assessing Customer Wants and Needs

It is important for operations managers to know what product features and delivery terms critical customers consider important, what they are willing to pay, and what they consider acceptable. These product-specific traits can be classified into one of three categories:[1]

LO2-3 Describe customer-desired outcomes in terms of order winners, order qualifiers, and order losers.

- **Order winners**. These product traits cause customers to choose a product over a competitor's offering; for example, better performance or lower price. These are traits on which the operations management system must excel.
- **Order qualifiers**. These are product traits such as availability, price, or conformance quality that must meet a certain level in order for the product to even be considered by customers. The firm must perform acceptably on these traits (i.e., the products must meet certain threshold values of performance), usually at least as well as competitors' offerings.

order winners Product traits that cause a customer to select one product over its competitors.

order qualifiers Product traits that must be met at a certain level for the product to be considered by the customer.

[1]Terry Hill, *Manufacturing Strategy: Text and Cases* (New York: McGraw-Hill/Irwin, 2000).

GET REAL

Huffy Bikes Targets Its Critical Customer

Huffy Bikes markets a line of inexpensive, durable bicycles sold through mass merchandising channels (e.g., Toys R Us, Meijers, Walmart) to a wide range of customers (parents, students, young children). To succeed in this very crowded and competitive market, Huffy recognized that its critical customer was not the end user—the person who bought the bike. Buyers of Huffy bikes are not particularly concerned with the Huffy brand; what they buy is determined more by availability and price. Two groups of managers determine availability—the store manager (who determines what products are stocked), and the purchasing manager (who determines what product lines will be bought). Consequently, Huffy has targeted these two groups as their critical customers. They have tried to make the purchasing manager's job easier by reducing the transactions and effort required to buy from Huffy. In addition, they have focused on communicating to the store manager the financial benefits of selling Huffy bikes, including improved sales and profits, and fewer returns because of the ease with which Huffy bikes are assembled. By focusing on these critical customers, Huffy has strengthened its market position in a very competitive field.

order losers Product traits that, if not satisfied, cause the loss of either the current order or future orders.

- **Order losers**. Poor performance on these product traits can cause the loss of either current or future business. For example, when an online retailer fails to deliver an order in a timely manner, a customer might cancel the order and refuse to place orders in the future.

student activity

Think about a recent purchase you made. What were the order-winning traits that influenced your decision? What traits were necessary for you to even consider buying one product over another?

In reviewing these categories, there are several factors to remember. First, order winners and order qualifiers form the basis for customers' expectations. Order losers, in contrast, result from customers' actual experiences with the firm and its operations management processes. They represent the gap between what the firm delivers and what customers expect. Second, order winners, order qualifiers, and order losers vary by customer. An order winner to one customer may be an order qualifier to another. Third, these traits vary over time. An order winner at one time may become an order qualifier at another point in time. As can be seen in the Get Real box on the next page about the Bosch CS20 circular saw, being able to identify and act on order winners offers the firm a critical strategic advantage.

Value Propositions and Competitive Priorities

value proposition A collection of product and service features that is both attractive to customers and different than competitors' offerings.

To attract critical customers, the firm must formulate and implement a **value proposition**, a statement of product and service features that the firm offers to its customers. A value proposition needs to be both attractive to customers and different from what is offered by the firm's competitors. For example, Walmart's value proposition has been to offer everyday low prices on a wide variety of products. The value proposition is critical because it not only defines how the firm competes, it also determines the types of products that the firm will (and will not) offer.

GET REAL

Bosch CS20: Finding a New Order Winner by Changing the Way Customers Cut Straight Lines

Managers at Bosch Power Tools faced a challenging problem—how to design and deliver a better circular saw. Such saws are found in nearly every handyman's workshop, and over the years their designs had become fairly standard. Consequently, there were few features except price to differentiate competing products. Bosch managers looked at circular saws from an outcome perspective. They saw that many of the circular saws on the market did a poor job of helping users attain a simple but critical outcome—cutting straight lines. Customers were frustrated because the lines were inevitably covered up by either sawdust or by the footplate of the saw itself. Bosch's solution? First, they installed a powerful fan to vacuum dust off of the cut line. Second, they replaced the steel footplate with an acrylic one that allowed users to see the line as they cut. The result: an award-winning product that customers want to buy.[2]

[2]For more information about this innovative product, see: www.newwoodworker.com/reviews/bcs20rvu.html.

A well-designed value proposition has four characteristics:

1. It offers a combination of product features that customers find attractive and are willing to pay for.
2. It differentiates the firm from its competition in a way that is difficult to imitate.
3. It satisfies the financial and strategic objectives of the firm.
4. It can be reliably delivered given the operational capabilities of the firm and its supporting supply chain.

The value proposition reflects the order winners, order qualifiers, and order losers for a critical customer segment. Thus, the combination of traits contained in the value proposition greatly influences the competitive priorities for all the related operations across the supply chain. In order for operations managers to reliably deliver a given value proposition, they must appropriately align these product outcomes into operational competitive priorities. They need to clearly specify what the operations management system must do better than its rivals, what it must do at least as well as its rivals, and what it must avoid doing (because it will jeopardize customer satisfaction and orders). Competitive priorities, along with associated performance measures and targeted objectives, provide a language for managers to communicate the value proposition in operational terms.

Typically, competitive priorities address both product-related outcomes and process-related capabilities. Once these priorities are established, they form the basis for performance measurement.

Product-Related Competitive Priorities

LO2-4 Explain what profuct-related and process-related operational competitive priorities are, and how they are related to competitive advantage.

Product-related priorities address the customer's problem to be "solved" and are communicated in terms of the quality, timeliness, and cost of the product "solution." As Table 2-2 shows, each of these three product-related competitive priorities involves various dimensions. There are many different aspects of quality that may be important to customers, for example. Each dimension potentially appeals to different types of customers; each also

TABLE 2-2 Dimensions of Product-Related Competitive Priorities

Quality	Timeliness	Cost
Performance (superior attributes)	Reliability (on-time)	Purchase (price)
Features (unique attributes)	Speed (lead time)	Transaction (acquisition costs)
Conformance (no defects)	Availability (always on or in-stock)	Maintenance/repair
Reliability (long time to failure)		Operating (cost of consumables)
Durability (long useful life)		Salvage/disposal
Aesthetics (appeal)		
Service/support (ancillaries/ intangibles)		
Perceived quality (image)		

may require different capabilities of supply chain operations. Because it is difficult, if not impossible, to simultaneously deliver the highest levels of all of these product attributes, operations managers need to communicate which attributes are of highest priority and lowest priority, respectively, in accordance with the order winners and qualifiers of the targeted critical customers. These priorities form the basis on which performance measures can be formulated and implemented.

Quality

quality A product's fitness for consumption in terms of meeting customers' needs and desires.

A product's **quality** is its fitness for consumption by the customer who bought it. It is an assessment of how well the customer's expectations are met. Some dimensions of quality are often viewed by customers as minimum requirements (order qualifiers) for most products. For example, poor conformance quality (many defects) is not tolerated in most markets. At the same time, superiority in other dimensions of quality can significantly differentiate a product. For example, a well-known brand can create a perception of quality that differentiates a product. Firms that produce high-quality products have many advantages including improved company reputation and easier selling, the elimination of time-consuming activities and costly resources required to correct quality-related problems, and employees who are motivated by the knowledge that they produce great products.

Timeliness

timeliness The degree to which a product is delivered or available when the customer wants it.

lead time The amount of time that passes between the beginning and ending of a set of activities.

time to market The total time that a firm takes to conceive, design, test, produce, and deliver a new or revised product for the marketplace.

Dimensions of product **timeliness**, the degree to which the product is delivered or available when the customer wants it, can serve as order winners or qualifiers, depending on the situation. On-time delivery of a product is in many cases an order qualifier (or order loser, if the product is late). Similarly, availability of a good or service is usually a qualifier. For example, grocery store customers expect products to be on the shelf. On the other hand, **lead time**, the amount of time that passes between the beginning and ending of a set of activities, is often an order winner, especially for nonstandardized products. There are two types of lead time that are typically important. The first, **time to market**, is the total time that a firm takes to conceive, design, test, produce, and deliver a new or revised product for the marketplace. This lead time is a once-in-product-life-cycle event. That is, a firm may spend 18 months designing a car and getting the supply chain ready for production, but once production has been ramped up and the cars begin rolling off the assembly line, there is no significant design product lead time needed to make subsequent copies of that car. Time to market can be an order winner if the new product offers features or performance that is not available in other products.

The other type of lead time is **order-to-delivery lead time** for an existing product. This encompasses the time interval starting at the moment that the customer places an order for a product, including the time required to place and fulfill an order, and ending at the moment that the customer takes delivery of the product. In services, customers often judge the value of a service largely on the operation's order-to-delivery performance. For example, a dining experience is marred by slow service, or it is irritating when a salesperson seems to have gotten lost in the back room. Order-to-delivery lead time is also important for highly customized, made-to-order products; a piece of customized jewelry, for example.

order-to-delivery lead time The time that passes from the instant the customer places an order for a product until the instant that the customer receives the product.

Cost

It is well known that people like to get things cheaply but they do not like "cheap things." This statement describes both the attraction and the problem of emphasizing cost as the firm's major source of value. Customers typically want at least the same product performance for a lower cost, not simply less for less. A competitive priority placed on **cost** usually treats certain dimensions of quality and timeliness as givens and focuses on reducing cost.

cost The expenses incurred in acquiring and using a product.

Different types of costs may be more or less important to customers, depending on the product type. Purchase cost (price) is usually most important for consumer goods. However, maintenance and operating costs are often much more important for customers buying long-life items such as industrial machinery. Disposal costs are becoming more important considerations for durable goods (cars, washing machines) due to environmental concerns.

sustainability

Process-Related Competitive Priorities

LO2-4 Explain what profuct-related and process-related operational competitive priorities are, and how they are related to competitive advantage.

While product-related competitive priorities focus on the outcomes that customers experience directly, process-related competitive priorities pertain to how supply chain operations are run over time. In addition to managing for cost, timeliness, and quality, operations managers place priorities on longer-term initiatives affecting areas such as flexibility, innovation, and sustainability. Capabilities developed in these areas contribute to supply chain operations' abilities to create new solutions and to respond effectively to changes in technology, competition, and the overall operating environment.

Innovation

Innovation refers to both radical and incremental changes in processes and products. Especially in highly industrialized countries, innovation is an important way to create new demand. Through the creation of new and improved products, firms can appeal to new market segments, or take away business from competitors. Innovation is a response to emerging customer needs, or it can even be a way to create new needs. For example, with the creation of the iPod, Apple combined existing technologies in a way that created a new business for selling online music and other content.

innovation Both radical and incremental changes in process and products.

Traditional views of innovation tend to distinguish between product innovations and process innovations. In reality, product and process innovation are usually interrelated. Product innovations sometimes arise from process innovations, and process innovations (at least incremental ones) are usually required to support any new product innovation. Accordingly, operations managers located in various functions throughout the supply chain typically have two sets of innovation-related priorities: support product innovation and drive process innovation. In companies that pursue a low-cost strategy, most innovation tends to be incremental in nature, whereas technology-leading companies tend to pursue more radical product and process innovations.

It is important to realize that process innovations can be technological or organizational in nature. Operations managers are always looking for new technologies to enhance their capabilities. However, organizational innovations can also be effective in creating new efficiencies or new market opportunities. IKEA provides a good example of a company

GET REAL

IKEA: Growth through Supply Chain Innovation[3]

IKEA is a franchise-based chain of household furnishing stores that does business in 31 countries. At the heart of IKEA's success is a simple but powerful value proposition: "We shall offer a wide range of well-designed, functional home furnishing products at prices so low that as many as possible will be able to afford them." To achieve this proposition, IKEA's designers have focused on delivering products that can be assembled by the customer; this is done by selling the products in "knocked-down" form, which is cheaper to store and ship. For example, an unassembled, knocked-down bookcase is more compact and cheaper to ship than a preassembled bookcase. In addition, by using flat-pack distribution methods, the products can be easily transported by either car or public transport (e.g., bus) from the store to the consumer's home. This innovation required changes in product designs, but it also required changes in suppliers, transportation modes, and scopes of responsibilities. Some of the supply chain responsibility has been shifted to the customer, for example.

[3]For more information, see www.ikea.com © INTER IKEA Systems B.V. 2003–2009.

that has developed a strong value proposition by changing the organizational relationships in the supply chain that affect how its products are stocked and shipped (see the Get Real box above).

Flexibility

flexibility An operation's ability to respond efficiently to changes in products, processes (including supply chain relationships), and competitive environments.

Flexibility is generally defined as an operation's ability to respond efficiently to changes in products, processes (including supply chain relationships), and competitive environments. The words *respond efficiently* mean that an operation can cope with a wider range of changes faster or with less cost than competitors can.

With decreasing product life cycles, rapidly changing technologies, and growing pressure to meet localized, specific customer needs, flexibility has become an important priority for many companies today. Firms that have flexible operations have many opportunities to create value for their customers in unique ways. The potential for niche marketing is increased when operations can produce in small lots and deliver unique specifications quickly and inexpensively. Firms can command premium prices when their operations can be tailored to meet specific needs or when they can accommodate last-minute changes in demand.

There are many types of flexibility, including short-term, operational flexibilities such as labor flexibility, as well as longer-term, strategic flexibilities such as the ability to introduce new products quickly. Consequently, it is important for operations managers to clearly define and focus on the types of flexibility they want to develop.

sustainability Maintaining operations that are both profitable and nondamaging to society or the environment.

risk management Developing operations that anticipate and deal with problems resulting from natural events, social factors, economic issues, or technological issues.

Sustainability and Risk Management

sustainability

In recent years, operations managers have begun to address *sustainability* and *risk-related* issues more explicitly as competitive priorities. With **sustainability**, the focus is on maintaining operations that are both profitable and nondamaging to society or the environment. A primary focus of **risk management** is to build operations that anticipate and

GET REAL

Seven Cycles: Building a Bicycle Your Way

"One bike. Yours." This isn't simply a slogan. It represents the heart of Seven Cycles' philosophy about who they are and what they do. And nowhere is this philosophy more apparent than in their manufacturing processes. At Seven Cycles, each craftsperson focuses on only one bike at a time. Unlike most bikes, which are produced on an assembly line or in batches—destined for a warehouse or a shop's inventory—a Seven Cycles bike is created specifically for a given customer: one machinist; one welder; one finisher; one bike.

Frame building at Seven Cycles is both an art and a science, requiring a special harmony between creative enthusiasm and manufacturing discipline. However, there's no room for interpretation when it comes to quality. Each stage in manufacturing—from materials selection to the application of the frame's finish—employs standards for precision unparalleled in the industry.

Seven Cycles owns several proprietary technologies that allow them to hold tolerances at much stricter levels than their competition. In addition, they have extremely rigorous quality inspection routines and supporting technologies. By developing these capabilities, Seven Cycles is aiming at delivering a riding experience that is different, and unmatched by any competitor.

Source: www.sevencycles.com/home.php. Copyright © 2009 Seven Cycles, Inc.

deal with problems resulting from natural events (e.g., earthquakes), social factors (e.g., strikes), economic issues (e.g., a bankruptcy of a critical supplier), or technological issues (e.g., finding a major flaw in software). In addition to these operational types of risks, safety and security are growing key concerns, especially as supply chain operations become more global and dispersed. A famous example is provided by Mattel in 2007. The company recalled over nine million toys because of concerns over lead in the paint that was introduced by the actions of a lower-tier supplier located in China. Firms that provide food and drugs are intensely concerned with contamination, either accidental or intentional.

Nancy Nord, commissioner of the U.S. Consumer Product Safety Commission, announces the Mattel toys recall. Mattel is the world's largest toy company.

Governments, social groups, and consumers are placing increasing demands on companies to be more socially responsible. In response, operations managers must place priorities on preventing environmental or human damage as a result of operations. This means an increasing emphasis on reduction of biohazards, and on using materials and processes that use less energy, require less input, and generate less waste. Operations managers also want to ensure that workers are treated fairly and given a safe work environment. These priorities have serious implications for decisions affecting all aspects of operations, beginning with supplier selection and buying decisions, and ending with product disposal.

The increasing importance of sustainability has caused many companies to adopt a **"triple bottom line"** approach to performance measurement. Using this approach, managers prepare three different measures of profit and loss. The first is the

student activity

Examine the websites of companies such as Heineken and Sweet Leaf Tea (of Austin, Texas), or pick a company of your interest. What elements do they include in their "triple bottom line" measures?

triple bottom line An approach to corporate performance measurement that focuses on a company's total impact measured in terms of profit, people (social responsibility), and the planet (environmental responsibility). Also referred to the as the **TBL**, the **3BL**, or the **3Ps**.

traditional measure of performance—monetary profit; the second is an assessment of its "people account"—how socially responsible the firm has been throughout its operations; the third is the company's "planet account"—how environmentally responsible the firm has been. Together, these three Ps (Profit-People-Planet) capture the total impacts of a firm's business.

Capabilities: Strengths and Limitations of Supply Chain Operations

capabilities Unique and superior operational abilities that stem from the routines, skills, and processes that the firm develops and uses.

The third element of delivering value, as identified in Figure 2-2, is capabilities. **Capabilities** are unique and superior operational abilities that stem from the routines, skills, and processes that the firm develops and uses. As we stated earlier, it is difficult for an operations system to simultaneously deliver high levels of performance on many different dimensions. Thus, it is important to develop capabilities in the few areas that are of greatest strategic value for the firm.

It is difficult to describe capabilities directly without describing them in terms of outcomes such as quality, flexibility, and so on. Usually, abilities to deliver superior performance come from investments and developmental efforts in one or more of the following areas:

- *Processes*—specialized routines, procedures, and performance measurement systems that guide operational activities.
- *Planning systems*—access and development of sources of information, and use of proprietary decision support systems and processes.
- *Technology*—proprietary usage of hardware or software that enables the firm to do things differently and/or better than competitors.
- *People and culture*—skills, associated training programs, and cultural norms for the company that produce better motivation and performance. The impact of culture must be recognized at both a corporate and at a national level.
- *Supply chain relationships*—unique and exclusive relationships with customers and suppliers that are unmatched by competitors.

core capabilities The skills, processes, and systems that are unique to the firm and that enable it to deliver products that are both valued by the customer and difficult for competitors to imitate.

The Seven Cycles operation discussed in the Get Real box on the previous page presents a good example of how both company culture (philosophy) and special technologies can create unique capabilities.

Honda Airplane Powered by Honda Jet Engine

Sometimes certain capabilities become so unique and valuable to a firm that they are considered to be "core," that is, central to the very existence of the firm. **Core capabilities** are the skills, processes, and systems that are unique to the firm and that enable it to deliver products that are both valued by the customer and difficult for competitors to imitate. These are strategically critical, and are often the source of a stream of new products and market opportunities. For example, over the years Honda has developed successful products in a wide range of very different markets—motorcycles, power generators, cars, marine engines, lawn mowers, snow blowers, and now jet airplanes. In each market, Honda moved from being an outsider to become one of the major players. Honda succeeded because its core capability is its ability to design and build high-efficiency, low-vibration motors and engines. Such engines are common to each of the markets that Honda has entered.

Other examples of core capabilities include Apple's focus on ease of use and system integration, 3M's specific knowledge of substrates, coatings, and adhesives, and Pixar's creativity in using visual technologies to tell interesting stories.

It goes without saying that every firm should have at least one core capability. Furthermore, it should be aware of what its core capabilities are. Finally, it should seek to refine and exploit its core capabilities.

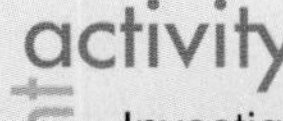

student activity

Investigate recent developments such as the Honda Jet Engine and the new Honda Insight. What is common about these developments? What is different?

Maintaining the Fit between Customer Outcomes, Value Propositions, and Capabilities

At the heart of operations strategy is the notion of **fit**. Fit exists when operational capabilities support the value proposition and the outcomes desired by critical customers. If strategic planning processes are neglected, over time the dynamics of changing market trends, technologies, and competition can destroy the fit between customer-desired outcomes, value propositions, and capabilities. A company can find itself with capabilities and value propositions that no customers care about, either because it made improper investments, or because existing customers changed, or both. For example, a firm may find itself using technologies that have become obsolete. Under such conditions, management has three options: (1) live with the mismatch (which means reduced profits and potential opportunities for the competition); (2) change the critical customers to those who value the solutions provided by the firm; or (3) change the operational capabilities. Each option requires top management involvement, resources, and time. Most often, changing operational capabilities is the hardest of the changes to make because the development of capabilities typically takes large investments made over long periods of time. Developing effective strategic planning processes that maintain fit is therefore imperative for a firm's survival over time.

fit The extent to which there is alignment between the firm's operational capabilities, its value proposition, and the desires of its critical customers.

The Get Real box below provides an excellent example of how Five Guys Burgers and Fries has maintained the fit between its capabilities, customers, and value proposition by refusing to offer products that are inconsistent with its core capabilities.

Prepare

How do operations managers execute their strategies?

Organize

Deploying Operations Strategy: Creating Value through Execution
- Feedback/Measurement: Communicating and Assessing Operations Strategy
- The Strategic Profit Model
- The Balanced Scorecard
- The Supply Chain Operational Reference Model

DEPLOYING OPERATIONS STRATEGY: CREATING VALUE THROUGH EXECUTION

Once managers have established the objectives and goals of operations strategy, they must convert them into operating realities. Strategy deployment consists of two interrelated activities:

- *Execution*—to carry out plans and initiatives in order to deliver the realized value to customers.
- *Feedback/measurement*—to assess, communicate, and manage performance in ways that capture lessons learned and focus attention on areas needing improvement.

GET REAL

Don't Expect a Salad at Five Guys Burgers and Fries

Don't expect to have chicken, milk, or a salad at Five Guys Burgers and Fries—it won't happen. That is not what is at the heart of this fast-growing restaurant chain. Founded in 1986, Five Guys began franchising in 2002. By the end of 2011, Five Guys had grown to almost 1,000 stores and over $1 billion in sales. The secret to its success: offer the customer

Continued

Continued

a great hamburger truly done his/her way (with over 15 different toppings) and lots of fresh French fries. Also encourage employees to be personable and to avoid scripted greetings. Trust the cook to know when the burger is done, not some system. Finally, keep everything simple and stress the details. With a simple menu, errors or poor quality become obvious. Chicken and salad are considered distractions and not what Five Guys sells. Milk—well, when kids go out for a Five Guys burger, they want a treat. As the founder, Jerry Murrell, observed, Five Guys does not serve milk because kids don't actually like milk; kids like Five Guys because it is a pleasure.

Operations strategy is ultimately defined by what is done over time, not by what is written down as plans. Managers have to assign resources to tasks, identify the relative priorities of competing orders, and monitor the progress of orders and work as they flow through the system. In addition, managers have to devise and implement strategic initiatives needed to make planned changes to supply chain operations a reality. For example, an operations strategy might depend heavily on making changes such as installing new equipment or systems, implementing a training program, adopting a new management approach, acquiring or divesting facilities, or downsizing the workforce.

relationships

Strategic initiatives typically address operations that are spread across internal functions as well as across organizations making up the supply chain. Initiatives need to be coordinated across internal supply management, logistics, marketing, sales, and engineering groups in order to ensure that consistent decisions are made. Similarly, including supply chain partners in strategic planning and execution creates opportunities to exploit the complementary skills and assets of the partnerships. However, this also increases the complexity of planning and reduces the amount of direct visibility and control that managers have over operational outcomes. Thus, decisions and strategic initiatives must be formed in ways that integrate the concerns of internal operational activities with the concerns of suppliers and customers, without creating too much dependence on external partners. Decisions must also address the physical, structural elements of operations as well as the intangible, infrastructural elements. Table 2-3 lists decision areas that define how an operations strategy is deployed. Taken together, these decisions define the operations management system of the firm, how it is structured, how it operates, and how it is evaluated. These decisions are discussed in more detail in various chapters throughout this book.

The first four decision categories presented in Table 2-3—*capacity, facilities, technology,* and *supply chain network*—are *structural* in nature. They affect strategy and the physical operations management system. Once made, decisions in these areas act as constraints, determining what the operations management system can and cannot do well. Altering these decisions often requires significant investments and lots of time—often years. The remaining four decision areas—*workforce, production planning and control, product/process innovation,* and *organization*—are *infrastructural* in nature. Decisions in these areas determine what is done, when it is done, and who does it. The decision areas are closely interrelated. For example, decisions regarding the supply chain network also affect the type of information technology that must be in place, how activities are scheduled, and how people are recruited and evaluated. Because these areas are interrelated, managers who make a decision affecting one area must consider the impacts of the decision on the other areas. Equally important, decision makers must consider how operations decisions affect decisions in other areas such as marketing, finance, and human resources. Table 2-3 indicates some of the other functional areas likely to be affected by each of the decisions in operations management.

LO2-5 Explain how strategic performance can be assessed both operationally and financially by using the strategic profit model, the balanced scorecard, and the supply chain operational reference model.

Feedback/Measurement: Communicating and Assessing Operations Strategy

Performance measurement plays very important roles in operations strategy. First, performance measures communicate strategic intentions, as formulated at the corporate/SBU/functional level, to operational personnel. Second, performance measures control operations. By establishing metrics, a performance measurement system establishes how

TABLE 2-3 Strategic Decision Areas in Operations Management

Decision Domain	Operations Management Issues Considered	Other Functional Groups Involved
Capacity	Amount of capacity, timing of changes in capacity, type of capacity used	Finance, Marketing
Facilities	Size of facilities, location of facilities, specialization of what the facilities do	Finance, Marketing
Technology	Hardware: equipment types, automation, linkages Information systems and software: equipment, type, purpose of packages, interfaces/linkages	Finance, Engineering, Information Technology, Human Resources
Supply chain network	Supply network: sourcing policies, level of vertical integration/outsourcing, network structure and assignment of responsibilities, supplier relation-ships, segmentation of supply base Customer/distribution network: transportation modes, network structure and assignment of responsibilities, customer relationships, sales and delivery channels	Finance, Engineering, Marketing, Sales
Workforce	Skill level, training, wage policies, employment security, incentives and reward systems	Human Resources
Production planning and control	Planning procedures and decision rules; controls on cost, workflow, and quality; performance measurement; market orientation (make-to-order, make-to-stock)	Finance, Human Resources
Product/process innovation	Improvement programs, problem-solving procedures, knowledge management, change management, new product launches, management of intellectual property	Engineering, Human Resources
Organization and management	Centralization, authority hierarchy, roles of staff people, intra-firm relationships, performance metrics	Human Resources, Marketing

performance is measured, the standard against which performance is to be compared, and the consequences of exceeding or not meeting the standard. In doing so, performance measures tell workers what things they need to do well, and how well they need to do them. In these ways, performance measures help to ensure alignment between the actions of operations managers and the objectives stated in corporate/SBU/functional strategies.

relationships

Different functional groups tend to measure performance in different ways. For example, finance and top managers look at performance using financial measures (e.g., return-on-sales, asset turnover); operations managers look at performance using operational measures (e.g., lead time, quality, cost). Consequently, performance measurement must include a mix of financial and operational measures. In the following sections, we examine three different measurement approaches frequently used in operations strategy.

The Strategic Profit Model

Also known as the DuPont Model, the **strategic profit model (SPM)** shows how income and balance sheet data are interrelated, and how operational changes affect the overall performance of a business unit. Thus, the SPM converts operational changes (often measured in time, defects, labor hours, etc.) into financial impacts (measured in dollars and returns).

strategic profit model (SPM) A model that shows how operational changes affect the overall performance of a business unit.

As Figure 2-3 shows, the SPM focuses on return on assets (ROA), a metric that indicates how profitably a firm uses its assets. ROA is calculated by multiplying the net profit margin (defined as a percentage) by asset turnover. The net profit margin measures the percentage of each dollar that is kept by the firm as net profit. The asset turnover measures how efficient management was in using its assets. For example, an asset turnover of 4 indicates that for every \$4 of sales, management had invested only \$1 in assets. The net profit margin and asset turnover capture different aspects of performance. Net profit margin is influenced by issues such as sales volume, operating costs, and expenses. Asset turnover reflects issues such as the amount of inventory needed (a key concern of operations managers, and one of the major assets controlled by operations). In general, the higher the ROA, the better the level of performance.

The SPM is useful for evaluating both operational and marketing-based plans and actions, and answering "what-if" questions such as: What if we reduced fixed expenses by

FIGURE 2-3 Strategic Profit Model[4]

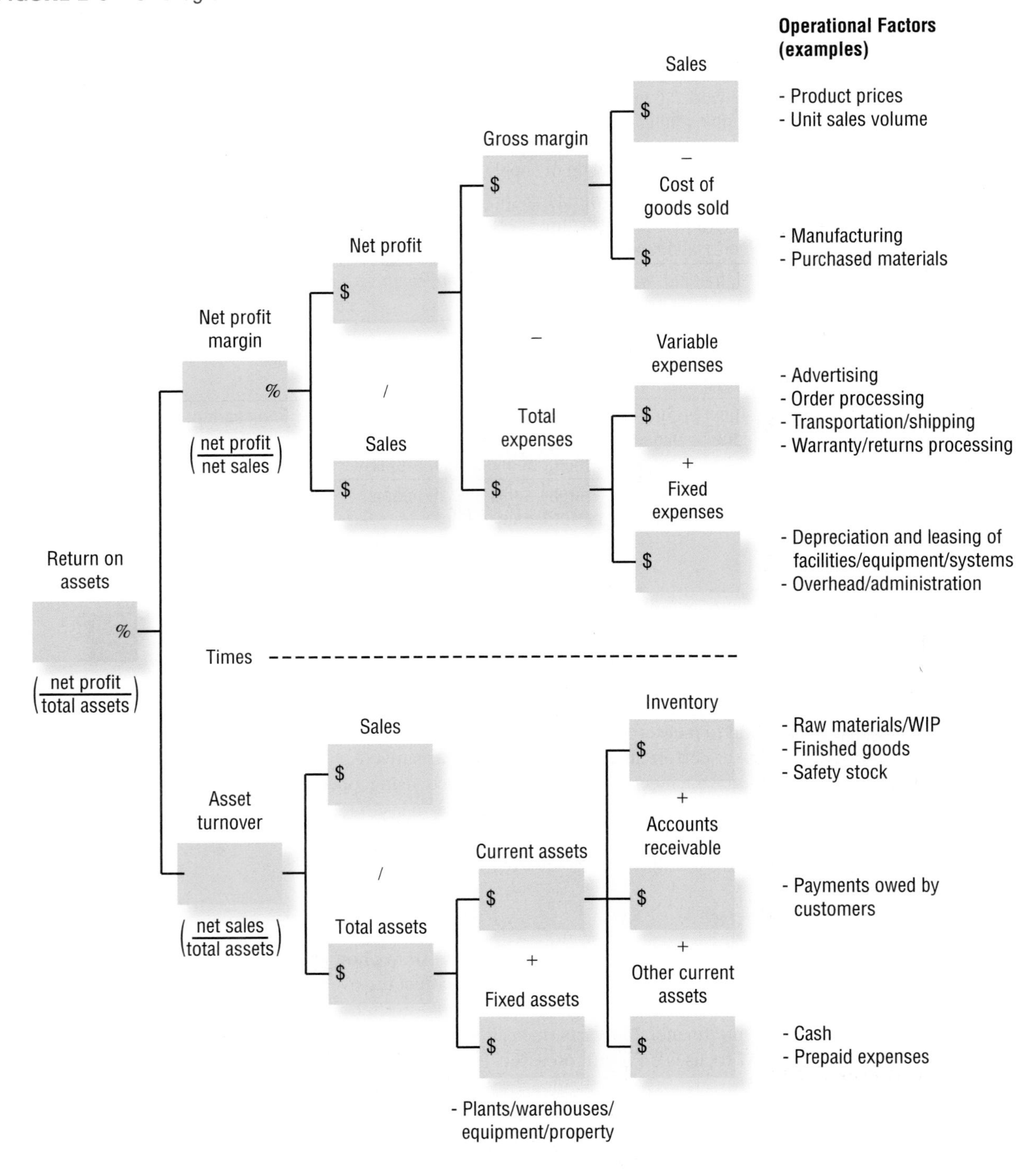

[4]Note that in the SPM, *cost of goods sold* refers to the actual costs incurred in procuring and making products and services, while *expenses* refers to the costs of supporting sales and business transactions.

10 percent? What would be the overall impact on ROA? To answer this question, we would enter the dollar values of operational changes in the categories shown on the right side of the SPM. The calculations in the SPM then reflect the impacts of these changes on financial measures shown on the left side of the SPM (which are of interest to top managers). Consider the following example of this type of analysis.

EXAMPLE 2-1

Suppose that the director of marketing has approached you, as a member of the top management team, with a suggestion that appears very attractive. The proposal begins by noting that because demand is down, the firm (and its supply chain) has much unused capacity. Happily, the marketing group has identified a new potential customer segment. Unlike existing customers (who are price sensitive and who buy large quantities of fairly standard products), these new customers will likely order smaller quantities more frequently. The new customers are also likely to want to make last-minute changes to order sizes, due dates, and product mix. Your current operating system is not really set up to accommodate such changes. However, the marketing director feels that the prices these customers are willing to pay will provide gross margins (30% as compared to the 10–15% currently being given by existing customers) that should be high enough to offset any operational problems. The chief financial officer has stated that, in order to enter any new market, it must be expected to generate at least a 25 percent return on assets (ROA).

Given the information provided below, would you recommend accepting the marketing director's proposal?

Category	Estimated First Year Impact	Comments
Sales	$420,000	
Cost of Goods Sold	$294,000	30% gross margin
Variable Expenses	$45,000	Need more for small batch shipping and expediting
Fixed Expenses	$40,000	More inspections needed
Inventory	$200,000	Need safety stock to ensure timely delivery
Accounts Receivable	$120,000	Customers tend to pay on longer cycles
Other Current Assets	$0	No change
Fixed Assets	$15,000	Need special fixtures and tooling

The strategic profit model is well suited for this type of analysis. A gross margin of 30% seems attractive. However, to make a good decision we need to factor in other required changes. By entering the data into the SPM (as can be seen in Figure 2-4 on next page), we find that expected ROA is 20.19%—less than the 25% hurdle rate. Consequently, we would recommend that the marketing request be rejected.

The SPM model is relatively simple and straightforward to use. The data required for the model are readily available in most firms with well-developed financial and accounting systems. The model reduces all aspects of performance into one number, ROA, making it simple to compare performance across different time periods and different divisions. It helps direct management's attention to those areas that represent opportunities or problems. Since the SPM is a system of metrics, it shows how performances in different areas of the firm are related. This helps managers avoid decisions that might improve performance in one area to the detriment of other areas.

FIGURE 2-4
SPM Analysis for Example 2-1

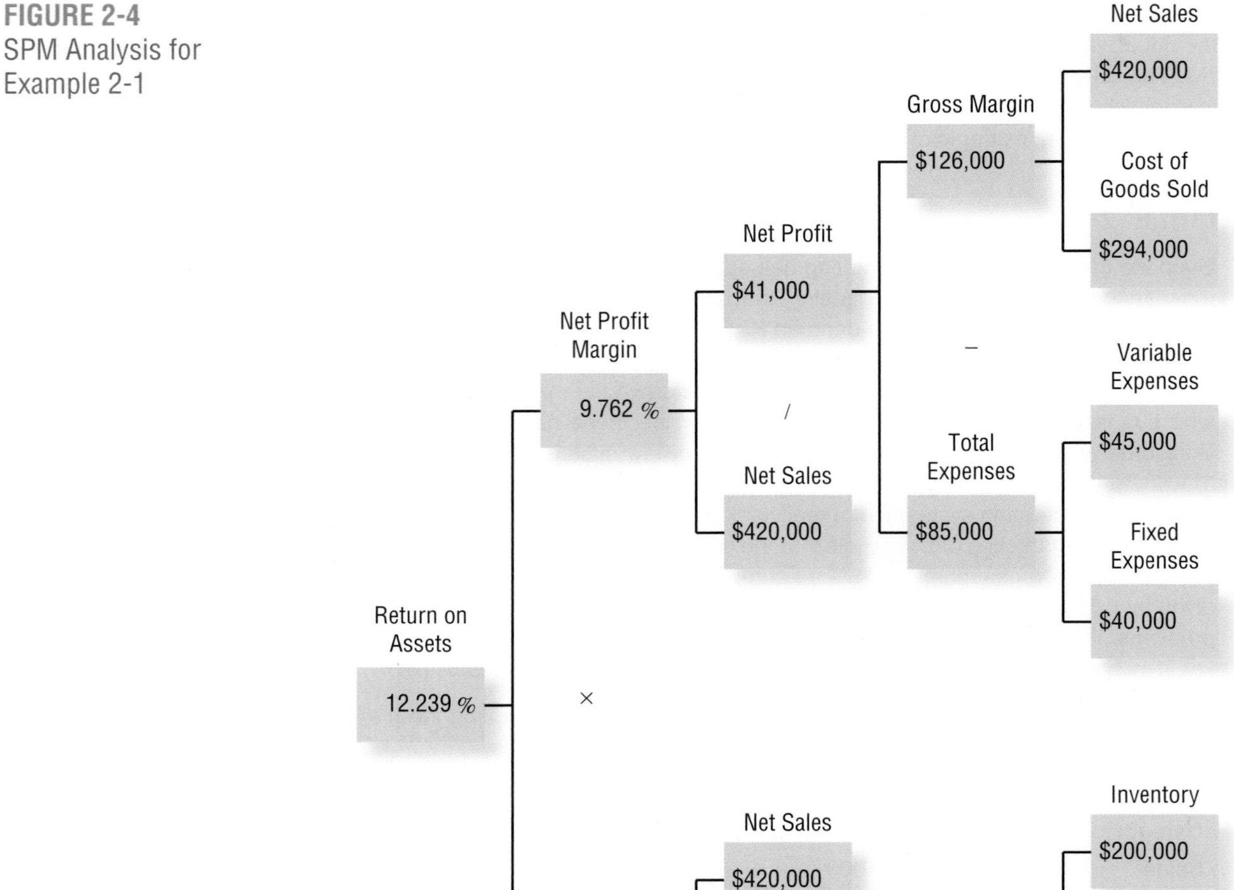

The Balanced Scorecard

balanced scorecard An integrative approach for developing strategic, organizational-level metrics.

Like the strategic profit model, the **balanced scorecard**[5] is an integrative approach for developing strategic, organizational-level metrics. Unlike the SPM, the balanced scorecard encourages the use of a mix of financial metrics and nonfinancial, operational metrics. The balanced scorecard seeks to integrate these various metrics into a meaningful whole, creating a strategic framework for action. The balanced scorecard approach assumes that success is based on balanced management of activities in four major areas: financial, internal

[5]Robert S. Kaplan and David Norton, "The Balanced Scorecard—Measures That Drive Performance," *Harvard Business Review*, January/February 1992, pp. 71–79.

business processes, learning and growth, and customer satisfaction. In each of these areas, metrics should address a central question (see Figure 2-5). For each question, the balanced scorecard approach requires the development of objectives, measures for each objective, target performance levels for each measure, and planned initiatives for reaching each target.

The balanced scorecard approach can be used as both a strategic planning tool and a strategy deployment tool. That is, it provides a mechanism by which focused short-term plans and improvement initiatives are aligned with long-term strategic objectives. As a framework for translating strategy into operational terms, the balanced scorecard helps to:

- Set direction and communicate specific objectives and goals.
- Define measures that indicate degree of achievement of specific objectives.
- Determine the relative importance of the targets of opportunities for improvement.
- Maintain consistency and alignment between the corporate-level objectives and the operational initiatives, and the objectives/initiatives and strategic objectives and annual goals.

As Figure 2-5 suggests, the balanced scorecard helps to create a cycle of planning, action, assessment, and feedback. It also prevents management from focusing on one area (e.g., financial performance) to the detriment of the other three areas. To succeed financially, the firm must focus on serving its critical customers through appropriate processes. It must also invest in the future because what works today may not work in the future.

The Supply Chain Operational Reference Model

With the advent of supply chain management, managers have increasingly sought to coordinate activities spanning customer and supplier organizations. In the late 1990s a group of industrialists from about 70 leading companies created an organization called the "supply chain council." Working together they developed the **supply chain operational reference model** (commonly known as the SCOR model).[6]

supply chain operational reference model (SCOR) A model for assessing, charting, and describing supply chain processes and their performance.

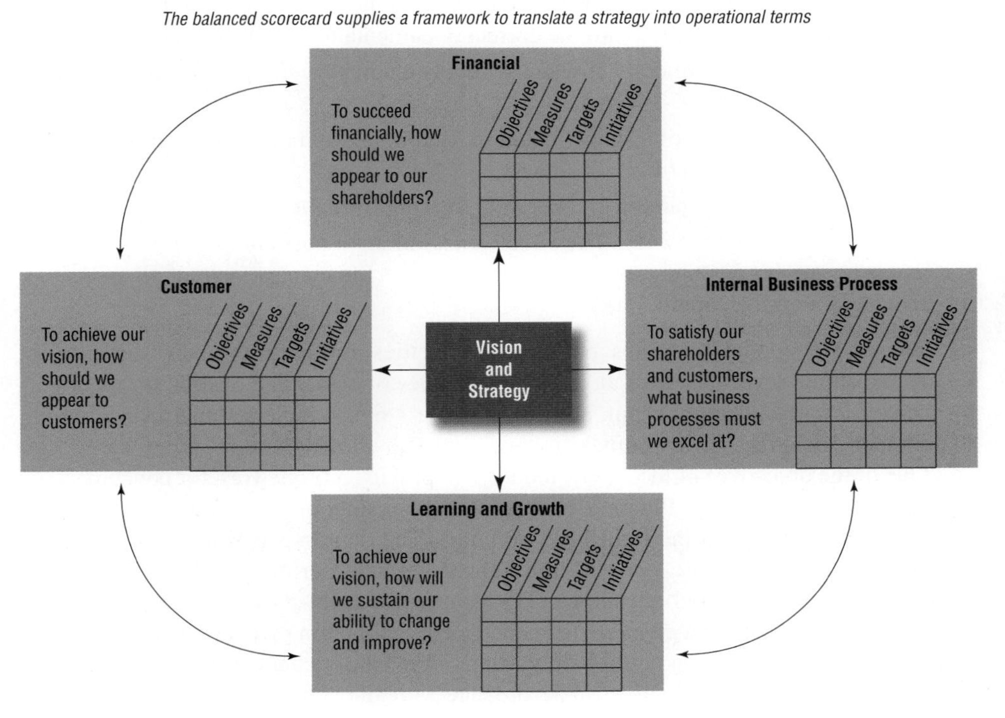

FIGURE 2-5 Balanced Scorecard

Source: Robert S. Kaplan and David Norton, *The Balanced Scorecard* (Cambridge, MA: Harvard Business School Press, 1996). Reprinted with permission of Harvard Business School Press from Robert Kaplan and David Norton, *The Balanced Scorecard—Measures That Drive Performance,* © 1996 by the Harvard Business School Publishing Corporation. All rights reserved.

[6]See www.supply-chain.org for more information on the supply chain council and the SCOR model.

FIGURE 2-6
Performance Metrics in the SCOR model

Source: Elaine Reichardt and Lindsay Jackson Nichols, "SCOR Your ISO Certification," *Quality* 42, no. 2 (February 2003), p. 44. Copyright © 2003 American Society for Quality. All rights reserved.

	Performance Attribute or Category	Level of Performance Metrics	Actual	Performance Versus Competitive Population: Parity Median of statistical sample	Advantage Midpoint of parity and superior	Superior 90 Percentile of Population	Value from Improvements
EXTERNAL	Supply Chain Delivery Reliability	Delivery Performance to Commit Date	61%	85%	90%	95%	$30mm revenue
		Fill Rates	66%	94%	96%	98%	
		Perfect Order Fulfillment	51%	80%	85%	90%	
	Supply Chain Responsiveness	Order Fulfillment Lead Time	27days	7 days	5 days	3 days	$30mm revenue
	Supply Chain Flexibility	Supply Chain Response Time	97days	82 days	55 days	13 days	Key enabler to cost and asset improvements
		Production Flexibility	45days	30 days	25 days	20 days	
INTERNAL	Supply Chain Cost	Cost of Goods	78%		63%	57%	$22m indirect cost
		Total Supply Chain Cost	19%	13%	8%	3%	
		SG&A Cost	20%	20%	17%	14%	
		Warranty / Returns Processing Costs	8%	4%	2%	1%	
		Value Added Employee Productivity	$122K	$156K	$306K	$460K	
	Supply Chain Asset Management Efficiency	Cash-to-Cash Cycle Time	196 days	80 days	46 days	28 days	$7m capital charge
		Inventory Days of Supply	77 days	55 days	38 days	22 days	
		Asset Turns	6.10	8.00	12.00	19.00	
SHARE-HOLDER	Profitability	Gross Margin	26%	34%	43%	51%	
		Operating Income	11%	13%	17%	21%	
		Net Income	3%	6%	10%	14%	
	Effectiveness of Return	Return on Assets	9.6%	18%	22%	27%	

The SCOR model includes more than just metrics; it provides tools for charting and describing supply chain processes. It also describes supply chain management best practices and technology. However, we will focus only on the metrics portion of the model.

The SCOR model identifies basic management practices at different levels of operation. For example, "level 1" processes include plan, source, make, deliver, and return. One of the basic tenets of the SCOR model is that metrics should cascade hierarchically from one level to the next. At each of the levels addressing the supply chain, SCOR addresses five basic dimensions of performance. They are:

- *Delivery reliability:* The performance of the supply chain in delivering the correct product, to the correct place, at the correct time, in the correct condition and packaging, in the correct quantity, with the correct documentation, to the correct customer.
- *Responsiveness:* The velocity at which a supply chain provides products to the customer.
- *Flexibility:* The agility of a supply chain in responding to marketplace changes to gain or maintain competitive advantage.
- *Costs:* The costs associated with operating the supply chain.
- *Asset management efficiency:* The effectiveness of an organization in managing assets to support demand satisfaction. This includes the management of all assets: fixed and working capital.

The SCOR model identifies performance metrics for each of these dimensions. Figure 2-6 shows level 1 metrics along with examples of actual and desired levels of performance for a given supply chain. Note that Figure 2-6 also includes metrics addressing shareholder concerns such as profitability and return on assets.

One of the objectives of the SCOR model is to provide a framework for benchmarking and for deploying strategy. Figure 2-6 illustrates the results of a benchmarking analysis with the data provided in the right-hand columns. The data indicate the level of performance necessary to be on a par with the industry middle performers, as well as levels required to gain differential advantage. The data in the right-most column indicate the impact of improvement in a given performance metric, either on revenues, costs, or investments. This type of analysis could help partners in a supply chain to plan and prioritize operational improvement initiatives in accordance with an overall business strategy.

CHAPTER SUMMARY

This chapter has introduced the operations strategic planning process within the context of supply chain management. In discussing this process, the following points were made within this chapter:

1. Strategic planning defines the specific types of value that the firm will deliver to its customers. It takes place at three levels. Corporate strategy identifies the business units to be included in the firm. Business unit strategy defines how the business will compete. Operations strategy identifies the priorities, capabilities, and resource deployments needed to support the business strategy and associated value proposition. These three levels of strategic planning should be integrated, with planning taking place from the top down, while execution takes place from the bottom up.
2. Operations strategic planning is driven by the business model—an integrative, systematic view of how the SBU generates value. This planning process begins with the critical customer. It translates the demands of this customer into meaningful terms, using the concepts of order winners, order qualifiers, and order losers.
3. The business model and operations strategy bring together three critical elements: critical customers, value propositions, and operations capabilities. The fit between these elements defines the effectiveness of the strategy.
4. Competitive priorities address product-related issues (quality, lead time, cost) and longer term process-related issues (innovation, flexibility, sustainability, and risk management).
5. In developing the future capabilities of the supply chain, operations managers must know what their firm's existing core competencies are (because these must be protected).
6. Extending strategy development to multiple functions and supply chain partners, operations managers must make critical strategic decisions about what is to be done, with what resources, when activities are to take place, and who is responsible.
7. Critical to strategic success is the ability of the firm to effectively integrate and maintain fit among the desires of critical customers, the firm's value proposition, and its operational capabilities.
8. Strategic assessment tools like the strategic profit model (SPM), balanced scorecard, and supply chain operational reference model (SCOR) help link and integrate strategic plans, operations strategies, operational actions, and performance.

KEY TERMS

order-to-delivery lead time 33
order winners 29
quality 32
risk management 34
strategic business unit (SBU) 27
strategic profit model (SPM) 39
supply chain operational reference model (SCOR) 43
sustainability 34
SWOT 27
timeliness 32
time to market 32
triple bottom line 36
value proposition 30

DISCUSSION QUESTIONS

1. Why should the firm never outsource its core capabilities? What happens if the firm is approached by a supplier who is willing to supply goods and services based on these core capabilities at a significantly lower price? What should the firm do?
2. Apply the corporate/SBU/functional planning hierarchy introduced in this chapter to your university/college or business. What would be the equivalent to corporate planning? SBU planning? Functional planning?
3. How would you define capabilities within a school or business?
4. When can a consumer be a critical consumer? In other words, when does it make sense to focus on consumers such as retail stores, distributors, or buyers, rather than on the end consumer?
5. A critical concept introduced in this chapter was that of the value proposition. Explore two competing products (e.g., RIM's the BlackBerry, and Apple's iPhone). Identify the underlying value propositions present in these products and how this proposition is evident in the resulting products.
6. Core capabilities are critical issues in operations management. Are there any instances in which a firm's core capabilities can be a liability rather than an asset?
7. Fit is critical to the development and maintenance of a successful operations strategy. Suppose that we are faced with a firm in which there is a lack of fit between the outcomes desired by the critical customer, the value proposition, and the firm's capabilities. What options are available to the firm in the short term when dealing with this lack of fit? What is the impact of the lack of fit? What are the implications of the firm trying to improve the fit?
8. Suppose that you are the owner of a pizzeria that is located near a university or college. How could you use the concepts of order winners, order qualifiers, and order losers to help develop and implement an attractive business model?
9. Why should metrics be regarded as primarily methods of communication? Think about the relationship between a metric, the strategy, and the task being carried out by an operations person.
10. A metric consists of three elements: the measure, the standard (what is expected), and the reward. Why are all three elements critical? What happens to the effectiveness of a metric when one of these three elements is missing?
11. What is the impact of sustainability on the business model? How does it affect issues such as the order winners, order losers, and order qualifiers? How does it affect the identification of the critical customer? When addressing this question, look up such products as Chrome or Timbuk2 for bags or Teva or Timberland for shoes.
12. Why is there a need for the four dimensions of the balanced scorecard?

13. As North American firms increasingly turn to product innovation, the management and protection of intellectual property becomes an important issue. Discuss how intellectual property considerations can affect such areas in supply chain strategy as:
    a. Supplier relationships.
    b. Supplier contracts.
    c. Supplier location.
    d. Attractiveness of vertical integration.
14. Elm Furniture Company, a medium-sized, publicly traded manufacturer of wood-based office and home furniture systems, has agreed that its major goal should be to "Become recognized as a value and social leader in the wood furniture industry." Consistent with this macro goal, Elm Furniture has identified the following specific objectives:
    - Become recognized as a leader in the use and application of environmentally responsible practices and systems.
    - Achieve sales growth averaging 5 percent more than that of the industry average.
    - Keep stock price stable relative to that of the industry average.
    - Reduce cost and waste at all levels of the firm.
    - Be recognized as a design leader.

    Using these goals and the balanced scorecard approach, what would the corresponding goals and metrics be for the following?
    a. Operations management/manufacturing.
    b. Product engineering and design.
    c. Sales and marketing.
    d. Purchasing/supply chain management.
15. In this chapter, you were introduced to Huffy Bicycles. You were also told that the critical customers were store managers and purchasing managers. Now, assume that Huffy decided to target first parents and then children as their critical customers (using the information provided below). What impact would this shift in critical customer have on you—how would you design the resulting operations management system (including the supplier base)?

Critical Customer	Order Winners	Order Qualifiers
Parent	Acquisition price Durability (has to be passed down) Ease of maintenance (does not cost much to maintain over the summer)	Safety Availability
Child	Style (colors) Can be easily customized Newness (I have the first one on the block) Imitation (it is what I see others having on television)	Availability Maintenance

16. Using a SWOT analysis, can the operations management system be a strength? Can the operations management system be a weakness? Provide examples.

SOLVED PROBLEM

Suppose you have been asked to determine the return on net worth for Great Northwest Canoe and Kayak, a small manufacturer of kayaks and canoes, located near Seattle, Washington. For this task, you have been given the following information:

Categories	Values
Sales	$32,000,000
Cost of goods sold	$20,000,000
Variable expenses	$ 4,000,000
Fixed expenses	$ 6,000,000
Inventory	$ 8,000,000
Accounts receivable	$ 4,000,000
Other current assets	$ 3,000,000
Fixed assets	$ 6,000,000

What is the return on assets for Great Northwest Canoe and Kayak?

Solution:
To address this question, we must first calculate net profit margin and the asset turnover. This can be done using the structure for the SPM found in Figure 2-3.

Gross Margin = 32,000,000 − 20,000,000 = 12,000,000
Total Expenses = 6,000,000 + 4,000,000 = 10,000,000
Net Profit = Gross Margin − Total Expenses = 2,000,000
Net Profit Margin = Net Profit/Sales = 6.25%

Current Assets = Inventory + Accounts Receivable + Other Current Assets = $15,000,000
Total Assets = Current Assets + Fixed Assets = $21,000,000
Asset Turnover = Sales/Total Assets = 1.52

Return on Assets = Net Profit Margin × Asset Turnover = 6.25 × 1.52 = 9.5

What areas should we as operations managers focus on if our goal is to improve ROA?

Solution:
We can see that the largest asset under our control is inventory. By reducing inventory we can improve the ROA. (It is left up to the student to prove this. One way of doing this is to examine the impact on ROA of a $1 million reduction in inventory or a $1 million increase in inventory.)

PROBLEMS

1. Given the following information:

Categories	Values
Sales	$48,000,000
Cost of goods sold	$24,000,000
Variable expenses	$ 8,000,000
Fixed expenses	$ 8,000,000
Inventory	$ 6,000,000
Accounts receivable	$ 3,000,000
Other current assets	$ 4,000,000
Fixed assets	$10,000,000

   a. What is the net profit margin for this firm?
   b. What is the asset turnover?
   c. What is the return on assets?
   d. What is the size of the total assets used by the firm?

2. You are the operations manager for a small kayak and canoe manufacturer (Valley Kayaks) located on the Pacific Northwest (Oregon). Lately your company has experienced product quality problems. Simply put, the kayaks that you produce occasionally have defects and require rework. Consequently, you have decided to assess the impact of introducing a total quality management (TQM) program. After discussing the potential effects with representatives from marketing, finance, accounting, and quality, you arrive at a set of estimates (contained in the following table). Top management has told you that they will accept any proposal that you come up with PROVIDED that it improves the return on assets measure by at least 15 percent. Would you go forward with this proposal to improve quality?

Category	Current Values	Estimated Impact of TQM
Sales	$2,000,000	5% + (improvement)
Cost of goods sold	$1,500,000	0%
Variable expenses	$ 300,000	8.25% − (reduction)
Fixed expenses	$ 100,000	0%
Inventory	$ 300,000	25% −
Accounts receivable	$ 100,000	0%
Other current assets	$ 500,000	0%
Fixed assets	$ 400,000	0%

3. As the operations manager for Valley Kayaks (as described in the previous problem), you find yourself faced with an interesting situation. Marketing has informed you that they have lost a number of sales because of a lack of inventory. Kayaks, being seasonal in nature, have to be in stock at your dealers if they are to be sold (customers are not willing to wait). The director of marketing proposes that you increase inventories by 25 percent (a major investment to you). She has also given the information in the following table (top next page). How would you assess this proposal from marketing? Would the projected change in ROA justify the inventory investment?

Category	Current Values	Proposed Impact of Inventory Increase
Sales	$2,000,000	25% + (improvement)
Cost of goods sold	$1,500,000	0%
Variable expenses	$ 300,000	10% − reduction (why?)
Fixed expenses	$ 100,000	15% + (increase)
Inventory	$ 300,000	25% +
Accounts receivable	$ 100,000	0%
Other current assets	$ 500,000	0%
Fixed assets	$ 400,000	0%

4. Noble Bicycles of Glen Arbor, Michigan, is a small batch manufacturer of high-end bicycles. That is, it typically builds bicycles in batches of one to three units. Quality is high, only to be expected when the typical bicycle frame costs $2,500 and up. Yet, profits have not kept pace with top management's expectations. Management has set a goal of generating a minimum of 25 percent return on assets. As a result of a corporate SWOT analysis, management has identified one critical threat: the costs at Noble are simply too high—and one important opportunity: because of the flexibility of operations and the experience of the design team, many of whom are either professional or serious amateur bicyclists, Noble is well positioned to become an innovation leader. A top management team consisting of the marketing director, the finance director, the corporate vice president, the purchasing director, and the director of operations management has developed two alternative strategies: (1) focus on reducing costs through the application of lean systems and procedures (Chapter 8), and (2) focus on product innovation (Chapter 4). To assess the two approaches, the team has generated the following table.

Category	Current Values	Lean Proposal	Innovation Proposal
Sales	$12,500,000	$12,500,00	$16,000,000
Cost of goods sold	$10,625,000	$9,375,000	$12,000,000
Variable expenses	$ 750,000	$ 650,000	$ 800,000
Fixed Expenses	$ 750,000	$ 600,000	$ 750,000
Inventory	$ 1,250,000	$ 900,000	$ 1,500,000
Accounts Receivable	$ 600,000	$ 500,000	$ 600,000
Other Current Assets	$ 600,000	$ 600,000	$ 750,000
Fixed Assets	$ 600,000	$ 600,000	$ 600,000

a. What is Noble Bicycles' current ROA?
b. How does the lean proposal affect operations at Noble Bicycles?
c. How does the innovation proposal affect Noble Bicycles (why)?
d. Which proposal would you recommend to top management? Why?
e. How much of a change in sales would be required in order to make the returns of the two proposals equivalent?
f. What are the strategic risks of these proposals?

CASE

Otis Toy Trains Explores the Supply Chain

Otis Toy Trains of Minneapolis, Minnesota, was a landmark company in the toy business. Since the 1900s, it had been responsible for building electrical and steam-driven toy trains. Since the 1950s, Otis trains had developed a major presence on children's television shows. Every person (especially boys) knew about Otis toy trains and nearly everyone wanted one. For many kids growing up in the 1960s to the 1980s, waking up on Christmas day and finding an Otis toy train set under the tree was a dream come true. However, the 1990s had not been good to Otis Toy Trains. The preferences of many children had changed. Instead of toys, what many children wanted was a game playing system (like Sony's PS2 or Microsoft Xbox or Nintindo's GameBoy Advanced). After a lot of investigation and assessment, the management at Otis had decided to reorient the product and the market. Consequently, it decided to target the adult male customer in the 30 to 50 year age bracket. This market was selected for several reasons. First, they had grown up with Otis toy trains and, as a result, Otis had excellent brand recognition among these buyers. Second, since Otis had decided to maintain the bulk of its production facilities in the areas around Minneapolis (the major production facility was located in Rochester, Minnesota), it needed a buyer who was willing to pay the premium now demanded by Otis Toy Trains for its products. Adult males in the 30 to 50 year age bracket typically had the income that supported luxury buys such as the Otis toy trains. Finally, the new target market was attractive because they tended to buy more than one system and they tended to buy a large number of accessories with their toy train purchases.

To sell to this new market, Otis introduced in 1995 the Otis Premium Trains of the Past series. This was a line of highly detailed, highly accurate trains drawn from critical points in North American history. The first launch consisted of the De Witt Clinton Rocket (the first train operated in the United States), the Abraham Lincoln train (a train model based on the train coaches that were used to transport the body of the recently assassinated President Lincoln from Washington, DC, to Springfield, IL, for final burial), the Zephyr (the famous streamlined train that ran between Chicago and Denver during the 1930s), and the Orange Blossom Special. Launched in limited numbers, this first series was an unqualified success. Subsequent launches were almost as successful. Over this time, the designers at Otis Toy Trains developed and refined the skill of identifying attractive train series and of designing products that were detailed, attractive, accurate, and highly evocative of past times.

By 2010, however, Otis Toy Trains found itself faced by the challenge of dealing with increasing labor costs. It was during this time period that the Joyous Luck Prosperity Toy Company (JLPTC) of China approached the management of the Otis Toy Train Company with a proposal that had already secured the support of Otis corporate accountants. They proposed to work closely with the designers of the Otis Toy Train Company with the goal of taking over the bulk of production of the Otis Premium Trains of the Past series. What JLPTC offered Otis was a landed price per unit that was between 40 and 60 percent lower than current manufacturing costs. This was a price that was too good to pass up.

Questions

1. Assume that you are hired as a consultant to help Otis Toy Trains. What recommendations would you give to the management of Otis regarding the attractiveness of this proposal?
2. Assume that Otis decided to accept this proposal. Identify and discuss the most appropriate relationship that you would recommend for Otis and JLPTC. What risks are present in this proposal? How could Otis protect itself from these risks?

CASE

Steinway & Sons Piano

Steinway pianos have long been the premier brand among serious pianists. Franz Liszt called his Steinway "a glorious masterpiece." Gioacchino Rossini, a 19th-century composer, described the Steinway sound as "great as thunder, sweet as the fluting of a nightingale." In short, Steinway's product is the piano of choice for the vast majority of concert artists.

From the beginning, Steinways were a work of art. Jose Feghali, a classical pianist, illustrated this point when he remarked, "With the best pianos, you can walk into a room with 10 pianos and it's like playing 10 different instruments." The prices of the 5,000 or so pianos that Steinway produces each year range from $10,000 for an upright to $62,000 for a special-order concert grand piano.

In the 1990s, Steinway & Sons encountered some problems. John and Robert Birmingham purchased the firm in a $53.5 million leverage buyout deal. John's previous experience involved making plastic windows for envelopes. Robert's most recent experience was with a mail-order business selling products with bear themes. Robert Birmingham said that they were delighted with the purchase because they viewed Steinway as a "great opportunity" given the firm's "great name and great tradition."

Steinway's craft-driven organization had not fared too well under its previous owner, CBS. The turmoil resulting from frequent management changes had reduced the consistency of Steinway's cherished reputation. Dealers complained that Steinways weren't of the same quality any more—they were often badly tuned and had sloppy finishes. Finally, in 1978, CBS hired a long-time piano industry executive who helped restore much of Steinway's reputation.

Now, a new set of outsiders owned them. That the owners liked classical music did not assure Steinway's 1,000 employees that they knew how to make classic quality pianos. To make matters worse, the Birmingham brothers were now talking about using their "extensive manufacturing experience" to streamline operations. One commented that the operation was "too reliant on a few craftsmen."

Soon modern manufacturing methods crept into the Steinway operation. A computer control system was introduced to keep track of parts and inventory. Eight million dollars was invested in new equipment to make the quality of small parts, such as piano hammers, more consistent. The loose-leaf binders that specified how pianos were to be built were replaced with engineering drawings. By the late 1980s, Steinway had entered the 20th century. John Birmingham lamented: "The music industry is made up largely of people enamored of music and the instruments they make, but they don't necessarily have great management skills."

As Steinway became more scientific, some stakeholders began to be concerned. Many of the older craftsmen found the new work environment not to their liking, and they left. Equally important, some within the industry began to be concerned that Steinway pianos were losing their personality. Some dealers and their customers even began to question the quality of Steinway's latest pianos. One classical pianist fumed that he had to use a 30-year-old Steinway because he could not find a new one he liked. Another dealer hired a consultant to review the quality of the pianos he had purchased from Steinway. He claimed that the soundboard, a key contributor to a piano's quality, had developed cracks. The consultant reported that this problem "indicated inadequate or improper controls over wood moisture content during various stages of manufacture." Subsequent study indicated that Steinway's new production quotas might have caused workers to pull wood from the conditioning rooms before it was ready to be bent, say, into a piano.

Questions

Assume that you are hired as a consultant to help Steinway deal with these latest problems. How could you use a value-driven approach to help this firm address these problems? What would you recommend?

CASE

Trail Frames Chassis

Trail Frames Chassis (TFC) of Elkhart, Indiana, is a major manufacturer of chassis for the motor home and van markets. Since it was founded in 1976 by two unemployed truck-manufacturing engineers, TFC has grown into one of the major suppliers in this market. Success in the motor home and van markets is difficult because of the constant rate of change taking place. Increasingly, motor homes and vans are bought by people in their late 40s to 60s. What these people want is a motor home that rides like a car. They are willing to pay for innovations such as ABS (antilock breaking systems), assisted steering, GPS, voice-activated control, and computer-balanced suspension. TFC produces a pusher type of chassis. This is one powered by a diesel engine in which the engine is located in the rear. While expensive to build, this design offers the customer a large number of advantages (no tunnel for the transmission, reduced engine noise, better handling). However, these chassis are used in motor homes that are very expensive ($150,000 and up). TFC builds its chassis for the large manufacturers—companies such as Winnebago, Airstream, and Gulf Stream. In general, these companies place orders for small quantities (5 to 10 in a batch). Many of the units in a batch are customized to a specific customer's requirements.

TFC has become successful because of its ability to develop new lines of designs in a timely fashion. These designs build on TFC's extensive experience with motor home users. They also build on TFC's knowledge of new technological advances and its ability to incorporate these advances into its designs. As a result, TFC has become the technological leader in this market. It is generally recognized that no one in the industry can match TFC's design and marketing knowledge base.

TFC is proud of its ability to design and build highly customized chassis. As John Stickley, its young and aggressive chief operating officer, is proud of pointing out, "Trail Frames has never met a customized chassis it didn't like." Complementing this focus on customization and speed, TFC has developed a culture of doing anything necessary to meet the needs of the customer. Changes are often introduced on the fly with an engineer taking a change down to the assembly line. In many cases, the bills of materials (the recipes for what goes into a given chassis) that were generated initially in engineering do not agree with the components and parts actually put into the chassis.

This approach has served TFC well for a number of years. However, recently sales for TFC have begun to level off. After visiting numerous customers in the field, John Stickley identified what he thought was the reason for this leveling off—the market for high-end, customized motor home chassis had been effectively saturated. There were only just so many customized motor homes that people wanted. Several of the major customers for TFC had strongly hinted that there was another market that TFC could enter that was consistent with its design strengths and its reputation.

Many of TFC's customers had noticed that there was a significant gap between the high-end motor homes that TFC served and the low-end market. The high-end consisted primarily of "pushers," and it began at $150,000; the low-end consisted of "pullers," and these products sold for between $35,000 and $70,000. That is, a motor home manufacturer would take an existing truck body (which consisted of the front end and the cab) and mount on it a motor home body. As can be seen, there was a significant gap between the two markets.

One of TFC's major customers, Gulf Stream, approached TFC with an interesting proposal. It wanted TFC to design and build a low-end pusher chassis for this market. This chassis would go into a motor home that would cost between $75,000 and $90,000. In contrast to the current line of products, this chassis would not be customized. Rather, once the chassis was designed, it would not be changed. Production runs would go up from batches of five to batch runs of 100. Critical to success in this market would be cost and conformance to the schedule. If TFC could be the first to produce such a chassis, it would own the market. The financials were very attractive. Theoretically, it seemed easy for TFC to enter this market. All that had to be done was to take an existing chassis and to take out the "costs" by using less-expensive components. While TFC had never built such a chassis, there was no reason why it should not work. The only danger that the people at TFC could identify was that once it entered this market, it would be potentially competing with such firms as Ford, GM, and Toyota (major suppliers of the existing chassis). However, these firms supplied pullers (a chassis with the engine in front)—not pushers, like the proposed TFC product. In light of these issues, John was not sure whether this was the right market for TFC.

Questions

1. Compare the order winners, order qualifiers, and order losers for the customized chassis and for the proposed TFC chassis. To what extent are these factors similar?

2. What type of strategic consistency would you expect to find in TFC for its existing customized chassis? Would this be the same type of consistency that you would find with the proposed chassis?
3. Evaluate the proposal for this new line of chassis. Is this a business that TFC should get into? If yes, why? If no, why not?
4. What would you recommend to John Stickley that TFC should do to increase its sales and to stimulate demand?

SELECTED READINGS & INTERNET SITES

Fine, C. H. *Clockspeed.* New York: Perseus Books, 1998.

Hayes, R.; G. Pisano; and S. Wheelwright. *Operations, Strategy, and Technology: Pursuing the Competitive Edge.* Hoboken, NJ: John Wiley & Sons, 2005.

Hill, T. *Manufacturing Strategy: Text and Cases.* New York: McGraw-Hill/Irwin, 2000.

Mckeown, M. *The Truth About Innovation.* London: Frances Pinter, 2008.

Melnyk, S. A.; E. W. Davis; R. E. Spekman; and J. Sandor. "Outcome Driven Supply Chains." *Sloan Management Review* 51, no. 2 (2010): 33–38.

Ulwick, A.W. *What Customers Want: Using Outcome-Driven Innovation to Create Breakthrough Products and Services.* New York: McGraw-Hill, 2005.

Apple Inc. **www.apple.com**

General Electric Company **www.ge.com**

Honda Motor Company, Inc. **www.honda.com**

Honda Aircraft Company, Inc. **www.hondajet.com**

Inter IKEA Systems B.V. **www.ikea.com**

Seven Cycles, Inc. **www.sevencycles.com**

PART 2

FOUNDATIONS OF OPERATIONS MANAGEMENT

		relationships	sustainability	global
3	Managing Processes and Capacity	X	X	
	Supplement: Process Mapping and Analysis	X	X	
4	Product/Process Innovation	X	X	X
5	Manufacturing and Service Process Structures	X		X
6	Managing Quality	X	X	X
	Supplement: Quality Improvement Tools			
7	Managing Inventories	X		X
8	Lean Systems	X		X

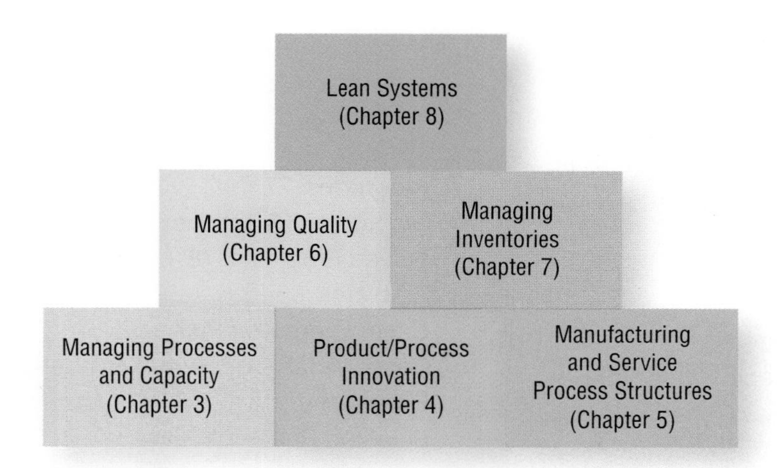

Just how do organizations work? If you had to name the six things that every operations manager should know, what would they be? The chapters in Part 2, Foundations of Operations Management, explain the basic principles of how organizations operate. Each chapter addresses a fundamental building block of knowledge that describes how to design and manage operational processes.

A process is a system of structured activities that use resources to transform inputs (such as energy, materials, and information) into valuable outputs.

As the figure above indicates, the first three chapters in Part 2 of the book are about processes. **Chapter 3** discusses the principles that govern how processes work, and the accompanying supplement provides tools for analyzing any process. **Chapter 4** describes how product designs and supporting operational processes are invented and developed. **Chapter 5** describes how resources and technologies are typically organized in different types of processes.

The other three chapters in Part 2 discuss fundamentals and ways to manage resources in operations so that objectives are achieved. The two overarching goals of operations management are to do things effectively and to do things efficiently. **Chapter 6** describes ways to ensure high product quality, a measure of effectiveness. The accompanying supplement shows tools and techniques for analyzing and improving product quality. **Chapters 7** and **8** describe ways to improve the efficiency of materials usage (inventories) and of process execution (systems). Together, these three chapters identify cutting-edge ways to make materials, people, and processes as effective and efficient as possible.

3 Managing Processes and Capacity

CHAPTER OUTLINE

LEARNING OBJECTIVES *After studying this chapter, you should be able to:*

LO3-1 Understand the importance of processes and process thinking to operations and supply chain management.

LO3-2 Define the various components that make up processes, including types of inputs and outputs.

LO3-3 Distinguish between operational, tactical, and strategic capacity planning.

LO3-4 Estimate the capacity and utilization of a process.

LO3-5 Explain the impacts of bottlenecks, variance, and other factors on process performance.

LO3-6 Describe process improvement methodologies such as business process reengineering and Kaizen Events.

CLEANING UP DRY CLEANERS

You take your clothes into your neighborhood dry cleaners; they are tagged and taken away. To most customers, the dry cleaning process is a mystery, and customers are often dissatisfied with the end results. The shops are bland, smelly, and dark, and clothes are often returned with stains still in them. The dry cleaning process has changed little since the 1930s, when cleaners began using a cleaning agent called perchloroethylene or "perc." While perc is especially good at dissolving oil-based stains, the Environmental Protection Agency (EPA) has classified it as a toxic air pollutant and potential human carcinogen. Consequently, the EPA has mandated that cleaning businesses located in residential buildings phase out perc by the end of 2020. Some states such as California, Illinois, and New Jersey are looking to end its use earlier and more broadly. Switching to safer alternative solvents is costly, requiring that dry cleaners buy new machines costing between $45,000 and $100,000.

This is not the only change taking place at your local dry cleaner. Procter & Gamble research recently discovered that many dry cleaning customers are dissatisfied. Seeing this as an opportunity, they have introduced Tide Dry Cleaners stores, which use new processes to offer consumers quite different dry cleaning experiences. The stores have valets to carry clothes to and from the customers' cars, lockers with customized passwords where customers can drop off or pick up clothes after hours, and bar codes that keep track of customer data and preferences. Some stores will even pick up clothes from customers' homes. In addition, Tide offers a range of stain removal/color protection/color restoration services, and reattachment of lost/damaged buttons free of charge. The stores are bright and open with machines and the dry cleaning process highly visible. Gone are the chemical smells and mysterious back office processes that characterized most dry cleaning facilities.

Tide's process changes extend beyond the cleaning process itself to comprehend the entire consumer experience, from drop-off to pick-up. By improving the process from end to end, Tide Dry Cleaners aims to improve convenience and performance for its customers, while also minimizing negative environmental impacts. The well-known Tide brand name instills trust, and the new processes ensure quality (all products are returned clean and fresh smelling) and service (24-hour drop-off and pick-up, pleasing store surroundings), all wrapped up in a process that is environmentally responsible.

Source: Ray A. Smith, "The New Dirt on Dry Cleaners.," ***Wall Street Journal,*** July 28, 2011.

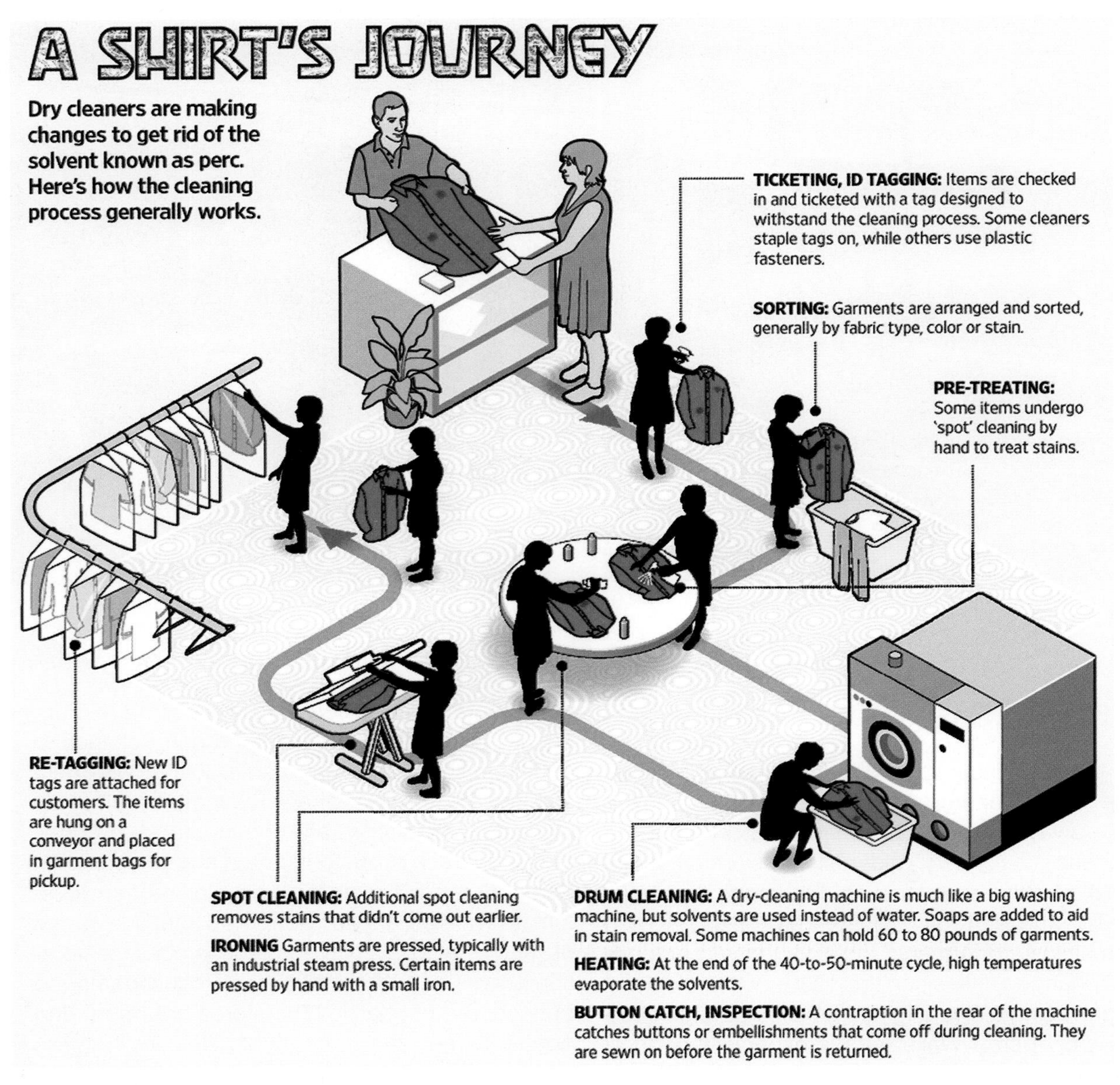

From Ray A. Smith, "The New Dirt on Dry Cleaners," Wall Street Journal, July 28, 2011.

Prepare

What is a process and why is process thinking so critical to operations management?

Organize

Processes and Process Thinking

Revolutionary process changes in the dry cleaning industry offer an example of the importance of processes in operations management. Processes determine the specific types of products that an organization can offer to its customers, as well as the timeliness and quality of those products. When customers' requirements change or when a company wants to offer its customers something very different, then it must change its processes. In a supply chain, operations managers must recognize that they are fundamentally process managers. Consequently, they must understand the principles that govern processes and process thinking.

PROCESSES AND PROCESS THINKING

process A system of structured activities that use resources to change inputs (energy, material, information, labor, knowledge) into valuable outputs.

A **process** is a system of structured activities that use resources to transform inputs (such as energy, materials, and information) into valuable outputs. Every process has structural and resource constraints that limit the range of outputs it can produce. Each process has a structure that defines, orders, and links the activities included in the operation. Usually, it also has procedures, monitoring and control structures, and feedback mechanisms.

LO3-1 Understand the importance of processes and process thinking to operations and supply chain management.

Process thinking is a way of viewing activities in an organization as a collection of processes (as opposed to departments or functional areas). This way of thinking focuses one's attention not only on an operation's outputs, but also on the processes responsible for these outputs. Outputs become viewed as the result of the process; if you don't like the outputs, then change the process.

process thinking A way of viewing activities in an organization as processes rather than as departments or functions.

Using process thinking, operations managers design, document, manage, and change business processes located throughout the supply chain, with the goal of ensuring that these processes make the desired results inevitable. Process thinking causes managers to address critical process elements, including activities, inputs, outputs, flows, structure, resources, and metrics.

At the heart of process thinking is **Juran's Law**. Joseph M. Juran (1904–2008) was one of the leading quality gurus of the 20th century. He once observed that *15 percent of operational problems are the result of human errors; the other 85 percent are due to systemic process errors.* Accordingly, to improve operations we should focus our attention on processes first.

Juran's Law A key premise of process thinking: 15% of operational problems are the result of human errors; the other 85% are due to systemic process errors.

Viewing supply chain operations as a collection of processes, rather than a collection of departments, functions, or companies is important because this perspective helps managers to break down organizational barriers that can impede operational performance. By focusing on managing processes, operations managers can better ensure that the operational capabilities and outcomes they create are more fully consistent with the firm's strategy. In addition, process thinking causes managers and workers to view operational activities from a customer's perspective. Processes are the means by which customers' needs are satisfied.

Note that the notion of a *process* is much more general than just *manufacturing processes.* As can be seen in Table 3-1, process thinking can be applied to any operation that involves transformations of materials, information, currencies, or even people. These high-level processes consist of smaller and more focused subprocesses. Between every pair of subprocesses, an interface must be maintained. Often these interfaces cross departmental boundaries. For example, a customer service process might involve personnel from sales, manufacturing, logistics, and other departments. In the same way, processes often span the organizational boundaries of different firms in a supply chain.

TABLE 3-1 Major Types of Business Processes

Business Process	Inputs	Outputs
Strategic planning	Competitor data, market assessments, internal capability assessments, economic forecasts	Strategic vision, long-term objectives and plans
Innovation	Technological developments, customer needs, production capabilities	New products, new production technologies
Customer service	Customer orders and requests, complaints, demand forecasts, priorities	Entered orders, delivery commitments, resolved problems
Resource management	Strategic objectives, resource costs, availability of existing resources	Capacity plans, facilities plans
Human resource management	Strategic objectives, skill requirements, demand requirements by area, staffing requirements and shortfalls	Hiring plans, training programs (both at time of hire and subsequently), staffing plans, employee development plans
Supply management	Supplier capabilities, raw materials, customer orders, demand forecasts	Fulfilled orders, production schedules, goods and services
Performance measurement	Raw information, benchmarks, standards	Performance variances, trends

Prepare

What are the various components that make up a process?

Organize

Anatomy of a Process
- Activities of a Process
- Inputs, Outputs, and Flows
- Structure
- Management Policies

ANATOMY OF A PROCESS

Processes involve structured activities and resources that are guided by performance metrics. A particular process can be defined by its:

1. Activities
2. Inputs/outputs/flows
3. Process structure
4. Management policies

LO3-2 Define the various components that make up processes, including types of inputs and outputs.

Activities of a Process

A process usually consists of many different activities. For example, at McDonald's the activity of moving hamburger patties to the cooking area is different from the activities of cooking the patties or assembling a sandwich. Activities usually fall into five distinct categories:

operation (change) An activity that changes an input.

transportation (move) An activity that moves an input from one place to another without changing any of its other characteristics.

inspection (check) An activity that checks or verifies the results of another activity.

delay (wait) An unintentional stoppage of the flow of work.

storage (inventory/store) An activity that intentionally stops flow of work items and places them under formal control.

1. An **operation** is any activity that transforms an input. For example, operations occur when a part or person is physically transformed, when information is organized, when a transaction is made, or when planning and calculations take place. For the most part, operations are the major source of value creation in processes.
2. **Transportation** is any activity that moves an input from one place to another without transforming its other characteristics.
3. An **inspection** checks or verifies the results of another activity. For example, an inspector might examine a part to compare it against a standard. A planner might check the progress of a part to see if it is on track.
4. A **delay** occurs when the flow of an input is unintentionally stopped as a result of interference. You experience a delay when you wait in line to check into a hotel. Delays usually take place because of insufficient operating capacity, or because other needed inputs (information or materials) or resources are not available. For example, transportation delays occur when passengers are missing or when equipment breaks down. In practice, delays are unplanned, often difficult to predict, and sources of variance in process performance. Delays can also be a source of great frustration to customers (as described in the Get Real box on the next page).
5. **Storage** is an activity where items are inventoried *under formal control.* Access to stored items requires authorization. For example, when you put money in a bank, you put money into storage. In manufacturing, inventory storage occurs in many places including stockrooms, warehouses, and holding/receiving areas.

Inputs, Outputs, and Flows

sustainability

Process activities create outputs from inputs through a series of flows. Most processes involve two basic types of flows: information flows and material flows. Information flows can include data communicated in many forms (e.g., speech, binary code, written words or pictures, currency). Material flows involve physical products, including people. Inputs are items that come from outside the process and are acted upon or consumed by the process. Even simple processes usually involve a wide range of inputs including materials, energy, information, capital, and even people (in the case of a service process). Resources such as facilities, equipment, and labor are also inputs to a process. For example, an inspection activity requires floor space for storing the items to be inspected, and it consumes either a machine or a person's time to actually do the inspection. Outputs include both intended and unintended products of the process, including physical goods, services, and information. Intended outputs usually have value for customers. Unintended outputs are often undesirable by-products. For example, an important part of process management is to minimize pollution and environmental waste.

GET REAL

States Reduce Waiting Times for Car License Renewals and Registrations

State officials across the United States are attempting to reduce the amount of time customers spend waiting for license renewals and car registrations. The horror stories of people waiting for hours to get their licenses renewed are the source of a great deal of voter frustration and anger. Officials in states such as Michigan, California, Virginia, New York, and Rhode Island (to name a few) are changing process steps and technologies for renewing licenses and registering cars. For example, in Michigan, license renewals can now be done over the Internet or by fax. In Rhode Island, a study of the processes found that delays were caused by the lack of critical equipment. Some delays are avoided by providing better information to customers. For example, some states are using the Internet to post answers to frequently asked questions and to provide forms that can be downloaded and completed at home. State employees frequently act as greeters, welcoming incoming customers—and checking to see if they have the necessary forms and information. Operating hours have been extended to allow more customers to come in after or before work. The results: significant reductions in delays and waiting times. In Rhode Island, for example, the average waiting time in March 2003 was 81 minutes; by October, it had fallen to 23 minutes.

Structure

Structure deals with how inputs, activities, and outputs of a process are organized. Process managers define a process's structure by sequencing activities, by physically positioning them, and by linking them. Ideally, the sequencing, positioning, and linking of process activities should be closely tied to the priorities that process managers place on various performance outcomes. The structure limits the **process capabilities**—that is, the types of outputs that the process is able to produce, the specific types of problems that the process can best address, and the levels of performance the process is able to attain. For example, a process designed to minimize product delivery speed might be structured quite differently from a process that minimizes operating costs. Processes that have many parallel activities are typically faster and more flexible than more serial processes. On the other hand, because resources are often duplicated in parallel processes, they tend to be less completely utilized, thus making the process more costly.

process capabilities The specific types of outputs and levels of performance that a process can generate.

How activities are positioned and linked is also important for process performance. Locating two activities closer to one another reduces the time needed to move materials and tools between them. Dedicated physical links such as conveyor belts can be used to reduce transfer time and variability, resulting in lower material handling costs. However, building physical links requires capital investment and fixed operating costs, and they can make it more costly to change the flows within a process. Specialized information links are subject to the same trade-offs.

Over the years, a number of typical process structures have evolved. Each of these structures (project, job shop, batch shop, assembly line, continuous flow) represents a scheme of supportive choices regarding the sequencing, positioning, and linking of activities in a process. Chapter 5, "Manufacturing and Service Process Structures," discusses these process types.

Management Policies

Any effective process has to be designed and managed so as to satisfy some customer requirement (e.g., to produce a product of a certain quality within a certain amount of time). How these requirements are specified, measured, and evaluated by managers can have great effects on the overall performance of the process. In addition, the policies that managers use to control resources, especially human resources, are very important. For example, worker compensation policies can have a huge effect on process outcomes. Paying a worker for a rate of output (pay by the piece) tends to motivate the worker to produce higher quantities. However, other aspects of performance may suffer, for example, quality, safety, and so on. Paying workers by the hour or paying them a straight salary has other advantages and disadvantages. It is important to design the management aspects of a process, including metrics, rewards, and controls, so that they are consistent with the overall mission.

Prepare

How do operations managers plan for capacity changes? How can they achieve economies of scale?

Organize

Process Capacity and Utilization
- Capacity Planning
- Economies and Diseconomies of Scale

PROCESS CAPACITY AND UTILIZATION

Process **capacity** refers to the limit on the amount of output that a process can produce given an amount of inputs and resources made available to the process (i.e., machine hours, labor hours, tools, or square feet of floor space available). Process capacity is usually specified with respect to some unit of time, such as "this process can produce 100 units per hour." The term *capacity* is also used to denote size or storage limits. For example, a warehouse has a certain storage capacity limited by its square footage. Operations, transportation, and inspection activities are usually defined by output capacity, where delays and storage activities are defined by storage capacity.

capacity The limit on the amount of output per period of time that a process can generate or store given a level of inputs and resources available.

The capacity of a process is determined by the limits of its resources. For example, the capacity of a circuit board assembly operation is limited by the types of tools, machines, and labor it employs; the capacity of a transportation activity is limited by the size of its equipment; and so on. Table 3-2 gives examples of the capacity-limiting resources associated with the five types of process activities.

Operations managers usually express amounts of capacity in terms of either resource availability (e.g., available machine hours, labor hours, number of tools, or storage space) or potential output rate (e.g., number of parts that the process can produce in a day, dollars worth of products it can produce in an hour). Different types of business operations use different units of capacity measurement. Restaurants measure capacity in terms of the number of diners or meals that can be served during a day or specific mealtime. An amusement park assesses the number of patrons that can safely visit the park per day. A delivery company measures the number of packages that can be delivered per day. A manufacturing company may count the number of units (TVs, bicycles, tables, etc.) that it can make per day, or it might measure the amount of dollars of sales that it can support in a day. Capacity can also be measured in terms of inputs used. For example, a neighborhood bakery might measure the number of oven baking hours it has available, or simply measure the pounds of flour it can consume.

LO3-4 Estimate the capacity and utilization of a process.

Capacity limits are often expressed in two different ways: *maximum capacity* and *effective capacity.* **Maximum capacity** is the highest output rate that an activity or a process can achieve under ideal conditions in the short term. This assumes that all equipment and workers are fully operational for the maximum amount of available time. For equipment this is also known as rated or design capacity; it is an engineering assessment of maximum output, assuming continuous operation except for normal maintenance and repair time. Usually, producing at a rate of maximum capacity can only be sustained for a

maximum capacity The highest level of output that a process can achieve under ideal conditions in the short term; also known as *design capacity.*

TABLE 3-2 Capacity and Process Activities

Process Activity	Associated Resources That Limit Capacity
Operation	Tools, labor, machine capacity, supplier capacity
Transportation	Pallets, carts, fork-lift trucks, trucks, trains, airplanes
Inspection	Inspectors, inspection stations, gauges, robots, or machine-vision equipment
Delay	Space on the shop floor, bins, carts, racks
Storage	Floor space, racks, bins, stockrooms, stockroom clerks

relatively short time, because things do not always operate perfectly. When operations managers take into account the potential for disruptions in process flows, worker fatigue, machine breakdowns, preventive maintenance, and so forth, they can estimate the **effective capacity** that the process can sustain. The sustainable effective capacity of a process may only be 70–80 percent of the maximum designed capacity, for instance. It is the effective capacity estimate that operations managers use when they make plans for how they will satisfy customer demand, though they may plan output that exceeds effective capacity levels for short periods of time (such as during periods of peak demand).

effective capacity The level of capacity or output that the process can be expected to produce under normal conditions; what management plans for under normal conditions.

Both design capacity and effective capacity are planning concepts (different types of planning are described in greater detail later on in this book). As a measure of performance, operations managers often compare planned capacities with what was actually produced. **Utilization** is defined as the percentage of process capacity that is actually used. Utilization can be calculated as the ratio of the actual output rate to the capacity. Alternatively, utilization is sometimes calculated as the percentage of available resource time that is actually used. Very low utilization rates suggest that equipment or employees are being underused, while extremely high utilization rates suggest overuse and a corresponding danger that problems may occur if demand continues to exceed available capacity. Example 3-1 shows how the various types of capacity are calculated.

utilization The percent of process capacity that is actually used.

EXAMPLE 3-1

A distribution center for an Internet bookseller can handle a peak demand of 200,000 orders in a single day, under ideal conditions. However, the facility was designed to handle up to 120,000 orders per day during normal operating conditions. Orders processed for the first two weeks of December averaged 150,000 per day. Calculate the utilization of the distribution center relative to both maximum capacity and effective capacity.

SOLUTION

Maximum capacity = 200,000 orders per day

Effective capacity = 120,000 orders per day

Actual orders = 150,000 orders per day

Utilization of maximum capacity = (150,000/200,000) × 100% = 75%

Utilization of effective capacity = (150,000/120,000) × 100% = 125%

This example illustrates that the Internet bookseller can accommodate high periods of demand by utilizing maximum capacity (e.g., by using overtime work) in the short run. However, if this high demand continued for more than a few weeks, it should consider increasing its effective capacity by expanding its distribution center and/or hiring more workers.

Amazon distribution center.

Operations managers are usually concerned when effective capacity is greater than actual production (i.e., what we planned to make is greater than what we actually made, or the number of customers we planned to serve is less than the number we actually served). For either external or internal reasons processes are often not able to achieve desired levels of capacity utilization. External reasons include insufficient demand or supplied inputs. Internal reasons include lack of resource availability (machines break down or workers are absent), efficiency problems (workers are slowed by product changeovers, training, or unforeseen difficulties), and quality problems (some portion of the products do not meet requirements). In some contexts, there may be an insufficient yield rate. **Yield rate** is the percentage of good units produced as a percentage of total units begun. For example, a yield rate of 80 percent means that out of 100 units begun, only 80 were successfully completed; the remaining 20 units must be scrapped (thrown away) or reworked. It is the job of operations managers to minimize these sorts of difficulties in order to make the process as productive as possible.

yield rate The percentage of units successfully produced as a percentage of inputs.

Operations managers are also concerned when actual production exceeds effective capacity for a long period of time. Most processes can exceed their effective capacities in the short run by working faster than normal, or by working longer than normal (overtime). Such overproduction is usually not sustainable, however. Typically, when workers are pushed beyond normal limits, errors and accidents become more frequent. People become fatigued and safety issues emerge. Similarly, machines that are utilized for too long will break down if they are not properly maintained. It is the job of operations managers to maintain the balance between making sure that capacity is fully utilized and avoiding unsustainable overutilization.

sustainability

Capacity Planning

LO3-3 Distinguish between operational, tactical, and strategic capacity planning.

Capacity decisions are important because demand, products, technology, and the competitive environment shift over time. Managers must consider these shifts to determine when and how much to change capacity. Typically, cross-functional teams make decisions about how much capacity is needed and when it should be added or removed. Too much capacity in a supply chain means that resources are underutilized, so costs increase. For example, after years of rapid expansion, Starbucks increased its capacity too much. In 2008, because of sagging sales, Starbucks announced it was closing 600 stores. Too little capacity in a supply chain can be a problem, too. When Nintendo first introduced its Wii© gaming console system, capacity problems at one of its suppliers led to empty store shelves, upset customers, and lost sales.

There are three general strategies for determining when to change capacity relative to demand. Some companies use a capacity lead strategy by adding capacity assuming that demand will grow. Apple used this strategy very effectively for its iPad© tablet computer as described in the Get Real: "Capacity Planning Contributes to iPad's© Success." A lead strategy ensures sales will not be lost and helps companies gain market share during the early stages of a product's life cycle. However, this strategy can result in costly underutilization if sales do not grow as expected. Other companies add or remove capacity to correspond to average demand. This approach balances the risks of having too much capacity and missing out on sales. A third approach, a capacity lag strategy, is to wait to add capacity until after demand is actually known. This strategy, often used as products mature, lowers the risk of overexpansion, but results in lost sales.

Capacity changes involve increasing or decreasing key resources such as facilities and space, equipment, and labor within the supply chain. Capacity changes can be strategic, tactical or operational as summarized in Table 3-3. Strategic capacity changes take a long time to implement and often include large increases or decreases in capacity, such as building a new retail mall or manufacturing plant or outsourcing customer service operations to a supplier. Tactical capacity decisions occur in the medium term (6 to 24 months) and may be medium-sized capacity changes, such as buying equipment and leasing space. Finding and qualifying an additional supplier or distributor is a tactical decision. Some tactical capacity decisions may be smaller changes, such as hiring specialized labor such as

Capacity Planning Contributes to iPad's© Success

Although much of the credit for the iPad's© success goes to its innovative product design, effective capacity planning helped Apple to capture over 75 percent of the tablet computer market. Apple used a capacity lead strategy to tie up suppliers' capacities for key components such as the touch screen in anticipation of strong sales. In addition, Apple committed to use a large amount of the capacity of its contract manufacturer, Foxconn, which assembles the iPad in China. These moves helped Apple attain economies of scale, lowering costs, and left its competitors scrambling to purchase key tablet computer components.

TABLE 3-3 Capacity Decisions Addressing Different Time Frames

Time Frame (time required for changes)	Limiting Resource	Types of Capacity Change	Examples
Short term (0–6 months)	Low-skilled labor	Overtime, part-time, temporary labor, layoffs	Restaurant wait staff, bank tellers, production line workers
	Equipment, space	Rental, leasing	Landscaping equipment, temporary storage
Medium term (6–24 months)	Specialized labor	Hiring, firing, contract labor	Engineers, accountants, machine operators, physicians
	Equipment, space	Leasing, subcontracting, equipment installation and renovation	Distribution/warehousing, fast-food restaurant rebuild, production line renovation
Long term (more than 2 years)	Physical plant	New building, outsourcing	Automotive plant open or closure, new office building

physicians or engineers. Operational capacity decisions occur in the short term (zero to six months) and typically require small changes to low-skilled labor, equipment, and space. The use of temporary employees at retail stores and distribution centers for the holidays is an example of an operational capacity change.

Economies and Diseconomies of Scale

With the addition of capacity, some types of processes offer **economies of scale**. As production volumes increase with additions of capacity, the unit cost to produce a product decreases until some optimal level is reached. The left side of Figure 3-1 on the next page illustrates economies of scale. In some industries such as consumer electronics, operations managers install enough production capacity in a single manufacturing plant to meet global demand so that they can achieve economies of scale.

economies of scale As production volumes increase with additions of capacity, the unit cost to produce a product decreases to an optimal level.

FIGURE 3-1 Economies and Diseconomies of Scale

There are several reasons for economies of scale.

1. *Allocation of fixed costs,* which include things like depreciation of equipment, rent, taxes, insurance, utilities, and managers' salaries. Because fixed costs do not vary over a wide range of volumes, for accounting purposes they can be spread over more units as output grows, reducing the cost per unit.
2. *Equipment and construction costs* do not increase proportionally with size. For example, when the size of a storage tank in an oil refinery doubles, its cost only increases by about 1.5 times.
3. *Lower costs for purchases* because of higher volumes. When buying more, firms have more power to ask suppliers for lower prices. When volumes increase for suppliers, they gain their own economies of scale, and can pass some of the savings on to customers by lowering prices.
4. As volume increases, *learning* occurs; this is a phenomenon called the **learning curve**. With practice, employees become more efficient at their jobs and find ways to improve processes. Learning is higher in assembly processes and for new products. Learning is lower in automated processes, and the rate of learning diminishes as employees gain experience making the product.

learning curve As the production volume doubles, the labor hours required decrease by a constant proportion.

If the size of an operation increases beyond some point, costs per unit can increase and **diseconomies of scale** can occur, as shown on the right side of Figure 3-1. For example, hospital costs per patient decrease with the number of beds, up to a point; then costs begin to increase as more beds are added. A study in the U.K. suggested that the optimal size of a hospital was 400–600 beds, and beyond 600 beds, costs increased.[1] Several factors can cause diseconomies of scale. Overtime may be used more frequently and routine maintenance may be delayed, thereby increasing breakdowns. Use of overtime may not be sustainable in the long run. Too much overtime puts stress on employees and can cause safety problems.

diseconomies of scale Occur when the cost per unit increases as an operation's size increases.

LO3-5 Explain the impacts of bottlenecks, variance, and other factors on process performance.

PRINCIPLES OF PROCESS PERFORMANCE: THE THEORY OF CONSTRAINTS

Since processes are spread across the many organizations that make up a supply chain, it is important for all managers (even in marketing and finance) to understand the basic operating principles of processes. One way of expressing these principles is through a management system known as the **Theory of Constraints (TOC)**.[2] The principles offered by the

Theory of Constraints (TOC) The overall management system that strives to improve system performance by identifying, focusing on, and managing constraints.

[1] J. Posnett, "The Hospital of the Future: Is Bigger Better? Concentration in the Provision of Secondary Care," *British Medical Journal* 319, no. 7216 (1999), pp. 1063–65.

[2] The theory of constraints was initially forwarded by Eli Goldratt. His popular book, *The Goal,* explains the basic principles in the context of a fictional story.

Theory of Constraints apply universally, whether the processes are located in a manufacturing plant, a service facility, a sales office, or in a financial planning office. The principles serve to simplify process management by focusing managers' attentions to the important constraints that limit the performance of a process. There are five basic principles at the heart of TOC:

1. Every process has a constraint.
2. Every process contains variance that consumes capacity.
3. Every process must be managed as a system.
4. Performance measures are crucial to the process's success.
5. Every process must continually improve.

Prepare

How do bottlenecks, variance, and other factors impact process performance? How can we estimate the capacity of a process?

Organize

Principle 1: Every Process Has a Constraint

The overall operating capacity of a process is limited by one or more constraints. As indicated in Table 3-2, a constraint is a physical limitation applied by a person, by equipment, or by facilities. The constraining activity in the process that limits the overall output is called a **bottleneck**. Over time the output of a process can be no greater than the output of its bottleneck activity.

Let's use the bottleneck principle to calculate the maximum capacity in a process. How we calculate capacity is strongly influenced by the structure of the process. A process can be serial/sequential or parallel. In a **serial/sequential structure**, the activities in the process occur one after the other; in a **parallel structure**, an activity is done by two or more resources simultaneously (e.g., two or more bank tellers serving customers). Example 3-2 describes a serial process while Example 3-3 describes a parallel process.

EXAMPLE 3-2

Figure 3-2 below shows a circuit board assembly process with four serial operations. The maximum capacity for this process, 275 boards per hour, is based on the capacity of Operation C, which has the lowest capacity. Although Operation B can produce 400 boards per hour (125 more per hour than Operation C), the process cannot exploit this excess capacity because Operation C can accept only 275 boards an hour. Thus, Operation C is the bottleneck in this process.

bottleneck An activity or resource that limits or constrains the output of a process.

serial/sequential structure A process structure where the activities occur one after the other in sequence.

parallel structure A process where there are two or more resources doing the same task simultaneously.

Awareness of bottlenecks is critical. To improve the overall output of a process, operations managers must identify the bottleneck and ensure that it is always busy. An hour of lost output at the bottleneck equates to an hour of lost output for the entire process. For this reason, operations managers often keep an inventory of work waiting in front of the bottleneck activity so that it will never be "starved" for work. Managers also closely monitor and maintain the operation of the bottleneck to ensure that it is working correctly. Finally,

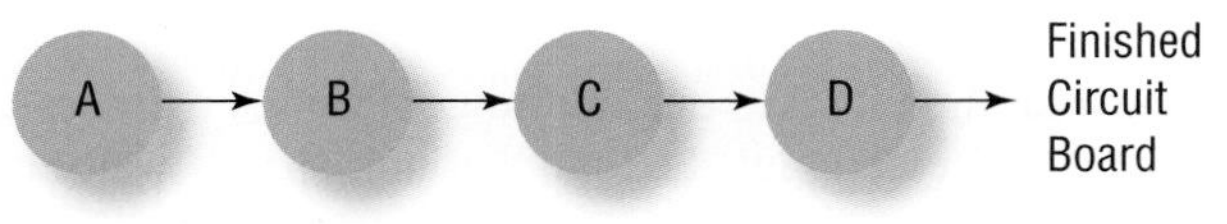

FIGURE 3-2 Maximum Capacity in a Serial Process

EXAMPLE 3-3

If a process contains parallel resources that do the same type of activity, then the total capacity of the set of parallel activities simply equals the sum of the individual resource capacities. Figure 3-3 revises the circuit board assembly process to show a second operational stage made up of three parallel operations, each performing the same type of task. The total capacity for this second stage is not 90 boards (the single-operation minimum) but 400 boards (the sum of the capacities of Operations E, F, and B). The maximum capacity for the overall process remains at 275 boards per hour, however, because the work must still flow through Operation C.

FIGURE 3-3 Maximum Capacity in a Parallel Process

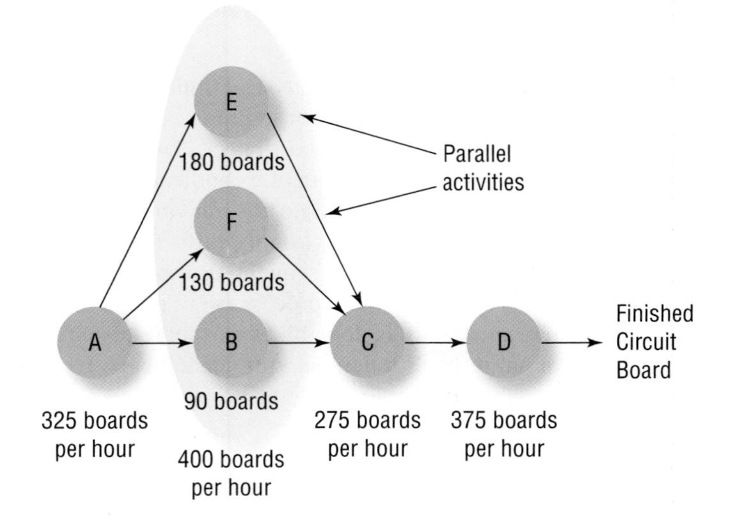

awareness of bottlenecks is important because it affects investment strategies. Investing money or effort to improve the capacity of a nonbottleneck activity is actually a waste of time and money, since it has no effect on overall output.

The notion of bottlenecks is simple to understand. In practice, however, bad decisions are often made simply because operations managers do not have a clear view of how bottlenecks constrain their operating processes. The same situation applies in a supply chain context. Take another look at Figure 3-2, but this time imagine suppliers and customers in place of the four serial activities shown in the process. Ultimately, if Supplier B adds to its capacity, it does not help the overall supply chain, as it will always be limited by the capacity of Supplier C. Because various suppliers and partners in a supply chain are often unaware of capacity differences and have little control over them, isolated investments in capacity can be ineffective as far as the overall supply chain is concerned.

A bottleneck affects more than capacity in a process. It also impacts the timeliness of outputs produced, as well as cost and quality. The bottleneck determines the time that an input unit spends in a process because the bottleneck ultimately determines the rate at which units are processed. Little's Law[3] helps us to understand this relationship. **Little's Law** shows how flow time (F) is related to the inventory (I) and throughput rate (TH) of a process.

Little's Law An empirically proven relationship that exists between flow time, inventory, and throughput.

(3.1) $$F = I/TH$$

flow time The time it takes one unit to get through a process.

Flow time is the total time it takes one unit to get through a process; that is, the time that a unit spends being processed plus the time that unit spends waiting to be processed.

[3] John D.C. Little, "A Proof for the Queuing Formula: L = λW," *Operations Research* 9, no.3 (1992): 383–87.

The time that a unit spends being processed at a given operation in the overall process is called the **cycle time**. The throughput rate, or capacity, of a process is simply the reciprocal of the cycle time at the bottleneck operation. For example, if it takes 10 minutes for an operation to process a unit (the cycle time), then the throughput rate is one unit every 10 minutes, or six units per hour.

cycle time The time that it takes to process one unit at an operation in the overall process.

Little's Law indicates that the flow time for a given unit is dependent on the inventory that is in front of the unit, and the rate at which that inventory is processed (throughput rate or capacity). Recall from the preceding examples that the throughput rate for a given process is determined by the throughput rate of the bottleneck operation in that process. Because in most processes the time a unit spends waiting far exceeds the time it spends being processed, identifying the causes of waiting and reducing or eliminating them can create fundamental improvement in the process. In most processes, a bottleneck is ultimately the cause of waiting time and the attendant costs and quality problems. Example 3-4 shows how Little's Law can be used to set process times for a theme park ride.

EXAMPLE 3-4

A theme park (like Disney World in Orlando, FL, Cedar Point in Sandusky, OH, or Canada's Wonderland in Toronto, ON) plans to introduce a new thrill ride. At present, about 18,000 people come to the park every day, and the park is open for 12 hours. If managers want everyone in the park to have at least one chance to experience the ride, what should the maximum cycle time for the ride be? To process all 18,000 people (I) in 12 hours (F), the ride would need to "process" them at a throughput rate (TH) of 18,000/12 = 1,500 per hour. If the ride holds 100 people each time it runs, then it must run at a rate of 15 times an hour, or once every four minutes. The cycle time must be no more than four minutes. That is, the time needed to load the ride (get the people on the ride), provide proper safety instructions, let the ride experience occur, and then unload the ride, can take no longer than four minutes.

Inventory due to bottlenecks creates requirements for longer total operating time, and for more space to store inventoried items. Labor is needed to track and control this inventory. All of these factors increase costs. Quality also suffers. As inventory grows, more units are susceptible to damage, and problems in production are not as easily detected. In addition, insufficient capacity tends to encourage process workers to hurry, which in turn leads to mistakes. As one manager said, "quality is the first victim of insufficient capacity."

The supplement to this chapter gives steps for diagramming a process and analyzing its capacity, lead time, and cost.

student activity

What symptoms would you look for that would indicate the presence of a bottleneck? Go to a fast food restaurant and see if you can identify the bottleneck resource or operation.

Estimating Capacity Requirements

Operations managers use their understanding of bottlenecks in capacity planning. They estimate capacity requirements for a process by using a forecast of each product's demand, its processing requirements, and any setup time that is needed when switching between products. The capacity requirements are determined by dividing the sum of the total time needed to make the products and the total setup by the operating time that is available. Example 3-5 gives us an example of how a manager might go about the task of estimating capacity requirements.

EXAMPLE 3-5

Table 3-4, shows the annual demand forecast and the processing time for four different styles of desk chairs that can be assembled on the same assembly line. Assume that there is no time required to set up when changing over from making one type of chair to another. Multiply the annual demand for each chair by its processing time to estimate the processing time per year for each type of chair. Then, add these times together to get the total processing time for all four chairs. In this example the total processing time is 468,500 minutes.

The total processing time required for all chairs is divided by the total operating time that is available to determine the number of assembly lines needed. To ensure there is enough capacity, always round up to the next unit of capacity. In this example, the firm operates one eight-hour shift 250 days per year.

Total operating time available (minutes/year) = 250 days/year × 8 hours/day × 60 minutes/hour

= 120,000 minutes/year

Number of assembly lines = (Total processing time required)/(Total operating time available)

(468,500 (minutes/year))/(120,000 (minutes/year))

= 3.9 assembly line, so round up to 4 assembly lines.

If time is required to set up, this must be considered when determining capacity requirements. Let's recalculate the capacity requirements for the desk chair assembly assuming that setup time is needed. Table 3-5 shows the setup time and lot size for each chair. The number of setups per year is determined by dividing the annual demand for each chair by its lot size. Multiply the number of setups for each chair type by its setup time to get the total annual setup time per chair. The annual setup times are summed together to get the total setup time required per year.

The setup time is added to the total processing time, and this value is divided by the total operating time available to determine the capacity required.

Number of assembly lines = (Total processing time required + Total setup time required)/(Total operating time available)

(468,500 (minutes/year) + 6,500 (minutes/year))/(120,000 (minutes/year))

= 3.96 assembly lines rounded-up to 4 assembly lines

In this example, the setup time did not increase the overall number of assembly lines needed. However, in some cases, setup time consumes a large amount of capacity. By reducing setup time, the capacity requirements and an organization's resource requirements and costs can be reduced.

TABLE 3-4 Estimating Capacity Requirements for Chairs

Chairs	Demand Forecast (chairs/year)	Processing Time (minutes/chair)	Processing Time Required (minutes/year)
A	2,000	20	40,000
B	3,800	45	171,000
C	2,500	33	82,500
D	5,000	35	175,000
		Total Processing Time (minutes/year)	468,500

TABLE 3-5 Estimating Capacity Requirements for Chairs with Setup Time

Chairs	Demand Forecast (chairs/year)	Lot Size (number of chairs)	Number of Setups/year	Setup Time (minutes/setup)	Setup Time/Chair (minutes/year)
A	2,000	10	200	5	1,000
B	3,800	19	200	8	1,600
C	2,500	10	250	10	2,500
D	5,000	25	200	7	1,400
				Total Setup Time (minutes/year)	6,500

Principle 2: Every Process Contains Variance That Consumes Capacity

The second principle governing all processes is that every process has variance. Variance, or variability, exists in outputs, inputs, or in the process activities themselves.[4] Table 3-6 summarizes the effects that different types of variability have on process capacity. Essentially, variability of different sorts introduces complexity and uncertainty into processes, which in turn increase the difficulty of efficiently and fully utilizing resources. In addition, resources must be dedicated to managing complexity and uncertainty. For example, more support personnel are needed to plan and control activities that often do not contribute directly to producing outputs (inspection and storage, for example). These activities take away from the total productive capacity of the process.

In addition to consuming capacity, variance increases process congestion and increases flow times because jobs must sit in queues and wait. This phenomenon is specified by

TABLE 3-6 Types and Effects of Process Variability

Type of Variability	Example of Effects on Capacity
Output—product variety	As one facility is used to produce a wider range of products, more process changeovers are required. Each changeover requires time that could otherwise be used to create output.
Output—variable schedule	As demand and production schedules vary, they become more complex and coordination becomes more difficult. Different activities become bottlenecks at different times (especially if product variety is large and if production batches are large). This increases the potential for bottleneck activities to be poorly scheduled and left idle.
Process—quality variance	Defective product subtracts from the effective capacity of the process. In addition, productive resources are consumed by quality control and rework activities.
Process—resource availability variance	Absent employees and broken-down machines hold up production.
Process—variance in processing speed	As processing speed at an activity becomes more variable, upstream activities are blocked from clearing work from their areas and downstream activities are starved for needed inputs more frequently. This increases idle time, thereby reducing output.
Input—variance in quality	Poor quality results in unexpectedly insufficient quantities of needed inputs (e.g., materials, energy, information). It also introduces variance into the process that may result in poor final product quality.
Input—variance in delivery	As delivery variability increases, there is greater potential for process activities to be halted because they are missing needed components.

[4]The impact of variability on process performance is also discussed in the Lean Systems chapter.

FIGURE 3-4 Effects of Process Variability on Wait Time

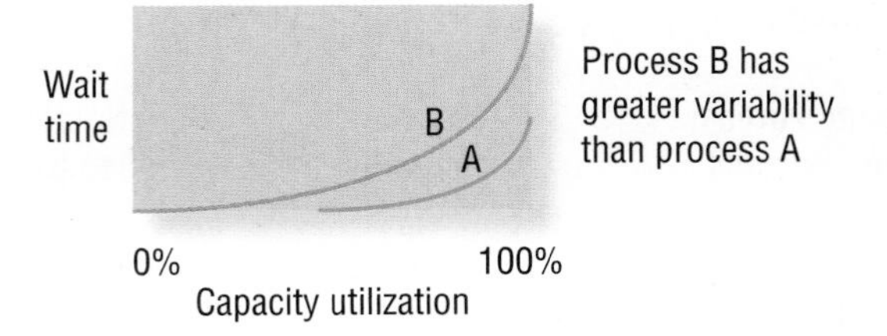

wait time The amount of time that an item spends waiting.

equation (3.2). For a single operation, this equation quantifies the effects on a unit's **wait time** that result from both the level of variance and the level of utilization. This formula, developed from queuing theory, can be used to examine the interaction of utilization and variance.

(3.2)

$$Wait\ time = \left(\frac{c_a^2 + c_p^2}{2}\right)\left(\frac{u}{1-u}\right)t_p$$

c_a = coefficient of variation (standard deviation divided by the average) of job arrival times

c_p = coefficient of variation of job processing times

u = utilization of the work center

t_p = average processing time (cycle time) for jobs

In equation (3.2), the terms c_a and c_p represent variability in the arrivals and in the processing of jobs in the work center. Figure 3-4 illustrates the relationships specified in equation (3.2). As one can see, the effect of variance on wait time is nonlinear; it increases at an increasing rate. In addition, the impact of variability on wait time is worsened as utilization levels are increased. The use of the wait time calculation is illustrated in Example 3-6.

EXAMPLE 3-6

Suppose you are the manager of the Accounts Receivable department in your university. Recently, you have been hearing complaints from the students about having to wait too long in line before they can discuss their bills with one of the counselors. After discussing the situation with your boss, you decide that students should expect an average wait time of 20 minutes. With this standard in mind, you collect the following information during periods of high demand (i.e., the start of term).

Average arrival rate = 5 minutes
Standard deviation of arrivals = 10 minutes
Average time to discuss bill = 3 minutes
Standard deviation of discussion time = 4.5 minutes
Utilization = 85 percent

Based on this information, you can use equation (3.2) to determine that the expected average wait time is as follows:

$$\text{Wait time} = (((10/5)^2 + (4.5/3)^2)/2) \times (.85/(1 - .85)) \times 3 = 53.125 \text{ minutes}$$

You now understand why students are so upset about having to wait so long. To improve this situation, you are left with a number of options:

- Reduce the variance in student arrival times (this can be done by telling students when the busiest and least busy times are so that they can decide to arrive during the least busy periods).
- Reduce utilization by having more staff.
- Reduce the processing times by improving the efficiency of the current processes.

For example, the target wait times can be achieved if the average utilization can be reduced from 85 percent to 68 percent (by having more counselors available during peak periods). Use equation (3.2) to verify this result.

GET REAL

Storyboarding: The Key to Success at Pixar

Few people can deny the success of Pixar. This company has the enviable record of a string of hit movies, including *Toy Story, A Bug's Life, Finding Nemo, The Incredibles, Cars, Toy Story 2, WALL-E, Up,*—and Pixar's latest hit—*Brave.* Critical to this success is the practice of storyboarding. Storyboarding was first developed at the Walt Disney studio during the early 1930s. It involves developing a series of illustrations displayed in sequence for the purposes of previsualizing a motion graphic or media sequence. It allows users to experiment with changes in storylines to evoke stronger reactions or interest. It also facilitates brainstorming. Pixar has adapted this process to fit with computer animation. A storyboard is the blueprint of the movie, beginning with the concept and ending with the finished product. One of the reasons that Pixar has been so successful is that they focus intensely on this practice. About three-quarters of the film's development at Pixar is spent in the story and in the storyboard. To better understand this process, see www.pixar.com/howwedoit/index.html.

Because variability can create severe problems for a process, managers spend a great deal of time and effort in managing and responding to variability. There are three basic ways to deal with variability in a process. The first is to *reduce it.* This means finding sources of variability in process activities and eliminating or controlling them. For example, experimentation with the settings of a production machine might uncover ways to reduce its inherent variability. The second way to deal with variation is to *buffer it.* By placing safety stock (buffer inventories) before and after highly variable activities, one can reduce some of the bad effects on resource utilization. Finally, managers deal with variation by designing processes that *flexibly respond to it.* By investing in flexible technologies and cross-training of labor, managers can create processes that quickly react to unplanned situations so that, once again, the detrimental effects of variation are minimized.

Principle 3: Every Process Must Be Managed as a System

relationships

Operations management is by its very nature a system management activity. As discussed earlier, the elements of the "system" include process activities, input and output flows, structure, and management policies. All of these elements need to be aligned to the needs of the customers that the process serves. Activities within a process are connected, so that what happens in one area of a process can affect what happens elsewhere. This is very much the case when dealing with variance and bottlenecks. Because of interdependencies in the system, variances tend to be amplified throughout the system. If activity B is dependent on activity A, then B cannot work faster than A works. In addition, delays due to variability in activity A are passed on to activity B.

Changing one element of a process in isolation can lead to unpredictable results. Every change made to a given activity needs to be evaluated in light of how it relates to other activities in the process. The application of this principle has contributed to the success of

student activity

Compare the Pixar process for story development with that used by Dreamworks (its major competitor). This process can be found at www.dreamworksanimation.com. What differences can you find? What similarities?

entertainment companies such as Pixar (see the Get Real box about Pixar—"Storyboarding: The Key to Success at Pixar" on the preceding page). As we noted earlier, adding capacity to an activity will have different effects on the overall process performance depending on that activity's role in the overall process (i.e., whether or not it is a bottleneck). Similarly, changes to one management element of a process will have effects on many other elements. For example, changing the way that employees are evaluated and rewarded will affect behaviors and process outcomes.

Principle 4: Performance Measures Are Crucial to the Process's Success

metric A measure, a standard, and a consequence that work together to close the gap between what is valued by the customer and what is intended by the organization.

relationships

Because almost all processes involve human beings, performance measures are important drivers of process success. Process performance measures, or **metrics**, need to address the aspects that are important to the customer as well as to the organization. Simply stated, a metric consists of three important elements: the measure, the standard against which the measure is compared, and the consequence associated with the measure's meeting or not meeting the standard. A metric should be designed to close the gap between what is valued by the customer and what is intended by the organization. Metrics should be *verifiable* and *quantitative* and they should be computed using a clearly specified method that uses objectively gathered data.

Equally important are the standards and rewards associated with metrics. The standard defines what an acceptable level of process performance is. The reward, which can be either positive or negative, serves to motivate behaviors. Metrics (measures, standards, and consequences) communicate a firm's strategy and priorities related to the process. These aspects of management provide a language for communicating process performance to workers, customers, and top managers. They also provide the basis by which managers can monitor, control, and improve process performance by directing everyone's efforts and all decisions toward the same set of corporate objectives.

Understanding the Importance of Metrics: Insights from Business Experts

You get what you inspect, not what you expect.

—Oliver Wight

A strategy without metrics is just a wish. And metrics that are not aligned with strategic objectives are a waste of time.

—Emery Powell

If you are not keeping score, then you are only practicing.

—Tom Malone

Several steps can be taken to insure that metrics motivate process behaviors in ways that increase customer value. The first is to identify and prioritize the customers served by the process. Processes typically serve many potential customers, some of whom may be internal to the operation. For example, a school serves its students as "customers" who consume education. At the same time, the school serves many other customers including the students' parents, recruiters who hire the students, and even the community as a whole. Different customer groups rarely have identical wishes, and it is rarely possible to completely satisfy all customers. Consequently, managers must identify the critical (most

TABLE 3-7 Six Types of Critical Processes

Process Type	Why Critical?
Bottleneck	Limits output; increases lead time; adversely affects cost, quality, and flexibility.
Visible to the customer	Affects how the customer views not only the process but also the firm.
Core capability	A process that incorporates a critical strategic skill set that is difficult for the competition to copy. Must be guarded, managed, and improved continuously because it is the major source of our firm's value.
Feeder process	A process that feeds a number of alternative processes coming out of it. A problem in this process (e.g., delay) can affect many downstream outcomes.
Greatest variance	Variances are amplified by sequential steps in processes. To reduce variance, managers should identify those steps that are sources of greatest variance.
Most resources consumed	We focus on these processes because they offer the "biggest bang for the buck."

important) customers. Second, they have to prioritize the requirements of these critical customers, while not losing sight of less critical groups. Third, they must pick a limited number of critical requirements and provide meaningful operational definitions (metrics) for them. These metrics should be consistent with the specific types of value that the firm provides within the marketplace and with the ways that the firm differentiates itself from its competitors. Having established metrics, managers can then assess the adequacy of the current process, and establish objectives for a redesigned process as needed.

Principle 5: Every Process Must Continuously Improve

LO3-6 Describe process improvement methodologies such as business process reeingineering and Kaizen Events.

Operations managers do not work in a static world. Technology is always changing, the competition is changing, and customers (and their expectations) are changing. Consequently, processes (especially the critical processes identified in Table 3-7) should also be changing. They must be evaluated and changed when the level of value that they provide is no longer acceptable to customers.

There are a number of specific tools that can be used to aid process improvement efforts, including process flow analysis (covered in detail in the supplement to this chapter) and Kaizen Events.

Kaizen Events: Small Process Changes Made Quickly

One approach for continually improving processes makes use of **Kaizen Events**. A Kaizen Event is a short-term project aimed at improving an existing process, or an activity within a process. It is characterized by the following traits:

Kaizen Event A short-term (i.e., lasting one week or less) approach to enhancing efficiency that focuses on improving an existing process or an activity within a process.

- *Team-oriented:* The responsibility for an event is placed in the hands of a cross-functional team consisting of employees from the process being studied, employees outside of the process, management, and in some cases, supplier representatives. The entire team is responsible for all the Kaizen steps. As a result, the team members develop greater ownership of the changes.
- *Short-term and focused:* Kaizen Events usually take between one and four days from start to finish, and focus on a tightly bounded process or activity. During this period, team members are introduced to the process analysis tools that they will use. They then study the process, identify opportunities for improvement, implement them, assess the impact, redo the cycle, and present their results to management.
- *Action-oriented:* An interesting feature of Kaizen Events is the immediacy of action. Any change that is identified and approved by the team is immediately implemented. The only major constraint is that the changes not require any major funding or capital requests. After the changes have been implemented, the new system is run and

relationships

GET REAL

Delta Faucet Uses a Kaizen Event to Improve Quality and Reduce Scrap

Delta Faucet designs and builds premium faucets. Managers determined that during a cooling process in one of the plants, the faucets seemed to develop surface defects that resulted in either increased rework or scrap. They decided to set up a Kaizen Event team to focus on this process-related problem. To execute this Kaizen Event successfully, the management team followed these steps:

1. *Define the desired outcome and associated metrics.* The desired outcome was to reduce rework and rejects due to process problems. Their metric was "to maximize the percent of faucets acceptably finished the first time." Management was convinced that an acceptable standard was a minimum of 95 percent of all the faucets finished correctly the first time.
2. *Establish the Kaizen Event team.* Management assigned a team consisting of one facilitator, two people who were experts with the process, one customer representative, one supplier representative, and one person who was completely unfamiliar with the process (that person's role is to question everything about the process).
3. *Set the contract of the Kaizen Event.* The time period for the Kaizen Event and the goals of the event were reviewed with the facilitator. The event was targeted for four days.
4. *Implement the Kaizen Event.* The facilitator introduced the team to the problem, the desired outcome, and the metrics. Next, the members of the team were introduced to the necessary tools: value stream mapping, cause and effect diagramming, and Pareto analysis). They then studied the process to understand why the problems were occurring. As opportunities for improvement were identified, they were implemented immediately to see if these "solutions" worked. At the end of four days a new process emerged.
5. *Present the results.* In the presentation of the results, the team described what the problem was, discussed the underlying causes of the problems, the solutions evaluated, and the new, "improved" process. Finally, the team presented management with the *action list*—a list of opportunities for improvement that were identified over the course of the event but that could not be explored because they fell outside of the scope of the event. These actions became the basis for future events.

the resulting performance is documented and compared with the old system. As one American manager put it, the motto of a Kaizen Event is "Ready, Fire, Aim."

- *Repetitive:* Once begun, Kaizen Events are regularly repeated. Each event generates an action list or a list of opportunities for improvement identified by the team in areas that they could address within their event. These items, in turn, become the focal point for future Kaizen Events.

To understand both the attraction of Kaizen Events and their impact on operations performance, consider the experiences of Delta Faucets. Their personnel applied the Kaizen Event approach to resolve a quality/scrap problem (as described in the Get Real box above).

Along with Kaizen Events, operations managers may occasionally use more radical approaches for improving processes. Managers typically decide what types of approaches to use depending on the size of the gaps between the current process capabilities, competitors' capabilities, and customers' requirements. Substantial gaps justify major process renovations, whereas small gaps encourage incremental improvements through Kaizen Events.

CHAPTER SUMMARY

Processes are the critical building blocks of operations across the supply chain. The importance of processes is emphasized in the following critical lessons:

1. Every business is defined by its various processes. These processes determine capabilities including what the organization can and cannot do regarding the types of product value delivered to customers.
2. A process is a collection of activities that uses resources to convert various inputs into outputs that customers value. Inputs used by processes include materials, energy, information, management, technology, and labor. Outputs consist of products, information, and experiences.
3. Processes are characterized by activities (i.e., operations, decisions, storage, transportation, delays, and inspections), flows (inputs and outputs), structures (organization schemes of activities), resources, and metrics.
4. Capacity within the supply chain should be managed strategically. Key decisions include when capacity should be added or deleted, which supply chain member should have capacity, and how much capacity is needed.
5. In many situations, as output volume increases, economies of scale and reductions in cost per unit are encountered until an optimal level is reached. If volume increases too much, the cost per unit can increase because of diseconomies of scale.
6. The maximum level of output from any process is determined by the activity with the lowest capacity, known as the *bottleneck*. Attempts to increase output and decrease lead time must focus on bottleneck activities.
7. Capacity requirements are estimated by considering the sum of total processing time and the total setup time for products divided by the total operating time available.
8. Variability in processes also consumes capacity, cost, and lead times.
9. Processes need to be continuously improved, and sometimes entirely renovated or replaced. Kaizen Events are appropriate when intensive, focused modifications in the current process are desired.

KEY TERMS

DISCUSSION QUESTIONS

1. Describe the various operations within an amusement park that are most likely to become a bottleneck. How might an amusement park influence demand to better fit available capacity?
2. What are the primary resources that determine the capacity of each of the following?
   a. A grocery store.
   b. A hospital emergency room.
   c. A company that assembles appliances.
3. How can a university attain economies of scale? What impact might this have on quality and flexibility?
4. How would you define the maximum capacity for the front desk of a hotel? What is meant by the effective capacity? Define the difference in these two terms relative to the number of customers that can be checked into the hotel in a given period.
5. Which would require a larger amount of excess capacity, a hospital emergency room or a doctor's office? Why?
6. Discuss the challenges that an operations manager can expect to encounter when applying the principles of process performance to the upstream (supply-based) section of a supply chain.
7. Which of the five activity categories is represented by each of the following actions?
   a. A person taking an order from you at a restaurant.
   b. A conveyor belt carrying your order to you at a store.
   c. Work waiting at a workstation.
   d. Parts in a bin that an operator is working on.
   e. The safe at your bank.
   f. A person setting up a workstation to process parts.
   g. The advisor at your college checking your transcripts over to make sure that you have enough credits to graduate.
8. Under what conditions could inspections, storages, and transports be considered value-adding?
9. How would you define the capacity of your school? In what way does capacity influence the value of your college experience?
10. Under what conditions would you use a Kaizen Event?
11. Why is it important to begin with the metrics rather than to start by looking at the process?
12. Interpret Juran's Law from a process thinking perspective. How would this change your approach to problem solving?
13. If your goal is to reduce variance within a supply chain (especially if the variance is most evident in your supply), under what conditions does it make sense to focus first on the customer side of the supply chain?

SOLVED PROBLEMS

1. **Process Capacity at Zug Island Steel**

   Zug Island operates a mill that makes steel for a variety of uses. You have been hired as a consultant to evaluate the current state of operations of the coking oven, blast furnace, and basic oxygen furnace (BOF) departments. In the first stage of the process, a coking oven changes coal from a nearby coal dump into coke. The coke is left to cool in a heap and then moved to a pile near the blast furnace. Currently, the coke oven has a design capacity of 71,000 tons of coke per year.

The blast furnace converts coke from the pile and iron pellets, also from a nearby pile, into pig iron. The pig iron is moved to a staging area to cool. The blast furnace uses 1.5 tons of coke and 2.3 tons of iron pellets to make every ton of pig iron, with a design capacity of 55,000 tons of pig iron per year.

In the next step, the BOFs convert pig iron into steel, which is taken to a soaking pit to await the next stage of processing. The BOFs require 0.8 tons of pig iron and 1.2 tons of scrap and chemicals to produce a ton of steel. They have a design capacity of 68,000 tons of steel per year.

Over the last year, the plant produced 60,000 tons of steel. You have been asked to calculate the capacity of the production process at Zug Island, stating results in tons of finished product (i.e., tons of steel). Also, the company is considering increasing the capacity of the blast furnace from 55,000 tons to 70,000 tons of pig iron per year, citing two major reasons. First, managers see a need to balance capacity across processes. Second, the change seems very attractive economically, with a return on investment significantly above the firm's requirement. What is your evaluation of this proposed change?

Solution

Initially, this problem seems complex with many different activities and capacities stated in varying units such as pig iron tons, steel tons, and coke tons. The following four steps show how the problem can be analyzed.

1. Figure 3-5 lays out three operations (the coking oven, the blast furnace, and the basic oxygen furnaces) and six storage activities within the steel-making process. The process is organized sequentially, as the coking oven feeds the blast

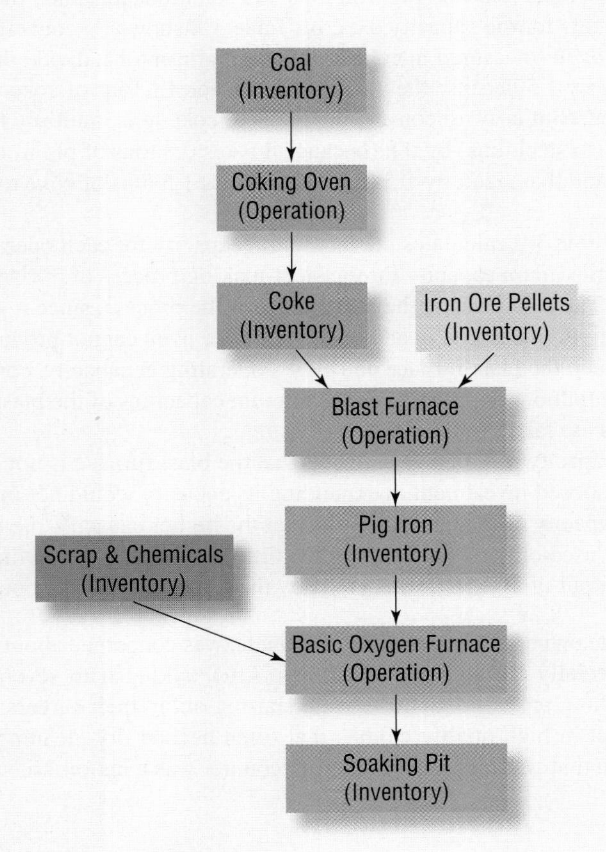

FIGURE 3-5 Process Flow for Zug Island Steel

TABLE 3-8 Converting between Different Units of Capacity Measurement

Unit of Capacity	To Convert to Coke Tons	To Convert to Pig Iron Tons	To Convert to Steel Tons
Output of coke oven (CO)	No conversion	(CO output)/1.5	(CO output)/(1.5*.8)
Output of blast furnace (BF)	BF output * 1.5	No conversion	BF output/.8
Output of basic oxygen furnace (BOF)	BOF output * 1.5 * .8	BOF output * .8	No conversion

TABLE 3-9 Calculating Maximum Capacity

Unit of Capacity	Maximum Coke Tons	Maximum Pig Iron Tons	Maximum Steel Tons
Output of coke oven (CO)	71,000	47,333.33	59,166.67
Output of blast furnace (BF)	82,500	55,000	68,750
Output of basic oxygen furnace (BOF)	81,600	54,400	68,000

furnace that feeds the basic oxygen furnaces. Therefore, the overall capacity for this process depends on that of the lowest-capacity activity.

2. The most appropriate time period for the capacity calculation is one year because all data are stated in annual units.
3. To establish a common unit of measure, the calculation must convert the first two units—coke tons and pig iron tons—to steel tons to satisfy the company's requirements for the capacity data. As Table 3-8 shows, to convert the output of the coke oven (measured in coke tons) into pig iron tons, divide the number of coke tons by 1.5 because the blast furnace needs 1.5 tons of coke to create a ton of pig iron. Similarly, to convert steel tons to coke tons, multiply the output of the BOF (in steel tons) by 0.8 (because it takes 0.8 tons of pig iron to make a ton of steel) and that result by 1.5 (because it takes 1.5 tons of coke to make a ton of pig iron).
4. Finally, Table 3-9 calculates the maximum capacity for each operation. This shows a maximum capacity for the steel-making process of 59,166.67 steel tons per year. The coke oven is the bottleneck for the process, since it generates the lowest output, measured in any units. The coke oven cannot produce enough coke to keep the blast furnace and BOFs operating at capacity, constraining the overall output of the process. The maximum capacities of the blast furnace and the BOFs are fairly well-balanced.

   This capacity calculation indicates that the blast furnace is not the bottleneck, so the proposed investment in expanding its capacity would not improve the overall capacity of the process. In fact, at the higher capacity, the blast furnace would be used only 67.6 percent of the time, found by dividing the coking oven's output of 59,166.76 steel tons by the new blast furnace output of 87,500.

2. Terry Ilgen, the owner of Nu-Clean Dry Cleaners, was concerned about customer waiting time, especially during peak/rush times. After talking with several of her target customers (young professionals who were starting out in their careers and were more likely to invest in high-quality clothes that often needed dry cleaning), she came to the conclusion that waiting time at the front counter was a major issue. Her customers

were willing to wait up to five minutes before they started to become upset; they were not willing to wait any more than 10 minutes.

Peak periods were from 8 a.m. to 10 a.m. and from 4 p.m. to 6 p.m.

Terry undertook a process study with the help of her front counter staff. They collected data for two weeks and obtained the following:

Average arrival rate at peak	1 arrival every two minutes
Standard deviation of arrivals	1 minute
Average time to process an order	2 minutes
Standard deviation of process time	3 minutes
Total amount of time for peak	56 hours
Time that clerks were busy	36 hours

Given this information, what is the expected waiting time for a customer during the peak period?

To answer this question, we have to get the information needed in the equation for wait time [equation (3.2)]:

$$\textit{Wait time} = \left(\frac{c_a^2 + c_p^2}{2}\right)\left(\frac{u}{1-u}\right)t_p$$

Coefficient of variation of job arrivals (arrival time at peak and standard deviation of arrivals) $\left(c_a^2\right)$ is 1/.5 = 2

Coefficient of variation for procession $\left(c_p^2\right)$ is 3 (standard deviation of processing time) / (average time to take an order) = 1.5

Utilization (u) is 36/56 = .64

Average processing time (t_p) = 2

Plugging these numbers into the equation, we get:

$$\textit{Wait time} = \left(\frac{2^2 + 1.5^2}{2}\right)\left(\frac{.65}{.38}\right)2$$
$$= 11.11 \text{ minutes}$$

We can see that the average expected waiting time is greater than the 10-minute maximum desired by customers. In reviewing this analysis, one of Terry's employees suggested, why not use bar code tags for frequent customers? Terry estimated that this change would reduce the average processing time from 2 minutes to 1.5 and the standard deviation from 3 to 2. Further analysis also indicated that the total time that the clerks would spend working should fall from 36 hours to 25 hours. Should Terry consider this suggestion?

The suggestion changes c_p^2, u, and t_p.

$$u = 25/56 = .45$$

$$c_p^2 = \left(\frac{2}{1.5}\right)^2 = 1.78$$

$$\textit{Wait time} = \left(\frac{2^2 + 1.33^2}{2}\right)\left(\frac{.45}{.55}\right)1.5$$
$$= 3.54 \text{ minutes}$$

This is a good suggestion since it not only reduces the average waiting time, it also helps Terry to keep the average waiting time in a range that is acceptable to her critical customers.

TABLE 3-10 Skateboard Demand, Processing Time and Setup Time

Skateboard	Demand Forecast (units/year)	Processing Time (minutes/unit)	Lot Size (# of boards)	Setup Time (minutes/setup)
Pro	5,000	90	10	15
Trickster	8,000	75	10	25
Traverse	12,000	45	25	10

3. The X-Games Skateboard Company is planning to introduce three new skateboards, the Pro, the Trickster, and the Traverse. The boards can all be made in the same type of work cell. The manufacturing plant operates two 8-hour shifts, 250 days per year. Given the demand forecast, processing time for each skateboard type, and setup time information shown in Table 3-10, how many skateboard work cells are needed?

Solution

First, determine the total processing time for the skateboards. Multiply the annual demand for each skateboard by its processing time to estimate the processing time per year per skateboard. Then, sum these times to get the total processing time for all three skateboards.

Skateboard	Demand Forecast (units/year)	Processing Time (minutes/unit)	Processing Time Required (minutes/year)
Pro	5,000	90	450,000
Trickster	8,000	75	600,000
Traverse	12,000	45	540,000
	Total Processing Time (minutes/year)		1,590,000

Next, determine the number of setups required by dividing the annual demand for each skateboard by its lot size. Multiply the number of setups for each skateboard type by its setup time to get the annual setup time per skateboard. The annual setup times are summed to get the total setup time required per year.

Skateboard	Demand Forecast (units/year)	Lot Size (# of boards)	Number of Setups/year	Setup Time (minutes/ setup)	Setup Time/ Board (minutes/year)
Pro	5,000	10	500	15	7,500
Trickster	8,000	10	800	25	20,000
Traverse	12,000	25	480	10	4,800
			Total Setup Time (minutes/year)		32,300

Determine the total operating time available.

$$\text{Total operating time (minutes/year)} = 250 \text{ days/year} \times 2 \text{ shifts/day} \times 8 \text{ hours/days} \times 60 \text{ minutes/hour)}$$
$$= 240{,}000 \text{ minutes/year}$$

To determine the number of work cells, the total setup time is added to the total processing time, and this value is divided by the total operating time available.

Number of work cells = (Total processing time required + Total setup time required)/Total operating time available
(1,590,000 (minutes/year) + 32,300 (minutes/year))/(240,000 (minutes/year))
= 6.7 work cells, so round up to 7 work cells.

PROBLEMS

1.

Operation	No. Equipment	Design Capacity (by equipment)	Planned Utilization (overall)
A	1	400 units/hr	80%
B	4	100, 80, 150, 125	77%
C	1	350 units/hr	95%
D	2	190, 235	72.5%

With the process information provided in the preceding table, when the sequence of flow is A → B (any machine can be used if available)→ C → D (any machine can be used if available), calculate the overall flow rate for:

a. Maximum capacity
b. Effective capacity

2. You are given the following information. Which of the statements below can you support with this information?

Maximum capacity (labor hours): 480 hours per week

Effective capacity ratio: 85%

Actual time worked: 380 hours per week over the last two weeks

On-time delivery %: 75 percent of the jobs are being completed on time

a. More capacity needs to be added in the short term to improve performance in the system.
b. We need to look at variability in the rate at which jobs enter the shop.
c. Our workforce is not working hard enough.
d. Our workforce may be waiting on delayed arrivals of inputs needed to do the work.

Describe the reasons why you selected the specific option(s) that you did.

3. Electronics Assembly Inc. is a contract manufacturer that assembles consumer electronics for a number of companies. Currently, the operations manager is assessing the capacity requirements as input into a bid for a job to assemble cell phones for a major global company. The company would assemble three models of cell phones in the same assembly cell. Setup time between the phones is negligible. Electronics Assembly Inc. operates two 8-hour shifts for 275 days per year. Use the information in the table to determine the capacity requirements.

Cell Phone	Demand Forecast (phones/year)	Processing Time (minutes/phone)
Mars	15,000	15
Saturn	8,000	18
Neptune	12,000	16

4. Penny's Pies is a small specialty supplier to a national coffee-house chain. Penny's makes three types of pies (apple, cherry, and pecan). Penny's operates 250 days per year with a single eight-hour shift. Capacity is controlled by the number of production lines within the bakery (a line consists of mixing equipment, rolling and cutting equipment, an oven, and packaging equipment). Based on the information provided in the table, determine the number of production lines Penny's should have.

Pie	Demand Forecast (pies/year)	Processing Time (minutes/pie)	Lot Size (# of pies)	Setup Time (minutes/setup)
Apple	60,000	2	600	10
Cherry	30,000	4	200	15
Pecan	20,000	3	200	30

5. Best Bicycles manufactures three different types of bikes: the Tiny Tike, the Adult Aero, and the Mountain Monger. Given the information in the table, calculate the required capacity for this year's production. Note that the times are given for assembly lines, so capacity calculations should be in terms of the number of lines necessary. Assume that Best Bicycles operates two shifts, each with 2,000 hours per year.

Bike	Demand Forecast (units/year)	Processing Time (minutes/unit)	Lot Size (# of bikes)	Setup Time (minutes/setup)
Tiny Tike	14,000	8	10	50
Adult Aero	16,000	10	10	80
Mountain Monger	19,000	12	25	40

6. Doog's Donuts produces five varieties of pastries, which are sold to a national grocery chain: muffins, donuts, cookies, cream puffs, and fritters. Assuming that Doog's operates a single shift for 1,800 hours per year, calculate the required capacity. The processing time per unit, setup time per lot, the annual demand, and lot size are given in the table. Assume that the times given are for a work cell of four workers each, so required capacity should be in terms of the number of work cells needed.

Pastry	Demand Forecast (units/year)	Processing Time (minutes/unit)	Lot Size (# of pastries)	Setup Time (minutes/setup)
Muffins	440,000	0.1	400	20
Donuts	600,000	0.1	300	5
Cookies	1,000,000	0.05	1,000	10
Cream Puffs	240,000	0.2	200	20
Fritters	180,000	0.2	300	15

7. Spartan Redi-Care is a small urgent care facility located near the University. Because of the high competition for student business, the manager of Spartan has decided that the most effective way of competing is to emphasize short wait times. Spartan Redi-Care has even gone so far as to adopt the slogan, "Get in, Get better, Get out." As the facility manager, you have decided that this slogan translates into an average customer wait time of 30 minutes. You have collected the following data taken from a three week period of typical demand:

$c_a = 3$
$c_p = 1$
$u = 70$ percent
$t_p = 6$ minutes

a. What is the expected average waiting time for Spartan Redi-Care?
b. If the expected average waiting time is greater than what you have promised, what are some actions that you could introduce to correct this imbalance (be specific)?

8. New Time Videos (NTV) is a new online video rental service. In the field, it is trying to compete by offering its customers access to all of the major new video releases in one business day. That is, if you order a video from NTV, you can expect it in one business day from the time when you placed the order. When you are done with the video, you simply drop it in the prepaid mailing envelope and return it. All videos arrive in a sorting facility located in the Midwest where envelopes with the videos are opened, checked (right video with the right sleeve, no scratches, no cracks, no dirt on the videos), and made ready to be sent out again. As the manager of this facility, your goal is to turn the returned videos around in 6 hours (a shift is 8 hours long). You have the following information:

Inventory of videos:	450,000 per shift
Throughput:	325,000 per shift

a. Calculate the expected average flow time (hint: Use Little's Law).
b. What changes would you recommend to meet the goal of processing a returned video within 6 hours?

9. PizzaTime Restaurants is building a new pizza place and needs to determine how big to make the various parts of its facility. It wants to be able to accommodate a maximum of 500 customers per hour at its peak times. PizzaTime has collected the following information: the average time to place and receive an order is 1.1 minutes, 20 percent of the customers have cars and require parking spots, and the average length of time at the restaurant is 20 minutes per customer. Assuming a capacity cushion of 20 percent, find:

a. The number of cash registers required. (assume an average of 4 customers per group)
b. The number of parking spaces needed.
c. The number of seats/tables needed. (assume 4 seats per table)
d. Which of these operations are likely to be bottlenecks?

10. Mike operates a hair-cutting salon that specializes in providing quick walk-in service for just about any type of haircut. He deals with customers as they walk in the door. This includes writing down the customer's name and what they desire in terms of haircut, wash, dry, and so on. This process usually takes two minutes. If no hair stylist is available, the customer then goes to the waiting area, where he/she is processed on a first-come, first-serve basis. The salon has five hair stylists who work eight hours each day. It takes, on average, 25 minutes for a stylist to greet the customer, wash and/or cut his hair, and wish him a fond farewell. Then Mike completes the process by taking the customer's money and telling him about the satisfaction guarantee offered by the shop. This final set of steps takes two minutes on average.

a. Assuming that the waiting area always has at least one customer in it, how many customers on average can Mike's salon process in a day (assuming no problems in utilization, quality, or efficiency)?
b. Suppose that you need an "average" haircut, and as you walk into the salon you see three people sitting in the waiting area. You notice that another person is just sitting down in one of the stylists' empty chair, and the other stylists are all busy with customers. Assuming you choose to wait, how long would you expect it to be before you are ready to leave the salon?

11. Cooper's Copy Shop is considering two different processes for completing copying jobs brought in by customers. Process A uses one person to set up the job and do the copying. If this approach is used, an experienced person can complete an average of 20 jobs per day. Process B uses two people. One person does the setup and the second person does the actual copying. Setup on one job can be done while copying is being completed on another but copying must be completed on a job before the copying machine can start copying the next. After some practice, this second process can be completed with a standard time of 10 minutes for setup and 15 minutes for actual copying. In either case, assume an 8-hour day, 5 days per week, 250 days per year.
    a. Assuming ideal conditions, what is the maximum capacity of process B?
    b. How long would it take to process 200 jobs using process A (assume only one worker and one machine)?
    c. How long would it take to process 200 jobs using process B (assume only one "production line")?
    d. If Cooper is primarily interested in providing low cost to customers, which process should he put in place?
    e. If Cooper is primarily interested in providing quick service to customers, which process should he put in place?
12. Metal Hoses Inc. (MHI) is a major manufacturer of metal braided hoses for industry. These products are used in everything from cars to tanks to motorcycles. MHI's products can even be found on the Space Shuttle. At first glance, it may seem that MHI's products are mature and compete on the basis of cost alone. However, recently, the management at MHI have identified that there is a market segment that demands (and is willing to pay for) speed in delivery. That is, these customers are willing to pay if MHI can receive, process, and deliver orders quickly. From talking with its customers, the management at MHI has determined that the customers are most sensitive to order lead times of one week or less (from time of receipt to time of delivery). In studying their processes, management has determined that order entry is the major bottleneck. This process consists of the following steps: (1) the order is received from the customer; (2) it is moved to accounting where it is checked and entered; (3) it next goes to engineering for evaluation and acceptance; (4) purchasing is next for material assessment; and (5) it is scheduled by operations. These five steps are separated physically since the order has to move to the departments where these activities are carried out. Analysis of the situation has indicated that under the current process it takes an order two weeks to complete this process. However, when errors are uncovered, the process can take up to five weeks (since the problem order has to return to the steps where the problem was first created). Management has determined that order entry should take no more than four hours.
    a. Identify appropriate metrics for both the order entry process and the overall order fulfillment process for MHI.
    b. Use process thinking to re-engineer the order entry process
        - With technology.
        - Without technology (management has determined that MHI should not spend its way out of this problem).
13. "This should be a simple issue. You know that our average weekly sales are $2,000 and the flow time is one day. Surely with this information, you should have no problem maintaining an inventory level of $200 to serve the sales."

    With these words, the director of finance leaves your office. Now, you have a challenge before you—that of determining whether the analysis carried out by the director makes sense.
    a. Using Little's Law, determine anticipated flow time and compare it with the expected flow time. (*Hint:* the flow time is in days, the sales in weeks; use a common unit of measure.)

b. Keeping the flow times and throughputs constant, determine if the process as currently described can be supported by $200 of inventory. If not, what options should you consider?

14. You have been asked to determine the average wait time for a process that has caused problems for the management of your company. From data you collected over a two-week period (which you feel are representative), you have determined the following:

Average process utilization:	80 percent
Average processing time:	10 minutes
Average job arrival rate:	10 minutes
Processing time, standard deviation:	50 minutes
Arrival rates, standard deviation:	100 minutes

a. What is the average wait time?
b. If management wants to promise its customers an average wait time in the system of no more than 24 hours, what recommendations would you provide management on how to change the operation of the process of concern?

CASE

Evergreen Products

The top managers of Evergreen Products of East Lansing, MI, have asked you to act as a consultant on a problem plaguing the entire company. Evergreen Products manufactures decorated containers and care tags for a market consisting primarily of small- to medium-sized florists and grocery stores. The containers are relatively inexpensive to make, but they are sold at a high markup (60 percent). The same is true for the tags. Because of the targeted market segment, management feels that it must be able to provide its customers with quick delivery and quality. However, this has not been happening lately.

To understand what happens, it is useful to first follow the course of an order received from the customer. Orders are placed in one of two ways at Evergreen. First, customers may notice that their stocks are getting low. They call the Evergreen sales department with an order, which is received by one of three clerks. The clerk records on a sheet the customer number, the type of product, and the quantity needed. At this point, a customer due date is set based on the customer's needs. However, the clerks try to encourage a due date that is about five working days out (there is no hard-and-fast rule for this procedure).

Once a day, the sales account manager picks up all sales orders. He is responsible for ensuring that all orders are complete and accurately entered and that the customer's credit rating is OK. If it is, the order is put into another pile where it is picked up once every morning. If the order is not acceptable or if there are errors, the order is returned to the person who took the order. That person is then responsible for correcting the problem within a reasonable period of time. When the order has been corrected, the process is repeated. It takes about half a day to move from phone order to sales account manager and about an hour to clear the sales account manager. Forty percent of the orders experience some form of error.

The second way that an order can be placed is through the company's own traveling salespersons that stop in on accounts and check their inventory stocks. When they see that an item is low, they fill out an order. They then phone the order into the plant (about once every day—this varies depending on how busy they are). Since each salesperson is rated on the total dollar sales he generates, there is a built-in incentive to be very concerned about clients' inventory stocks. When the order is turned over to the sales account manager, the process is identical to the one previously described. On average, the delay for entering orders through the salesperson is about half a day (but it can range up to two days).

Once the order clears the sales account manager, it goes to accounting where it first is put into the day's pile. It is then entered into the accounting system. This step marks the beginning of the billing process. It takes an average of half a day to clear accounting (but this can range up to two days). From here, it goes to the shop floor scheduler.

The shop floor scheduler reviews all orders for accuracy and completeness. Any problem orders are set aside and returned to the sales account manager for correction. About 15 percent of the orders are typically set aside each day. The rest of the orders are released to the shop floor. It typically takes one day to clear the shop floor. The time can vary depending on the time of year. Christmas, Valentine's Day, Easter, Mother's Day, and other similar holidays put a great deal of pressure on the shop floor (which runs on average at 80 percent utilization). The shop floor is held accountable for meeting all quoted customer due dates.

Top management is concerned over the poor performance of the shop floor. Inventories are high and growing; overtime is excessive; on-time delivery performance is poor; and customer dissatisfaction is growing. The top manager has asked you if he should replace the current shop floor planner.

Questions

1. What are the desired outcomes for Evergreen? What should Evergreen wish to accomplish with its order entry system? How do we know if the order entry system is working well or poorly? How is it doing now?
2. What do the customers want from Evergreen? What types of problems do the existing customers pose for Evergreen? Why?
3. Apply the process for incorporating value through process thinking to this problem. What metrics would you apply to this process? What insights into the process did you obtain?
4. How would you improve the operation of the current order entry process at Evergreen? Be specific.

Hints

1. Make sure that you identify and understand the various customers. To simplify the analysis, focus on the florists as the critical customer.
2. Bound the process by focusing only on the orders that come into the system by telephone.
3. Make sure that you establish metrics at the outset.
4. Assume no errors in the process.

CASE

Midas Gold Juice Company

You are the purchasing director for Midas Gold Corporation, a small Midwestern fruit-juice company that produces a line of premium, limited-run fruit juice (Slogan: Midas Juice—You'll be touched by the Gold). As one of your responsibilities, you review all requests for capital equipment that costs $10,000 or more. Recently, you have received a request from the production department to purchase an additional stamping machine. This machine will double the capacity of the tin shop from its current level of 80,000 lids (design capacity) to 160,000 lids. Every can needs two lids. Production managers also claim that the new machine will balance the line and improve output dramatically.

In reviewing the request, you decide to examine the production process. You find a fairly straightforward process that starts by squeezing the juice from the fruit and storing it in tanks. On average, these tanks hold 4,000 gallons available at any time. Under ideal circumstances, this amount fills 40,000 cans per month.

The can-making process has two stages. In the first, the cans are made in two steps involving two departments. The tin department makes lids with a current capacity of 80,000. The stamping department converts sheets of tin into the can bodies. The tin department uses 4,000 sheets of tin per month, and each sheet produces 12 can bodies. The bodies and lids are assembled in the filling department where they are filled and sealed. The design capacity of the filling department is 50,000 cans per month.

Questions

1. What is your response to the request for the new machine?
2. Identify any concerns that you have. (*Hint:* Think about the process and its design capacities when answering this question.)

Hints

1. Make sure that you express all the capacity in the same units.
2. You may want to use the process mapping and analysis techniques described in the supplement to this chapter.

CASE

American Vinyl Products

To: Brad Hadley, President, American Vinyl Products (AVP)

From: Bev Trudeau, Director of Purchasing, American Performance Car, CA

Subject: Customer Service at American Vinyl Products

Our two companies have basically had a good relationship over the last two years. We have generally been pleased with both the quality of the products as well as the price offered. These features, while important, are not critical. What is critical to our future relations is customer service. This is one area where you have recently fallen down. Our staff has persistently experienced delays in getting through to your staff by phone. When we do, we experience further delays in getting answers. Our needs are few but simple. We want to contact American Vinyl quickly. We want to get through to a person quickly. We want to place orders, confirm status and change requirements quickly. Three days ago, Brad Allenby from our purchasing department spent 20 minutes waiting to get through. He had a critical problem that had to be resolved. He kept waiting. All the time, all he heard was how it was important that he remain on the line and that he would be answered in the order in which he was received. He finally gave up and called Joan in your marketing department. Even then, it took 24 hours before he got an answer. This is unacceptable. Unless you adequately resolve the problems with your phone system, we will take our business elsewhere. As you are aware, your contract with American Performance Car is going to be up for review in six months. Your product is not so unique that we cannot quickly find an alternative supplier. I am sorry for the angry tenor of this letter. However, this note reflects the frustration that we have experienced. It is totally unacceptable that we cannot even get hold of anyone at American Vinyl after 3 p.m. our time here in California. Your company must become more customer-oriented. Or else. You have 90 days to provide us with an acceptable resolution to the current situation.

As Tom Adamson put down the fax and looked at Brad, the president, Tom knew that things were not good. The phone system had been a persistent source of problems for American Vinyl Products (AVP). Tom knew that this complaint was not an isolated event. He also knew that Brad had commissioned a local telecommunications company to do a study on AVP's phone system. Their recommendation was that a new system be put in that offered more lines and more staff capacity. Brad thought that this might be the answer. Tom also knew that he would be asked to come up with recommendations for improving the current system.

As Tom got up and left the office, he reviewed the information that he had recently gathered. AVP was a small manufacturer of vinyl and plastic products, including vinyl car products (e.g., decals and pin striping for cars), plastic after-market products (e.g., new brake lenses for cars designed to make the car look more sporty) and decals for the recreational market (AVP sold name decals to Four-Winns in the boating marketing and to Bombardier in the ski-doo and sea-doo markets). Located in Charlotte, Michigan, this company had experienced a great deal of recent growth. Part of the reason for this growth could be traced to the excellent customer service that AVP gave its customers.

AVP sold primarily to three groups of customers. The first were the do-it-yourselfers (DIY). These typically bought vinyl striping from a local retail or car accessory store. As a rule, their purchases were very small yet they needed a great deal of information. Often, they would call AVP asking for a catalog of products, information on how to use AVP's products (or information on how to correct a problem with an AVP product), or information on where they could get AVP products. As a rule, DIYs were very price sensitive. The second market consisted of professional users. These were the people who used AVP products as part of their business (e.g., in a body shop). While buying a moderate amount of product, they were often more interested in getting very technical information pertaining to the use of an AVP product. They were often considered to be very demanding with the result that only the most experienced sales staff worked with them. Finally, there were large corporate accounts, accounts such as American Performance Car. These accounts would call AVP typically to place orders, to determine the status of current orders, and to see if they could change the status of current orders (i.e., change the due date, the order quantities, or the product mix). Typically, their calls were short and to the point. The differences between the three groups are summarized in the table on the next page.

Customer Type	Average Calls per Day	Average Time per call (min.) Range in ()	Average Revenue per call
DIYs	200	20 (min of 5, max of 35)	$5.00 per call (estimated)
Professional users	40	10 (min of 5, max of 20)	$40.00
Large corporate accounts	20	5 (min of 1, max of 10)	$400

The same phone process served all three customers. All three customers called into the same 1-800 number. Once they called, their calls went into a queue area where they waited until a service representative was available. The calls were answered on a first-come, first-served basis. In this phone-bank area, the current system would periodically remind them that: (1) their call was important, and (2) their calls would be answered in the order received. When the calls were answered, a representative would try to determine the type of customer and then determine what was needed to answer the call. Typically, the representatives would fill in a form (in the case of a catalog request), look up locations of outlets selling their products (done using a large book centrally located), and look up possible solutions from a tips file or generate a follow-up form (in the case of a customer requested change or status query). When done, the information would be placed in a large basket for processing. Finally, the representatives would then give the customer a best guess of when they could expect an answer (if further information was needed). Because of the great diversity in the types of calls and the demands of the callers, training and staffing was considered a major obstacle. At present, the line was staffed with 10 representatives on average over an 11-hour period (however, over the two-hour staggered lunch, there were fewer representatives). The department was open from 7:00 a.m. until 6:00 p.m. The rate at which the calls came in was difficult to predict. However past experience was that it was never level. Finally, since 1995, 40 percent (and growing) of the sales came from California, Washington, Nevada, and Oregon. Unlike Michigan, which is in the Eastern time zone, these states were located three time zones away.

Questions

1. You have been asked to help Tom. What recommendations would you give him about how to improve the operation of the phone system?
2. Tom has a recommendation for increasing the capacity of the phone system. Is this recommendation adequate to help address the problems facing AVP? Make sure that your answer is supported by the appropriate analysis.

SELECTED READINGS & INTERNET SITES

Andrews, D. C., and S. K. Stalick. *Business Reengineering: The Survival Guide.* Englewood Cliffs, NJ: Yourdon Press, 1994.

Imai, M. *Gemba Kaizen.* New York: McGraw-Hill, 1997.

Madison, D. *Process Mapping, Process Improvement, and Process Management.* Chico, CA: Paton Press, 2005.

Melan, E. H. *Process Management: Methods for Improving Products and Service.* New York: McGraw-Hill, 1993.

Miller, H. "Apple Has Edge on Tablet Rivals with iPad Costs, Report Says." BusinessWeek.com, March 2, 2011.

Rummler, G. A., and A. P. Brache. *Improving Performance: How to Manage the White Space on the Organization Chart.* San Francisco, CA: Jossey-Bass Publishers, 1990.

Sengupta, S. "A Plan for Building a New Supply Chain." *Supply Chain Management Review* 12, no. 1 (January/February 2008), pp. 46–52.

Shapiro, B. P.; V. K. Rangan; and J. J. Sviokla. "Staple Yourself to an Order." *Harvard Business Review* 70, no. 4 (July/August 1992), pp. 113–22.

Smith, H., and P. Fingar. *Business Process Management: The Third Wave.* Tampa, FL: Meghan Kiffer Press, 2006.

Womack, J. P., and D. T. Jones. *Lean Thinking: Banish Waste and Create Wealth in Your Corporation.* New York: Simon and Schuster, 1996.

3 Chapter Supplement: Process Mapping and Analysis

CHAPTER SUPPLEMENT OUTLINE

LEARNING OBJECTIVES *After studying this supplement, you should be able to:*

LO3S-1 Work through the various steps in process mapping and analysis.

LO3S-2 Assess a process to determine how effective it is in achieving its desired outcome(s).

LO3S-3 Determine to what type of activity each step in a process belongs.

LO3S-4 Understand when and how to apply the various tools of process mapping.

LO3S-5 Change a process to make it more effective and efficient by either refining the current process or designing a new replacement process.

Process mapping and analysis is a technique for documenting activities in a detailed, compact, and graphic form to help managers understand processes and highlight areas for potential improvements. The technique generates a process blueprint that supplies nearly all of the information needed to effectively evaluate a process. As the name implies, process mapping and analysis helps managers improve the effectiveness and efficiency of processes by first mapping (diagramming) the process, and then analyzing it to identify and eliminate sources of waste or inefficiency.

process mapping and analysis
A technique for graphically documenting the activities in a process with the goal of identifying opportunities for improvement.

LO3S-1 Work through the various steps in process mapping and analysis.

THE "PROCESS" OF PROCESS MAPPING AND ANALYSIS

Process mapping and analysis consists of six steps:

1. Determine the desired outcome for the process and the associated metrics needed to evaluate its performance.
2. Identify and bound the critical process.
3. Document the existing process (the "current state" map).
4. Analyze the process and prioritize opportunities for improvement.
5. Recommend appropriate changes to the process (the "future state" map).
6. Implement the changes and monitor improvements.

The remainder of this supplement describes the steps by way of an example. The example illustrates how process mapping and analysis can be used to uncover problems and to improve efficiency and effectiveness of the affected processes.

Prepare

How do managers document and analyze processes?

Organize

The "Process" of Process Mapping and Analysis
American Health and Medical Products (AHMP)
Step 1: Identify the Desired Outcomes in Advance
Step 2: Identify and Bound the Critical Process
Step 3: Document the Existing Process
Step 4: Analyze the Process and Identify Opportunities for Improvement
Step 5: Recommend Appropriate Changes to the Process
Step 6: Implement the Changes and Monitor Improvements

AMERICAN HEALTH AND MEDICAL PRODUCTS (AHMP)

American Health and Medical Products (AHMP) is a major designer, innovator, manufacturer, and supplier of medical and health supplies for hospitals, nursing homes, medical facilities, and doctor/dentist offices. One of AHMP's major product lines consists of sterilizers, more commonly known as autoclaves. AHMP is the market leader in autoclaves; its products are viewed as the most sophisticated of all competitors. Customers buy AHMP autoclaves expecting to receive a well-designed, quality product, quickly delivered. In fact, order-to-delivery lead time is very important to the customers. Typically, AHMP promises its customers that they will receive delivery of an ordered autoclave within 16 weeks. Allowing one week for shipping, this means that AHMP has 15 weeks for order entry, material acquisition and delivery, and manufacturing. Recently, a competitor advertised that it would deliver a standard autoclave in as little as 10 weeks. Managers at AHMP felt that they had to respond.

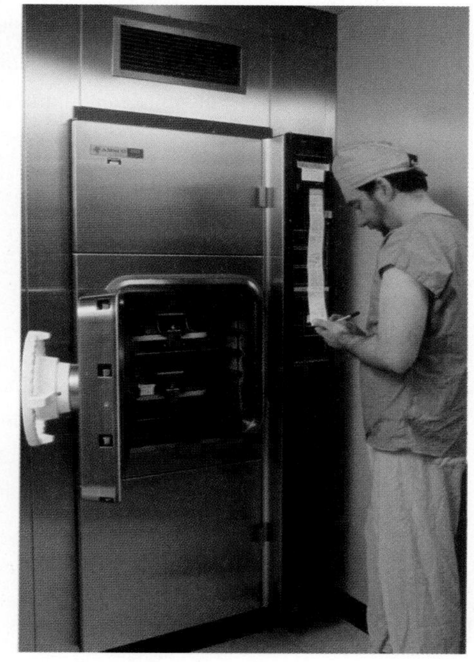

The managers carried out a series of process studies with the goal of determining whether the existing process could be reduced from 16 weeks to six weeks, including shipping. If successful, they felt that this significant reduction in lead time would meet the competitive threat. An initial study indicated that the internal manufacturing process could be accomplished in two to four days *provided* that the necessary orders, capacity, and materials were in place. A second, purchasing-oriented study determined that components could be procured within two weeks of order placement. Thus, allowing two weeks for procurement, one week for manufacturing, and one week for shipping, the remaining question was whether or not the order entry and approval process could be completed in two weeks. Order entry managers estimated that the average actual lead time for order entry was four weeks, with a range of one to six weeks. This is the process element that we will study as our example.

LO3S-2 Assess a process to determine how effective it is in achieving its desired outcome(s).

Step 1: Identify the Desired Outcomes in Advance

Before making any change to a process, it is important to clarify what the process should achieve. These are the critical customers' desired outcomes, as discussed in Chapter 2. Objectives may include lowered costs, decreased lead times, improved quality, more reliable deliveries, or other outcomes. Metrics are critical in making these desired outcomes meaningful to those involved with the process. Table 3S-1 contains some of the more commonly used output metrics (measured at the end of the process) and process metrics (traits of the process that affect the outcomes being pursued).

Applying Step 1 to AHMP

AHMP's goal was to deliver a standard autoclave to the customer in no more than six weeks. Further discussion led managers at AHMP to determine that they would like to

TABLE 3S-1 Examples of Commonly Used Measures

Desired Outcomes	Output Measures	Process Measures
Cost	Actual cost per unit Actual cost vs. standard cost Target prices—relation of actual costs to target or desired costs Percentage cost savings achieved Reduction of administrative/overhead costs	Number of steps in the process (more steps should lead to higher costs) Number of people involved in the process (more people involved, the higher the costs) Average setup costs (higher setup costs should lead to larger batch quantities, which should increase costs) Percentage of unique components (the more unique items, the higher the costs)
Quality	Total Cost of Quality (discussed in Chapter 6) Percentage of products done right the first time Actual yield rates vs. standard yield rate Percentage of work reworked or rejected or held for further inspection Defective parts per million (PPM) Customer quality incidents Factory quality incidents Percentage and number of defect-free shipments	Number of times an item is handled (more handling creates more opportunities for quality problems) Number of steps in the process The number of times that the item is allowed to stop or to go into inventory (more times, more opportunities for quality problems) Number of inspections (more inspection—an indication of quality concerns) Number of steps in the process (more steps increase the probability of more quality defects).
Availability	Amount of inventory Order fill-rates Fill-rate by line On-time arrivals Number of lines/customers shut down because of supply shortages	Number of delays in the process (more delays create more unanticipated stoppages)
Lead time	Actual lead time to build a unit Actual lead time vs. standard lead time Percentage reduction in lead time	Number of steps (the more steps, the longer the lead time) Average setup time (as setup times increase, order quantities go up, and total lead times are increased) Distance covered by the process (the greater the distance, the longer the transport time) The number of people who touch the order (more touches create more costs, time, and potential errors

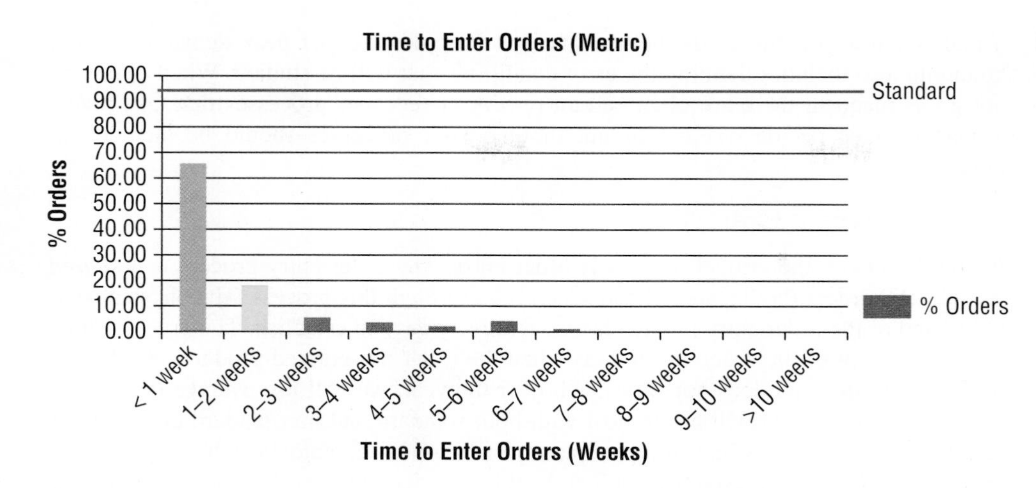

FIGURE 3S-1
Using a Metric for Time to Enter Orders

see 95 percent of all standard autoclave orders to be entered and approved within one week, with no order taking more than two weeks. Thus, the desired outcome for the process is to *maximize the percentage of orders going through order entry that are completed within one week from the time that they are received, with 95 percent being an acceptable level of performance.* This desired outcome may now be translated into a metric, consisting of three elements: the measure (to answer the question of "how are we doing"); the standard (what is an acceptable level of performance); and the reward (what happens if we do better than expected and what happens if we fail to meet the standard).

For AHMP, the measure is the percentage of the total orders within a given time period that are completed by order entry within one week of receipt. The standard is 95 percent. Also, taking more than two weeks to enter an order is considered unacceptable. Performance can be color coded using three colors: green if the order is completed within one week; yellow if order entry takes more than one week but not more than two weeks; and red if order entry for the specific order takes more than two weeks. Finally, we can put the standard of 95 percent into the figure and create a metric that conveys a great deal of information quickly to the user (as done in Figure 3S-1).

Step 2: Identify and Bound the Critical Process

The second step involves identifying and bounding the process that is most important to our desired outcome. As noted in Chapter 3, a critical process typically exhibits at least one of the following traits:

1. It is a bottleneck process—one that limits capacity for the overall system.
2. It is visible to the customer—one that directly affects customers' perceptions of value.
3. It consumes the largest amount of resources—one that offers the greatest potential for cost savings.
4. It is a shared process—one that feeds multiple downstream processes.
5. It exhibits the greatest level of variance—one that offers potential for improved reliability and capacity gains.
6. It is a process that is related to a unique skill or core competency—one that serves to differentiate us from competitors.

It is important to bound, or define the limits, of the critical process. Without bounds, a process study runs a real risk of never being completed. Bounding includes defining the physical starting and ending points for process analysis, as well as defining the operating conditions or demands to be considered in the analysis. A manager has to decide whether to study the process under low demand, average demand, or peak (highest) demand conditions. For example, if the process involves a perishable product such as a service, then it makes sense to focus on the performance of the process under peak demand. Process bounding also includes defining the error conditions that will be studied. When things do not go as planned, there are often certain rework or recovery processes that take place. Managers must decide whether or not these rework processes should be included in the analysis.

Applying Step 2 to AHMP

In AHMP's case, the critical process is order entry. The order entry process is a *shared* process. All orders (both standard and special) go through this process. The physical/spatial bound of the order entry process is also relatively easy to establish. The process starts with the receipt of the order and it ends when the order has entered production scheduling. Because demand does not vary much over the year, we will use average demand as the demand setting. AHMP has to deal with both standard and nonstandard orders (typically nonstandard orders have unique features or finishes—an autoclave done completely in stainless steel is a nonstandard order). In this case we will limit the process mapping exercise to standard orders. Finally, to keep things simple we will deal with the "best-case" scenario (no problems with the order).

Step 3: Document the Existing Process (the "Current State" Map)

current state The state of the process in its current or "as is" state.

LO3S-3 Determine to what type of activity each step in a process belongs.

Describing the **current state** of a process can be difficult. Inefficiencies and poor designs in the process may reflect poorly on particular managers or workers, so they may be reluctant to offer process information. It is important for the analyst to speak directly with the people who actually perform the process, not just those who manage the workers. Otherwise, the analyst might develop a distorted view of the "actual" process. Finally, the analyst must be aware that their presence near the workers can alter the way in which work is performed (for various reasons), thus making it difficult to develop an accurate picture of the process.

An effective way to document and communicate the current state of a process is to develop a process map, or diagram. By using a set of symbols in such a map, the analyst can graphically present how the inputs, outputs, flows, and activities of a process are linked together. Table 3S-2 lists five types of process activities that were defined in Chapter 3, along with each activity type's symbol. These categories can be used to classify nearly all activities in a process.

Process mapping and analysis can potentially be complex and time-consuming, but there are some general guidelines that can make this task simpler and easier to manage.

Identify Minimum Acceptable Levels of Detail

A process analyst must decide whether to show small activities separately in a map or to show them collectively as larger, more aggregated activities. This decision weighs the benefit of including an activity against the cost in time and effort to handle such minute detail.

TABLE 3S-2 Process Activity Types

Activity Classification	Symbol	Major Action/Result
Operation	O	Decides, produces, does, accomplishes, makes, uses
Transportation	⇒	Moves, changes location
Inspection	□	Verifies, checks, makes sure, measures
Delay	D	Blocks, starves, interferes, temporary stop
Storage	∇	Keeps, safeguards

As a general rule of thumb, include the least amount of detail necessary to understand the process. As problems in one specific part of the process are identified, that section can be documented in greater detail. The documentation of a process is similar to the act of peeling an onion—begin with a very general picture of the process and then peel away successive layers of detail if necessary until you reach a sufficient level of understanding of the process.

Use Different Process Mapping and Analysis Techniques

Use as many different display formats as necessary to provide a complete picture of what is taking place within the process. Pictures, physical layouts or blueprints, work routing sheets, and other documents might be needed to give a better overall description of the process. If interdepartmental coordination issues are critical, it is sometimes useful to enhance a process map by color coding or repositioning front office and back office activities, or activities that are the responsibility of different departments.

Watch Out for Hidden Steps in a Process

It is often easy to overlook certain types of activities, especially delays. Sometimes there might be confusion or disagreement about the sequence of activities. One useful approach to make sure that all activities are correctly identified is to "Staple Yourself to an Order."[1] In this useful (and sometimes fun) approach, you pretend that you are the workpiece (e.g., an order, a part, a piece of information) moving through a process. As you go from activity to activity, you record what happens to you (taking pictures is a good idea) and you ask questions of the workers performing the activities (e.g., what are you doing? how often do you do this task?). This approach frequently provides insights into the process that don't normally arise from simple descriptions given by process workers.[2] Keep in mind, however, that your presence might influence the ways that people working in the process behave.

student activity

"Staple Yourself to an Order." Pick a process and *become* the order within it. What steps were involved? How long did it take for the process to complete operations? What did you learn? What surprises did you uncover?

When documenting the current state of a process, the analyst should try to capture all the relevant aspects, including the following attributes:

1. Number of steps in the process (broken down by category).
2. Distance covered by workpieces in the process (both vertically and horizontally).
3. Time required for activities (minimum, maximum, average, variance).
4. Value orientation of the activities (value-adding or not).[3]
5. Number of departmental boundaries crossed by workpieces.
6. Number of departments involved in each activity.
7. Number of people who touch or come into contact with the workpiece or activity.

After the existing process (the current state) has been mapped, it should be verified by reviewing it with the people involved.

To help meaningfully map a process, analysts often make use of three basic charting and analysis tools:

1. Process flow table
2. Physical layout diagram
3. Process summary table

---

[1]For a deeper look at tracing and analyzing order management cycles, see B. P. Shapiro; V. K. Rangan; and J. J. Sviokla, "Staple Yourself to an Order," *Harvard Business Review* 70, no. 3 (July/August 1992), pp. 113–22.

[2]As Chapter 8, Lean Systems, points out, the approach of studying the process as it takes place in its actual environment is referred to as "Gemba." Gemba often means "the actual place" or "the real place."

[3]This aspect of process mapping is discussed in greater detail later on in this supplement.

Applying Step 3 to AHMP

The order process for AHMP is currently carried out as follows. The order is received by an order entry person via fax, mail, or phone. An order form is placed into a pile where it waits until the orders are moved by a person to the engineering department. This is done twice a day. There, all of the orders are checked to determine what type of engineering work is required. For a standard autoclave, one of the engineers checks the order and its specifications (verification only) and then signs off on it (this takes no more than 10 minutes). The standard order is then put in another pile to wait until it is moved to the marketing office. Once it arrives there, it goes into a pile to wait for the marketing accounts manager to review and approve it. It usually takes no more than five minutes to process an individual order. Once it is approved, it goes next to accounting for entry (five minutes per order) and from accounting it goes to production scheduling.

process flow table A technique that records process activities, their key attributes, and their sequence.

A **process flow table** systematically records process activities, their key attributes, and their sequence (see the example given in Table 3S-2). The user fills in the required information and designates the appropriate symbol for each activity on one line of the table and then connects the symbols to show the flow through the process. The completed chart also records several important pieces of information for each activity:

- *Distance and time:* The chart reports the physical distance a workpiece covers in each activity and the amount of time it takes measured as a standard time, mean observed time, or range or standard deviation of observed times. These statistics indicate the reliability or predictability of the activity. Users could also record setup or changeover times associated with activities.
- *Activity symbol:* One simply circles or marks the appropriate symbol.
- *Number of people:* Staffing needs for an activity can indicate overall costs. Sometimes analysts indicate the numbers of direct workers and indirect (overhead) workers.
- *Value code:* Analysts classify each activity as one that (1) adds value (V), (2) generates waste (W), (3) adds no value but remains necessary (N) (e.g., equipment setup or an inspection required by a customer), or (4) is uncertain in terms of its impact on value (indicated by a question mark or ?). We discuss the rules for determining the value content of an activity in greater detail later.
- *Activity description:* Along with the activity description, the table might indicate the analyst's recommendation to keep the activity as is, eliminate it entirely, combine it with another similar activity, or rethink it.

The process flow table is handy for identifying activities, describing their organization and sequence, and categorizing them for detailed study. It gives less information regarding spatial relationships, however. Physical layouts can be important to consider when evaluating the distance that each workpiece must cover and its lead time, handling requirements, costs, and quality.

physical layout diagram A technique that documents both the horizontal and vertical movements of work within the process.

The **physical layout diagram** documents both the horizontal and vertical movements of workpieces from one area to another, recording process performance in units of time and distance. Labels on the physical layout diagram indicate areas or activities that correspond to the list on the process flow table, creating a strong, complementary relationship between these tools.

Figure 3S-2 presents an example physical layout diagram for the office complex at AHMP. This diagram shows the physical flows across offices involved in the order entry process. As can be seen from this diagram, one of the challenges facing AHMP is a series of long moves (the moves are identified as 1, 2, 3, and 4 and correspond to the four moves in the order in which they are noted in Table 3S-3). A manager looking at this figure would see that there is an opportunity to reduce time by locating the office areas closer together (thus reducing the physical distance covered by the order while also improving the quality and frequency of communication between the groups).

Analysis of a physical layout diagram looks for excessive and unnecessary movements, such as long moves between activities, crossed paths, repeated movements or

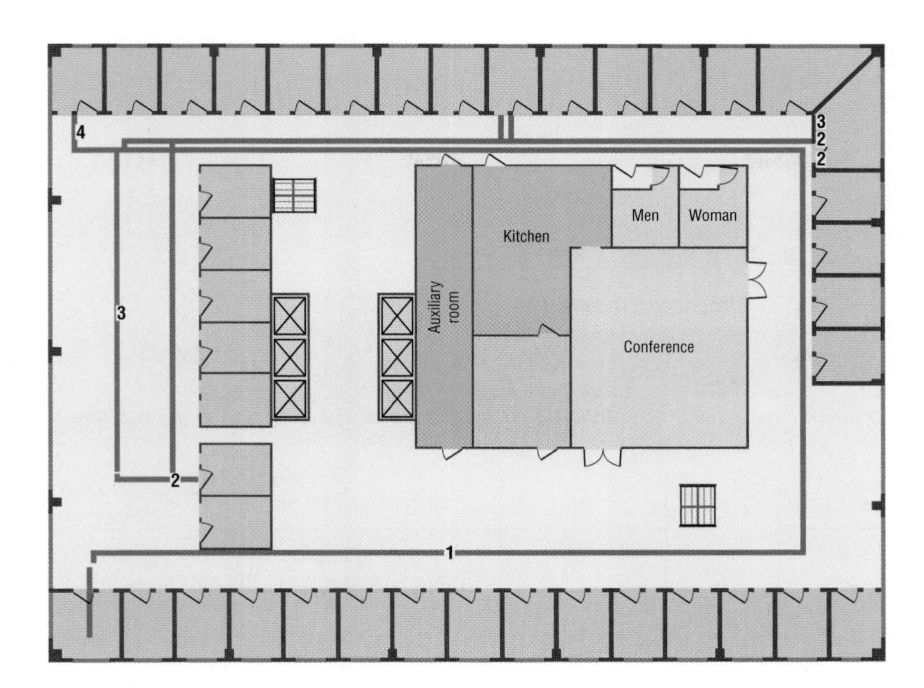

FIGURE 3S-2 Physical Layout Diagram

activities, or illogical or convoluted flows. An effective, efficient process eliminates criss-crosses and locates sequential, high-volume activities close together to minimize move times and improve communication.

Step 4: Analyze the Process and Identify Opportunities for Improvement

LO3S-4 Understand when and how to apply the various tools of process mapping.

In this step, we are interested in determining if the process requires minor or radical changes to it. If the current process is basically acceptable in its structure and operation, all that may be needed are repositioning and alterations of existing activities (i.e., a minor change). Alternatively, if managers decide that the process requires major changes, it is sometimes better to throw out the current process and to design a new one starting with a clean slate (i.e., a radical change is required). Whether minor or radical process changes are anticipated, it is always a good idea to keep in mind the goal of improving the value that a process delivers to its customers. The following paragraphs describe a three-stage analysis for generating improvement ideas: assessment, dispositioning, and repositioning.

Assessment—Mapping Value

Ideally, every activity in a process should create value as it is defined from the customer's perspective. Hence, we must assess every step in the process in terms of the extent to which it adds value or adds waste. In this type of assessment, an analyst can classify each activity into one of four different categories: *value-adding, necessary but not value-adding, waste generating,* and *question mark.*

A **value-adding activity** moves the product (be it a good or a service) closer to the form or location that the customer desires. In general, operations and transportations tend to most often contribute to value, but not all do. For example, an operation that creates scrap is not value-adding. Similarly, a transportation that temporarily moves a workpiece to storage only to later move it back again does not add value. Other activities may create value only under certain conditions.

value-adding activity Any activity that moves the product closer to the form or location desired by the customer.

An inspection only creates value for a customer when the customer demands it, or when it somehow differentiates the product. For example, at Steinway, a pianist plays the piano coming out of manufacturing to determine its tone and "voice," because different tones are best suited for playing different types of music. In this case, "inspection" adds value. One simple way to assess the value-adding extent of an activity is to ask, "Would a fair-minded customer be willing to pay for this activity?"

TABLE 3S-3 Process Flow Table for AHMP Order Entry Process

Process Flow Table

Page __1___ of ___1__

Overall Description of Process Charted:

Date Charted: ____________________ Charted by: ____________________

Check appropriate box: Current Process: (X) Proposed Process: ( )

Dist Meters	Average Time (range)	Symbol	Pers Invol.	Value Code V/W/N/?	Description of Activity (indicate outcome)
	15 min	● ⇒ D □ ∇	1	V	Order received by operator
	120 min (1-240)	O ⇒ ◗ □ ∇		W	Order placed in pile, waiting to be moved. Orders picked once in the morning, once in the afternoon.
200	60 min	O ➡ D □ ∇	1	?	Order moved to engineering
	45 min 1-180	O ⇒ ◗ □ ∇		W	Order waits in pile until an engineer can check it.
	5 min	● ⇒ D □ ∇	1	N	Engineer decides whether the order is standard or special.
	10 min	O ⇒ D ■ ∇	1	?	Engineer verifies the technical specifications for the standard autoclave order.
	120 min 1-240	O ⇒ ◗ □ ∇		W	Wait in pile waiting to be picked up for Marketing. Two pickups per day.
300	30 min	O ➡ D □ ∇	1	?	Move to Marketing.
	7 days 1–15	O ⇒ ◗ □ ∇		W	Wait until the Marketing Accounts Manager has a chance to review the order.
	5 min	O ⇒ D ■ ∇	1	N	Review the order.
	120 min 1-240 min	O ⇒ ◗ □ ∇	1	W	Wait to be picked up. Two pickups per day.
200	30 min	O ➡ D □ ∇	1	?	Move to accounting.
	5 min	● ⇒ D □ ∇	1	N	Enter order into accounting system.
	120 min 1-240 min	O ⇒ ◗ □ ∇		W	Wait to move to scheduling.
250	30 min	O ➡ D □ ∇	1	?	Move to scheduling.
	30 min	O ⇒ ◗ □ ∇		?	Wait in pile
	5 min	● ⇒ D □ ∇	1	N	Schedule autoclave order.
Totals: 950 m	8.54 days[4]	4 4 7 2 0	11	1 (V); 4 (N) 6 (W); 6(?)	

[4]Order entry at AHMP is done during the day shift, Monday to Friday. Consequently, it is assumed that 8 hours or 480 minutes equals one day.

Some activities are **necessary but not value-adding activities**; that is, some activities do not add value directly, yet they are necessary to enable a value-adding activity. For example, consider a process setup that prepares equipment for a task. Measuring performance, entering data into the accounting system, and generating reports for managers may also be non–value-adding but necessary activities.

necessary but not value-adding activity Any activity that does not add value directly but is necessary before a value-adding activity can take place.

A **waste-generating activity** consumes resources and time without returning some form of value. Inspections and transportations are often waste-generating activities. One can view an inspection activity as an admission that there are problems within the process that we have not been able to eliminate or control. Similarly, transportation can be considered wasteful if it is redundant or a result of problems in the physical layout of the operations management system. Waste-generating activities offer prime opportunities for process improvement.

waste-generating activity Any activity that consumes resources and time without returning any form of value.

Sometimes it is not easy to identify the extent to which an activity contributes to waste or value. At that point, it is essentially an unknown and can be categorized as a **question mark activity**, at least temporarily. One procedure that often helps analysts move an activity from a question mark activity to one of the other categories is to ask "Why" until the root cause for the activity is uncovered. For example:

question mark activity Any activity that cannot be easily categorized into one of the prior categories (value, necessary but not value-adding, waste).

1. Why are we inspecting part #4567? Answer: To see if it conforms to spec.
2. Why are we checking to see if it conforms to spec? Answer: To see if the machine is under control.
3. Why are we seeing if the machine is under control? Answer: Because the machine output is highly variable.
4. Why is the machine output highly variable? Because its operating procedures are not adequately specified and the operator is not well trained.

In this case, we can label the inspection as a wasteful activity that could be eliminated after giving adequate training to the machine operators.

Dispositioning

Dispositioning involves deciding what to do with each specific activity at the time of analysis. In general, there are four disposition options available: *keep, combine, rethink,* and *eliminate.*

- **Keep**—Leave the activity intact.
- **Combine**—Join an activity with others that do the same or similar things to improve the efficiency of the process.
- **Rethink**—Reevaluates an activity that produces a favorable outcome (value added or non–value added but essential), but does so inefficiently.
- **Eliminate**—Usually appropriate for wasteful activities.

dispositioning A disposition decision to leave the activity "as is" in the short term.

combine A disposition decision to join the activity with others that do the same or similar thing.

rethink A disposition decision to reevaluate the activity with the goal of improving its efficiency.

eliminate A disposition decision to drop the activity because it generates waste.

Repositioning

Repositioning looks at where (i.e., on which path) an activity should be positioned within the overall process. Within every process there are two types of paths: critical paths and noncritical paths. The critical path is the set of sequential activities with the largest total activity time. This path is critical because it determines the overall lead time of the process. By moving activities from critical to noncritical paths one can shorten the total order lead time for the process.

repositioning Deciding where to position an activity in the overall process—either on the critical path or off the critical path.

Another potential improvement comes from shifting work or resources from one activity to another activity so that bottleneck constraints are broken and the workload is balanced. Yet another way to improve process performance is to break a single path of activities into two parallel paths. Many times these types of changes are not possible because of technical constraints (i.e., one activity must precede another) or resource constraints (e.g., making parallel paths would increase the number of workers required). Nevertheless, it is important to question why each activity is positioned where it is, and whether moving it could improve process performance.

TABLE 3S-4 Principles of Process Improvement

1. Design the process to produce at the rate of customer demand.
2. Produce each product in a mix of products at a rate proportional to the customer demand.
3. Eliminate or reduce process interruptions, uncertainties, variability, or any other instabilities that lead to delays or storage.
4. Break a series of activities into parallel paths if you can do so without increasing resources.
5. Process workpieces on a first-in, first-out (FIFO) basis.
6. For each resource, sequence activities to minimize setups, distance, or other activity transition costs.
7. Add resources only to bottleneck (least capacity) activities on critical paths.
8. Use redundant resources and parallel copies of activities to reduce throughput time and increase route flexibility. Use single resources and serial activities to minimize cost.
9. Minimize cross-departmental handoffs.
10. Keep non–value-adding but necessary activities (e.g., measurement) off the critical path.
11. Co-locate activities that share resources or information.
12. Try to limit the number of entry points of workpieces into the process.
13. Develop the ability to economically make every part every day (i.e., make setup times as minimal as possible).
14. When processing a variety of different items, group them into "families" of items with similar processing requirements and dedicate resources to each family (i.e., create work "cells").
15. Capture data at its source. Minimize translations of data.
16. Change the product design to facilitate process improvements.

Principles of Process Improvement

Improvement opportunities are unique to each process, but there are certain principles that one can draw upon when making the process evaluation. Typically, managers get better at identifying improvement opportunities as they gain experience in multiple process mapping and analysis projects. Table 3S-4 lists some important principles of process improvement.

Applying Step 4 to AMHP

As previously noted, the overall order fulfillment standard was to be six weeks, with 95% of order entries taking no more than one week. In reviewing the current state, the team came up with the following observations:

- The current process could not meet the standard set by management on a regular, consistent basis. The average lead time for order entry was 4 weeks. The best-case scenario of one-week order entry was not very likely to occur regularly.
- The order entry process consisted of 17 steps: 4 operations, 4 transportations, 2 inspections, and 7 delays. Several of the activities were especially bothersome since they exhibited a very high level of variance. Furthermore, there was only 1 value-adding activity, 6 wasteful activities, 4 necessary-but-not-value-adding activities, and 6 question marks. The process appeared to be confused, highly variable, and not effective.
- What bothered the team was the nature of the delays. How long the order stayed in a delay appeared to be dictated by various informal scheduling practices. For example, the reason for the relatively short delay in moving orders from accounting to scheduling was the accounting practice of running the orders down to scheduling once an hour. In contrast, the marketing manager wanted to build up enough orders so that he could spend the entire morning (or afternoon) reviewing them. It was his view that checking the orders was time-consuming and compromised his ability to do other more "valuable" activities.

- The marketing review was really only necessary for new customers or customers who had some special problem.
- There was no real need for engineering to review the technical specifications of standard autoclaves. This review requirement was a carryover from the time when all orders in AHMP were engineered to order.

Step 5: Recommend Appropriate Changes to the Process (the "Future State" Map)

Once a list of possible changes for improvement has been made, it is important to bring together representatives from the various stakeholder groups to evaluate and prioritize the changes. Stakeholders in a process include the suppliers to and customers of the process, workers and support personnel involved in the process, and various functional managers. The prioritization of possible improvements to the process often classifies them into one of three basic categories:

relationships

1. Make the change immediately.
2. Postpone the change until sufficient resources or capabilities become available.
3. Determine that the change is not ultimately desirable or feasible.

LO3S-5 Change a process to make it more effective and efficient by either refining the current process or designing a new replacement process.

Many times desirable process changes are not implemented (category 2 above) because resources such as capital, skills, or machinery are not currently available. All too often changes are not implemented because the organization's internal culture or politics will not support the change. In any event, it is important to document the potential benefits of such changes and to schedule reevaluations when future conditions are likely to be more conducive to the change.

An effective way to communicate the impacts of a potential process change is to represent the changes in a new process flow table, or a new process map, called the **future state** map. By comparing and contrasting the future state map with the current state map, decision makers can more easily identify the impacts on resources, flows, and other process elements.

future state The new or proposed process that the changes in the existing processes are intended to achieve.

Applying Step 5 to AHMP

The process analysis team proposed a process redesign as specified in the new future state process flow table shown in Table 3S-5. First, standard autoclave orders for existing customers in good standing would be quickly identified and separated out. Second, accounting and scheduling representatives would be moved and co-located in the same office so that orders would be quickly transferred (it was recognized that in the near future this manual system could be replaced by a computerized, online system). These changes reduced the expected order entry lead time from about seven days to only 24 minutes for standard orders. Since most orders were for standard autoclaves, the new process made the strategic objectives for AHMP now possible. The team recognized that more work could be done to streamline the order entry for nonstandard orders.

To communicate these changes effectively, the team developed a **process summary table**. This type of table summarizes the current process, the proposed new process, and expected improvements from proposed changes (Table 3S-6). It indicates at a single glance the major problems in the existing process, measured in activity time, frequency of occurrence, or total time. Improvements are indicated by the presence of fewer activities, less distance, fewer people, and/or less time.

process summary table A table that summarizes the current process, the proposed new process, and identifies the expected improvements offered by the proposed process.

Step 6: Implement the Changes and Monitor Improvements

Process improvement is usually an iterative, trial and error activity. Consequently, feedback mechanisms should be put into place whenever a significant process change is implemented so that managers can evaluate its impacts and make adjustments as needed. In

TABLE 3S-5 Future State Process Flow Table for AHMP

Process Flow Table

Page ___1__ of __1___

Overall Description of Process Charted:

Date Charted: ____________________ Charted by: ____________________

Check appropriate box: Current Process: ( ) Proposed Process: (X)

Dist Meters	Average Time (range)	Symbol	Pers Invol.	Value Code V/W/N/?	Description of Activity (indicate outcome)
	15 min	● ⇒ D □ ∇	1	V	Order received by telephone operator.
	1 min	● ⇒ D □ ∇	1	N	Order reviewed to see if it is standard or special.
	1 min	● ⇒ D □ ∇	1	N	Order reviewed to see if customer is existing customer in good standing.
2	1 min	O ➡ D □ ∇	1	?	Order moved within same room to the accounting representative.
3	1 min	O ➡ D □ ∇	1	?	Move to scheduling representative (located in same room).
	5 min	● ⇒ D □ ∇	1	N	Schedule autoclave order.
Totals: 5 m	24 min	4 2 0 0 0			

TABLE 3S-6 Process Summary Table for AHMP

Activities	Current #	Current Total Time	Proposed #	Proposed Total Time	Difference #	Difference Total Time
Operations (O)	4	30	4	22	0	8
Inspections (□)	2	15	0	0	2	15
Transportations (⇒)	4	150	2	2	2	148
Storages (∇)	0	0	0	0	0	0
Delays (D)	7	3915	0	0	7	3915
Distance (feet/meters)	950		<15		935	

relationships

some cases a pilot study might be done to verify the benefits of a process change. In others, a wholesale, radical change might be attempted very quickly to shake up existing infrastructures and to overcome barriers to change that often arise. It is important to get agreement from all important stakeholders, and to make sure that all important resources needed to support the change are identified and secured.

OTHER PROCESSING MAPPING TOOLS

In addition to the techniques introduced in this supplement, there are several other approaches that can be used.

Process flow diagramming is commonly used to indicate the general flow of plant processes and equipment. This procedure shows the relationship between major equipment but not the minor detail such as piping and such. An example of this technique being used to diagram the process of converting corn to fuel-grade ethanol is shown in Figure 3S-3.

Value stream mapping is a mapping technique that analyzes the flow of material and information currently needed to bring a product to a customer. Value stream mapping is used to assess the extent to which the current process adds value (as a percentage of the total time) and to identify opportunities for reducing lead time. It is more comprehensive and complex when compared to the process mapping approach introduced in this supplement. In some implementations, value stream mapping requires the use of over 25 different symbols (as compared to the five discussed in this supplement).

Service blueprinting (discussed in Chapter 5) is used to map an entire service system, so that the process can be analyzed, monitored, and improved in terms of its ability to satisfy the needs of the customer. It maps out and assesses all of the various interactions and actions that occur when the customer and the company (and its process) meet.

Swim lanes can be used as a visual element in process flow diagrams or flowcharts that organizes the activities into groups based on the major types of tasks being carried out or on who is responsible for those activities. The major attraction of swim lanes (also known as ***functional bands***) is that it helps organize the processes into functional

process flow diagramming A technique used to indicate the general flow of plant processes and equipment.

value stream mapping A mapping technique that analyzes the flow of material and information needed to bring a product to the customer.

service blueprinting A technique for mapping an entire service system, so that the process can be analyzed, monitored, and improved in its ability to satisfy the needs of the customer.

swim lanes A visual element used in process flow diagrams or flowcharts that organizes the activities into groups based on the major types of tasks being carried out or on who is responsible for those activities.

FIGURE 3S-3 Process Flow Diagram: Dry-Mill Ethanol Process for Converting Corn to Fuel-Grade Ethanol[5]

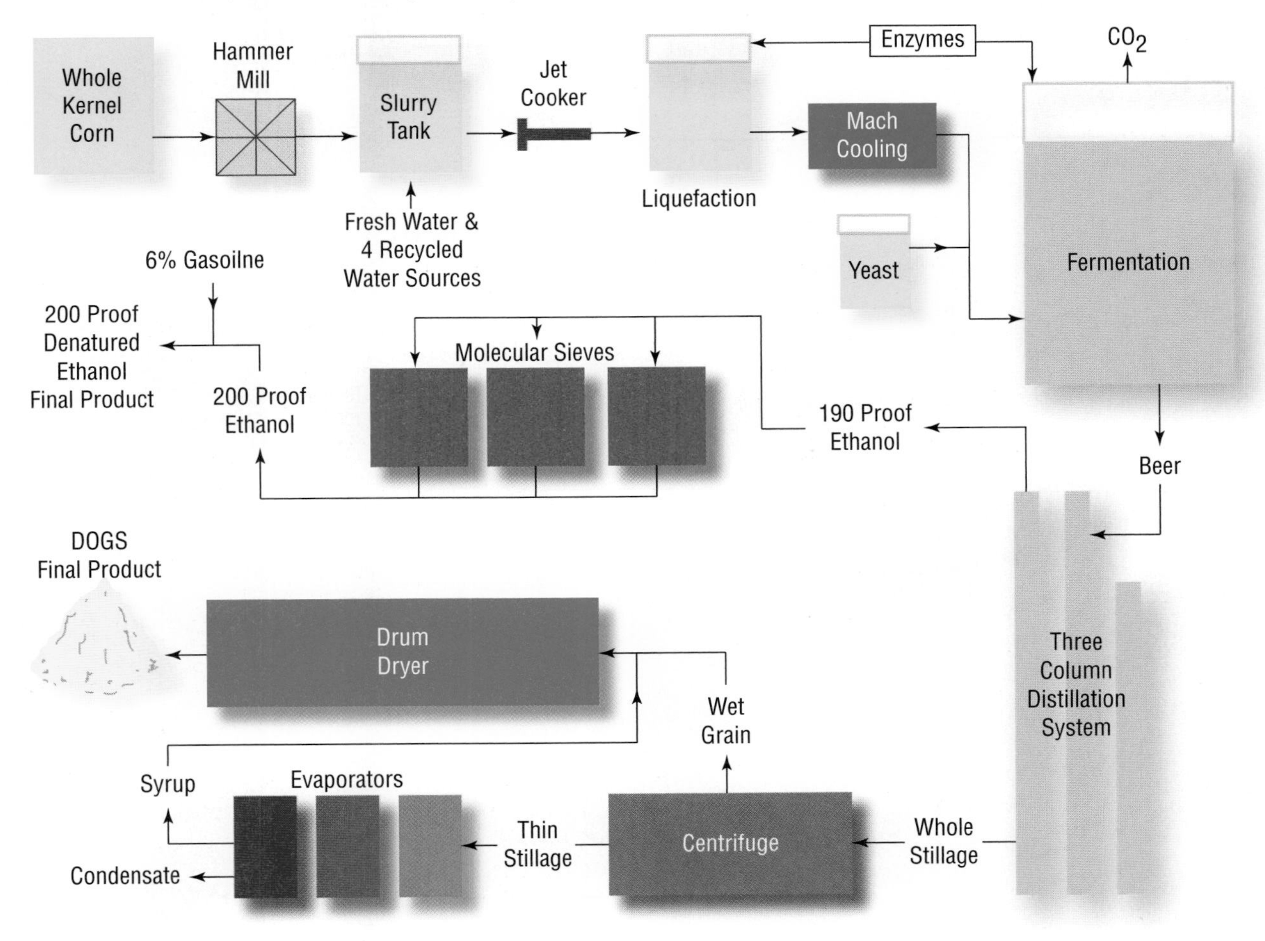

[5]http://www.6solutionsllc.com/drymill_lg.php. © 2010 6 Solutions LLC.

or organizational blocks (and responsibilities). Figure 3S-4 provides an example of swim lanes. Here we can see that the overall process consists of five major activities: order entry, division, warehouse, credit, and customer—each potentially managed by a different group. This means that if we want to improve or change the process presented in Figure 3S-4, we have to coordinate our activities with up to five different groups.

FIGURE 3S-4 Swim Lanes for an Order Fulfillment Process[6]

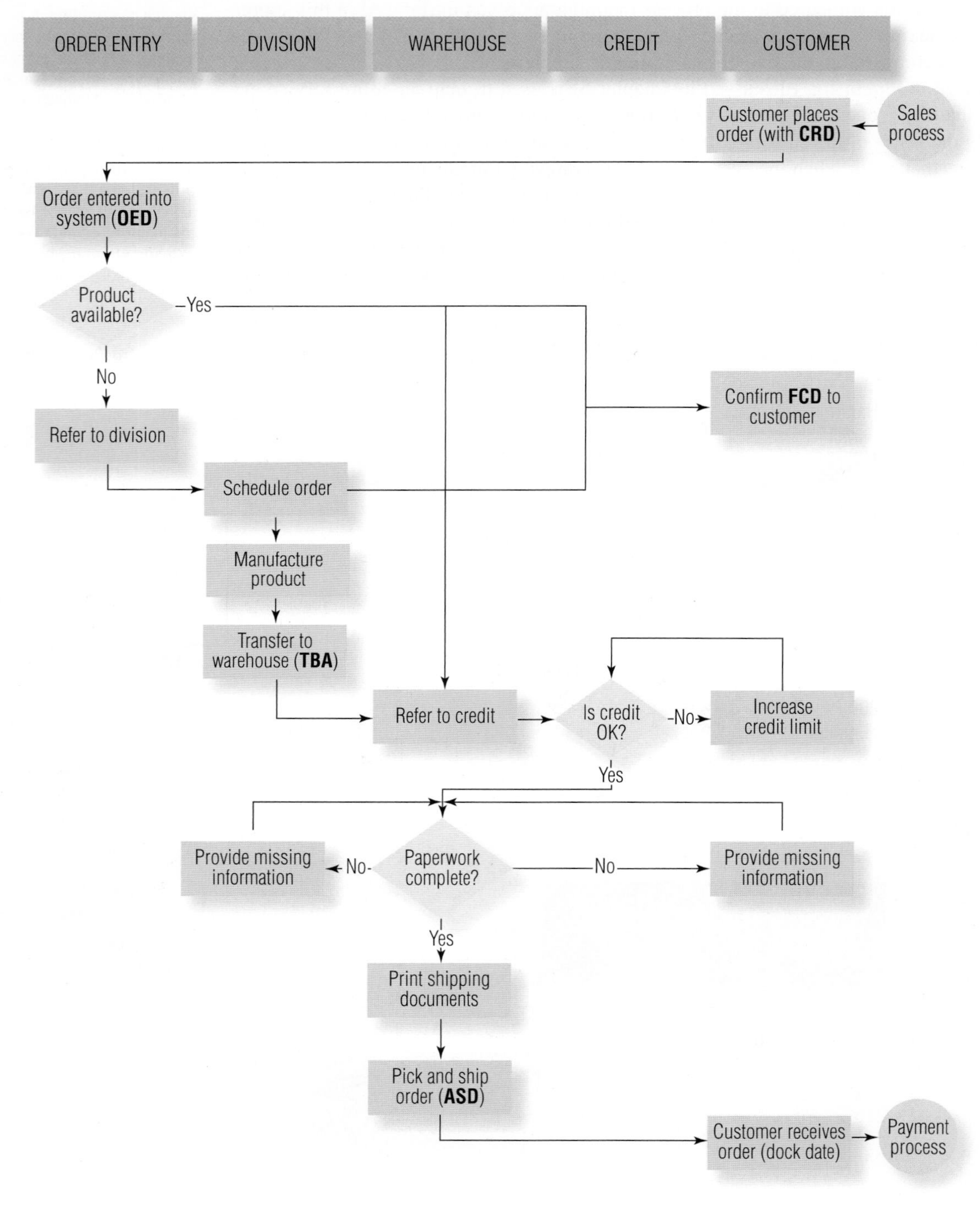

[6]Schneiderman, A. M. 1996. "Metrics for the Order Fulfillment Process (Part 1)." *Journal of Cost Management* 10, no. 2 (Summer 1996), pp. 30–42.

SUPPLEMENT SUMMARY

Process mapping and analysis tools provide the means for process improvements that can have great performance impacts. This supplement illustrates the process mapping and analysis method, including the following important points:

1. Process mapping and analysis involves six major steps: (1) determine the desired outcome for the process and the associated metrics needed to evaluate its performance; (2) identify and bound the critical process; (3) document the existing process (the "current state" map); (4) analyze the process and prioritize opportunities for improvement; (5) recommend appropriate changes to the process (the "future state" map); and (6) implement the changes and monitor improvements.
2. Processes are characterized by six basic types of activities (i.e., operations, decisions, storage activities, transportation activities, delays, and inspections).
3. Process mapping and analysis is a graphic technique to study and improve processes using symbols, diagrams, and tables to map process flows. Process analysis tools include the process flow table, physical layout diagram, process map, and process summary table. These tables and charts describe the number and types of activities in a process, their organization, the time they require, and the distance they cover.

KEY TERMS

combine 101
current state 96
dispositioning 101
eliminate 101
future state 103
keep 101
necessary but not value-adding activity 101
physical layout diagram 98
process flow diagramming 105
process flow table 98
process mapping and analysis 93
process summary table 103
question mark activity 101
reposition 101
rethink 101
service blueprinting 105
swim lanes 105
value-adding activity 99
value stream mapping 105
waste-generating activity 101

PROBLEMS

1. You are making your weekly trip to your local grocery story. Use a process flow diagram chart to describe your decision-making process about what to buy and where to buy it. What inputs did you use in helping you make these weekly decisions? How could an advanced consumer information system have made your process easier?
2. Your eyeglass frame-making firm is considering one of two distribution alternatives. The first is to make all shipments from your Chicago plant to one of three regional warehouses located in Philadelphia, Chicago, and Reno. All orders from eyeglass retailers would be shipped from these sites. The second alternative would be to create one warehouse in Memphis, Tennessee, and ship all orders via Federal Express.
   a. Prepare a process flow diagram of each alternative.
   b. What additional information would you need to ascertain which alternative will provide the best value to your customers?
   c. Is this different from a lower cost solution? Why?

3. Murphy's Bagel Shops (MBS) is a chain of bagel eateries supported by a central bakery. Most raw materials are delivered to MBS's bakery where the ingredients are inspected for quality and then stored in the raw materials warehouse, which is located on the bakery's second floor. The second floor is also where the ingredients are measured into batch quantities before being inserted into the bagel dough blender. Two hundred-pound batches of each bagel blend are mixed for about one hour. The mixed dough is then extruded into bagel shapes and placed on flat baking pans. The full pans are placed in "shipping racks," which are then sent about fifty yards to the shipping area.

   Each day, the shops order bagel blanks in increments of the number on each flat baking pan. The shipping department rearranges the number of each type of bagel on each shipping rack to assure that the number shipped to a given bagel shop matches the number ordered. Each shop's filled shipping racks are segregated by the delivery department to assure that the incoming trucks can be accurately and quickly loaded. Loading a truck requires approximately 20 minutes.

   The bagel dough rises during the transportation process for about 40 minutes. The trucks are scheduled to arrive at each bagel shop at 5 o'clock in the morning. There the bagel shop crew unloads each shipping rack, places any surface ingredients (i.e., poppy seeds) on the bagel trays as needed, and then places them either into the shop's ovens or the raw bagel storage area. It takes approximately 40 minutes to cook most bagels. Trays of cooked bagels are removed from the ovens and placed in the bagel cooling area.

   Once sufficiently cooled, the fresh bagels are placed into the retail area displays that are designed to send bagel-scented air in the direction of the customer-seating area. Fresh bagels are cooked each morning as needed. Unsold bagels are packaged into six-pack bags and sold at a discount after 2 p.m.

   a. Prepare a process flow diagram of the above business.
   b. Indicate the operations in which value is being added.

CASE

Midwestern Lighting[7]

"I can't see why you have to spend so much time looking at our processes. Hey, we have everything under control. It has been over five years since we got our last EPA inspection and nearly six years since we got our last major citation and fine. Things are going really smoothly and I really don't see why you have to look at the process. Now, why don't you go out and get me some cost savings? Every time I can save a penny per finished lighting assembly, I get that much better a chance to keep my business with the big boys."

With those words, Barry Jamieson, the plant manager of Midwestern Lighting's Light Fixture Plant (LFP) dismissed Tim Bryant. Tim had been hired some six months ago to help improve overall operations at LFP. Initially, he had been brought in by corporate to identify opportunities for cost reduction and for reducing scrap and landfill related costs. When he arrived at LFP, located in New Hudson, Michigan, Tim found a plant that was operating under a siege mentality. Everyone knew that they had to reduce costs and improve operating efficiencies if they hoped to win another contract from their three major customers. LFP was unique in that it was one of the few plants in the automotive industry that built light fixtures for GM, Ford, and Daimler-Chrysler. While LFP was noted for its superb quality, it was also recognized as not being very cost efficient. The managers of Midwestern Lighting had tried to convince the plant manager at LFP to consider QS9000 certification. That effort was a disaster and ultimately resulted in the dismissal of the plant manager. It was that dismissal that gave rise to the hiring of Barry Jamieson. Since arriving at LFP, Barry had developed a reputation for being a hard-nosed manager. To Barry, if you couldn't reduce cost, then you didn't have anything to say of importance. Barry was not really excited by Tim's presence. To Barry, Tim represented nothing more than increased overhead.

The Production Process Described

Since arriving at LFP, Tim could not help but feel that there were too many "diamonds in the rough" to ignore. Typical

[7]This case is prepared for the purpose of class discussion rather than to illustrate either effective or ineffective handling of an administrative situation. Ford Motor Company supplied the data. Some of the data have been modified to protect proprietary information. The writers of the case are fully responsible for the information within the case.

was the process for making the tail light assemblies for the Dodge Ram, one of the best selling trucks in the market. The process began with the back plate. This was long black piece of extruded ABS plastic (produced in another part of the plant) that contained two concave depressions–one for the turn light and one for the backup light. These were withdrawn from a temporary storage location found near the assembly line. Each back plate was first checked for cosmetic defects. Those that failed this step were placed in a bin where they were eventually used as a source of raw material for regrinds. Any plate passing this test was placed in a metalization chamber where nickel metal particles were sprayed on using a high-pressure water-based system. Because of the nature of the process, only half of the material ever reached the back plate. The rest either fell to the bottom of the chamber or was vented out. Periodically, the chamber had to be taken off line and cleaned out. This process took 1 to 2 days and effectively shut down production of the tail light.

After the parts were metalized, they were removed from the chamber and checked for completeness and evenness of the coverage. Any rejected parts were placed in a bin. Because of the presence of the metal coating, the back plate could not be recycled, so it had to be landfilled. The accepted parts went into a rack where they waited for the arrival of lenses from a supplier. A plastic-wrapped film covered the lenses. Each lens, as it arrived from the supplier, was checked for surface flaws. Any rejected lenses were then put into a recycle bin, where they were used as inputs for any parts requiring low-grade black plastic.

The next step in the process was mating. At this stage, each lens was mated to a back plate. This was accomplished by placing the back plate and the lens into two fixtures. These fixtures were then fed into an automated gluing machine. The machine placed a bead of glue on the lens, waited for 10 seconds and then placed the lens onto the back plate. Periodically, the gluing machine had to be purged and cleaned. This was typically done twice a shift; each instance required 30 minutes. This process was fairly messy and required several globs of glue to be expressed through the nozzle. After this was done, the last glob of glue was then expressed and the nozzle was removed. The machine had four nozzles. The residual glue and nozzles were then thrown into an old 55-gallon barrel. Because this barrel was used as a receptacle for all sorts of scrap (including floor sweepings and cigarette butts), the only disposal option was a landfill.

After mating, the back light assembly was next tested for leaks. Placing the body into a tank of water and then shooting a burst of air through it completed the testing. Again, any assemblies that failed this test were put into a bin for eventual disposal in a landfill site. Those that passed this stage next proceeded to the finishing assembly. It was here that two light bulb assemblies were first made. These assemblies required one receiver and one light bulb each. Both the receiver and the light bulbs were provided by outside suppliers. After they were assembled, the assemblies were inserted into the appropriate holes in the car body. The light assembly was then inspected for performance and surface blemishes. Any problem assemblies were put aside for rework. Those that could not be reworked were set aside for disposal (again landfilled). The remaining "good" assemblies were packed into a cardboard box and shipped out to the Dodge Ram Assembly plant.

The current practice at the LFP was to allocate the total production cost to the number of good assemblies produced. By working with the material requirements planning system at LFP, Tim and others were able to track the following costs associated with waste in the process. For the tail light assemblies, the line produced 3,600 lot size/shift. Labor and overhead costs were considered to be fixed.

Current Process	Molding	Metalization	Inspection
Direct materials waste	.05	.001	.000
Other waste (materials and labor)	.058	.023	.048
Production cost/piece	.093	.042	.023
Total cost/piece	1.15	1.216	10.727

Questions

1. Assess the production process for the Ram light assembly. How efficient is it?
2. Develop a process map for this operation.
3. Where are the largest opportunities to reduce waste and associated costs?
4. What strategy/approach would you use for making recommendations to Barry Jamieson?

SELECTED READINGS & INTERNET SITES

Jacka, J. M. *Business Process Mapping: Improving Customer Satisfaction.* New York, NY: Wiley, 2002.

Lovelle, J. "Mapping the Value Stream." *IIE Solutions* 33, no. 2 (February 2001), pp. 26–33.

Melan, E. H. *Process Management: Methods for Improving Products and Service.* New York: McGraw-Hill, 1993.

Rother, M., and J. Shook. *Learning to See: Value Stream Mapping to Create Value and Eliminate Muda.* Brookline, MA: The Lean Enterprise Institute, Inc., 1999.

Rummler, G. A., and A. P. Brache. *Improving Performance: How to Manage the White Space on the Organization Chart.* San Francisco, CA: Jossey-Bass Publishers, 1990.

4 Product/Process Innovation

CHAPTER OUTLINE

LEARNING OBJECTIVES *After studying this chapter, you should be able to:*

LO4-1 Explain why product/process innovation is an important contributor to a firm's performance.

LO4-2 Contrast different types of innovation strategies and projects.

LO4-3 Describe new product/process design and development objectives and project phases.

LO4-4 Explain why cross-functional integration is needed in product and process design.

LO4-5 Apply tools and techniques for integrating customer needs and supply chain considerations into product/process design and development.

Want a Coke? We've Got 100 Different Kinds.

Ever had one of those moments where all you wanted was a Diet Black Cherry Vanilla Coke, but all that the fountain could offer you was regular old diet? Coca-Cola has solved that problem by introducing a new beverage dispenser, the Coca-Cola Freestyle. A single machine can dispense more than 100 regular and low-calorie branded beverages. Pick what you want, and the Freestyle mixes it on the spot—including many varieties of waters, sports drinks, lemonades, energy drinks, and sparkling beverages that previously were not widely available. Even with all these options, the machine uses the same amount of space as typical six- or eight-valve fountains.

The Freestyle offers a great example of an innovation that creates an exciting new customer experience while also providing tremendous operational advantages. Coca-Cola succeeded in bringing this product to market by working with new partners to combine previously unlinked technologies in a novel way. The fountain has an intuitive and easy-to-use touchscreen developed by BSQUARE. "We worked closely with the Coca-Cola Company and studied consumer feedback to provide the software that would ultimately power Coca-Cola Freestyle," says BSQUARE CEO Brian Crowley. The flavors are mixed by "PurePour" technology, which was originally developed to measure extremely precise amounts of dialysis and cancer drugs. Radio-frequency-identification (RFID) scanners are used to match cartridges to dispensers and to track inventory levels of each flavor, and the onboard computer powered by Windows Embedded confirms that everything is in place.

The Freestyle dispensers are certainly more expensive to produce than old-style fountains, but Coca-Cola managers expect operational savings to far exceed any added costs. Existing soda fountains use five-gallon concentrate bags and require lots of backroom space and labor. Now all that is required is a highly concentrated 46-ounce cartridge inside a self-contained machine. The built-in communications software provides other important supply chain management capabilities. The dispenser sends business data back to Coke's headquarters in Atlanta, continuously providing details on beverage consumption, peak times, and popular locations. In addition to providing valuable insight into consumer behavior, these data make it easy to track and efficiently restock inventory levels within each fountain dispenser. Each Freestyle also notifies maintenance personnel as to when and how it needs to be serviced. Coke can also talk back to the machine, letting it know if a particular flavor needs to be discontinued or recalled, and causing it to stop serving the drink immediately.

According to Gene Farrell, Coca-Cola Freestyle vice president and general manager, the Freestyle creates ". . . an unprecedented beverage experience for consumers." The system also creates fantastic operational efficiencies. In these ways, Coca-Cola's innovation creates a winning advantage for itself and its retail partners.

Prepare

How does product/process innovation affect a firm's performance, and what roles do supply chain operations managers play in making innovations successful?

Organize

The Role of Product/Process Innovation in Supply Chain Operations Management
- The Product Life Cycle
- How Product/Process Innovation Affects Firm Performance

This chapter is about managing product and process innovations. The Coca-Cola Freestyle story illustrates some of the unique opportunities associated with bringing a new product to market. When a business succeeds in closely linking new product innovations to its supply chain's operational capabilities, it often sees dramatic benefits in terms of profits and competitive advantages.

Innovative changes made to products and processes can be large or small. Continuous improvements to existing operational processes happen in all areas of the supply chain, and these types of innovations are discussed throughout the chapters of this book. In this chapter, however, we focus on operational approaches for developing new products and processes. In addition, the chapter describes tools used to integrate product design and supply chain process design decisions.

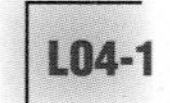

LO4-1 Explain why product/process innovation is an important contributor to a firm's performance.

THE ROLE OF PRODUCT/PROCESS INNOVATION IN SUPPLY CHAIN OPERATIONS MANAGEMENT

new product design and development projects The transformation of a new market opportunity and/or new product technology into a set of specifications that define a product.

new process design and development projects The transformation of product specifications and new process technology into a new or revised production system.

In today's rapidly moving world, managers throughout the supply chain are continually thinking about how to exploit new technologies to improve their products and processes. Most of the time, these development efforts are done in the form of projects.

New product design and development projects transform a new market opportunity and/or new product technology into a set of specifications that define a product. Coca-Cola's introduction of the Freestyle was the culmination of a new product design and development project.

New process design and development projects transform product specifications and new process technology into a new or revised production system.[1] Examples are the design and installation of a new production line in a factory or a new information system in a bank.

You might think that product development is mainly a marketing and engineering activity, while process development is more of an operations management activity. Actually, operations managers get involved in both types of development projects in at least two different ways.

First, all development projects are actually operational processes. Operations managers bring their project management skills to bear as a business seeks to improve the speed, quality, and productivity of its innovation development efforts. This chapter explains operational approaches that can be used to improve development projects.

Second, in most settings new product and new process development activities are closely linked together. For example, in the steel industry new grades of steel often result from newly designed or refined production processes. In services, such as a hospital or a hotel, the process *is* the product, so product development and process development are essentially the same thing. Even when a product is mostly a tangible good, product design decisions usually have huge impacts on all aspects of internal operations (facilities, equipment, layout, workforce) as well as on suppliers' roles and logistical requirements. For this reason, operations managers located throughout the supply chain have a large stake in how product design decisions are made, and they usually play important roles in supporting product development tasks.

Ultimately, product/process design and development can be viewed as part of the resource/technology supply chain. These activities *supply* performance requirements and technology specifications as inputs to operations managers located throughout the supply chain, who turn these specifications into goods and services for customers. This chapter discusses ways that managers coordinate product and supply chain process development activities and decisions.

---

[1] Types of goods and service production systems are described in Chapter 5, "Manufacturing and Service Process Structures."

The Product Life Cycle

Most products go through periods of sales growth and decline that necessitate changes in a firm's operational capabilities. For a given product, this pattern of changes is known as the **product life cycle**. Figure 4-1 illustrates the role of innovation throughout a product's life cycle.

product life cycle A pattern of sales growth and decline over the period in which a product is offered.

The product life cycle has four phases: launch, growth, maturity, and decline.

- *Launch*—A new product launch to the marketplace is usually the culmination of an intense product design and development effort. Supply chain process innovation may be required too, if the product does not make use of existing process technologies and capacities.
- *Growth*—As the product is introduced and sales begin to grow, customer responses give the firm information about how to refine the product specifications. Product modifications continue until standardized forms of the product begin to emerge. During this growth stage, major investments in process innovation are postponed. Operating processes in the supply chain must be flexible in accommodating a high mix of low-volume product orders, and they must be able to rapidly increase capacity in order to avoid losing sales.
- *Maturity*—Once demand stabilizes and product refinements become less frequent, costs become more critical because low-cost competitors often enter the market. Process innovation is usually needed in this stage to increase supply chain efficiencies. Process innovation is justified because the product specifications are fairly stabilized, and early profits have generated funding for process investments.
- *Decline*—Product maturity may last for many years, yet eventually products enter a decline stage as customer needs change or as new technologies supplant existing ones. As demand declines, operations process managers across the supply chain face intense pressures to reduce cost and to efficiently decrease capacity. Firms often try to avoid the decline phase by using incremental product design and development projects to revitalize products with new or better features, or to replace them with next generation products (examples: new versions of the iPod, new types of credit cards, and new types of guided tour packages).

Product life cycles can be very short (months) or very long (many years). For example, sales for a trendy new toy (like "Angry Birds: Knock on Wood Game") might grow and decline very quickly, whereas products like certain breakfast cereals (like "Cheerios") have been in the maturity stage for decades. Operations managers use the product life cycle concept to plan the initial design and periodic changes to supply chain processes.

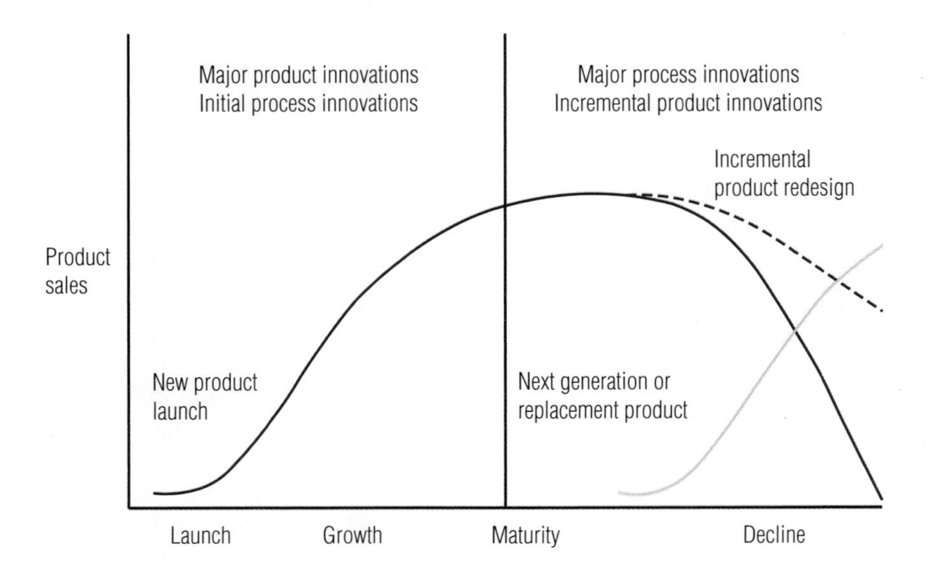

FIGURE 4-1
Innovation Across a Product's Life Cycle

How Product/Process Innovation Affects Firm Performance

relationships

Throughout a product's life cycle, product and process innovation affect a company's growth as well as its profitability. Excellent innovation projects translate customer desires and technology-based opportunities into product and process designs that operations managers can deliver reliably and efficiently. It is widely believed that 80 percent of a product's total supply chain costs are determined by decisions made in product design. To make good product design decisions, managers need to integrate inputs from many different functions and groups located within a firm and across its supply chain. In particular, these groups play important roles in new product development:

- Customers communicate their needs and desires.
- Financial managers help evaluate and select the most promising innovation opportunities.
- Marketing managers understand and communicate customers' needs, competitive opportunities, and marketing strategies.
- Engineers and designers use technological knowledge and creativity to turn needs into product and process specifications.
- Various operations managers located across the supply chain determine how to best source, produce, and deliver the product to meet the firm's objectives based on their operational capabilities.

The best innovative firms have well-defined processes for integrating the inputs of these various groups at appropriate times throughout design and development projects. A later section of this chapter discusses integrated design and development approaches in detail.

Numerous studies have shown that more-innovative firms consistently outperform their rivals. Firms that have developed strong innovation competences grow at rates that are three to six times the rate of their competitors, and typically create profits that are 20 to 150 percent greater than the profits of their competitors. Why are innovative firms so successful? They gain the following advantages from being faster, better, and more efficient innovators.

LO4-2 Contrast different types of innovation strategies and projects.

Fast innovators:

- Capture additional sales by getting their new products to market more quickly than their competitors do.
- Are able to react quickly to competitors' product introductions, thus capitalizing on the development and promotional efforts of their competitors.
- Produce a more continuous stream of new product introductions that create a greater and more constant market awareness of their brands.

High-quality innovators:

- Have fewer problems in launching new products and fewer failures in the marketplace.
- Satisfy customers more effectively, building strong brand image and customer loyalty.

Efficient innovators:

- Are able to fund more new design and development projects than other firms.
- Can sell at lower prices or lower the total sales needed for a new product to pay back its initial development costs.

student activity

Each year *BusinessWeek* magazine publishes a special issue that profiles the most innovative companies in the world. Examine the issues from the past few years. What do most of these innovative companies have in common?

Finally, product/process innovation projects also contribute to a firm's competitiveness in ways that go beyond the immediate creation of new products or processes. Every innovation project, successful or not, involves learning—learning about new markets, new technologies, new methods, new suppliers, and even new personnel. These lessons learned often lead to new innovation opportunities that create competitive advantages.

OPERATIONAL PRODUCT/PROCESS INNOVATION COMPETENCIES

To effectively coordinate all of the inputs from the various functional contributors to innovation processes located across the supply chain, a firm has to have a strong overarching innovation strategy, as well as operational competencies in the areas of idea development, project selection, project management, and organizational learning. As Figure 4-2 shows, one can view innovation as a "funnel." While many new product and process ideas may be initially considered, the best innovators are good at pursuing a portfolio of ideas that have high potential impacts and also fit well with the firm's strategy and capabilities. Strong innovators are also good at managing projects needed to bring new product and process ideas to fruition. Finally, they are good at launching new products and then learning from successes and failures. Note that firms often involve customers and suppliers as innovation partners. Operations managers play key roles in establishing these partnerships and in making decisions at each stage of the funnel.

Prepare

What operational skills does a firm need to have in order to be an outstanding innovator?

Organize

Operational Product/Process Innovation Competencies
- Idea and Opportunity Development
- Innovation Portfolio Planning
- Innovation Project Management
- New Product/Process Launch and Learning
- Codevelopment

Idea and Opportunity Development

Some firms are better than others at finding and developing new ideas and opportunities for innovation. Excellent firms have a culture that motivates workers in all areas of the firm's operations to constantly be looking for new ways to improve processes and to please customers. Firms foster an innovative culture through by the following practices:

- *Hiring the best and the brightest.* Companies such as McKinsey (consulting), Microsoft, Google, IBM, and BMW are known for their emphasis on hiring top students in their respective fields.
- *Having an effective reward system in place.* Many firms have electronic forums or other venues where employees can submit ideas. Employees are paid for ideas based on their merits.

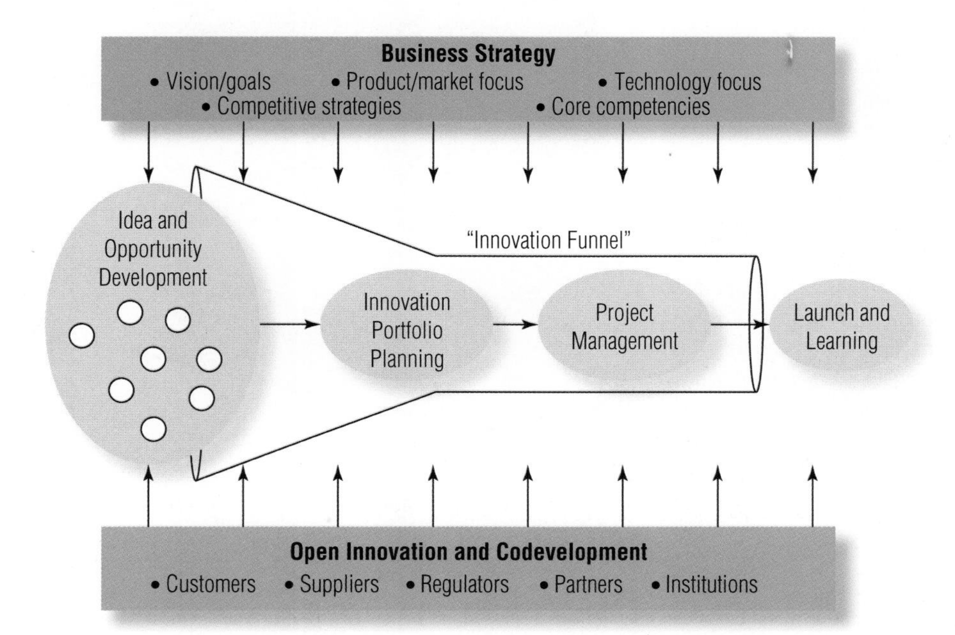

FIGURE 4-2 Competencies for Product/Process Innovation Management

global

- *Allocating adequate resources.* Firms that are dedicated to innovation typically set aside a significant amount of money and worker time to the development of new ideas. Most large firms have separate R&D organizations dedicated to innovation. Where the average U.S. firm allocates about 2 percent of its revenues to R&D, innovative firms may allocate as much as 10 percent, or more, to this purpose.

open innovation An organizational effort to capture ideas and resources from sources outside the firm for use in innovation efforts.

In addition to developing ideas internally, some firms have taken extraordinary steps to solicit ideas from external networks including customers, suppliers, universities, and even competitors to develop new products and processes. This approach is known as **open innovation**. Pharmaceutical companies such as Eli Lilly, for example, have created Web sites where scientists from around the world can quickly enter new product formulation ideas, and where the company can publish requests for help in solving certain medical problems. Firms that are good at idea and opportunity development typically have many such systems in place that scan various environments for useful market, technological, and competitor intelligence. The Get Real box below describes an open innovation approach for idea generation used at Procter & Gamble.

relationships

Innovation Portfolio Planning[2]

Most firms have more innovation ideas than they have the resources to pursue. It is important for new ideas to be formally screened to identify those that are most promising and most consistent with the firm's business strategy and development capacity. The screening

GET REAL

global

Procter & Gamble's Connect + Develop Process

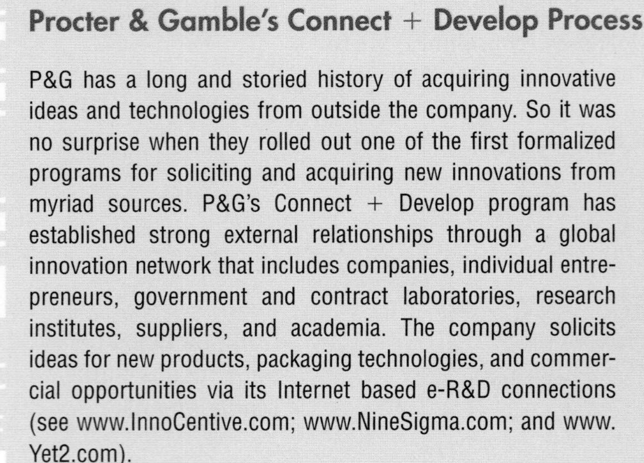

P&G has a long and storied history of acquiring innovative ideas and technologies from outside the company. So it was no surprise when they rolled out one of the first formalized programs for soliciting and acquiring new innovations from myriad sources. P&G's Connect + Develop program has established strong external relationships through a global innovation network that includes companies, individual entrepreneurs, government and contract laboratories, research institutes, suppliers, and academia. The company solicits ideas for new products, packaging technologies, and commercial opportunities via its Internet based e-R&D connections (see www.InnoCentive.com; www.NineSigma.com; and www.Yet2.com).

Procter & Gamble accelerates its internal research and development efforts by leveraging the ideas, talents, and innovation assets of partners. The Connect + Develop approach allows them to rapidly create products to best meet the performance and cost needs of the world's consumers. One example of the many successes yielded by this approach is Crest White-strips. P&G innovation managers worked with experts in oral hygiene, fabric and home care, and thin-film technology to develop the new product concept for Crest Whitestrips.

Crest Whitestrips is one of the most successful products developed from P&G's Connect + Develop process.

[2] Methods for project evaluation and selection are discussed in Chapter 15, "Project Management."

process, known as **innovation portfolio planning**, analyzes estimated market share (by customer segment and channel), revenues, profits, investment, and development time requirements. These factors must be compared with the firm's marketing and technology strategies in order to ensure that design and development projects move the firm in the right direction. The screening must also compare the resource needs of a potential development project to the resources available, while considering the needs of other ongoing and planned projects. This type of aggregate innovation planning helps establish the priority and role of every project within the overall business strategy.

innovation portfolio planning The process of selecting and prioritizing innovation projects to ensure that they are consistent with the firm's strategy and development capacity.

Figure 4-3 compares four primary types of innovation projects:

LO4-2 Contrast different types of innovation strategies and projects.

- *Research and advanced development projects* are aimed at finding new core products or processes; for example, a project by an auto company to develop a hydrogen fuel cell vehicle.
- *Radical breakthrough development projects* develop products or processes that will employ some entirely new technology, perhaps one developed through an advanced development project; for example, the initial development of digital cameras employed a new core technology.
- *Next generation or platform development projects* develop new product platforms using mostly existing technologies. Apple's iPod provides a good example of a new platform product, as it essentially brought together some existing technologies under a new overall architecture. If successful, platform innovations provide starting points for follow-on derivative products.
- *Enhancements, hybrid, and derivative development projects* refine and improve selected features of existing products. Adding a peanut butter flavor or a new color to M&Ms candy amounts to a derivative project. The scope of such a project is much narrower than the other, more ambitious innovations.

Operations managers can play different kinds of roles in each of these project types. A new supplier or technology vendor may play a very central role in advanced development and radical product development projects, especially if product and process technologies are highly interrelated. For example, Gillette employed the services of equipment vendors to develop a radical new welding technology for production of the first flexible, moving head shaving razors. Platform and derivative development projects tend to rely more upon existing process technologies. In these projects, supply chain operations managers typically play consulting roles by clearly communicating the existing capabilities of processes to product designers.

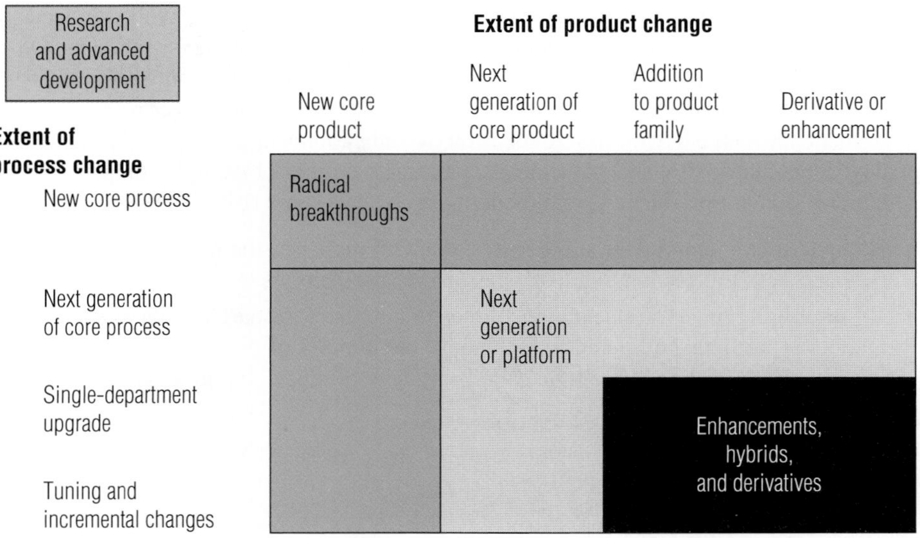

FIGURE 4-3
Types of Development Projects

Source: S.C. Wheelwright and K.B. Clark, *Revolutionizing Product Development* (New York: Free Press, 1992).

Innovation Project Management

In innovative firms, product/process design and development projects are marked by two key competencies: discipline and flexibility. Innovation projects often involve uncertainty relating to customers' responses, competition, technology, and resource availability. Good innovation project teams clarify and reduce uncertainty as much as possible, and build flexibility for situations where uncertainties persist.

- A disciplined innovation project has well-defined process steps, consideration and inclusion of all relevant stakeholders and decision makers, and well-thought-out metrics and incentives.
- A flexible innovation project includes rigorous risk analysis and contingency plans; planned evaluation and decision points where the project may be killed, redirected, or continued; and extra resources (funds, people, equipment) that can be quickly redeployed.

Operations managers are usually directly responsible for planning and executing product/process innovation projects. Because this is such an important task, most of the remainder of this chapter is dedicated to the discussion of approaches and tools that can be used to make innovation projects more disciplined, flexible, and ultimately more successful.[3]

New Product/Process Launch and Learning

Beyond the management of each individual project, the *progression* of innovation projects needs to be managed. After a new product is launched or a new process is brought online, it is important to capture the lessons learned from the project. A continual chain of innovation projects adds to a firm's overall capabilities when the knowledge gained in one project is captured and exploited in the next project.

Codevelopment

relationships

A single firm rarely possesses all of the knowledge and resources it needs to bring a major new product to market, or to bring a major new process online. Consequently, firms often partner with other firms to codevelop the new product or process. A codevelopment relationship may involve joint ownership of the new product design, or the development partner may participate strictly on a contract basis.

Operations and supply managers play important roles in helping to identify partners with high potential. Many firms ask production suppliers to participate directly in their product development processes. This practice is referred to as **early supplier involvement (ESI)**. By being involved early, suppliers of all kinds of services can influence design decisions so that products can be produced and delivered more efficiently. They also can plan for changes that they need to make in their own production processes and supply chain networks. In fact, suppliers often develop parts and even complete systems for their customers' products. On the Boeing 787, for example, a supplier developed the fuselage using carbon fibers rather than a metal exterior, a radically different approach from that of other passenger planes. Supplier involvement allows the buying firm to focus on overall systems integration and product functionality, rather than getting lost in the detailed technical designs of multiple complex systems.

early supplier involvement (ESI) A codevelopment approach in which suppliers participate directly in product design activities.

Codevelopment produces several benefits, as well as some risks. The benefits:

- By opening up its innovation processes, the firm increases the number of sources for new and better ideas, leading to higher-quality products.
- By leveraging the expertise and resources of suppliers, research firms, universities, and other partners, companies can increase the number of products they successfully launch, and reduce the time it takes to bring new products and processes online.

[3] In addition, Chapter 15 discusses tools and techniques that can be applied to any type of project.

- When companies work together to codevelop new products, they often share the financial and legal risks of development.

Some of the risks:

- By including more partners, a firm risks losing control over intellectual property. Either intentionally or accidentally, a codevelopment partner may leak secret plans or technical knowledge to competitors or other parties who might use this information against the firm.
- The firm can lose control over the goals and timing of the innovation project if it becomes too dependent on partners.

Managers have to weigh these pros and cons as a part of their overall innovation strategy. As more and more firms increase their levels of open innovation and codevelopment activities, the roles of internal operations managers and external supply managers become more and more important. Operations and supply managers work together with other functional groups to evaluate the benefits and risks associated with innovation partnership opportunities and to comprehend the technical capabilities and innovation competencies of their potential partners.

GET REAL

Codeveloping with a Competitor: Clorox Aligns Its Business Model with P&G

A few years ago, Clorox (famous for its Clorox brand bleach) acquired the Glad brand from SC Johnson. The Glad product line includes baggies, food wrap, and trash bags. It is a strong brand, but Clorox managers soon realized that they had no technological advantage needed to create follow-on products in this category. Thus, they feared that the Glad products would eventually become commodities. Clorox eventually learned that scientists at Procter and Gamble were developing and market testing two important technologies: Press'n Seal and Force Flex. Both developments looked very promising, but at the time P&G lacked the financial resources needed to launch and distribute a new brand highlighting these technologies.

At first glance, this looked like a match made in heaven. P&G had innovative technologies; Clorox had an existing brand and financial wherewithal. However, Clorox and P&G had also been long-time competitors. Both companies saw big risks in a partnership in which P&G licensed the technologies to Clorox. Clorox could simply sit on the technologies (not use them), thus killing the potential gains for P&G. P&G could license the technologies to Clorox, but withhold important information that Clorox would need in order to embed the technologies into its products and manufacturing processes.

The two companies eventually agreed upon a joint venture arrangement in which both companies held a significant stake in the success of new products using the technologies. The venture has been a huge success. In fact, Clorox subsequently approached P&G for another deal in which P&G would take some of Clorox's other brands into Asian markets, where P&G has strong distribution channels and Clorox does not. This new option would never have emerged had either Clorox or P&G been unwilling to take on the risks of their initial deal. This story clearly shows how codevelopment benefits can extend far beyond the profits associated with a single joint product development effort.

Source: Henry Chesbrough and Kevin Schwartz, "Innovating Business Models with Co-development Partnerships," *Research-Technology Management* 50, no. 1, (January/February 2007), pp. 55–59.

Prepare

How do operations managers ensure that new products meet customer requirements while also making the most of the capabilities of supply chain operational processes?

Organize

PRODUCT/PROCESS DESIGN AND DEVELOPMENT

There are many ways to describe the activities included in an innovation project. The most common approach is to think of stages through which the project must progress. Table 4-1 describes six major stages in product design and development. These stages can be collapsed into fewer phases or expanded into more detailed steps depending on the nature of the product and market environments and the planning needs of the company. Service innovation projects follow similar stages.

The Stage-Gate Process

Some firms use a disciplined **stage-gate™ process** developed by Robert G. Cooper[4] to manage costs and risks in product/process innovation projects. Resources are committed to the project only on a stage-by-stage basis.

stage-gate™ process A disciplined approach that defines specific criteria for each project stage that must be completed before proceeding to the next stage.

LO4-3 Describe new product/process design and development objectives and project phases.

TABLE 4-1 Stages of Product/Process Innovation

Stage	Activities and Decisions
Concept Development	• Identify core product concept • Conduct market, technical, and financial assessments • Identify the target values of the product attributes, volume, and price • Determine the primary product architecture, including product variants and components sharing plan • Propose and investigate production process concepts
Product and Process Planning	• Decide which components will be designed versus off-the-shelf • Identify who will design, produce, and assemble the components • Specify the types of processes to be used to produce the product and the structure of the supply chain • Identify who will develop and supply needed process technologies • Develop early prototypes and system-level simulations
Detailed Design and Development	• Determine the values of the key design parameters • Perform detailed design of the components including material and process selection, assembly precedence, and tooling requirements • Build full-scale prototypes and detailed simulations
Product and Market Testing	• Conduct full-scale product performance tests and simulations • Conduct customer tests • Design and test critical tools and production procedures • Refine details of product design
Commercialization	• Evaluate pilot production units • Establish market channels and an order fulfillment system • Train sales force and field service personnel
Market Introduction	• Ramp-up production volume • Fill distribution channels • Launch promotion and advertising campaigns • Evaluate field experience with product

[4] http://www.stage-gate.com/index.php

Near the completion of each stage, the project is reviewed by senior managers and a go/no-go decision is made to determine if the project should be continued. If the decision is go, then resources are provided to allow the project to continue into the next stage until the next gate is reached. At the next gate, the project is reviewed again and another go/no-go decision is made. If the decision is no-go then the project may repeat the stage, or it may be terminated and its resources reassigned to other projects. The discipline imposed by the stage-gate approach has been shown to increase teamwork, reduce product development time and cost, and identify problems earlier. This approach also helps to identify and reduce risks, as it allows managers give more scrutiny to the project's progress before additional resources are committed.

Integrated Product/Process Design and Development: Concurrent Engineering

LO4-4 Explain why cross-functional integration is needed in product and process design.

relationships

concurrent engineering The simultaneous design and development of all the processes and information needed to produce a product, to sell it, to distribute it, and to service it.

Some stages of product/process design and development naturally follow other stages, yet the stages do not have to be executed in a purely sequential way. For example, when developing a new laundry detergent using a sequential approach, the formula would be developed, then the production process would be designed, then the product packaging would be designed, and then the sales and advertising plans would be developed. Each development step would be performed by a different functional group that knows the most about doing that step. In reality, however, many activities in each of these steps can be overlapped using an approach known as **concurrent engineering** (CE) (see Figure 4-4). Concurrent engineering is defined as the simultaneous design and development of all the processes and information needed to produce a product, to sell it, to distribute it, and to service it. Other terms sometimes used in place of CE include *simultaneous engineering* and *integrated product development.* By getting different groups to work together, concurrent engineering integrates and facilitates cross-functional communication, leading to better decision making and faster development.

Operations managers located across the supply chain play very important roles in concurrent engineering product development projects because they get involved in design and development activities much earlier than in conventional projects. Consider the two product development projects depicted in Figure 4-5 on the next page. The overall resources spent in new product/process development can be split into three categories:

- Development costs—spent to fund the design, development, and testing activities in the development project.
- Sustaining and warranty costs—spent to make changes to the product design and to production processes needed to solve problems uncovered both in production and in the field. This includes costs to repair and replace defective products for customers.
- Production and sales support costs—spent to promote, sell, produce, and distribute the product.

In the functional/sequential development project shown in Figure 4-5, the design and development stages are pursued sequentially, without much interaction among various functional groups. This approach can lower the development costs because each functional

Advanced Research
Opportunity
Concept Development
Product/Process Planning
Detailed Design/Development
Development Project
Testing
Testing
Testing
Commercialization
Production and Sales Support
Market Introduction

FIGURE 4-4 Overlapped Product Development Activities: Concurrent Engineering

FIGURE 4-5 Comparing Resource Expenditures in Functional and Integrated Product Development Projects

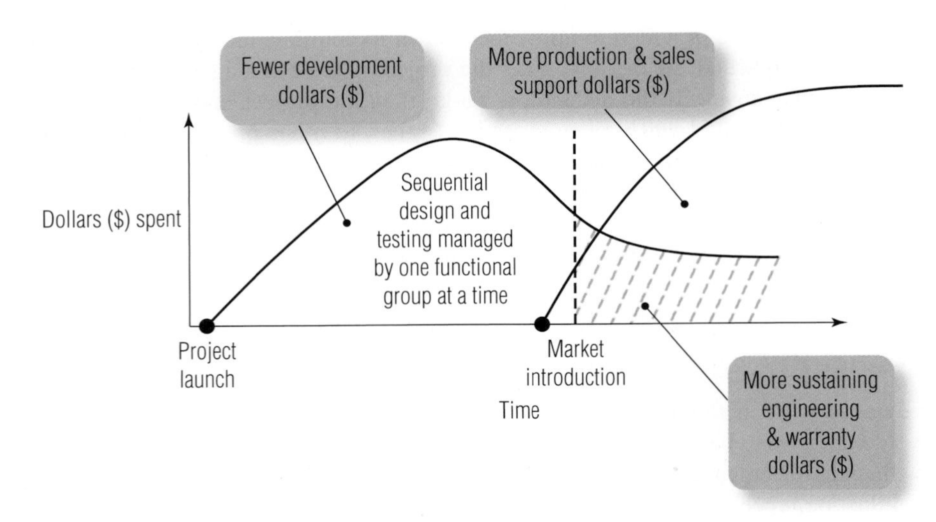

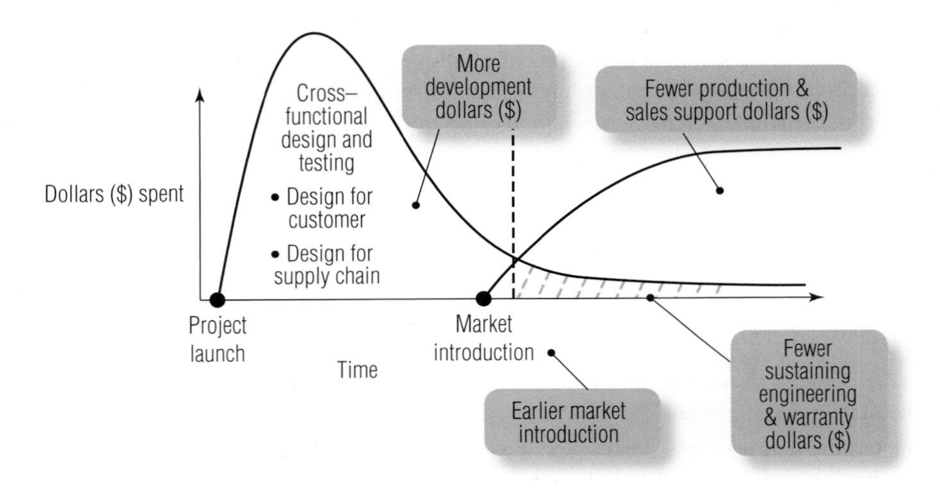

group focuses only on its specific development tasks. However, interdependencies in design decisions at different stages are often not fully considered. For example, what if a small change in laundry detergent formulation could have a large impact on manufacturing cost without affecting its washing performance? Product designers involved in a sequential development project may never be prompted to consider such a change because they are focused only on product performance.

The integrated/concurrent engineering approach overlaps the development activities (as shown in Figure 4-4), and many functional representatives work together in collocated teams. Internal operations managers and suppliers from all parts of the supply chain participate alongside marketing personnel and design engineers to codesign the product and its supporting processes. When product and process designs are developed simultaneously, the interdependencies in design decisions become more apparent and are more fully considered.

The integrated/concurrent engineering approach often requires more up-front commitments of development resources in order to evaluate a larger set of design issues earlier in the product development project. This concentrated and more thorough design and development effort provides several important benefits, as illustrated in Figure 4-5:

- First, by overlapping development phases, managers are usually able to complete the project faster and introduce the product sooner. Speed to market can be especially valuable if there are many competitors or if the market window of opportunity is limited.

- Second, by identifying and solving more product- and process-related problems before market introduction, product sustaining and warranty costs can be drastically reduced. It is usually much cheaper to solve problems in design before expensive commitments to tooling, production, and other commercialization processes have been made.
- Finally, by considering product performance specifications and process design alternatives simultaneously, concurrent engineering teams are usually able to design supply chain processes that are more cost effective. Thus, the production and sales support costs can be lowered over the life of the product.

The following sections describe procedures that make concurrent development activities most effective. Some are aimed at ensuring that designs meet customers' needs, and others are more concerned with the constraints and capabilities of supply chain operations. All of these approaches involve cross-functional teams made up of marketing, engineering, and supply chain operations personnel.

Design for the Customer

LO4-5 Apply tools and techniques for integrating customer needs and supply chain considerations into product/process design and development.

To be successful, a product must meet the targeted customer's needs. There are several techniques that are used to ensure that the product has the right product features and performance at the right price.

Voice of the Customer

The **voice of the customer (VOC)** is a term used to describe a research effort that typically takes place in the early phases of a new product or process concept development. The effort uses customer interviews, focus groups, surveys, and other means to gather detailed data describing customers' wishes, needs, likes, and dislikes regarding specific product features and functionalities. In addition to working directly with key customer representatives, many companies use the Internet to understand what product features customers like by allowing them to create customized virtual products. For example, the Web sites of most major car companies allow you to select and view the features and colors you want in a customized car. In industries such as software development, lead customers use prototype versions of the software and provide feedback to developers, a process known as **beta testing**.

voice of the customer (VOC) Research efforts that gather detailed data describing customers' wishes, needs, likes, and dislikes regarding specific product features and functionalities.

beta testing An approach in which customers use product prototype versions and provide feedback to developers

All of these approaches are aimed at acquiring and implementing the best new ideas and technologies as quickly as possible. Both qualitative and quantitative data are organized and prioritized so that product feature alternatives can be assessed by cross-functional teams who evaluate their benefits and costs. The information developed in a VOC process provides the key input for setting the detailed design specifications using a process such as quality function deployment.

Quality Function Deployment

Quality function deployment (QFD) is widely regarded as a useful tool for translating ordinary language used to describe customer needs into engineering language used to set product and process design parameters. Using QFD, a cross-functional team identifies all of the major customer requirements for a given product (possibly through a VOC effort) and evaluates how well the current product and process designs meet or exceed those requirements. Four linked information matrices are completed in QFD (see Figure 4-6):

quality function deployment (QFD) A method for translating ordinary language used to describe customer needs into engineering language used to set product and process design parameters.

1. The **customer requirements planning matrix**, also known as the **House of Quality**, identifies customer requirements and translates them into a set of technical product features.
2. The **technical features deployment matrix** translates the technical product features into product design specifications for critical product components.
3. In the third step, QFD translates the design specifications into the process parameters and control limits that define the processes that will deliver the product components.
4. In the fourth and final step, QFD translates critical process parameters into specific instructions to be performed by operations personnel.

customer requirements planning matrix or House of Quality A template that guides identification and translation of customer requirements into product features.

technical features deployment matrix A template that guides the translation of product features into technical product specifications.

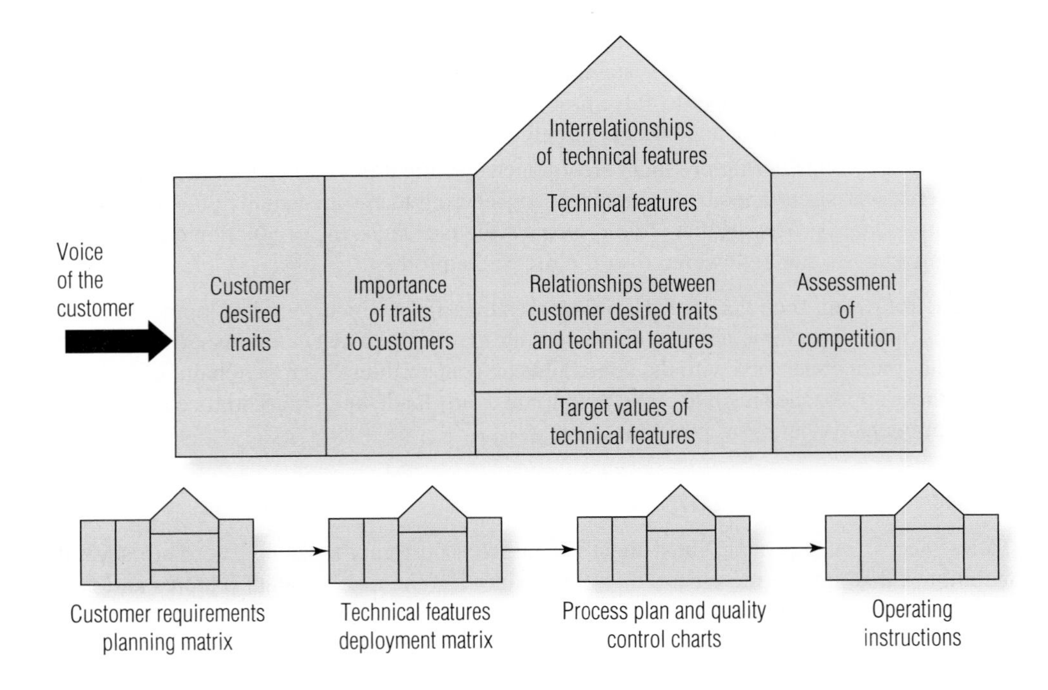

FIGURE 4-6 Quality Function Deployment—the House of Quality

At each step, the QFD process generates requirements (listed in the rows of the matrixes) and translates these requirements into supporting specifications and actions (listed in the columns of the matrixes). This series of steps provides a systematic way to ensure that all important customer needs are identified and translated into product and process specifications. The analysis usually requires several iterations to arrive at an acceptable design.

QFD has proved useful in both manufacturing and service firms. For example, Ritz-Carlton Hotels coupled QFD with process analysis to improve their housekeeping operations. They cut the average time to clean a room in half, reduced interruptions by one-third, and improved productivity by 14 rooms per worker. Law offices, hospitals, and even not-for-profit institutions such as higher education have also benefited from QFD.

We can use a hotel example (shown in Figure 4-7 on the next page) to understand how a customer requirements planning matrix (House of Quality) is constructed:

Customer desired traits. The information filling the rows of the matrix under customer desired traits defines what the hotel needs to do well in order to satisfy customers. This information is usually developed from research including surveys, focus groups, and other efforts to acquire the voice of the customer. In our example, customers have communicated that they want their valuables to be secure (the trait receiving the highest importance rating), they don't like to wait for their rooms, they want consistent service, and so on. Note that management has also added "Reduce Housekeeping Cost/Labor" as a desired trait. While customers might not identify this trait directly, management realizes that it is an important goal that interacts with the other traits.

Assessment of competition. Data on the right-hand side of the matrix provide a comparison of how well the hotel is doing on each customer desired trait, relative to its competitors. This information might come from the hotel's own survey combined with intelligence gathering efforts—hotel employees might even visit competitors' facilities to gather such intelligence. These data give an indication of the traits in which the hotel has an advantage, and where it needs to improve. The hotel appears to do quite well in having rooms ready when customers arrive. They need to improve the consistency of service, however.

Technical features and target values. The top and bottom columns of the matrix define the "hows" related to delivering the customer desired traits. In the design of a tangible product, these columns would contain engineering characteristics that are related to the delivery of various product functions. For example, the number of gears on a bike (a technical feature) determines how easy the bike is to pedal (a customer desired trait). In the hotel example, the technical features are service process characteristics that define how

FIGURE 4-7
House of Quality for Housekeeping Services

	Customer desired traits (WHAT's) / Technical Features (HOWs)	IMPORTANCE RATING	Defect Rate (Random sample)	Room Cycle Time	Possible Number of Interruptions	Occupied Interruptions	Honor Bar Discrep. Allowance Rate	No. Guest Room Doors Open at One Time	Housekeeping Productivity	Customer perceptions of performance (Poor 1 2 3 4 5 Excellent)
	DIRECTION OF IMPROVEMENT		↓	↓	↓	↓	↓	↓	↑	
Guest requirements housekeeping	Fully stocked room	4	◉				○			X A B
	Room serviced right the 1st time	5	◉		○	○	○			A X B
	Few if any interruptions	3			◉	◉				A B X
	Short interruptions when they occur	4		◉					△	A X B
	Consistent service provided	5	◉				○			X A B
	Room ready when I arrive	5		○					○	B A X
	Room cleaned at my convenience	4		○		◉			○	X AB
	Honor bar billing correct & timely	5	△				◉			XAB
	My things should be safe/secure	6		△				◉		B X A
Hotel	Reduce housekeeping cost/labor	6		◉					◉	A B X
	TARGETS		<5 defects (110 items)	<20 minutes	<4 per guest-day	<1 per guest-day	<5 per 1000 guests	<4 doors open	>24 rooms' keeper	

X - Our Hotel
A - Competitor A
B - Competitor B

ROOF		MATRIX		WEIGHTS	ARROWS	
Strong Pos.	◉	Strong	◉	9	Maximize	↑
Positive	○	Medium	○	3	Minimize	↓
Negative	×	Weak	△	1	Normal	○
Strong Neg.	⋇					

housekeeping services might be delivered and controlled. The data at the bottom of the matrix give target performance ranges for each service technical feature. For example, the target time to complete room cleaning is less than 20 minutes.

Interrelationships. The symbols in the remainder of the matrix define relationships. First, the symbols in the body of the matrix show how customer traits are related to technical features. For each desired trait, these relationships indicate the specific, directly observable measures of technical features, that are good indicators of customer satisfaction. For example, room cycle time is at least weakly related to five of the customer desired traits. The second set of symbols, found in the "roof" of the matrix, shows the relationships among the various technical features. These data help identify trade-offs among various dimensions of performance. For example, there appears to be a strong trade-off making it difficult to maintain high housekeeping productivity while maintaining a low defect rate. Establishing all of the interrelationships shown in the matrix is the heart of the product/process design activity.

Process plans and instructions. The next step for operations managers would be to translate the performance targets into process specifications. For example, hotel operations managers would use the 20-minute room cleaning target and quality requirements to develop procedures defining the cleaning and inspection steps, cleaning tools to be used, employee training programs, and so on.

In order to complete a House of Quality analysis, marketing, engineering, and operational personnel typically must have many discussions regarding the interpretations of customer inputs and the pros and cons of various technical options for meeting customer desired traits. These discussions ultimately produce better product designs. The QFD process is simply a tool for facilitating a more thorough design analysis and richer cross-functional interactions.

Failure Modes and Effects Analysis

failure modes and effects analysis (FMEA) A procedure for identifying and correcting potential quality problems inherent to product or process designs.

One of the important goals of innovation is to identify and eliminate potential quality problems early during design. These problems can affect both product performance and process reliability; that is, the ability to consistently produce a good or deliver a service that conforms to design specifications. **Failure modes and effects analysis (FMEA)** is a procedure for identifying and correcting potential quality problems inherent to product or process designs. FMEA is team-based; it brings together representatives from such groups as engineering, manufacturing, purchasing, quality, research and development, and field service. The FMEA team is tasked with answering two basic questions:

- How can this product design (or process design) fail to do what it is supposed to do?
- What should we do to prevent these potential failures?

Answering these questions involves five major steps from problem identification to resolution:

1. *Determine what portions of the product or the process are to be analyzed.*
2. *Identify types of potential failures, modes for each failure type, causes and effects of each failure mode.* For example, a failure for a coffeemaker could be that the coffee is the wrong temperature. This failure has two modes; the coffee could be too hot or too cold. Each of these failure modes has potentially different causes, and different effects on customer satisfaction.
3. *Prioritize the failure modes.* For each failure mode, rate the frequency or probability of its occurrence, the severity of its effects, and the inability to detect the problem early. Then prioritize failure mode causes and identify the critical ones requiring action. To simplify the process of prioritizing, a **risk priority number (RPN)** is calculated as

risk priority number (RPN) A rating used in FMEA to indicate the combined probability, severity, and undetectability of a failure mode.

$$\text{RPN} = \text{Occurence Rating} \times \text{Severity Rating} \times \text{Undetectability Rating}$$

4. *Create plans to deal with each critical failure mode.* The consequences of a failure mode can be alleviated by eliminating it, by reducing its severity, by reducing its occurrence, and/or by increasing its detection in advance.

relationships

EXAMPLE 4-1

FMEA

In examining a proposed design for a new coffeemaker, the heating element (that part of the coffeemaker that keeps the coffee warm and at a constant temperature) is a potential area of concern. After studying the problem, a cross-functional team developed the FMEA found in Table 4-2. The table indicates two possible failures pertaining to the heating element. Of these, the more serious is the problem of a malfunctioning regulator causing the coffee to be too hot. Its high severity and undetectability gave it the highest RPN. Having burned hands or a burned mouth is a much greater consequence than having to throw away a pot of coffee because it is too cold. The last column in Table 4-2 shows the team's recommended actions. The goal here is to find the most cost-effective way to minimize the overall risk (RPN) by lowering either the severity, occurrence, or undetectability. The team decided to take no action regarding the potential for a broken heating element. They believed that the consequences of this cause of failure were small enough to be acceptable, given the cost of dealing with this problem.

TABLE 4-2 FMEA for Coffee Heating Element

Name	Function	Failure Mode	Effect	Cause	Severity (S)	Occurrence (O)	Undetectability (U)	RPN = S × O × U	Recommendation
Heating Element	Keep coffee at constant temperature	Coffee cold	Coffee thrown out	Broken connection	3	6	6	108	Reinforce connection guides for protection
				Broken heating element	3	4	3	36	No action
		Coffee too hot	Mouth or hands burned	Malfunctioning regulator	8	4	8	256	Swap current regulator for new, redesigned one provided by supplier

5. *Implement the plans, measure their impact, and repeat the analysis as needed.* Like other design tools, FMEA is very much an iterative procedure. As critical failure modes are eliminated or reduced, other failure modes may be targeted for action. This process continues until the design is viewed as being sufficiently reliable.

In addition to improvements to product reliability and safety, FMEA has been found to reduce development costs and time, provide insights for product testing and maintenance, and serve as a means for tracking and communicating design activities throughout the organization.

Value Engineering/Value Analysis

Another process for developing improvements in product and process designs is known as **value engineering/value analysis**. In a typical value engineering project suppliers meet with internal cross-functional teams, bringing together critical information about a new product concept, its function, its marketing appeal, and its production methods. Value analysis uses the same approach for existing products, including the following steps:

value engineering/value analysis A method to improve the benefits and costs of a product through a detailed examination of its function.

1. *Identify the functional purposes of a product or component.* Describe what the product does, not what it is. Describe each function using a two-word phrase (one verb and one noun). For example, a function of a pencil is to "make marks."
2. *Separate the various functions into two categories, those that make the product work, and those that make it sell.* For example, a drill motor's housing protects the user from the motor and gears; this helps to make it work. A housing with an especially comfortable handle makes the drill easier to use; this helps to sell the product.
3. *Estimate the value (benefits and costs) of each function.* Rate each function (high, medium, low) according to a typical customer's assessment of the importance of the function and the cost of providing that function.
4. *Compare the importance of each function with its cost.* Asking certain questions can improve the analysis; questions such as: Can the function be eliminated entirely? Can the function be provided in some other way? Can the product be simplified or standardized? What changes will reduce costs or speed up production?

5. *Implement changes to the product design that maximize the value of the product.* Verify the team's conclusions by gathering information from customers and suppliers, whoever has a stake in the success of the product. Then make the changes and measure the results.

A value analysis of electric drill motors prompted a redesign of the housing, replacing cast steel housings with plastic ones. While plastic proved less durable than steel, it was cheaper and faster to make. A plastic housing also made the drill motor lighter and more comfortable to hold, reducing user fatigue. Also, plastic does not conduct electricity, so it reduces the safety risk of electrical shock as compared to steel housings, thus eliminating the need for electrically grounding the tool.

Design for Supply Chain Operations

The foregoing approaches focus on the value and performance quality of goods and service designs. Other product design improvement programs focus squarely on attributes that affect the efficiency or effectiveness of supply chain operational processes. Each of the following "design for" methods focuses on a specific area of supply chain management. By matching the designs of products to the operational capabilities that exist throughout the supply chain, products can be made and delivered faster, cheaper, and with better quality.

Design for Manufacture

design for manufacture (DFM) An umbrella term that describes methods and tools that focus design activities on improving the ease with which products can be produced.

producibility A measure of the speed, ease, cost efficiency, and reliability with which a product can be produced.

Design for manufacture (DFM) is an umbrella term that describes any of a host of methods and tools that focus design activities on improving product **producibility**. Producibility is a measure of the speed, ease, cost efficiency, and reliability with which a product can be produced. DFM efforts make use of many tactics for communicating and highlighting the needs and limitations that process capabilities impose on the product design. One tactic is to publish design rules such as:

- Reduce the total number of unique parts in the product.
- Reduce the number of fasteners used.
- Eliminate the need for specialized tools.
- Design all assembly tasks to come from one direction.

While DFM often focuses on aspects of product fabrication, this type of analysis can address many processes throughout the supply chain such as:

design for assembly Focus on minimizing the number of parts in a product and easing the assembly processes.

design for product serviceability Focus on easing product disassembly and reusing product components.

design for Six Sigma Focus on systematically evaluating the consistency with which a good or service can be produced or delivered given the capabilities of the processes used.

robust design Focus on designing products that can be made consistently even with varying inputs and operating conditions.

- **Design for assembly**—designers focus on minimizing the number of parts in a product and on easing assembly processes.
- **Design for product serviceability**—designers focus on easing product disassembly and maintenance, and on the reuse of product components. For example, cars, computers, and other equipment usually have modules that can be easily swapped out and recycled.
- **Design for Six Sigma**[5]—designers systematically evaluate the consistency with which a good or service can be produced or delivered given the capabilities of the processes used.
- **Robust design**—designers use experiments and simulation models to design products that can be produced consistently, even when production processes vary greatly. For example, designers of corn flakes cereal develop a recipe that yields the same consistency of product, regardless of the source of the corn, the humidity or temperature in the production plant, and so on.

DFM involves design review meetings between product engineers and manufacturing workers. Meetings in early phases of design and development typically focus on product architectural decisions such as the number of product variants envisioned, the potential for

[5] Design for Six Sigma is described in Chapter 6, "Managing Quality."

reusing existing or standardized parts across different products, and the role of modularity in the product design. As the product design becomes more detailed and prototypes become available, design review meetings focus more on specific component and feature issues such as dimensional tolerances, use of fasteners or other means of assembly, and part geometry issues (e.g., shape and symmetry).

DFM efforts have been credited with improving the quality of products while saving firms thousands or even millions of dollars. For example, Mattel Toys saved over $40 million in production costs in a single year due to the implementation of DFM (see the Get Real box on the next page describing the impact of DFM on a Mattel product).

components standardization Reusing part designs across multiple products in order to reduce development and production costs.

Components Standardization

A way to reduce development and production costs and to increase product quality is to standardize the parts and components used across various product designs in a product family. Instead of designing a new part for each product, designers reuse parts from existing products. **Components standardization** produces several advantages. Fewer new designs must be created, reducing development cost and time. Fewer unique parts in an operations system simplifies inventory management because there are fewer parts to order, warehouse, and control. This produces savings in overhead, personnel, and storage space. With fewer parts, purchasing leverage can be increased because the volume per part is increased, lowering prices per unit (through quantity discounts). Supply management is also made less complex because fewer parts must be ordered.

sustainability

Environmental management is simplified as well. Until recently, for example, Chrysler used over 40 different plastic films for protecting, wrapping, and storing items. This meant that the company had to have a different set of environmental procedures for each plastic film, and frequent problems were encountered when it came time to separate the films for recycling. Chrysler reduced these 40 films to one standard film, which enabled them to reduce the number of suppliers from eight to two. Other benefits included elimination of floor space needed for storing and sorting the various plastics, reduction in environmental management procedures, elimination of charges made by recyclers who had to re-sort incorrectly sorted plastic films, and a reduction in purchase price.

PowerShot: SX200, ELPH, A-Series, E-Series (in various colors)

EOS: XTI, EOS 50D, Rebel XT (silver), Rebel XSI

Four platforms for Canon cameras. Each row represents a separate platform.

Modular Product Designs

For some products, customers demand a wide array of features. Take digital cameras, for example. A company like Canon designs cameras for many different customer groups, each of which wants a different combination of camera features. Some customers want a simple "point and shoot" camera while others want advanced features. Rather than design an entirely new product variant for each customer group, it is much more efficient for a company like Canon to design a few basic product platforms, and then to design modules that can be added or subtracted from these platforms to create different combinations of product features.

This approach, designing products as combinations of standardized components and processes, is known as **modular product design**. Canon can switch out different lens assemblies and digital logic control systems in a common camera platform (the camera body) to produce many different product variants with various levels of functionality and cost. This modular approach is used in hundreds of different products, both goods and services. For example, a company that provides guided tours might design basic packages that can be supplemented with special events to tailor the experiences to the desires of particular tour groups. By using modular product designs, operations managers can create all kinds of efficiencies in supply chain processes, while at the same time satisfying a wide variety of customer needs.

modular product design Using combinations of components with standardized product interfaces to create different product variations.

GET REAL

Mattel's Serious Approach to DFM for Toys

The creator of Barbie dolls and other children's toys should be in a fun business. In reality, it's a cutthroat, mature business that requires a cost minimization strategy to remain competitive. Hence, Mattel manufactures in many low-labor-cost countries.

Because there are limits to the benefits of cheap labor, Mattel created a "Design for Competitive Advantage" program to streamline costs. They started off right by setting up a training program to teach DFM principles to their engineers. To begin, they created a computerized data bank to help them identify similar or redundant parts. This system also helped them establish standardized part tolerances. The result? Lower costs and a shorter product design cycle.

To illustrate their new approach, Mattel selected Color Spin, an existing product that helps a toddler develop "visual awareness and action–reaction motor skills." The product retails for about $13 and is designed for babies six months and older. The existing product design called for 55 parts to be made, purchased, and assembled. The schematic of the parts and their location in the final product is shown here. After applying simple DFM principles, the Mattel team reduced the number of parts by 50 percent while increasing quality and performance. The improved product also is shown here. How did they do it? Mostly by redesigning parts to snap together. In other cases, plastic welding replaced fasteners. An in-house software system analyzed the cost effectiveness of design alternatives.

Mattel was able to shave 38 percent from the cost of Color Spin—an annual savings of $700,000. When asked what advice they would give to others, they responded:

- Make sure it's a team effort, with designers aboard as allies.
- Choose a leader who has experience on both sides, design and manufacturing.
- Get support from as high up in the company as possible.
- Assure recognition for DFM achievements and stimulate continued interest.
- Maintain an understanding of what the customer wants, and exceed their expectations.

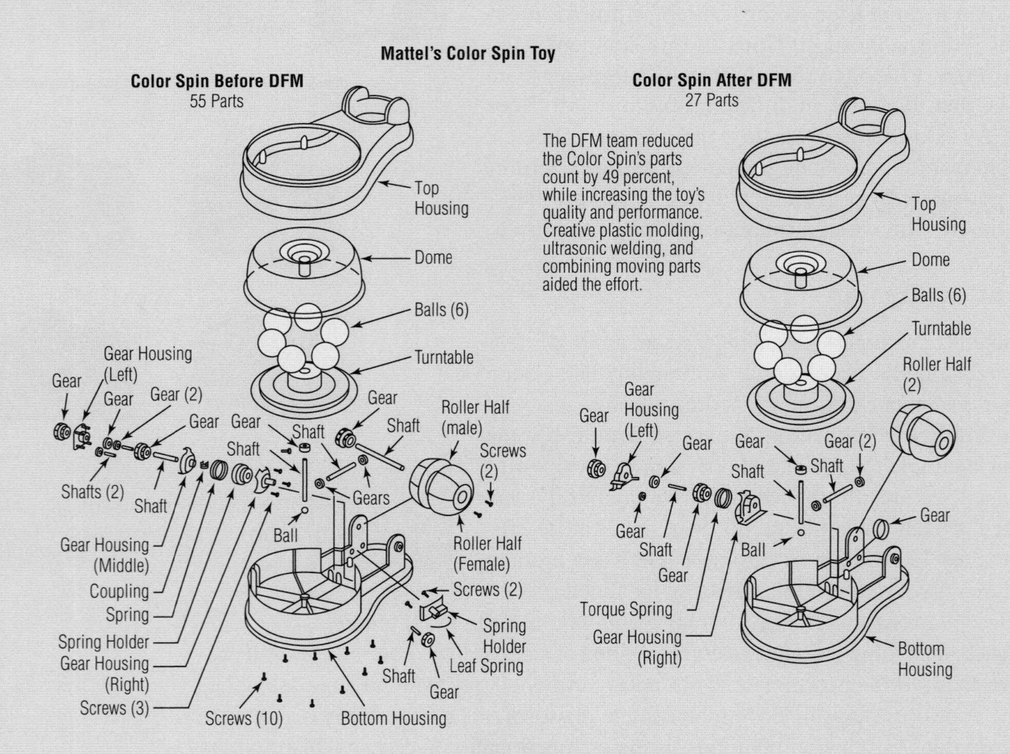

SOURCE: D. Gardner, "DFM Adds Sparkle to Toy Line," *Design News*, July 7, 1991, pp. 62–64.

Design for Logistics

Design for logistics focuses on minimizing the packaging, handling, and shipping costs for products. Logistical operations managers, both internal and from supply partners, work with designers to reduce product size and weight, as both factors tend to drive logistics costs. In addition, by redesigning the product's packaging orientation, managers can sometimes increase the amount of product that can be stored in a given facility or transportation vehicle. For example, the packaging for recent versions of the iPhone is half the size that it was for the original iPhone shipped in 2007. Thus, almost twice as many product boxes fit on each shipping pallet. Yet another typical analysis addresses the taxes and duties associated with procurement, storage, and distribution alternatives for a product. For example, if a product is designed to be more modular, then this might create more options for the sourcing and assembly of its components. By sourcing from low-tax regions, and by importing components rather than finished assemblies, import taxes and duties might be decreased. Finally, design for *reverse-logistics* is becoming more and more important. The concern here is to design products so that they can be easily returned and refurbished or recycled after use. For example, makers of ink cartridges for printers often include return envelopes in product boxes, and they design the cartridges to be easily cleaned and refilled.

design for logistics Focus on minimizing packaging, handling, and shipping costs for products.

design for environment Focus on minimizing the detrimental environmental impacts of product and process designs across all stages of a product's life.

Design for Environment

Design for environment seeks to minimize the detrimental environmental impacts of product and process designs across all stages of a product's life. Typical design-for-environment analyses would evaluate product material and packaging choices to minimize the use of energy and hazardous materials, and to maximize the potential for product reuse and recycling. Analyzing the carbon dioxide impact of products is of special and growing importance as more and more countries impose pollution taxes or caps on a company's outputs of carbon dioxide and other greenhouse gases. The Get Real box on the next page tells how Texas Instruments redesigned a manufacturing plant to minimize environmental impacts.

sustainability

ENABLING TECHNOLOGIES FOR PRODUCT/PROCESS INNOVATION

Prepare

How do computer-aided technologies help to improve the quality, speed, and efficiency of innovation processes?

Organize

Enabling Technologies for Product/Process Innovation

Information technology and computerization have greatly enhanced innovation processes by speeding up design activities, by improving computational power, and by enhancing communications among design partners. Here we very briefly describe some of the more important technological developments that are improving the speed and quality of design and development activities.

Computer-aided design (CAD) systems automate many aspects of the design process, especially the development of drawings and technical specifications. Design rules (DFM rules, for example) and best-practices can be embedded into CAD systems. Data captured in these systems can be accessed by persons located around the world for use in product design, process planning, and computer-aided manufacturing.

Computer-aided engineering (CAE) tools are frequently linked to CAD systems in ways that reinforce good design practices. These sophisticated systems create and analyze three-dimensional models of parts and assemblies, reducing the need to build expensive and time-consuming physical prototypes. For example, linked CAD/CAE systems can automatically analyze assembly designs to identify areas of potential interference between parts. Further, many CAD systems embed process information and design

computer-aided design (CAD) Systems that automate the development of drawings and technical specifications.

computer-aided-engineering (CAE) Systems that create and analyze three-dimensional product models, reducing the need to build physical prototypes.

GET REAL

TI Builds a Green Wafer Factory

While other semiconductor manufacturing companies are moving their factories to China and Taiwan, Texas Instruments recently built a completely new silicon wafer manufacturing plant near their headquarters in Richardson, Texas. Their goal was to build a plant for $180 million less than the cost of their most recent plant built seven years earlier and six miles away. Even more stunning was their aggressive goal to lower the operating costs of the plant while making it as energy efficient and environmentally friendly as possible. A typical wafer fabrication plant uses the same energy as 10,000 homes.

Through intense cross-functional efforts with design partner the Rocky Mountain Institute, TI achieved its goals, ultimately spending 30 percent less capital on plant construction . . . and lowering projected production costs more than $4 million per year—due to a 20 percent energy reduction, 35 percent water-use reduction, and 50 percent emissions reduction. They started with a radical innovation in architectural design. Conventional wafer factories have at least three floors because of the need to surround the manufacturing process with cooling and other support systems. The design team developed a plan with only two floors, saving all the associated infrastructure and energy costs. Numerous other innovations included:

- A reduction in the number of elbows in water pipes and air ducts, thus reducing friction and enabling the use of smaller pumps.
- Use of passive solar technologies including reflective concrete and a plastic roof covering that reflects 85 percent of the sun's radiation.
- Design of windows and reflection systems to maximize natural lighting.
- Use of native plants for landscaping and recycled water for irrigation and cooling.
- Recycling of almost 90 percent of construction waste.

Operations managers sometimes believe that it costs more to build and operate green (environmentally friendly) processes, but TI showed that it isn't necessarily so. Well-designed processes can be *green* and *lean.*

Silicon wafer.

group technology A coding system that allows designers and manufacturing planners to identify product components that have similar design or processing characteristics.

product life cycle management (PLM) A software-facilitated process used to capture and share all the information needed to define products throughout their life.

rules directly into the design software so that it may be linked to certain design features. For example, when a designer draws a hole, she can then select a pull-down window of information providing a list of processes that could create the hole, typical dimensional tolerances, defect rates associated with each process, and any other design rules related to the feature.

Some companies have developed CAE systems that aid the evaluation of design choices using virtual prototypes of products. These systems can analyze both product and process functionalities, including physical stresses and thermal patterns, mechanical assembly steps, printed circuit board design, and so on. The technology for developing virtual prototypes is still emerging, but as it is refined it is expected to play a major role in design and development.

In large organizations, designers often waste time and resources by unknowingly re-creating existing designs. CAD systems can be linked with product databases that contain information on preferred components, existing designs from other products, and suppliers of purchased items. Classification and coding systems enable designers to easily search design databases for existing designs that meet their current needs. Similarly, databases that list preferred components and vendors can speed up a designer's search for suitable parts. These databases frequently make use of **group technology**, a coding system that allows designers and manufacturing planners to identify "families" of parts that have similar design or processing characteristics. These approaches reduce design time and reap enormous benefits in manufacturing because fewer unique parts must be fabricated and inventoried, less special tooling is needed, production scheduling is simplified, and less disruption is experienced.

Product life cycle management (PLM) is a process, facilitated by computer software and databases, used to capture and share all the information needed to define products throughout their life. PLM is used during all phases of development, product launch, production, and disposal. By capturing development information, development of next generation and derivative products that reuse much of the design of current or former products can be accomplished much faster. The benefits include increased collaboration, because all groups involved in design and development can access and share the same information. Learning within the organization is facilitated since the information is captured in the organization rather than staying with an individual.

3-D CAD model of the BMW 645i.

CHAPTER SUMMARY

New product/process innovation activities define the products and markets that a firm will pursue. Operations managers in the supply chain play critical roles in bringing product and process innovations to reality. They also help their firms find competitive advantages by developing codevelopment partnerships, fast time-to-market capabilities, high development efficiency, and design creativity. The following points offer important considerations and tools for managing innovation projects:

1. Innovative firms gain advantages over their competitors by virtue of their innovation competencies in areas including idea and opportunity development, project portfolio planning, project management, and postproject learning.
2. More and more, innovation is a supply chain activity in which a firm involves its customers, key suppliers, and other partners. This process of open innovation and co-development leads to higher quality products developed faster and more efficiently.

3. A typical innovation project has stages of development including concept development, product and process planning, detailed design and development, product and market testing, commercialization, and market introduction.
4. Innovation project stages can be executed sequentially or concurrently, using an approach called concurrent engineering, depending upon the requirements of the particular project.
5. A key challenge in managing an innovation project is the integration of the many interrelated product/process design issues. A number of methods and tools are useful for managers who want to encourage teamwork and cross-functional communication among project workers. These methods include voice of the customer, early supplier involvement, quality function deployment, failure modes and effects analysis, value analysis, design for manufacture, components standardization, and modular design.

KEY TERMS

beta testing 123
components standardization 129
computer-aided design (CAD) 131
computer-aided engineering (CAE) 131
concurrent engineering 121
customer requirements planning matrix 123
design for assembly 128
design for environment 131
design for logistics 131
design for manufacture (DFM) 128
design for product serviceability 128
design for Six Sigma 128
early supplier involvement (ESI) 118
failure modes and effects analysis (FMEA) 126
group technology 133
House of Quality 123
innovation portfolio planning 117
modular product design 129
new process design and development projects 112
new product design and development projects 112
open innovation 116
producibility 128
product life cycle 113
product life cycle management (PLM) 133
quality function deployment (QFD) 123
risk priority number (RPN) 126
robust design 128
stage-gate™ process 120
technical features deployment matrix 123
value engineering/value analysis 127
voice of the customer (VOC) 123

DISCUSSION QUESTIONS

1. Describe a situation where the functional/sequential approach to product development might be more appropriate than the integrated/concurrent engineering approach.
2. Operations personnel tend to favor product component standardization while design and marketing personnel tend to resist it. Why is this true? What are the potential disadvantages to standardization?
3. Why are discipline and flexibility both needed in new product/process innovation? Are these two capabilities in conflict with each other?

4. What major differences would you expect to find in the management approaches used for breakthrough innovation projects versus those used for derivative or enhancement projects?
5. Discuss the pros and cons of open innovation.
6. Under what circumstances might concurrent engineering (overlapping the stages of design and development) be a bad idea?
7. Discuss the roles that personnel from warranty/field service and the manufacturing shop floor might play when conducting an FMEA.
8. In which stages of a new product design and development project are supply chain operations managers most likely to have the greatest impact? Why?

PROBLEMS

1. Refer back to the QFD for housekeeping services shown in Figure 4-7.
   a. What seem to be the biggest opportunities for improvement, relative to competitors' levels of performance?
   b. Which technical feature is most strongly related to the goal of protecting the safety and security of guests' possessions?
   c. Why would room cycle time and defect rate be negatively correlated?
   d. Which technical feature has the strongest associations with the largest number of guest requirements?
2. Given the FMEA data provided in the table below:
   a. What is the RPN for each failure cause?
   b. Which failure cause would be of least concern?
   c. Which failure cause would be of greatest concern?
   d. For the failure of greatest concern, would your recommended action be aimed at reducing failure severity, occurrence, or undetectability? On what other information would your answer depend?

Failure Cause	Severity	Occurrence	Undetectability
M	5	2	1
N	3	4	9
X	2	2	3
Y	7	3	2
Z	9	1	5

3. Identify three or four important failure modes for a cellular phone.
4. Conduct an FMEA for a simple service or tangible product with which you are familiar. Identify a few failure modes, estimate the RPNs, and recommend possible improvements.
5. Complete a value analysis for the following products:
   a. Paper clip
   b. Textbook
6. Make a list of customer desired traits for an MP3 player.
7. Document the steps that someone using the House of Quality procedure might follow in developing:
   a. A new mountain bicycle.
   b. An introductory operations management course.
   c. A new candy bar.

CASE

The ALPHA Timer Development Project (A)

Roger Terry hurried down the hallway toward the planning meeting for the ALPHA timer product development project. Terry had served as project manager for the initial stage of the ALPHA single-block product development, and he was now preparing to start the follow-on development activities.

The ALPHA timer development project was a major effort for Doorley Controls, Inc., to develop a new platform design for its washing machine timer control mechanism. The project was started with a conscious strategy to gain market position with Doorley's key customers: Whirlpool, Maytag, and Frigidaire. The idea was to create a new core product design to take advantage of the recently increased sales volume to Whirlpool. Doorley planned to replace multiple existing timers with a lower cost, single product platform with enhancements. While existing timers were made with numerous plastic and metal parts requiring a lot of hand assembly, the ALPHA would be made mostly of molded plastic parts, assembled by automation. The product concept also included a unique feature called *quiet cycle-select,* which allowed the user to index the control shaft quietly. The idea for it came out of Doorley's internal quality function deployment analysis (QFD). The results of the ALPHA QFD analysis are shown below.

Questions

1. What features of the timer design appear to offer Doorley the strongest advantages over its competitors' products? What features are apparent weaknesses?
2. Which manufacturing methods are most strongly related to the goal of producing a flexible drive system? Do any of these methods conflict with each other?
3. Which design parameter has the strongest dependence on any of the manufacturing methods?
4. What evidence is there that the ALPHA team has used a DFM approach?

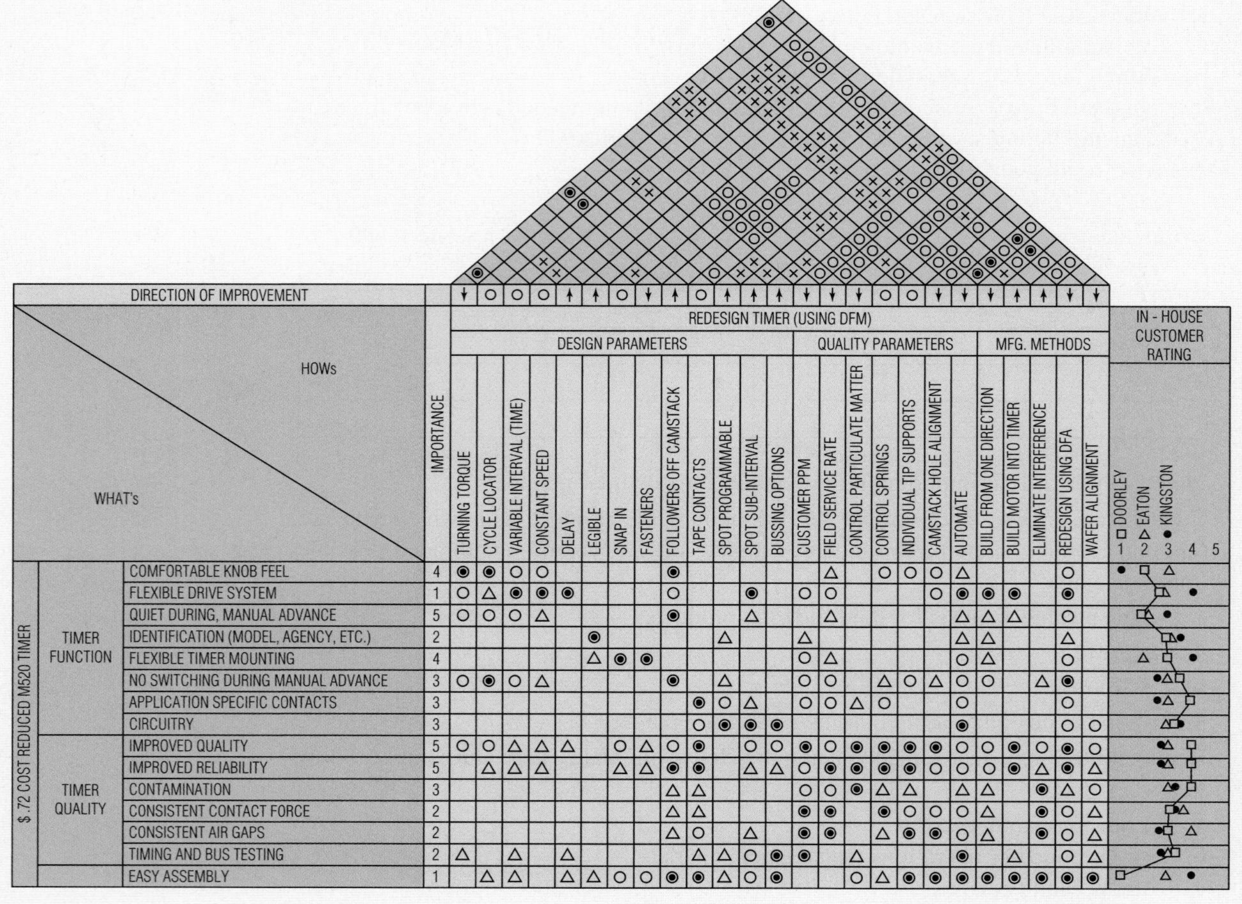

CASE

The ALPHA Timer Development Project (B)

The ALPHA single-block timer development project had not gone exactly as planned. The product development time-to-market was 48 months instead of the planned 30 months, and capital expenditures for the project were at least 30 percent over budget. On the other hand, quality levels for the timer were much better than before, and assembly labor costs were reduced by 25%.

Near the end of the first year of the project, difficulties began to arise. Changes in the appliance industry occurred as governmental pressures for more energy-efficient washers favored more horizontal-axis machines, requiring more complex timing devices. A marketing manager complained, "Even if we would have gone to our customers and asked them what they wanted in a new timer, I doubt that they could have told us at that time." It also soon became clear that a more complex, double-block version of the timer would be needed for top-of-the-line washers. This surprised the project team. As a team member explained, "We expected that customers would use more electronics or hybrids in the top-of-the-line appliances. We didn't really realize at the time that our customers still considered mechanical timers to be very important for the top end of the line. The *quiet cycle-select* was a very nice feature that they wanted to have in the top of the line, and if we couldn't provide that feature in double-block designs, they didn't want to use it anywhere."

An engineer from the program recalled other problems in the development process: "We were testing a new rigid material for the timer housing, which Whirlpool had approved. However, our initial testing showed that it could not be molded at the wall thickness that our supplier told us we could produce. We lost several months in development as a result. The alternative material we finally selected required some major production tool changes that also took more time. Manufacturability problems with the combsets in the timer also caused delays, requiring another four-month redesign."

Finally, the first timer samples were delivered to Whirlpool for evaluation. They were rejected. An engineer explained, "We knew all along that Whirlpool was concerned about the damaging effects of SPRAY'n WASH on some plastics. We did SPRAY'n WASH testing here and had all our plastic suppliers do SPRAY'n WASH testing. Unfortunately, we tested the parts using the manual pump version of SPRAY'n WASH, not the aerosol version, which is the problem product. We lost a good six months in development figuring out a new material to use."

Project manager Roger Terry had mixed feelings as he walked back to his office after the double-block planning meeting had ended. The meeting had gone well, and it seemed that everyone was enthusiastic about the program. Terry knew that the success of the new double-block platform project depended on his ability to analyze the single-block experience and to apply the lessons they had learned.

Questions

1. Assess the outcomes of the Alpha project. Was the project a success?
2. Were the problems encountered in the development project typical, or could they have been avoided?

CASE

The ALPHA Timer Development Project (C)

As he stopped to refill his coffee mug, Roger Terry began to recall some of the comments he had heard from various members of the single-block product development team (see the comments reproduced below).

The following comments were gathered from informal conversations with ALPHA program team members after the project's completion.

"Very large portions of time were lost because of having to go back and reinvent the wheel and make ALPHA something it was never proposed to be."

"We struggled with the project because of our relationship with Whirlpool. They wanted exclusivity. We were trying to maintain secrecy, working only with them, when we really needed the whole market to speak out. We don't have any real marketing department, we have a sales department that takes care of the ongoing business."

"Part of the problem is that you end up with two masters here. You've got the engineering guy who is always worried about the material content and uniqueness of design, and you've got an operations guy who's only worried about the automation and the labor content. The structure and incentives in the organization sometimes pit functions against one another."

"The design for manufacture efforts in the beginning included quality and tooling people from operations at headquarters, but plant manufacturing people only first heard of the ALPHA concept after parts had been designed, and tooling orders were about to be released."

"I don't know what we could have done to try harder—I mean, we made people available, and tried to schedule sessions with all the appropriate functional areas and people who where in the know, and participate and critique and give us their feedback. Even though we made all those efforts to get input, as time goes on and people change, and the complexity of it unfolds, and you've got people at Whirlpool saying we didn't do our homework—we did not ask them what they wanted. But we came and asked and asked and asked!"

"There is a culture within the company of limited information sharing. When things went wrong, instead of dealing with facts, things were rearranged to make it seem a little bit better for whatever reason. A lot of doubt was generated within the company and then a lot of doubt was generated in 'customer-land.' It just started building—this great big wall of doubt. Our customers asked us if we were having design problems, and we said 'No.' They knew better."

"No one person was responsible for the entire project. Operations did their thing; engineering did their thing, but early on no one coordinated things. When push came to shove, when a decision had to be made quickly, then one person needed the authority to get the plant people, operations people, quality people, engineering people, and sales people together to decide once and for all what to do."

"We really didn't have the kind of input into equipment design and manufacturer choices that we needed to have. The headquarters group always had the final say. Consequently, there are several changes that we will make to get further cost reductions and quality improvements in the next few years that we could have had right off the bat."

Questions

1. How would you describe the team members' morale at this point? What are their primary concerns?
2. Given the team members' comments, what advice would you give Roger Terry regarding the forthcoming double-block timer development effort?

SELECTED READINGS & INTERNET SITES

Cargille, B., and C. Fry. "Design for Supply Chain: Spreading the Word Across HP." *Supply Chain Management Review,* July/August 2006, pp. 34–41.

Chesbrough, H. W. *Open Innovation: The New Imperative for Creating and Profiting from Technology.* Boston: Harvard Business School Press, 2003.

Cooper, R. G., and E. J. Kleinschmidt. "Stage-Gate Systems for New Product Success." *Marketing Management* 1, no. 4 (1993), pp. 20–29.

Dodgson, M.; D. Gann; and A. Salter. "The Role of Technology in the Shift Towards Open Innovation: The Case of Procter & Gamble." *R&D Management* 36, no. 3 (June 2006), pp. 333–46.

Hauser, J. R., and D. Clausing. "The House of Quality." *Harvard Business Review,* May–June 1988, pp. 62–73.

Huston, L., and N. Sakkab. "Connect and Develop." *Harvard Business Review* 84, no. 3 (March 2006), pp. 58–66.

Petersen, K. J.; R. B. Handfield; and G. L. Ragatz. "Supplier Integration into New Product Development: Coordinating, Product, Process, and Supply Chain Design." *Journal of Operations Management* 23, no. 3/4 (April 2005), pp. 371–88.

Swink, M. "Product Development—Faster, On Time." *Research-Technology Management,* July–August 2002, pp. 50–58.

Swink, M. "Building Collaborative Innovation Capability." *Research-Technology Management,* March–April 2006, pp. 37–47.

Swink, M., and V. Mabert. "Product Development Partnerships: Balancing Manufacturers' and Suppliers' Needs." *Business Horizons* 43, no. 3 (May–June 2000), pp. 59–68.

Ulrich, K. T., and S. D. Eppinger. *Product Design and Development.* 2nd ed. New York: McGraw-Hill, 2000.

Wheelwright, S. C., and K. B. Clark. *Revolutionizing New Product Development.* New York: Free Press, 1992.

Product Development Management Association
www.pdma.org

Quality Function Deployment Institute
www.qfdi.org

5 Manufacturing and Service Process Structures

CHAPTER OUTLINE

LEARNING OBJECTIVES *After studying this chapter, you should be able to:*

LO5-1 Compare and contrast the seven process structures: project, job shop, batch, repetitive process, continuous process, mass customization, and cellular manufacturing.

LO5-2 Compare and contrast the goals and challenges associated with a service factory, a mass service, a service shop, and professional services.

LO5-3 Describe how each of the operations layouts, fixed-position, functional, product, and cellular, is designed to meet the demands placed upon it.

LO5-4 Analyze a product layout using line balancing.

LO5-5 Explain how technology is used in the supply chain and the benefits and drawbacks of process automation.

LO5-6 Use indifference analysis in process selection decisions.

Process Design Is the Key to Success at Noodles & Company

Founded in 1995, Noodles & Company is an innovator in fast-casual dining. The company's goal is to provide guests (customers) with quick, fresh, high-quality noodle dishes, soups, and salads. So how do they do it? Every part of a Noodles restaurant—the lobby, dining area, and kitchen—is designed to enhance the guest experience while ensuring fast, efficient service.

A repetitive process structure, creating efficient line flows for guests and in the kitchen, is one of the keys to Noodles & Company's success. Guests choose from a wide variety of fresh ingredients, spices, and sauces to create a noodle dish that is right for them. As an important part of the process, guests receive "training" when they enter the queue to place their orders. A sign "how to noodle" explains how to select from the Asian, Mediterranean, or American menu choices. To keep the process running smoothly, each guest should be able to place an order in about 30 seconds.

The managers at Noodles & Company have the kitchen process down to a science and know exactly how long each step should take so that each guest's order is ready from start to finish in about five minutes. In the kitchen, ingredients are arranged in a line flow to make assembly fast and easy. The specially designed stove cooks food quickly and so that the sautéing process is completed in about 3½ minutes. Clearly, the executives at Noodles & Company understand how process design helps them to meet their organization's strategic objectives.

Whether an operation is manufacturing-oriented, service-oriented, or some combination of the two, the capabilities contained within its supply chain drive its ability to compete on quality, time, cost, or flexibility. This chapter describes some of the key decisions about manufacturing and service structures that determine an organization's operations and supply chain capabilities. For example, at Noodles & Company the process is designed for flexibility, efficiency, and consistency. They achieve these goals by paying attention to the process structure decision areas discussed in this chapter: process selection, operations layout, and technology selection.

Prepare

What are the differences among the types of process structures: project, job shop, batch, repetitive process, continuous process, mass customization, and cellular manufacturing? What are the four market orientations? Which process structures are likely to be used with each?

Organize

Process Structures
- Product-Process Matrix
- Aligning Process Structure and Market Orientation

PROCESS STRUCTURES

Managers must design processes based on *what kind* of work needs to be done. Different process structures provide different capabilities. Process structure determines how inputs, activities, flows, and outputs of a process are organized. Within a supply chain, each organization must select the process structures that are appropriate considering their competitive priorities of quality, timeliness, cost, flexibility, and innovation.

Product-Process Matrix

To better link a product's life cycle and marketing decisions with operations capabilities, Hayes and Wheelwright developed the **product-process matrix**. They observed that processes progress through a life cycle just as products do. Although developed for manufacturing, the product-process matrix also describes many service processes. To achieve high performance, a firm's process structure must be aligned with its competitive priorities and marketing strategies.

product-process matrix Categorizes processes into structures based on output volume and variety.

The matrix shows five process structures along the diagonal based on output volume and variety: project, job shop, batch, repetitive process, and continuous process (see Figure 5-1). Often within a single company, different process structures are

FIGURE 5-1
Product-Process Matrix
Source: Adapted from R. Hayes and S. Wheelwright, *Restoring Our Competitive Edge: Competing Through Manufacturing* (New York: John Wiley & Sons, 1984).

LO5-1 Compare and contrast the seven process structures.

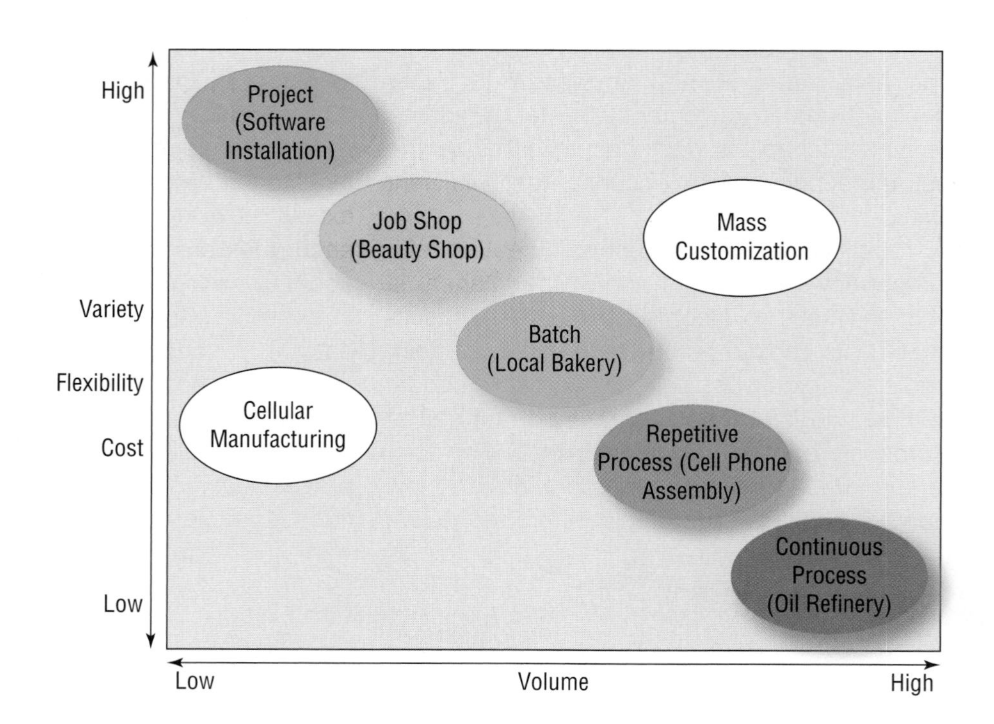

TABLE 5-1 Comparison of Process Types

Process Type	Output Characteristics	Example	Process Characteristics
Project	Unique One of a kind	Custom home Designing a video game	Unique sequencing High complexity Employees and equipment must be flexible Activities are often outsourced to specialists
Job shop	Customized, low volume	Auto repair Beauty salon Copy shop	High variety of inputs and process flows Job sequencing is challenging High work-in-process inventory Highly skilled, flexible workers General-purpose equipment
Batch	Moderate volume and variety	Bakery Automotive parts Cinema	Dominant flow patterns Some common inputs Setup time can be high Moderately flexible employees and equipment
Repetitive process	Standard products with a range of options	Appliances Automobiles Buffet restaurant	All products follow the same sequence Standard methods and materials are used Low-skilled workers specialize in completing a limited number of activities
Continuous process	Commodities with high volume, little variety	Aluminum cans Laundry detergent Gasoline	Products follow sequence Operations often run 24/7 Line stoppages are very costly Highly specialized equipment Low-skilled operators

used for different products. An entire supply chain typically has each of these process structures. Let's examine the characteristics of each of the process structures, as summarized in Table 5-1.

Project

A **project** produces a unique, "one of a kind" output. Examples of projects include building a custom home, designing a video game, or planning a wedding. Because the outputs are customized, the customer is highly involved in the design process. The type, sequencing, and complexity of activities change from project to project, so employees and equipment must be flexible. To maximize flexibility, a project manager plans and organizes the project, and activities are often outsourced to suppliers. For example, a wedding planner consults with a bride and groom to determine their preferences for flowers, music, photography, and food. The planner then hires and manages the florist, musicians, photographers, and caterers. Chapter 15 discusses the management of projects in more detail.

project A one-time or infrequently occurring set of activities that create outputs within prespecified time and cost schedules.

relationships

Job Shop

job shop A flexible process structure for products that require different inputs and have different flows through the process.

Automobile dealers' service shops, beauty salons, copy shops, and department stores use **job shop** process structures. Outputs are customized and produced in low volumes. Products are typically made to order for a specific customer. Each order or "job" can involve different inputs and sequencing of activities, and thus have different flows through the process. Because of the high variety of inputs and activities, planning and scheduling the jobs is challenging. Products can spend a lot of time waiting to be worked on, thus work-in-process inventory is high and expediting is often necessary.

Because of the differences from order to order, the equipment used in a job shop is general purpose, and employees must be skilled and flexible enough to handle a wide range of tasks. Job shops are typically more labor than capital intensive. Equipment and employees capable of doing similar activities are typically located together in departments or groups.

Batch Process

batch process A process in which goods or services are produced in groups (batches) and not in a continuous stream.

A local bakery that produces cookies, cakes, and pies uses a **batch process** structure. Many interior parts for automobiles such as the center console are made using batch processes. Cinemas offer movies in batches. A batch process structure works well when products have moderate levels of volume and variety. A batch structure is a good choice for products that have basic models with several different options.

Although there may be some differences between the flow patterns of each batch, there are dominant flow patterns. Equipment and employee flexibility are important, but the range of flexibility needed is less than with projects or job shops. Cleaning and setup are usually required between each batch, reducing the available capacity.

Repetitive Process

repetitive process A process in which discrete products flow through the same sequence of activities.

When there are many customers who want a similar product, such as automobiles, appliances, cell phones, or lunch at a buffet restaurant, a **repetitive process** structure is used. Some standard options, such as a range of colors, features, or menu items are offered, but the range of choices is limited and determined by marketing in advance of the customer's order.

Products made using a repetitive process are typically made to stock. Discrete products flow through the same sequence of activities, and equipment can be specialized to each specific task. Operations managers usually focus on developing standard methods and procedures to continuously improve quality and reduce costs.

Employees who work on the line may not be highly skilled, but they become very efficient in completing one small task. For example, in assembling a car, one employee may install the front seats. Employees can become bored doing the same activity repeatedly. Job rotation can lessen this problem.

Continuous Process

continuous process A single-flow process used for high-volume nondiscrete, standardized products.

Standard, nondiscrete products such as gasoline, chemicals, laundry detergent, aluminum cans, and cereal are produced using **continuous processes**, in which products always flow through the same sequence of production steps. Check and mail processing also are examples of continuous processes. These made to stock products offer customers very little variety and are considered as commodities. Differentiation typically occurs at the end of the production process. For example, laundry detergent comes in different sizes or aluminum cans are printed with different labels.

These processes use highly specialized automated equipment, which often runs 24 hours a day, seven days a week. Economies of scale reduce unit cost, but it is very

student activity

Companies focusing on different competitive priorities can use different process structures for the same type of product. One example is clothing, off-the-rack compared to custom tailored. Identify a product and competitors who are using different competitive priorities. What position on the product-process matrix would you expect for each?

costly to stop or change the product because the specialized equipment is expensive. Low-skilled employees monitor equipment while highly skilled engineers and maintenance employees work to minimize downtime and improve processes.

Mass Customization

When the product-process matrix was developed in the 1970s, the processes on the diagonal were thought to lead to the best performance. Today, changes in management practices and technologies have created more options. One way to get the cost advantages of high-volume continuous and repetitive processes while increasing variety is **mass customization**. With mass customization, customers "design" a product by choosing from a range of options. Dell Computers is perhaps the best-known example of mass customization. Selecting from a range of components and warranty options described at the Dell Internet site, customers can quickly design a computer system to meet their performance and price needs, and have delivery within about a week.

mass customization Uses advanced technologies to customize products quickly and at a low cost.

Process flexibility is essential for mass customization. Products are designed to be assembled from standard modules that can be stored in inventory, reducing the elapsed time from order to delivery. The exact product configuration is postponed until a customer order is received. Companies also use **flexible manufacturing systems (FMS)** that can produce a wider range of products in a wider range of volumes than is economically feasible with conventional equipment. FMS reduce the time required to set up between different products, so lot sizes are smaller.

Flexible manufacturing systems (FMS) combine automated machines, robots, and material handling systems that are all controlled by a single computer.

The Internet and other technologies facilitate mass customization. For example, customers design their own high school or college class rings at Jostens by choosing band style, metal, stone, and carvings. In doing so, each customer can trade off features and price. Mars Inc. used the Internet and new printing technology to mass customize M&Ms, creating a whole new market segment as discussed in Get Real: "Personalized M&Ms" on the next page.

Cellular Manufacturing

At the other end of the product-process matrix, the flexibility of job shop and batch production is retained but costs are lowered through use of **cellular manufacturing**. The complexity of job shop and small batch production environments can be reduced and efficiency increased by producing products that have similar processing characteristics using small assembly lines referred to as *work cells*. The cellular approach also works well in services where information or customers needs can be grouped by their similar processing characteristics. The cellular process structure will be further discussed later in this chapter in the section on operations layout.

cellular manufacturing The production of products with similar process characteristics on small assembly lines called *cells*.

Aligning Process Structure and Market Orientation

By now, you may have noted that different process structures involve different decisions about whether a product is designed and produced before a customer order is placed or after the order is placed. This decision determines how the firm competes in the marketplace. There are four different marketing orientations; each delivers a different level of service in terms of lead time and customization. To be effective, an organization's process structure must fit with its marketing orientation.

Products that firms **engineer to order (ETO)** are designed for individual customers and generally have long lead times. Examples include a custom-built house, a cruise ship, specialized industrial equipment, and a customized employee training program. Because each ETO product requires an entirely new design, a customer must place an order before work begins. Firms that anticipate orders often carry raw materials inventory to reduce lead times. Products that are ETO typically use either project or job shop process structures.

engineer to order (ETO) Unique, customized products.

The basic design of **make to order (MTO)** products covers the needs of broad groups of customers, but allows for some customization during production. Like ETO,

make to order (MTO) Products that have similar designs but are customized during production.

GET REAL

Personalized M&Ms

Who would have thought that a mature candy brand introduced in 1941 would be a candidate for mass customization? Standard M&Ms are produced using a continuous process and are packaged for distribution through grocery stores and other retail outlets all over the world.

Engineers at Mars developed a breakthrough in printing technology that enabled the introduction of personalized M&Ms in 2005. Now, customers can even put their own faces on M&Ms after uploading their own images at my.m&ms.com.

Personalized M&Ms follow the same continuous process as standard M&Ms, until the printing process. Then, the customer's choice of M&M colors are printed using the images provided by the customer. The M&Ms are then filled into packages selected by the customer and sent directly to the customer's home or business address. However, based on the price per ounce, you may not want to have these for an everyday snack.

http://www.mymms.com/

a customer order triggers activities at the very early stages of production. Because the design does not start from scratch, the lead time for MTO is less than for ETO. A jet airplane, a meal at an elegant restaurant, a haircut, and a trip to the emergency room are examples of MTO operations. MTO products typically use job shop, batch, and cellular process structures.

assemble to order (ATO) Products that are produced from standard components and modules.

The designs of the components and modules in **assemble to order (ATO)** products are standardized and do not change with customer orders. However, the components and modules can be assembled in different ways to create end product configurations that meet individual customer needs. Raw materials and components are produced and stored in inventory, but final assembly is postponed until the customer orders. For example, paint stores mix coloring agents with a white base paint after the customer orders, to provide many color options. Subway Restaurants assemble sandwiches to order from prepared ingredients, including freshly baked bread. Repetitive processes are used for ATO products, and many firms have developed mass customization processes for their ATO products.

make to stock (MTS) Finished goods that are held in inventory in advance of customer orders.

Groceries, retail clothing, books, electronics and cars are examples of **make to stock (MTS)** products. So that products are immediately available, finished products are made in advance of customer orders and held in inventory. Thus, firms must make products based on forecasts of customer demand. MTS items are typically standardized, mature products. Repetitive assembly lines and continuous processes are typically used for MTS products.

UNIQUE ASPECTS OF SERVICE PROCESSES

Prepare

What are the differences among service factories, mass services, service shops, and professional services? How do front- and back-office processes differ?

Organize

Unique Aspects of Service Processes
- Service Process Matrix
- Managing Front-Office and Back-Office Processes
- Service Blueprinting

Although the product-process matrix can be used to describe services, it does not address the fact that customers often participate in service processes. **Customer contact** refers to the presence of the customer in a service process. Services range from those with high customer contact, such as a haircut, to those with low customer contact, such as package delivery. Contact with the customer creates unique challenges in designing, controlling, and operating service processes. Thinking back to the opening vignette, Noodles & Company manages customer contact with the "how to noodle" instructions. These reduce the number of questions that employees must answer as well as the order time.

customer contact The presence of the customer in a process.

service process matrix Categorizes service processes based upon the degree of customization/customer interaction and labor/capital intensity.

LO5-2 Compare and contrast the goals and clhallenges associated with a service factory, a mass service, a service shop, and professional services.

Service Process Matrix

Building on the concept of the product-process matrix, Schmenner developed the **service process matrix** shown in Figure 5-2 that categorizes services based upon the degree of customization/customer interaction and labor/capital intensity involved. Services in the same industry can compete in different ways by adopting process structures specified in this matrix.

Professional Services. Lawyers, doctors, consultants, and accountants interact closely with clients to deliver customized services. Professional services tend to be time-consuming and costly because providers are highly skilled and educated. However, by reducing the degree of customization, some firms have reduced time and costs. Stores such as Target, Walmart, and CVS have medical clinics staffed with nurse practitioners. These clinics treat minor ailments quickly and at a much lower cost than a traditional family doctor. Other organizations use technology to outsource engineering design, data analyses, and medical diagnoses to professionals in lower wage regions such as India and Mexico.

Service Factory. Trucking companies, airlines, and hotels are examples of service factories. Customer contact, customization, and labor intensity are low while investment in facilities and equipment is high. A range of standard services is offered to customers who tend to value low price above all else. Operations managers in service factories are mainly concerned with utilizing equipment and facilities to a maximum extent, because these fixed assets account for the majority of operating costs. Matching capacity and demand to keep equipment and facilities busy is important to both competitiveness and profitability.

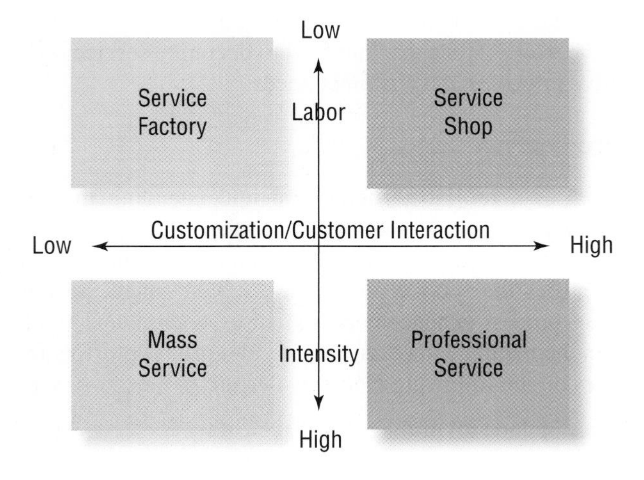

FIGURE 5-2
Service Process Matrix
Source: R.W. Schmenner, "How Can Service Businesses Survive and Prosper?" *Sloan Management Review* 27, no. 3 (1986), pp. 21–32. Copyright © 1986 by Massachusetts Institute of Technology. Reprinted with permission.

Service Shops. Automobile repair shops and hospitals are examples of service shops, which have a high degree of capital intensity and high customer interaction/customization. Keeping up-to-date on new technology and scheduling to ensure effective utilization of technology are key operations issues. For example, auto repair shop operations typically have large spikes in demand on Mondays, making scheduling a challenge. Some organizations have specialized to reduce the variety of services offered to move from service shops to mass services (described next). For example, muffler replacement and oil changes are mass services.

student activity

Think of the last service you purchased. What category of service was it? Can you suggest changes in product features or delivery technologies that would move the service to another category? What could be the advantages of such a change?

Mass Services. Mass services, such as retail banks, gas stations, and other retail outlets, meet the standard needs of a large volume of customers. These services have low customer interaction/customization and high labor intensity. Through automation, some mass services have reduced costs and improved customer service availability. Using ATMs or the Internet, customers can do routine banking activities 24/7. Paying at the pump reduces the wait time for gasoline customers. Many mass services have been automated through Internet technologies.

Managing Front-Office and Back-Office Processes

front-office processes Processes that have contact with the customer.

back-office processes Processes that are not seen by the customer.

While some processes within a company require customer involvement and interaction, others do not. Processes involving customer contact are referred to as the **front-office processes**. Those that are behind the scenes are called **back-office processes**. In a formal restaurant, the front office is the dining room where the host and servers interact with the customer, and the back office is the kitchen. Clearly, the front-office and back-office processes require different employee skill sets, equipment, and physical layouts.

Depending upon the nature of the service, front-office and back-office processes can be decoupled or separated from each other. With decoupling, each process can be managed separately, creating opportunities for efficiency gains. For example, consistent quality and economies of scale occur when back-office operations from different locations are combined. Some chain restaurants use this approach by preparing meals at a centralized location, and then doing final preparation in each individual restaurant's kitchen.

global

The ability to decouple services allows different processes to be done by different supply chain members who are dispersed globally. Decoupling through use of the Internet allows a physician in India to analyze an MRI to diagnose the illness of a patient in the United States. These approaches do not always work out as planned, however. For example, the outsourcing of activities such as call centers has resulted in complaints about customer service. The decision of what and how to decouple service operations should be driven by competitive priorities and customer needs.

Service Blueprinting

service blueprinting An approach similar to process mapping that analyzes the interface between customers and service processes.

Service blueprinting is a tool that focuses on understanding the interfaces between customers and service providers, technology, and other key aspects of the process. The approach is similar to process mapping described in the supplement to Chapter 3. A cross-functional team identifies the service process to be blueprinted, documents the process step-by-step, analyzes process enhancements or causes of problems, implements improvements, and monitors the results. However, service blueprinting differs from process mapping in that it focuses on the following elements that are particular to services:

- *Customer actions* include all of the steps that customers take as part of the service delivery process.
- *Front-office/visible contact employee actions* are the actions of frontline contact employees that occur as part of a face-to-face encounter with customers.

- *Back-office/invisible contact employee actions* are nonvisible interactions with customers, such as telephone calls, as well as other activities employees undertake to prepare to serve customers.
- *Support processes* are all activities carried out by employees who do not have direct contact with customers, but whose functions are crucial to the service.
- *Physical evidence* represents all of the tangibles that customers see or collect during their contact with a company.

For example, at a retail clothing store, customer actions include looking at clothing, selecting clothing, trying on clothing, and making a purchase. The visible part of the store includes the clothing displays and dressing rooms. Behind the scenes would be receiving and storage. Physical evidence would include the store décor, the displays and merchandise.

In addition to evaluating existing services, blueprinting can help a new service design team identify the critical aspects of the process, and find opportunities for innovation. The service blueprint itself is a tangible, visual document that lays out where and how customers and companies interact. Good blueprints require inputs from all supply chain members, including customers. Figure 5-3 shows a service blueprint for a hotel stay.

Service blueprinting of a houseboat resort in Lake Powell, Arizona, showed key reasons why guests were not returning: they were doing a lot of work during their vacations. Guests had to shop for groceries and supplies, and carry these and luggage onto their boats. To remedy these problems, resort managers added a series of new services, including grocery buying and onboard chefs. As a result, the company experienced a 50 percent drop in complaints, while repeat business jumped 12 percent.

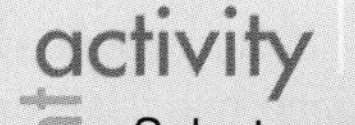

student activity

Select a service on campus and create a service blueprint for this service. How did the service blueprint help you to understand the process? What process improvements do you recommend?

FIGURE 5-3 Service Blueprint for a Hotel Stay

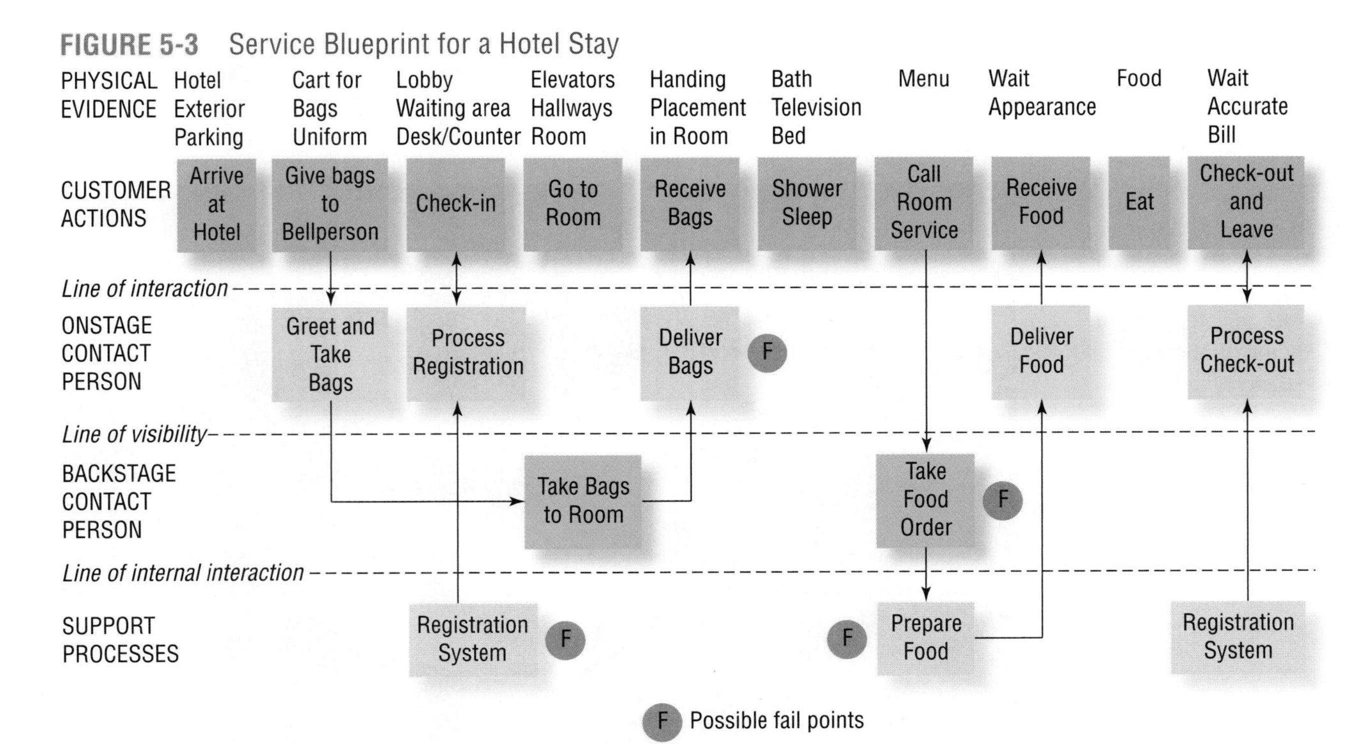

Sources: http://knowledge.wpcarey.asu.edu/article.cfm?articleid=1546; and M.J. Bitner, A.L. Ostrom, and F.N. Morgan, "Service Blueprinting: A Practical Technique for Service Innovation," California Management Review 50, no.3 (Spring 2008), p. 66.

Prepare

What are the characteristics of each of the operations layouts: fixed position, functional, product, and cellular? How is a product layout analyzed using line balancing?

Organize

OPERATIONS LAYOUT

The type of process structure selected influences the physical layout of the operation, including arrangement of the equipment, employees, inventory, and aisles for movement. When managers decide to build a new facility, develop a new product, implement new process technology, or make changes to accommodate changes in demand, they must make layout decisions. Layout has a major impact on performance, especially cost, time, and flexibility. There are four basic types of layouts: fixed-position, functional, product, and cellular.

Fixed-Position Layout

When a product cannot be moved during its production, a **fixed-position layout** is used. Fixed-position layouts are typically used for projects involving large products such as homes, buildings, bridges, large ships, airplanes, and spacecraft.

fixed-position layout The layout used when the product cannot be moved during production.

With a fixed-position layout, all of the resources and inputs must come together at the product's location. During a visit to your family physician, a fixed-position layout is used because the nurse, doctor, and any needed treatments are brought to you.

One of the supply chain challenges associated with a fixed-position layout is ensuring that all the right people, equipment, and materials arrive at the work site at the right time. Scheduling is very complex, and project management software tools are often used to manage the process. Scheduling methods are discussed in Chapter 15.

Functional Layout

functional layout A layout that groups together similar resources.

LO5-3 Describe how each of the operations layouts, fixed-position, functional, product, and cellular, is designed to meet the demands placed upon it.

Multiple copies of similar resources are grouped together in a **functional layout** (sometimes called a *departmental* layout). Fitness centers and copy shops use a functional layout. Retailers such as Macy's use a functional layout with different departments for shoes, jewelry, women's clothing, men's clothing, and cosmetics. In manufacturing, one area of a plant may do stamping, another welding, and a third assembly. Job shops and batch processes often use a functional layout where work centers using the same types of equipment are grouped together. For example, in a salon the bowls for hair washing are grouped together as are the workstations for doing nails.

In a functional layout, workers weld parts on a door frame at the Volvo truck assembly line in Dublin, Virginia.

There are several benefits to using a functional layout. By grouping general-purpose equipment together, a functional layout offers many different routes for a given job or customer so each has a unique flow through the process. A problem occurring at a single workstation does not usually stop production, because other similar workstations are located nearby. Learning and collaboration increases because employees with similar skills work together.

The functional layout also has several drawbacks. Because each job or customer takes a unique route through the process, scheduling, planning, and control are difficult. Processing times and work-in-process inventory tend to be high as jobs or customers wait to be processed in different departments. Consider the time you spend traveling and waiting when shopping at multiple stores within a shopping mall. Also, a significant amount of time is usually needed to clean and set up workstations when changing from one job or customer to another. In manufacturing, materials handling costs are high when jobs are moved from department to department.

In designing functional layouts, a common goal is to arrange the departments so that the time and cost of moving materials and people are minimized. To select a low-cost layout, managers compare the estimated number and cost of interdepartmental movements for all possible layouts. The complexity of this calculation increases rapidly with the number of departments involved in the decision, so facility layout software is typically used to determine functional layouts.

In retail layouts, an additional goal is usually to increase sales. Big box retailers are looking for ways to overcome some of the drawbacks of functional layouts. In large stores, customers grow tired of going from department to department looking for the items they need. Some retailers such as Target have rearranged merchandise by purchase type rather than by item type. For example, all the key items that new parents might need, such as baby clothes, diapers, and strollers, are located in the same department.

Product Layout

A **product layout** arranges resources according to a regularly occurring sequence of activities in the process. An automotive assembly line, a Taco Bell kitchen, Noodles & Company, a buffet line, and an insurance claims office all use product layouts. Repetitive processes and continuous processes typically use a product layout. Product layouts minimize processing times and simplify planning, scheduling, and control because work centers are positioned in a sequence that mirrors the steps needed to assemble the product or serve the customer.

product layout A layout where resources are arranged according to a regularly occurring sequence of activities.

In a product layout, the flow of products or customers is visible and easy to trace. Operations managers sometimes use Kanban systems (discussed in Chapter 8, "Lean Systems"), to pull material from one workstation to the next just when it is needed. This approach minimizes the inventory of parts and components needed to support the process. In high volume situations, workstations are often linked by conveyors so that products can be automatically transported from one workstation to the next.

Automobile assembly lines use a product layout.

Lack of flexibility and low work variety for employees are drawbacks to product layouts. Because activities are linked, a problem at any single workstation can cause the entire line to stop. Think about your frustration when you are behind an indecisive person in a buffet line. This is one reason why automotive assemblers demand on-time delivery and high quality from their suppliers. A quality problem with any supplied part can shut the entire assembly line down. At an automobile assembly plant, this can cost tens of thousands of dollars per minute.

Line Balancing in Product Layouts

LO5-4 Analyze a product layout using line balancing.

line balancing Used to assign tasks so that idle time and the number of workstations are minimized.

In designing a product layout, the goal is to have a smooth, continuous flow through the process. **Line balancing** is used to assign individual tasks to workstations for a desired output rate. Idle time and the number of workstations are minimized. Let's review a simple example of line balancing for assembling a deli fresh sausage and pepperoni pizza. In manufacturing, most line balancing problems will be much more complex than this example.

Example 1

precedence relationships Presents the order in which tasks must be completed.

First, identify the time required for each task and the order in which the tasks must be done—the **precedence relationships** (Table 5-2). Some tasks physically cannot be done until others are completed. The dough must be formed before it is topped with sauce. However, either sausage or pepperoni can be added after the cheese. Both sausage and pepperoni must be added before the pizza is packaged. Visually, Figure 5-4 shows the precedence relationships.

Next, determine the maximum total task time allowable at each workstation. Recall from Chapter 3 that the time it takes one unit to go though a workstation is the cycle time. The actual work time at each station must not exceed the cycle time that is allowed, referred to as **takt time**. If customer demand changes then the takt time must be recalculated.

takt time The maximum allowable cycle time at each workstation.

(5.1) *Takt time = Available production time per day/output needed per day*

Operations run continuously for 8 hours per day, so 480 minutes are available and the demand is for 200 pizzas per day.

Takt time (T) = 480 minutes/200 pizzas = 2.4 minutes per workstation

FIGURE 5-4
Precedence Diagram for Sausage and Pepperoni Pizza Assembly

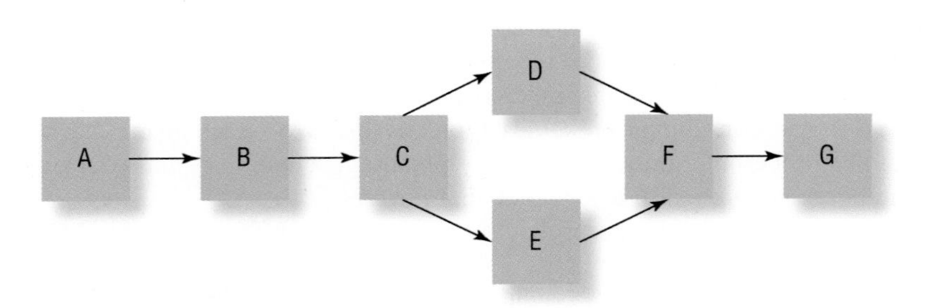

TABLE 5-2 Precedence Relationships for Sausage and Pepperoni Pizza Assembly

Task		Predecessors	Time (minutes)
A	Shape the dough to form the crust	None	2
B	Add the pizza sauce	A	1
C	Add the cheese	B	2
D	Add the sausage	C	0.75
E	Add the pepperoni	C	1
F	Package the pizza	D, E	1.5
G	Label the package	F	0.5
		Total Time	8.75

TABLE 5-3 Workstation Assignments for Pizza: Balanced Using the Longest Task Time

Workstation	Tasks in Order	Workstation Time (minutes)	Idle Time (minutes)
1	A	2	0.4
2	B	1	1.4
3	C	2	0.4
4	E, D	1.75	0.65
5	F, G	2	.4

The next step is to determine the theoretical minimum number of workstations. This would be the minimum possible number of stations; the balanced line may have more stations. When determining the number of stations, *round up* to the next whole number, otherwise there will not be enough time to make all the products to meet customer demand.

(5.2) *Theoretical number of stations (N) = Total of all task times/takt time*

N = (2 min. + 1 min. + 2 min. + .75 min. + 1 min. + 1.5 min. + .5 min)/
2.4 min. per station = 3.7 so 4 stations

Assign as many tasks as possible to each workstation such that the sum of the task times does not exceed the takt time. The sum of the task times may be less than the takt time. Sometimes, more than one task can be done, so you have to decide which task to assign first. For example, once a pizza is topped with cheese, either sausage or the pepperoni can be added next.

To make this decision, you can use rules or guidelines that lead to a good, but not necessarily the best, solution. Two commonly used rules are to first enter either the task with the most number of followers or the task with the longest task time. With a complex process there may be several different ways to balance the line, so select the alternative that provides the highest efficiency. In this example, because both steps D and E have the same two followers, using the longest task time rule, add the pepperoni first (Step E) (see Table 5-3).

(5.3) *Efficiency = [Sum of all task times/(Actual work stations × takt time)] × 100*

Efficiency = [(2 min. + 1 min. + 2 min. + .75 min. + 1 min. + 1.5 min. + .5 min.)/
(5 stations × 2.4 min./station)] × 100 = 73%

As with the functional layout, as the number of tasks increases so does the complexity of the line balancing problem. Bottlenecks, as described in Chapter 3, are constraints that have lower output than other workstations on the line, slow the process, and reduce efficiency. To improve efficiency, reduce time at the bottleneck workstation. For example, perhaps split tasks into smaller work elements, change technology to reduce the time required, or deploy more workers at the bottleneck.

Cellular Layout

In situations with mid-range volume and variety, a cellular layout combines the flexibility of a small, focused job shop with the efficiency of a repetitive line. A cellular layout arranges workstations to form a number of small assembly lines called *work cells*. Workstations within each individual work cell are arranged using product layout principles. The first step in designing a cellular layout is to use group technology to identify products that have similar processing requirements, called **product families**. Product families may have similar shapes, sizes, process flows, or demand. Each work cell can be dedicated to make a product family.

product families Groups of products that have similar processing requirements.

FIGURE 5-5
Product, Functional, and Cellular Layouts

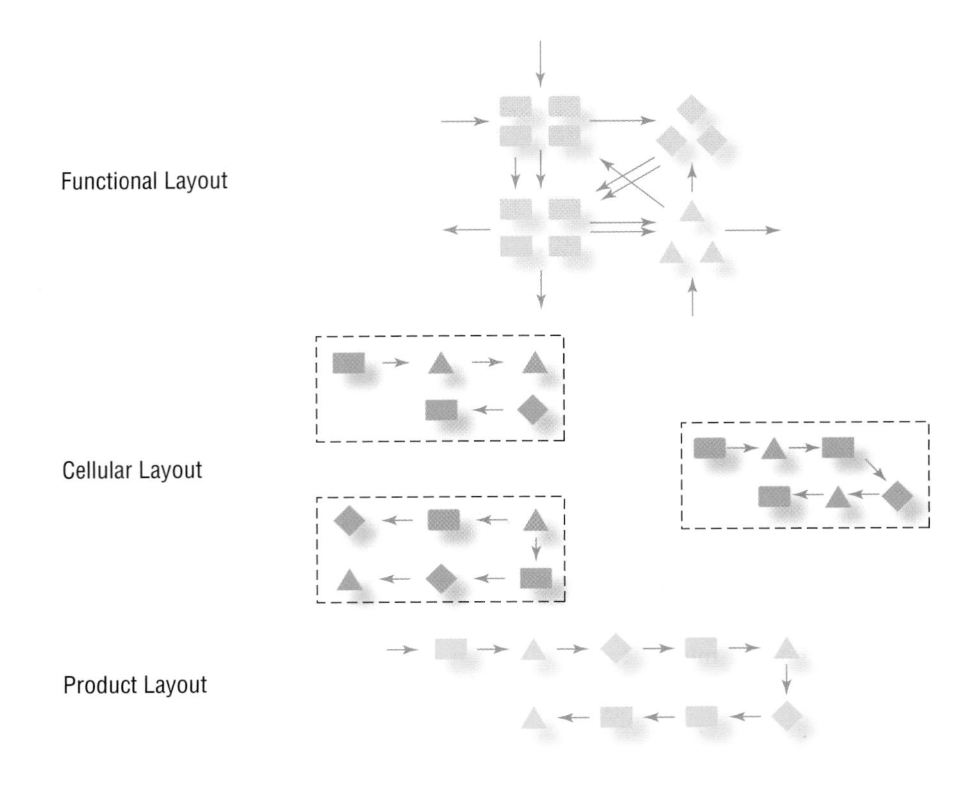

Workers are typically dedicated to a cell and are trained in all of the activities within a cell, increasing process flexibility. As they become intimately familiar with the product and demand requirements of the cell, the workers as a team identify opportunities for improvement, and take on larger roles including planning, maintenance, and quality inspection.

Cells can make job shops or batch processes more efficient, or increase the flexibility of repetitive processes. Processing time, inventory, material flow distance, and setup times are reduced, and scheduling is less complex than with functional layouts. For example, with the war in Afghanistan, Babcock Marine could not meet the British army's demand for weapons-mounted patrol vehicles. By outsourcing, eliminating non–value-adding steps, and rearranging the departmentalized functional layout into 12 cells, production increased to meet the army's demand of one vehicle per day. Similarly, insurance firms and banks have increased efficiencies by grouping together workers and activities that were formerly isolated into different departments.

LO5-5 Explain how technology is used in the supply chain and the benefits and drawbacks of process automation.

Converting a product layout into cells creates more options in how products might be routed from cell to cell, increasing flexibility. When converting a product layout to a cellular layout, managers must determine where customization will be added to the product line. This indicates where the line should be broken, what activities should be included in each cell, and how the cells should relate to each other. Product, functional, and cellular layouts are shown in Figure 5-5. Each shape represents a different type of activity.

Prepare

How is technology used in the supply chain?

What are the benefits and drawbacks of using technology to automate processes?

Organize

Capability Enabling Technologies

CAPABILITY ENABLING TECHNOLOGIES

Technology has a major impact on operations and supply chains, so deciding how to use technology to enhance value for customers is an important managerial decision. Table 5-4 shows some of the technologies that are used in operations and supply chain management. Technology can reduce variation, increase efficiency, and improve safety by replacing human involvement and decision making with process automation. New capabilities can also be created through the use of technology. For example, advances in information technology and communications have dramatically improved operational

TABLE 5-4 Types of Supply Chain Operational Technologies

Type of Technology	Capabilities	Examples
Decision support systems	Provide computing power and data management to make higher-quality decisions faster.	• Advanced planning and scheduling (Chapter 14) • Supply chain network design (Chapter 11) • Transportation management system (TMS) • Warehouse management system (WMS) • Manufacturing execution system (MES)
Processing technologies	Automate material and data processing to provide 24/7 resource availability, faster processing, greater consistency, lower cost.	• Computer-aided design (Chapter 4) • E-procurement (Chapter 10) • Industrial robots • Flexible manufacturing systems (FMS) (Chapter 5) • Automated storage and retrieval systems (AS/RS) (Chapter 11) • Point of sale (POS) bar code scanners • Radio frequency identification (RFID) (Chapters 7 and 11)
Communications technologies	Create greater connectivity and speed flow of richer forms of information.	• The Internet • Electronic data interchange (EDI) (Chapter 10) • Communication satellites • Fiber optic cables • Radio frequency data communications (RFDC)
Integrative technologies	Combines data management, communications, decision support, and processing capabilities.	• Enterprise resource planning (ERP) (Chapter 14) • Product life cycle management (PLM) (Chapter 4) • Customer relationship management (CRM) (Chapter 9) • Supplier relationship management (SRM) (Chapter 10) • Collaborative planning, forecasting, and replenishment (CPFR) (Chapter 12) • "Cloud" computing

processing, data management, visibility, and coordination across global supply chain networks. Successful business models such as iTunes, PayPal, Orbitz, Amazon, and Facebook were made possible because of advances in information technology.

Figure 5-6 illustrates how technologies improve overall supply chain operations. As sales are made in retail stores, the sales and inventory information is automatically captured by point of sale (POS) bar code or RFID scanners. The data are then conveyed through the Internet to a central control point. An enterprise resource planning system (ERP) then shares this information with first tier suppliers' systems so that inventory records are updated and replenishment orders are generated. Inventory replenishment orders that are sent from warehouses to the retail stores are scheduled and monitored using warehouse management systems (WMS) and transportation management systems (TMS). These decision support systems optimize the sequencing and routing of material flows throughout the distribution network.

Meanwhile, the production of replacement inventories at suppliers and manufacturing plants is scheduled using manufacturing execution systems (MES) and accomplished by robots and flexible manufacturing systems (FMS). Flexible manufacturing systems

FIGURE 5-6
Technology and the Supply Chain

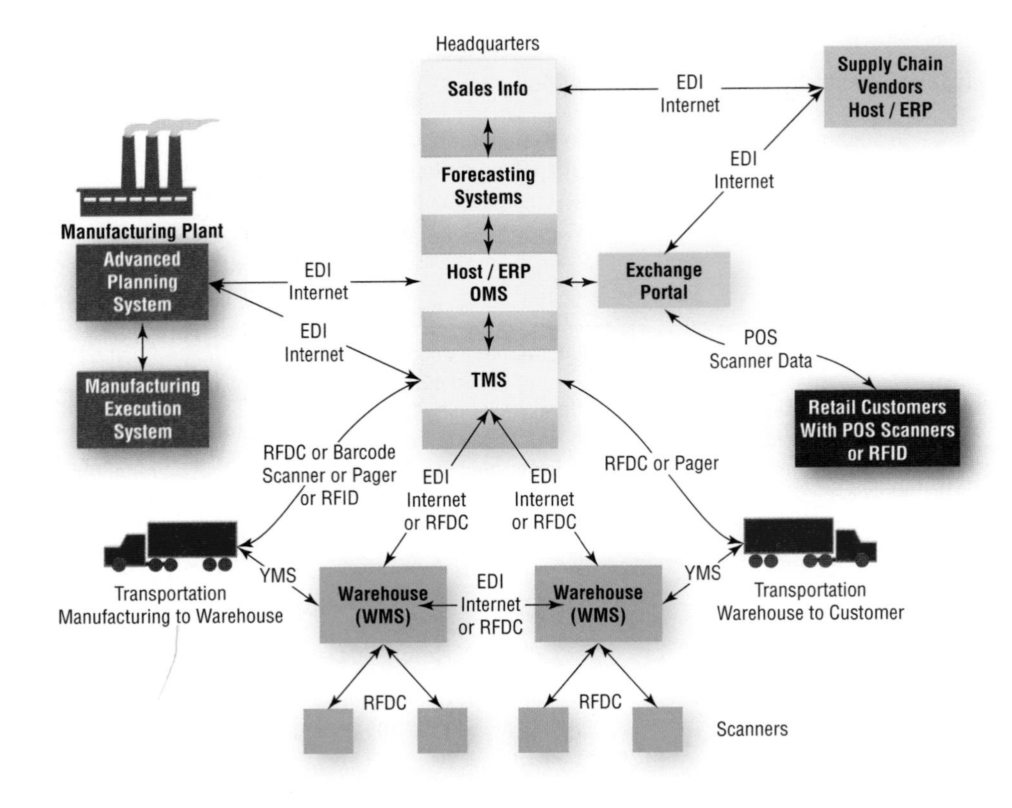

combine automated machines, robots, and material handling systems that are all controlled by a single computer. Fast, automated setups allow FMS to produce a wide variety of products. Repetitive tasks such as picking and placing parts are also done by FMS. Automotive assembly lines use robots for hazardous activities such as welding, and painting, thus increasing safety for workers. For example, the Automotive Alliance plant in Flat Rock, Michigan, has 380 robots that perform over 2,000 welds on cars such as the Ford Mustang. Throughout the entire process, automated storage, retrieval, and materials handling systems manage the movement of materials from station to station. All of these activities are monitored and controlled by supply chain partners who are interconnected by various communications technologies.

sustainability

Apps are changing the way companies interact with customers and manage operations.

Using technology to automate existing processes can increase productivity, lower direct labor costs, improve quality by reducing variation, increase worker safety, and improve customer service. When automating processes, the direct labor costs per unit decrease because fewer employees are needed to perform operations and less supervision is needed. The availability of processes 24/7 through the Internet and mobile apps increases customer service by allowing customers access and flexibility. Smart phones and tablet computers such as Apple's iPad create mobility, where information previously stored in desktop computers can be accessed in real time and exactly where it is needed for decision making. For example, companies such as Procter and Gamble access process manuals and procedures using iPads. NFL teams, including the Cincinnati Bengals, Baltimore Ravens, and the Denver Broncos, have replaced their paper playbooks with iPads. The rich media possible with mobility also enables firms to contact new customers, to offer different and broader value

GET REAL

Starbucks Weighs the Pros and Cons of Automation

A few years ago, Starbucks invested in automatic espresso machines. These machines improved the speed of service as well as the consistency of the coffee drinks delivered. In addition, labor productivity increased because baristas were able to multitask, taking and delivering other orders while the machines did the work.

In the end, however, Starbucks replaced the automated machines with the old style manual ones because the automated process negatively affected the customer experience. First, customers could no longer watch baristas make their drinks because the machine was too tall. This destroyed the intimate experience shared by the customer and the barista. Some customers even felt that the coffees tasted like they were of lower quality, since they were no longer handcrafted. Finally, the baristas themselves felt less a part of the theater that makes up the Starbucks experience. In this instance, Starbucks' management team decided that the customer experience was paramount, so they chose to preserve the experience while losing the efficiencies offered by automation.

propositions, and to interact more closely with their critical customers. Using apps, for example, hotels such as the St. Regis allow guests to chat with concierges, in real time.

However, there are drawbacks to process automation. Purchasing and installing information systems, software, and automated equipment requires a high capital investment, increasing an organization's fixed costs. Thus, limits on an organization's ability to obtain credit to finance these investments may impact its ability to automate processes. Managing and maintaining automated systems requires highly skilled IT professionals, process engineers, and maintenance employees, increasing indirect labor costs. In addition, automated equipment cannot learn or come up with new, innovative ideas for process or product improvement like humans can.

As production volumes increase, automation becomes more cost effective. Indifference analysis, discussed in the next section, determines the production volume needed for automation to be cost effective. However, if demand drops, an automated process may no longer be cost effective, making it difficult to compete with more efficient companies. Typically automation reduces flexibility, making it more difficult to change a product's design. Thus, process automation can be a risky investment for products with short life cycles.

Finally, automation of service processes can impact the customer's perception of service quality as was the case at Starbucks (see the Get Real box above). Consider how frustrating it can be to end up in an automated system when calling a company's customer service phone number. In general, the efficiency gains offered by automation need to be balanced against potential financial risks, losses in flexibility, and detriments to the aesthetic aspects of product quality.

Prepare

How is Indifference analysis used to examine profits and costs in process selection decisions?

Organize

Selecting Processes with Indifference Analysis

LO5-6 Use indifference analysis in process selection decisions.

indifference analysis
A cost-based quantitative decision-making tool that identifies the production volume at which the total costs of two processes are equal.

SELECTING PROCESSES WITH INDIFFERENCE ANALYSIS

How do managers choose which process structures to use, and when to change processes? One quantitative tool that they can use in decision making is **indifference analysis**, an approach based on estimates of total costs. Other operations and supply chain decisions such as selecting locations, evaluating new products, and making insourcing/outsourcing decisions can be supported by indifference analysis. One drawback is that indifference analysis focuses only on costs without considering other important factors.

The indifference point for a given process structure occurs at the sales volume where total cost (fixed plus variable costs) for two processes is equal. To do an indifference analysis, set the total costs of each process equal to each other, then solve for sales volume.

Indifference analysis can compare an automated process to a more labor-intensive process. Automated processes are generally capital intensive and have high fixed costs. Fixed costs include equipment depreciation, maintenance, and engineering costs. Labor-intensive processes have lower fixed costs because of less investment in equipment, but have higher variable costs because of the wages of employees. At lower volumes, labor-intensive processes are typically more profitable, but as volume increases, capital-intensive processes become more profitable.

Example 2

Let's examine how indifference analysis is used for process selection using an example of Pollyeyes Pizza. The company currently mixes and shapes all of its pizza dough by hand. This is a labor-intensive process. The variable costs (VC) for this process are \$3.00 per pizza, and the fixed costs (FC) are \$30,000 per year. The average selling price is \$8.00 per pizza. Pollyeyes' owner Pat Polly is considering investing in an automated process to make and shape the dough. With the new process, fixed costs increase to \$42,000 per year but variable costs decrease to \$2.00 per pizza.

Pat can determine the sales volume needed to make the more capital-intensive process a good investment. This is calculated by determining the sales volume where the total cost between the two processes is equal; this is called the indifference point. Above this sales volume, investing in the capital-intensive process is a good decision. Below this sales volume, Pat should stay with the current, more labor-intensive process.

$$\text{Total Cost}_{\text{process 1}} = \text{Total Cost}_{\text{process 2}}$$

$$(\$30{,}000 + (\$3.00/\text{pizza} \times V)) = (\$42{,}000 + (\$2.00/\text{pizza} \times V))$$

$$(\$3.00/\text{pizza} \times V) - (\$2.00/\text{pizza} \times V) = (\$42{,}000 - \$30{,}000)$$

$$\$1.00/\text{pizza} \times V = \$12{,}000$$

$$V = 12{,}000 \text{ pizzas}$$

The use of indifference analysis for process selection needs to be repeated when situations change. For example, many organizations have used lean and quality improvement programs to reduce fixed and variable costs. These changes can move the indifference point for a process.

CHAPTER SUMMARY

This chapter describes some of the key decisions about manufacturing and service process structures that impact an organization's capabilities.

1. The product-process matrix classifies processes based on output volume and variety. The process types are: project, job shop, batch, repetitive process, and continuous process. Two contemporary process structures are mass customization and cellular manufacturing.
2. Services can be categorized based on customization/customer interaction and labor/capital intensity. A framework shows four classifications: professional service, service factory, service shop, and mass service.
3. The front office of a service process that is in contact with the customer has different requirements than the back office of a process that is not visible to the customer. Decoupling often creates efficiencies in both the front-office and the back-office processes.
4. Layout is the physical arrangement of resources in a process. The type of layout is closely related to the type of process. Layout types are product, functional, cellular, and fixed-position.
5. Advances in information and communications technologies have enabled new business models and supply chain improvements. Process automation can reduce variation, increase efficiency, and reduce direct labor costs. However, automation requires a high capital investment and highly skilled support staff, and may not be able to adapt to major product changes.

KEY TERMS

assemble to order (ATO) 146
back-office processes 148
batch process 144
cellular manufacturing 145
continuous process 144
customer contact 147
engineer to order (ETO) 145
fixed-position layout 150
flexible manufacturing system (FMS) 145
front-office processes 148
functional layout 150
indifference analysis 158
job shop 144
line balancing 152
make to order (MTO) 145
make to stock (MTS) 146
mass customization 145
precedence relationships 152
product families 153
product layout 151
product-process matrix 142
project 143
repetitive process 144
service blueprinting 148
service process matrix 147
takt time 152

DISCUSSION QUESTIONS

1. Airlines allow customers to purchase tickets, select seats, and check in online. How does this process differ from a check-in process at an airline ticket counter?
2. Think of two companies in the same industry that use different process structures. Why is this the case? Is one process structure a better choice than the other? Why, or why not?

3. Consider several members of the supply chain of a company that makes plastic toy cars and trucks. Which of the processes described in the product-process matrix is likely to be used by the following supply chain members? Why?
   a. The company that assembles the toys.
   b. The company that produces the parts that go into the toys.
   c. The company that produces the plastic.
4. Provide an example of how technology has made it possible to use processes that are not on the diagonal of the product-process matrix.
5. Are some process structures inherently safer or more environmentally friendly than others?
6. In which of the service categories would you put a large state university? Why? Would a small private university be in the same category? Why, or why not?
7. Some upscale restaurants have their kitchens visible to their customers, changing the traditional view of front-office and back-office processes. What are the benefits and drawbacks to this approach?
8. Think about three of your favorite fast-food restaurants. What type of layout is used in the food preparation area of each? Are these layouts a good fit with the organization? Why, or why not? Should the layout be changed and if so, how?
9. Provide an example of technology that enhances customer service and one that reduces customer service. Why is this the case?

SOLVED PROBLEMS

1. Using the information in Table 5-5, balance the assembly line for the Tourist T-Shirt Company. The operations run continuously for eight hours per day. Each day, 80 T-shirts must be produced to meet customer demand.
   a. Draw the precedence diagram.
   b. What is the takt time?
   c. What are the theoretical number of workstations?
   d. Assign tasks to workstations using the longest task time rule.
   e. What is the efficiency of the balanced line?

TABLE 5-5 Precedence Relationships for Making a T-Shirt

Task		Predecessors	Time (minutes)
A	Put the pattern on the material	None	5
B	Cut out the pattern	A	3
C	Hem the neck slit opening	B	2
D	Sew the sleeve seams	B	1
E	Hem the sleeves	D	2
F	Sew the side seams of the tunic	C	3
G	Sew the sleeves to the tunic	E, F	4
H	Hem the bottwom of the shirt	F	5
		Total Time	25

Solution

a. Precedence diagram.

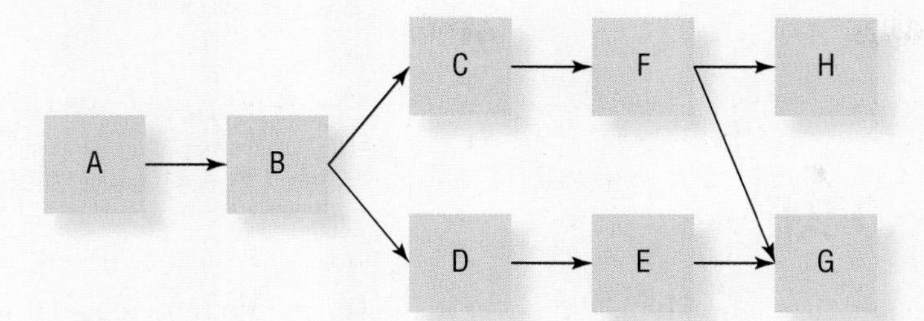

b. Takt time (T) = Production time per day/output needed per day.

Takt time (T) = 480 minutes/(80 T-shirts/day) = 6 minutes/workstation

c. Theoretical minimum number of stations (N) = Total of all task times/takt time.

N = (25 minutes)/(6 min./station) = 4.2 so 5 stations

d. The tasks are assigned to each station in order of precedence, assigning as many tasks as possible to each station. When you can choose among multiple tasks, for example, C or D, choose the task with the longest operating time.

Workstation	Tasks in Order	Workstation Time (Min.)	Idle Time (Min.)
1	A	5	1
2	B, C, D	6	0
3	F, E	5	1
4	H	5	1
5	G	4	2

e. Efficiency = [Sum of all task times/(Actual workstations × takt time)] × 100.

Efficiency = [(25 minutes)/(5 stations × 6 min./station)] × 100 = 83%

2. A small manufacturer that produces outdoor furniture is considering increasing the automation on the production line that makes its most popular metal patio chairs. The current process has fixed costs of $150,000 per year and variable costs of $20 per chair. The more automated process that is being considered will increase fixed costs to $250,000 annually but variable costs will decrease to $10 per chair.

a. What sales volume is the indifference point between these two processes?

b. If the estimated annual sales volume for metal chairs is 18,000 chairs, should the owner invest in the new process? Why, or why not?

Solution

a. To determine the sales volume that is the indifference point, set the total cost for the two processes equal to each other and solve for sales volume (V).

$TC_{\text{process 1}} = TC_{\text{process 2}}$

$\text{Fixed Cost}_{\text{process 1}} + \text{Variable Cost}_{\text{process 1}} = \text{Fixed Cost}_{\text{process 2}} + \text{Variable Cost}_{\text{process 2}}$

(\$150,000 + (\$20/chair × V)) = (\$250,000 + (\$10/chair × V))

(\$20/chair × V) − (\$10/chair × V) = (\$250,000 − \$150,000)

\$10/chair × V = \$100,000

V = 10,000 chairs

b. Since the expected volume of 18,000 chairs exceeds the indifference point, the company should implement the new, more automated process. The total costs will be lower for the automated process when sales volumes exceed 10,000 chairs.

PROBLEMS

1. An assembly line currently has five workstations, and the time required for each is shown below.

   a. What is the current cycle time?
   b. What is the efficiency of the process?
   c. Customer demand is 80 units per hour. What is the hourly production rate of the current process?
   d. What does the cycle time need to be to be able to meet demand (what is the takt time)?
   e. What changes to the process are needed?

2. An insurance company uses the following tasks to process paperwork. Forty claims need to be processed in an *eight-hour work day.*

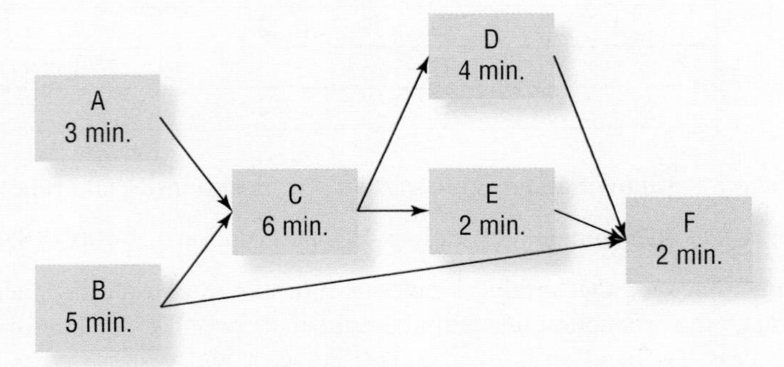

   a. What is the takt time?
   b. What is the theoretical number of workstations?
   c. Assign the tasks to the workstations to balance the line using the longest operating time rule.
   d. What is the efficiency of the balanced line?

3. Swoosh Snowboard Company must set up an assembly line for snowboards. Forecasts show that 600 units per day should be produced. The plant operates *two eight-hour shifts each day* and runs the line continuously during both shifts. The tasks required, task times, and precedence relationships are as follows:

Task	Time (seconds)	Predecessors
A	40	–
B	27	A
C	30	A

D	35	–
E	30	B
F	40	D
G	55	C, E, F
H	39	G

a. Draw the precedence diagram.
b. What is the takt time?
c. What is the theoretical number of workstations?
d. Assign the tasks to the workstations to balance the line using the longest operating time rule.
e. What is the efficiency of the balanced line?

4. The Carry-on Luggage Company must set up an assembly line for a wheeled carry-on bag. Forecasts show that 60 units per hour should be produced. The tasks required, task times, and precedence relationships are as follows:

Task	Time (seconds)	Predecessors
A	30	–
B	50	A
C	25	A
D	10	B
E	25	B
F	15	B
G	10	C, E, F
H	30	D, G

a. Draw the precedence diagram.
b. What is the takt time?
c. What is the theoretical number of workstations?
d. Assign the tasks to the workstations to balance the line using the longest operating time rule.
e. What is the efficiency of the balanced line?

5. Wild Widget must set up an assembly line for widgets. Forecasts show that 50 units per hour should be produced. The tasks required, task times, and precedence relationships are as follows:

Task	Time (seconds)	Predecessors
A	10	–
B	30	A
C	15	A
D	35	C, B
E	25	D
F	10	D
G	35	E, F

a. Draw the precedence diagram.
b. What is the takt time?
c. What is the theoretical number of workstations?
d. Assign the tasks to the workstations to balance the line using the longest operating time rule.

e. What is the efficiency of the balanced line?
f. If demand decreased to 40 units per day, what changes would be needed, if any?

6. Golf Carts Inc. must set up an assembly line for golf carts. Forecasts show that 10 units per day should be produced. The plant operates *one eight-hour shift* each day and runs the line continuously during the shifts. The tasks required, task times, and precedence relationships are as follows:

Task	Time (minutes)	Predecessors
A	12	–
B	10	–
C	16	–
D	24	A, B
E	14	C
F	30	D
G	15	E, F

a. Draw the precedence diagram.
b. What is the takt time?
c. What is the theoretical number of workstations?
d. Assign the tasks to the workstations to balance the line using the longest operating time rule.
e. What is the efficiency of the balanced line?
f. If demand increased to 12 units per day, what changes would be needed, if any?

7. Williams Motor Manufacturing assembles small motors for sale to major appliance manufacturers around the world. Average demand for its best-selling motor is 600 units per day. The assembly line operates continuously during a single eight-hour shift. The tasks required, task times, and precedence relationships are:

Task	Time (seconds)	Predecessor
A	12	–
B	22	–
C	20	–
D	20	A
E	18	C
F	30	B, D
G	17	E
H	25	F, G
I	20	H

a. Draw the precedence diagram.
b. What is the takt time?
c. What is the theoretical number of workstations?
d. Assign the tasks to the workstations to balance the line using the longest operating time rule.
e. What is the efficiency of the balanced line?
f. If demand increased to 650 motors per day, what changes would be needed, if any?

8. A privately owned company manufactures metal seat frames that are used to make automobile seats. Its customer, the seat manufacturer, forecast that 50,000 frames will be needed next year. The seat frame manufacturer must determine which process to install. One process is more labor-intensive with fixed costs of $400,000 and variable costs of $90 per frame. The second process has fixed costs of $850,000 and variable costs of $75 per frame. Which process do you recommend? Why?
9. An insurance company is evaluating a new software system designed to reduce the time for claims processing. The fixed costs with the new system are $120,000 per year. The average variable costs with the new system are $20 per claim. The current system being used by the company has fixed costs of $80,000 and variable costs of $35 per claim. What is the indifference point between these two processes? If the company expects to process 3,500 claims per year, which process would you recommend? Why?
10. Party Pools LLC assembles pool pumps for residential in-ground swimming pools. Fixed costs to produce model P07 pump are $75,000 per year. Variable costs per pump for this model are $40. The company is evaluating a new process that would increase fixed costs to $150,000 per year but will reduce variable costs to $15/pump. What sales volume is needed to justify this investment?
11. The Jazzy Java Company is considering upgrading its espresso machine to reduce the time to make each cup of coffee. The current machine has fixed costs of $3,000 per year and variable costs of $.75 per cup of coffee. With the new machine, fixed costs increase to $7,000 per year and variable costs are $.40 per cup of coffee.
    a. What is the indifference point between the two processes?
    b. If the forecast is for 12,500 cups of coffee to be sold each year, which process should be used? Why?
12. The process used by the Gourmet Food Company to produce dressings has annual fixed costs of $240,000 and variable costs of $0.50 per bottle. The company just entered into an agreement with a major national grocery store chain to sell its dressings. Sales volumes are expected to increase. Two new processes are being explored. The first has a fixed cost of $320,000 per year and variable costs of $.30 per bottle. The second has fixed costs of $400,000 per year and variable costs of $.25 per bottle.
    a. What are the indifference points between the processes?
    b. If sales are expected to be 1,000,000 bottles, which process should be used?

CASE

Coffee Roasters

Once considered a commodity product, many small boutique coffee companies are luring customers with promises of high quality and unique flavors. How do the processes used by the small companies compare with those of the major coffee processors? Coffee producers purchase green coffee beans, which have been processed through several steps. At the manufacturer, green coffee beans are screened to remove debris, and then roasted for up to 30 minutes. A roaster is typically a rotating drum in which the beans are heated. The length of time spent in the roaster impacts coffee flavor. The longer the time spent in the roaster, the richer the coffee flavor. Following roasting, beans are sprayed with water, cooled, and screened to remove any remaining debris. Once roasted, coffee is ground to the size required for the brewing process and packaged.

Ohori's Coffee is an example of a boutique coffee company. Established in 1984, Ohori's Coffee is located in Santa Fe, New Mexico. This privately owned business microroasts 32 types of coffee from Africa, the Saudi peninsula, Indonesia, the Pacific Rim, and North and South America. In batch sizes of 30 pounds or less, coffee beans are roasted in natural gas-fired rotating drum roasters carefully monitored by highly skilled "master roasters." To maintain quality, Ohori's depends on humans, not computer controls in the roasting process. Online and in its Santa Fe location, Ohori's sells whole beans and 10 different grinds ranging from Percolator to Turkish style. (Source: http://ohoriscoffee.com.)

Folgers Coffee was purchased from Procter & Gamble in 2008 by the J.M. Smucker Company in a deal reportedly worth $3.3 billion. Folgers coffee accounts for over 30 percent of the U.S. packaged coffee market, with over $2 billion in sales. Sales growth is estimated to be 2–3 percent per year.

Folgers' largest roasting and blending facility is in New Orleans, with 550 employees. It also has manufacturing operations in Kansas City, Missouri, and Sherman, Texas. The distribution center for Folgers is near New Orleans in Lacombe, Louisiana. Its coffee is sold in a single grind type. The company sells three Classic blends, seven blends in its Coffee House product line, five types of flavored ground coffee, and 10 flavors of Folgers Gourmet Selections.

Folgers has introduced an enhanced roasting process for its Classic products. The coffee beans are preconditioned to reduce moisture and improve consistency before the final roasting. (Source: www.folgers.com.)

Think about the production processes used by Ohori's and Folgers.

Questions

1. Using the product-process matrix, which processes are likely to be used by Ohori's and Folgers? Why?
2. Explain how the choice of process supports each organization's competitive priorities.
3. Is the operations layout likely to be the same or to be different at Ohori's and Folgers? Why?
4. What changes would Folgers need to make to compete directly with Ohori's? Why?

CASE

Sonnie's Gourmet Sandwich Café

Sonnie's Gourmet Sandwich Café, a popular new fast casual restaurant, serves high-quality, made-to-order sandwiches. Located in a local outdoor shopping center, parking in front of Sonnie's is limited. However, there are many parking spaces available behind the café within a five-minute walk. The café has an inviting, bright, and open interior with deli cases, blackboards listing specials, and oak tables and chairs.

The café's popularity at lunch is a concern for Sonnie. During the prime lunch time between 11:30 a.m. and 1:30 p.m. Monday through Friday, the waiting line is often out the door. On average Sonnie would like to serve 40 customers per hour at lunch. Working professionals, who typically spend more than other customers at lunch, are on busy schedules, and do not have time to wait in line. Sonnie estimates that currently some customers go to other restaurants because of the line.

The menu at Sonnie's includes nine standard sandwiches such as roast beef, pastrami and rye, and a B.L.T. Many customers choose to build their own sandwiches, selecting from eight types of bread, 25 meats, 12 cheeses, and 20 different vegetables. Sandwiches are served with chips or a choice of four types of salad.

Order Placement

When customers enter the café, they walk past a large deli counter displaying meats and cheese on their left and stop in front of a counter to place their orders. An employee greets the customer, asks for each customer's name, then takes his or her order by filling out a two-part paper form. Because of the number of choices, customers take, on average, 1 minute and 20 seconds to place their orders. However, those ordering standard sandwiches complete the order in about 1 minute. The employee gives the top part of the order form to the customer (10 seconds) to take to the cashier and the other is handed to the next employee in line, who starts working on the order. The employee who took the order then fills the customer's beverage order and hands it to the customer (30 seconds). The customer then walks about 15 feet to the cashier and pays, which on average takes 1 minute and 30 seconds. Then the customer selects a table and waits for his or her name to be called when the order is complete.

Order Fulfillment Process

Three employees work in the food preparation area, which uses a product layout. The first employee in the food preparation line puts the choice of side on a plate (35 seconds) then assembles the sandwich from pre-sliced bread, meat, and cheese, a task that takes about 1 minute and 20 seconds. The sandwich is handed off to the next employee, who adds toppings and sauces (45 seconds), and slices the sandwich (10 seconds). The last employee checks the order for accuracy (15 seconds), moves the sandwich to the pick-up area, and calls the customer by name (20 seconds).

Questions

1. Compared to a fast-food restaurant such as McDonald's, where would Sonnie's sandwich shop be placed on the service process matrix? What challenges and opportunities does this position create relative to McDonald's? Why?
2. How many customers is the current process able to accommodate per hour?
3. Use line balancing and service blueprinting to redesign the process at Sonnie's. What changes do you recommend? Why?

SELECTED READINGS & INTERNET SITES

Ford Mustang
http://media.ford.com/press_kits_detail.cfm?presskit_id=1232&item_id=#3839&press_section_id=2879

Jostens, Inc.
www.jostens.com

M&Ms
www.marthastewart.com/article/mandm-factory-tour
www.mymms.com

Noodles and Company
www.noodles.com

Berman, B. "Should Your Firm Adopt a Mass Cust omization Strategy?" *Business Horizons* 45, no. 4 (2002), pp. 51–61.

Bitner, M.; A. Ostrom; and F. Morgan. "Service Blueprinting: A Practical Technique for Service Innovation." *California Management Review* 50, no. 3 (2008), pp. 66–94.

Bulik, B. S. "Waiting Game: Consumers Clamor for Wii." *Advertising Age* 78, no. 9 (2007), p. 21.

Chappell, L. "Kia's New U.S. Plant Is No Windfall for U.S. Suppliers." *Automotive News* 80, no. 6196 (2006), pp. 1–39.

Chase, R. B., and D. A. Tansik. "The Customer Contact Model for Organizational Design." *Management Science* 29, no. 9 (1983), pp. 1037–50.

Das, A., and R. Narasimhan. "Process-Technology Fit and Its Implications for Manufacturing Performance." *Journal of Operations Management* 19, no. 5 (2001), pp. 521–40.

Elmer-DeWitt, P. "Charlie Wolf Has Second Thoughts about Apple's iPad." *CNNMoney,* July 12, 2012.

Harrington, L. "Change Drivers: Navigating the New Auto Supply Chain." InboundLogistics.com, February 2007.

Hayes, R., and S. Wheelwright. "Link Manufacturing Process and Product Life Cycles." *Harvard Business Review* 57, no. 1 (1979), pp. 133–40.

Hayes, R., and S. Wheelwright. *Restoring Our Competitive Edge: Competing Through Manufacturing.* New York: John Wiley & Sons, 1984.

Hibbert, L. "War on Waste." *Professional Engineering* 21, no. 3 (2008), www.profeng.com.

Hudson, K., and A. Zimmerman. "Big Boxes Aim to Speed Up Shopping." *The Wall Street Journal,* June 27, 1984, p. B1.

Isidore, C. "Ford to Cut Up to 30,000 Jobs: No. 2 Automaker to Close 14 North American Manufacturing Plants in Effort to Stem Losses." *CNNMoney.com,* January 23, 2006.

Lummus, R.; R. Vokurka; and L. Duclos. "The Product-Process Matrix Revisited: Integrating Supply Chain Trade-offs." *SAM Advanced Management Journal* 71, no. 2 (2006), pp. 4–10, 20, 45.

Posnett, J. "The Hospital of the Future: Is Bigger Better? Concentration in the Provision of Secondary Care." *British Medical Journal* 319, no. 7216 (1999), pp. 1063–65.

Safizadeh, M., and L. Ritzman. "An Empirical Analysis of the Product-Process Matrix." *Management Science* 42, no. 11 (1996), pp. 1576–95.

Sampson, S., and C. Froehle. "Foundations and Implications of a Proposed Unified Services Theory." *Production and Operations Management* 15, no. 2 (2006), pp. 329–43.

Schmenner, R. "How Can Service Business Survive and Prosper?" *Sloan Management Review* 27, no. 3 (1986), pp. 21–32.

Schmenner, R. "Service Businesses and Productivity." *Decision Sciences* 35, no. 3 (2004), pp. 333–47.

Selladurai, R. "Mass Customization in Operations Management: Oxymoron or Reality?" *Omega* 32, no. 4 (2004), pp. 295–301.

Sohel, A., and R. Schroeder. "Refining the Product-Process Matrix." *International Journal of Operations and Production Management* 22, no. 1 (2002), pp. 103–25.

Verma, R. "An Empirical Analysis of Management Challenges in Service Factories, Service Shops, Mass Services, and Professional Services." *International Journal of Service Industry Management* 11, no. 1 (2000), pp. 8–25.

Verma, R., and K. Boyer. "Service Classification and Management Challenges." *Journal of Business Strategies* 17, no. 1 (2000), pp. 5–24.

Zellner, W. "Airlines: How Ugly." *BusinessWeek,* January 14, 2002, p. 124.

6 Managing Quality

CHAPTER OUTLINE

LEARNING OBJECTIVES *After studying this chapter, you should be able to:*

LO6-1 Explain what the concepts of *product quality* and *quality management* entail.

LO6-2 Explain the roles that operations and other functional managers play in determining product quality.

LO6-3 Apply the core values and typical practices associated with quality management.

LO6-4 Perform a cost of quality analysis.

LO6-5 Compare and contrast various quality standards and certification programs.

LO6-6 Apply the Six Sigma DMAIC approach to quality improvement.

Brand Turnaround at Hyundai

For most of its history, Hyundai cars were widely considered to be of low quality. This Korean manufacturer achieved sales growth mainly by offering low prices. In 1999, Chairman Chung Mong Koo decided to refocus the company on catching Japanese rival Toyota in quality. Toyota's reputation for quality has given it levels of customer retention that few companies could match, and has given cachet to its luxury nameplates. Consistent with this change in focus, Hyundai made the following changes to improve quality:

- Increased the number of workers on the quality control team from 100 to more than 850.
- Instituted mandatory seminars for all workers on the importance of quality.
- Invoked the direct involvement of its CEO in twice-monthly meetings comparing Hyundai quality with that of its rivals.
- Made capital investments in problem areas, including $30 million invested in a computer center to test electronic systems.

By 2012, Hyundai had compiled an impressive track record of quality:

- According to Kelley Blue Book , brand loyalty for Hyundai surpassed that of Honda and Toyota to take the No. 1 spot.
- Cars.com recently ranked five Hyundai cars among its "Best Bets" for safety, reliability, and fuel efficiency.
- By introducing its Sonata and Genesis models, Hyundai has become a strong competitor in the luxury market, where excellent quality is imperative.
- In 2010 and 2011 it was the fastest-growing carmaker and in 2012 it became the fourth-largest manufacturer in the world.

During the past four years, Hyundai models have achieved consistently strong levels of dependability. However, initial negative quality perceptions are difficult to change. Given that quality is a primary consideration for car buyers, Hyundai will have to continue its journey toward achieving excellence in the dimensions of product quality that consumers care most about.

Quality is an integral focus of operations management. As we can see from the experiences of Hyundai, quality offers firms a way of enhancing their competitiveness and strategic position in the marketplace. The reality in today's market is that no firm can afford to forget quality; no firm can afford to compromise on quality. Quality is expected; quality must be delivered. To be delivered, it must be understood, and that is the focus of this chapter.

This chapter describes how operations managers and their supply chain partners improve and ensure the quality of products that the company delivers. First, we define the dimensions of product quality and the roles that different functional groups across the supply chain play in delivering quality. The "quality" of a product is a large and multidimensional concept; it encompasses all the aspects of what a product is—beginning with its design and including how it is delivered and supported in the field. Next, the chapter explores the core values of quality management to help you understand why quality is so important, and how companies are continually improving all processes involved in the design and delivery of products. The final sections of the chapter describe how national quality awards, international quality standards, and the "six-sigma" approach to quality management apply many of the core values and practices associated with quality management. The supplement to this chapter provides an explanation of many of the data analysis and statistical tools used in quality management programs.

LO6-1 Explain what the concepts of product quality and quality management entail.

Prepare

What is product quality, and how do operations management and other business functions help firms attain high levels of quality? What core values and concepts are central to quality management?

Organize

Defining the Dimensions of Quality
- Functional Roles in Quality Management
- Core Values and Concepts of Quality Management

DEFINING THE DIMENSIONS OF QUALITY

Quality management can dramatically impact business success. Over a decade ago, for example, Hewlett-Packard found defects in 4 of every 1,000 soldered computer components. Through better quality management, the company originally hoped to cut defects in half; it was ultimately able to reduce the defect rate to 2 defects per 1 million soldered components! The impact of this improvement was significant and widespread—fewer product returns in the field, less internal rework, fewer inspections, improved reputation with customers, less inventory, reduced lead times, less floor space (for inspections and rework), and ultimately, lower costs. Quality management programs can create equally dramatic improvements in all types of service industries. Some services offer outstanding consistency in their quality of service, McDonald's restaurants for example. Others, such as Ritz-Carlton Hotels (see the accompanying Get Real box), offer premium quality experiences.

As we discussed in Chapter 2, product quality can be broadly defined by the following terms:

product quality A product's fitness for consumption in terms of meeting customers' needs and desires.

design quality A measure of how well a product's designed features match up to the requirements of a given customer group.

conformance quality A measure of whether or not a delivered product meets its design specifications.

quality management A management approach that establishes an organizationwide focus on quality.

Product quality is a product's fitness for consumption in terms of meeting customers' needs and desires. Fitness for consumption is determined by both a product's design quality and its conformance quality.

Design quality is a measure of how well a product's designed features match up to the requirements of a given customer group.

Conformance quality is a measure of whether or not a delivered product meets its design specifications.

Quality management is a management approach that establishes an organization-wide focus on quality, merging the development of a quality-oriented corporate culture with intensive use of managerial and statistical tools.

Fitness for consumption is a very broad definition of quality. Operations managers must define quality in more specific terms that are relevant for their products and intended customers. In Chapter 2 we noted various aspects of product quality, addressing product design and conformance. Aspects of design quality address product functions, features, and characteristics. This includes how well the product does what the consumer needs, but it also includes ancillary aspects such as how environmentally friendly the product is, or how socially responsible the providing company is. Conformance quality is measured by how well an actual delivered product matches the dimensions and traits specified in its design.

sustainability

Ritz-Carlton: Where Quality Is Always First and Foremost

The Ritz-Carlton is a hotel chain that prides itself on offering its guests an extraordinary experience during their stay. The Ritz's goal is to exceed customers' expectations, rather than simply meeting them. Their commitment to quality has made them highly successful in achieving this goal. The Ritz-Carlton is one of only two American companies to have won the Malcolm Baldrige Quality Award twice (the Malcolm Baldrige Award is the "Oscar" of quality).

Management at the Ritz-Carlton has integrated quality into every activity. Every morning, the performance of every department in every hotel is compared to metrics in the Ritz's Service Quality Index (SQI). Every one of the 14,000 employees of the Ritz-Carlton knows the Ritz's "Gold Standards" of customer service, consisting of the Credo, the Three Steps of Services, the Motto, and the Twenty Basics. All employees carry laminated pocket versions of the Gold Standards with them.

Information regarding The Ritz-Carlton and its Gold Standards is available for review at the corporate site of the Ritz-Carlton Web site (www.ritzcarlton.com).

TABLE 6-1 Dimensions of Quality for Goods and Services

Dimension of Product Quality	Description for a Tangible Good	Description for an Intangible Service
Performance	The degree to which the product meets or exceeds certain operating characteristics	
Features	Presence of unique product characteristics that supplement basic functions	
Reliability	Length of time a product performs before it must be repaired	Ability to perform the promised service dependably and accurately
Durability	Length of product life or the amount of use one gets before a product deteriorates	
Conformance	The degree to which a product meets its design specifications	
Aesthetics	Subjective assessment of a product's look, feel, sound, taste, or smell	Appearance of physical facilities, equipment, personnel, and communication materials
Support/Responsiveness	Competence of product support in terms of installation, information, maintenance, or repair	Willingness to help customers and provide prompt service
Perceived Quality (Reputation/Assurance/Empathy)	Subjective assessment based on image, advertising, brand names, reputation, or other information indirectly associated with the product's attributes	Subjective assessment of the knowledge and courtesy of employees and their ability to convey trust and confidence Subjective assessment of the caring, individualized attention paid to customers

Source: Adapted from A. Parasuraman, V. A. Zeithaml, and L. L. Berry, "SERVQUAL: A Multiple Item Scale for Measuring Customer Perceptions of Service Quality," *Journal of Retailing,* April 1992, pp. 57–71; R. B. Chase and D. M. Stewart, "Making Your Service Fail-Safe," *Sloan Management Review* 35, no. 3 (Spring 1994), pp. 35–45; and D. A. Garvin, *Managing Quality.* New York: Free Press, 1988.

These quality traits were originally developed with tangible goods in mind. However, they apply equally well to services. In addition, face-to-face services require an expanded notion of product quality that considers interpersonal interactions, and customers' perceptions throughout the service experience. Table 6-1 provides a summary of dimensions of product quality that have been identified for goods and services, respectively. Note that the service quality dimensions go beyond the specifics of the service task. Service quality is affected by the environment surrounding the service as well as by the interpersonal communications and experiences involved. These aspects can have huge effects on customers' perceptions of service quality.

It is easy to draw parallels between the quality dimensions for tangible products and those for service products. Notions of performance, features, reliability, durability, and conformance can be applied to the task portion of the service quality dimension. For example, the durability of a service might be associated with how well a service is performed (how often do you have to get your hair "permed"?). Both tangible good and service quality dimensions contain some aspects that are fairly easy to measure objectively, and others that are mostly subjective and very difficult to assess. For example, aesthetics and perceived quality dimensions are both difficult to quantify, mainly because judgments vary widely from customer to customer and from situation to situation.

Surprisingly, quality is poorly understood and weakly defined in some firms. Managers in different functions sometimes emphasize different dimensions of quality. Marketing managers tend to care a lot about product aesthetics and perceptual aspects such as brand image. Design engineers tend to focus on aspects such as performance, reliability, and durability. Operations personnel, on the other hand, often focus on conformance quality. While each functional group has its primary area of focus, it is important for all managers in a given firm to understand all of the dimensions of quality that are important to customers.

Functional Roles in Quality Management

LO6-2 Explain the roles that operations and other functional managers play in determining product quality.

Quality management is fundamentally a *business* management approach, in that it encompasses many functional areas and activities both within and across companies in the supply chain. Table 6-2 provides examples of some of the ways that decisions made by managers in various functions might impact product quality. Note that some of these decisions might be made in places and times that are far away from actual production and delivery operations. Sometimes it is difficult to anticipate how decisions about markets or facilities, for example, might affect product quality outcomes in the future. Managers who are far removed from operations activities might not even be aware of how their decisions impact product quality. This is why the development of a culture of quality awareness is such a fundamentally important beginning to quality improvement programs within a business.

student activity

Ask a marketing professor, an operations professor, a finance professor, and an engineering professor to give you their definitions of *product quality.* Compare and contrast the definitions you receive.

relationships

It is not enough that managers within a given firm practice quality management principles; they need to permeate throughout the supply chain (for example, see the Get Real box on tracing quality in food supply chains on page 174). Quality is an important consideration when selecting suppliers. Practices such as single sourcing and full partnerships with suppliers can be used to extend quality management practices upstream and downstream. Some large companies help their suppliers understand and implement quality management practices. Similarly, companies work closely with their customers in order to clearly define customers' specifications of quality. Ultimately, the customer decides whether a "quality" product has been delivered.

Core Values and Concepts of Quality Management

LO6-3 Apply the core values and typical practices associated with quality management.

Some of the philosophical elements of quality management have been around since the industrial revolution. However, events in Japan made that country a fertile ground for the development and refinement of these elements. World War II devastated the Japanese economy. Japan had such a reputation for building inferior products that the phrase "Made in Japan" was synonymous with shoddy workmanship. After World War II, Japanese managers searched for ways to restructure their firms and the country's economy as a whole. Thought leaders like W. Edwards Deming, Joseph Juran, and others brought the seeds of a management philosophy to Japan as they worked as part of the American Occupation Force. W. Edwards Deming and Joseph Juran complemented each other as they worked

global

TABLE 6-2 Functional Influences on Product Quality

Functional Personnel	Decisions and Activities with Potential Impact on Product Quality
Marketing managers	Choices of markets to pursue and product features to offer
	Design of advertising and other programs that communicate product attributes to customers
	Development of new product testing programs
Sales managers	Setting of sales targets
	Interactions with customers
	Interpretations of customers' needs and desires
Product engineers	Design of product specifications, service elements, dimensional tolerances, etc.
	Design of product prototyping procedures
Process engineers	Design of manufacturing and service processes
	Choices of technology and associated capabilities and capacity limits
	Design of quality assurance tests and procedures
Finance and accounting managers	Setting of restrictions for equipment purchases
	Establishing goals for utilization of facilities and working capital
	Design of measures used to assess efficiency and productivity
Human resources managers	Design of hiring criteria, training and development programs
	Setting of compensation schemes and incentives
Manufacturing and service operations managers	Design and execution of processing procedures
	Design of work policies
	Interactions with customers
	Management of facilities and equipment
	Scheduling of work
Supply managers	Description of purchase requirements
	Selection of suppliers
	Establishment of contracts and associated incentives and penalties
	Management of and interactions with suppliers
Logistics managers	Selection of transportation providers
	Development of tracking and other information systems
	Design of packaging, storage, and material handling processes
	Management of and interactions with transportation providers

relationships

to spread the word of quality: Deming focused his message on top management, while Juran emphasized the tactical/operational side of quality. These leaders advocated merging certain core management values with statistical techniques and other management tools. The resulting "total quality management," or TQM, approach helped to transform Japan's

GET REAL

sustainability global

Food Safety in Global Supply Chains—A REAL Challenge

Quality problems in our food supply are often in the news. Rather than becoming less frequent, recent trends suggest that food safety problems are occurring even more often. In fact, five of the largest food recalls in history have occurred since 2007:

Menu Foods Pet Food—In 2007 Menu Foods Inc. recalled several brands of dog and cat food. Wheat gluten, an ingredient provided by a Chinese company, contained melamine, an industrial chemical used in the making of plastics. In the end, two Chinese companies and their owners were indicted in U.S. federal court over the incident, as well as a U.S.-based wholesaler.

Hallmark/Westland Meat Packing—In February 2008, the culmination of an investigation into slaughter practices resulted in the recall of 143 million pounds of beef, much of it destined for school lunch programs.

Peanut Corporation—This company shipped products containing salmonella a dozen times between 2007 and 2008. The shipments were later linked to eight deaths, and they sickened over 600 people in 46 states and in Canada.

Wright County/Hillandale Farms—Salmonella was the cause of a 2010 recall of over a half billion fresh eggs. The Centers for Disease Control noted over 1,900 reports of illness connected with the outbreak.

Cargill—Cargill issued a recall of over 35 million pounds of ground turkey in August 2011 due to contamination. The contaminated meat was responsible for one death and the sickening of over 75 people.

While there are likely many root causes to these quality failures, a growing concern is the lack of traceability of products as food manufacturers in industrialized countries increasingly source their ingredients from distant, low-cost countries. Many of these countries do not have the same sanitary standards for production, especially in the case of seafood and fresh produce. Sourcing products and ingredients internationally provides cost savings and the ability to source products all year long. On the other hand, the global supply chain adds complexity to an already complex system of food safety, quality, and logistics.

Tracing the sources and flows of ingredients throughout the supply chain is very difficult in global, complex supply chains. In China, for example, crops and seafood are typically combined from millions of small parcels managed by individual farmers, and there are often many intermediaries involved in the various stages of getting food from the farm to the table. There is sometimes little control over the chemicals and pesticides that may be used by these sources, and longer distances affect food freshness and quality, often necessitating the use of additional preservatives and dyes.

The size of the challenge is already huge, and it is growing. For example, in 2010 over 80 percent of fish and seafood consumed in the United States was imported. It is up to supply chain managers, working with government regulators and health officials, to find ways to ensure food safety and quality without substantially raising costs. These same challenges exist in many other supply chains as well, including pharmaceuticals, toys, and home and personal care products.

economy, making it an industrial powerhouse. Since then, this approach has spread to the United States and the rest of the world. Table 6-3 summarizes the contributions of the major quality gurus.

Prepare

What does the word *total* in total quality management (TQM) mean? What are the factors that influence the successful deployment of TQM across the firm and the supply chain?

Organize

TQM: A "TOTAL" VIEW OF QUALITY

Total quality management (TQM) is an integrated business management strategy aimed at embedding awareness of quality in all organizational processes. The word *total* in total quality management has several important connotations. First, a product's quality is ultimately determined by the customer's acceptance and use of the product. Accordingly, any discussion of product quality issues should always start with a focus on all of the attributes, the total package that targeted customers will care most about. Second, quality management is a total, organizationwide activity, rather than a technical task. Quality assurance is not simply the responsibility of product inspectors. Every employee in a company has a stake in product quality, and almost everyone has some direct or indirect influence on it. Consequently, the responsibility for quality belongs to everyone. Third, quality improvement

TABLE 6-3 Contributions of Quality Management Thought Leaders

Deming	Juran	Crosby	Imai
Holistic view of responsibility for quality	Broadened definition of product quality	Quality is free	Kaizen system of continuous improvement
Variability as the source of most problems	Focus on change management	Zero defects	Intense process-oriented view
Importance of customer	Cost of quality analysis	Focus on incremental change	Heavy dependence on frontline workers' insights.
			Emphasis on training and worker development
Deming's 14 Points	Juran's Universal Breakthrough Sequence	Crosby's 14 Steps for Quality Improvement	Kaizen Steps
1. Create consistency of purpose for continual improvement of goods and services.	1. Proof of Need. Create awareness by showing the costs of not changing.	1. Management commitment. Make quality a high priority for the firm.	1. Standardize an operation.
2. Adopt the new philosophy for economic stability.	2. Project Identification. Pick an initial project that has the highest, most visible payoffs.	2. Quality improvement teams. Cross-functional teams guide and achieve improvements.	2. Measure the standardized operation.
3. Cease dependency on inspection to achieve quality.	3. Organize for Improvement. Put in place the resources, top management, employees, and work policies needed to ensure success.	3. Quality measurement. Clear measures that relate to individual activities.	3. Gauge measurements against requirements.
4. End the practice of awarding business on price tag alone.	4. Diagnostic Journey. Identify and understand the critical few problems and their causes.	4. Cost of quality evaluation. Assess prevention, appraisal, and failure costs.	4. Innovate to meet requirements and increase productivity.
5. Improve constantly and forever the system of production and service.	5. Remedial Action. Identify and implement necessary corrective actions.	5. Quality awareness. Formal programs for creating awareness.	5. Standardize the new, improved operations.
6. Institute training on the job.	6. Resistance to Change. Overcome resistance by encouraging wide participation and by giving people sufficient time to understand and accept the changes.	6. Corrective action. Teams identify, study, and resolve problems.	6. Continue cycle *ad infinitum.*
7. Adopt and institute modern methods of supervision and leadership.	7. Holding Onto the Gains. Prevent a return to the "old" ways of doing things by establishing new standards, increasing training, and developing new control systems.	7. Zero defects planning. Move from correcting problems to totally eliminating them.	
8. Drive out fear.		8. Employee education. Employees at all levels trained to fulfill their proper roles.	
9. Break down barriers between departments and individuals.		9. Zero defects day. Event to signal a new, higher standard of performance.	
10. Eliminate the use of slogans, posters and exhortations.		10. Goal setting. New goals to guide performance and to keep quality in the forefront.	
11. Eliminate work standards and numerical quotas.		11. Error cause removal. Moves from correcting problems to removing the underlying causes.	
12. Remove barriers that rob the hourly worker of the right to pride in workmanship.		12. Recognition. Appreciation of employees whose actions have helped the firm achieve its quality objectives.	
13. Institute a vigorous program of education and retraining.		13. Quality council. Team leaders meet regularly to share experiences and plans.	
14. Define top management's permanent commitment to ever-improving quality and productivity.		14. Do it all over again! Repeat the steps at a higher level.	

total quality management (TQM) An integrated business management strategy aimed at embedding awareness of quality in all organizational processes.

requires a total commitment from all employees. A quality product results from good design combined with effective production and delivery methods. Because almost everyone in a company has some role either directly or indirectly related to design, production, or delivery, commitment to high quality is required of everyone in the firm. To make good decisions, people from all affected functions should be involved. Consequently, TQM has a heavy emphasis on decision making in cross-functional teams.

LO6-4 Perform a cost of quality analysis.

cost of quality (COQ) A framework for quantifying the total cost of quality-related efforts and deficiencies.

prevention costs Costs associated with efforts to prevent product defects and associated failure and appraisal costs.

appraisal costs Costs resulting from inspections used to assess quality levels.

internal failure costs Costs associated with quality failures uncovered before products are delivered to customers.

external failure costs Costs associated with quality failures uncovered after products reach customers.

Recognizing the Total Impacts of Quality Performance

In addition to affecting sales and other direct measures of business performance, poor product quality can have hidden or indirect effects. For example, poor quality can affect inspection, rework, and warranty costs—elements often buried in a company's overhead expenses. A focus on quality management demands that the total costs and benefits of quality performance be first understood by everyone in the organization. This usually requires a quite involved and far-reaching analysis. An operations management framework known as a **cost of quality (COQ)** analysis was developed by Feigenbaum[1] to help clarify the cost impacts of poor conformance quality. COQ identifies and assesses four major cost categories:

- **Prevention costs** result from efforts to prevent product defects (nonconforming products), and from efforts needed to limit both failure and appraisal costs. Such costs include resources spent on planning, new-product reviews, investments in more capable processing equipment, training, process control, and quality improvement projects.
- **Appraisal costs** result from inspections used to assess products' quality levels. Such costs include resources spent on incoming material inspections, product and process inspections, inspection staff salaries, test equipment, and development of test procedures.
- **Internal failure costs** result from defects that are found in products prior to their shipment to customers. These costs include scrapped materials, salvage and rework, excess material inventories, and other costs of correction.
- **External failure costs** result from defects that are found only after products reach customers. These costs include complaint settlements, loss of customer goodwill and future sales, returned materials, warranty work, and field service or repairs.

Prevention costs are the costs of activities aimed at eliminating the potential causes of product defects, or failures, while appraisal costs are the costs of activities aimed at ensuring that defective products are identified and not delivered to customers. Failure costs include both the internal costs of defects found inside the company and the external costs of defects found by customers.

Fill level tolerances, by law, are very narrow when it comes to permissible underfilling. However, business profitability demands that overfill be kept to a minimum, too. Machine vision systems can check fill level to verify minimum product requirement and alert when overfill results in excessive product giveaway.

[1] A.V. Feigenbaum, "Total Quality Control," *Harvard Business Review* 34, no. 6, (November–December 1956), pp. 93–101.

Cost of Quality Analysis Applies to Both Services and Manufacturing

The following table provides recent cost of quality data for two different companies. The left side of the table provides costs as a percentage of revenues for a hotel restaurant; the right side shows average costs of quality across 11 manufacturing plants owned by a single large company.

Comparing these two analyses points out some interesting differences in how services and manufacturing firms may apply the cost of quality approach. First, note that total costs of quality range from about 7 percent to 16 percent of revenues. These are fairly typical values. For a large company, costs of quality at this level could amount to hundreds of millions or even billions of dollars! In both cases, the total costs of quality went down from year 1 to year 2, especially for the restaurant, where total costs decreased from 16 percent of revenues to

Continued

Comparing Costs of Quality for a Hotel Restaurant and Manufacturing Plants

	Percentage of Revenues			Percentage of Revenues	
Hotel Restaurant	**Year 1**	**Year 2**	**Manufacturing Plant**	**Year 1**	**Year 2**
Prevention costs:			*Prevention costs:*		
Design menu	0.70%	1.12%	Design engineering	0.38%	0.27%
Equipment maintenance	0.30%	0.70%	Preventive repair / maintenance	0.43%	0.31%
Training	0.75%	1.76%	Training	0.13%	0.14%
Vendor evaluation	0.25%	0.42%	Process engineering	0.32%	0.38%
			Quality engineering	0.70%	0.91%
Total prevention costs	2.00%	4.00%	Total prevention costs	2.00%	2.00%
Appraisal costs:			*Appraisal costs:*		
Inspection of production	0.90%	0.65%	Manufacturing inspection	0.41%	0.32%
Product-testing (equipment)	1.15%	0.56%	Design analysis	0.24%	0.17%
Product-testing (labor and material)	1.70%	0.63%	Product acceptance	0.77%	0.63%
Incoming products inspection	0.25%	0.40%	Receiving inspection	0.24%	0.22%
			Lab audit	0.42%	0.40%
Total appraisal costs	4.00%	2.00%	Total appraisal costs	2.00%	1.70%
Internal failure costs:			*Internal failure costs:*		
Scrap	2.20%	1.30%	Scrap	2.84%	2.43%
Rework	1.50%	0.85%	Rework	0.58%	0.42%
Breakdown maintenance	0.80%	0.35%	Process engineering	0.15%	0.18%
Total internal failure costs	4.50%	2.50%	Total internal failure costs	3.57%	3.03%
External failure costs:			*External failure costs:*		
Returned meals (room service)	0.70%	1.10%	Returned material	0.20%	0.29%
Customer support	0.50%	0.20%	Marketing	0.05%	0.05%
Discount due to defects	1.80%	0.70%	Process engineering	0.07%	0.08%
Lost sales	2.50%	1.50%	Repair	0.02%	0.01%
			Travel	0.03%	0.03%
Total external failure costs	5.50%	3.50%	Total external failure costs	0.37%	0.46%
Total cost of quality	16.00%	12.00%	Total cost of quality	7.98%	7.24%
			Defect rate (per million units)	3.307	1,332

Sources: C. Ramdeen; J. Santos; and H. K. Chatfield, "Measuring the Cost of Quality in a Hotel Restaurant Operation," *International Journal of Contemporary Hospitality Management* 19, no. 4 (2007), pp. 286–95.

Venky Nagar and Madhav V. Rajan, "The Revenue Implications of Financial and Operational Measures of Product Quality," *The Accounting Review,* 76 no. 4 (2001), pp. 495–513

12 percent of revenues. Restaurant managers attributed this improvement to the increased investments that they made in prevention—note that they spent twice as much on prevention in year 2. This supports the quality management principle that prevention is better than cure.

A second difference is in the kinds of costs tracked by the restaurant versus the manufacturing plants. While the four cost of quality categories are used by just about everyone in business, most companies need to include or exclude specific costs in accordance with the nature of their business. For example, the manufacturing plants include more engineering-related costs. Also note the differences in drivers of total costs. External failure costs make up a much larger share of the total costs of quality in the restaurant than they do in the manufacturing plants. This attests to the fact that it is much more difficult to provide remedies for service failures than for failures in tangible goods—it is hard to "repair" bad service! External failure costs can vary a great deal across different manufactured products too, depending on their durability and warranty policies.

It is important to note that, as a product progresses from one stage to the next in the supply chain, a defect found in later stages is much more costly than a defect found in earlier stages. In later stages more resources have been invested in the product, and there is sometimes less ability to rework the product. Costs are highest when a defect is uncovered by the customer. Repair costs are relatively large, but often more importantly the costs of lost sales and tarnished product image can be very large. Lincoln Electric, one of the most visible users of TQM, uses COQ. They estimate that a quality problem that costs $1 to repair internally (i.e., internal failure) costs $8 to repair once it is in the hands of the customer (i.e., external failure).

Some of the costs contained in these four categories are identifiable in expense reports, yet others are hidden in overhead and other administrative accounts. For example, it may be difficult to establish the percentage of production engineering and management salaries (an overhead expense) that is attributable to solving quality problems. Similarly, some percentage of safety stock inventories may be needed to cover quality problems, but this is rarely explicitly identified.

relationships

A thorough COQ analysis usually requires quite a bit of digging, and cooperation by accounting and operations personnel. They often find that the cost of poor quality is surprisingly large! Once a COQ analysis helps managers quantify the monetary impact of quality on their company's performance, they are typically highly motivated. The COQ analysis points out the magnitude of the opportunity, and gives managers a stronger basis for financially justifying investments in quality improvement initiatives.

An Inverted View of Management

A focus on quality management turns a conventional view of management on its head. Traditional management views make sharp distinctions between managers and workers, often elevating the importance of managers. That is, the workers are present to support the activities of management. This view is illustrated by the pyramid shown on the left-hand side of Figure 6-1. The base of the pyramid consists of frontline workers who interact routinely with customers and operational processes, so they deal with the daily problems and difficulties of running the business. In doing so, frontline workers can be seen as supporters of smaller and smaller layers of management. In this view of the organization, managers are thought to be the decision makers and "owners" of operating processes and, therefore, they are seen to have primary responsibility for product quality.

A progressive quality management approach challenges this view, arguing that it is the workers on the front lines of business who should actually have primary "ownership" of operating processes. Further, managers should support workers, not the other way around. Frontline workers have the closest contact with customers and operational processes; therefore, they ultimately determine the quality level that the firm offers, and how customers view the firm. In addition, they know more than anyone about the firm's problems and the best ways to solve them. In total, quality management advocates believe that the entire organization should support the frontline workers, as the right-hand side of Figure 6-1 illustrates. This idea of elevating and empowering frontline workers is a core value of total quality management.

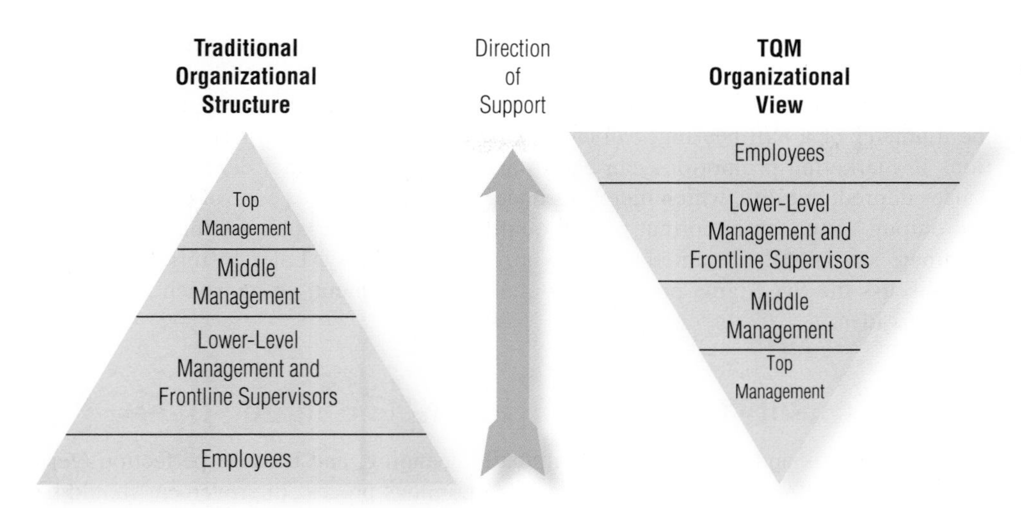

FIGURE 6-1 Traditional versus Quality Management View of Organizational Structure

What does employee *empowerment* actually mean? Several elements are required in order for employees to be empowered to actively manage the quality of an organization's products. First, frontline workers must be given both the responsibility and authority to make decisions. This is sometimes the hardest change for both managers and frontline workers to accept. Both groups have to clearly define and recognize the enlarged scope of decisions for which frontline workers are responsible, and then managers have to relinquish control and actively encourage these frontline workers to take charge. Measurement and incentive systems may also need to be changed to motivate frontline worker involvement.

Second, frontline workers need to have the knowledge required to make good decisions. Empowerment usually requires education and cross-training (job rotation) of employees on all technical issues related to their job environments. Equally important, employees need training on quality management concepts and in the use of problem-solving tools. If frontline workers are to set appropriate priorities and make good business decisions, they also need an understanding of the organizational strategy and current objectives.

Finally, frontline workers must have the resources required to make quality improvements. Such resources usually include data, tools and systems, money for investments, and time.

Process-Oriented Focus on Prevention and Problem Solving

Quality management approaches view products as the outcomes of processes. All organizations, functions, and activities involved in the design, production, and delivery of a product, good, or service should be viewed collectively as parts of a process. This extended process view includes suppliers and customers, making quality management principles very consistent with the overall supply chain management perspective. Quality problems are often only solvable through the involvement of suppliers, because their inputs may be related to problem causes. Suppliers can also help determine the costs and feasibility of changes required to address quality problems. As stated above, it is almost always more efficient to solve problems at as early a supply chain stage as possible, rather than trying to find a remedy or workaround at some later stage. Involving customers can clarify requirements needed to define acceptable levels of quality.

In TQM, problem prevention is emphasized, rather than an emphasis on fixing problems after they occur. It is better to eliminate the causes of problems than it is to only find and sort out defectives before they go to customers. In the long term, prevention is almost always cheaper than correction. Sometimes managers refer to this prevention-oriented approach as *quality at the source* as opposed to *quality through inspection.* Furthermore, problem solving is most effective when decisions are based on the analysis of actual data, as opposed to conjectures or opinions. The supplement to this chapter illustrates a number of analytical tools that have been developed to collect and analyze data. Use of these tools along with a data-led, or fact-based, approach helps managers to detect and solve problems in processes.

Variability in repeated activities is noted as the major source of problems for all operations processes. For example, variability in the time it takes to complete a task often disrupts work flows. Variations in a purchased material characteristic, such as in the diameter of a ball bearing, can cause unreliability in product performance. Variations in marketing promotions can cause large swings in product demand. Variability causes unpredictability, which increases uncertainty and reduces control over processes and outputs. Thus, an important task in quality management is to continually find and eliminate sources of unwanted and uncontrolled variability. Later in this chapter we will discuss the Six Sigma program for quality management, an approach that builds upon this idea.

Viewing Quality Management as a Never-Ending Quest

Because products and processes are continually changing, and because perfection (zero defects) is deemed to be an appropriate goal, continuous process improvement should be a part of every person's job. A widely used improvement process known as Kaizen, or Continuous Improvement, is based on the notion that the long-term survival and success of any organization occurs only when everyone in the firm actively pursues opportunities to identify and implement improvements every day. Chapter 3 discussed the practice of Kaizen for process improvement. Pursuit of small improvements keeps people thinking about the process and its current operation. Furthermore, small improvements are often gained without needing large investments of capital. In many cases, these improvements can be gained with little or no required investment.

Building an Organizational Culture Around Quality

relationships

An organizational culture is reflected in the values and behavioral norms that guide the decisions and interactions of people within an organization. Culture is shaped by the actions of the organization's leaders, by the environment, and by the collective experiences of the people in the organization. For example, think about the values and norms that exist among members of a sports team. Team members' goals and beliefs are shaped by what the coach says and does, but they are also shaped by what their teammates say and do. Experiences also play a role. Consider the effects on team culture that result from a series of close wins or losses. Close wins can build a sense of confidence and a winning spirit. Close losses can be disheartening.

Managers have to recognize that their actions, more than their words, help to shape culture. At the same time they have to recognize that they are not completely in control of the firm's culture. Both past experiences and external forces, such as the economic environment, labor union influences, and governmental controls, can have big impacts.

The culture within an organization can have tremendous effects on the success or failure of quality improvement initiatives. History contains many cases of companies whose quality initiatives were rendered ineffective by an incompatible culture. Most often cultural barriers to change are created by perceived inequities that have created a mistrust of management, or by incentive systems that motivate behaviors at odds with the values of quality management (e.g., when management pays for output irrespective of the quality).

It is critical for managers to continually assess the dynamics of culture in their organizations that may be creating values and norms of behavior that are supportive, or damaging, for quality management initiatives. Through communications, actions, measures, rewards, and incentives, managers should seek to build the values of total quality management into their corporate culture. Table 6-4 lists the values we have discussed in this section, along with some of the factors that have contributed to the creation of a TQM culture. Note that the success factors are not guarantees of success, but their absence will hinder successful implementation.

TABLE 6-4 TQM Values and Success Factors

Values that Characterize TQM	Factors Affecting the Success of TQM
• Holistic view of product quality and its impacts	• Strong, charismatic leadership
• Emphasis on customer requirements	• Trust between labor and management
• Extended process view of operations	• Crisis situation or compelling reason for change
• Emphasis on prevention rather than inspection	• Adequate resourcing of training and improvement projects
• Disdain for variability	• Clear, well communicated, uncomplicated change process
• Data-based decision making (not opinion-based)	• Unquestionable success of early efforts
• Employee empowerment	
• Top management support	
• Supplier involvement	
• Continuous improvement	

The core values of quality management are fleshed out in various quality improvement methodologies, certification standards, and awards criteria. In the following sections, we describe several methodologies and standards that you are likely to encounter, namely:

- Plan-Do-Check-Act Cycle
- Six Sigma Approach to Quality Improvement
- ISO 9000 Series: An International Quality Standard
- Malcolm Baldrige Award

plan-do-check-act cycle (PDCA) A process for improving quality that describes the sequence used to solve problems and improve quality continuously over time; also known as the *Deming Wheel* or *Deming Cycle.*

GUIDING METHODOLOGIES FOR QUALITY MANAGEMENT

Plan-Do-Check-Act Cycles (Deming Wheel)

A popular methodology used to guide problem identification and solution is the **plan-do-check-act cycle (PDCA)**, also known as the *Deming Wheel* or *Deming Cycle* (in honor of W. Edwards Deming, the man who frequently used it). The PDCA cycle (see Figure 6-2) describes the sequence used to solve problems and improve quality continuously over time.

The PDCA cycle consists of four separate but linked activities:

- *Plan.* Identify a problem by studying the current situation to detect a gap between it and the desired future situation. Identify actions to improve the situation (i.e., close the gap). Formulate a plan for closing the gap (e.g., a plan for reducing the number of defects coming from a specific process).
- *Do.* Having formulated a plan, implement it.
- *Check.* Use performance metrics to monitor and inspect the results. Identify unplanned problems elsewhere in the system or previously hidden problems uncovered by the changes.
- *Act.* Review information collected in the check step and take corrective actions to prevent reoccurrence of problems. Institutionalize changes (through revised procedures and associated training) as a starting point for the next PDCA cycle.

Prepare

What are the various methodologies that are used for quality management, and what are their goals and roles in the quality management process?

Organize

FIGURE 6-2
PDCA in Action

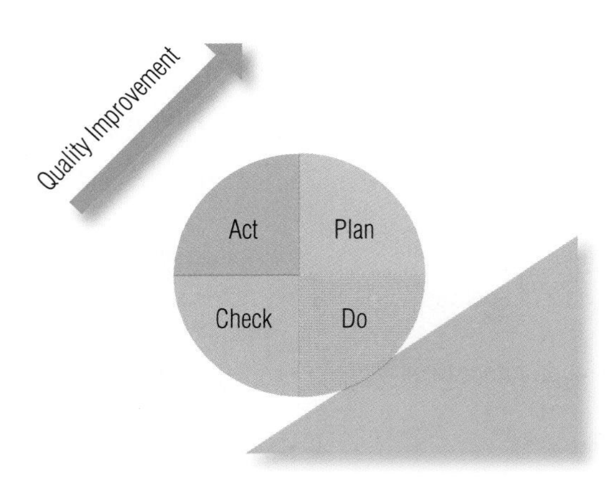

The PDCA method is simple, giving all employees the impetus and guiding structure for attacking problems on a daily basis. Workers at all levels can be trained in the PDCA process and in the use of the quality tools referenced above.

Six Sigma: A Systematic Approach to Quality Management

In addition to general methods for quality improvement that can be applied by all workers, companies often need to organize specific quality improvement projects. In recent years, the **Six Sigma** program for quality and process improvements has been adopted by many of the larger firms around the world. Six Sigma is a management strategy that seeks to improve the quality of process outputs by identifying and removing the causes of defects and variation in the various processes.

Six Sigma A management program that seeks to improve the quality of process outputs by identifying and removing the causes of defects and variation in the various processes.

standard deviation A measure of the variability or dispersion of a population, data set, or distribution.

The term *sigma* refers to the Greek symbol, σ, that represents the standard deviation of values for the output of a process. The standard deviation is an indicator of process variability (inconsistency). In statistics, **standard deviation** is a measure of the variability or dispersion of a population, a data set, or a probability distribution. A low standard deviation indicates that the data points tend to be very close to the same value, typically the mean, while high standard deviation indicates that the data are spread out over a large range of values. As standard deviation increases, there is greater uncertainty about the exact outcome. As previously noted in this chapter, variability is regarded as a source of quality failures. A primary objective of the Six Sigma method is to design and improve products and processes so that sources of variability are reduced.

That explains the *sigma* in Six Sigma, but what about the *six?* One of the issues in quality improvement is deciding how far variability reduction efforts should go. In a Six Sigma approach, the goal is to achieve a process standard deviation that is 12 times smaller than the range of outputs allowed by the product's design specification. In this case, the design specification encompasses *six* process output standard deviations on each side of its center point.[2] Consider Example 6-1 on the next page.

Curious students often ask, "Why is *six* sigma the goal? Why not *five* sigma, or *seven* sigma?" Good question. Early developers of the Six Sigma approach at Motorola originally chose six sigma as an appropriate goal because of the nature of their products and manufacturing processes. A six sigma rated process, where upper and lower product specifications are set 12 standard deviations apart, will produce at most only 3.4 product defects per million outputs. Is this goal suitable for other products? It all depends on the costs of quality. If the costs of failure outweigh the costs of prevention and appraisal, then pursuing greater levels of conformance (more "sigmas") is probably justified. However, for some products there is a point at which the size of potential failure cost savings does not justify

[2]This relationship between product specification and process variation is illustrated in the supplement to this chapter, "Quality Improvement Tools," in the section describing process capability.

EXAMPLE 6-1

You operate a trucking company that delivers products to distribution centers for a large retailer such as Walmart. Distribution centers are very busy places. Consequently, they schedule deliveries in very tight windows of time. Walmart often requires that deliveries arrive within a 15-minute window, that is, no more than 7.5 minutes before or after a scheduled time. A Six Sigma approach would seek to make truck arrivals so consistent that the standard deviation of arrival times is no more than 1.25 minutes (15 minutes/12). If this level of consistency were achieved, it would be highly unlikely that a truck would ever arrive too early or too late.

How would you reduce driving time variability this much? The Six Sigma approach provides a systematic process for first identifying sources of variability and then reducing them. For example, you might start by thinking of all the possible causes of early and late arrivals (weather, traffic, breakdowns, and so on). Then you would brainstorm ways to prevent these causes or to overcome them. If variability cannot be reduced sufficiently, another option would be to widen the specifications; that is, to negotiate wider delivery windows with Walmart.

the investments required to achieve them. For example, Six Sigma quality is arguably not justified for a product such as an inexpensive ballpoint pen, because the internal and external failure costs are low once a reasonable level of quality has been achieved. On the other hand, Six Sigma quality may be too low a goal for products such as drugs and medical devices, where the cost of a single failure can be very high (someone's life!).

Table 6-5 shows the levels of quality associated with other sigma levels, along with some of the quality levels seen in our everyday lives. In truth, very few business operations ever attain a Six Sigma level of quality. More important than the absolute goal are the quality improvement processes that comprise a Six Sigma program.

TABLE 6-5 How Quality Relates to Sigma

Sigma Level	Defects per Million Units
2 σ	308,537
3 σ	66,807
4 σ	6,210
5 σ	233
6 σ	3.4

The Classical View of Quality "99.9% Good" (3.8σ)	The Six Sigma View of Quality "99.99966% Good" (6σ)
• 20,000 lost articles of mail per hour.	• Seven lost articles of mail per hour.
• Unsafe drinking water almost 15 minutes each day.	• One minute of unsafe drinking water every seven months.
• 5,000 incorrect surgical operations per week.	• 1.7 incorrect surgical operations per week.
• 2 short or long landings at most major airports daily.	• One short or long landing at most major airports every five years.
• 200,000 wrong drug prescriptions each year.	• 68 wrong drug prescriptions each year.
• No electricity for almost 7 hours each month.	• One hour without electricity every 34 years.

DMAIC An acronym for the five steps at the heart of the Six Sigma process: define, measure, analyze, improve, and control.

DMAIC: The Six Sigma Process

At the heart of the Six Sigma approach is a five-step process: define, measure, analyze, improve, and control (DMAIC). Figure 6-3 describes the **DMAIC** process. For any given good or service, members of a cross-functional team usually work through these steps together to complete a quality improvement project. The focus of the DMAIC improvement process is initially on the product outcome; then it shifts to the underlying processes needed to produce and deliver the product.

student activity

For a candy such as M&Ms, identify the important critical-to-quality characteristics. How would you measure these characteristics objectively? Which of these measures pertain to the physical product itself? Which of these measures relate to the packaging or the services surrounding the good?

As project teams work through the DMAIC process, they focus on several objectives:

LO6-6 Apply the Six Sigma DMAIC approach to quality improvement.

1. Each *critical-to-quality* (CTQ) characteristic should be defined from a customer's perspective and in a way that it can be measured as objectively as possible.
2. It is important to determine and consider the future market and technology strategies for the product, as well as the strategies for the processes that are involved in delivery of the CTQ characteristics.

FIGURE 6-3 The DMAIC Process

Source: Copyright © 2009 Dynamic Diagrams.

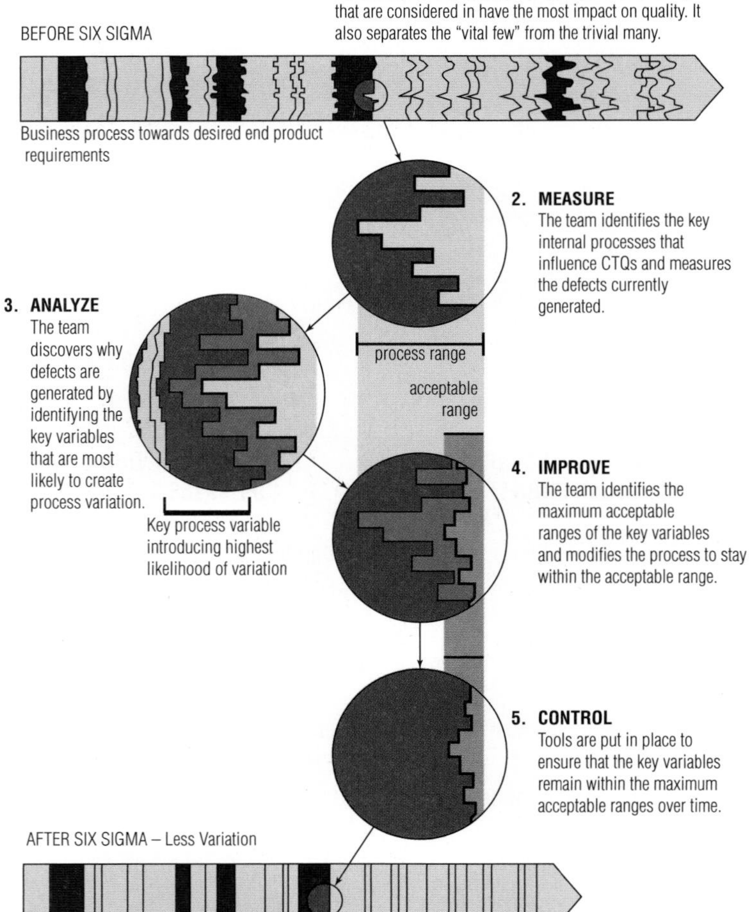

3. The quality improvement tools described in the supplement to this chapter are especially useful in the analyze, improve, and control steps of the process.
4. If the data do not already exist, the project team needs to develop a way to measure important outcomes on a frequent and regular basis.
5. The lessons learned from the process should be documented, and the final problem solution should be implemented in all applicable areas.

The Get Real box page 186 presents an example of how DMAIC can be successfully used to resolve quality problems.

Design for Six Sigma

The DMAIC process is usually aimed at improving existing products and their supporting operational processes. A similar approach has been developed to guide design decisions made in the creation of new products. **Design for Six Sigma (DFSS)** is an approach in which a cross-functional team designs products and processes in a way that balances customer requirements with the constraints and capabilities of the supporting manufacturing and service processes. The primary difference between DFSS and DMAIC is that DFSS takes place in the development phase, whereas DMAIC usually takes place after a new product has been launched. DFSS makes use of design engineering tools that may be used to simulate and evaluate different product/process design scenarios, whereas DMAIC ideally works with actual product and operational data. Other "design-for" processes and tools similar to DFSS are described in Chapter 4.

Design for Six Sigma (DFSS) A design approach that balances customer requirements with the constraints and capabilities of the supporting manufacturing and service processes.

Implementing Six Sigma

Organizations often view Six Sigma as an improvement program aimed at gaining greater consistency and efficiency throughout the organization. The most common approach for implementing Six Sigma is to start by training key leaders in the organization in quality management philosophies and tools. Then these initial leaders train others, who then train others, and so on. Usually there are two to three levels of training targeted for various employees in the organization. Persons completing the levels of training are given names taken from the Asian martial arts tradition. For example, persons who complete the highest levels of training are called Black Belts, or even higher-level Master Black Belts. Black Belt personnel have usually completed at least several quality improvement projects. Master Black Belts may even work full-time in training others in Six Sigma processes. Employees who complete the basic level of training are often called Green Belts.

To achieve Green Belt status, employees usually must complete a project that applies the Six Sigma process to a product in their own areas of work. These projects often must satisfy certain operational or financial performance goals (e.g., the project will achieve a 25 percent reduction in lead times, or the project will generate a minimum 25 percent return on investments). The cost savings from such projects can be used to pay back the costs of training for the Six Sigma program. Numerous companies have shown tremendous benefits from implementing Six Sigma. Yet, some companies are finding that Six Sigma has limitations as well. Under certain conditions, managers are finding that the use of Six Sigma can be a deterrent to innovation. That is the point raised in the Get Real box on page, 187 "Does Six Sigma Stifle Innovation?"

CERTIFYING PROGRESS IN QUALITY MANAGEMENT

Prepare

What is the role of certification in quality management? What are goals and benefits of various quality certification standards?

Organize

The TQM and quality initiatives we have discussed up to this point are company specific; project improvements and their evaluation varies from company to company. Operations managers often want to know how their operational quality processes compare to others. In addition, prospective customers often want assurances that a given supplier has achieved some level of quality performance. External audits in the forms of certifications and

GET REAL

Applying DMAIC to Cough Drops

A British food company used DMAIC to improve operations in its cough drop production line. Before the DMAIC project, the line suffered from high rates of machine downtime, scrap and rework, and chronically late order deliveries.

- *Define:* The project team mapped out the production process, identified a probable cause of their defined problem—variability in the size of the cough drops—and calculated the costs associated with this problem. Too much variance in the size of a cough drop may seem incidental, but larger tablets were more likely to chip and introduce abrasive sugar dust into the machinery causing breakdowns. That problem, along with slowdowns in packaging and the added maintenance, was estimated to cost £485,000 (783,000 USD) per year.
- *Measure:* The cough drop team found that the existing measuring techniques were not precise enough, so they did their own process measurements. They found that the process was not within specifications: almost 20 percent of the cough drops were too large, while almost none were too small.
- *Analyze:* The team measured the accuracy of the syrup base extrusion system and found it to be accurate. They then determined that air bubbles forming in the tablets somewhere in the process was the culprit. The team investigated possible process steps where air could enter the product, finally settling on three possible steps.
- *Improve:* The team experimented with changes in product temperature, machine lubrication and other factors to prevent air bubbles from forming. Implementing these changes caused cough drop variability to fall within process specifications. Even so, the team noted that the process was still fairly low in capability. They suggested adding an additional wrapping line with wider tolerances for larger tablets.
- *Control:* The process changes included training for personnel and the installation of new monitoring systems to ensure that the variability improvements were maintained.

The financial impact of this project was dramatic. By decreasing the variability and increasing the wrapping tolerance for larger sizes the company was able to save £290,000 (470,000 USD) per year in waste, maintenance, downtime, and late orders. The cost of the DMAIC project team was only £13,000 (21,000 USD). The return on investments—2,230.8 percent!

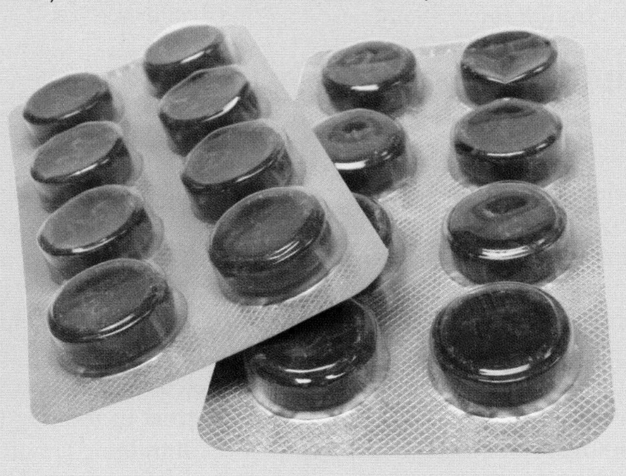

LO6-5 Compare and contrast various quality standards and certification programs.

awards programs help to provide universal standards that managers and customers can use to gauge a company's quality progress. In this section, we focus on two such programs: ISO 9000 and the Malcolm Baldrige Quality Award.

ISO 9000: An International Quality Standard

ISO 9000 A set of internationally accepted standards for business quality management systems.

ISO 9000 defines a set of internationally accepted standards for business quality management systems. It was initially developed by the International Organization for Standardization to facilitate international trade. Since its inception in 1987, the standard has been revised several times. The newest version is referred to as the ISO 9000:2008 standard. National bodies from over 120 countries now support this standard.

As a standard, ISO 9000 is applicable to all forms of organizations, irrespective of size or product offerings. Certifications have been attained by banks, consulting operations, manufacturing plants, software development firms, tourism operations, and even universities. The essential purpose of ISO 9000 is to ensure that operating processes are well documented, consistently executed, monitored, and improved. ISO 9000 certification provides essentially the same function for business processes as financial accountants provide when they audit a company's financial transactions.

GET REAL

Does Six Sigma Stifle Innovation?

Traditionally, 3M has prided itself on being a center for excellence in innovation. The corporate culture allowed workers time and grant money to work on their own projects and invited scientists to take risks. This level of innovation allowed 3M to routinely meet its goal of having one-third of its sales come from products introduced in the previous five years. However, at the end of the 1990s 3M stock price had stagnated at a time when the rest of the market was experiencing rapid expansion. To get the company back on track, 3M hired former General Electric (GE) executive James McNerney in December 2000. McNerney brought with him GE's Six Sigma playbook, including DMAIC (short for design, measure, analyze, improve, and control) and design for Six Sigma (DFSS), which stress waste elimination and process control, even during product innovation.

In the short term, these process innovations produced excellent financial returns. However, in the four-and-one-half years of McNerney's tenure the R&D budget was held flat, many rigid new constraints were put on lab activities, and many workers who had enjoyed the entrepreneurial atmosphere they had known at 3M left or were let go. Today only about one-fourth of sales come from products introduced in the last five years, and 3M's creative reputation has suffered.

3M's struggles highlight the possible tension between innovation, which requires trial and error, slack resources, and a tolerance for failure, and Six Sigma, which seeks to wring any slack resources, including time devoted to personal research, out of the system as waste. 3M's current CEO, George Buckley, is attempting to chart a more balanced course than his predecessor. Buckley has relaxed many of the Six Sigma program constraints for laboratory scientists, while still attempting to hold on to the benefits of Six Sigma on the production floor.

Source: B. Hindo, "At 3M, A Struggle between Efficiency and Creativity: How CEO George Buckley Is Managing the Yin and Yang of Discipline and Imagination," ***BusinessWeek*****, June 11, 2007.**

Attaining ISO 9000 Certification

Over one million organizations have been independently certified to ISO 9000. To attain certification, an organization must be audited by an external, authorized party. Certification states that the firm's processes meet the requirements in the ISO 9000 standards. Typically, an organization first conducts an internal audit to determine whether its processes are consistent with the standards. Then, it contracts with a registrar (an external and independent body)[3] to perform a formal audit. Attaining ISO 9000 certification is usually quite demanding and time-consuming. The process can take anywhere from 3 to 24 months, depending on the initial level of compliance of the firm's systems. If the organization passes the audit, its certification is recorded by the registrar.

The standard itself consists of five sections. Table 6-6 provides a brief description of each section. The standard emphasizes many of quality management's core values.

- First, it is customer-oriented, with a great emphasis placed on defining, meeting, and achieving customer satisfaction.
- Second, it emphasizes the need to make improvements on a regular basis.

[3]It is possible to self-certify a system to be ISO 9000 compliant. However, such an action does not carry the weight and credibility of external certification.

TABLE 6-6 The ISO 9000: 2008 Certification Structure

Section	Focus/Description
4	**Quality Management System Requirements**
4.1	Establish your quality system—Develop, implement, and improve the system.
4.2	Document your quality system—Develop, prepare, control, and maintain quality system documents.
5	**Management Requirements**
5.1	Support quality—Promote the importance of quality. Develop, implement, and improve the system.
5.2	Satisfy your customer—Identify, meet, and enhance customer requirements.
5.3	Establish a quality policy—Define and manage your organization's quality policy.
5.4	Carry out quality planning—Formulate your quality objectives and plan for the system.
5.5	Control your quality system—Define responsibilities, appoint management representatives, and support internal communications.
5.6	Performance management reviews—Review the system and examine review.
6	**Resource Requirements**
6.1	Provide quality resources—Identify and provide quality resource requirements.
6.2	Provide quality personnel—Use and support competent personnel.
6.3	Provide quality infrastructure—Identify, provide, and maintain the needed infrastructure.
6.4	Provide quality environment—Identify and manage the needed work environment.
7	**Realization Requirements**
7.1	Control realization planning—Plan and develop the product realization process.
7.2	Control customer processes—Identify and review customers' product requirements. Communicate with your customers.
7.3	Control product development—Plan, design, and develop the product development cycle, including inputs, outputs, review process, design verification process, and the design and development change process.
7.4	Control purchasing functions—Control, document, and verify the purchasing process.
7.5	Control operational activities—Control, validate, and identify production and service provision.
7.6	Control monitoring devices—Identify monitoring and measuring needs. Select, calibrate, protect, validate, and use monitoring and measuring devices.
8	**Measurement, Analysis, and Improvement Requirements**
8.1	Perform remedial processes—Plan and implement remedial processes.
8.2	Monitor and measure quality—Monitor and measure customer satisfaction. Plan and perform regular internal audits. Monitor and measure quality processes. Monitor and measure product characteristics.
8.3	Control nonconforming products—Develop a procedure to identify, document, and control nonconforming products and verify that nonconforming products that were corrected.
8.4	Analyze quality information—Define quality management system, collect quality management system data, and provide quality management information.
8.5	Make quality improvements—Improve quality management system and correct actual nonconformities and prevent potential nonconformities.

- Third, it recognizes the importance of product design to quality by including product realization (i.e., all the processes and activities a firm undertakes to design, develop, and build a new product) in the standard.
- Finally, the standard emphasizes the definition, measurement, and documentation of processes.

In general, the standard is fairly flexible in that it tells management what to do, not necessarily how to do it.

Businesses are motivated to seek ISO 9000 certification for several reasons. Increasingly, firms are required to be certified to sell products in most major markets. Virtually every major industrial nation in the world has accepted these standards. Certification at least gives the appearance that a company will be a reliable supplier. Beyond appearances, ISO 9000-certified firms benefit from internal improvements as a result of the certification. To pass the audit, employees usually must reexamine and critically challenge their practices. The certification process can also improve communication links between functional areas within the firm. It forces people to forge agreements on important issues such as the firm's definition of quality and its identification of its target market. The success with ISO 9000 has caused the ISO organization to extend the focus of business issues covered by such standards. For example, in 1996 ISO introduced the ISO 14000 standard for environmental systems. This standard is discussed in greater detail in Chapter 16.

Industry Interpretations of ISO 9000

While the guidelines in ISO 9000 can be applied just about anywhere, each organization needs to carefully interpret them for their context. In some cases industry groups have created interpretations for their specific requirements. Table 6-7 shows some examples of common interpretations of ISO 9000.

The Malcolm Baldrige Quality Award

Over the years, increased awareness of the importance of quality has inspired the introduction of numerous quality awards, at the city, state, and international levels. At present, some 40 U.S. states have their own quality awards programs in place. These quality award programs have helped formalize the ways that firms consistently design, produce, and deliver high-quality products. The **Malcolm Baldrige National Quality Award** is the foundation on which many of the current state, national, and international awards are based. It is a national quality award bestowed by the United States National Institute for Standards and

Malcolm Baldrige National Quality Award A national quality award bestowed by the United States National Institute for Standards and Technology (NIST) in recognition of superior quality and performance excellence.

TABLE 6-7 Industry-Specific Interpretations of ISO 9000

Standard	Industry
TickIT	Interpretation of ISO 9000 produced by the UK Board of Trade for the information technology industry (specifically software development)
AS9000	Interpretation developed by major aerospace manufacturers (e.g., AlliedSignal, Allison Engine, Rockwell-Collins, Boeing, Lockheed-Martin)
ISO/TS 16949:2009	Interpretation developed and agreed to by major American and European automotive manufacturers
TL 9000	Interpretation developed by the telecom consortium QuEST forum.
ISO 13485:2012	Interpretation developed by medical industry
ISO/IED 90003:2004	Application of ISO 9000 to computer software
ISO/TS 29001	Quality management system for products in petroleum, petrochemical, and natural gas industries.

Technology (NIST) in recognition of superior quality and performance excellence. The Baldrige Award was originally designed to strengthen American competitiveness by:

1. Helping improve organizational performance practices, capabilities, and results.
2. Facilitating communication and sharing of "best practice" information among all organizations.
3. Serving as a working tool for understanding and managing performance and for guiding planning and opportunities for learning.

Separate awards are given to organizations in manufacturing, services, small business, education, and health care. The list of past winners (see www.quality.nist.gov) includes many firms from the elite of American industry. Each award provides other companies with a way to benchmark their quality progress. In addition, award winners can serve as role models for firms seeking to improve.

Table 6-8 shows the seven award examination categories and the scoring system used by the NIST to evaluate award applicants. The categories and weights assigned to each

TABLE 6-8 Malcolm Baldrige National Award Categories and Item Point Values, 2007

Criteria		Points
1 Leadership		**120**
1.1 Senior Leadership	70	
1.2 Governance and Social Responsibilities	50	
2 Strategic Planning		**85**
2.1 Strategy Development	40	
2.2 Strategy Deployment	45	
3 Customer and Market Focus		**85**
3.1 Customer and Market Knowledge	40	
3.2 Customer Relationships and Satisfaction	45	
4 Measurement, Analysis, and Knowledge Management		**90**
4.1 Measurement, Analysis, and Improvement of Organizational Performance	45	
4.2 Management of Information, Information Technology, and Knowledge	45	
5 Workforce Focus		**85**
5.1 Workforce Engagement	45	
5.2 Workforce Environment	40	
6 Process Management		**85**
6.1 Work Systems Design	35	
6.2 Work Process Management and Improvement	50	
7 Results		**450**
7.1 Product (Good and Service) Outcomes	100	
7.2 Customer-Focused Outcomes	70	
7.3 Financial and Market Outcomes	70	
7.4 Workforce-Focused Outcomes	70	
7.5 Process Effectiveness Outcomes	70	
7.6 Leadership Outcomes	70	
TOTAL POINTS		**1,000**

Source: www.quality.nist.gov.

category have changed over time as the reviewers have become aware of the changing requirements of business. For example, the emphasis on supplier partnering is recent and reflects the increasing importance of the supply chain. As you can see, the core values of TQM are well represented in these evaluation categories.

CHAPTER SUMMARY

In this chapter we have explored the concept of quality management by tracing its origins and philosophical elements, and by describing how its core values have been fleshed out in quality standards and improvement programs today. We can summarize the important points of this chapter as follows:

1. Quality management strives to achieve a sustainable competitive advantage by focusing company actions on customer satisfaction, employee empowerment, and powerful management and statistical tools to achieve superior quality.
2. It is important to integrate quality management into the firm's strategic activities by ensuring that the voice of the customer is heard. The Six Sigma approach to quality is a corporatewide system to integrate the elements of the customer, strategy, value, processes, statistical tools, and metrics. This approach has been successfully implemented in many firms.
3. Formal certification to quality standards such as ISO 9000 indicates that a firm has passed a rigorous audit to confirm that its major processes have been documented, that everyone associated with those processes understands correct procedures, and that people routinely follow these procedures. ISO 9000 seems likely to make certification a near-universal order qualifier in important markets around the world.
4. Many firms use the Malcolm Baldrige National Quality Award guidelines to assess the performance of their quality management systems.
5. Quality management in face-to-face services must take into consideration the interpersonal interactions of service providers and customers. Sometimes customers' perceptions of quality vary widely as they are potentially influenced by many different aspects of the operating system.
6. Regardless of the form of quality improvement program that a firm pursues, the core values of total commitment, cross-functional decision making, continuous improvement, and data-based decision making are the critical aspects to making quality improvement a success.

KEY TERMS

appraisal costs 176
conformance quality 170
cost of quality (COQ) 176
design for Six Sigma (DFSS) 185
design quality 170
DMAIC 184
external failure costs 176
internal failure costs 176
ISO 9000 186
Malcolm Baldrige National Quality Award 189
plan-do-check-act cycle (PDCA) 181
prevention costs 176
product quality 170
quality management 170
Six Sigma 182
standard deviation 182
total quality management (TQM) 174

DISCUSSION QUESTIONS

1. Pick a product (good or service) that you are interested in consuming sometime in the near future (for example, a textbook, apartment rental, cell phone, etc.). Analyze the offerings of two competing firms. How do the products compare on various dimensions of quality? From these differences, what can you infer about each company's strategy and the customers that they seem to be targeting?
2. Employee empowerment is an essential element of quality management, especially in services. From your own experience, cite instances where a service provider empowered its employee to go the extra mile to delight you. Then indicate an instance where the opposite happened.
3. You have been commissioned to create a local equivalent of the Malcolm Baldrige National Quality Award for your college's campus. The winner will receive free campus parking for one academic year. Prepare a list of criteria for use in deciding who on your campus is most worthy of this award. How would you propose that these factors be measured? Should they be?
4. You have been appointed head of quality control for your organization (a firm you have worked at or at your college). During the first month, you interview disciples of Deming, Juran, and Crosby. Each seems to be equally affable and competent. Which consultant would you hire for your organization? Why?
5. Why are most quality awards based on the Malcolm Baldrige National Quality Award program? Why not the ISO 9000 standard?
6. It has been said that quality management is really a "people" system, more than a technical system. If this is true, what conditions must first be in place for a firm to be successful with quality management? What are the possible repercussions for the firm if the employees aren't committed to the quality management program?

PROBLEMS

1. Given the following cost information for company XYZ, calculate:
   a. Total appraisal cost
   b. Total prevention cost
   c. Total cost of internal failures
   d. Total cost of external failures
   e. Total cost of quality

Cost item	Total for the year
Quality assurance	$450,000
Equipment maintenance	$205,000
Product redesign	$310,000
Product warranty and repair	$550,000
Product testing and inspection	$372,000
Training	$250,000
Process improvement/Kaizen	$120,000
Material scrap	$230,000
Rework labor	$426,000
Incoming materials inspection	$323,000
After sales customer support	$150,000
Travel to suppliers/process certification	$ 75,000
Travel to customers/problem solving	$ 80,000

2. Rachel loves to bake cookies, but she has an old oven that has trouble maintaining a constant temperature. If the acceptable temperature range for making the cookies is 350 plus or minus 5 degrees, what is the allowable standard deviation in the temperature of her oven in order to achieve a Six Sigma level of quality?
3. Six Sigma quality (3.4 defects per million units produced) is probably a bit much to ask of Rachel's old oven.
   a. What would the standard deviation in the temperature of her oven need to be if she settled for a "Three Sigma" level of quality?
   b. If her oven exactly meets this quality level, what percentage of the time would her oven be operating at a temperature outside the acceptable range? (Hint: see Table 6-5.)
4. Suppose that the Dallas School District wants to achieve Six Sigma quality levels of performance in delivering students to school. They have established a 20-minute window as an acceptable range within which buses carrying students should arrive at school.
   a. What is the maximum allowable standard deviation of arrival times required in order to achieve this standard of quality?
   b. If they achieve this standard, about how many times out of a million deliveries will a bus deliver students either too early or too late?

CASE

Aqua-Fun

Roberta Brown sat at her desk and looked through the preliminary slide deck she had prepared. This presentation had to be good. In two weeks she would be giving the presentation to the top management team of Aqua-Fun. The goal: to secure their commitment to a new program aimed at improving quality. Improvements were to come through a new (to Aqua-Fun) corporatewide program to implement Six Sigma. Involvement in this program was the principal reason that Roberta had been hired by Eric Tremble, the vice-president of operations/supply chain management at Aqua-Fun, some six months earlier.

Demand for Aqua-Fun's products had grown from an emerging interest in home swimming pools over the past few decades. During that time, the founders of Aqua-Fun recognized that there was a need for good quality, fun water toys and swimming pool accessories. Since then, Aqua-Fun had grown to its current state of $195 million in annual sales, employing some 650 employees. The secret to its growth: a fair price, reliable products, and the ability to design and introduce interesting and fun new toys and accessories quickly. However, in the last two years, there was evidence that Aqua-Fun's reputation was suffering. Sales growth had slowed, and, as some of the accessories (such as pool automatic cleaners) became more sophisticated, warranty claims had grown dramatically. Top management's best estimate of the costs of dealing with poor quality in the field was about $6.7 million. However, Eric Tremble was convinced that Aqua-Fun's managers did not fully comprehend the total costs associated with managing quality and quality failures.

Before joining Aqua-Fun, Roberta Brown had worked for two years in a firm that had successfully improved quality, reduced costs, and increased revenues by implementing a companywide Six Sigma program. Roberta had been part of the Six Sigma planning and deployment team; she had gone through Green and Black Belt training; and she had successfully carried out three high visibility Six Sigma projects. Now, she was being asked to introduce a similar approach at Aqua-Fun. For both Aqua-Fun and Roberta, the time seemed right for Six Sigma.

The Presentation

Critical to this presentation was Roberta's CoQ analysis (shown in the table following). She worried that the analysis was missing important cost categories. She was also unsure regarding which costs should be included. Items with question marks "????" in the CoQ were items that she either did not have data for, or she was unsure about including. For example, she wasn't sure how the marketing managers would feel about including marketing research as a category in the CoQ, though she knew that this was a large expense for the company, well above $10 million per year. Other missing categories could be quite substantial as well. Besides, Roberta still felt that there might be even more "hidden" costs of quality not captured in the analysis.

As Roberta reviewed the presentation, she noted points that she wanted to make, and questions she still needed to answer:

- Aqua-Fun had tended to underestimate the true costs of quality. For example, the external failure cost estimate of $6.7 million neglected lost sales and damaged customer goodwill that might occur from poor quality products.
- The initial costs of training for a Six Sigma program (between $20,000 and $30,000 per Green Belt) and Black Belts ($40,000–$50,000) were high. In typical Six Sigma implementations, companies trained 2 to 5 percent of employees as Black Belts and they trained 50% to 100% of employees as Green Belts.
- There were significant benefits to be gained by such investments. Other firms had achieved 10 to 20 percent reductions in the CoQ each year for the first few years of the Six Sigma program.
- To be successful, this program had to be corporate-wide. It had to involve everyone from top managers to the people working on the floor. It had to involve not only operations, purchasing, logistics, and supply chain areas but also finance, personnel, training, marketing, engineering, and accounting.

Questions

1. Review the CoQ Analysis. Should marketing research and other similar cost categories be included? What other cost categories should be included? Where should Roberta go to get estimates for these other costs? Who else might need to be involved?
2. If Aqua-Fun implements Six Sigma, what costs might be expected to go up, at least in the short term? What costs should be expected to go down? Can this program be financially justified? How?
3. Thinking about the core values of quality management, what factors should Roberta encourage the management team to consider as they design a Six Sigma implementation?

	Estimated Annual Cost	**Total Category Cost**
I. Prevention costs		$ 9,507,000
A. Marketing/customer/user		
1. Marketing research	????	
2. Customer/user perception surveys/clinics	????	
B. Product/service/design development		
1. Design quality progress reviews	$ 1,300,000	
2. Design support activities	900,000	
3. Design qualification and test	3,600,000	
C. Purchasing		
1. Supplier reviews, ratings, and certifications	564,000	
2. Purchase order tech data reviews	260,000	
3. Supplier quality planning	????	
D. Operations (manufacturing or service)		
1. Operations process validation (planning and equipment design)	750,000	
2. Operations support quality planning	25,000	
3. Operator quality education	95,000	
4. Operator SPC/process control	623,000	
E. Quality administration		
1. Administrative salaries and expenses	1,330,000	
2. Quality program planning and reporting	????	
3. Quality education	25,000	
4. Quality improvement projects	20,000	
5. Quality audits	15,000	
6. Other prevention costs	????	
II. Appraisal costs		8,612,000
A. Purchasing appraisal costs		
1. Receiving or incoming inspections and tests	2,260,000	

2. Measurement equipment (annualized cost)	856,000	
3. Qualification of supplier product	????	
4. Source inspection and control programs	????	
B. Operations (manufacturing or service) appraisal costs		
1. Planned operations inspections, tests, audits	3,950,000	
2. Inspection and test materials	225,000	
3. Process control measurements	325,000	
4. Laboratory support	145,000	
5. Outside endorsements and certifications	????	
C. External appraisal costs		
1. Field performance evaluation	-	
2. Special product evaluations	75,000	
3. Evaluation of field stock and spare parts	$ 776,000	
D. Review of tests and inspection data	????	
E. Miscellaneous quality evaluations	????	
III. Internal failure costs		$ 12,639,000
A. Product/service design failure costs (internal)		
1. Design corrective action	1,230,000	
2. Rework due to design changes	560,000	
3. Scrap due to design changes	3,650,000	
B. Purchasing failure costs		
1. Purchased material reject disposition and rework costs	1,330,000	
2. Purchased material replacement costs	230,000	
3. Supplier corrective action	????	
4. Uncontrolled material losses	????	
C. Operations (product or service) failure costs		
1. Material review and corrective action costs	356,000	
2. Operations rework and repair costs	1,700,000	
3. Re-inspection / retest costs	23,000	
4. Extra operations	????	
5. Scrap costs (operations)	3,560,000	
6. Downgraded end product or service	????	
7. Internal failure labor losses	????	
D. Other internal failure costs	????	
IV. External failure		6,695,000
A. Complaint investigation/customer or user service	845,000	
B. Returned goods	1,200,000	
C. Recall costs	650,000	
D. Warranty claims	3,250,000	
E. Liability costs	750,000	
F. Customer/user goodwill/lost sales	????	
G. Other external failure costs	????	
	Total CoQ	$ 37,453,000

CASE

A Comment on Management Attitude[4]

I visited my old pal Dinsmore recently. He had called to let me know that he had taken over as general manager of the Flagship hotel about six months ago, and thought that I might be interested in seeing a real hotel from the inside. He also indicated that I might learn something about the hotel business.

When I drove up to the front door, a steady rain kept me inside the car for 10 to 15 minutes. During that time, I noticed that the doorman was peering at me from inside the lobby. Sensing that the rain was not going to quit, I made a dash for the doors and pushed my way in, dripping on the carpet in the process. The doorman told me that I could only leave the car there for about 10 minutes because it was a no-parking zone, but that the hotel garage in the next block would be glad to store it for me. He offered to lend me his umbrella in order to unload the trunk.

Accepting his offer, I retrieved my suitcase and clothes bag to drop both at the front desk. Announcing myself as Mr. Dinsmore's guest didn't seem to make much of an impression on the clerk, who was chatting with the cashier. She seemed a little irritated at my interference.

There was no reservation for me, but they said they could fix me up since I had said the general manager had invited me. After only three rings of the "front" bell, the bellhop came to lead me to my room, which, as it turned out, wasn't made up. He commented that it was only 3 o'clock and the room would probably be fixed up by the time I returned from my business. I tipped him, dropped my bags, and remembered the car.

It wasn't necessary to worry because the police had just towed the vehicle away. The doorman said that he had waved to the tow truck but they hadn't been able to see him for the rain. He assured me that I could pick up the car in the morning with no problem. A cab could take me to the police lot, and the fine was only $25 plus the towing charge. The garage charged $6. He noted that it was interesting how they could move a car like that without having the key. Said they would make good thieves.

I found Dinsmore's office on the third floor. One of the elevators wasn't working so I took the brisk walk up the stairs. His secretary nodded and suggested that I move some magazines off that bench and sit down as "Elmer" would be with me as soon as he got off the telephone. She went back to her book.

After a few minutes, she seemed to notice my presence again, and offered me some coffee from the percolator in the corner of the reception room. (She didn't like the hotel coffee, and neither, apparently, did Elmer.) I accepted with thanks, telling her I was still damp, having not been able to shower and change because the room was not prepared. She said I really shouldn't expect much else because, although checkout time was noon, they didn't like to push their guests out on rainy days like this. I said I thought that was very considerate of them.

I asked about my automobile, and she repeated the information I already had about the $25 fine and towing charges. Happens all the time, she indicated. The police have no class.

Dinsmore emerged from his office and greeted me effusively. Now, he told me, I was going to see how a hotel should be run. He took me into his office, cleared some reports off a chair, and offered me a cigar. After remarking on my trip, and how fortunate it was of him to catch me in an off moment, he asked me how I liked the place so far.

I told him about the car, the doorman, the room clerk, the room, the bellhop, and the elevator. He told me how to get the car back and dismissed the other incidents as growing pains.

Then, lowering his voice, he asked me if I would mind checking out the restaurant for him. He would pay, naturally. But he wasn't sure if the restaurant manager was really operating the place right. She didn't seem to get along with the other department heads and barely spoke to Elmer. Something funny is going on, he thought. Also, the hotel occupancy had been dropping steadily. He was sure that this had something to do with the food.

Then, straightening his tie, rolling down his sleeves, and putting on his favorite old hunting jacket, he took me on a tour of the hotel. He emphasized that I had only seen the front side of hotels in my travels. He was going to show me the real guts.

In the maid's room, nine or ten women were involved in a discussion with the housekeeper about their assignments. Those of the lower floors had to wait until the vacuum cleaners were available from the upper floors, so naturally everyone wanted to work on the upper floors. Dinsmore suggested that they might vacuum every other day; then they could share the machines on a rotating basis. The maids thought that this was a great idea, although the housekeeper didn't seem too pleased.

Dinsmore remarked to me about the lack of some people's decision-making ability. He sighed that he had to make more and more decisions each day because his staff seemed reluctant to take the initiative.

We toured all the floors. I mentioned the number of room service trays that seemed to be standing in the hall. Dinsmore said that this was a normal part of the hotel scene. The guests didn't mind because it reminded them that room service was available.

[4]Phillip Crosby, *Quality Is Free* (New York: McGraw-Hill, 1979).

The cigar and newspaper stand looked like it belonged in the subway. The old man behind the counter offered some stale alternatives to the cigars I requested. He was very pleasant about it. Only a few magazines could be seen. "Guests don't go in for magazines anymore," Dinsmore told me. With a nudge, he reminded me that I didn't understand the hotel business.

The restaurant seemed to belong to a different world. It was packed. The maitre d' rushed over, bowed, seated us at a window, and took our drink orders. An atmosphere of quiet efficiency seemed to blanket the room. Two drinks appeared before us while attractive menus were deftly placed to our left. Elmer didn't seem happy. The restaurant, he told me, was a concession left over from the previous owners. He was trying to buy out the leases so he could turn it into a real moneymaker. At present, it made only about 10 percent net. I mentioned that most hotels lose money on their restaurants. He countered by showing me how many people were there even on that rainy day. He insisted that raising the prices while cutting back on the help was bound to increase the take.

The next morning, I retrieved my car, placed it firmly in the hotel garage, and returned for a farewell meeting with Dinsmore. He asked my opinion concerning his stewardship. He commented on the failing standards of today's workers, noted that he had ever-increasing difficulty in getting people who wanted to do quality work, and bemoaned the fact that the big grand hotels like his were losing out to the motels.

Questions

1. How would you rate Dinsmore's hotel? What evidence would you provide to support your position?
2. What are some of the most interesting examples of quality found in the case? How does Dinsmore view these examples? How would you, as the customer, view these same instances?
3. What do you think of Dinsmore's handling of the dispute involving the vacuums?
4. What would you recommend to Dinsmore about the manager of the restaurant?
5. If you were hired as a consultant by the owners of this hotel, what would you do? Why?

SELECTED READINGS & INTERNET SITES

American Society for Quality **www.asq.org**

ISO—Organization for Standardization **www.iso.org**

Macolm Baldrige National Quality Award information **www.nist.gov**

Antony, J. "Six Sigma for Service Processes." *Business Process Management Journal* 12, no. 2 (2006), pp. 234–48.

Breen, M.; B. Jud; and P. E. Pareja. *An Introduction to ISO 9000.* Dearborn, MI: Society of Manufacturing Engineers, Reference Publication Division, 1993.

Breyfogle III, F. W.; J. M. Cupello; and B. Meadows. *Managing Six Sigma: A Practical Guide to Understanding, Assessing, and Implementing the Strategy That Yields Bottom-Line Success.* New York: John Wiley & Sons, Inc., 2001.

Crosby, P. B. *Quality Is Free.* New York: McGraw-Hill, 1979.

Deming, W. E. *Out of Crisis.* Cambridge, MA: MIT Center for Advanced Engineering Study, 1986.

Furterer, S., and A. K. Elshennawy, "Implementation of TQM and Lean Six Sigma Tools in Local Government: A Framework and a Case Study." *Total Quality Management & Business Excellence* 16, no. 10 (December 2005), p. 1179.

Garvin, D. A. *Managing Quality.* New York: Free Press, 1988.

Goetsch, D. L., and S. B. Davis. *Quality Management,* 5th ed. Englewood Cliffs, NJ: Prentice Hall, 2005.

Hoyle, D. *ISO 9000 Quality Systems Handbook,* 5th ed. New York: Butterworth-Heinemann, 2005.

Imai, M. *Kaizen: The Key to Japan's Competitive Success.* New York: Random House, 1986.

Juran, J. M., and F. M. Gryna, Jr. *Quality Planning and Analysis.* New York: McGraw-Hill, 1980.

Kotter, J. P. "Leading Change: Why Transformation Efforts Fail." *Harvard Business Review* 85, no. 1 (January 2007), p. 96.

Pyzdek, T. *The Six Sigma Handbook: A Complete Guide for Greenbelts, Blackbelts, and Managers at All Levels,* 2nd ed. New York: McGraw-Hill, 2003.

Stevenson, W. J., and A. E. Mergen. "Teaching Six Sigma Concepts in a Business School Curriculum." *Total Quality Management & Business Excellence* 17, no. 6 (July 2006), pp. 751–56.

Swink, M., and B. Jacobs, "Six Sigma Adoption: Operating Performance Impacts and Contextual Drivers of Success," *Journal of Operations Management* 30, no. 6 (2012), pp. 437-53.

Yeung, A. C. L. "Strategic Supply Management, Quality Initiatives, and Organizational Performance." *Journal of Operations Management* 26, no. 4 (2008), pp. 490–502.

6 Chapter Supplement: Quality Improvement Tools

CHAPTER SUPPLEMENT OUTLINE

LEARNING OBJECTIVES *After studying this supplement, you should be able to:*

LO6S-1 Apply quality management tools for problem solving.

LO6S-2 Identify the importance of data in quality management.

OVERVIEW

Quality management programs make managers and employees better problem solvers by giving them the tools and procedures to measure and improve processes, to identify potential problems, and to describe these problems to others. These tools can help managers determine whether processes are under control or whether they are capable of meeting certain performance specifications needed to make products acceptable to customers. In this supplement, we use an example situation to illustrate the applications of some of the more important quality management tools and the types of problems they are designed to solve. While this supplement focuses on quality issues, these tools are universal and applicable to almost any process setting.

STANDARD PROBLEM SOLVING APPROACH

LO6S-1 Apply quality management tools for problem solving

LO6S-2 Identify the importance of data in quality management

Chapter 6 introduced two problem solving approaches: (1) the Six Sigma improvement process known as Define, Measure, Analyze, Improve, and Control (DMAIC) and (2) the Plan-Do-Check-Act cycle (PDCA) process. Both approaches are good at standardizing improvement processes and giving everyone in the organization a common language for describing problems and related improvement efforts. A standard problem solving process also ensures that all employees use systematic, data-driven methods. While problem solving processes may vary from company to company, most follow the same fundamental steps represented in the DMAIC and the PDCA cycle. Most of the tools described in this supplement deal with the measure, analyze, improve and control steps of the DMAIC, or alternatively, steps P, D, and C of the PDCA cycle.

QUALITY IMPROVEMENT TOOLS

Prepare

What quality improvement tools are available? How are they used to help operations managers improve quality?

Organize

The major goal of quality improvement is to move from uncovering symptoms of problems to determining the underlying root causes of problems in a structured and logical manner. In this process, quality management decisions should be based on data whenever possible. Data fall into one of two categories: variable data or attribute data. **Variable data** measure quantifiable conditions such as speed, length, weight, temperature, density, and so forth. **Attribute data** measure qualitative characteristics of a process output (pass/fail, go/no go, good/bad). All variable data can be transformed into attribute data. However, it is not possible to transform attribute data into variable data.

Consider the following example. To ensure safety, amusement parks have minimum height requirements for riders of roller coasters. At the Cedar Point amusement park, guests must be at least 52 inches tall to ride the Top Thrill Dragster®. The park could measure and record the actual height of each guest, gathering variable data. Instead, only those guests whose height is in question are measured. Their height is compared with a standard set at 52 inches; each guest is either tall enough to ride or not. Thus, Cedar Point is measuring an *attribute,* as opposed to a *variable.*

The various quality tools are just that—tools. They are used to address a specific question and to help managers understand what is taking place in operational processes. Table 6S-1 gives a summary of the tools and their usages.

The applications of quality improvement tools are best understood within the context of an example. In the next section we will illustrate the application, objectives, and outcomes of the various tools by using them to address problems faced by Pear Computers.

variable data Measures quantifiable or numerical conditions.

attribute data Measures qualitative dimensions or conditions.

TABLE 6S-1 Quality Improvement Tools

Quality Tools	Typical Usage
Histogram	To uncover underlying patterns (range and frequency) in data variability.
Cause-and-effect analysis	To uncover possible contributors to an observed problem; to facilitate group brainstorming.
Check sheets	To identify the frequency and location of problem causes.
Pareto analysis	To identify the most critical (relatively frequent) causes of problems.
Scatter diagrams	To determine if two variables are related to each other (do the two variables move together in some predictable manner).
Process flow analysis	To graphically display and analyze the steps in a process.
Process capability analysis	To predict the conformance quality of a product by comparing its specification range to the range of its process variability.
Process control charts	To monitor process outputs and determine whether a process is operating according to normally expected limits.
Taguchi method/design of experiments	To evaluate and understand the effects of different factors on process outputs.

Pear Computers: Using Quality Tools to Improve Performance

Pear Computers is a small Midwestern manufacturer of personal computers and data collection devices specifically targeting usages in the medical and dental fields. Pear has been successful in serving the needs of this market and in fending off the forays of larger computer makers such as Dell, Lenovo, and HP by relying on a strategy that emphasizes constant innovation, flexible product configurations, on-time delivery and extremely high levels of quality.

Recently, however, quality has slipped. Given where Pear Computers are used (which is often in literally life and death situations), this issue has become a major management concern. Increased final inspections have revealed that an unacceptably high number of computers are leaving final assembly DOA (dead on arrival—not working properly). Some computers have refused to boot up; others begin the startup procedure only to stop and restart continuously without finishing the bootup. Still others have started up and then become frozen at the startup screen. Bob Feller, the operations manager in charge of the assembly line, has been charged with the task of eliminating these problems and ensuring that Pear delivers a computer that its customers can rely on.

Histograms

histogram A graphical representation of the distribution of values.

Variance exists in every activity or process. A **histogram** graphically displays a distribution of values in data of one variable to show the extent and type of variance. To create a histogram, one needs at least 30 observations, but more are better. Also, the analyst must determine the number of ranges or categories for grouping the data. The number of ranges is typically between 5 and 20, increasing with the number of observations.

Figure 6S-1 shows examples of histograms (each number identifies the frequency of occurrence of a given outcome). Histograms help problem solvers recognize and understand three critical traits of distributions:

- *Center:* The theoretical or desired mean (μ) should fall at the center of the distribution. Any gap between the observed mean and μ may indicate bias.

FIGURE 6S-1 Common Histogram Shapes

Histrogram Distribution	Implications
Bell-shaped	This is the typical or normal distribution that we expect to see when dealing with variable data. It is centered and symmetrical about the mean. This can be viewed as the baseline to which the subsequent histograms are compared.
Double or twin-peaked	Often indicates that two normal distributions have been combined (signifying that we may have more than one process at work).
Plateau	Often the result of combining multiple data sets, where the data sets themselves are moving.
Comb	Typically occurs if there are errors in the process, faulty measurement, error in data collection, rounding errors, or poor grouping of data into categories.
Skewed	A symmetrical pattern of data, typically indicating that there is some limit that is restraining the process on one side of the distribution. Skewed can either be positively skewed (with the tail extending to the right as shown here) or negatively skewed (with the tail extending to the left).

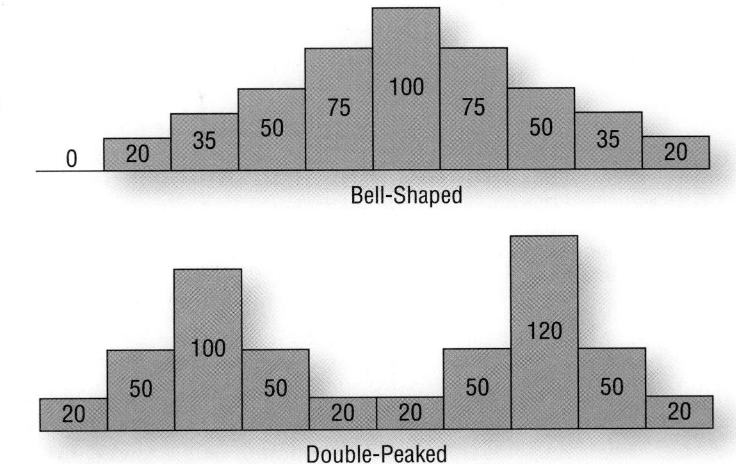

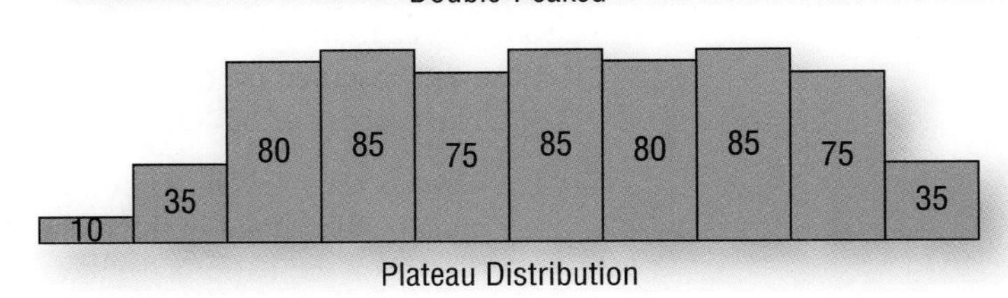

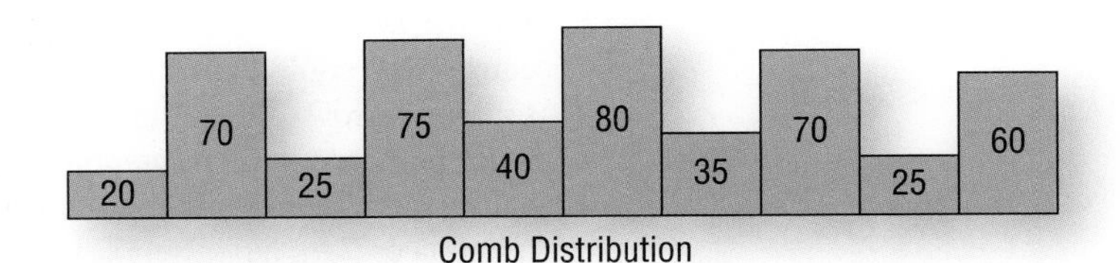

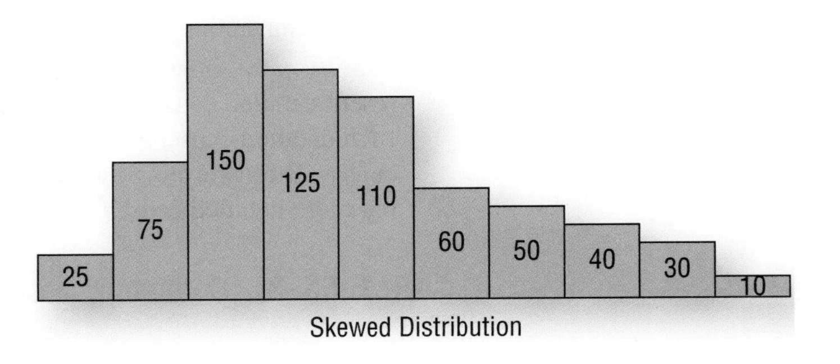

- *Width:* The range (the difference between the highest and lowest values) is shown graphically by a histogram. The width indicates the predictability of the process (i.e., the wider the distribution, the less predictable it is).
- *Shape:* The overall shape of a distribution can indicate problems in the data or influences on the overall distribution.

Examine the five different distributions shown in Figure 6S-1. Most students are familiar with the first, normal, bell-shaped distribution. However, the other four distributions contain important information that can be used to uncover the potential underlying problems and to improve the performance of the system.

For Bob Feller, histograms can provide a great deal of useful information. For example, Bob decides to collect initial time-to-failure data. When the computer goes through initial burn-in (test), we would like to see the frequency with which failures occur throughout the test. If the failure times are normally distributed, or skewed left or right, this information would give us an idea of the timing and stage where most failures occur. However, if Bob were to see distributions that were either double-peaked or exhibiting a plateau, then this would indicate that multiple factors may be affecting performance.

Cause-and-Effect Diagrams

cause-and-effect diagrams (CEDs) Diagrams that show the causes of certain outcomes. Also known as *fishbone diagrams* or *Ishikawa charts.*

The **cause-and-effect diagram (CED)** examines complex interrelationships, identifies the root causes (which are often hidden) of problems, and links them to the symptoms (which are often very visible). The CED is also known as a *fishbone diagram* (because a completed diagram looks like a fish skeleton), or an *Ishikawa chart,* in honor of Dr. Kaoru Ishikawa, who first developed this tool. In practice, CEDs offer users several important advantages. First, they are useful as brainstorming tools. They are best developed by a group of people who represent a variety of perspectives. Second, they discourage the presence of *management myopia*—"I know the root cause; don't confuse me with data." That is, CEDs help managers to see all of the potential causes, rather than limiting their attention to only a few. Third, they help to uncover the logic chain that leads from the root causes to the effects, thus showing how the various factors interact with each other to cause the observed problems.

The process of building a CED diagram consists of the following steps:

1. *Identify the problem to examine.* State the symptom or the effect (outcome) that must be explained in the form of a variance statement (e.g., reject rates are too high). Placed on the extreme right of the diagram, an arrow is next drawn from left to right. This arrow denotes the root effect—the link between the effect and the root causes.
2. *Identify the major categories of causes.* Identify the major categories of potential causes that could contribute to the effect. Represent them as main branches off the problem arrow, indicating the name of each category at the end of its branch. These main branches gather potential causes into categories and begin to structure the cause and effect relationships. The categories often reflect universal issues such as manpower (i.e., labor, work methods), materials, machines, and measurement. Firms often introduce additional categories that are appropriate to the situations and problems being studied. Table 6S-2 lists some commonly used categories.
3. *Identify more specific causes.* On each main branch, place smaller branches to represent detailed causes that could contribute to the primary categories of causes. For each detailed cause, ever-smaller branches represent still more specific and detailed causes. Brainstorming methods are used to identify major categories of causes and the more detailed causes.

TABLE 6S-2 Commonly Used Categories of Causes

Minimum Set	6 Ms (used in manufacturing)	7 Ps (used in service industry)	5 Ss (used in service industry)
People	Machine (technology)	Product=Service	Surroundings
Machine/Equipment	Method (process)	Price	Supplies
Methods/Processes	Material	Place	Systems
Material	Manpower/Mindpower	Promotion	Skills
	Measurement (inspection)	People/Personnel	Safety
	Mother Nature (environment)	Process	
		Physical Evidence	

4. *Circle likely causes.* After the diagram has been developed to show all potential causes, review all of the causes and circle the most likely ones. Further analysis and data collection can then focus on those causes.
5. *Verify the causes.* After identifying the most likely causes, use the other tools to ensure they really are the root cause of the problem.

To understand how a CED can be developed, let's return to Bob Feller and Pear Computers.

Bob still faces the problem of how to reduce the high failure rate of the new generation of Pear computers. An initial study has determined that CPUs are being damaged during assembly. To uncover causes of the damage, Bob assembled a group consisting of a process engineer, a maintenance technician, a line employee, and an inspector. From the resulting group brainstorming session, Bob was able to construct the CED found in Figure 6S-2.

In developing this diagram, Bob and the team discussed each category to drill down into root causes. For example, Bob asked "Why does the CPU chip lead to the CPU being damaged during assembly?" He received multiple answers from different participants. These are shown in Figure 6S-2 as arrows coming out of the CPU category arrow (e.g., received defective, pins not aligned). Bob then went through each one of these explanations asking why, until each logic chain answered at least five levels of why. This is illustrated in Figure 6S-2 where the main problem is the first why. The CPU chip category is the second why. The pins not aligned is the third why. Poor design is the fourth why. And, in answer to his question "Why does poor design lead to pins not being aligned?" Bob was told the fifth why, that "the specifications are not precise." Consequently, Bob was able to understand the line of logic that led from imprecise specifications to the problem of CPUs being damaged during assembly. With the insights generated from the CED, Bob is now able to collect data to determine if the insights gained from the CED are correct; he is also able to formulate, introduce, and evaluate the effectiveness of a corrective action program aimed at correcting the potential problems uncovered by the CED.

Check Sheets

A **check sheet** is a simple tool used to collect, organize, and display data to reveal patterns. An attribute check sheet consists of categories such as problem types, problem categories, or time. The categories could come from a cause-and-effect analysis. These categories typically represent factors that are seen as playing an important role in explaining what

check sheet A tool for collecting, organizing, and displaying data with the goal of revealing underlying patterns.

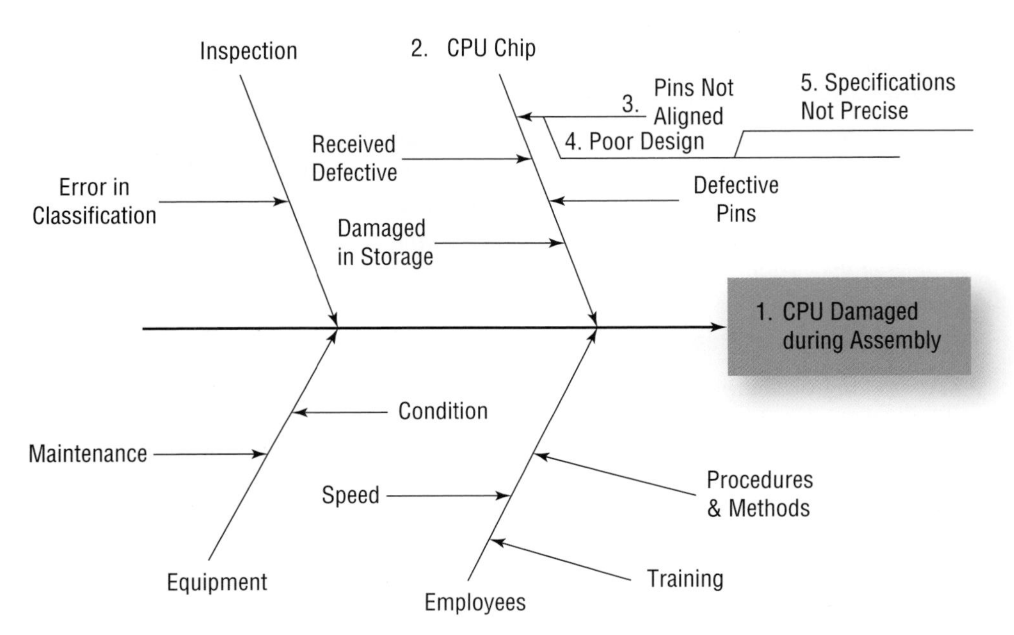

FIGURE 6S-2
Cause-and-Effect Diagram for Pear's CPU Damage Problem

FIGURE 6S-3
Example of Attribute Check Sheet

Reason for Reject	Number Rejected
Item damaged	✓✓✓✓✓✓✓✓✓✓✓✓✓
Wrong case shipped	✓✓✓✓✓✓✓✓
Part does not work	✓✓✓✓
Component(s) missing from part	✓✓✓✓✓✓✓✓✓✓✓✓✓✓✓✓✓✓✓✓✓✓✓✓
Not properly marked (no bar code on inside of case)	✓✓✓✓✓✓✓✓✓✓✓✓✓✓✓✓✓✓✓✓✓✓✓✓✓✓✓✓✓✓✓✓✓ ✓✓✓✓✓✓✓✓
Scratches found on case	✓✓✓✓✓✓✓✓✓✓✓✓
Other (factors not noted above)	✓✓✓✓

is happening. The goal of the analyst in collecting this data by category is to determine if there is a tendency for the data to be systematically associated with certain categories.

Figure 6S-3 shows a check sheet developed by Bob Feller to explore the reasons for rejecting component shipments received from a supplier (in this case, he is tracking problems with computer cases supplied by a vendor). Every time we reject a shipment, we examine it and determine the reason for the rejection (as is done in Figure 6S-3). The most frequent reason for rejecting a shipment is that it is not marked properly. With this information, we could work with the supplier to determine why this problem is occurring. More detail can be used in the check sheet classification scheme. For example, time of day could be added, if relevant. We could have added extra columns to represent time of day and collected the data to see if the time of day had any impact on rejects.

Pareto Analysis

Pareto analysis A technique for separating the critical few causes of problems from the trivial many.

Pareto analysis sets priorities for action based on the assumption that roughly 80 percent of problems typically result from 20 percent of the possible causes. Thus, not all possible causes of problems are equally important. Pareto analysis identifies the most critical (most frequent) causes to problems so that improvement efforts can be focused where the investment of time, effort, and money will yield the largest return.

Pareto analysis consists of a four-step procedure:

1. *Identify categories about which to collect information.* For example, specify categories that describe possible causes or types of defects. Such categories could come from a cause-and-effect analysis.
2. *Gather the data and calculate the frequency of observations in each category for an appropriate time period.* A check sheet could be used to guide data collection.
3. *Sort the categories in descending order based on their percentages.*
4. *Present the data graphically and identify the vital few categories that account for most of the variation.*

Pareto Analysis at Pear Computers

While working on the problems discussed previously, Bob Feller has become aware of problems involving the new Pear 6000 model. Performance analysis of the Pear 6000 has indicated that performance has not been up to the levels expected. Furthermore, insights have indicated that many of the computers are endlessly cycling during startup. After talking with assembly workers, Bob Feller, the operations manager in charge of the assembly line, has identified possible causes of these problems and gathered information about the frequency of problems. Over a four-week test period, 15,000 computers were assembled. Table 6S-3 shows the defects that were identified.

TABLE 6S-3 Frequency of Problems Occurring in Pear Computers Assemblies

Problems Type	Number of Occurrences	Percent	Rank
Chips inserted incorrectly	43	3.97	8
CPU chip/memory chips popping out during burn-in	117	10.79	4
Traces cut on motherboard (during assembly)	78	7.20	6
Loose power connections	150	13.84	3
Connections not made on motherboard	34	3.14	9
Dust getting into critical areas of the computer	90	8.30	5
Wrong components put on computer	51	4.71	7
Motherboard incorrectly seated	15	1.38	10
Motherboard damaged during installation	245	22.60	2
CPU damaged during assembly	261	24.08	1
	1,084	100.00	

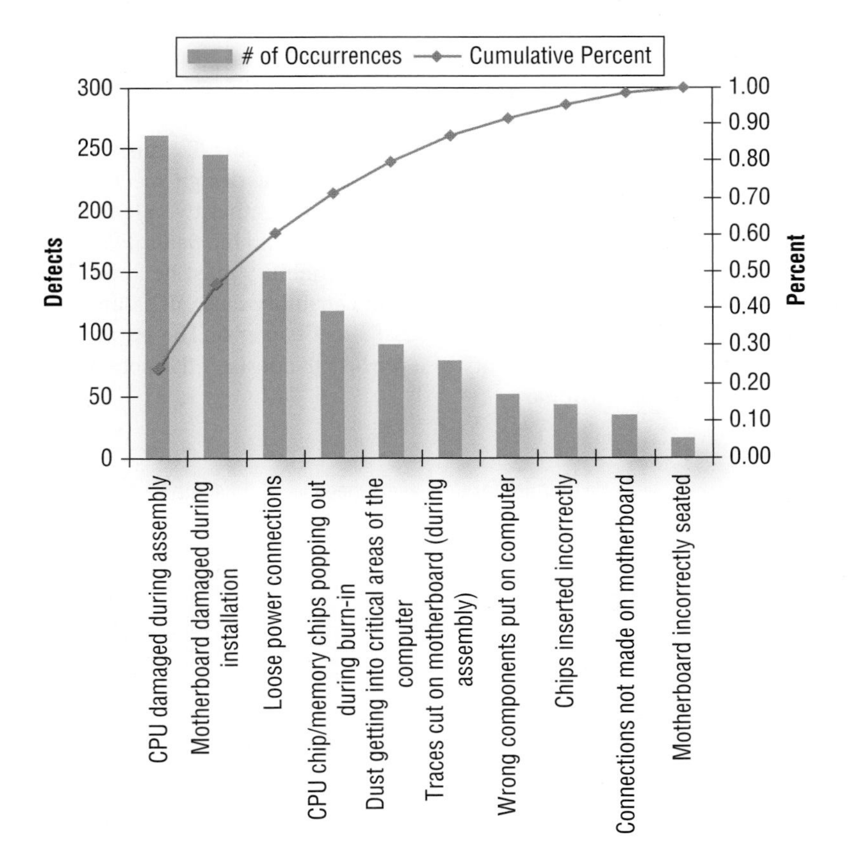

FIGURE 6S-4
Pareto Analysis for Pear Computers

Figure 6S-4 charts the data constructed using Pareto analysis. The chart shows that the last two causes together account for about 47 percent of all defects. This chart suggests that Bob should begin his improvement efforts in these two areas. Just by eliminating these two problem types, he could reduce defects from 1,084 per 15,000 assemblies to 578.

Scatter Diagram

scatter diagram A graphic illustration of the relationship between two variables.

A **scatter diagram** graphically illustrates data points that indicate the relationship between a pair of variables, such as how the number of defects per batch relates to changes in the speed of the production line, or how production time per unit relates to hours of training. This information can help to confirm or deny hypothetical causes of observed effects.

Pear Computers offers a medical equipment cart. This cart requires piping (which is cut internally) for the frame. Figure 6S-5 shows a scatter diagram that compares the speed of a conveyor line and the lengths of cut metal tubing. The diagram weakly suggests there is a positive relationship between the conveyor speed and the cut length; an increase in conveyor speed seems associated with longer pieces. The relationship does not seem strong, as indicated by the large space covered by the points. To determine the significance of the relationship between conveyor speed and cut length, further analysis would include a statistical test.

Process Flow Diagram

process flow diagram A graphic technique for mapping activities and their interrelationships in an operating process.

A **process flow diagram** uses symbols to represent the activities and interrelationships contained in an operating process. By diagramming a process, you can study its details and uncover potential causes of variance and opportunities for improvement. The basic symbols and procedures used in process flow diagramming are fully discussed in Chapter 3 (which looks at processes) and the Chapter 3 supplement (where the application of the tools is explored).

Process Capability Analysis: C_p and C_{pk}

process capability analysis A tool for assessing the ability of a process to consistently meet or exceed a product's design specifications.

One critical question that a manager like Bob Feller at Pear would like answered is whether a process is capable of consistently meeting or exceeding the design specifications set for a given product. The notion of process capability brings together two elements: the tolerances allowed by product or service design specifications, and the natural variability in the process. For a process to be "capable," limits on its variability must be less than the range defined by the product design tolerances. Process capability analysis is an essential part of the Six Sigma improvement approach discussed in Chapter 6. The purpose of **process capability analysis** is to assess the ability of a process to consistently meet or exceed a set of specifications set by the customer.

FIGURE 6S-5 Scatter Diagram for Conveyor Speed and Cut Length

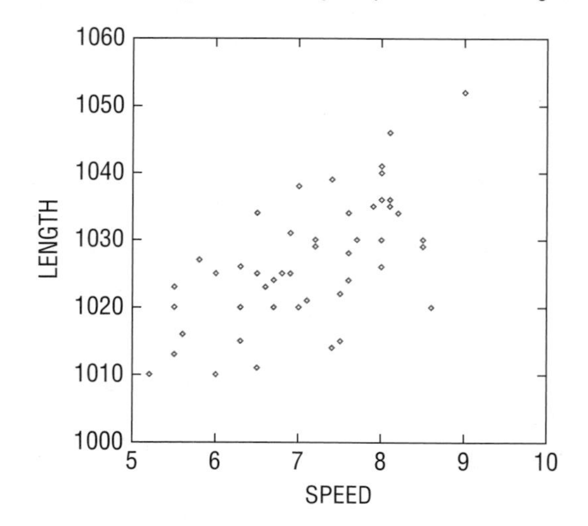

Consider the tubing for the medical equipment carts that Pear Computers sells. As Figure 6S-5 shows, it is not possible to cut each tube to *exactly* the same length. The design tolerances for tubing parts designate how much the lengths can vary yet still fit together properly in the cart assembly. Suppose the design specification for a tube length is 1030 millimeters ± 10 millimeters. This would allow tubes to be usable if they ranged from 1020 millimeters to 1040 millimeters. This range is referred to as the *specification width* (*S*). The specification width may be based on product functionality requirements (e.g., cereal boxes cannot be closed if there is too much cereal in them), or it might be based on economic considerations (e.g., customers don't want to pay for boxes of cereal with too little cereal in them).

Processes have natural variation. When cutting a metal tube, machine vibration, cutting tool wear, worker experience, and metal characteristics can cause variations in the length. *Process width* (*P*) denotes the actual range of outcomes generated by the production process itself. If the cutting process can maintain length from 1025 millimeters to 1035 millimeters, it is *capable* since $P \leq S$. Alternatively, if much of the process output is longer or shorter than the specification allows, then it is not capable. If the process is not capable, then either the process variability must be reduced through improvements, or the product design tolerances must be widened (if allowable) in order to avoid an unacceptable number of defective outcomes.

Mathematically, process capability is represented by the capability index, C_p (and its associated measure, C_{pk}). The C_p is essentially the ratio of the specification width to the process width. It is calculated as follows:

C_p A measure of process capability that compares the specification width with the process width—not adjusted for lack of process centering.

$$C_p = \frac{\text{Specification width}}{\text{Process width}} = \frac{S}{P}$$

where:

S = Upper specification limit − Lower specification limit

$P = 6\sigma$

σ = Standard deviation of process output

P is expressed as a function of σ because most process output distributions are open-ended; that is, there is some probability, albeit small, that any output value could be produced. By convention, managers in the past have chosen to set $P = 6\sigma$ because six standard deviations define a range that covers about 99.7 percent of the output for processes that vary according to a normal distribution. Thus, a C_p value less than one would indicate that more than 0.3 percent of produced units will not meet design specifications.

To illustrate the application of C_p, consider Figure 6S-6. Returning to Bob Feller and his problems at Pear Computers, we find him considering a proposal regarding different quality improvement options for the metal tube cutting process. Recall that the tube has a design specification of 1030 +/− 10 millimeters, so the specification width, *S,* equals 20 millimeters. Figure 6S-6 shows the existing tube cutting process in distribution A. The resulting C_p value of 0.67 indicates an incapable process (product would meet specifications only about 94 percent of the time). Distribution B, representing some incremental improvements in the process, shows that the process would be barely capable, with a C_p value of 1.0. Any slight disruption or movement of the process distribution would send it outside acceptable limits. Finally, distribution C, representing the anticipated results of a comprehensive process redesign, is capable because a C_p value of 1.67 indicates that it can deal with many unplanned but short-term variations in *P.*

In selecting between the three options, Bob would need to weigh the costs of making the proposed process improvements against the costs associated with having defective parts. If the costs of defective parts are low, or they can be corrected quickly, then he may decide that the second proposal (resulting in distribution B) is good enough. However, if the costs of defective parts are high, or it is difficult to quickly repair the problems, then he may opt for the higher performance offered by distribution C.

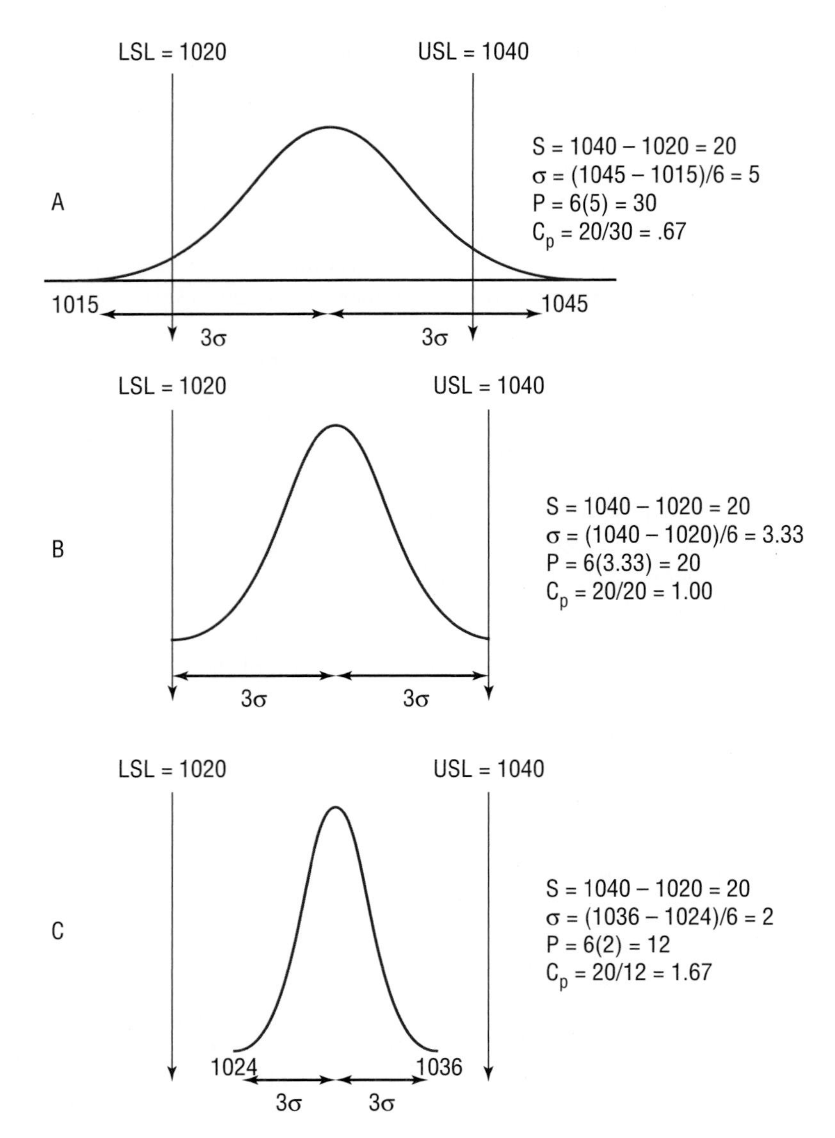

FIGURE 6S-6 Sample Distributions and their Associated C_p Measures

Distribution A identifies a process that is *incapable* of meeting the customer specifications.

Distribution B identifies a process that is *just capable.*

Distribution C identifies a process that is *capable.*

C_{pk}: Improving on the C_p Statistic

The C_p value effectively measures process capability *only* when a process is centered; that is, when the center of its output distribution is the same as the center of the product specification range. This is not the case for the distribution found in Figure 6S-7. In this figure the process width and specification width are the same as in distribution C from Figure 6S-6, so both distributions have the same C_p value. However, while distribution C showed a highly capable process, the distribution in Figure 6S-7 is not capable. It is clear that many of the units of output from this distribution will have values that are outside the specification range. To deal with noncentered process distributions, we must use an adjusted version of the C_p metric known as the C_{pk}.

C_{pk} A measure of process capability that compares the specification width with the process width—adjusted for lack of centering.

Mathematically, the C_p and C_{pk} can be written as follows:

(6s.1) $$C_p = S/P = (\text{USL} - \text{LSL})/6\sigma$$

(6s.2) $$K = \frac{|D - \overline{X}|}{S/2}$$

(6s.3) $$C_{pk} = (1 - K) * C_p$$

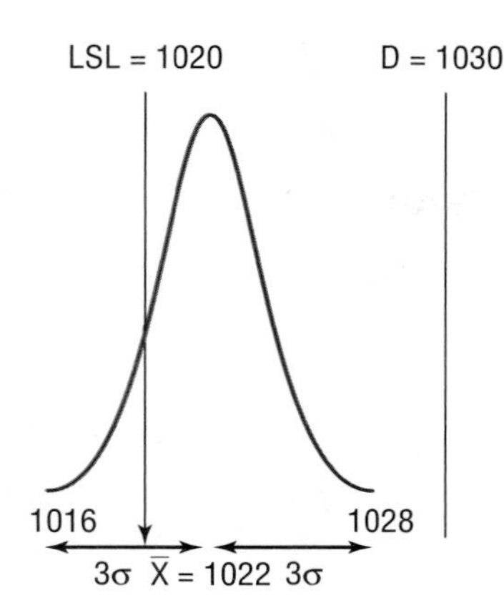

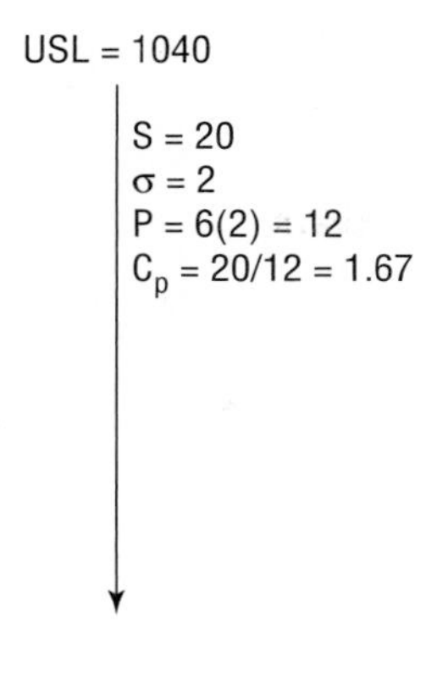

FIGURE 6S-7
Deceptive C_p Value: The Problem of Lack of Centering

where: USL = upper specification limit
LSL = lower specification limit
D = Center of the product specification range = (USL + LSL)/2
$\overline{X}$ = Mean of the process output distribution
K = Adjustment for differences between the specification center and the process mean

The C_{pk} and C_p are almost the same, except for the correction term, $(1 - K)$. The calculation of K involves a new parameter, D, which is the design center of the specification width S. D is the target value for performance data, while $\overline{X}$ is the process average. When D equals $\overline{X}$ then C_{pk} is identical to C_p.

There is another way of thinking about these two measures. C_p deals with the extent to which the process is *consistent,* while C_{pk} looks at the extent to which the process is *centered.* Consider the following example: Suppose you enjoy playing basketball and you want to become better at making shots. The hoop is 18 inches in diameter, while the basketball is 9.39 inches in diameter. If you become so good that your shots land within 5 inches of where you aim (that is, they land within a 10-inch range), then you will have become quite consistent—this is what is measured by C_p. However, as you practice, you might find that on average, your shots are mostly landing on the left side of the rim—they are not centered. That is what is measured by C_{pk}. Thus, you may have the consistency to make most of your shots, but if your aim is off center, you will still miss a lot of baskets. To prevent defects, you need to develop a process that is both consistent and centered.

Returning to the process for Pear Computers shown in Figure 6S-7, given that the process mean $\overline{X} = 1022$, we calculate the Cpk value as follows:

$$C_p = 1.67$$

$$D = (1020 + 1040)/2 = 1030$$

$$K = \text{abs}(1030 - 1022)/(20/2) = 0.8$$

$$C_{pk} = (1-0.8)\,(1.67) = 0.33$$

Since this value of C_{pk} is less than 1, it indicates an unreliable process that cannot reliably meet design specifications. Table 6S-4 shows the number of defective parts per million produced at different levels of C_{pk}.

TABLE 6S-4 *Cpk,* PPM, and Process Management

C_{pk}	PPM Defective	Process Implications
0.50	133,610	Process is incapable; 100% inspection may be needed
1.00	2,700	Process capable, normal sampling would be typical
1.33	64	
1.50	7	
2.00	0.00198	For values of 2 or more, no inspection may be needed; process is very stable.

Alternative Method for Computing C_{pk}

The C_{pk} formula presented in the preceding section emphasizes the need to adjust C_p for the difference between the process mean and the center of the product specification limits. C_p and C_{pk} can also be calculated using the following formula:

$$c_p = (\text{USL} - \text{LSL})/6\ \sigma$$

(6s.4)
$$C_{pk} = \min\ [(\text{USL} - \overline{X}) / 3 * \sigma, (\overline{X} - \text{LSL}) / 3 * \sigma\ ]$$

The alternative calculations for C_{pk} are frequently found in discussions of Six Sigma. Either is acceptable.

Process Control Charts

Once a process is determined to be capable, it should be monitored over time to ensure that it remains stable. Sometimes things can change such that the range of process output changes, or the mean (i.e., centering of the process) shifts. **Process control charts** are tools used to monitor process output to detect such changes. The terms *statistical process control (SPC)* and *process control charts* are often used synonymously.

process control chart A statistical tool used to monitor a process output to detect significant changes.

A control chart plots values for samples of process output collected over time. The plotted outputs are compared to a set of limits for the upper and lower boundaries of the process width (see Figure 6S-8), as defined by a confidence interval (usually 99 percent

FIGURE 6S-8
Process Control Limits

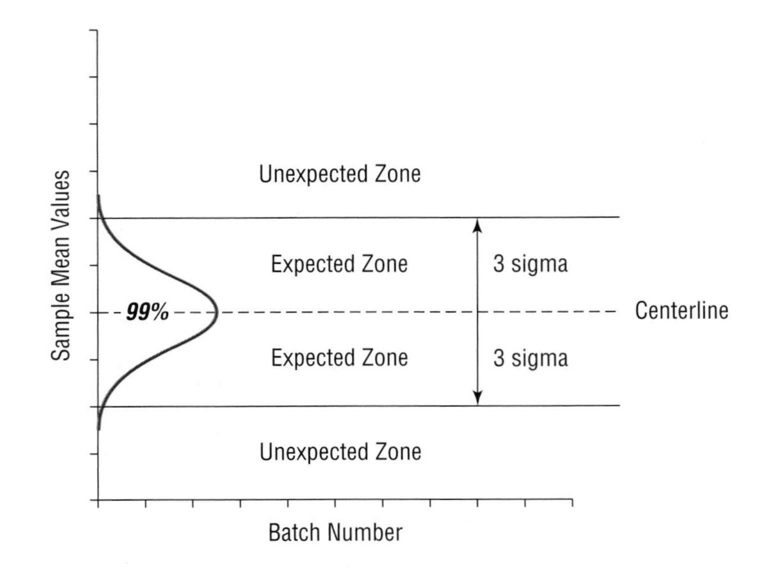

or 3σ). Any output sample value that lies between the upper and lower limits is within the expected normal random variation of the process. However, points that fall outside these limits are not likely to have occurred by chance, suggesting that the process may have changed. Thus, process control charts identify when a process has deviated from its normal operation (i.e., when it is "out of control"). Such a change prompts the process operator to stop, investigate, and correct the process. For example, over time a saw blade may wear, causing a change in the distribution of process output. A process control chart would indicate when a blade needs to be replaced. In services, one might use a control chart to track the order completion times for services (say, a drive-through window at McDonald's).

Process control charts are similar to process capability studies (C_p and C_{pk}) in that both tools evaluate the variability of processes. However, there are some important differences between these two tools. Process control charts are used to regularly monitor the output of a process to ensure that output lies within the *expected variation limits of the process.* Process control compares summary statistics (e.g., mean and range) for samples of output against predetermined process limits. Process capability studies, on the other hand, evaluate the extent to which process output lies within *design specification limits.* Process capability studies look at the variation in a large population of output, rather than the variation of sample means and ranges. It is important to understand that the use of process control charts only ensures that the process is operating normally; it does not ensure that product output meets design specifications. Evaluating consistency with design specifications is the the purpose of a process capability study.

There are five common types of control charts, listed in Table 6S-5. Each type of chart is used with a particular type of data. In the following sections, we will explain the $\bar{x}-R$ control chart, which deals with variable data, and the p control chart, which deals with attribute data. These are the most commonly used control charts.

Constructing an $\bar{x}-R$ Chart

$\bar{x}-R$ **chart** A technique used to monitor the mean and range values for samples of variable data describing a process output.

This control chart is really the combination of two charts. The first is the $\bar{x}$ chart, which compares an output sample mean $\bar{x}$ against the upper and lower control limits to determine whether a process has shifted to the point that it is no longer "in control." The R chart plots the value of the range for each output sample and compares this range to a control interval to determine whether the width of the process distribution is in control. Since the $\bar{x}$ chart plots only average values, we also need to use the R chart to evaluate the gap between the largest and smallest observations in each sample. The following section illustrates the procedure for constructing and using $\bar{x}-R$ charts.

TABLE 6S-5 Types of Control Charts and Data Covered[1]

Type of Data	Control Chart Used	Types of Data
Variables—Continuous/ Nondiscrete	$\bar{x}-R$	measurement (inches, mm) volume product weight power consumed
Attributes—Discrete	p (probability of defect)	number of defects
Attributes	p	fraction defective
Attributes	U	number of pin holes in pieces of plated sheet, differing in area (area/ volume is not fixed)
Attributes	C	number of pin holes in a specified area (area is fixed)

[1]Kaoru Ishikawa, *Guide to Quality Control,* Second Revised Edition (Tokyo: Asian Production Organization, 1982). Reprinted with permission.

Constructing and Using $\bar{x}-R$ Charts for Pear Computers

Bob Feller of Pear Computers wants to track hard disk seek times to make sure that the process of building the disks is under control. To make this assessment, he builds an $\bar{x}-R$ chart using the following steps:

1. *Collect data to calculate control limits.* To calculate control limits for both charts, data samples should come from a process known to be under control (not experiencing problems). An adequate amount of data (about 100 observations is typically considered adequate) is needed. Table 6S-6 shows data from 20 samples of 5 observations each. The sample size, n, should balance the cost of sampling against the added confidence that comes from larger samples. In this case the sample size is $n = 5$.
2. *For each sample, calculate the sample mean.* For each sample, calculate the sample mean using the following formula:

(6s.5)

$$\bar{x} = \frac{\sum_{i=1}^{n} x_i}{n}$$

For the first sample from Table 6S-6, the first sample mean is 12.3. Repeating this calculation for each sample gives the 20 sample means.

TABLE 6S-6 Hard Disk Seek Times (milliseconds)

Nominal Mean Seek Time = 12 ms Sample #	1	2	3	4	5	$\bar{x}$	R
1	12.2	12.3	12.4	11.8	12.7	12.3	0.9
2	12.3	12.1	11.8	12.2	12.3	12.1	0.5
3	12.4	12.7	12.3	12.5	12.3	12.4	0.4
4	12.5	12.3	12.3	12.1	12.1	12.3	0.4
5	12.1	12.4	11.9	12.0	12.3	12.1	0.5
6	12.6	11.8	12.2	11.9	11.9	12.1	0.8
7	11.8	12.1	12.5	12.8	12.5	12.3	1.0
8	12.5	12.8	12.0	12.5	11.9	12.3	0.9
9	12.1	12.3	12.0	11.9	12.1	12.1	0.4
10	11.2	12.3	11.8	11.7	11.9	11.8	1.1
11	11.7	12.2	12.2	11.7	12.1	12.0	0.5
12	12.4	12.2	12.1	12.1	12.1	12.2	0.3
13	11.7	12.1	11.9	11.8	11.9	11.9	0.4
14	11.8	12.2	12.2	12.1	12.2	12.1	0.4
15	11.9	12.3	11.8	11.9	12.1	12.0	0.5
16	12.3	12.4	13.0	12.3	12.2	12.4	0.8
17	11.9	12.6	12.6	12.9	12.1	12.4	0.9
18	11.9	12.0	12.7	12.7	11.9	12.2	0.8
19	11.4	11.6	12.4	11.9	11.8	11.8	1.0
20	11.6	11.8	12.4	12.3	11.2	11.9	1.2

3. *For each sample, find the range, R.* The range measures the difference between the largest and smallest values. For the first sample in Table 6S-6, R equals 12.7 minus 11.8 = 0.9.
4. *Calculate the overall "grand" mean, $\bar{\bar{x}}$.* Summing the sample means, $\bar{x}$, and dividing by the total number of samples gives the mean for the entire data set. From the data in Table 6S-6, the sample means sum to 242.7, so the overall mean equals 12.14 (242.7 / 20). This number defines the centerline for the control chart. We expect future sample mean values to vary normally around this centerline.
5. *Calculate the mean range* ($\bar{R}$). The R chart needs a centerline as well. To define this line, sum the R values from all of the samples and divide by the number of samples to arrive at the mean R, or $\bar{R}$ The range values for the data samples in Table 6S-6 sum to 13.7, so $\bar{R}$ is 0.69 (13.7/20). We expect future sample range values to vary normally around this centerline. Besides defining the centerline for the R chart, $\bar{R}$ also helps to estimate the upper and lower control limits, since the range gives a proxy measure of the standard deviation for samples ($\sigma/\sqrt{n}$).
6. *Compute control limits and construct the charts.* To calculate the values of the control limits, enter values for A_2, D_3, and D_4 found in Table 6S-7 into the equations below:

   Equations for the $\bar{x}$ and R control charts:

   $\bar{x}$ chart:

(6s.6) $$\text{Central line} = \bar{\bar{x}}$$

(6s.7) $$\text{Lower control line} = \bar{\bar{x}} - A_2\bar{R}$$

(6s.8) $$\text{Upper control line} = \bar{\bar{x}} + A_2\bar{R}$$

TABLE 6S-7 Values for Setting Control Limit Lines

n = number in each sample	A_2 = $\bar{x}$ limits for 99.7% (3 sigma)	D_4 = R upper limit	D_3 = R lower limit
2	1.88	3.27	0
3	1.02	2.58	0
4	0.73	2.28	0
5	0.58	2.12	0
6	0.48	2.00	0
7	0.42	1.92	0.08
8	0.37	1.86	0.14
9	0.34	1.82	0.18
10	0.31	1.78	0.22
11	0.29	1.74	0.26
12	0.27	1.72	0.28
13	0.25	1.69	0.31
14	0.24	1.67	0.33
15	0.22	1.65	0.35
16	0.21	1.64	0.36
17	0.20	1.62	0.38
18	0.19	1.60	0.39
19	0.19	1.61	0.40
20	0.18	1.59	0.41

R control chart:

$$\text{Central line} = \overline{R} \quad (6s.9)$$

$$\text{Lower control limit (LCL)} = D_3\overline{R} \quad (6s.10)$$

$$\text{Upper control limit (UCL)} = D_4\overline{R} \quad (6s.11)$$

Table 6S-8 gives the control chart parameters for the data in Table 6S-6. The control charts are shown in Figure 6S-9 on the next page. By convention, the centerline appears as a solid line and the control limits appear as broken or dashed lines.

7. *Plot new $\bar{x}$ and R values on the control charts.* With the centerline and control limits established, the control charts are ready to be used. After installing the new control charts on the hard disk production line, Bob Feller recorded the 12 sample means and ranges in Table 6S-9. When they were plotted (Figure 6S-9), Bob noticed that the sample mean for batch 10 was outside of the upper control limit. In practice, this would have triggered an immediate reaction—production would have been stopped with the goal of identifying the reasons for the problem. In flagging the out-of-bounds value for sample 10, Bob also realized something important: This value was a symptom; it indicated that something was wrong, but it did not tell Bob what was wrong. For Bob to uncover the underlying root causes, he and the team responsible for the hard disk production line would have to make use of tools such as the cause-and-effect diagram (previously discussed) in order to uncover possible root causes.

TABLE 6S-8 Control Limits Calculated for the Example Control Chart

Data Points	$\bar{x}$ Chart	*R* Chart
Central Line	12.14 ms	0.69
Lower Control Limit (LCL)	12.14 − 0.577*0.69 = 11.74	0
Upper Control Limit (UCL)	12.14 + 0.577*0.69 = 12.54	2.115*0.69 = 1.459

TABLE 6S-9 Sample Means and Ranges for Hard Disk Drives

Sample	Sample Mean ($\bar{x}$)	Sample Range (*R*)
1	11.82	0.30
2	11.90	0.92
3	12.10	0.86
4	11.95	1.23
5	12.32	1.40
6	12.20	1.30
7	12.50	0.56
8	11.86	0.89
9	12.30	1.10
10	12.60	1.32
11	12.49	1.01
12	12.30	0.42

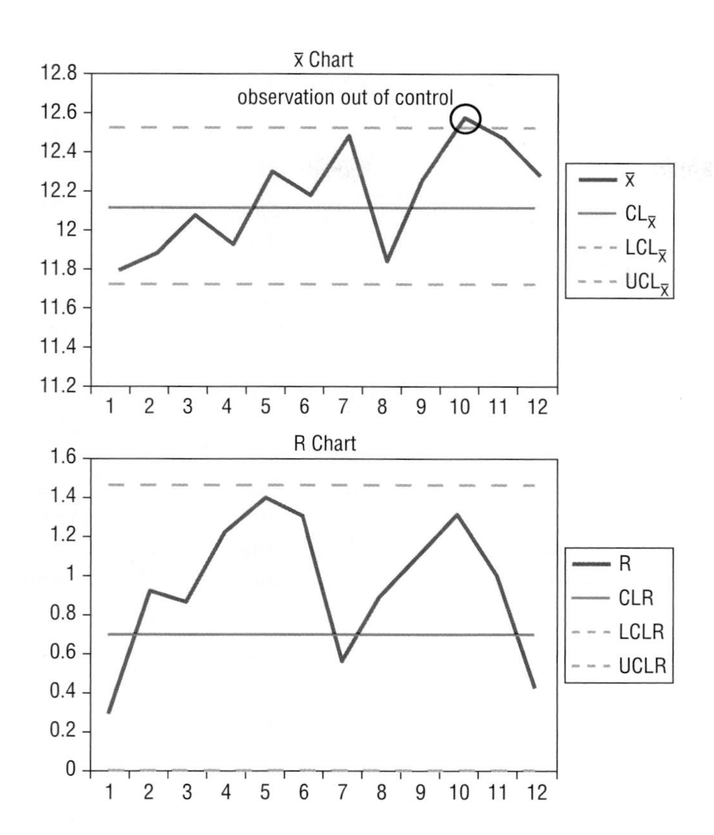

FIGURE 6S-9
$\bar{X}$ and R Chart for the Example Data

p Attribute Control Chart

$\bar{x}-R$ charts analyze samples of data for continuous variables. In some cases, the observed data are attributes. Such cases occur when we are dealing with pass/fail, live/die, or good/bad outcomes. In these cases, managers are usually interested in determining if the proportion of nonconforming product is stable and if the process generating such products is under control. To answer these questions, we use an **p attribute control chart**.

p attribute control chart A technique used to assess if the proportion of nonconforming product is stable. Applied to attribute data.

Consider the data presented in Table 6S-10. Bob Feller has been informed that the research team at Pear Computer has introduced the Mercury HD 6900, a new video graphics board for its top end computers. Since this product is new, Bob decides to construct a p attribute control chart. He is interested in whether the process can produce fewer than 5 percent defects, a minimum standard considered acceptable at Pear.

To carry out this analysis, Bob uses the following procedure:

1. *Collect and organize the data under normal operating conditions:* Table 6S-10 shows the data that were collected when the production line was running normally and presumably under control. Note that we are using constant sample sizes.
2. *Compute control limits and construct the chart:* To calculate the $\bar{p}$ and control lines, we use the following equations:

(6s.12) $$\bar{p} = (\text{Number of Defects/Total Parts Inspected})$$

(6s.13) $$\text{Upper control line} = \text{UCL} = \bar{p} + 3\sqrt{\bar{p}(1-\bar{p})/n}$$

(6s.14) $$\text{Lower control line} = \text{LCL} = \bar{p} - 3\sqrt{\bar{p}(1-\bar{p})/n}$$

where n = sample size. If the sample size varies from batch to batch, then an average sample size can be used.

Note that here, the 3 is the control limit. In this example, we have essentially specified the mean ($\bar{p}$) +/− 3σ. The value of 3 can be changed to increase or decrease this interval.

For the Mercury HD 6900 data:

$$\overline{p} = 67/2000 = 0.0335$$

$$\text{UCL} = 0.0335 + 3\sqrt{0.0335\ (1-0.0335)/100} = 0.0335 + 0.0540 = 0.0875$$

$$\text{LCL} = 0.0335 - 3\sqrt{0.0335\ (1-0.0335)/100} = 0.0335 - 0.0540 = \sim 0$$

(we cannot have a negative LCL)

3. *Create the control chart and begin monitoring results:* The parameters computed in the preceding step create a *p* chart with which Bob can monitor and control future production batches. Table 6S-11 shows data for 20 samples that Bob drew from production after creating the control chart, and Figure 6S-10 plots the number of defects from each sample. The chart shows that the process is under control (i.e., no samples are outside the control limits). However, the defects seem to exhibit *cycling.* That is, there seems to be a pattern of the defects going up and down in a consistent pattern. This is not the kind of random behavior that one would expect from a process. Bob should initiate an effort to uncover root factors contributing to this outcome (applying a technique such as cause-and-effect diagrams). Cycling indicates that something systematic (rather than random) is affecting the underlying processes.

TABLE 6S-10 Reject Rate Analysis for Mercury HD 6900

Batch	Sample Size	Defectives	Fraction Defective
1	100	5	.05
2	100	6	.08
3	100	2	.02
4	100	4	.04
5	100	6	.06
6	100	2	.02
7	100	3	.03
8	100	7	.07
9	100	1	.01
10	100	3	.03
11	100	2	.02
12	100	4	.04
13	100	4	.04
14	100	1	.01
15	100	1	.01
16	100	3	.03
17	100	2	.02
18	100	4	.04
19	100	5	.05
20	100	2	.02
Totals	2000	67	Average .0335

TABLE 6S-11 Sample Data Collected

Sample Number	Sample Size	Number Defectives
1	100	3
2	100	3
3	100	4
4	100	5
5	100	6
6	100	7
7	100	8
8	100	7
9	100	6
10	100	4
11	100	3
12	100	2
13	100	2
14	100	1
15	100	2
16	100	2
17	100	3
18	100	4
19	100	5
20	100	6

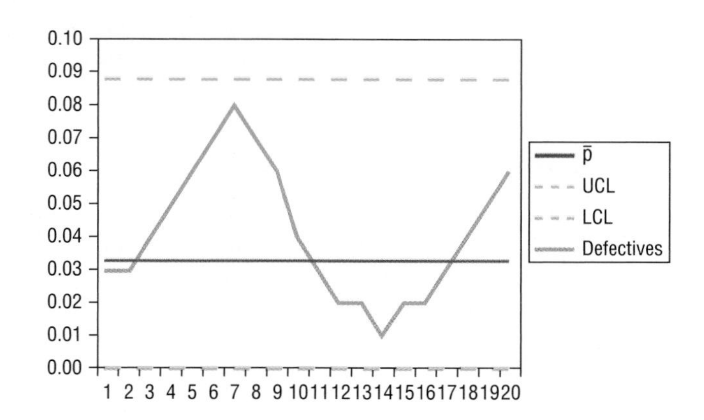

FIGURE 6S-10 Np Control Chart for the Mercury HD 6900 – Sample Evaluation

Interpreting Control Charts

A process is out of control whenever the sample means or range values appear outside the control lines. This signals managers or workers to stop the process to identify and correct the underlying problems that caused a change in the process. Control charts may also indicate a need for intervention in the process in four conditions: trends, runs, hugging, and periodicity.

Trends. A control chart indicates a trend when successive points seem to fall along a line moving either upward or downward. A trend in control chart data indicates some continuing change in the process. This signal may warrant intervention before the trend line crosses control limits.

Runs. Truly random variations should not form any pattern in the distribution of data around the central lines. A run of points above the central line followed by a run of points below indicate systematic changes in the process that require attention.

Hugging. Hugging occurs when various points appear so closely grouped around the central line that they seem to show no variation. Hugging usually indicates some external intervention in the process to limit or eliminate variation (thus masking the problems). This intervention might be the action of some employee who wants the process to look good. With hugging you cannot judge whether the process is really operating under control or if some outside force is taking unusual measures to produce acceptable results.

Periodicity. If the plotted points show the same pattern of change over equal intervals, it is called *periodicity.* It looks much like a uniform roller coaster of the same size ups and downs around the centerline. This process should be watched closely as something is causing a defined uniform drift to both sides of the centerline.

Taguchi Methods/Design of Experiments

One of the first quality researchers to recognize the importance of linking product design to process improvement was Professor Genichi Taguchi, director of the Japanese Academy of Quality and four-time recipient of the Deming Prize. He recognized that managers could eliminate the need for mass inspection by building quality into both the products and the processes at the design stage.

Taguchi methods Statistical methods for improving the design of a product and the processes used to produce it.

Taguchi developed a straightforward, well-integrated system (now called the **Taguchi methods**) for improving the design of both a product and the process used to produce it. The objective of this system is to identify easily controllable factors and their settings that can minimize variation in product features while keeping the mean values (or "response") of these features on target. Taguchi developed a methodology for designing experiments than can help managers identify the optimal settings of product specifications and process controls. One result of identifying these settings is that a product can be made robust with respect to changes in its operating and environmental conditions. Ultimately, this results in more stable, "process capable" designs. In other words, by focusing on both the product and the process and using well-developed designs, managers can develop products and processes that are properly centered and that have performance distributions with reduced spread.[2]

Other Quality Control Tools

This supplement has provided only a brief introduction to the wide range of quality control tools that are available to operations managers. In addition to the tools discussed, there are other tools that you might want to explore either in other courses, or by reading about them. Some other important tools include:

1. Acceptance sampling.
2. Operating characteristics curves.
3. Taguchi loss functions.
4. CTQ tree (critical to quality—a tool used to decompose broad customer requirements into more easily quantified requirements).
5. Quality storyboards (a visual method for displaying a quality control story that helps the personnel go from plan and problem definition to actions).

[2] For more information on this system, see N. Logothetis, *Managing for Total Quality* (Englewood Cliffs, NJ: Prentice Hall, 1992), Chapters 11–14.

SUPPLEMENT SUMMARY

1. Effective quality management is data-driven. Data can be quantitative variable data such as length and width or it can be attribute data (good/bad). The appropriate data analysis tool depends upon the type of data.
2. Tools such as the histogram, check sheet, and Pareto analysis are graphical techniques that help to identify and prioritize problems.
3. Cause-and-effect diagrams and scatter diagrams are used to explore relationships and understand underlying causes of problems.
4. Process capability indicates if a process is able to meet the customer's quality requirements. Process control is used to monitor if a process has changed. Taguchi's system for the design of experiments can be used to identify the settings of process factors that make a process capable.

KEY TERMS

attribute data 199
cause-and-effect diagram 202
check sheets 203
C_p 207
C_{pk} 208
histogram 200
p attribute control chart 215
Pareto analysis 204
process capability analysis 206
process control chart 210
process flow diagram 206
scatter diagram 206
Taguchi methods 218
variable data 199
$\overline{X}-R$ chart 211

SOLVED PROBLEMS

1. Given the information presented in Figure 6S-11 on the next page, calculate the process capability.

Solution:

$C_p = S/P = (20 - 10)/(16 - 10) = 10/6 = 1.667$
$K = \text{abs}\ [D - \overline{X}] / (S / 2) = \text{abs}\ [15 - 13] / 5 = 0.40$
$C_{pk} = (1 - K)\ C_p = (0.4)/1.667 = 1.00$

2. You have been given the following data for a production process that is responsible for filling bags of flour.

Production specifications:	$10.00 \pm .20$ pounds
Process standard deviation (σ):	0.05 pounds
Process distribution centered at:	10.10 pounds
Specification width (S):	$10.20 - 9.80 = .40$
Process width (P):	we need 99% or 3σ on each side or $10.10 - .15 = 9.55$
	$10.10 + .15 = 10.25$
	$10.25 - 9.55 = .30$

FIGURE 6S-11
Calculating C_{pk}

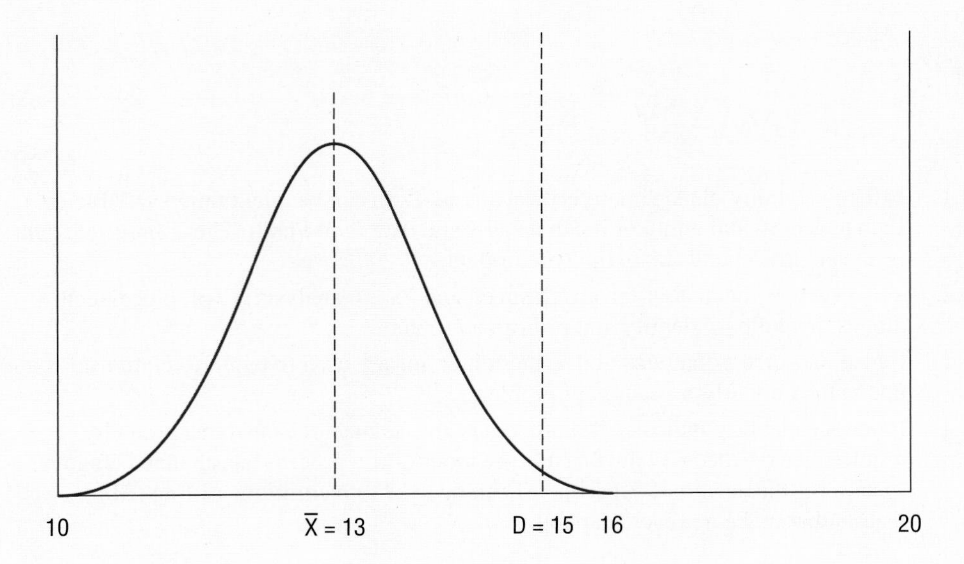

With this data, you have been asked by management to determine the answers to two questions:

- Is the process capable?
- If it is not, then what has to be done to bring the process back on control (i.e., make it capable again)?

Solution:

$C_p = S/P = .40/.30 = 1.333$

Based on the C_p value alone, the process is capable . . . but barely.

$K = |D - \overline{X}| / (S/2) = |10.00 - 10.00| / (.40/2) = .10/.20 = .5$

$C_{pk} = (1 - K) * C_p = .5 * 1.333 = .667$

This indicates that the process is not capable. The first step for management is to recenter the production process. That is, the center of the production process must be shifted from 10.10 to 10.00. This action, while improving things, is not enough. The next is to reduce the variance of the process. The two actions, when combined, should result in a process that is now capable.

3. You have been given the following data taken from 20 samples, where each sample consists of five observations. You have been asked to calculate the limits for the $\bar{x}-R$ charts.

Sample Number	Sample Mean ($\bar{x}$)	Range (R)
1	12.25	4.50
2	12.75	5.00
3	10.63	0.50
4	15.88	1.00
5	12.00	4.00
6	14.75	4.00
7	13.25	3.00
8	13.48	8.00
9	15.50	3.00
10	15.25	7.00

11	15.75	5.00
12	13.13	4.50
13	11.88	3.00
14	15.00	6.00
15	14.30	4.50
16	14.50	6.00
17	17.65	9.00
18	14.88	3.50
19	12.63	4.00
20	16.88	4.00
Means	14.15	4.45

Solution:

Calculating the control limits for the $\bar{x}$ chart:

Upper control limit $= \bar{x} + A_2 * \bar{R} = 14.15 + 0.58 * 4.45$ (0.58 taken from table where $n = 5$) $= 16.73$

Lower control limit $= \bar{x} - A_2 * \bar{R} = 14.15 - 0.58 * 4.45 = 11.57$

Note: as long as $\bar{x}$ remains between 11.57 and 16.73, this data is under control. Calculating the control limits for R charts:

Upper control limit $= D_4 * \bar{R}$ (where D_4 taken from table) $= 2.11 * 4.45 = 9.39$

Lower control limit $= D_2 * \bar{R} = 0 * 4.45 = 0.0$

Note: as long as R remains between 0 and 9.39, then the sample is under control.

4. Dick Ross, the plant manager for ABC Housing Tiles, was concerned about the on-time delivery performance of one of his departments. This department manufactures bathroom tiles specifically for large "big box" home improvement stores (such as Home Depot, Menards, Lowe's and Rona (Canada)). The buyers from these various customers were sending strong signals that they expected consistent on-time delivery (with future pressure to be on improving the level of on-time delivery).

Solution:

To help assess whether the department's on-line delivery was consistent, Dick collected two years' worth of information for calculating the parameters of the p control chart. The data are summarized as follows:

Month	Period	Sample	On-Time	p
January	1	250	230	0.921
February	2	250	229	0.916
March	3	250	229	0.918
April	4	250	228	0.915
May	5	250	228	0.912
June	6	250	230	0.923
July	7	250	226	0.905
August	8	250	223	0.892

September	9	250	228	0.913
October	10	250	226	0.905
November	11	250	227	0.908
December	12	250	228	0.912
January	13	250	228	0.912
February	14	250	233	0.932
March	15	250	230	0.921
April	16	250	227	0.911
May	17	250	229	0.918
June	18	250	224	0.896
July	19	250	226	0.905
August	20	250	230	0.923
September	21	250	227	0.910
October	22	250	227	0.908
November	23	250	229	0.916
December	24	250	228	0.914
Averages		250	227.92	0.913

Using this information, he calculated the overall $\overline{p} = 0.913$
He also calculated the UCL and LCL:

$$\text{LCL} = 0.913 - 3 \times \sqrt{\frac{0.913(1 - .913)}{250}} = 0.913 - 0.054 = 0.859$$

$$\text{UCL} = 0.913 + 3 \times \sqrt{\frac{0.913(1 - .913)}{250}} = 0.913 + 0.054 = 0.967$$

He also did a quick plot to see if these 24 months were really in stable (they are; you can do it yourself to check). With these control parameters, he next took the on-time delivery data for the current 12 months (see the following table):

Month	**Period**	**Sample**	**On-Time**	p
January	25	250	224	0.896
February	26	250	229	0.916
March	27	250	235	0.940
April	28	250	220	0.880
May	29	250	221	0.884
June	30	250	234	0.936
July	31	250	223	0.982
August	32	250	230	0.920
September	33	250	231	0.924
October	34	250	233	0.932
November	35	250	233	0.932
December	36	250	235	0.940

These data are plotted on the following control chart:

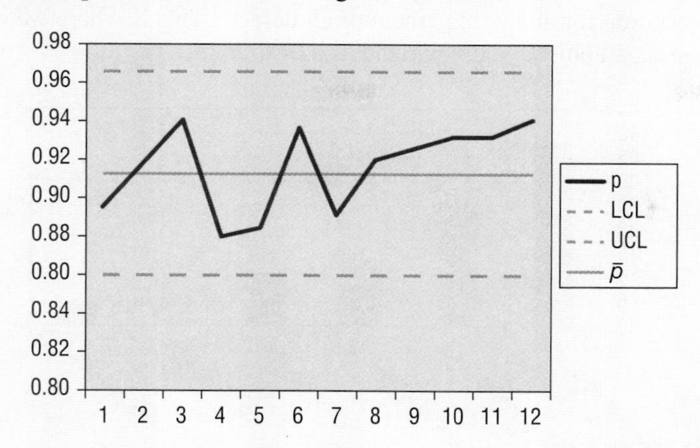

In reviewing these data, Dick noted that the process was under control. However, beginning in August there was an upward trend. Such a trend is problematic as it indicates that a systematic change is taking place. Dick took note of this so he could talk with the area supervisor. These data told Dick that his process delivers on time about 92 percent of the time. However, it did not tell him how late the late orders were. This would require further analysis.

5. You are responsible for the production of *Always Bright* bicycle flashers (the lights that we put on our bicycles to ensure that drivers see us). Recently, top management has noted that customers have been complaining about the quality of these products. Consequently, you decide to collect some data so that you can better understand the problem. You collect production data and rejects over a one-week period (see following table). A "v" indicates a defect. You have decided to organize the data by type of defect and by time of day (you have a feeling that some of the problems might be worse at certain times of the day).

Orders	7 a.m. - 9 a.m.	9 a.m. - 11 a.m.	11 a.m. - 1 p.m.	1 p.m. - 3 p.m.	3 p.m. - 5 p.m.	Sum
Insufficient plating	vvvvvvvv		v		vvvvvv	15
Inability to meet heat specs	vvvvvv	vvvvvvvvv	vvvvvvvvvv	vvvvvvvvv	vvvvvvvv	42
Scratched lens	vvvvvvvvv	vv	vvvv	vvv	vvvvvvvvvv	28
Failed leak test	vv	vv	v	vvv	vv	12
Glue on lens			vvv	vvv	v	7
Cracked body	v	vv		vv		5
	27	16	18	20	28	109

Solution:

a. Carry out a Pareto analysis on the types of defects irrespective of time of day. Here, we would first organize the data in terms of number of occurrences going from most frequent to least frequent.

Defect Type	Number	Percentage	Cumulative Percentage
Inability to meet heat specs	42	38.53	38.53
Scratched lens	28	25.69	64.22
Insufficient plating	15	13.72	77.98
Failed leak test	12	11.01	88.99
Glue on lens	7	6.42	95.41
Cracked body	5	4.59	100.00

What this analysis tells us is that were we to focus on the first three items, we would account for about 78 percent of all defects. This is where we should start. This can be graphically summarized as a histogram:

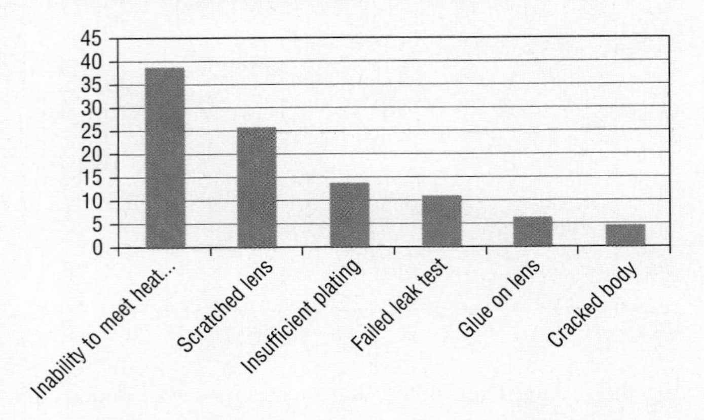

b. Does the time of the day have any impact?
Yes for insufficient plating and scratched lenses (both are more likely to occur before 9 a.m. or after 3 p.m.) and glue on lens (which is most likely to occur from 11 a.m. to 3 p.m.). These observations might be good candidates for CEDs.

PROBLEMS

1. The time students entered the classroom of OM 390, Introductory Operations Management, was recorded by the professor in the table below for five class meetings. Create and analyze a histogram of this data. Please note that a negative time means that the student arrived after the start of class.

Minutes Arrival Before Class (class starts at time 0)	Class 1	Class 2	Class 3	Class 4	Class 5
15	3	4	6	1	4
14	0	0	2	1	3
13	1	2	0	3	1
12	1	0	0	1	0
11	1	1	2	1	0
10	2	0	0	1	1
9	4	2	0	2	0
8	0	1	4	3	0
7	1	5	1	0	3
6	1	1	2	1	2
5	5	6	2	4	5
4	6	1	7	4	6
3	0	0	3	2	0
2	3	2	0	5	0
1	2	2	0	0	4

0	1	2	0	0	1
−1	0	0	0	0	1
−2	0	0	0	0	0
−3	0	0	0	1	0
−4	0	0	0	0	0
−5	0	1	0	0	0
−6	0	0	0	0	0
−7	0	0	0	0	0
−8	0	0	1	0	0
−9	0	0	0	1	0
−10	0	0	0	0	0

2. The injection-molded caps of disposable ballpoint pens must meet tight specifications to fit snugly on the pen. One specification that is tracked is the cap's weight, which should be 0.2 g. A sample of 100 pens is taken each day. Make a histogram of the data for one day's production, given the data in the table below.

Weights of Molded Caps in Grams									
0.225	0.243	0.239	0.231	0.228	0.215	0.161	0.161	0.207	0.177
0.190	0.186	0.203	0.230	0.228	0.180	0.230	0.194	0.243	0.177
0.210	0.210	0.185	0.225	0.204	0.152	0.245	0.231	0.152	0.150
0.161	0.171	0.208	0.208	0.170	0.204	0.250	0.178	0.205	0.236
0.159	0.229	0.173	0.228	0.184	0.223	0.240	0.193	0.170	0.241
0.161	0.193	0.165	0.154	0.192	0.214	0.189	0.208	0.227	0.169
0.163	0.196	0.181	0.197	0.248	0.238	0.205	0.207	0.244	0.208
0.200	0.207	0.225	0.162	0.229	0.151	0.224	0.169	0.220	0.182
0.214	0.233	0.194	0.181	0.208	0.249	0.220	0.197	0.204	0.247
0.216	0.160	0.210	0.222	0.157	0.174	0.173	0.240	0.203	0.247

3. The specifications for the diameter of an injection-molded part are 25 mm ± .5 mm. The actual average and standard deviation from 250 parts sampled is 25.01 and 0.1 mm, respectively. What are the C_p and C_{pk}?
4. The specification for the weight of a box of cereal is 16.2 oz ± .1 oz. The actual mean and standard deviation from a sample of 200 boxes is 16.1 oz and 0.05 oz, respectively. What are the C_p and C_{pk}?
5. A professor who teaches the Introduction to Management course has noticed that 20 percent of the students in her sections receive a grade lower than 2.0 on a 4.0 scale. This is the first management course that any of these students have taken. The text for the course is a standard survey text, which is used at many other colleges and universities. All of the students in the class are first semester junior, business students. The students work in teams to manage a simulated factory. As part of this they must use a computer spreadsheet to do simple income statements, balance sheets, and cash flow problems. Prepare a cause-and-effect diagram (CED) to analyze the problem: "Why do students in OM 301 receive low grades?" For the main branches of the CED, use the titles of student, books, faculty, and equipment.
6. Create a check sheet to organize the data in problem 1 above.
7. Create a check sheet to analyze the data in problem 2 above.
8. In an apparel factory, every time a sewing machine breaks, the symptom is recorded. In the past 30 days, all of the sewing machine breakdowns were recorded in the table below. Create a check sheet to organize and analyze this data.

Day	Machine Number	Reason for breakdown
	1	217 Dull knife
	1	145 Skip stitch
	1	193 Stuck pedal
	1	187 Skip stitch
	1	234 Breaking needles
	2	165 Air pressure low
	2	192 Breaking needles
	2	217 Thread breaks
	2	217 Skip stitch
	2	165 Skip stitch
	2	181 Breaking needles
	2	201 Dull knife
	2	172 Breaking needles
	2	195 Stuck pedal
	3	187 Skip stitch
	3	234 Breaking needles
	3	165 Air pressure low
	3	192 Breaking needles
	3	151 Skip stitch
	4	187 Skip stitch
	4	234 Breaking needles
	5	195 Stuck pedal
	5	187 Skip stitch
	6	165 Air pressure low

Day	Machine Number	Reason for breakdown
	6	192 Breaking needles
	6	165 Other
	6	192 Breaking needles
	6	217 Thread breaks
	6	217 Skip stitch
	7	165 Skip stitch
	7	195 Stuck pedal
	7	187 Skip stitch
	7	234 Breaking needles
	7	165 Air pressure low
	8	192 Other
	8	234 Breaking needles
	8	165 Air pressure low
	9	192 Breaking needles
	9	217 Thread breaks
	9	151 Other
	9	187 Skip stitch
	9	234 Breaking needles
	9	151 Breaking needles
	10	234 Skip stitch
	10	165 Air pressure low
	10	192 Breaking needles
	10	187 Skip stitch
	10	131 Other

9. The quality inspectors at Windows Inc. visually inspect each sheet of 4 ft × 8 ft glass when it is through with the annealing process. They record all of the defects onto a form. The defects that have been found this week are given in the table below. Use this data to create a location check sheet.

Corner	Body	Defect
Left upper		chipped corner
	center	indentation
Left upper		chipped corner
Right lower		scratch
	left of center	bump
Left upper		chipped corner
Left upper		chipped corner
Left lower		scratch

Corner	Body	Defect
	center	scratch
Left upper		chipped corner
Right upper	chipped corner	
Right lower		scratch
	right of center	indentation
Left upper		chipped corner
Left lower		scratch
Left upper		crack

10. Use the data in problem 8 to create a Pareto diagram.
11. Use the data in problem 9 to create a Pareto diagram.

12. For the following check sheet, assume that o indicates a surface scratch, x a blowhole, D a defective finish, * improper shape, and ? others. How would you go about analyzing the following check sheet?

	Worker	Mon	Mon	Tue	Tue	Wed	Wed	Thur	Thur	Fri	Fri
		AM	PM	AM	PM	AM	PM	AM	PM	AM	PM
Mach 1	1	oox*	ox	oxx	oooxxxo	oooooxxxo	ooxx	oooo	oxx	Oo	oDxx
Mach 2	2	oxx*	oooxx*	oooooxx	oooxx	oooooooxx*	ooooox*	ooooxx	ooox**	Ooxx*	ooooo

For this problem, analyze the data using Pareto analysis. Is stratification appropriate for this type of a problem? How would you stratify the data? That is, identify those variables that you think have an important effect on the observed results.

13. Construct an $\bar{x}$–R chart for the following data set.

Sub group No	6:00	10:00	14:00	18:00	22:00	$\bar{x}$	R
1	14.0	12.6	13.2	13.1	12.1	13.00	1.9
2	13.2	13.3	12.7	13.4	12.1	12.94	1.3
3	13.5	12.8	13.0	12.8	12.4	12.90	1.1
4	13.9	12.4	13.3	13.1	13.2	13.18	1.5
5	13.0	13.0	12.1	12.2	13.3	2.72	1.2
6	13.7	12.0	12.5	12.4	12.4	12.60	1.7
7	13.9	12.1	12.7	13.4	13.0	13.02	1.8
8	13.4	13.6	13.0	12.4	13.5	13.18	1.2
9	14.4	12.4	12.2	12.4	12.5	12.78	2.2
10	13.3	12.4	12.6	12.9	12.8	12.80	0.9
11	13.3	12.8	13.0	13.0	13.1	13.04	0.5
12	13.6	12.5	13.3	13.5	12.8	13.14	1.1
13	13.4	13.3	12.0	13.0	13.1	12.96	1.4
14	13.9	13.1	13.5	12.6	12.8	13.18	1.3
15	14.2	12.7	12.9	12.9	12.5	13.04	1.7
16	13.6	12.6	12.4	12.5	12.2	12.66	1.4
17	14.0	13.2	12.4	13.0	13.0	13.12	1.6
18	13.1	12.9	13.5	12.3	12.8	12.92	1.2
19	14.6	13.7	13.4	12.2	12.5	13.28	2.4
20	13.9	13.0	13.0	13.2	12.6	13.14	1.3
21	13.3	12.7	12.6	12.8	12.7	12.82	0.7
22	13.9	12.4	12.7	12.4	12.8	12.84	1.5
23	13.2	12.3	12.6	13.1	12.7	12.78	0.9
24	13.2	12.8	12.8	12.3	12.6	12.74	0.9
25	13.3	12.8	12.0	12.3	12.2	12.72	1.1
					Σ of $\overline{X}$	323.50	33.8
					Grand Mean ($\overline{\overline{X}}$)	12.94	1.35

14. You are responsible for managing a process that manufactures electronic capacitors. This process has experienced an unacceptable level of rejects. Consequently, you asked that the people responsible for the process that manufactures these products collect data regarding defects and the reason for these defects. This information has been collected in the following table (assume that the data is representative).

Observation	Reject Cause	Observation	Reject Cause	Observation	Reject Cause
1	Corrosion	2	Oxide defect	3	Contamination
4	Oxide defect	5	Oxide defect	6	Misc
7	Oxide defect	8	Contamination	9	Metallization
10	Oxide defect	11	Contamination	12	Contamination
13	Oxide defect	14	Contamination	15	Contamination
16	Contamination	17	Corrosion	18	Silicon defect
19	Misc	20	Contamination	21	Contamination
22	Contamination	23	Contamination	24	Contamination
25	Misc	26	Doping	27	Oxide defect
28	Oxide defect	29	Metallization	30	Contamination
31	Contamination	32	Oxide defect	33	Contamination

What conclusions can you draw from this data? What techniques would you use? How would you manage the data?

15. As a result of a Six Sigma exercise, the process described in the preceding question has been modified. Data has been again collected and summarized in the following table. To what extent have the improvements introduced by the process modification been successful in improving the process?

Failure Cause	Number Observed
Doping	0
Corrosion	2
Metallization	4
Misc	2
Oxide defect	1
Contamination	8
Silicon defect	2

16. Big Turkey Burger Farms (BTBF) produces a large turkey burger that is world famous. This burger is known not only for its quality, but also its size and consistency. They produce a turkey burger that on average is 12 ounces large (with a standard deviation of 0.10 ounces). Currently, BTBF has been approached by two major restaurant chains: Monarch Burgers and Audrey's.
    a. Monarch wants a turkey burger that is between 11.77 and 12.23 ounces.
        i. For this supplier, calculate the C_p.
        ii. Calculate the C_{pk} value.
        iii. How well would BTBF's products meet the demands of Monarch Burgers?
    b. Audrey's, in contrast, wants a turkey burger that is 11.95 ounces on average with a tolerance of 0.30 ounces.
        i. For this supplier, calculate the C_p.
        ii. Calculate the C_{pk} value.
        iii. How well would BTBF's products meet the demands of Audrey's?
    c. If BTBF had a choice of restaurant chains to serve (it can only pick one), which one should it select? Why?
17. In an article in *Quality Engineering,* a research article presented individual measurement data on sand compactibility, as follows:

46	43	41	42	40	44	40	41	40	42
41	41	43	43	40	38	45	42	41	43
42	43	39	44	44	45	43	42	41	46
41	39	40	40	42	44	42	40	43	

For this data, the author reported that the lower and upper specifications for sand compactibility are 38 and 46, respectively. Use this information to calculate the C_p and C_{pk} values.

18. Calculate the C_p and C_{pk} for a process characterized by the following data:
    Production specifications: 1.00 +/− 0.08 cm
    Process standard deviation: 0.005 cm
    Process distribution centered at 0.95 cm.
19. Suppose that you collect data for 15 samples of 30 units each, and find that on average, 2.5 percent of the products are defective. What are the UCL and LCL for this process?
20. Peerless Windows is a major manufacturer and installer of windows into new homes. Currently, management has found that it has experienced a large number (about 15% of all orders placed) of customer claims against Peerless. These customers, often builders, are claiming that they are receiving shipments of windows that are built to the wrong specifications. Correcting these errors has cost Peerless a great deal in terms of time, resources, and disrupted schedules. To determine if the order entry process is at fault, management has collected orders from the last two years. For each month, 100 orders were withdrawn and reviewed. The results are summarized in the table below. Experience with this product has resulted in the mean defect rate being 7.5 with the LCL being 0 and the UCL being 15. As an analyst, you have been asked to review the order entry process with the goal of assessing whether this process is causing the problems.

Month	Number of Orders Reviewed	Number of Orders with Errors
1	100	11
2	100	10
3	100	6
4	100	14
5	100	8
6	100	10
7	100	9
8	100	12
9	100	2
10	100	14
11	100	18
12	100	7
13	100	12
14	100	12
15	100	14
16	100	13
17	100	11
18	100	10
19	100	8
20	100	6
21	100	19
22	100	17
23	100	25
24	100	24

21. You are concerned about the quality of parts that you are receiving from your supplier. Consequently, you decide to take 25 batches of samples (where each sample

consists of 50 units) and to do 100% inspection on these samples. The results are summarized below.

Batch number	Defectives	Sample size (n=50)
1	5	50
2	6	50
3	5	50
4	6	50
5	3	50
6	3	50
7	6	50
8	5	50
9	3	50
10	5	50
11	5	50
12	7	50
13	8	50
14	10	50
15	10	50
16	6	50
17	5	50
18	4	50
19	5	50
20	5	50
21	6	50
22	5	50
23	6	50
24	3	50
25	4	50
Totals	136	1250

This forms the basis for your further analysis. Next, you collect information about 20 recent orders that you have received from your supplier in the last month. By the way, it is important to note that your supplier is aware that your firm is concerned about the quality of its parts. These are summarized below:

Sample Data – June		
Sample Number	**Sample size**	**Number of Defects**
1	50	3
2	50	2
3	50	3
4	50	4
5	50	1
6	50	2
7	50	4
8	50	3
9	50	1

10	50	1
11	50	2
12	50	2
13	50	3
14	50	1
15	50	3
16	50	3
17	50	4
18	50	5
19	50	5
20	50	5

a. Given the information in this problem, calculate the $\overline{p}$, UCL, and LCL from the baseline data. Use these parameters to construct an p control chart.
b. Plot the data from the June samples on the p chart derived in (a). What issues, if any, does this analysis reveal? What management actions would you recommend and why?
c. You receive a telephone call from your supplier informing you that they (the supplier) have significantly changed the production process for your orders at their facility. How would this affect the previous analysis (p control chart)?

CASE

The Tragedy of R.M.S. Titanic

On the evening of Sunday, April 14, 1912, R.M.S. Titanic, while on her maiden voyage, struck an iceberg about two days from New York City. Within three hours, she was gone (Monday, April 15, 1912). On this voyage, there were 2,201 passengers and crew members, of which 711 survived. Initially, it was thought that the survivors came primarily from the first class compartments (with some from the second class). After all, the passengers in first class had paid the most to travel on the Titanic's maiden voyage (in some cases paying in excess of $100,000 in today's dollars). These people were closest to the lifeboats. They represented some of the most important people in 1912 society—John Jacob Astor IV and his wife Madeleine Force Astor, industrialist Benjamin Guggenheim, Macy's owner Isidor Straus and his wife Ida, Denver millionaire Margaret "Molly" Brown (who became known later on as the "Unsinkable Molly Brown"), Sir Cosmo Duff Gordon and his wife Lucy, and silent film actress Dorothy Gibson. In contrast, the third class was located the furthest away from the lifeboats. Also, as a result of the U.S. immigration requirements, the gates that would have given the third class passengers access to the lifeboats were locked when Titanic left Southampton.

You have been asked to study the passenger list for Titanic and to determine if the premises stated in the previous paragraph really did occur. Specifically, consider the following:

1. Using the Excel Spreadsheet, Titanic.xlsx on the text website (www.mhhe.com/swink2e), analyze the data to determine what type of person would be most likely to survive. Least likely to survive?
2. Read about the Titanic and develop a CED to explain why so many people died on this ship.

CASE

The Bully Boy Bagging Line

Things were not going well at Bully Boy Products (BBP). BBP was a regional producer of organic fertilizer, potting soil, growing loam, and various gardening products for the discriminating gardener. It had been founded in 1976 when two agriculture students had decided that something had to be done to provide better supplies for gardeners. As one of the founders said, "Living better chemically may be great for chemicals but it has no place when it comes to gardening supplies."

Since their founding, BBP had grown by always remembering their core competencies—quality, variety, and innovative organic groups. As a result of this growth, the managers of BBP decided in 2011 to expand their production facilities, including installation of a new automated bagging line. This system was designed to provide quick product changeovers, something critical to BBP given their wide and ever-changing product line. The bagging system was brought on line at the start of 2012. After four weeks of debugging, the system was thought to be ready for full-scale production. Yet, as soon as it started up, problems became evident. These problems took a variety of forms: bagging seams were poorly made at the top; some bags were overfilled, while other bags were underfilled; and some bags experienced various forms of rips (the most common form of defect). Whenever a bagging problem occurred, the standard operating procedure was to stop, clear the problem, write up the issue, and then restart production. Top management had decided that the situation in the bagging line was no longer acceptable—something had to be done. To that end, they asked Lisa Vickery to determine whether the bagging problems were random or systematic in nature.

Lisa reviewed the production on the firm's large bag packaging line. There seemed to be much more variation in quality than she would normally expect. After calling for a summary of the data from production control, she received the BullyBoyBag.xlsx data (www.mhhe.com/swink2e) collected over the last 16 work weeks.

1. What does this data tell you?
2. Which tools did you use to determine what is happening? (Hint: consider looking at the impact of staffing and day of the week.)
3. What management actions are appropriate? What would you recommend to Lisa Vickery?

SELECTED READINGS & INTERNET SITES

American Society for Quality (ASQ)
www.asq.org

Six Sigma
www.isixsigma.com

AT&T. *Statistical Quality Control Handbook,* 11th ed. Charlotte, NC: Delmar Publishing, 1985.

Deming, W. E. *Out of Crisis.* Cambridge, MA: MIT Center for Advanced Engineering Study, 1986.

Garvin, D. A. *Managing Quality.* New York: Free Press, 1988.

Gitlow, H.; S. Gitlow; A. Oppenheim; and R. Oppenheim. *Tools and Methods for the Improvement of Quality.* Homewood, IL: Irwin, 1989.

Ishikawa, K. *Guide to Quality Control.* White Plains, NY: Quality Resources, 1982.

Ishikawa, K. *What Is Total Quality Control? The Japanese Way.* Englewood Cliffs, NJ: Prentice Hall, 1985.

Juran, J. M., and F. M. Gryna, Jr. *Quality Planning and Analysis.* New York: McGraw-Hill, 1980.

Nelson, L. S. "Technical Aids." *Journal of Quality Technology* 16, no. 4 (October 1984), pp. 238–39.

7 Managing Inventories

CHAPTER OUTLINE

LEARNING OBJECTIVES *After studying this chapter, you should be able to:*

- **LO7-1** Define the different types and roles of inventory in the supply chain.
- **LO7-2** Explain the financial impact of inventory on firm performance.
- **LO7-3** Explain and compute asset productivity and customer service–related measures of inventory performance.
- **LO7-4** Calculate inventory policy parameters to minimize total acquisition cost in continuous review, periodic review, and single period models.
- **LO7-5** Determine the cost of a company's service level policy.
- **LO7-6** Explain the advantages and disadvantages of different inventory location strategies.
- **LO7-7** Describe practical techniques for inventory planning and management.

Inventory Improvements at PolyOne Corp.

PolyOne Corp. is a global provider of specialized polymer materials, services, and solutions (such as metallic-look vinyl used in home appliances, the soft-touch plastic on the handle of your razor, and medical-grade polymers for tubing). A few years ago, it appeared that the company might have to file for bankruptcy. Instead, the company recently generated $218 million of free cash flow and reduced its net debt by $223 million. During this time its stock share price has risen 580%. How did the company increase cash flow in such a short time, and during one of the worst economic recessions in history? Largely through supply chain management improvements in two areas: better efficiencies in manufacturing facilities and much improved inventory management practices.

Inventory management improvements began when top managers formed a global inventory management team. The team's goal was to reduce inventory levels across businesses and regions while maintaining on-time delivery performance to customers. The effort included a two-day Kaizen (continuous improvement) event in which employees identified opportunities to reduce inventories throughout the supply chain. In doing so, they also focused on reducing cash-to-cash cycle times. Implemented ideas from the event included consolidating operations into a smaller number of facilities, identifying and focusing on the highest total cost items, working with key suppliers on delivery reliability, and adjusting inventory reorder points. In one year, inventory management actions reduced inventory levels by $152 million—freeing up much needed cash while nearly doubling inventory turns.

Source: Adapted from: Thomas Kedrowski, "Driving a Turnaround in Tumultuous Times," *Supply Chain Management Review* 14, no. 3 (May/June 2010), pp. 14–16,18–21.

Prepare

What are the different types and roles of inventory?

Organize

Types and Roles of Inventory
- Types of Inventory
- The Roles of Inventory

As the PolyOne story suggests, inventory management is critical to a firm's financial success. In recent years firms have been very focused on reducing inventories, both within their organizations and across their supply chains. From a supply chain perspective it does little good for one firm to reduce its inventory if the change requires another firm in the supply chain to increase its inventory holdings. Understanding the planning and management of inventory is critical to virtually all aspects of operations management.

TYPES AND ROLES OF INVENTORY

LO7-1 Define the different types and roles of inventory.

In general, **inventory** is a supply of items held by a firm to meet demand. The demand may come from an external customer, or it may come from internal operations, such as the need for parts on an assembly line to complete production or for paper to produce copies of a report. It is useful, however, to think more specifically about different types of inventory that a firm might hold.

inventory A supply of items held by a firm to meet demand.

Types of Inventory

raw materials and components parts Items that are bought from suppliers to use in the production of a product.

work in process inventory Inventory that is in the production process.

finished goods inventory Items that are ready for sale to customers.

MRO inventory Maintenance, repair, and operating supplies.

transit inventory Items being transported from one location to another.

In a manufacturing firm, considerable quantities of inventory may be held to support the manufacturing process itself. **Raw materials and components parts** are items that are bought from suppliers to use in the production of a product. Once these items enter the production process, they become classified as **work in process inventory**. Finally, when the manufacturing is completed and products are ready for sale to a customer, they become **finished goods inventory**. Retailers and wholesalers also hold finished goods inventory; in fact, their fundamental purpose is to have finished goods available for customer purchase.

There are other types of inventory that are held by all types of organizations. These items are generally referred to as **MRO inventory** or maintenance, repair, and operating supplies. MRO items include everything from office supplies and forms, to toilet paper and cleaning supplies, to tools and parts needed to repair machines. The need to manage MRO inventories makes the subject of inventory just as critical to service organizations as it is to manufacturing. Consider, for example, the vast quantity of paper used at your college to make copies of syllabi or exams in the courses you take. Also think of the supplies (such as food, water, blankets, and blood) held by the American Red Cross to support its ability to respond to disasters such as hurricanes or earthquakes.

It is also useful to consider one other category known as **transit inventory**. This consists of items that are in the process of being transported from one location to another, such as from a warehouse to a retail store. This category is particularly important because during the time that inventory is in transit, it cannot actually be used to meet an organization's needs!

Any given item may fall into several different categories, depending on who has it and for what purpose. For example, when copy paper comes off the production line at Mead Corporation, it becomes finished goods at Mead. When sold to your university it next becomes transit inventory as it is being transported to your university. Once it arrives, the same copy paper becomes part of your university's MRO inventory.

Some executives have gone so far as to suggest that holding any inventory at all is bad for an organization. Such a suggestion ignores the important roles that inventory plays in the supply chain. But it does emphasize the critical desire to minimize investments in inventory, as long as an organization can effectively meet its objectives.

The Roles of Inventory

There are several reasons that holding inventory is not necessarily bad. In fact, inventory has several important roles in a supply chain.

Balancing Supply and Demand

Holding inventory allows an organization to intermittently produce batches of products. Inventory is used to satisfy demand for a product during the periods when it is not being produced. This may be needed when a firm produces several products using the same equipment and has to switch between producing the items from time to time. In addition, inventory allows a firm to deal efficiently with seasonality of either supply or demand, as is the case with many agricultural products. For example, a potato farmer harvests potatoes only once each year and stores those potatoes in inventory, taking them out of storage when orders are received from customers.

Buffering Uncertainty in Demand or Supply

Managers rarely know with absolute certainty the amount of future demand for a product. Nor do they know for sure how long it will take to replenish inventory when more is needed. Consequently, companies frequently hold extra inventory to meet unexpected demand or delays in replenishment. Best Buy, for example, never knows how many units of a particular television model will be sold on a given day. There is also some uncertainty concerning exactly how long it will take to be resupplied with an item after an order is placed with the supplier. Therefore, Best Buy may carry more inventory than it actually expects to sell in any specific time period. Just about all organizations hold such extra inventory of at least some products to guard against these potential uncertainties in demand or supply. This extra inventory is frequently referred to as **buffer (or safety) stock**. Much of the attention in inventory management in recent years has focused specifically on reducing the quantity of safety stock needed.

buffer (or safety) stock Extra inventory held to guard against uncertainty in demand or supply.

Enabling Economies of Buying

For several reasons, supply managers may buy more inventory than they immediately need. Often, suppliers offer price discounts to encourage customers to purchase larger quantities at one time. Likewise, buying in large quantity may result in economies associated with transporting larger quantities at one time. Also related to the economics of buying are speculative holdings of inventory when supply managers buy ahead of need because they believe that prices may increase in the future or that that there may be supply disruptions or shortages.

Enabling Geographic Specialization

Supply locations and demand locations are rarely the same. For example, Kimberly-Clark makes paper towels in only a small number of production facilities, but those paper towels are demanded virtually everywhere. It would be infeasible to locate production facilities in every demand location. Instead, it holds inventory in distribution centers near major customer demands zones located around the world. Inventory frequently must be stored in such centers to quickly meet the demand of customers in different locales.

THE FINANCIAL IMPACT OF INVENTORY

Prepare
What is the financial impact of inventory?

Organize
The Financial Impact of Inventory
Balance Sheet Considerations
Costs Related to Inventory

Although most businesses recognize that inventory has many important roles, the primary reason that some executives think inventory is "bad" is that inventory has significant financial impact on an organization. From the standpoint of financial accounting, inventory represents both an asset on the balance sheet and a cost that impacts the profitability of any firm.

Balance Sheet Considerations

Just as a manufacturing plant, a warehouse, or a retail store represents money invested in assets, so too does inventory. In fact, for many firms, and particularly for wholesalers and retailers, inventory represents a very significant portion (30 percent or more) of the company's total assets. Naturally, the funds for this investment must come from either the owners of the firm or through some sort of debt. Because most owners/stockholders prefer to keep their investment and their debt as low as possible, they prefer to keep inventories low. Additionally, a reduction in inventory frees up cash that can then be invested in other assets or used to reduce debt or returned to shareholders.

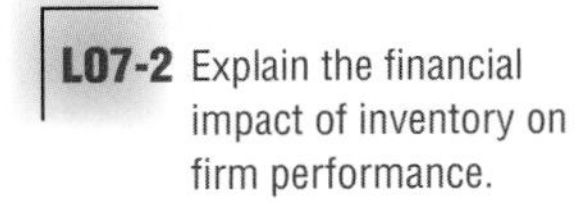
LO7-2 Explain the financial impact of inventory on firm performance.

Costs Related to Inventory

product cost The amount paid to suppliers for products that are purchased.

There are a number of costs and expenses a company incurs due to the fact that it holds inventory. First there is **product cost**. Product cost is simply the amount paid to suppliers for the products that are purchased.

Carrying Cost

carrying (or holding) cost Several expenses that are incurred due to the fact that inventory is held.

A very significant cost related to inventory is **carrying cost (or holding cost)**. Carrying cost actually encompasses a number of different expenses, which include the following:

- Opportunity cost, including the cost of capital.
- Cost of owning and maintaining storage space.
- Taxes.
- Insurance.
- Costs of obsolescence, loss and disposal.
- Costs of materials handling, tracking, and management.

Many companies drastically underestimate the opportunity costs associated with inventory and consider only the cost of capital in that category. In fact, there are other opportunity costs associated with inventory that are not immediately obvious. Holding large amounts of inventory frequently obscures other problems in an organization such as inefficient receiving processes or inefficient production process. In effect, the inventory leads to failure to identify potential improvements in the company, such as implementation of lean and just-in-time initiatives (as discussed in Chapter 8). Excess inventories also have societal costs. Disposal of unused inventories can contribute to air pollution, increased landfills, and hazardous wastes.

sustainability

Most companies state carrying cost as a percentage of the value of the inventory that is held. It is not unusual for a company to value its annual carrying cost as high as 25 to 30 percent of product value. Consider the following example:

EXAMPLE 7-1

If a firm holds, on average, $100 million of inventory and its carrying cost percentage is 25 percent, it incurs $25 million annually in carrying cost. Reducing that inventory to $80 million would result in annual carrying cost of $20 million, a savings of $5 million, which basically drops straight to the bottom line as increased profit.

Carrying cost is also frequently translated into a monetary amount per unit of a product per unit of time. For example, suppose Whirlpool Corporation determines that its inventory carrying cost is 30 percent of product value annually. A particular refrigerator that Whirlpool makes and holds as finished goods has a value (cost) of $1,000. Whirlpool may then consider that its annual inventory carrying cost on one unit of the refrigerator is $300 ($1,000 × .30) or $25 per month ($300 / 12).

Order and Setup Cost

order cost The expenses incurred in placing and receiving orders from suppliers.

setup cost Administrative expenses and the expenses of rearranging a work center to produce an item.

Order cost is a transaction cost associated with replenishing inventories. It includes the expenses incurred in placing and receiving orders from suppliers: order preparation, order transmittal, order receiving, and accounts payable processing.

Conceptually, **setup cost** is similar to, but slightly different from order cost. The difference lies in the fact that inventory is produced internally. In addition to administrative expenses, setup cost also includes the expenses of changing over or rearranging a work center to get it ready to produce an item. For example, Hershey may produce several different types of candy utilizing the same production equipment. After producing a batch of

Hershey production line making candy.

chocolate bars containing nuts, the equipment must be completely cleaned and sanitized, and prepared for production of a different type of candy. The costs related to the time required and other costs required to set up for production of a different item can be quite substantial.

Both order costs and setup costs are typically considered to be "fixed," irrespective of the size of the order or production batch. However, total annual order/setup cost varies with the number of orders (or setups) performed each year. If, for example, order cost is \$100 per order, placing ten orders per year results in \$1,000 annual order cost. Five orders per year results in \$500 annual order cost. Similarly, the cost of a setup may be fixed, but annual setup costs vary according to the number of times inventory is replenished.

Stockout Cost

Stockout (or shortage) cost is incurred when a company does not have inventory available to meet demand. A company may never know the actual amount of stockout cost for a product, because it does not know the actual amount of demand. In self-service retailing, for example, a consumer who can't locate an item may simply leave the store or buy a substitute item. Thus, one of the potential stockout costs is the cost of a lost sale (e.g., lost profit). In addition, the consumer who leaves the store may be so dissatisfied that she never returns to the store, and so the company loses future sales (and profits) as well. In cases where stockouts are known to exist, a company can incur significant back ordering and expediting costs. Stockouts also cause disruptions of materials flows in the supply chain. For example, if a production plant runs out of a component part needed to produce finished goods, the resulting cost of having to shut down the production line could run into the thousands or even hundreds of thousands of dollars.

stockout (or shortage) cost Cost incurred when inventory is not available to meet demand.

student activity

Using your library's electronic databases or a Web browser, find three articles that describe specific companies and their efforts to reduce inventory. Summarize the different reasons given for the desire to reduce inventory.

Prepare
How is inventory performance measured?

Organize
Measures of Inventory Performance
- Asset Productivity: Inventory Turnover and Days of Supply
- Service Level

MEASURES OF INVENTORY PERFORMANCE

There is a saying in business, "If you don't measure it, you can't manage it." Thus, measuring inventory performance is critical to provide information for effective management and control of inventory levels. There are two basic categories of inventory performance metrics. One category addresses issues of asset productivity, typically measured by *inventory turnover and days of supply.* The other addresses effectiveness in terms of meeting demand requirements, referred to as *service level.*

Asset Productivity: Inventory Turnover and Days of Supply

LO7-3 Explain and compute asset productivity and customer service-related measures of inventory performance.

Given the financial implications of inventory, companies are extremely concerned with the amount of inventory they hold. Two common measures of inventory asset productivity are inventory turnover and days of supply.

Inventory Turnover

inventory turnover The ratio between average inventory and the level of sales.

Inventory turnover measures the ratio between the average amount of inventory the company holds and its level of sales. There are, in fact, three different ways to measure inventory turnover, shown in the following three equations:

(7.1a) Inventory turnover = Cost of goods sold/Average inventory @ cost

(7.1b) Inventory turnover = Net sales/Average inventory @ selling price

(7.1c) Inventory turnover = Unit sales/Average inventory in units

Equation (7.1a), in cost values, is by far the most common method and is used almost universally. The second equation (7.1b) tends to be used primarily by retailers who use an accounting methodology known as the retail method of inventory valuation. The third equation (7.1c) may be a more accurate measure in situations where both the cost of an item and its selling price vary significantly during a year, such as gasoline.

EXAMPLE 7-2

As an example of calculating inventory turnover, suppose a firm has an annual cost of goods sold of $500 million and its average inventory level during the year is $80 million at cost. Then,

Inventory turnover = Cost of goods sold/Average inventory level = $500/80
= 6.25 turns.

This can also be expressed as turning its inventory every 58.4 days (365 days in a year divided by the turnover rate of 6.25 times).

Table 7-1 provides data concerning inventory levels, turnover rates, and inventory carrying cost at 10 well-known business firms. While the data assume an inventory carrying cost of 20 percent for all 10 companies, it illustrates the importance of inventory to all types of companies. In reality, the carrying cost differs among companies due to differences in capital cost and other expenses. Even service organizations such as Hyatt Hotels and Starwood, both well-known hotel and resort companies, carry significant inventories and can benefit from improved inventory management.

Companies that achieve high turnover rates enjoy several advantages, including:

- Increased sales volume due to having rapid flow of new or fresh items.
- Less risk of obsolescence or need to mark down or discount prices.

TABLE 7-1 Example Inventory Levels, Turnover, and Carrying Cost (Fiscal Year 2011, $ figures in millions)

Company	Cost of Goods	Beginning Inventory	Ending Inventory	Average Inventory	Inventory Carrying Cost*	Inventory Turnover
Boeing	$55,867.00	$24,317.00	$32,240.00	$28,278.50	$5,665.70	1.98
Deere	22,034.40	3,063.00	4,371.00	3,717.00	743.40	5.93
Ford	113,345.00	5,917.00	5,901.00	5,909.00	1,181.80	19.18
Hewlett-Packard	97,529.00	6,466.00	7,490.00	6,978.00	1,395.60	13.98
Kellogg	7,750.00	1,056.00	1,132.00	1,094.00	218.80	7.08
Procter & Gamble	40,768.00	7,379.00	6,384.00	6,881.50	1,376.30	5.92
Target	48,306.00	7,596.00	7,918.00	7,757.00	1,551.40	6.23
Wal-Mart	335,127.00	36,318.00	40,714.00	38,516.00	7,703.20	8.70
Hyatt Hotels	2,957.00	100.00	87.00	93.50	18.70	31.63
Starwood	4,994.00	802.00	812.00	807.00	161.40	6.19

*Inventory Carrying Cost calculation assumes a 20% annual rate for all calculations.

- Decreased expenses related to holding inventory.
- Lower asset investment and increased asset productivity.

However, there is a danger of having an inventory turn rate that is too high. These possible dangers include:

- Possible lowered sales volume due to running out of needed items (see the discussion of stockouts).
- Increased cost of goods sold due to inability to produce or purchase in quantity.
- Increased purchasing, ordering, and receiving time, effort, and cost.

Firms may differ in their inventory performance because of different circumstances in their supply and demand chains, or because they have different strategies. Food retailers, for example, in general have higher turnover rates than appliance retailers due to the fast-moving nature of their products. Within the food retailing industry, however, turnover ratios differ between firms based on their financial strategy, on their marketing strategy related to meeting customer demand, and on their operational effectiveness.

Days of Supply

Inventory turnover is often considered a backward-looking measure because it looks at the company's performance in managing inventory during a previous time period, such as the previous year. Another common way that companies think about their inventory investment is in terms of days of supply, which is considered a forward-looking measure. **Days of supply** (also called *days of sales* or *days of inventory*) is the number of days of business operations that can be supported with the inventory on-hand, given that no more inventory is bought or produced.

days of supply The number of days of business operations that can be supported with the inventory on-hand.

Days of supply is most meaningful when it is expressed in terms of future expected demand, or daily rate of usage. The daily sales or usage rate may come from forecasts or may be computed from the most recent actual sales/usage experience. For example, inventory of finished automobiles is frequently stated as the number of days of consumer demand that could be satisfied from the existing inventory, based on the most recent daily sales rates. The general expression for computing days of supply is

(7.2) Days of supply = Current inventory/Expected rate of daily demand

EXAMPLE 7-3

Suppose there are currently 2,000,000 finished automobiles sitting in dealer or manufacturing facility lots. If expected sales of automobiles are 25,000 units per day, then days of supply = 80 days (2,000,000/25,000).

Of course, the calculated 80 days of supply for automobiles presumes that the existing inventory consists of automobiles that consumers actually want to buy. If consumers want to buy hybrid electric cars and the existing inventory consists primarily of cars with V-8 gasoline engines, the 80 days of supply would be extremely misleading. In inventory management, it is frequently more meaningful to measure performance for specific items rather than for overall inventory holdings.

The preceding calculation for days of supply can also be calculated in terms of costs or selling prices, rather than units.

student activity

Choose three companies who are competitors in an industry of interest to you. Find their most recent annual reports. Compute and compare the inventory turnover ratios. Explain the financial and marketing implications of the differences in inventory turnover rates for each of the three companies.

Service Level

service level A measure of how well the objective of meeting customer demand is met.

stockout An event that occurs when no inventory is available.

Since inventory exists in order to meet demand, companies need **service level** metrics to track how well this objective is accomplished. There are several different ways to measure service level. Many of these will be discussed more specifically in Chapter 9, "Customer Service Management." At this point, it is sufficient to think of service level in terms of a **stockout**, the situation that exists when there is demand for an item and no inventory is available. When companies experience stockouts of raw materials or component parts, production processes must be halted, with considerable potential cost implications. Stockouts of finished goods result in lost sales and potential customer dissatisfaction. Stockouts of MRO items may also have significant consequences. Consider, for example, what would happen if your university had no copy paper so your professor couldn't give you an exam on the scheduled date!

It is common to measure stockouts in terms of the number or percentage of inventory items for which there is no inventory on hand. For example, studies of retail stores across many industries consistently find that stockouts average about 8 percent of the items a store commonly offers for sale, at all times. Even more surprising is that for items that are specifically being advertised and promoted by a store, stockouts average about 16 percent![1] In another study, catalog retailers were found to have stockout levels that averaged more than 15 percent.[2] The Get Real box "How Amazon Aims to Keep You Clicking" describes the efforts at Amazon to overcome this problem, which has plagued the catalog retail industry.

student activity

The next time you go shopping prepare a list of the exact items you want to buy (brand, size, etc.). Visit a store that, in your experience, normally carries these items. Keep a record of how many of the items on your list are out of stock. Does your experience match with the data cited above concerning retailer stockouts?

[1] Tom Gruen and Daniel Corsten, "Improve Out-of-Stock Methods at the Shelf," *Chain Store Age* (July 2006), p. 35.

[2] John C. Taylor and Stanley E. Fawcett, "Catalog Retailer In-Stock Performance: An Assessment of Customer Service Levels," *Journal of Business Logistics* 25, no. 2 (2004), pp. 119–35.

GET REAL

How Amazon Aims to Keep You Clicking

Amazon has gotten many ideas from trying to address customer complaints. One gripe from years past was that popular items were at times out of stock. The last thing Amazon wants is for a frustrated shopper to then head to another site or the mall.

During the past two years, Amazon developed new programs to keep hot items in stock and ready for quick delivery. One initiative is something Amazon calls the Milk-Run. Instead of waiting for suppliers to deliver to Amazon's warehouses, Amazon sends its own trucks out to pick up top-selling goods. That reduces the number of late or incomplete orders the company receives from suppliers. The program is "very forward-thinking," says Simon Fleming-Wood, vice president for marketing at Pure Digital Technologies, whose Flip camcorder has been included in the weekly Milk-Runs. Jeff Bezos, Amazon's CEO, says, "Our vision is to have every item made anywhere in the world in-stock and available for delivery."

Amazon's concern for in-stock performance extends beyond its own merchandise to include the outside merchants who sell through its Web site. The company has long let customers rate their experience with merchants and has instituted many internal safeguards to track the behavior of merchants. Amazon also uses metrics such as how often customers complain about a merchant and how often a merchant cancels an order because the product isn't in stock. Partners who have this problem with more than 1 percent of their orders can get booted off the site.

Source: Adapted from Heather Green, "How Amazon Keeps You Clicking," *BusinessWeek,* March 2, 2009, pp. 37–40.

Keeping merchandise in-stock in this warehouse is a passion of Jeff Bezos, Amazon's CEO.

INVENTORY MANAGEMENT SYSTEMS

Prepare

What different systems are used to manage inventory?

Organize

Inventory Management Systems

In this section we explain how to use inventory cost and service level parameters to determine how much inventory is required to support an operational process. The ultimate objective of any inventory management system is to minimize all inventory costs while meeting the organization's targeted service (product availability) objectives.

We first must distinguish between two different types of inventory management systems. **Independent demand inventory systems** are used when the demand for an item is beyond the control of the organization. This is typically the case for customer demands of end-items and repair parts. **Dependent demand inventory systems** are used when the demand for an item is derived from the demand for some other item.

independent demand inventory systems Inventory management systems used when the demand for an item is beyond the control of the organization.

dependent demand inventory systems Management systems used when the demand for an item is derived from the demand for some other item.

To understand the distinction, think of a John Deere assembly plant. The demand for tractors and other agricultural equipment is somewhat unpredictable and outside the manufacturer's control, despite their best efforts to accurately forecast how many new pieces of equipment will be wanted by their customers. It is also extremely difficult to forecast how many tractors may break down while in use and therefore need to be repaired. Thus, managing inventory of finished goods and for repair parts is best accomplished with independent demand systems. However, when John Deere has established a production schedule for tractors (typically based on a forecast), then it knows how many of each component

continuous review model Inventory is constantly monitored to decide when a replenishment order needs to be placed.

periodic review model The management system is built around checking and ordering inventory at some regular interval.

it will need to fulfill that schedule. The inventory of these components is managed with dependent demand systems. Chapter 14 discusses dependent demand inventory systems. Here, we explain independent demand inventory planning.

The major independent demand inventory systems can be broken into two types: the **continuous review model**, where inventory is constantly monitored to decide when a replenishment order needs to be placed, and the **periodic review model**, where the management system reviews and orders inventory at some regular interval.

THE CONTINUOUS REVIEW MODEL

Two basic questions must be answered in planning inventories. First, how much should be ordered when an order is placed? For example, a John Deere dealer has to decide how many tractors to order from Deere to have them available for its customers. Second, when should an order be placed? The Deere dealer also has to decide in advance exactly when or at what level of remaining inventory it needs to order more tractors to replenish its inventory. Again, the objective is to minimize inventory-related costs.

Prepare

What are the elements of inventory policy? How do managers calculate inventory policy parameters using a continuous review model? How do they determine the cost of a company's service level policy?

Organize

The Continuous Review Model
- The Case of No Variability
- How Much to Order: Economic Order Quantity
- When to Order: The Reorder Point
- EOQ Extensions
- Enter Variability and Uncertainty
- Determining the Standard Deviation of Demand During Lead Time
- Determining a Service Level Policy
- Revisiting ROP and Average Inventory

To answer these questions we must first have a demand forecast. Chapter 12 explains how to develop demand forecasts. With a forecast of demand in hand, inventory planning then depends on whether a company has the capability to continuously monitor its inventory levels or whether it relies on a periodic review of its inventory. Because most (but not all) major organizations today maintain a computerized perpetual record of inventory on-hand, we will first look at the continuous review model, and how this system answers the "how much" and "when" questions.

The Case of No Variability

It is easiest to understand the basics of inventory management by first making a very naïve and unrealistic assumption. In this first case we will assume that both the demand for an item and the supplier's lead time to replenish it are constant and known, with no variation. Later we will make adjustments to deal with variability.

For the next several pages, assume that you own a retail store that sells computer games. One particular game is Trexoid, a very popular fantasy game for which you pay your supplier $20.00 per copy, regardless of how many copies you buy. Each day you sell exactly 10 copies of Trexoid and the store is open 300 days per year; thus, annual demand is forecasted at 3,000 copies. In addition, you have done a detailed analysis of your costs and have determined that it costs $50.00 each time an order is placed. You also have determined that your inventory carrying cost is 20 percent of the item purchase cost annually. Suppose, finally, that when you place an order, it always takes exactly nine days for your supplier to get the shipment to you. How should you determine how much to order and when to order in a way that minimizes the total annual inventory cost?

LO7-4 Calculate inventory policy parameters to minimize total acquisition cost.

How Much to Order: Economic Order Quantity

total acquisition cost (TAC) The sum of all relevant inventory costs incurred each year.

The quantity you order will impact your **total acquisition cost (TAC)**, the sum of all relevant inventory costs incurred each year. In this case the cost to purchase or produce the product is the same regardless of the quantity you order, so product cost isn't relevant to the decision. Stockout cost isn't relevant either because we have assumed no variability in the system. Because we know with certainty both the demand and lead time, there should never be any stockouts. TAC in this case is simply the sum of your annual inventory carrying cost and annual ordering cost. Example 7-4 shows the impact of ordering 500 units each time.

EXAMPLE 7-4 Calculating Total Acquisition Cost

Suppose that you arbitrarily decide to order 500 copies of Trexoid every time you place an order. This order quantity requires that you place six orders during the year to acquire the needed 3,000 units.

$$N = D/Q = 3{,}000/500 = 6 \quad (7.3)$$

where

N = number of orders placed each year
D = annual demand
Q = order quantity

Figure 7-1 below illustrates the pattern of your ordering and inventory levels and is referred to as a **saw-tooth diagram**. Notice that the average inventory you will hold is 250 units. When no safety stock is held, the average inventory held across the year is one-half of the order quantity, or

saw-tooth diagram An illustration of the pattern of ordering and inventory levels.

$$\bar{I} = Q/2 \quad (7.4)$$

where

$\bar{I}$ = inventory

We can now determine the TAC of your decision by determining the sum of the annual order cost and annual inventory carrying cost. The annual order cost is the number of orders per year (6) times the order cost ($50.00), or $300. The annual inventory carrying cost is the average inventory in units (250) times the unit value ($20.00) times the inventory carrying cost percentage (20%), or $1,000. Thus, the TAC of your inventory management policy is $1,300.

$$\begin{aligned} \text{TAC} &= \text{annual ordering cost} + \text{annual carrying cost} \\ &= C_o\,(D/Q) + UC_i\,Q/2 \quad (7.5) \\ &= \$50\,(3{,}000/500) + \$20\,(20\%)\,500/2 \\ &= \$1{,}300 \end{aligned}$$

where

C_o = order cost
U = unit cost
C_i = inventory carrying cost percentage per year

What happens to TAC if you decide on a different policy? After all, ordering 500 was purely an arbitrary decision. Example 7-5 (next page) illustrates another policy.

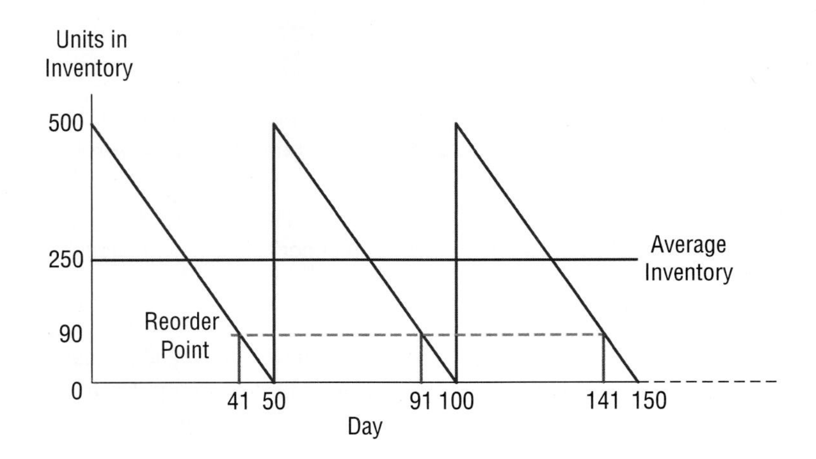

FIGURE 7-1
Trexoid Inventory Saw-Tooth Diagram: Order Quantity 500

EXAMPLE 7-5

Suppose you decide to order 200 units each time. This pattern, illustrated in Figure 7-2, results in placing 15 orders per year and an average inventory of 100 units. Annual order cost will be $750 (15 orders times $50 order cost). Annual inventory carrying cost will be $400 (100 units average inventory times $20 times 20%). Thus, the TAC of this policy is $1,150.

FIGURE 7-2 Trexoid Inventory Saw-Tooth Diagram: Order Quantity 200

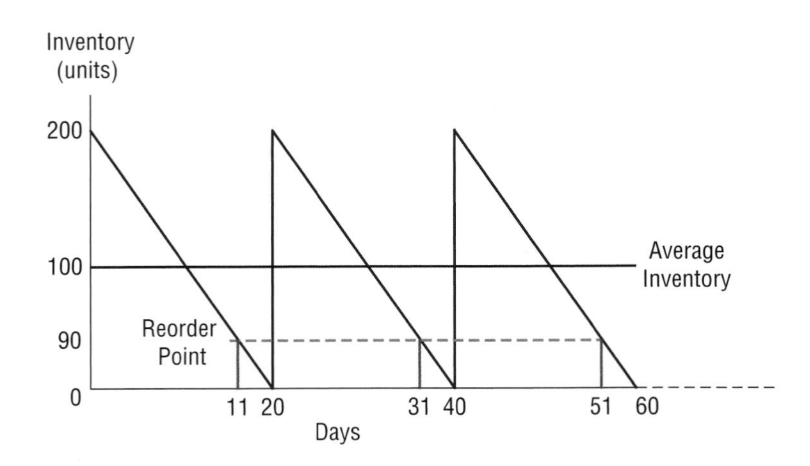

Ordering 200 units each time instead of 500 units each time saves you an expected $150 each year. How can you find the lowest cost ordering policy? Should you test every possible order quantity to determine the lowest TAC? Fortunately, that is not necessary. A formula exists that will solve the problem. This formula determines the order quantity that will yield the lowest TAC when the relevant costs are only annual inventory carrying cost and annual ordering cost. This order quantity is commonly known as the **economic order quantity (EOQ)**:

economic order quantity (EOQ) The order quantity that minimizes the sum of annual inventory carrying cost and annual ordering cost.

(7.6)
$$\text{EOQ} = \sqrt{\frac{2DC_o}{UC_i}}$$

EXAMPLE 7-6 Calculating the EOQ

Using the preceding formula, the EOQ for Trexoid is

$$\text{EOQ} = \sqrt{\frac{2 \times 3{,}000 \textit{ units/year} \times \$50/\textit{order}}{\$20/\textit{unit} \times .2}} = 273.86 \text{ units, or when rounded, } 274 \text{ units}$$

Given this order quantity, you will need to place 3,000/274 = 10.948 orders each year, rounded to 11 orders, and the average inventory of Trexoid will be 137 units. Thus,

TAC = order cost + inventory carrying cost = 11($50) + 137($20)(.2) = $550 + $548 = $1,098, which is less than either of the two previous alternatives.

You may have noticed in Example 7-6 that annual order cost and annual inventory cost using the EOQ are almost identical ($550 vs. $548). In fact, except for rounding, the two costs are equal. Essentially, the EOQ formula trades off the annual ordering cost and the

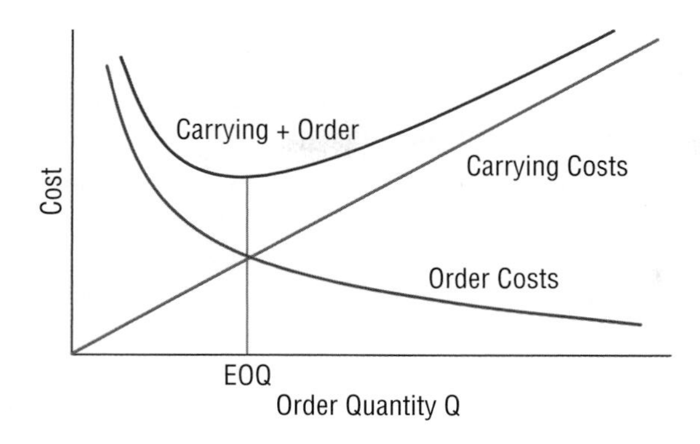

FIGURE 7-3
EOQ Cost Trade-Offs

annual inventory carrying cost and finds the quantity that yields the lowest combination. This is the order quantity at which annual inventory ordering cost and annual inventory carrying cost are exactly equal to each other. Figure 7-3 depicts the relationship between the two costs and the total cost.

It is important to think about the EOQ and TAC discussion as more than simple calculations. Think about the variables in the EOQ formula and the impact of changes in those variables. For example, what happens to order quantity if demand increases? Because demand is in the numerator of the formula, the order quantity (and average inventory) goes up. What about a change in ordering cost? If ordering cost goes down, for example, order quantity and average inventory also decrease. Inventory carrying cost has a major impact; if it increases, EOQ goes down. These relationships will be further explored later in the chapter when we discuss managerial approaches to managing and reducing inventory.

When to Order: The Reorder Point

Now that we know how much to order, the second decision is to decide when to place an order. In the continuous review model, the answer to "when" is actually an inventory amount. That is, at what amount of remaining inventory should a replenishment order be placed? The amount is known as the **reorder point (ROP)**. The reorder point is a level of inventory that triggers the need to order more. The ROP is easy to calculate when no variability or safety stock is involved. We know exactly how long it will take to receive the order from the supplier. Also, we know exactly how many we will sell each day while waiting for that order to arrive. This leads us to the simple formula:

reorder point (ROP) The minimum level of inventory that triggers the need to order more.

(7.7)
$$\text{ROP} = (\bar{d})\,\bar{t}$$

where:

ROP = reorder point
$\bar{d}$ = average demand per time period
$\bar{t}$ = average supplier lead time

EXAMPLE 7-7 Calculating the ROP

Because it will take 9 days to be resupplied and you sell 10 per day, you will need to initiate an order with your supplier when you have 90 copies remaining on hand. That way the new shipment will arrive just as you sell the last copy you have in stock. Refer back to Figures 7-1 and 7-2. Notice that this reorder point is indicated in both figures.

EOQ Extensions

There are several assumptions underlying the EOQ formulation that often do not hold true in practice. Primary among these are the following:

- No quantity discounts—Product cost (production cost and transportation cost) is constant regardless of quantity ordered.
- No lot size restrictions—It is possible to order a lot size equal to the EOQ (e.g., there are no minimum or maximum order size requirements and capital is unlimited).
- No partial deliveries—The product is produced and delivered in a single batch (e.g., the entire replenishment order of inventory becomes available all at the same time).
- No variability—Product demand and replenishment lead time are known and constant.
- No product interactions—Ordering of one product is not tied to ordering of some other product.

Because these assumptions are rarely met in real life, the EOQ formulation often needs to be modified. In the following sections we discuss modifications that can be made to accommodate the first four issues above. The issue of product interactions is quite complex and beyond the scope of this text.

Quantity Discounts

Quantity discounts are prevalent in the business world, so we will first explore how to extend the EOQ methodology when a supplier offers a discounted price for ordering larger quantities each time. The logic used for examining transportation discounts is similar and will therefore not be covered.

In general, the following steps must be taken to determine the order quantity when quantity discounts are available:

Step 1. Identify the price breaks offered by the supplier.

Step 2. Calculate the EOQ at each price break, starting with the lowest price possible.

Step 3. Evaluate the feasibility of each EOQ value. If the calculated EOQ for a given price is large enough to qualify for that specific price, then the calculated EOQ is feasible. If the EOQ calculated using the lowest price category is feasible, then it is the lowest TAC order quantity. If it is not feasible (as in the Trexoid example below where the EOQ for the $19 price is 281 units, but 1,000 units are required to qualify for that price), then go to Step 4.

Step 4. Calculate the TAC for each feasible EOQ and for the minimum quantity required to attain each price break.

Step 5. Pick the order quantity that has the lowest TAC.

Example 7-8 shows how quantity discounts would affect the order amount for Trexoid. As you can see from the example, sometimes it is worthwhile to order more than the EOQ in order to take advantage of price breaks for larger quantities.

Quantity discounts are present in many different inventory management situations. The Get Real box on page 250 about Pentagon purchasing illustrates quantity discounts in a defense spending environment.

student activity

Think about several instances where you have bought a larger quantity of an item than you normally buy. What factors influenced you to do so? Explain how those factors relate to the discussion of EOQ and TAC.

Lot Size Restrictions

How could the quantity discount approach be used to deal with the situation where products must be ordered in a particular batch size? For example, suppose that Trexoid must be purchased from the vendor in packs of 50 units each. In the case of the quantity discount (Example 7-8), this would pose no problem because 1,000 units is a multiple of 50. We would simply order 20 cases of the product. If there were no quantity discount, however, then from Example 7-6 we know that the EOQ of 274 would minimize costs. Unfortunately, we could not purchase exactly 274 units; we would need to purchase either 250 or 300. The simple solution is to calculate the TAC at an order size of 250 and at 300, and pick the order quantity that yields the lowest TAC.

EXAMPLE 7-8 Calculating EOQ with Quantity Discounts

Suppose the supplier of your video game Trexoid offers to sell the game to you for \$19 per unit if you purchase 1,000 units or more each time you buy. Does this price discount justify paying the inventory costs associated with a larger order size?

To answer this question, we first determine the total annual cost of the existing policy. Because there is a price differential being offered by the supplier, the *annual product cost* must now be included in the TAC. The TAC for the existing policy (Q = 274) is

$$\text{TAC} = \text{annual ordering cost} + \text{annual carrying cost} + \text{annual product cost}$$

(7.8) $$= C_O\,(D/Q) + UC_i\,Q/2 + UD$$

where:

U = unit cost

D = annual demand

For U = \$20:

Annual order cost = 3,000 units per year/274 units per order × \$50 per order = \$547

Annual inventory carrying cost = 274 units per order/2 × \$20/unit × .2 = \$548

Annual product cost = 3,000 units per year × \$20/unit = \$60,000

Therefore, the relevant TAC of the current policy is \$61,095.

As mentioned earlier, the annual order cost and annual inventory carrying cost are not exactly equal because we are using the rounded-up order quantity of 274 units, whereas the quantity that balances the two costs exactly is 273.86 units.

The next step is to determine the EOQ at the \$19 price:

$$\text{EOQ} = \sqrt{\frac{2 \times 3{,}000\ \textit{units/year} \times \$50/\textit{order}}{\$19/\textit{unit} \times .2}} = 280.98\text{, rounded to 281 units}$$

However, in order to receive the \$19 price, you must order 1,000 units. Thus, in this case, the EOQ of 281 units is not feasible because the price for 281 units is \$20. If the calculated EOQ at the discount price were higher than the quantity required (1,000 units in this case) we would continue the TAC analysis using that EOQ. *Because the calculated EOQ is not feasible, we need to determine the TAC at the smallest order size necessary to get the discount price; that is, an order size of 1,000 units.* At Q = 1,000, we can easily determine that the average inventory will be 500 units and the annual number of orders will be three.

Annual product cost = 3,000 units per year × \$19 per unit = \$57,000

Annual inventory carrying cost = 500 units × \$19 per unit × .2 = \$1,900

Annual order cost = 3 orders per year × \$50 per order = \$150

TAC = \$59,050

Thus, it is more economical to take advantage of the quantity discount offered by the supplier of Trexoid. Even though ordering 1,000 units is actually a larger order than the calculated EOQ, it does result in the lowest TAC. The annual savings of doing so are \$61,095 − \$59,050 = \$2,045.

Partial Order Deliveries—Production Order Quantity

Our previous EOQ models have assumed that inventory replenishments are produced and delivered in a single batch, and that an entire order is received and immediately available for use. In some situations, a replenishment order might be delivered in multiple shipments that occur as the product is produced. For example, a vendor may ship some product to us a little at a time, rather than making us wait until the entire batch is produced before the vendor ships anything. In this case, the first units in a replenishment order can be sold as the later units in the order are still being produced. In a production environment, units can be made available for sale immediately, one by one, as they are produced.

production order quantity The most economic quantity to order when units become available at the rate at which they are produced.

The EOQ modification used to deal with this situation is known as the **production order quantity**, the most economic quantity to order when inventory units become

GET REAL

Pentagon Buys Components in Bulk

The Pentagon is poised to start buying parts and materials in bulk for an upcoming V-22 Osprey multiyear production deal, according to Tina Jonas, the Defense Department's comptroller. The Navy will award Bell Helicopter Textron and Boeing an advance procurement contract that includes $169 million to buy components in bulk.

The contract moves the Pentagon closer to inking a major V-22 production deal later this year when the Osprey's first deployment to Iraq is under way. In Pentagon parlance, buying components in bulk to minimize costs is called economic order quantity (EOQ) procurement. The V-22 multiyear contract includes $166 million for EOQ, Jonas wrote. James Darcy, the Navy's V-22 spokesman, confirmed a contract award is expected this month. He declined to comment on the total value of the advance procurement contract, which may also fund other cost-cutting initiatives. By the end of the year, the Defense Department plans to finalize the multiyear production deal to buy 167 Ospreys between fiscal years 2008 and 2012.

Source: C.J. Castelli, "Pentagon Poised to Buy V-22 Components in Bulk for Multiyear Deal," ***Inside the Navy*** **20, no. 22 (June 2007).**

available at the rate of production, and they are sold as they are being produced. The basic concepts underlying the EOQ model can be applied to this situation. The difference is that replenishment inventory arrives or becomes available at the rate at which products are produced, (or delivered) while inventory is simultaneously being depleted at the rate of demand. Example 7-9 illustrates this situation.

You can see from this example that calculating the optimal order quantity in a production environment is very similar to calculating the optimal order quantity in a purchasing environment. The difference occurs because of the $(1 - d/p)$ multiplier on the carrying cost. This is necessary in the production environment to adjust for the fact that inventory is being depleted at the same time that it is being produced.

student activity

Verify for yourself the difference between the Q_p quantity and the EOQ. You can do that by using the standard EOQ formula and assuming that all items produced arrive simultaneously.

Enter Variability and Uncertainty

Life as an operations executive would be easy if it existed as we have described thus far, both demand and supplier lead time being constant and known. Unfortunately, these factors are both variable and at least somewhat unpredictable (despite the best efforts of forecasting). The way that we accommodate this uncertainty is to hold safety stock. The question that now must be answered is how much safety stock should be held?

To determine safety stock, two steps are required. First, the standard deviation of demand during the replenishment lead time must be calculated. Second, the company's policy on the desired service level must be determined. Let's start by examining the demand during the replenishment lead time.

Determining the Standard Deviation of Demand During Lead Time

Instead of the demand for Trexoid being 10 units per day, let's assume we have done a statistical analysis of past demand patterns and found that average demand is 10 units, but it

EXAMPLE 7-9 Calculating the EOQ with partial deliveries, AKA: the production order quantity

Consider the manufacturer of the Trexoid video games you have been ordering for your store. The manufacturer expects annual demand from all retailers to be 500,000 units of Trexoid games. It receives orders from retailers for, on average, 2,000 units per day (250 days per year). To change from production of another game to production of Trexoid requires a setup cost of $2,000. Once production of Trexoid units begins, it can produce 5,000 units per day. The cost to produce a unit of Trexoid is $10. Finally, the manufacturer has determined that its inventory carrying cost is 25 percent annually. The fundamental question to answer is how many units of Trexoid should be ordered in each production run? It is also useful to know the length of the production run in days.

Solving this problem requires a slight modification to the basic EOQ model discussed previously, using the following data:

Q_p = production order quantity (the same concept as EOQ)
D = annual demand = 500,000 units
d = daily rate of customer demand = 2,000 units
p = daily rate of production = 5,000 units
C_o = setup cost (the same concept as ordering cost in EOQ) = $2,000
U = unit cost = $10
C_i = annual inventory carrying cost percentage = 25%

The formula for determining production order quantity is

(7.9)
$$Q_p = \sqrt{\frac{2DC_o}{C_i U\left\{1 - \frac{d}{p}\right\}}}$$

Substituting in the formula,

$$Q_p = \sqrt{\frac{2(500{,}000)(\$2{,}000)}{.25(\$10)\left\{1 - \frac{2{,}000}{5{,}000}\right\}}}$$

$$Q_p = 36{,}514.84 = \text{(rounded to) } 36{,}515 \text{ units}$$

Because the most economic size of a production run is 36,515 units and the production rate is 5,000 units per day, the length of a production run is simply 36,515/5,000 = 7.3 days.

ranges from as few as 4 units to as many as 16 units, with a standard deviation of 1.5 units per day. A similar analysis of supplier lead times for replenishment reveals an average lead time of 9 days but a range from 3 days to 18 days with a standard deviation of 2.5 days. Thus, it is possible that while waiting for replenishment after you have placed an order, demand could range from as little as 12 units (lowest daily demand of 4 units × shortest lead time of 3 days) to as much as 288 units (highest possible demand of 16 units per day × longest lead time of 18 days). The amount of demand that occurs while you are awaiting receipt of your order is known as **demand during lead time**. Of course, demand during lead time has a statistical distribution with its own standard deviation. The formula for determining the standard deviation of demand during lead time is

demand during lead time The amount of demand that occurs while awaiting receipt of an inventory replenishment order.

(7.10)
$$\sigma_{ddlt} = \sqrt{\bar{t}\sigma_d^2 + \bar{d}^2\sigma_t^2}$$

where

σ_{ddlt} = standard deviation of demand during lead time
$\bar{t}$ = average lead time
σ_d = standard deviation of demand

$\bar{d}$ = average demand
σ_t = standard deviation of lead time.

EXAMPLE 7-10

Substituting our given information about Trexoid demand and lead time into the preceding formula, we find

$$\sigma_{ddlt} = \sqrt{9 \text{ days } (1.5 \text{ units})^2 + 10^2 \text{units } (2.5 \text{ days})^2} = 25.40 \text{ units}$$

The calculation of the standard deviation of demand during lead time is critical to determining the amount of safety stock that is to be carried. The next step is to determine a policy for customer service level.

Determining a Service Level Policy

service level policy Specification of the amount of risk of incurring a stockout that a firm is willing to incur.

A **service level policy** specifies the amount of risk of incurring a stockout that a firm is willing to incur. Ideally, this policy should weigh inventory carrying costs against stockout costs. However, because stockout costs are so hard to quantify, determining a service level

LO7-5 Determine the cost of a company's service level policy.

EXAMPLE 7-11

From our previous discussion, we know that, on average, demand by customers for Trexoid while waiting for replenishment from the supplier will be 90 units (the reorder point determined earlier). We now know that the standard deviation of demand during this lead time is 25.4 units. Suppose you have decided that you are only willing to have a 5 percent chance of being out of stock. Thus, your desired service level is 95 percent (100 minus the probability of a stockout while waiting for replenishment). Once you have made that decision, you can determine the required quantity of safety stock by

(7.11) $$SS = z\,\sigma_{ddlt}$$

where:
SS = safety stock
z = number of standard deviations (σ_{ddlt}) required for the desired service level
σ_{ddlt} = standard deviation of demand during lead time

The value of z can be determined from a table of cumulative probabilities of the normal distribution (we are assuming that demand follows a normal distribution, although that is not always an appropriate assumption). Table 7-2 displays some of the most commonly used standard deviations and probabilities in inventory management. A more complete table of the cumulative probability distribution of the normal distribution is included in Appendix A.

Table 7-2 indicates that, if you are willing to incur a 5 percent stockout probability, you must carry 1.65 standard deviations of safety stock because a 5 percent stockout probability is the same as a 95 percent probability of being in stock. Therefore, you must carry 42 units (1.65 standard deviations × 25.4 units) as safety stock.

How much does this decision cost you? You will, after all, incur inventory carrying cost on these units. Remember that we determined it was most economical to order Trexoid at a price of $19.

Safety stock inventory carrying cost = $19 × 42 units × 20% Carrying cost
= $159.60 per year

policy is usually a matter of managerial judgment, not a quantitative analysis. There are analytical methods that can help managers make more informed decisions. Essentially, the decision depends upon the company's willingness to take a chance of being out of stock of an item while waiting for it to be replenished. As managers' tolerance for being out of stock decreases, service level targets will be raised and the required safety stock will increase.

Table 7-3 displays the inventory carrying cost incurred across a range of different service level policies for Trexoid. Notice that the difference in inventory carrying cost is increasing at an increasing rate. To go from a stockout probability of 15 percent to a probability of 10 percent costs an incremental $26.60 ($125.40 − $98.80). From a stockout probability of 10 percent to a 5 percent probability costs another $34.20 ($159.60 − $125.40). But look at the cost differential to move from the stockout probability of 5 percent to 1 percent—this will cost an additional $64.60 ($224.20 − $159.60).

The general relationship between required inventory and increasing service level is depicted in Figure 7-4. As it shows, as companies attempt to offer higher levels of in-stock performance to their customers, inventory carrying costs become increasingly burdensome. The burden may not seem so large when you think about the inventory of a single item such as Trexoid, but consider that your store may carry hundreds of different computer games. Could you afford the extra expense of a 99 percent in-stock policy on all of them? Ultimately, the decision about how much safety stock to carry requires a balancing between these costs and management's best estimate of the cost and lost goodwill that will occur with those customers whose demand for an item cannot be filled at the time they want to purchase.

TABLE 7-2 Standard Deviations and Probabilities

Z = Number of Deviations Required	Probability of Being In Stock	Probability of Stockout
1	84.13%	15.77%
1.04	85	15
1.28	90	10
1.65	95	5
1.96	97.5	2.5
2.0	97.72	2.28
2.33	99	1
3.0	99.86	0.14

TABLE 7-3 Cost Related to Trexoid Service Levels

Std. Deviations of Safety Stock	Probability of In Stock	Probability of Stockout	Safety Stock Required	Safety Stock Inventory Carrying Cost
1	84.13%	15.77%	25	$95.0
1.04	85	15	26	98.8
1.28	90	10	33	125.4
1.65	95	5	42	159.6
1.96	97.5	2.5	50	190.0
2.0	97.72	2.28	51	193.8
2.33	99	1	59	224.2
3.0	99.86	0.14	76	288.8

FIGURE 7-4
Relationship between Inventory Investment and Product Availability

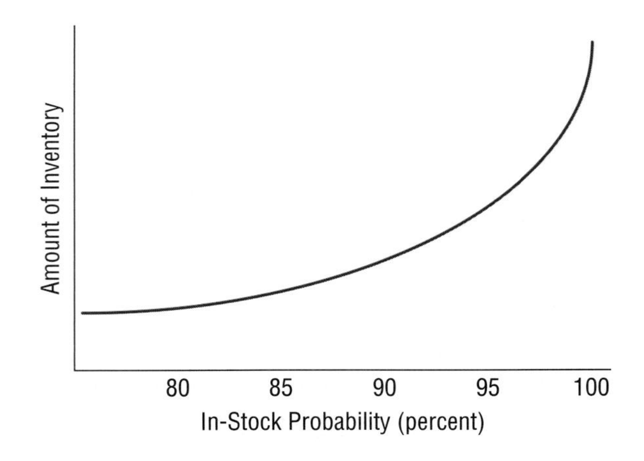

Revisiting ROP and Average Inventory

Two revisions to earlier statements are required when uncertainty and unpredictability exist. The addition of safety stock to a firm's inventory increases both the reorder point and the average inventory held by the firm in the following ways:

(7.12) $$\text{ROP} = (\bar{d} \times \bar{t}) + SS$$

(7.13) $$\text{and average inventory} = Q/2 + SS$$

where:

$\bar{d}$ = average daily demand
$\bar{t}$ = average lead time
SS = safety stock

cycle stock The portion of average inventory determined as order quantity divided by two.

order interval A fixed time period that passes between inventory reviews.

EXAMPLE 7-12

For Trexoid, assuming you chose a 95 percent service level, the ROP now becomes (10 units × 9 days) + 42, or 132 units. When on-hand inventory plus any units that may already have been ordered reaches 142 units, an order should be placed.

What we earlier called average inventory (the order quantity/2) is actually known as **cycle stock**. Calculating average inventory requires adding safety stock to cycle stock. Thus, for Trexoid, the average inventory will be 500 units of cycle stock + 42 units of safety stock, or a total of 542 units.

Prepare
What are the differences between a periodic review and a continuous review model? How do managers calculate the inventory policy parameters in a periodic review model?

Organize
The Periodic Review Model

THE PERIODIC REVIEW MODEL

While most large organizations use computerized inventory information systems, not all companies do. These companies usually rely on a periodic review model. Even when a company has the technology to use a continuous review, they may still choose a periodic review system because they want to place orders for multiple products at the same time. Remember that the continuous review system provides constant knowledge of the inventory status of an item, and an order of a fixed quantity is placed when the ROP is reached. In contrast, in the periodic review system an **order interval** is established. An order interval is a fixed time period that passes between each inventory review.

The quantity ordered in each review varies, depending upon how much inventory is on hand at the reorder time.

Let's evaluate the same scenario of ordering Trexoid from a supplier, this time using a periodic review system. For simplicity, assume that daily demand still has an average of 10 units with a standard deviation of demand of 1.5 units and lead time is constant at 9 days. The only difference is that now you have no system for continuous inventory status information. Suppose that, given the high importance you place on this item, you decide to check inventory status every 30 days. At that time, after you have determined the quantity on hand, you will place an order to replenish the inventory. How will you determine the amount to order?

LO7-4 Calculate inventory policy parameters to minimize total acquisition cost.

First, understand that this system has built into it an **uncertainty period,** a period of time in which you are uncertain about how much inventory is on hand. This time is determined by the order interval as well as the supplier's lead time. Expressed as an equation,

uncertainty period A period of time when an unknown amount of inventory is on hand.

(7.14) $$UP = OI + \bar{t}$$

where:

UP = uncertainty period
OI = order interval
$\bar{t}$ = lead time

The uncertainty period spans the time period between today, when we perform a review and place an order, and some future date, when the next order we place is expected to arrive. This is the period over which we are at risk of a stockout. Order quantity in the periodic review system is determined by the following computation:

(7.15) $$Q = \bar{d}\,(UP) + z\,\sigma_{ddup} - A$$

where:

Q = order quantity
$\bar{d}$ = average daily demand
UP = uncertainty period
z = standard deviations of safety stock desired
σ_{ddup} = standard deviation demand during the uncertainty period
A = amount of inventory on hand when the count is conducted

EXAMPLE 7-13

Given the data for Trexoid,

$$UP = 30 \text{ days} + 9 \text{ days} = 39 \text{ days}$$

Average demand during this time period will be 390 units (39 days × 10 units per day), but there will actually be a distribution of possible demands with a standard deviation. To determine a safety stock level, we have to determine the standard deviation of demand during the uncertainty period through the formula

(7.16) $$\sigma_{ddup} = \sqrt{(UP)\,\sigma_d^2}$$

Because the standard deviation of daily demand was determined to be 1.5 units, the standard deviation of demand during the uncertainty period is then

$$\sigma_{ddup} = \sqrt{(39)(1.5^2)} = 9.37$$

EXAMPLE 7-14

Suppose you have counted your inventory at the order review time and determine you have 105 units of Trexoid on hand. You now have to determine the order quantity. Assume that you desire to maintain the 95 percent service level. Your order quantity will be

$$Q = 10 \text{ units per day (39 days)} + 1.65 \text{ (9.37 units)} - 105 \text{ units}$$
$$Q = 390 + 16 - 105 = 301 \text{ units}$$

The periodic order system does not require investment in a computerized inventory information system and the maintenance that such systems generally require. However, it does require costs associated with monitoring and counting physical inventory on hand. The more frequently counts are conducted, the higher the associated costs. On the other hand, less frequent counts require higher levels of safety stock to maintain a given service level. Here, you can begin to see that trade-offs among inventory monitoring costs, ordering costs, and safety stock carrying costs can be complex.

Prepare

How do managers calculate inventory policy parameters when inventory is only used in a single period?

Organize

Single Period Inventory Model

SINGLE PERIOD INVENTORY MODEL

In many situations, managers must determine the order size for a one-time purchase, such as a retailer deciding the number of swimsuits to purchase to sell for the summer season. In these situations, there is no need or opportunity to issue a replenishment order. This situation requires a **single period inventory model**, because inventory is ordered and used only one time, and it may have little value after the period is over. The situation is frequently referred to as the *newsvendor problem,* named for the situation in which a newspaper vendor must determine an amount of papers to stock before actual demand is known. If the vendor doesn't buy enough papers to satisfy demand, a stockout cost will occur (C_{so}). The stockout cost includes lost profit lost due to lost sales and, possibly, lost future sales and lost customer goodwill. On the other hand, if the vendor stocks more newspapers than are demanded, there is a cost of being overstocked (C_{os}). The cost of being overstocked is the cost of the product itself, plus any costs associated with disposing of the extra product, less any salvage value of the excess.

There are several variations of the single period model. The method we describe requires estimates of an expected demand and a standard deviation. There are methods of analysis to use when this is not the case. However, if you understand the basic analytical approach shown in Example 7-15, you can easily understand the other methods as well.

single period inventory model Model used to determine the order size for a one-time purchase.

total system inventory The sum of the inventory held across all of the locations in a company.

Prepare

What is the impact of different inventory location strategies?

Organize

Impact of Location on Inventory

LO7-6 Explain the advantages of different inventory location strategies.

IMPACT OF LOCATION ON INVENTORY

In addition to determining *how much* inventory to order and *when* to order it, many companies must also determine *where* to stock inventories of different items. Many companies have several manufacturing plants, distribution centers, or other facilities that maintain inventories of the same items. Generally, firms hold stocks closer to customers so that they can satisfy demands more quickly. While each location may use the models described previously to plan its inventory of an item, the sum of the inventory held across all of the locations is of concern as well. It is this **total system inventory** that represents the company's asset investment, which must be financed and for which carrying cost will be incurred.

EXAMPLE 7-15

Suppose you open a kiosk at the mall every October to sell Halloween costumes. The most popular costume historically has been a skeleton costume. You can buy the costume for $10 and sell it for $30. Any costumes not sold have to be disposed of because the design changes each year and customers will not purchase a previous year's costume. Disposal and salvage costs are minimal and can be considered zero. Thus,

(7.17) C_{so} = Unit selling price − Unit cost = $30 − $10 = $20

C_{os} = Unit cost + Disposal cost − Salvage value

(7.18) = $10 + 0 − 0 = $10

The next step is to determine the **target service level (TSL)**. The target service level is the probability of meeting all demand for an item. We want the TSL to be set such that the expected cost of being out of stock of costumes is equal to the expected cost of having more costumes than needed. Mathematically,

target service level (TSL) The probability of meeting all demand for an item.

(7.19)

$$(1 - \text{TSL})(C_{so}) = \text{TSL}(C_{os})$$

where

TSL = target service level

C_{so} = cost of a unit stockout

C_{os} = cost of being overstocked by one unit

Solving the above equation we find that

$$\text{TSL} = \frac{C_{so}}{C_{so} + C_{os}}$$

Substituting data for your Halloween kiosk,

$$\text{TSL} = \frac{\$20}{\$20 + \$10} = \frac{\$20}{\$30} = .667$$

This TSL will provide a 66.7 percent chance of meeting all of the demand for skeleton costumes. Suppose that in the past, sales of skeleton costumes have averaged 200 units per year with a standard deviation of 15 units. How many costumes should be ordered this year given the TSL? By looking at the table of the cumulative normal distribution in Appendix A, we see that this target probability equates to .43 standard deviations. Thus, the target order quantity should be

(7.20) Order quantity = expected demand + *SS*

Q = 200 constumes + .43(15 costumes)

= 200 + 6.45 = 206.45, rounded to 206

Suppose a company is currently serving all of the demand in the United States for its product from a single location in Michigan. It has applied the principles discussed previously and, as a result, has decided to hold 1,000 units of safety stock. What would happen if the company decided to open a second warehouse in California? Each warehouse will serve half of the company's total demand. However, as a result of adding this location, the variation in demand that each location will face individually is greater than the variation in demand that was faced by serving the entire country from a single location. This occurs because from a single location, some of the variations in demand that exist across different markets are essentially offset by one another. Increasing the number of locations means that this offsetting does not occur. Thus, while the two locations will each carry safety stock that is less than required by a single location, the total safety stock carried by the firm will have to be increased to provide the same protection against stockouts. The impact of the change in the number of locations can be estimated by using the following formula, known as the **square root rule**:

square root rule A method of estimating the impact of changing the number of locations on the quantity of inventory held.

(7.21)

$$SS_n = \frac{\sqrt{N_n}}{\sqrt{N_e}} \times SS_e$$

where:

SS_n = system safety stock for the new number of locations
N_n = total number of new locations
N_e = number of existing locations
SS_e = system safety stock for the number of existing locations

It is important to note that the square root rule gives only a rough approximation of the impacts of inventory location strategies. It is based on the assumption that demands in different locations are independent (not correlated), and that inventories are not shared across stocking locations. In fact, if demands are correlated, then the square root rule might under-estimate the impact of consolidating stocks and overestimate the impact of increasing the number of stocking locations.

EXAMPLE 7-16

Because of opening a second warehouse, the company needs a total safety stock of

$$SS_n = \frac{\sqrt{2}}{\sqrt{1}} \times 1{,}000 \text{ units} = 1.41 \times 1{,}000 \text{ units} = 1{,}410 \text{ units}$$

Thus, the impact of adding the additional facility is an overall increase in total system inventory of 410 units. As additional locations may be added by the firm, the total system inventory will continue to increase, but at a decreasing rate, as shown in Figure 7-5.

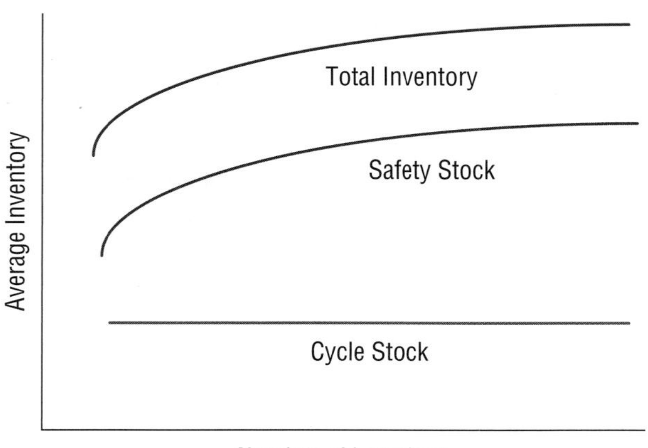

FIGURE 7-5
Inventory Related to Number of Locations

Prepare

What techniques can be used to manage inventory?

Organize

Managing Inventory
- Managing Cycle Stocks
- Managing Safety Stocks
- Managing Locations
- Inventory Information Systems and Accuracy
- Implementing Inventory Models

MANAGING INVENTORY

Planning and management of inventory levels is both an art and a science. The inventory models presented provide the foundation for order quantities and timing, but they do not provide understanding of how firms actually manage inventory. In practice there are numerous issues related to efforts to more effectively reduce, track, and manage inventory levels.

Managing Cycle Stocks

To reduce inventory it is useful to think about the causes of cycle stocks, safety stocks, and so on, and the variables that drive the different types. For example, the primary driver of cycle stock is the order quantity. One way to reduce total average inventory is to reduce the order quantity. Recall that the EOQ is a function of annual demand, order (or setup) cost, inventory carrying cost, and product price. If order costs can be reduced, order quantity declines, with a resulting decline in cycle stock. Order costs may be reduced through such techniques as online ordering, reducing receiving costs, or automated payment of invoices. Setup costs in production can be similarly reduced through automation and process improvements. All other things remaining the same, lowering order costs will lower the order quantity that provides the lowest total acquisition cost. For example, the original problem involving purchasing Trexoid from the manufacturer assumed an order cost of $50. If that order cost could somehow be reduced to only $1, the EOQ would be reduced to 39 units, resulting in average cycle stock of 19.5 units, as compared to the EOQ of 274 units and average cycle stock of 137 units in the original problem. This change moves the inventory management system toward a more lean operation, as described in Chapter 8.

Additionally, working more closely with suppliers to discourage quantity discounts (which typically result in larger order quantities) and instead offer the lowest possible price per unit regardless of order quantity would result in smaller order quantities. Companies that develop more JIT/lean processes may make longer-term commitments to suppliers in return for an agreement to deliver smaller quantities at the lowest price per unit.

Managing Safety Stocks

relationships

Much of the attention in reducing total inventory is focused on safety stock. Recall that the only reason that safety stock is required is that there is uncertainty (due to variability) in both demand and lead time. If you can reduce this uncertainty, then you reduce the need for safety stock. Better forecasting models may be developed in order to reduce the unpredictability of demand. Companies also use such techniques as marketing promotions and pricing incentives to reduce demand variability. These topics are covered in detail in Chapter 12, "Demand Planning." It is also critical to focus on lead times in attempting to reduce inventory. Average lead time impacts the amount of safety stock, as does the standard deviation of lead time. Both of these may be reduced by some combination of buying from a supplier located closer, using a more reliable method of transportation, and/or using a faster method of transportation.

A frequently used approach in managing safety stock is **ABC analysis**. This analysis requires that every item in inventory be ranked according to some criterion of importance. The purpose of ranking items is to focus on the most important items, as opposed to the less important ones. For finished goods, items can be classified according to their annual sales volume or annual item profit. Raw materials, component parts, and MRO items can be classified according to their cost, their annual usage in the organization, or the difficulty of acquiring the items.

ABC analysis The ranking of all items of inventory according to importance.

Once a ranking of items is accomplished, you will generally see the effect of **Pareto's law**: a small percentage of the items account for a large percentage of the sales (or profit, or importance, or difficulty). It is then common to classify the inventory items by assigning them an alphabetic code. For example, a small percentage of items (frequently 10 to 20 percent) which account for a large percentage of sales (often 70–80 percent) may be classified as A items; moderate volume items as B items; and the low volume items as C items. Frequently, the B items are about 30 percent of the total and Cs are about 50 percent of the total number of items. It should be noted that these percentages are offered as guidelines only, and that some firms actually use four or five classes rather than three.

Pareto's law The rule that a small percentage of items account for a large percentage of sales, profit, or importance to a company.

Figure 7-6 provides an example of ABC analysis. In this figure, A items account for about 70 percent of sales but are only 20 percent of the items carried; B items provide 20 percent of sales (30 percent of the items); and Cs provide only 10 percent of sales from the 50 percent of items they represent.

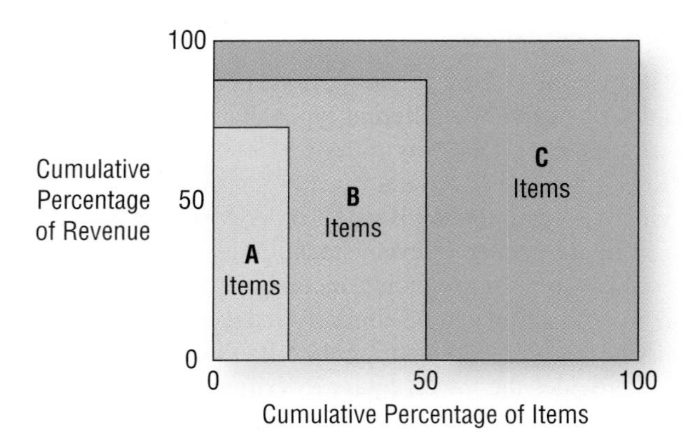

FIGURE 7-6 ABC Classification of Inventory

The general procedure for a quantitative ABC analysis is:

- Determine annual usage/sales for each item (units and/or value).
- Determine the percentage of the total usage/sales by item.
- Rank the items from highest to lowest percentage.
- Classify the items into ABC categories.

Without ABC analysis, companies frequently fall into a trap of assuming that all inventory items are of equal importance. Therefore, they establish the same safety stock policy for every item. ABC analysis can be used to establish different policies for different items. For example, A items usually have higher safety stock levels than B items. For C items, little or even no safety stock may be maintained. The result is a much smaller likelihood of stockouts on the most important items, yet the total amount of inventory in the company is less than would be required if all items had large safety stocks. This approach ensures that money (investment in safety stocks) is put to the best use.

EXAMPLE 7-17

Table 7-4 provides an example of how an ABC analysis might be conducted for finished goods inventory. In the table, 20 products have been ranked according to annual sales volume and percentage of total sales. Four of the 20 (20 percent) in this example are classified as A, as they (in total) account for 80 percent of the sales, 5 items (25 percent) are classified as B, and 10 (50 percent) of the items are classified as C because their combined sales volume is only slightly more than 5 percent of total sales. However, these quantitatively determined classifications may be modified by managerial judgment factors. For example, suppose item #76543 in the table is absolutely essential to the company's most important customers. Even though it only represents 0.7 percent of annual sales, managers may determine that it should be treated as an A item.

Operations policies for cycle stocks and other inventories may also be based on ABC analysis. More purchasing effort may be warranted for A items than B or C items. Additionally, more time and effort may be devoted to monitoring inventory levels (as discussed later in this chapter) of A items than the others.

TABLE 7-4 Example ABC Analysis for Finished Goods

Product ID	Annual Sales (in 000s)	% of Total Sales	Cumulative % of Total Sales	Class
12345	$90,000	30.0%	30.0%	A
23456	70,000	23.3	53.3	A
34567	50,000	16.7	70.0	A
45678	28,000	9.3	79.3	A
56789	18,000	6.0	85.3	B
67890	10,000	3.3	88.6	B
09876	8,000	2.7	91.3	B
98765	6,000	2.0	93.3	B
87654	4,000	1.3	94.6	B
76543	2,000	0.7	95.3	C
65432	2,000	0.7	96.0	C
54321	2,000	0.7	96.7	C
43210	2,000	0.7	97.4	C
43258	1,500	0.5	97.9	C
46598	1,500	0.5	98.4	C
57589	1,500	0.5	98.9	C
24367	1,000	0.3	99.2	C
89566	1,000	0.3	99.5	C
76888	1,000	0.3	99.8	C
21345	500	0.2	100	C
Total	$300,000	100		

Managing Locations

The discussion of location impact on inventory levels also has important managerial implications for inventory management. There has been a major effort in many firms to reduce the number of warehouses and distribution centers in their logistics networks. The driving force behind this effort is the substantial reduction in inventory that this consolidation of facilities allows.

Amazon Distribution Center

Chain retailers such as Walmart and Target utilize distribution centers to replenish inventory of individual stores. In effect, the distribution centers reduce, rather than increase, the total amount of inventory that is actually held by the companies. While this may seem counterintuitive at first, consider the alternative for the chains. The alternative is to treat each store location as a totally independent location, ordering inventory from far-distant suppliers, likely with very long and variable lead times. The result would be extremely large inventories required at each store location to service consumers. By utilizing distribution centers, many stores can draw on the stocks held at the local center and receive very rapid and consistent lead times, reducing the amount of inventory held at each location.

Similarly, consider the differences between Amazon and Barnes & Noble in the book industry. From a small number of distribution centers, Amazon can offer tens of thousands of different book titles with a relatively small inventory of each, as compared to the total inventory of a specific book title accumulated across all of the hundreds of Barnes & Noble store locations.

Another approach used in some situations is to share inventory among different locations within a firm. For example, dealers of Caterpillar equipment sometimes share repair parts and supplies among themselves. Thus, each dealer can reduce its inventory, knowing that there may be another dealer located close by who can provide a part if needed. This type of system can work particularly well when locations share information about what items are in stock.

Inventory Information Systems and Accuracy

LO7-7 Describe practical techniques for inventory planning and management.

Managing inventory requires an information system that provides operations managers with data concerning, among other things, quantities of inventory on-hand and expected arrivals of replenishment items. Any system is only as good as the data that it contains, and inventory systems are no different. Inaccurate inventory records create uncertainty in the trustworthiness of the information. Such uncertainty usually requires firms to hold additional safety stocks. As firms attempt to reduce inventory, it is even more imperative that the records can be trusted.

Item Identification

Global Trade Item Number (GTIN) An item identification system for finished goods sold to consumers.

An important step in developing an inventory information system involves establishing a system for identifying each individual item carried in inventory. While items may have names and descriptions, this is typically a very cumbersome way of maintaining inventory information systems. Notice in Table 7-4 that each of the 20 products has a product identification number. Numbering schemes are much more efficient for capturing and maintaining inventory data than are lengthy product descriptions.

The **Global Trade Item Number (GTIN)** is an item identification system for finished goods sold to consumers. There are several variations of GTIN, and it is a continuously evolving system, but the simplest example is also perhaps the oldest: the Universal Product Code (UPC) that is familiar to consumers in North America. A similar system, European Automatic Numbering (EAN), was developed at about the same time.

global

Manufacturers apply to an organization called the Uniform Code Council (UCC). The company pays an annual fee for the right to receive a UPC identification. In return, the UCC issues the manufacturer a six-digit manufacturer identification number and provides guidelines on how to use it. You can see the manufacturer identification number in any standard 12-digit UPC code. The photo on the next page shows the bar code from a 3-liter bottle of Diet Coke.

The UPC symbol has two parts. The manufacturer identification number is the first six digits of the UPC number—049000 in the photo. The next five digits, 01134, constitute the specific item number, in this case a 3-liter bottle of Diet Coke. A person employed by the manufacturer, called the UPC coordinator, is responsible for assigning item numbers to products. This person makes sure the same code is not used on more than one product, retires codes as products are removed from the product line, and so forth.

In general, every item the manufacturer sells, as well as every size package and every repackaging of the item, needs a different item code. So a 12-ounce can of Diet Coke needs a different item number than a 3-liter bottle of Diet Coke, as does a 6-pack of 12-ounce cans, and so on. It is the job of the UPC coordinator to keep all of these numbers straight!

The last digit of the UPC code is a check digit. This digit lets the scanner determine if it scanned the number correctly or not.[3] Assuming that the scanner determines that the

[3]The discussion and picture of UPC code is based on material from http://electronics.howstuffworks.com/upc1.htm.

Bar code for a three-liter bottle of Diet Coke.

number is correct, the computer system then looks up the price of the item in a separate file to determine how much the customer pays for the item.

The original 12-digit North American UPC system is undergoing a change to 14 digits (as is EAN) so it is compatible with other numbering systems in GTIN. What is so useful about UPC and the other GTIN variations is that all companies in a supply chain are able to use the same identification number for a specific item. No other item has the number 049000011340; it exclusively identifies a 3-liter bottle of Diet Coke.

GTIN and its variants are quite useful for finished goods, but standardized systems have yet to be developed for most raw material and component parts. A **part number** is a unique identifier of a part used by a specific company. Its purpose is to simplify referencing to that item within that company. For example, when specifying a screw, it is easier to refer to "HSC0424PP" than say "Hardware, screw, machine, 4-40, 3/4" long, pan head, Phillips." A business using a part will often use a different part number than the various suppliers of that part use.

part number A unique identifier of a part used by a specific company.

For example, when referring to a "Hardware, screw, machine, 4-40, 3/4" long, pan head, Phillips":

Supplier A uses part number 4-40-3/4"-pan-phil.

Supplier B uses part number 100-440-0.750-3434-A.

Supplier C uses part number TSR-1002.

A business using such a screw may buy screws from any supplier, because each supplier manufactures the screws to the same specifications. Therefore, the user typically devises its own part numbering system.[4] It is easy to see how keeping track of all the part number systems represented in the inventories of a large firm can be a fairly daunting task.

[4]http://en.wikipedia.org/wiki/Part_number.

GET REAL

American Apparel Introduces RFID

American Apparel's recent deployment of radio frequency identification (RFID) tags for item-level replenishment reinforced that the technology has granular benefits that extend from the supply chain to the store shelf. More surprisingly, it showcased that RFID can be cost-justified and rolled out with relative ease and expediency.

The company's business model calls for each store to maintain at least one piece of every size, color, and style on the sales floor at all times—that translates to roughly 40,000 pieces representing 12,000 to 13,000 unique items. Zander Livingston, American Apparel's research and development strategist and project manager for the RFID project, reported the item-level RFID system demonstrated 99.9 percent accuracy on inventory replenishment throughout the store.

Prior to RFID, this aggressive replenishment goal had sales associates running in circles and spending excessive hours manually counting and managing inventory. The pilot project showed American Apparel not only that RFID could work, but that employees could be significantly more productive because of the technology.

"We were seeing a huge savings in labor," noted Livingston. "Before the pilot, we were doing inventory twice weekly and it required four to six employees working up to six hours. Now we can maintain inventory accuracy on the floor and do inventory just once a week. Two employees walking around the store with handheld RFID readers can scan everything in the entire store in under two hours."

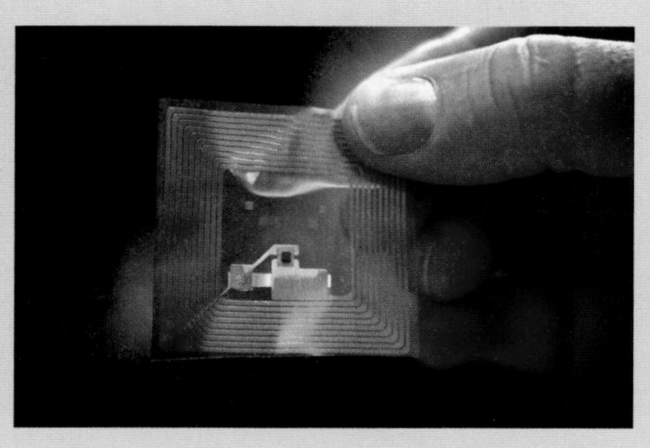

Source: Adapted from Connie Robbins Gentry, "RFID Speeds Replenishment," *Chain Store Age* 84, no. 6 (June 2008), pp. 54–55.

Inventory Record Accuracy

Once an identification system is in place, record accuracy is affected by a number of things. As items are received or produced, they must be logged into the system correctly and in a timely fashion so that the organization knows they are available. Technologies such as bar codes and electronic identification tags can help in this effort. Point-of-sale scanning systems help with accuracy and up-to-date information as well.

student activity

Contact the purchasing department at your college or university. Ask if they would be willing to allow a group of students to interview someone and/or tour the campus facility where materials and supplies are kept in inventory. If so, also ask them about the inventory information system and the methods used to ensure accuracy of the inventory information.

However, despite everyone's best efforts, records can and do become inaccurate. Human error or accidents can never be totally eliminated. Sometimes someone forgets to log in receipts of products, or makes an error in the entry. Consider, for example, a clerk at the checkout in a retail store. A customer arrives at the checkout with 10 three-liter bottles of Coca-Cola products. Some are Diet Coke, some are regular Coke, and perhaps some are Sprite. To save time, the clerk takes one bottle and scans it very rapidly 10 times. The clerk may think this is acceptable because all three items are the same price. However, the clerk may not realize (or even care) that the store inventory information system is now incorrect.

Inventory audits are important to ensure that entry and count errors are identified and corrected. Annual physical inventories can help, but these are expensive and lack the kind of frequency that most systems need. A common audit approach is **cycle counting**, where each item in inventory is physically counted on a routine schedule. An easy way to set these audit cycles is to use the ABC classification discussed earlier. For example, A item inventories might be checked every week, B items checked every month, and C items checked every quarter. These checks are then spread out over the audit cycle so that a little is checked each day.

cycle counting A process where each item in inventory is physically counted on a routine schedule.

The Get Real box on the opposite page describes how American Apparel has used a new technology, RFID tags, to aid in more rapid replenishment of inventory, introduce efficiency in the process of physically tracking the on-hand inventory, and obtain greater accuracy in inventory records.

Implementing Inventory Models

A final issue to understand regarding inventory models is that no one model is likely to be used exclusively in an organization. Because most companies stock many different inventory items that differ in importance and value, a mix of different models is usually required. The most critical products may be managed with the continuous review model, which is most likely to reduce stockouts. It may also be the most expensive inventory management model to implement due to the high cost of information technology and system administration.

Many items may be managed using the basic concepts of the continuous review model but without the need for high-level technology. For example, in a **two-bin system,** inventory of an item is stored in two different locations. Workers withdraw items as needed from one location until that location (or bin) is empty. When it is empty, workers immediately know that it is time to issue an order for more. This information is immediately given to purchasing, frequently by removing a form attached to the bin. While awaiting arrival of the order, inventory is taken from the second bin. The normal level of inventory in the second bin is determined as the ROP. When the order arrives from the supplier, the first bin is refilled and any remaining is put in the second bin. This system is frequently used in practice to manage inventory of low value but necessary items such as office supplies, and high-volume parts such as bolts, screws, and similar pieces.

two-bin system Inventory of an item is stored in two different locations.

MANAGING INVENTORY ACROSS THE SUPPLY CHAIN

Prepare

How is inventory value related to the supply chain? What are the bullwhip effect and vendor-managed inventory?

Organize

Managing Inventory Across the Supply Chain
- Inventory Value in the Supply Chain
- The Bullwhip Effect
- Integrated Supply Chain Inventory Management

Thus far, we have focused on the individual firm and fundamentals for inventory within that firm. However, a firm must also consider how its actions and decisions may impact inventory of other firms in the supply chain.

Inventory Value in the Supply Chain

As discussed earlier, an item that is considered a finished product for one firm may well be a raw material or component part for a downstream supply chain member. For example, Lear provides seats to General Motors assembly plants. To Lear, a completed seat for a Cadillac automobile is a finished good. When that seat arrives at an assembly plant, it is just one of many component parts that go into a finished Cadillac. It is also important to note that the further downstream an item is in the supply chain, the more expensive it is to stock that item. As an item moves in the supply chain, value is constantly being added to it. The seat received from Lear by the Cadillac plant has value added of transportation to the plant. Once installed, there is the added value of the labor and effort required to install it. Further, once it is installed, it becomes a part of a much more valuable product, the finished automobile. In fact, the finished automobile has a value that is much greater than the sum of its individual parts.

The Bullwhip Effect

bullwhip effect A small disturbance generated by a customer produces successively larger disturbances at each upstream stage in the supply chain.

relationships

The **bullwhip effect** occurs when a small disturbance in the flow of orders generated by a customer produces successively larger disturbances at each upstream stage in the supply chain. Bullwhip effects are of great concern. They incite excessive expediting (moving certain orders ahead of others), increased levels of inventory, uneven levels of capacity utilization (where plants go from being idle to working overtime), and, ultimately, increased costs.

To understand how a bullwhip effect is created, consider a hypothetical supply chain for a consumer product such as baby food. In this hypothetical chain, consumers buy baby food from a retailer, who, in turn, buys from a distributor. The distributor buys from the manufacturer. Under normal circumstances, the amount of baby food purchased by consumers ought to be fairly stable and predictable. It is easy to determine the number of babies who are at the appropriate age for consumption of baby food and the amount typically consumed per baby, per day, and so on.

Now, suppose that a large retailer decides to run an advertising promotion. In order to stock up for anticipated increases in sales, the retailer temporarily boosts orders to the distributor, as indicated in Figure 7-7 by an increase in order size in weeks 3 and 4. How should the distributor react? If it knows nothing about the retailer's promotional plan, the increased orders from the retailer come as a surprise. The distributor worries that it won't be able to fill future orders of this magnitude.

A natural response would be for the distributor to place even larger orders with the manufacturer. After all, as far as the distributor knows, the retailer might place even larger orders in the future. This phenomenon is replicated upstream, until finally the orders that the manufacturer places on its suppliers are quite large indeed. Once the retailer's promotion campaign is over, it returns to placing normal smaller orders. How might the distributor react? By now it has lots of excess inventory sitting around. As a result it will probably decide to reduce future orders drastically. And so this opposite effect cascades up the supply chain.

What are the root causes of this bullwhip effect? Without information, suppliers are likely to overreact to changes in order sizes from their customers, regardless of whether they are larger or smaller than expected. Also, differences in ordering policies (batch sizes and order timing) at different stages of the supply chain can create unevenness in the flows. The ultimate outcome is continual fluctuations of excesses and shortages of inventory in the supply chain. In order to reduce these effects, operations managers have developed several approaches for more integrated supply chain inventory management.

Integrated Supply Chain Inventory Management

relationships

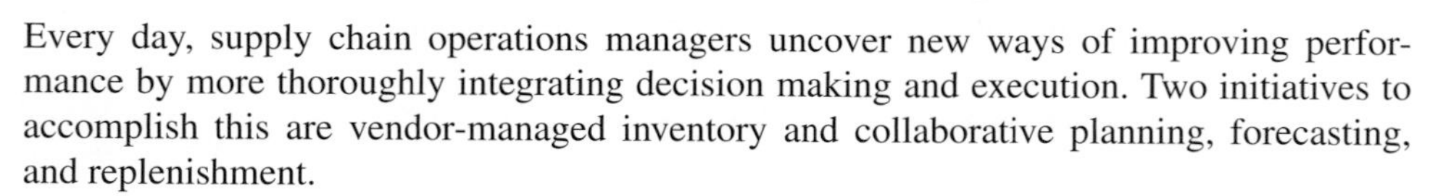

Every day, supply chain operations managers uncover new ways of improving performance by more thoroughly integrating decision making and execution. Two initiatives to accomplish this are vendor-managed inventory and collaborative planning, forecasting, and replenishment.

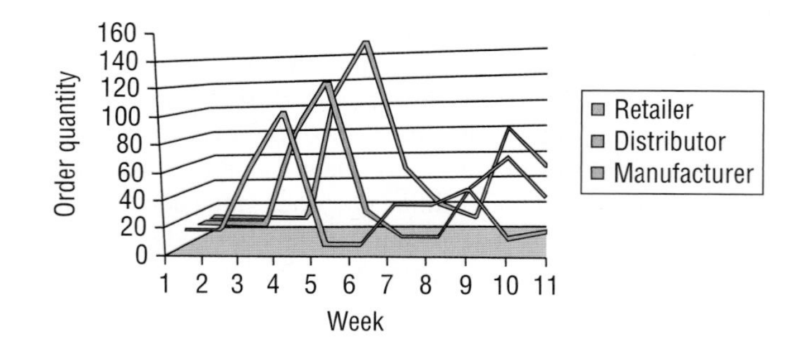

FIGURE 7-7
The Bullwhip Effect: An Example

In the past, it was standard practice for operations managers to own and manage all the inventories on their property. More recently, an increasing number of firms have implemented **vendor-managed inventory (VMI)** arrangements. As the name suggests, the vendor (supplier) is responsible for managing the inventory located at a customer's facility. The vendor stocks the inventory, controls its flow in and out of the facility, and places replenishment orders. Often the vendor owns the inventory until the customer uses it, and a vendor representative often is located at the site where the inventory is stocked.

vendor-managed inventory (VMI) The vendor is responsible for managing the inventory located at a customer's facility.

This approach offers several important advantages to both the customer and the vendor. The customer saves the costs associated with managing inventories, including the labor costs usually incurred by both the materials and purchasing managers. The customer also receives more responsive service from the vendor because the on-site vendor representative works directly with production schedulers and other production personnel, thereby gaining a better understanding of the customer's schedule and quality needs.

The vendor gains better insights into the customer's operations and, surprisingly, often does a better job of scheduling inventory replenishment orders than the customer does.

GET REAL

Vendor-Managed Inventory at Stryker Instruments

Staying in stock of the component parts for medical products such as this gurney was a major problem for Stryker Medical. Much of the problem was solved through a vendor-managed inventory system.

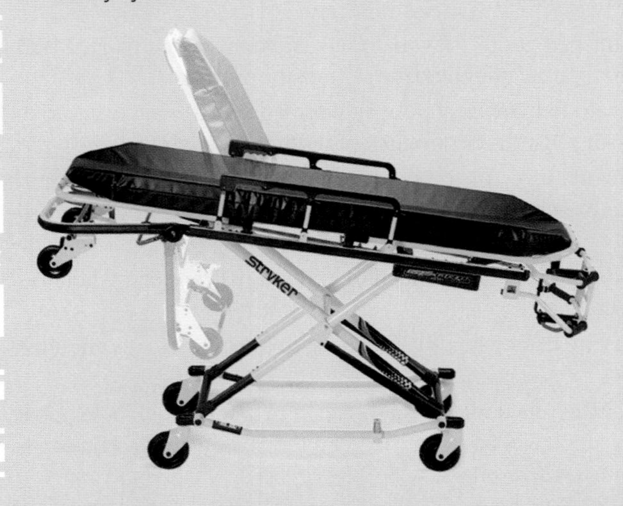

Stryker Instruments, a manufacturer of hospital equipment and instruments, had a classic inventory problem: It wasn't able to share real-time information with its key suppliers. Though inventory levels were too high, the company was hesitant to lower them for fear of stockouts.

Using an inventory management solution from TradeBeam Inc., Stryker instituted a new four-step process with its suppliers:

1. Stryker sets monthly inventory targets for each part number. Suppliers are responsible for keeping inventory within the target inventory range.
2. The inventory management system gives suppliers real-time visibility into Stryker's on-hand inventory levels, forecasts, current and future production schedules, and order commitments. More than 90` percent of Stryker's direct material supply is now managed through the vendor replenishment process.
3. Using this data, the system helps suppliers determine how and when to ship to Stryker to ensure that inventory remains within target levels.
4. Suppliers enter into the TradeBeam inventory management solution promises for future ship dates with projected quantities, and they also provide advance shipment notice (ASN) information for products shipped.

As a result, Stryker has seen a 30 percent reduction in direct material inventory for its manufacturing facilities in Michigan and Ireland. It also has seen a 30 to 40 percent reduction in finished goods inventory sent to Stryker distribution centers in the U.K. and Japan.

Source: Adapted from David Blanchard, "Stryker's 4-Step Inventory Reduction Process," ***Industry Week*** **256, no. 4 (April 2007), p. 48.**

By controlling the order schedule, the vendor can also accommodate the needs of its own internal operations. For example, the vendor has the liberty to batch orders to reduce costly production setups. In addition, the production personnel at the vendor site receive higher quality and more timely information because the person generating the information has the vendor's interests at heart. The Get Real box about Stryker Instruments on the preceding page provides an example of vendor-managed inventory.

VMI approaches often blur the boundaries between the vendor's and customer's operations management systems. If secrecy is a high priority, this lack of separation sometimes poses a threat to the customer or vendor. Successful VMI arrangements require a fairly long-term commitment from both parties. Consequently, most VMI partnerships are usually reserved for only a few, important vendor relationships.

collaborative planning, forecasting, and replenishment (CPFR) Supply chain partner firms share information and insights in order to generate better forecasts and plans.

Another well-known supply chain initiative is known as **collaborative planning, forecasting, and replenishment (CPFR)**. Using this approach, partner firms periodically share information and forecasts in order to jointly develop their production, distribution, and replenishment plans. Chapter 12 discusses the CPFR process in more detail.

We are not finished with our coverage of the subject of inventory in this book. As you will see, most of the remaining chapters reference inventory in some way.

CHAPTER SUMMARY

This chapter has discussed fundamental aspects of inventory and inventory management in supply chain and operations management.

1. Inventory can be held as finished goods, raw materials and component parts, MRO (maintenance, repair, and operating supplies), or as transit inventory.
2. The key roles of inventory are to balance supply and demand, buffer against variability and uncertainty, and assure that the economics of buying are maintained.
3. Inventory represents a financial investment by an organization as an asset. The costs related to inventory management include product cost, inventory carrying cost, ordering cost, and stockout cost.
4. Inventory policy involves determining how much of an item to order and when to place an order for replenishment.
5. Continuous review systems are used when the firm is able to continuously monitor inventory status.
6. Service level provided to customers depends on the level of safety stock held. Cost of different levels of safety stock can be quantified and then evaluated in relation to potential impact of stockouts on customers.
7. Periodic review systems are used when companies do not have this information and must, instead, rely on physically counting inventory levels on a predetermined schedule.
8. When inventory is held in many locations, total inventory increases because of location impact on demand and lead time uncertainty.
9. While the mathematical models explained in the chapter can be used to establish the critical inventory parameters, in a practical sense managers attempt to reduce inventory requirements by changing and managing the variables (demand and its variation; lead time and its variation) that are components of those models.

10. To properly manage inventory, each item must have a unique identification and accurate inventory records must be maintained. Several different numbering systems have been developed for item identification. Record accuracy requires careful entry of information and typically can be supplemented with a program of cycle counting.
11. The bullwhip effect occurs when a small change in demand at the end-customer level of a supply chain results in increasingly large changes in the upstream supply chain.
12. Vendor-managed inventory is one approach taken in some supply chains to reduce the bullwhip effect and to reduce overall inventory levels in a supply chain.

KEY TERMS

ABC analysis 259
buffer (or safety) stock 237
bullwhip effect 266
carrying (or holding) cost 238
collaborative planning, forecasting, and replenishment (CPFR) 268
continuous review model 244
cycle counting 265
cycle stock 254
days of supply 241
demand during lead time 251
dependent demand inventory systems 243
economic order quantity (EOQ) 246
finished goods inventory 236
Global Trade Item Number (GTIN) 262
independent demand inventory systems 243
inventory 236
inventory turnover 240
MRO inventory 236
order cost 238
order interval 254
Pareto's law 259
part number 263
periodic review model 244
product cost 238
production order quantity 249
raw materials and component parts 236
reorder point (ROP) 247
saw-tooth diagram 245
service level 242
service level policy 252
setup cost 238
single period inventory model 256
square root rule 258
stockout 242
stockout (or shortage) cost 239
target service level (TSL) 257
total acquisition cost (TAC) 244
total system inventory 256
transit inventory 236
two-bin system 265
uncertainty period 255
vendor-managed inventory (VMI) 267
work in process inventory 236

DISCUSSION QUESTIONS

1. Why do some executives believe that inventory is "bad"? Explain why this thinking is incorrect.
2. Explain the different types of costs related to inventory planning.
3. Explain the trade-offs involved in the economic order quantity. How do these change when quantity discounts are considered?

4. Why does total system inventory increase as a company increases its number of stocking locations?
5. Early in the chapter it was stated that planning inventory levels is both an art and a science. Explain in your own words why this is true.
6. A firm is presently using the basic EOQ model and is considering switching to the production order quantity model (i.e., receiving gradual deliveries over time). If all the cost and demand parameters stay the same, what changes should the firm expect?
7. Suppose you have been given the task of reducing inventory in your company, without negatively impacting customer service. What actions might you be able to take to accomplish this task?
8. What steps do you think companies can take to improve the accuracy of their inventory information systems?
9. Why should one company in a supply chain consider total supply chain inventory as well as its own inventory levels?

SOLVED PROBLEMS

1. Jiffy Print Shop, located close to a major university, does an enormous amount of printing of documents, papers, course packs, and dissertations for students and faculty. The shop uses an average of 20 cases of copy paper each day during the 320 days per year that it is open. Each case of paper costs $40.00. It conducts a count of its paper inventory at the end of every quarter of the year. Jiffy began the year with 1,200 cases of paper and at the end of each of the next four quarters had 800 cases, 1,050 cases, 950 cases, and 1,100 cases, respectively. Jiffy management has determined that its inventory carrying cost is 25 percent annually. What is Jiffy's average inventory for the year, inventory turnover rate, and annual inventory carrying cost for paper? Assuming that Jiffy expects demand for the next year to remain at an average of 20 cases per day, how long can Jiffy satisfy demand given its ending inventory (end of the fourth quarter) of 1,100 cases?

Solution

Annual demand for paper is 20 cases/day (320 days) = 6,400 cases
Each case cost $40.00, therefore cost of goods = 6,400 cases * $40.00 = $256,000

Average inventory = (1,200 + 800 + 1,050 + 950 + 1,100) / 5 = 1,020 cases
Average inventory cost value = 1,020 cases * $40.00 per cases = $40,800

Inventory turnover in this problem can be computed either in units or in dollars of cost:
Inventory turnover (units) = 6,400 cases used / 1,020 average inventory = 6.27 times
Inventory turnover (cost) = $256,000 cost of goods / $40,800 average inventory = 6.27 times

Annual inventory carrying cost = $40,800 average inventory * . 25 = $10,200
Days of supply of inventory for the next year = 1,100 cases / 20 cases per day = 55 days

2. Johnson Widgets Inc. is examining its inventory of maintenance supplies in its warehouse. It wants to conduct an ABC analysis of these supplies. It maintains inventory of 10 parts and the history of part usage is contained in the following table.

Item #	Item Cost	Annual Usage	Annual Value
G-507	$ .45	50,000	$ 22,500
G-680	.80	600	480
K-100	1.70	2,000	3,400
K-300	2.20	250	550
K-303	.90	8,000	7,200
K-601	.50	4,000	2,000
N-005	8.50	80	680
N-035	4.00	24,000	96,000
P-440	1.20	900	1,080
Z-212	.02	100,000	2,000
Total			$135,890

What would you recommend to Johnson Widgets?

Solution

In the table below, percentage of total annual value for each item has been calculated (shown for the first item) and items have been ranked by this percentage value.

Item #	Annual Value	% of Annual Value	Cumulative % of Usage Value
N-035	$ 96,000	(96,000/135,890) = 70.65%	70.65%
G-507	22,500	16.56	87.21
K-303	7,200	5.30	92.51
K-100	3,400	2.50	95.01
K-601	2,000	1.47	96.48
Z-212	2,000	1.47	97.95
P-440	1,080	0.79	98.74
N-005	680	0.50	99.24
K-300	550	0.40	99.64
G-680	480	0.36	100
TOTAL	$135,890		

As for specific recommendations, some judgment is required. It seems clear that item # N-035 should be classified as an A item. Beyond that, it could be argued that item G-507 may be an A or B item, while the remainder would most likely be classified as Cs. However, even these classifications based on the quantitative analysis may be modified by managerial factors. For example, notice that item Z-212 is a very low cost item and annual value is only 1.47 percent of the total. However, since it has the highest usage quantity of 100,000 units, it may be very important to overall operations at Johnson Widgets and therefore classified as an A or B item, thus maintaining higher safety stocks and/or receiving more managerial attention than some of the other items. The quantitative analysis is a very useful first step in ABC classification, but it must be tempered with other factors.

3. Foods Galore is a major distributor to restaurants and other institutional food users.
   a. Foods Galore buys cereal from a manufacturer for $20.00 per case. Annual demand for cereal is 200,000 cases, and the company believes that the demand is constant at 800 cases per day for each of the 250 days per year that it is open for

business. Average lead time from the supplier for replenishment orders is eight days, and the company believes that it is also constant. The purchasing agent at Foods Galore believes that annual inventory carrying cost is 10 percent and that it costs $40.00 to prepare, send, and receive an order. How many cases of cereal should Foods Galore order each time it places an order? What will be the average inventory? What will be the inventory turnover rate?

Solution

The economic order quantity for cereal is

$$\sqrt{\frac{2 \times 200{,}000 \times \$40}{\$20 \times .10}} = 2{,}828.47 \text{ or } 2{,}829 \text{ cases}$$

Average inventory will be

$$2{,}829/2 = 1{,}414.5 \text{ cases}$$

Inventory turnover will be

$$200{,}000/1{,}414.5 = 141.4 \text{ times per year}$$

b. Foods Galore conducts an in-depth analysis of its inventory management practices and discovers several flaws in its previous approach. First, they find that by ordering 10,000 or more cases each time, they can obtain a price of $18.00 per case from the supplier. What order quantity should Foods Galore place? Why?

Solution

The economic order quantity for the $18.00 price is

$$\sqrt{\frac{2 \times 200{,}000 \times \$40}{\$18 \times .1}} = 2{,}981.43 \text{ or } 2{,}982 \text{ cases}$$

However, Foods Galore is required to order 10,000 cases in order to receive the $18.00 price. Therefore, the total acquisition cost of ordering 10,000 cases must be compared to the total acquisition cost of ordering 2,829 cases at a time.
The TAC of ordering 2,829 cases is

Annual product cost = 200,000 × $20 = $4,000,000.00
Annual inventory carrying cost = 1,414.5 cases × $20 × .1 = $2,829.00
Annual ordering cost = (200,000/2,829) × $40 = $2,827.85
Total cost = $4,005,656.85

(*Note:* Annual inventory carrying cost and annual ordering cost are not equal in this case due to rounding.)

The TAC of ordering 10,000 cases is

Annual product cost = 200,000 × $18 = $3,600,000.00
Annual inventory carrying cost = 5,000 × $18 × .1 = $9,000.00
Annual ordering cost = (200,000/10,000) × $40 = $800.00
Total annual cost = $3,609,800.00

Foods Galore should order 10,000 cases of cereal each time because it will save a total of $395,856.85 per year by doing so.

c. In its analysis, Foods Galore determined that demand and lead time are not constant. In fact, demand has a standard deviation of 60 cases per day and lead time has a standard deviation of 1.5 days. Foods Galore management wants to evaluate two service level policies. One policy would incur a 5 percent risk of stockout while waiting for replenishment, the other only a 1 percent risk of stockout. What would be the cost of carrying the safety stocks for each of the two policies?

Solution

The standard deviation of demand during lead time for cereal is

$$\sqrt{8\ days\ (60\ cases)^2 + (800\ cases)^2\ (1.5\ days)^2} = 1{,}211.94 \text{ or } 1{,}212 \text{ cases}$$

A 5 percent risk of stockout is equal to a 95 percent probability of being in stock, which will require 1.65 standard deviations of safety stock, or 1.65(1,212) = 2,000 cases (rounded). Because the $18 price was determined to provide the lowest total acquisition cost, the cost of carrying the safety stock for this service level is (2,000 cases × $18 × .1) = $3,600.00.

A 1 percent risk of stockout is equal to a 99 percent probability of being in stock, which will require 2.33 standard deviations of safety stock, or 2.33(1,212) = 2,824 cases (rounded). The cost of this safety stock policy is (2,824 cases × $18 × .1) = $5,083.20.

4. Thomas Toys Ltd. uses a periodic review inventory management system. One important item for the company is building blocks, which sell, on average, five sets per day. However, the standard deviation of demand is two sets per day. The company checks the status of inventory for building blocks every 21 days. When blocks are reordered from the supplier, it takes 14 days to be replenished. Thomas has just checked its inventory and found that it currently has 160 sets in stock. The company desires to maintain a 97.5 percent service level. How many sets of building blocks should Thomas Toys order?

Solution

For building block sets, the uncertainty period is 21 days (the review period) plus 14 days (the lead time), or 35 days.
The standard deviation of demand during the uncertainty period is

$$\sqrt{2^2(35)} = 11.8 \text{ sets}$$

The order quantity for building blocks is

(5 sets per day)(35 days) + 1.96 (11.8 sets) − 160 sets = 175 + 24 − 160 = 39 sets

5. Johnson Plastics makes and sells, among many other things, specialty plastic display cases for retail stores. Johnson's expected demand for the display cases is 1,000 units, and average daily demand is 4 units. The production process is most efficient when 16 units per day are produced at a cost of $100 per unit. Setup cost is $50. Inventory carrying cost at Johnson is determined to be 10 percent annually. What is the best production order quantity, and how many days is a required production run?

Solution

The production order quantity is

$$Q_p = \sqrt{\frac{2(1{,}000)\$50}{.10(\$100)\left(1 - \frac{4}{16}\right)}} = 115.47 \text{ units or (rounded up) } 116 \text{ units}$$

Producing 116 units in a production run at a rate of 16 per day requires 116/16 = 7.22 days.

6. Concert Productions is planning an appearance of the top band Iggy Wiggy. They plan to buy custom designed T-shirts to sell at the stadium where the concert will take place. The T-shirt will sell for $25.00 and the cost per shirt is $8.00. Previous experience at Concert Productions suggests that after the concert is over, T-shirts can still be sold, but the selling price will only be $5.00 per shirt. Based on analysis of previous similar concerts, the company estimates sales of the T-shirt will be 6,000 units. However, the analysis also shows that the standard deviation in similar situations is 800 units. How many Iggy Wiggy T-shirts should the company order?

Solution

The cost for a stockout (C_{SO}) of a T-shirt = Unit selling price − unit cost = \$25 − \$8 = \$17
The cost of overstock (C_{OS}) of a T-shirt is = Unit cost + Disposal cost − Salvage value
= \$8 + 0 − \$5 = \$3

Target service level = $C_{SO}/(C_{SO} + C_{OS})$
Therefore, the target services level (TSL) for the T-shirts = \$17/(\$17 + \$3) = 0.85

This TSL will provide an 85% probability of meeting all demand for the Iggy Wiggy T-shirts. From the table of cumulative probability in Appendix A, we see that this target probability is closest to 1.04 standard deviations. Therefore, the target order quantity for T-shirts is:

Order quantity = Expected demand + Safety stock = 6,000 T-shirts + 1.04(800 T-shirts)
= 6,832 T-shirts

PROBLEMS

1. Akers Inc. maintains average inventory of \$1,000,000 (at cost). Last year, Akers' sales volume was \$10,000,000 and cost of goods sold was \$7,000,000. Akers has determined that its inventory carrying cost is 15 percent annually. What was the inventory turnover rate? How much was the inventory carrying cost for the year?
2. The following table contains data about the inventory for five items at Jones Corporation. Complete the missing items in the table.

Item #	Beginning Unit Inventory	Ending Unit Inventory	Average Unit Inventory	Annual Unit Sales	Inventory Turnover
1	150,000	120,000		400,000	
2	40,000	60,000		80,000	
3	85,000	97,000		190,000	
4	200,000	170,000		350,000	
5	50,000	60,000		165,000	
Total					

3. Suppose Jones Corporation in the above problem determined that its annual inventory carrying cost = 18 percent. The item unit cost was as follows:

   Item 1 = \$25.00
   Item 2 = \$60.00
   Item 3 = \$5.00
   Item 4 = \$10.00
   Item 5 = \$1.00
   Compute the dollar values for the information in the above table, determine the annual inventory carrying cost for each item, and the total annual inventory carrying cost.
4. Again, using the data for Jones Company in problems 2 and 3, suppose Jones believes that in the upcoming year, the rate of sales expected for each of the five items is as follows:

   Item 1 = 4,000 units per day
   Item 2 = 2,000 units per day
   Item 3 = 15,000 units per day
   Item 4 = 7,000 units per day
   Item 5 = 2,000 units per day
   Compute the days of supply for each item.

5. Complete an ABC analysis of the five items that Jones Corporation carries in inventory.
6. Suppose management of Foods Galore (in solved problem 3 above) found that it had drastically underestimated its annual inventory carrying cost. Rather than the 10 percent carrying cost assumed in the solved problem, carrying cost is actually 25 percent. Rework all parts of the solved problem assuming the 25 percent carrying cost.
7. Suppose Thomas Toys Ltd. (in solved problem 4) decides to reduce the review period from 21 days to 10 days. Rework the problem assuming everything else remains the same.
8. Suppose Johnson Plastics (in solved problem 5) reduces setup cost to $20. Rework the problem.
9. Ergonomics Inc. sells ergonomically designed office chairs. The company has the following information:

   Average demand = 20 units per day
   Average lead time = 30 days
   Item unit cost = $50 for orders of less than 200 units
   Item unit cost = $48 for orders of 200 units or more
   Ordering cost = $25
   Inventory carrying cost = 25%
   The business year is 250 days
   The basic question: How many chairs should the firm order each time? Assume there is no uncertainty at all about the demand or the lead time. There are many associated questions, such as what will the firm's average inventory be under each alternative? What will be the breakdown of costs for each alternative?
10. A sporting goods company has a distribution center that maintains inventory of fishing rods. The fishing rods have the following demand, lead time, and cost characteristics:

    Average demand = 100 units per day, with a standard deviation of 12 units
    Average lead time = 12 days with a standard deviation of 2 days
    250 days per year
    Unit cost = $25
    Desired service level = 95%
    Ordering cost = $50
    Inventory carrying cost = 20%
    The basic question: How many fishing rods should the distribution center carry to provide the desired service level? There are, of course, many other specific questions, such as EOQ? Average cycle stock?
11. A company experiences annual demand of 1,000 units for an item that it purchases. The rate of demand per day is very stable, with very little variation from day to day. The item costs $50 when purchased in quantities less than 100 and $48 for 100 or more. Ordering costs are $40 and the carrying cost is 25 percent. How much should the company buy each time an order is placed?
12. Meyer Stores carries a specialty line of flavored syrups. One of the most popular of these is raspberry syrup which sells, on average, 30 bottles per week. Meyer's cost is $8 per bottle. Meyer has determined its order cost to be $50 and inventory carrying cost is 20 percent. Meyer is open for business 52 weeks per year. What is the EOQ for raspberry syrup? If Meyer orders the EOQ quantity each time, what will be the inventory turnover rate for raspberry syrup?
13. Talbot Industries is evaluating its service level policy for a product that is considered critical to customers. Demand for the item averages 100 units per day and the lead time from the supplier of the item averages 6 days. An analysis of demand and lead time patterns has shown that the standard deviation of demand during lead time is 110 units. The existing service level policy allows for a stockout probability of 10 percent during the replenishment cycle. Marketing managers claim that the item is so critical that the firm should carry three standard deviations of safety stock. If the item cost is $60 and Talbot's inventory carrying cost is 20 percent, what is the incremental inventory carrying cost of the suggestion by marketing managers?

14. Johnson Corporation has the following information about a product that it carries in stock:

    Average demand = 40 units per day
    Average lead time = 15 days
    Item unit cost = $55 for orders of less than 400 units
    Item unit cost = $50 for orders of 400 units or more
    Ordering cost = $30
    Inventory carrying cost = 20%
    The business year is 300 days
    Standard deviation of demand = 2.5 units
    Standard deviation of lead time = 1.5 days
    Desired service level = 97.5%

    a. What is the annual total acquisition cost of ordering at the $55 price?
    b. What is the annual total acquisition cost of ordering at the $50 price?
    c. What level of safety stock should Johnson maintain for the item?
    d. If Johnson chooses the ordering policy that results in the lowest total annual acquisition cost, and maintains the safety stock level for 97.5 percent service, what will Johnson's average inventory be for this item?
    e. What will the annual inventory turnover rate be for this item?
    f. What will the reorder point be for the item?

15. Michigan State Figurine Inc. (MSF) sells crystal figurines to Spartan fans. MSF buys the figurines from a manufacturer for $10 per unit. They send orders electronically to the manufacturer, costing $20 per order and they experience an average lead time of eight days for each order to arrive from the manufacturer. Their inventory carrying cost is 20 percent. The average daily demand for the figurines is two units per day. They are open for business 250 days a year. Answer the following questions:

    a. How many units should the firm order each time? Assume there is no uncertainty at all about the demand or the lead time.
    b. How many orders will they place in a year?
    c. What is the average inventory?
    d. What is the annual ordering cost?
    e. What is the annual inventory carrying cost?

16. The supplier in the above scenario now decides to offer a volume discount. They will sell the crystal figurines at $8 per unit for orders of 250 units or more. Answer the same set of questions.

17. Freeport Corporation finds that demand for surfboards has average demand of 10 units per day, with a standard deviation of 3 units. Lead time from the supplier averages 12 days, with a standard deviation of 2 days. The item costs $50 and the inventory carrying cost is 30 percent.

    a. Suppose management decides to offer a 95 percent service level; that is, it is willing to experience a stockout probability of 5 percent during the order cycle. How much safety stock should be carried?
    b. How much is the annual inventory carrying cost of the safety stock because of this decision?
    c. You decide that you want this company to give better service to its customers. You decide that a 99 percent service level is appropriate. How much safety stock must be carried to offer this service level?
    d. What is the *additional* inventory carrying cost that will be incurred on this item because of your decision to increase the service level?
    e. What will the reorder point be for the company *if your decision is implemented?*

18. Suppose you are a corporate buyer. One of your suppliers delivers a particular part in 12 days on average, with a standard deviation of 3. The daily usage averages 20 units per day with a standard deviation of 4. What is the standard deviation of demand during lead time? If you use a continuous review policy, how much safety stock would

you want on hand to ensure at least 90 percent availability of the part while waiting for replenishment?

19. Korner Hardware manager Emerson Jones is interested in determining how many nativity scenes to order for the 10-day holiday season. Past experience indicates that demand for these nativity scenes averages eight per day during this 10-day period, with a standard deviation of two per day. Demand is approximately normal. Emerson purchases the nativity scenes for $15 per unit and sells them for $30 each during the season. After Christmas, they are marked down as sale items for $10 each. How many should Emerson order for the coming holiday season?
20. You have a one-time chance to purchase an item for $5. The item can be sold to customers for $30. After one day, the item has no salvage value because it becomes rotten at the end of the day. It will then cost you $15 to properly dispose of any unsold items. You think you can sell 1,000 units in one day, but you also know that the standard deviation of demand for the item is 50 units. How many units should you order?
21. Jasper's Grocery places an order for Monster every three weeks. Once the order is placed, delivery to the store typically occurs in one week. Average demand is 100 cases per week and the standard deviation of demand is 20 cases per week. The store policy is to stock an amount of inventory that allows for an average stockout condition of 10 percent while waiting for replenishment. It is time to place an order, and there are 420 cases on hand. How many units should be ordered?
22. Dreyfus Company has a policy of counting on-hand inventory of one of its products every 45 days. When a replenishment order for the product is placed with the supplier, lead time is 8 days. Demand for the product averages 6 units per day with a standard deviation of 1.5 units. It has just been determined that the company currently has 42 units on hand. How many units should the company order if it strives to maintain a 99% service level on this item?
23. You manage inventory for your company and use a continuous review inventory system to control reordering items for stock. Your company is open for business 300 days per year. One of your most important items experiences demand of 20 units per day, normally distributed with a standard deviation of 3 units per day. You experience a lead time on orders from your supplier of six days with a standard deviation of two days. If you order 1,000 units or less, you pay the supplier $5.00 per unit. Orders of 1,000 or more can be bought at a unit price of $4.75. Your ordering cost is $50. Your inventory carrying cost is 20 percent. You have established a service level policy of 97.5 percent on this item. What is your optimal order quantity? What is your reorder point? How much safety stock do you carry? What is your average inventory?
24. Suppose in problem 23, you were able to reduce your order cost to $10. What is the impact on all other variables?
25. After you reduce your order cost, as described in problem 24, the supplier in problem 23 changed its pricing policy to a standard $4.75 per unit, regardless of the order quantity. What would be the impact on all other variables?
26. You are the buyer for your university bookstore. One of the textbooks has a cost to you of $100 and you sell it to students for $140. Any copies of the book that you order and do not sell to students can be returned to the publisher for an average $80 credit. (Sometimes you can get full credit, but sometimes a new edition is published so you get no credit.) In one particular course, demand has averaged 400 books each semester, with a standard deviation of 40. What is your target service level? What is your target order quantity for the course?
27. In the same situation as described in problem 26, a text costs $100 and sells for $200. In this case, however, you cannot salvage any value from copies that do not sell because a new edition is published every semester. Demand for this text averages 80 copies each semester, with a standard deviation of 10 copies. How many should you order each semester?

28. Charles Cycles produces bicycles and tricycles. The setup cost when switching production from one to the other is $1,000. On average, retail customers order 150 tricycles per day (consider a 250-day year). The daily production rate for tricycles is 600 units. Unit cost of a tricycle is $60 and the company has determined inventory carrying cost to be 15 percent. What should the production order quantity be?
29. Bryson Carpet Mills produces a variety of different carpets. Changing from production of one carpet to another involves a setup cost of $1,000. One particular carpet costs $5 per yard to produce. Annual demand for this style is 120,000 yards. Bryson Carpet Mills produces carpet 300 days per year. The production process is most efficient when 4,000 yards per day are produced. Inventory carrying cost is estimated at 20 percent annually. What should be the production order quantity?
30. Suppose Bryson Carpet Mills develops a production process that is most efficient when 6,000 yards per day are produced at a cost of $4.50 per yard. Everything else remains the same. How does this affect the calculation in problem 29?
31. After implementing the change described in problem 30, Bryson Carpet Mills now finds that it can reduce setup cost to $500. Does this further change the calculations of production order quantity? How?

CASE

Inventory at Champion Electric

Champion Electric, a regional supplier of electrical and electronic components, keeps thousands of SKUs (stock keeping units) of various products on hand for its customers. A new operations manager, Barb Patterson, has just been hired to replace Bob, who resigned because of customer complaints and management pressure to keep inventories in check.

Gil, a longtime warehouse manager reporting to Barb, has been filling her in on past performance. "Bob was a good manager who always did what the bosses wanted him to do. He just couldn't do everything. Management was upset with Bob about customer service, the number of people we have working in this area, and more recently, with the overall level of inventory."

"Barb, I think you need to put some pressure on marketing to stop adding products, and while you're at it, we should get rid of many of the items that sell so infrequently that you have to dust the box off to read the label. We always have the higher volume, more profitable items in stock—we keep lots of safety stock so we never run out."

"We are always getting hammered because of customer complaints, and yet our records show that we have a fill rate of 99.9 percent. With over 30,000 SKUs, you can't get much better than that. None of our competition has that kind of service. At the same time, every other order has a request for some piddly item that we don't have in stock. Sometimes our system even shows we should have stock but we don't. When we don't have an item, we have to reorder it or expedite it or do something extraordinary to make sure the customer gets the product—and many times it's late. That takes people and time. It drives us crazy. We shouldn't sell all of these things. You just can't keep enough inventory."

Gil continues, "But adding product every day just makes it worse. Marketing always makes the case that it is our strategy to supply customers a 'full line' of supplies—that means we have to add a product if there is demand for it. Customers often decide they want a new and improved version of what we are stocking and we almost always try to get them what they need."

Barb questions, "How do we add these items—what's the process?"

"Sales makes an estimate of what they think they can sell and then we place an order. We try to determine the best 'economical' volume to buy of that item when we place the order. The problem is that even though customers say they want these new items, many times these things are never ordered after the first time. Would you believe that we have some 20 percent of our inventory classified as dead—it hasn't moved in over three months."

Later that day in President Campos's office, Barb gets some more information on her new mandate. "I have continued to invest money in inventory but there is a limit to how much we can afford. Customers are still complaining. I know that our inventories are higher than our competitors—I have backed that idea so that we could get a higher customer service rating than our competitors. But I'm not sure our service is any better; and, I know our inventory is higher. You have to get this thing under control."

Questions

1. Why, in your opinion, is senior management so concerned about the "high" inventory levels at Champion Electric?
2. What would you suggest to Barb as steps to take in addressing the concerns of President Campos?

CASE

Tasty Treats

Tasty Treats is a distributor of candy and snack products serving customers in a six state region of the midwestern United States. Bill Jones, chief operations officer, has been concerned about inventory levels and inventory performance at Tasty Treats for quite some time. In speaking with Jim Busfield, chief executive officer of Tasty Treats, Bill voiced some of his concerns. "Jim, we carry over 5,000 different items in inventory. I have a feeling that we just don't have a good handle on the proper approach to managing this part of our operations. We don't have any real analysis that tells us how much we should carry of each item. We just use simple rules of thumb to determine how much we should order from our suppliers. For example, we sell an average of 100 cases of Chocolate Chewies every day. When we order Chocolate Chewies from our supplier, it usually takes about 10 days for us to get the order. So, we order 1,000 cases of Chocolate Chewies every 10 days. I also try to keep an extra 200 cases on hand just in case something unexpected happens. Sometimes we run out of stock anyway and sometimes I look and see an enormous number of cases of Chocolate Chewies on hand. The same basic approach is used for every item we sell. There's got to be a better way."

Jim briefly thought over Bill's concerns before he replied. "I think you're right, Bill. As you know, my background is in finance, not operations, but I can tell you that we have a lot of money tied up in inventory and we spend a lot of money not just in buying it but in maintaining it, too. We pay insurance, taxes, and a lot of other costs just because of the amount of inventory. If we manage it better, we may be able to free up a lot of capital, too. There has to be a more sophisticated approach than what we are doing. I tell you what let's do. We have a summer intern who is majoring in supply chain management at State University. Let's turn her loose on this project."

Jim and Bill called the intern, Rachel Atkins, into the office and explained the situation to her. She happily accepted the assignment. She explained to Bill and Jim that she would need to gather a lot of information from them in order to complete the assignment. They agreed that she could have access to any data she needed and that they would tell other managers at Tasty Treats to cooperate with her in the project.

First, Rachel conducted a detailed analysis of demand for the past two years. For each of the 300 days per year that Tasty Treats ships to customers, she found that Bill was correct in saying that demand averaged 100 cases per day. However, in fact, the demand pattern had a standard deviation of 8 cases per day. She also looked at the supplier's performance and found that the 10-day lead time was a good average, but it also varied and had a standard deviation of 2 days.

From the supplier of Chocolate Chewies, Rachel learned that Tasty Treats paid $25.00 per case for Chocolate Chewies. The supplier's sales representative then remarked, "I've always wondered why Tasty Treats orders 1,000 cases every time. They've never asked about any of our discounts. If they order 3,000 cases, our selling price drops to $24.50. That's a 2 percent discount."

Rachel had several discussions with Jim and Bill. After explaining to them what "order costs" and "inventory carrying costs" consist of, they provided her with their estimates of each. Jim suggested that she should use 15 percent as the annual inventory carrying cost. Bill determined that a good estimate of order cost would be $100 per order.

As her final step in gathering information, Rachel talked with Jim, Bill, and the sales staff about the importance of customer service. She explained about service levels and stockouts, and their importance in inventory management. The sales staff was insistent that a 99 percent service level policy was needed. Jim and Bill were a little hesitant to accept that and suggested instead that Rachel consider a 95 percent service level. Rachel commented, "I'll do both and we can see what the difference is." Jim said, "That'll be great, Rachel. I'm scheduling a meeting of all senior managers for next Tuesday to hear your report. I'm looking forward to it."

Question

What recommendations should Rachel make in her presentation to Tasty Treats senior management?

SELECTED READINGS & INTERNET SITES

Inventory Operations Consulting

www.inventoryops.com/articles.htm

Supply Chain Brain

www.supplychainbrain.com/content/index.php

Bhattacharya, A.; B. Sarkar; and S. K. Mukherjee. "Distance-Based Consensus Method for ABC Analysis." *International Journal of Production Research* 45, no. 15 (2007), pp. 3405–20.

Boute, R. N.; S. M. Disney; M. R. Lambrecht; and B. Van Houdt. "A Win-Win Solution for the Bullwhip Problem." *Production Planning and Control* 19, no. 7 (October 2008), pp. 702–11.

Gruen, T., and D. Corsten. "Improve Out-of-Stock Methods at the Shelf." *Chain Store Age,* July 2006, p. 35.

Hung, K-T, and S. Ryu. "Changing Risk Preferences in Supply Chain Inventory Decisions." *Production Planning and Control* 19, no. 8 (December 2008), pp. 770–80.

Kator, C. "Inventory Costs Rise Dramatically." *Modern Materials Handling* 62, no. 7 (July 2007), pp. 9–10.

Taylor, J. C., and S. E. Fawcett. "Catalog Retailer In-Stock Performance: An Assessment of Customer Service Levels." *Journal of Business Logistics* 25, no. 2 (2004), pp. 119–35.

Trunick, P. A. "Get Down to Detail on Inventory." *Logistics Today,* September 2007, pp. 16–18.

Vollman, T. E.; W. L. Berry; D. C. Wybark; and F. R. Jacobs. *Manufacturing Planning and Control Systems for Supply Chain Management.* 5th ed. New York: McGraw-Hill, 2004.

Wang, C. X. "Random Yield and Uncertain Demand in Decentralised Supply Chains under the Traditional and VMI Arrangements." *International Journal of Production Research* 47, no. 7 (2009), pp. 1955–68.

Zipkin, P. H. *Foundations of Inventory Management.* New York: McGraw-Hill/Irwin, 2000.

8 Lean Systems

CHAPTER OUTLINE

LEARNING OBJECTIVES *After studying this chapter, you should be able to:*

LO8-1 Explain how the lean system approach improves value for internal operations and across the supply chain.

LO8-2 Describe the cultural changes, tools, and techniques needed to implement a lean approach.

LO8-3 Apply the concept of lean systems to product design.

LO8-4 Recognize the strengths and limitations of lean systems.

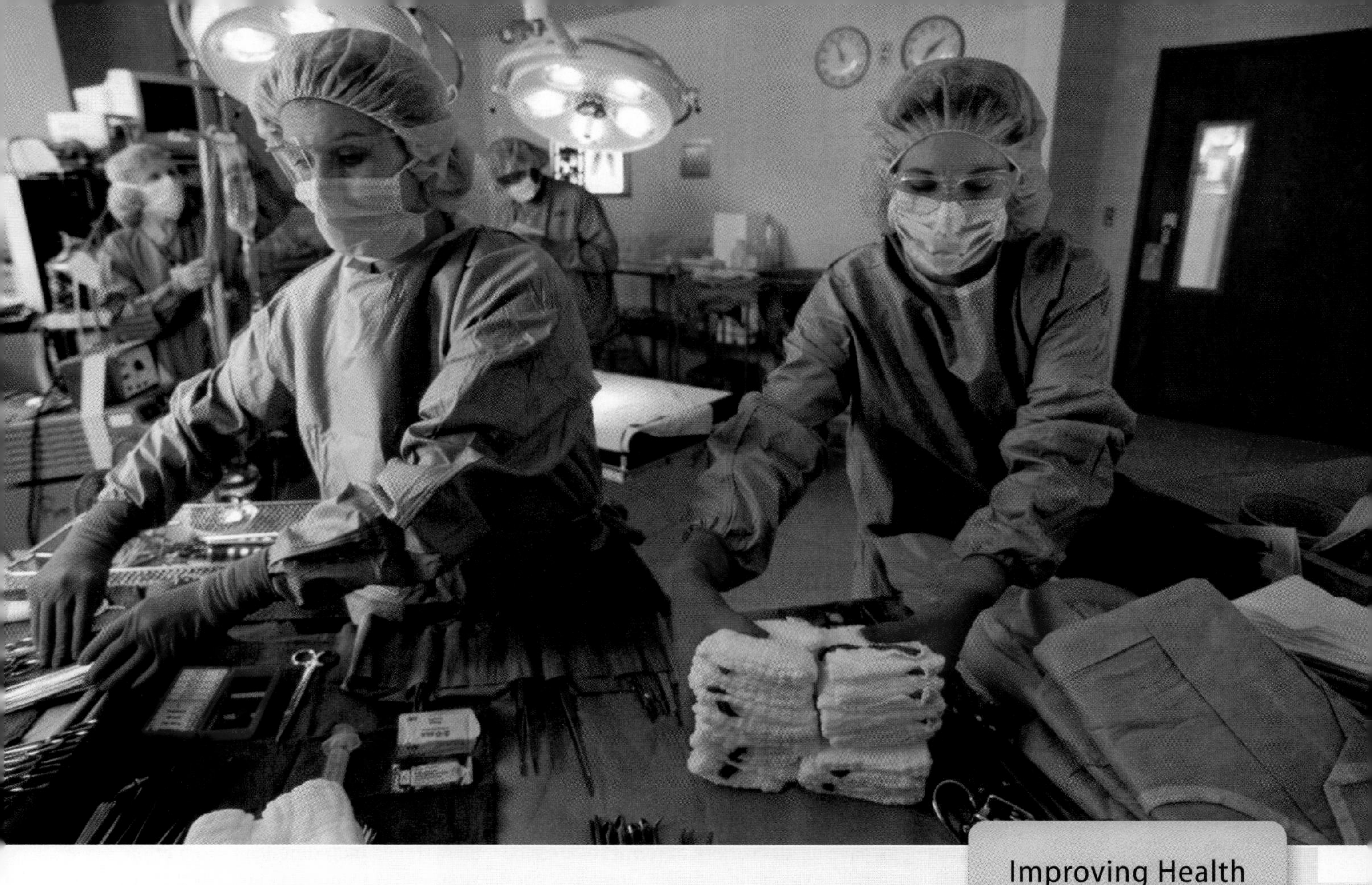

Improving Health Care through the Application of Lean Tools[1]

Imagine managing the operating room (OR) staff of a 250-bed community, not-for-profit medical center. How do you get more surgeries done per day without spending more money? In studying the problem directly through the use of ***gemba kaizen,*** a process improvement team discovered that capacity was being wasted through excessively long setups. It simply took too much time to change over operating rooms between surgical cases in the 11-OR-suite inpatient surgery department. Every minute saved in operating room changeover time could be used for more surgery or for ensuring better patient quality. Adding capacity in this way would help the staff improve both patient care and physician satisfaction.

To reduce changeover time, the team applied various lean tools such as process mapping, SMED (single minute exchange of dies—a process for setup reduction), and work standardization. The staff worked to streamline processes by identifying and moving work steps that had been internal to the changeover, and making these steps external (i.e., steps that could be done simultaneously with other activities). Visual indicators such as color coding were used to clarify the process and to standardize the OR changeover process. These and other changes were achieved through a four-day Kaizen Event. The impact: a reduction of operating room changeover time by 60 percent. Patient care has improved; nurses are more satisfied; and doctors feel that they have more time to focus on patient care rather than facility issues.

---

[1]http://leanhealthcareperformance.com/leancasestudies.html.

Prepare

What is a lean system and why is it important to today's operations management system? Why is the approach viewed as a philosophy of guiding principles rather than a technique or procedure?

Organize

Lean Systems Defined
- Origins of Lean Systems and Just-in-Time Production
- Strategic Benefit of Lean Systems
- Lean Systems Objectives, Culture, and Guiding Principles

The focus of this chapter is *lean*—a systematic approach that has been developed to help managers identify and reduce/eliminate waste and variance in the processes under their control. To many, lean is something that a manufacturer of cars and farm equipment would apply; it is not something that a restaurant owner would consider using. Yet, as can be seen from the medical center's experience in the opening story, the lean approach to managing operations across the supply chain is broad-based and it has been successfully applied in a wide variety of product and service operational settings. In addition to traditional high volume production settings and hospitals, lean systems have been applied to the production of unique, short-run collector dolls (Madame Alexander Dolls, see Figure 8-1), high-end designer luggage (Louis Vuitton), jet airplanes (Boeing), and in services (Jefferson Pilot Insurance Company, now known as Lincoln Financial Group). Starbucks (a leading maker and retailer of specialty coffees) uses lean principles and practices to enable its baristas (coffee preparers) to speed up drink preparation, while maintaining product quality. The principles, tools, and procedures that make up the lean management system are highly versatile.

In sectors such as automobiles and electronics, the lean system approach has become the dominant way that operations managers view their businesses. Because lean offers such a powerful way to eliminate wastes and variance in operational processes, it is important for all business professionals to understand its underlying principles and tools. This chapter focuses on what *lean* means, and how it can be applied in various settings.

global

LEAN SYSTEMS DEFINED

just-in-time (JIT) An older name for lean systems.

Toyota Production System (TPS) Another term for lean systems; refers to the specific lean system implemented at Toyota.

Managers have used a variety of terms to describe lean systems, including lean production, **just-in-time (JIT)** manufacturing, stockless production, zero inventories, and the **Toyota Production System (TPS)**. Currently, lean systems has become the term most commonly

FIGURE 8-1 Firms That Have Successfully Implemented Lean Systems

Madame Alexander Dolls®

Louis Vuitton luggage:

Boeing

Lincoln Financial Group

LO8-1 Explain how the lean system approach improves value for internal operations and across the supply chain.

used to describe the increasingly broad application of lean principles across manufacturing and service supply chain settings. While formal definitions of lean vary, this book uses the following definition:

> The **lean systems approach** is a *philosophy* of operations management that emphasizes the minimization of the amount of all the resources (including time) used in the various activities of the enterprise.[2]

lean systems approach A philosophy that emphasizes the minimization of the amount of all resources used in the various activities of the enterprise.

Just as a lean athlete has mostly muscle and little fat, operational processes can be described as being lean when they are very efficient and have few wasted resources. The elimination of *waste* is actually the defining objective of lean. More importantly, lean is also a philosophy—that is, a way of thinking and a way of viewing business activities and their associated resources. As a philosophy, lean offers managers guidelines that must be adapted to fit the firm's situation—the needs of its critical customers, the specific form of product value delivered, and the operations setting in which lean is deployed. Consequently, practices that work well in one setting may not work as effectively in another.

Origins of Lean Systems and Just-in-Time Production

Though elements of lean systems thinking have been around since the dawn of industrialization, credit is given to Taiichi Ohno of Toyota for organizing these elements into what eventually became the Toyota Production System.[3] Beginning in 1937, Ohno discovered that American laborers were nine times as productive as Japanese laborers. He borrowed important roots of lean systems thinking from two distinct American institutions: Henry Ford's mass production system, and the supermarket. The merging of these elements into what eventually became *lean* occurred during the 1950s when a delegation from Toyota led by Ohno visited the Ford plant at River Rouge (see Figure 8-2), then considered the most advanced car manufacturing system in the world.

global

At Ford, Ohno studied practices such as setup reduction, work standardization, focused factories, ongoing employee training, supply chain integration, and variance control and reduction. He also noted the presence of large amounts of inventory and rework. While he was greatly impressed with the operations at Ford, it was in the American supermarket that Ohno found his vision of the ideal operating system:

> We made a connection between supermarkets and the just-in-time system. . . . A supermarket is where a customer can get (1) what is needed, (2) at the time needed, (3) in the amount needed. From the supermarket, we got the idea of viewing the earlier processes in the production line as a kind of store. The later process

FIGURE 8-2 Ford's River Rouge Plant: Once a Symbol of American Mass Production, 1942

[2] *APICS Dictionary*, 9th edition, 1998.

[3] Yasuhiro Monden, *Toyota Production System* (Norcross, GA: Industrial Engineering and Management Press, 1983), p. v.

(the customer) goes to the earlier process (the supermarket) to acquire the required parts (the commodities) at the time and in the quantity needed. The earlier process immediately produces the quantity just taken (restocking the shelves). We hoped that this would help us approach our just-in-time goal, and . . . we actually applied the system to our machine shop at the main plant.[4]

From this vision, the idea of just-in-time manufacturing was born. Initially, many North American managers felt that Toyota's approach could not succeed in the United States. However, the publication of a three-year study of worldwide automobile manufacturing[5] ended the debate about whether lean systems created real, lasting benefits. Table 8-1 shows that in the 1980s, Japanese-owned automotive plants following lean were as much as 30 percent more productive than U.S.–owned plants using traditional methods—quite a turnaround from the situation in the 1930s. Furthermore, the Japanese plants delivered cars

TABLE 8-1 Performance Characteristics for Lean Systems

	Japanese in Japan	Japanese in North America	Americans in North America	All Europe
Performance				
Productivity (hrs/vehicle)	16.8	21.2	25.1	36.2
Quality (assembly defects/100 vehicles)	60.0	65.0	82.3	97.0
Layout				
Space (sq. ft. / vehicle / yr)	5.7	9.1	7.8	7.8
Size of repair areas (as % of assembly space)	4.1	4.9	12.9	14.4
Inventories (days for 8 sample parts)	.2	1.6	2.9	2.0
Workforce				
% of workforce in teams	69.3	71.3	17.3	.6
Job rotation (0 = none; 4 = freq)	3.0	2.7	.9	1.9
Suggestions/ Employee	61.6	1.4	.4	.4
# of job classes	11.9	8.7	67.1	14.8
Training of new production workers (hours)	380.3	370.0	46.4	173.3
Absenteeism	5.0	4.8	11.7	12.1
Automation				
Welding (% of direct steps)	86.2	85.0	76.2	76.6
Painting (% of direct steps)	54.6	40.7	33.6	38.2
Assembly (% of direct steps)	1.7	1.1	1.2	3.1

Source: *The Machine That Changed the World,* p. 92, by James P. Womack, Daniel T. Jones, and Daniel Roos. Copyright 1990.

[4]William H. Davidow and Michael S. Malone, *The Virtual Corporation* (New York: Harper Business, 1992), pp. 119–20.

[5]J. P. Womack, D. T. Jones, and D. Roos, *The Machine That Changed the World* (New York: Rawson Associates, 1990).

with fewer defects using facilities that required less floor space and lower inventories. The data showed that the Japanese lean effect was significant, whether the plant was located in Japan or in the United States.

Strategic Benefit of Lean Systems

The foregoing automotive comparison highlights the productivity and operational gains created by a lean approach. More importantly, lean can produce straegic benefits. As illustrated in Figure 8-3, by becoming lean a firm can significantly lower its break-even production quantity; that is, the minimum amount of output the firm needs to sell in order to make profit. It does this in two ways: by increasing the contribution margin (the difference between price and the firm's direct costs) and by reducing fixed overhead costs.

By eliminating wastes of all sorts in the system, the lean approach lowers variable production costs associated with labor, materials, and energy, thus raising the unit profitability of products. Since lean also emphasizes building exactly the products customers need, exactly when they need them, the contribution margin may also increase if the firm is able to charge higher prices. Lean also attacks waste associated with the fixed costs of facilities, equipment, capital, and support labor such as management, engineering, and so on. Together, improvements in the use of resources that affect both fixed and variable costs drive the production break-even point downward, enhancing the firm's flexibility. The firm can afford to produce smaller quantities, allowing niche marketing, and it can change outputs more quickly in response to changes in customer demand.

Lean Systems Objectives, Culture, and Guiding Principles

The objectives and principles of Lean Systems thinking are well established. They are to produce:

1. Only the products (goods and services) that customers want,
2. Only as quickly as customers want them,
3. With only features that customers want, and no others,
4. With perfect quality,
5. In the minimum possible lead times,
6. With no waste of labor, materials, or equipment, and
7. Using methods that reinforce the occupational development of workers.

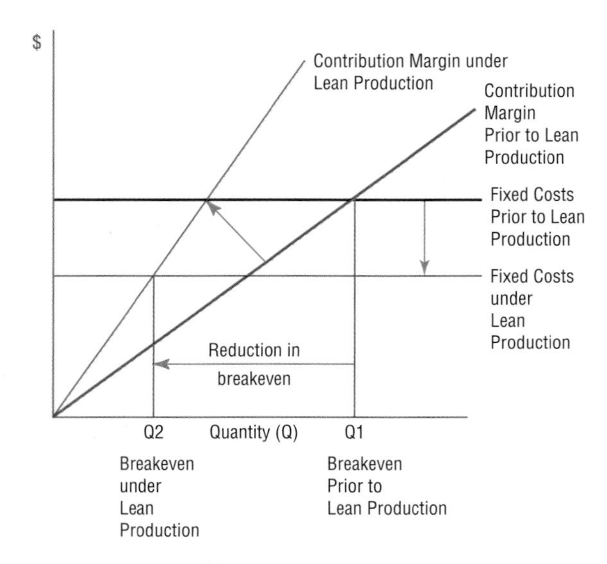

FIGURE 8-3 Changes in Cost Structure under Lean Systems

Note that the first three objectives emphasize producing exactly what customers want just-in-time; that is, building products at the same rate that customers demand them. If operations managers can *synchronize* their production with demand (i.e., building at the same rate as customers demand the products), they can eliminate many sorts of waste (which are discussed later). Objectives 4–6 emphasize the quality, timeliness, and cost elements associated with creating value for customers. For the first three objectives to be met, operational processes and their personnel must embrace objectives 4 through 6 (since these objectives describe the desired traits of the products and the associated processes). The last objective reflects lean's greater emphasis on employees as the primary agents for improving operations. For operations to become flexible and responsive, employees closest to the underlying causes of waste and variance must become active problem solvers.

As stated earlier, lean systems is not just a set of techniques; rather, it is a management philosophy that emphasizes the creation of value with minimization of waste. To achieve the objectives identified above, lean is guided by important shared cultural beliefs and values, by a common language, and by five important principles:[6]

Principle 1. Precisely specify value for each specific product.
Principle 2. Identify the value stream for each product.
Principle 3. Make value flow without interruptions.
Principle 4. Let the customer pull value from the producer.
Principle 5. Pursue perfection.

Principle 1, "precisely specify value for each specific product," maintains that the final consumer ultimately determines the value of a product or service. Consequently, the firm must . . . engage in a dialogue with the consumers of its products and services to determine which outcomes, features, functions and capabilities are most valuable. This dialogue provides the basis for continual improvement since it allows everyone to understand what attributes are valued and what attributes are "wasteful." As Henry Ford once noted, any action that does not generate value must ultimately be regarded as waste.

Principle 2, "identify the value stream for each product," suggests that a firm must clearly understand and link together all of the activities involved in product development, order processing, production, and delivery. A strong value is placed on viewing and organizing these activities as processes within an overall system. Operations analysts often map out these processes in order to identify value-adding and non–value-adding steps. This type of analysis identifies different types of *muda* (the Japanese word for waste) in the process.

Waste is viewed as a symptom of problems elsewhere. Wastes of all kinds can usually be categorized into one of **seven basic types of waste** (see Table 8-2).[7]

seven basic types of waste **A classification of wastes into one of seven basic categories.**

To reduce waste, workers must quantify its impact, uncover its underlying root causes, and then attack these root causes. For example, if inventory is too high, study the problem, uncover the root cause, and then attack it. As we can see from Table 8-2, high inventory (which is a symptom of overproduction) can be caused by several possible factors. If the root cause is long process setups, then the appropriate response is to attack setup time and cost. As workers begin to eliminate waste from internal value streams, they typically become aware of waste throughout the supply chain as well.

Principle 3, "make value flow without interruptions," means that the movements of materials and information in value streams should be swift and even. Sometimes operations managers use the saying "once in motion, always in motion"

student activity

See how many different wastes you can identify on your next visit to a doctor's office, hair salon, hotel, or restaurant.

[6]J. P. Womack and D. T. Jones, *Lean Thinking* (New York: Simon and Schuster, 1996).

[7]These seven basic types of waste are foundational. Some managers have expanded the categories to include areas such as "underutilization of the problem solving capabilities of employees."

TABLE 8-2 Seven Basic Types of Waste

Waste	Symptoms	Root Causes
Overproduction (processing more units than are needed)	• Extra inventory • Excessive floor space utilized • Unbalanced material flow • Complex information management • Disposal charges • Extra waste handling & treatment • High utility costs	• Product complexity • Misuse of automation • Long process setups • Unlevel scheduling • Overengineered equipment / capability • Lack of reuse & recycling • Poor market forecast
Waiting (resources wasted waiting for work)	• Underutilization of resources • Reduced productivity • Increase in investment • Idle equipment • Large waiting / storage rooms • Equipment running, not producing • Unnecessary testing	• Unbalanced workload • Unplanned maintenance • Long process setup times • Misuse of automation • Unlevel scheduling • Ineffective layout • Too much specialization
Transportation (units being unnecessarily moved)	• Extra handling equipment • Large storage areas • Over-staffing • Damaged product • Extra paperwork & hand-offs • Excessive energy consumption	• Mislocated materials • Unlevel scheduling • Unfavorable facility layout • Poor organization / housekeeping • Unbalanced processes
Processing (excessive or unnecessary operations)	• Extra equipment • Longer lead time • Reduced productivity • Extra material movement • Sorting, testing, inspection • Inappropriate use of resources • Excess energy consumption • Processing by-products	• Product changes without process changes • Just-in-case logic • Lack of communication • Redundant approvals and inspections • Undefined customer requirements • Stop-gap measures that become routine • Lack of reuse / recycling
Inventory (units waiting to be processed or delivered)	• Complex tracking systems • Extra storage & handling • Extra rework / hidden problems • Paperwork / documents • Stagnated information flow • High disposal costs • In-process packaging	• Just-in-case logic • Incapable processes (poor quality) • Unbalanced workload • Unreliable supplier shipments • Inadequate measurement & reward system
Motion (unnecessary or excessive resource activity)	• Reduced productivity • Large reach / walk distances • Excess handling • Reduced quality • People / machines waiting	• Poor ergonomics / layout • Machine / process design • Nonstandardized work methods • Poor organization / housekeeping
Product defects (waste due to unnecessary scrap, rework, or correction)	• Rework, repairs, & scrap • Customer returns • Loss of customer confidence • Missed shipments / deliveries • Hazardous waste generation • High disposal costs	• Lack of process control & error-proofing • Deficient planned maintenance • Poor product design • Customer needs not understood • Improper handling • Inadequate training

waste of overproduction Processing more units than are necessary.

waste of waiting Resources wasted waiting for work.

transportation waste Units being unnecessarily moved.

processing waste Excessive or unnecessary operations.

inventory waste Units waiting to be processed or delivered.

waste of motion Unnecessary or excessive resource activity.

waste from product defects Waste due to unnecessary scrap, rework, or correction.

GET REAL

"Picturing" Waste and Value: A Process Mapping Story

Process mapping (discussed in the Chapter 3 Supplement) is an invaluable tool for identifying waste. At one company, managers had every employee take pictures of every activity they performed. The pictures were used to create a pictorial flow chart. The chart surprised both the managers and employees because the process involved over 1,100 steps. As the employees then developed ways to eliminate each wasteful activity, they removed the photograph of that activity from the process flow collage and pinned it to a picture of a trashcan on another bulletin board. In this way the process improvement team was able to visually chart its progress as well as recognize those workers who had eliminated non–value-adding activities.

to characterize the ideal state of a lean system. The key indicator that this state is attained is very little inventory. Inventory is often sitting still; therefore, it represents an interruption to material flows. Even worse, inventory often hides or covers other types of waste. This effect of inventory is illustrated in Figure 8-4, where the "rocks" below the surface represent problems and wastes. Too much inventory allows production to continue in spite of these problems, and consequently they are never addressed.

Excess inventory in a system often removes the urgency needed to identify and address problems created by such root causes as poor quality, long process setups, and unreliable machines. Inventory is sometimes used to protect the operation just in case these kinds of problems occur. Though this use of inventory may be unintentional, it nevertheless makes flow-interrupting problems difficult to find and solve. Process managers are likely to use inventory to satisfy shortages caused by problems, and worry about addressing the root causes of the problems later when they have time (which, in many situations, is never).

Inventory serves as a measure of the health of an operating system (just like a thermometer measures a patient's temperature). The more inventory needed for the system to work, the less healthy the system is. While using some inventory as a buffer against uncertainty makes sense in some cases, it can be overdone. In a service setting, excess capacity and increased lead times are often the buffers that hide problems. Inefficiencies in the systems are hidden by having too many people and by allowing lengthy lead times.

pull system Activities in the operating processes are initiated by actual customer demands, and not by forecasted demands.

Principle 4, "let the customer pull value from the producer," is the source of the term, **pull system**. In a pull system, activities in operating processes are initiated by actual customer demands, not by schedules that are based on forecasts. In doing so, the

FIGURE 8-4 Inventory Hides Operating Problems

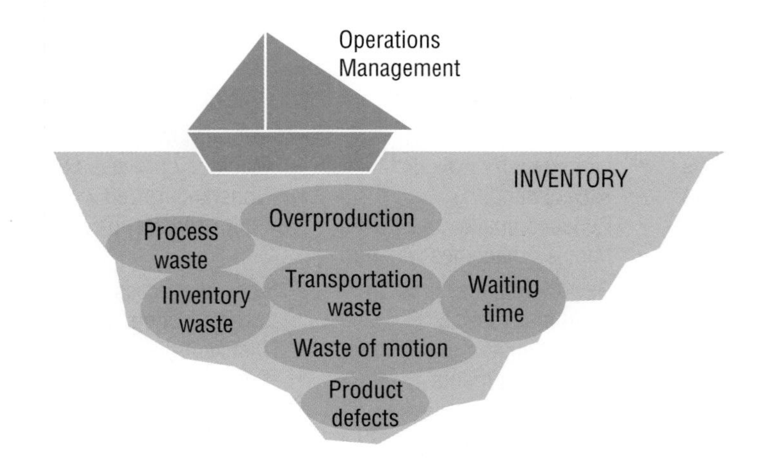

process produces only what customers want, when they want it, and where they want it. The pull system approach is discussed later in this chapter in the section, "Kanban-Pull Scheduling."

Principle 5, "pursue perfection," suggests that continuous improvement is always possible. As long as workers are implementing the first four principles, they will always uncover more opportunities to improve processes and eliminate waste. A part of the lean systems philosophy is the belief that everyone in the organization, from top managers to frontline workers, must be engaged in this ongoing effort to seek perfection.

Underlying the successful implementation of these five principles is the need for a **lean system culture**. The lean system culture places a high value on respect for people in the system. Employees must be empowered—given the training, tools, and authority to make continuous process improvements. Recall that the last major objective of lean systems is to produce "using methods that reinforce the occupational development of workers."

lean system culture The culture that is present in lean systems and that places a high value on respect for people in the system.

In the lean systems philosophy, employees are viewed as critical resources for success, for several reasons:

- *Acceptance:* Lean requires that everyone from top to bottom must buy into the goals and approaches underlying lean. Veteran employees must be willing to teach new employees through words and actions the basics of lean.
- *Source of flexibility:* At the heart of lean is an emphasis on building the flexibility to respond directly to customers' demands (pull system). This type of flexibility depends on employees who are multiskilled and cross-trained, workers who can move quickly to fill constantly changing demand requirements.
- *Working in teams:* Lean places a high value on teamwork. Problems are best solved when representatives from different functional areas, suppliers, and customers work together in a team environment. Employees must be able and willing to work in teams.
- *Power in their hands:* More commonly referred to as **employee empowerment**, the responsibility for improving product quality and flow lies with the frontline workers who are the most familiar with the processes that must be improved. These employees have the power to stop work, for example, should they see instances of problems emerging in the system. Managers and engineers must be willing to trust and work with frontline workers in a partnership.

employee empowerment Putting the responsibility for attacking waste with the employees directly involved in the processes.

The lean system culture is based on certain shared values and beliefs. Of these beliefs, the following are the most important:

- *Manage with data.* Problems and solutions are identified, solved, and evaluated with data (quantitative, objective information). Data analysis replaces opinions, and the focus is placed on process performance rather than personal feelings.
- *Waste is a symptom.* Inventory and other visible forms of waste are never attacked directly. Rather, they are seen as the results of problems elsewhere.
- *Goals are to be met.* Managers must set realistic, achievable goals. The expectation is that everyone will meet their goals. It is management's role to find out how to help everyone meet their goals.
- *Standardization is fundamental to performance improvement.* Standardization highlights variation and abnormalities. It simplifies problem solving. Under lean, the motto is "Without Standardization, There Is No Opportunity for Improvement."
- *Process orientation.* If you don't like the outcomes (the level of quality, the cost, the lead time), then you change the process. Lean involves attaining superior behavior by identifying the critical processes and changing them.

These values are inculcated into each person who works in a lean system. They become part of the belief structures that guide how everyone operates. It is important for managers to allow workers the time and social interactions needed to foster a lean culture.

Prepare

What are the various tools and techniques commonly used in lean systems and what are their purposes?

Organize

Implementing Lean Systems: Tools and Techniques
- Total Productive Maintenance (TPM)
- Group Technology—Cellular Manufacturing
- Focused Factories
- TAKT Time Flow Balancing
- Kanban (Pull) Scheduling
- Level, Mixed-Model Scheduling
- Setup Reduction
- Statistical Process Control
- Visual Control
- Quality at the Source
- Kaizen Events
- Process Analysis/Value Stream Mapping
- Poka-Yoke
- 5-S Program
- Simplification/Standardization

IMPLEMENTING LEAN SYSTEMS: TOOLS AND TECHNIQUES

Along with a common culture and language, lean encourages a common view of work processes and improvement techniques. Table 8-3 classifies lean tools and techniques according to their areas of primary operational impact. Some of the tools work together synergistically. For example, a 5-S program is usually an essential prerequisite to a setup reduction effort. Also note that there is a high degree of overlap between these tools and the procedures discussed in the quality improvement tools and techniques supplement to Chapter 6. Quality management programs and lean systems work well together.

Total Productive Maintenance (TPM)

Equipment breakdowns create variance and costs within operational processes, not to mention user frustration (think about the frustration that an out of order sign can cause). Equipment failures, setups, processing speed losses, and quality defects can often all be traced to a lack of preventive maintenance. **Total productive maintenance (TPM)** works to identify and prevent all potential causes of breakdowns to achieve an ambitious goal of zero unplanned downtime. Typical TPM programs emphasize shop floor organization, disciplined adherence to operating procedures, rigorous equipment design and upkeep, and a focus on preventing problems rather than fixing them. In addition to manufacturing equipment, TPM can be applied to computer networks and automated service kiosks.

total productive maintenance (TPM) The processes and systems that work to identify and prevent all possible equipment breakdown.

Group Technology—Cellular Manufacturing

In contrast to a functional layout (which puts the same types of equipment together in departments), or a product layout (which assigns workers to highly specialized, individual machines and tasks), **group technology (GT)** gathers in one location all of the equipment and work skills necessary for complete production of a family of similar products. Part families are created based on similarities in design features or in processing requirements. For each family, operations managers organize a work cell that lays out the equipment and facilities in the optimum sequence needed to build the items of the product family.

group technology (GT) An approach to work layout and scheduling that gathers in one location all of the equipment and work skills necessary to complete production of a family of similar products.

Focused Factories

The **focused factory** applies the same logic of group technology at the plant level. This approach reduces customer-induced variance by grouping together similar customers and then designing and implementing production systems (factories) to serve these specific customers (and no one else). The underlying logic is that a factory focused on a few specific tasks will outperform a factory that attempts to serve many disparate demands. A factory can be *market focused,* supplying a range of products to customers with similar or complementary demand patterns and value propositions, or it can be *product focused,* producing products that have similar technological processing requirements. Frequently, a "factory-within-a-factory" approach is used where two separate factories are housed within one overall building structure. Jefferson Pilot Insurance Company (as described in the Get Real box) provides a good example of this approach in a service organization.

focused factory Organizing operations systems by grouping together similar customers and then designing and implementing product systems to serve these specific customers.

LO8-2 Describe the cultural changes, tools, and techniques needed to implement a lean approach.

TAKT Time Flow Balancing

TAKT time flow balancing is a lean systems scheduling approach aimed at synchronizing the output rate with the rate of customer demand. *Takt* is a German word that means pace or rhythm of operations. Consider this example. Suppose that each week an insurance

TAKT time flow balancing A scheduling approach aimed at synchronizing the output rate with the rate of customer demand.

Applying the Focused Factory Idea to an Insurance Firm

Jefferson Pilot Insurance Company (a part of the Lincoln Financial Group) applied lean concepts to its application processing operations. Early on, managers noticed that differences in requirements created a high degree of variance in application processing times. One major difference in applications was that some required time-consuming attending physician statements, while others did not. The improvement team decided to create two processing lines, or "factories," one for each type of application. In this way, two steady moving streams of work were created. Fast-moving applications would no longer sit behind slow-moving applications waiting for physician statements. By making this change, along with other lean improvements, the company reduced application-processing time by 70–80 percent, and overall labor costs by 26 percent.

TABLE 8-3 Lean Systems Tools and Techniques

Area of Primary Impact		
Development of Facilities and Resources	**Operational Scheduling and Control**	**Continuous Process Improvement**
Total productive maintenance	TAKT time flow balancing	Quality at the source
Group technology	Kanban (pull) scheduling	Kaizen Events
Focused factories	Mixed model scheduling	Process analysis / Value stream mapping
	Setup reduction	Poka-yoke (fail-safing/mistake-proofing)
	Statistical process control	5-S program
	Visual control	Simplification/Standardization

company has 33 hours of operating time to process an average of 100 applications submitted. This means that the company should adjust its capacity to process applications at a TAKT time rate of about three applications per hour, or one application every 20 minutes. In order to achieve this output, the company needs to balance its processing line and ensure that the bottleneck (slowest) operation in the overall process can work at least at this rate. Chapter 5 shows calculations for this type of line balancing.

Kanban (Pull) Scheduling

In keeping with the principle of letting customers pull value from the producer, the lean approach uses a scheduling system that can immediately and clearly communicate the demands of the customer to the delivery system. A **kanban (pull) scheduling** system does this. *Kanban* is the Japanese term for a signal. Kanbans are most often a system of control cards that govern material movements through a process. However, empty bins, colored golf balls, lights, or other types of items have been used as kanban signals.

kanban (pull) scheduling A scheduling system that builds output in response to actual customer demand.

A common approach uses two basic types of kanbans: *production kanbans* and *withdrawal kanbans* (also known as *conveyance kanbans*). A production kanban authorizes a worker to replenish an empty bin, specifying the type of parts and the number to build. When an empty bin arrives at a workstation with a production kanban attached, it is a signal to build a new batch of items to fill the bin. A withdrawal kanban authorizes someone to withdraw a standard amount of specific parts from a container. If a worker

GET REAL

Using Kanbans to Schedule a Steel Mill

This picture shows a kanban system in use. Each cradle can store a steel coil; the cradles are organized by operation; the coils are organized in order of processing. Management can control the number of coils produced and stored by taping off the unneeded cradles. As we can see in this picture, a number of cradles are taped off. This tells everyone that we can produce steel coils until we reach the taped off cradles. At that point, we have to stop. Production is initiated as inventory is pulled, exposing open cradles; once these open cradles are filled, production stops. In this plant, the introduction of lean has resulted in a 50 percent reduction in lead times, improved on-time delivery, and a $5,000,000 per month improvement in profitability.

processing the job runs out of a part, the withdrawal kanban that accompanied the job gives that person the authority to take an empty bin to a replenishment area to exchange for a full bin.

These two kinds of kanbans control interactions between workstations such that no product is produced or withdrawn before it is needed at the downstream consuming work center. In a "push" system, by contrast, movements are controlled by a schedule that is based on forecasted demand and fixed operating times. Often, forecasted demands do not materialize and supposedly fixed operating times vary. Kanban scheduling provides the ability for the system to react to these uncertainties, as opposed to forcing movements according to a prearranged schedule. Further, the kanban system links work centers together in a way that eliminates the need for paperwork, complex computer technology, and order tracking. This aspect of the kanban system can be seen in the Get Real box "Using Kanbans to Schedule a Steel Mill."

Kanban (pull) scheduling can be effectively viewed as a complement to materials and requirements planning (MRP) systems (as discussed in Chapter 14). MRP tells the system what to produce and when the end items are needed; kanban determines the exact order and flow with which production is to be carried out.

push scheduling A system in which activities are initiated and products are moved according to a schedule, irrespective of whether or not the customer demands it.

Kanban pull scheduling can be contrasted with **push scheduling**, where a product is sent to the next stage of production or delivery irrespective of whether or not an actual demand for the product exists. Such deliveries are determined in advance by a schedule based on a forecast of demand, or simply by the fact that the preceding operation completed the item and wanted to send it on. With push scheduling, line imbalances or bottlenecks become hidden because production still takes place even though there is no demand for it. With pull scheduling, process problems become immediately visible (and urgent) because activities stop and wait until more demand initiates production. This difference is one of the factors that makes pull scheduling so attractive to many managers (especially when lean is used).

level, mixed-model scheduling The practice of leveling quantities of different product models produced over a period of time, with the goal of reducing batch sizes and lead times.

heijunka A form of level, mixed-model scheduling.

Level, Mixed-Model Scheduling

An important goal in lean systems is to schedule work so that flows are smooth and predictable. **Level, mixed-model scheduling**, also known as **heijunka**, is the practice of leveling production of different product models over a period of time, with the goal of reducing batch sizes and lead times. It consists of two linked steps: load leveling and mixed-model scheduling. *Load leveling* is essentially a calculation of the average rate of production needed for each item based on the overall TAKT time. Then, one uses *mixed-model scheduling* to decide how to distribute the production of different products over the workday.

The level, mixed-model scheduling approach apportions batches of each product to be produced evenly throughout the day. For example, in a plant that produces four products, small production runs of product A, B, C, and D (ideally one unit in each run) are sequenced again and again throughout the day. The number of occurrences of each product in the schedule is proportional to its relative demand.

Level, mixed-model scheduling promotes the lean systems goal of simple flows through relatively simple methods. The technique offers a way to achieve swift, even response to market demand, simpler coordination of supply because consumption is at a constant rate, more consistent production learning, and minimal inventories.

Setup Reduction

In order for level, mixed-model schedules to be efficient, changeovers required to switch from one product to the next must be minimized. In general, **setup reduction** lowers changeover times and costs and makes it possible to produce outputs in smaller batch sizes efficiently. Chapter 7, shows this relationship mathematically.

setup reduction The processes used to reduce setup and changeover times with the goal of making output of smaller batches more efficient.

Setup reduction efforts usually involve process mapping and analysis to identify steps that can be eliminated, executed faster, or done in parallel. Think about the ways that a pit crew works together to execute extremely fast tire changes and refueling for race cars. Operations managers in factories and service centers similarly make use of careful planning, process analysis, good housekeeping, specialized training, tooling and technologies, and teamwork to make setups faster.

The most commonly used approach for setup reduction is that of **single minute exchange of dies (SMED)**. This is a systematic three-stage procedure for reducing long setups:

single minute exchange of dies (SMED) A systematic three-stage procedure for reducing long setups.

- *Stage 1: Separate internal and external setups.* An *internal setup* includes any setup procedure that occurs while the equipment sits idle. In contrast, an *external setup* is any setup activity that workers complete while the equipment operates.
- *Stage 2: Convert internal setups to external setups.* Again, this is done by examining the flow process chart and developing a new process.
- *Stage 3: Streamline all activities in a setup.* This stage tries to eliminate any activities performed to make adjustments, calibrations, elaborate positioning, unnecessary tightening, or trial runs.

Statistical Process Control

Statistical process control (SPC) makes use of various statistical tools for analyzing the capabilities of a given process and for monitoring its performance. The essential goal of SPC is to put controls in place that help ensure the quality of production and give quick notice when unusual events occur that might lead to product or service defects. SPC tools are discussed in greater detail in the Chapter 6 Supplement, "Quality Improvement Tools."

statistical process control (SPC) The use of various statistical tools for analyzing the capabilities of a given process and for monitoring its performance, with the goal of flagging potential problems before they occur.

Visual Control

Visual control is like SPC in that its goal is to immediately make the status of an operation visible and continuously updated for all interested parties. Bulletin boards, SPC charts, large electronic displays, and lighting systems are some of the means used to make real-time performance metrics available to large numbers of people. The first Get Real box on page 297 provides an example of an andon board—one form of visual control. Visual control reduces waste by reducing reaction time and by maintaining a sense of urgency.

visual control Making current performance and potential problems immediately visually apparent.

Mobile technologies are creating new opportunities for visual control. With devices like the iPad or the Android-based tablet, firms are introducing new ways of interacting with operations data. Previously, a worker might have had to look at fixed computer screens or process boards in different locations to see what was taking place. Now, common procedures can be stored (with accompanying videos) and real-time status reports can be obtained on wireless, handheld devices. With such devices, workers need fewer resources and less lead time to identify, diagnose, and solve problems. Mobile access to information is changing the shop floor, transportation, and operations all across the supply chain.

quality at the source The practice of eliminating defects at their root cause origination points.

jidoka A focus on developing technological features of equipment and processes that automatically detect and flag problems.

stop-and-fix (or line-stop) system The practice by which an operator should stop the process and immediately fix problems, rather than allowing it to continue making poor-quality output.

Quality at the Source

Quality at the source (often abbreviated as Q@S) is an emphasis on eliminating defects at their origination points. Ensuring quality at the source reduces the potential for quality problems downstream, because the quality of the outputs of later stages of production depends substantially on the quality of their inputs. Three techniques are often associated with quality at the source: jidoka, stop-and-fix (or line-stop) systems, and andons (trouble lights).

Jidoka

Japanese for *autonomation,* **jidoka** represents a focus on developing technological features of equipment and processes that automatically detect and flag problems while the systems run. For example, a limit switch on a machine might monitor the contents of a feeding bin and light a signal or sound a tone when the bin becomes nearly empty, to alert the operator to refill it.

Stop-and-Fix (Line-Stop) Systems

A **stop-and-fix (or line-stop) system** works on the simple premise that an operator should stop the process and immediately fix any significant problem that arises, rather than allowing it to continue making poor-quality output. Besides guarding against low quality, such a system brings focused attention to the source of the problem because its failure has shut down the process in a highly visible and immediate way, perhaps disrupting other operations that depend on the problem activity.

Andons (Trouble Lights)

andons (trouble lights) The use of visual indicator systems such as flashing lights to help management assess current performance and quickly identify the location of current problems.

Programs to enhance quality at the source may rely on visual signals to identify the exact locations of problems in the system. Lean systems often combine these **andons (trouble lights)** with jidoka and stop-and-fix systems to make problems highly visible, allowing workers to develop visual control of a process. We can see an example of an andon system in the Get Real box at the bottom of the next page.

Kaizen Events

kaizen event A short-term, cross-functional team project aimed at improving an existing process.

A **kaizen event** is a short-term project (usually one to four days) aimed at improving an existing process. In that time period, cross-functional team members document a process, assess different options for performance, and develop and document the implemented process changes. This highly focused effort emphasizes fast action improvements, verifiable measures of improvement, and disciplined documentation of the ideas to be used in future improvement efforts.

gemba kaizen Managers and employees are obligated to see the problems and issues in person rather than relying on reports.

Critical to the success of the Kaizen Event is **gemba kaizen**. The term gemba (meaning "actual place") emphasizes the notion that managers and employees are obligated to see the problems and issues in person, rather than relying on reports. They must travel to where the problems are taking place. This may sound expensive, but a lean systems belief

Example of Visual Control in Action: Andon Board

Lines 1 and 3 indicate machines; lines 2 and 4 indicate what is taking place. For example, from this figure, we can see that machines 1C, 8, 9, 14, and 17 are experiencing problems with quality control (QC) being the issue at 1C, 9, and 17. The entire operations system and its status is immediately evident to the manager.

Source: www.pcmsigns.com/andon2.htm.

Source graphic: www.salescaster.com.

is that these expenses will pay off in terms of faster and higher-quality problem solving. More information about kaizen events is found in Chapter 3, "Managing Processes and Capacity."

Process Analysis/Value Stream Mapping

Process analysis/value stream mapping is a graphic mapping technique (as discussed in Chapter 3 and the Chapter 3 Supplement) that helps managers understand the material and information flows as a product makes its way through the process. Value stream mapping also considers factors such as capacity, quality, and variability. One of the major metrics/outputs of a value stream mapping exercise is to identify the percentage of the total lead time that is value-adding.

process analysis/value stream mapping A graphical technique that helps managers understand material and information flows as a product makes its way through the process.

GET REAL

Using an Andon Board to Spot a Problem

This andon board is used to help management assess the performance of a five-line plant. This board gives management a lot of useful information. It tells management what the output target is, what each line is doing, and if any line(s) are experiencing problems. From this board, we can see that lines 1 and 4 are under control, lines 2 and 3 are running slow (indicated by the yellow), and that line 5 has stopped. Because line 5 has stopped, this is where management should focus its attention.

Source: www.london-electronics.com/andon-displays.php.

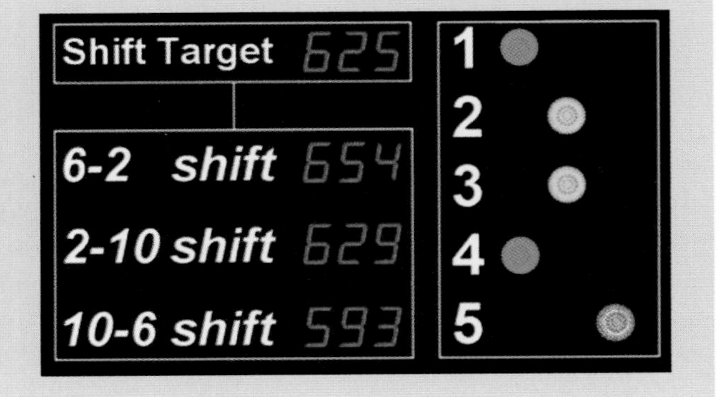

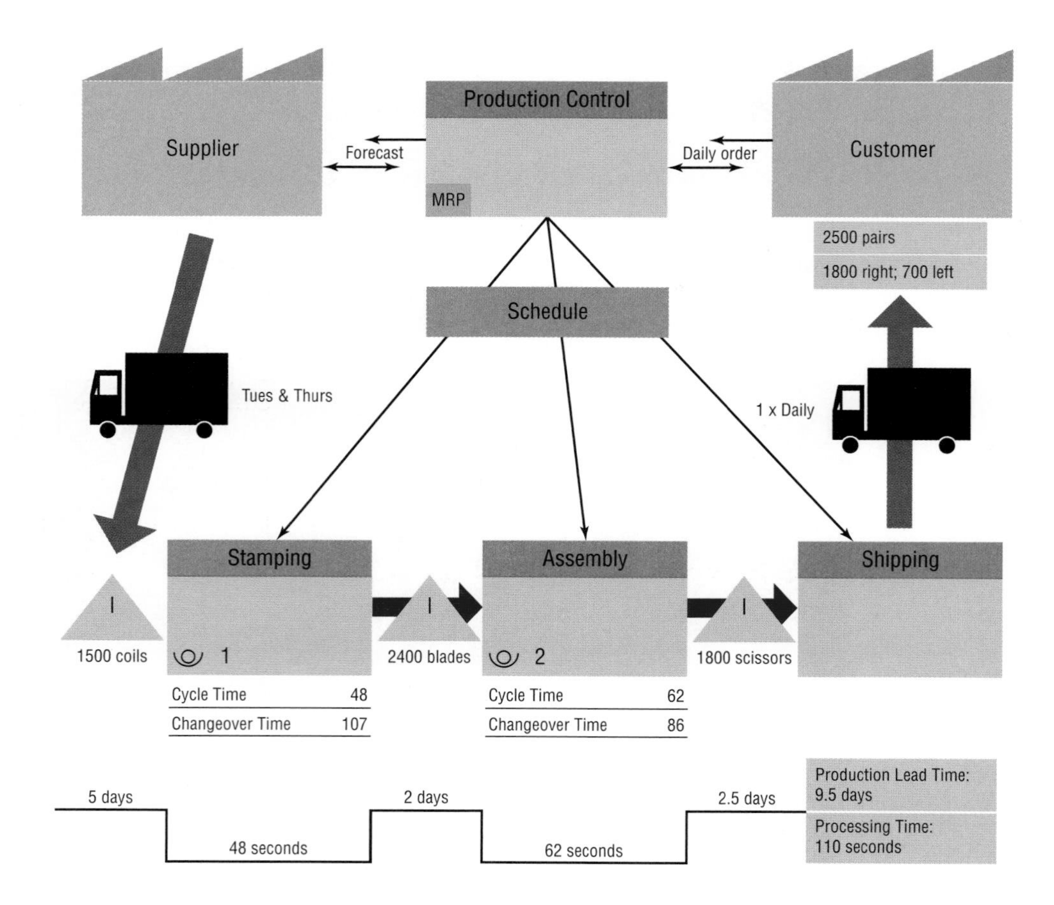

FIGURE 8-5 Value Stream Mapping: An Example of a Current State Map

Source: http://office.microsoft.com/en-us/visio/HA101130241033.aspx.

Value stream mapping generates two different process maps. The first is the "current state" map, which describes the value stream as it currently exists. Figure 8-5 presents an example of such a map. The second is the "future state" map. This map lays out the revised process designed to increase the percentage value metric by identifying and eliminating any non–value-adding steps in the process.

Poka-Yoke

poka-yoke (foolproofing) An emphasis on redesigning processes in such a way as to make mistakes either impossible or immediately apparent to the worker.

To produce perfect quality the first time and every time, managers and workers must develop processes and systems that make performing tasks correctly every time easy and inevitable. The Japanese term **poka-yoke** (also known as fail-safing or mistake-proofing) indicates an emphasis on redesigning processes in such a way as to make mistakes either impossible or immediately apparent to the worker. For example, before giving medicines or blood, a nurse checks bar codes on the item and on the patient's bracelet to ensure that the patient is receiving the right treatment.

5-S Program

5-S program A systematic program for effective housekeeping in operational processes.

sustainability

Effective housekeeping is an important discipline in lean systems. It prevents wastes of waiting and inventory by reducing the chances of lost tools, equipment breakdowns, and damaged goods. One popular housekeeping program is known as the **5-S program**. The term *5-S* refers to the first letters of the five Japanese words that describe the five major activities. Table 8-4 shows the Japanese words along with their English counterparts and a *5-C* equivalent program that is used in some companies. Some managers have added a sixth S to the list of 5-S activities — Safety. Safety has always been an important part of social responsibility for operations managers.

TABLE 8-4 Major Activities of the 5-S Program (and Its Variants)

5-S Elements (Japanese)	5-S Elements (English)	The 5-C Campaign	Intent
Seiri	Sort	Clear out	Red tag suspected unnecessary items. After a monitoring period, throw out unnecessary items.
Seiton	Straighten	Configure	Put everything in an orderly fashion so that it can be located—"a place for everything and everything in its place." This is frequently done using "footprinting," which creates a painted outline for each item.
Seiso	Scrub	Clean and check	Clean everything and eliminate the sources of dirt.
Seiketsu	Systematize	Conform	Make cleaning and checking routine. Set the standard, train and maintain.
Shitsuke	Standardize	Custom and practice	Standardize the previous four steps into one process and continuously improve it. Use visual control through performance boards, checklists, and graphs.

Simplification/Standardization

In lean systems, **simplification and standardization** are means used to reduce lead time and process variances of all sorts. *Simplification* has a focus on eliminating non–value-added activities in a process. *Standardization* is aimed at clarifying and documenting the steps in a process so that they are executed exactly the same way every time by every worker.

simplification and standardization
An emphasis on eliminating non–value-adding process steps and on executing process steps in exactly the same way each time by every worker.

LEAN SYSTEMS: RANGE OF APPLICATION

Table 8-5 (next page) describes the level of adoption and application of the lean approach in a number of different business environments. Lean has been applied in many manufacturing companies across many industrial settings. It has become the dominant manufacturing paradigm around the world. Service companies have also adopted a *lean services* approach, especially services that involve repeated processing of similar jobs, such as logistics services, airlines, banks, insurance firms, call centers, software development, hospitals, and law offices. Tools such as 5-S, visual control, pull systems, and poka-yoke (mistake-proofing) have been very successfully applied in service environments.

Prepare

How are lean systems concepts applied in different parts of the supply chain? What is the interaction between lean systems and innovation?

Organize

Lean Systems: Range of Application
- Applying Lean Systems Within the Firm
- Applying Lean Systems Across the Supply Chain
- Applying Lean Systems to Product Innovation

Applying Lean Systems Within the Firm

The application of lean systems needs to move beyond the shop floor in order to produce maximum benefits. In the most successful firms, all functions have adopted lean principles. The lean approach requires tight coordination of marketing, sales, and operations to increase communication and decrease order processing lead times. Some firms have achieved this coordination by

TABLE 8-5 The Extent of Lean Systems Applications

Operational Setting	Level of Lean Systems Application
In manufacturing	Heavy adoption
In services	Growing adoption
Within firms	Heavy adoption and application
Across supply chains	Growing application
In execution activities	Mature application
In design activities	Early application
In stable business environments	Optimal application
In moderately dynamic business environments	Application with some buffers
In turbulent business environments	Very limited application

relationships

creating integrated product teams responsible for marketing, sales, design, production, and distribution. Importantly, marketing managers must reassess promotional programs and sales incentives that can create large swings (high variance) in demand, as these shifts are inconsistent with the lean approach.

Human resources practices for recruitment and selection, training, and performance evaluation and compensation must reflect the goals of lean. Though the lean approach tends to empower workers, not all potential workers desire to work in a lean environment. Recruitment and selection must strive to hire engaged, self-motivated employees who have a strong interest in solving problems through process innovation. Employees must also be able to work effectively with others in teams. In addition, the design of training programs needs to be driven by lean objectives.

Applying Lean Systems Across the Supply Chain

Managers have also extended lean concepts to supply chain management. However, applications of the lean approach across the supply chain have experienced a mix of benefits and problems. In stable environments, lean can enhance the performance of the supply chain by reducing lead times (thus making the supply chain more responsive to customer demands), improving quality, reducing cost, and improving customer service. Many companies have deployed lean techniques jointly with their suppliers and customers, including Toyota, John Deere, Honda, Harley-Davidson Motorcycles, Nissan, Dell, Apple, Hewlett-Packard, Nike, SYSCO (food products), Cisco (IT), Gap/Limited (clothing), Walmart, and Boeing.

Lean supply chains strive to eliminate the need for inventory, lead time, and capacity buffers. This is best achieved if suppliers and customers work together as partners in streamlining the system. Visibility plays an important role. Partners must work together to develop an environment where suppliers can "see" into their customers' operations, and vice versa. This visibility enables the partners to better understand each other's needs and capabilities, so they can be more responsive with higher quality. Finally, lean supply chains require close coordination of processes and tight integration of the transportation system to ensure the constant flow of materials and information between supply chain partners. Applying lean principles to supply chain relationships leads to the following prescriptions:

global

- Buy to achieve the lowest total cost (as compared to the lowest unit price).
- Keep distances between partners short (in the case of Toyota, this has been restated as "buy in the country where manufacturing is performed").
- Minimize the number of suppliers.

TABLE 8-6 Types of Events Causing Problems for Lean Supply Chains

Category of Event	Examples	Real World
Operational/Technological	Forecast errors Capacity constraints IT disruptions	Nike—glitch in planning software in 2000 caused shortage of Air Jordans. Boeing 787, 2008—dealing with a new process that is being run lean with very little allowance for problems or startup issues.
Social	Labor strikes Sabotage	Strike at west coast ports in 2002 starved many manufacturing plants and retail stores.
Natural/Hazard	Fire, flood, monsoon, earthquake	Japan — March 12, 2011, an earthquake and tsunami severely impacted production and supply (especially in the computer industry). Thailand — March/April 2011, severe flooding delayed deliveries to companies such as Nikon, Sony, and Seagate.
Economy/Competition	Interest rate fluctuations Bankruptcy of supply partners	Problems with logistics firms in 2008 due to increasing fuel prices
Legal/Political	Lawsuits, wars, border customs, regulations	Mattel Toys and lead paint in toys, November 2007—lead found in paint on Fischer-Price, Barbie, Polly Pockets, Batman, and Cars toys; too little time to respond to problems.

LO8-4 Recognize the strengths and limitations of lean systems.

- When a problem occurs, treat the problem as a symptom and focus on what in the supply chain processes could have contributed to the emergence of that problem.
- Work with your suppliers and not against them; the firm is only as strong as the weakest supplier.

The lean supply chain produces benefits, yet it can also open up risks. Since lean supply chains are more tightly linked and have reduced buffers (in the form of excess capacity, inventory, and lead time), a problem that takes place anywhere in the supply chain can quickly and negatively affect the entire supply chain. A strike at a supplier's plant could starve the rest of the supply chain; a hurricane that destroys roads and rails can prevent shipments; a lightning storm can disrupt communications, preventing a critical order from being scheduled. Being lean can make a company more susceptible to these types of events. Additional examples are presented in Table 8-6. When protection from buffers is reduced to the lowest levels, the resulting supply chain becomes fragile; that is, when a breakdown occurs, then the supply chain stops performing. This concept is also discussed in Chapter 10, "Sourcing and Supply Management."

Applying Lean Systems to Product Innovation

LO8-3 Apply the concept of lean systems to product design.

Lean concepts can also be applied to product and process engineering and innovation. Choices made in product and process design have huge effects on the potential to achieve lean objectives. Engineers must ensure that product designs exploit any possible commonalities in processing methods or components, as these commonalities reduce the need for setups.

lean design The application of lean principles and tools to the task of designing products.

Lean design applies lean principles and tools to the task of designing products. Lean design has three major goals:

- Design products that exactly meet customers' needs (i.e., to generate real value).
- Design products that support corporate strategic objectives and that meaningfully differentiate the firm and its products from those offered by the competition.
- Design products that reduce/minimize the opportunities for waste.

Just as lean thinking seeks to reduce waste in operations, lean design seeks to reduce opportunities for product design waste. Table 8-7 lists some of the types of waste that can be reduced in lean design.

Product innovation can be radical or incremental. Radical innovations sometimes make existing business models and products obsolete. For examples, innovations such as the ballpoint pen, compact discs, jet engines, digital photography, and antibiotics all made their predecessors obsolete. Lean design approaches are most compatible with incremental innovation.

To be successful, radical innovation depends on unfettered idea generation with lots of exploration and testing. Employees are encouraged to generate as many new ideas as possible using new and different approaches and processes (something that runs counter to the strong emphasis on standardization found in lean systems). Furthermore, radical innovation demands the presence of slack—excess and unused resources. Slack is needed to free up time for outside-the-box idea generation, for debugging, to absorb the impact of innovation failures (not every idea works), and for pursuing unexpected opportunities. The radical innovation approach can be seen as "wasteful" from a lean perspective, because a primary goal of lean is to reduce slack.

Recognizing that a lean environment may not be consistent with the needs and demands of radical innovation raises an important fact of operations management. Not every system, such as lean systems and total quality management systems, works well in all settings. The task facing every operations manager is to identify the demands that they must satisfy and pick the system that works best in that setting.

TABLE 8-7 Reducing the Opportunity for Product Design Waste

Seven Wastes in Product Design	What Does It Mean?
Complexity	Many different processes; high quantity required to deliver the product's value both on the factory floor and in the customer's use.
Precision	Product design requires precision at the outer limits of our ability to produce the product or the customer's ability to use it.
Variability	Product specifications make it difficult to control processes on the factory floor, within our supply base, or in the customer's domain.
Sensitivity	Product design results in a situation where the resulting product can be easily flawed or damaged during factory operations (either internal or within the supply base) or in the customer's domain.
Immaturity	The use of the solution found within the product design has not been previously validated for a specific application (we are not sure whether the solution offered by the product design is either valid or valued by the customer).
Danger	The use of the product design may unintentionally expose users or the environment to potentially dangerous impacts.
High skill	Does the product design require processes or components that demand high degrees of training and experience (either within our internal factory or within our suppliers' operations)?

CHAPTER SUMMARY

Lean systems and techniques have now become integral to operations and supply chain management in many industries. In this chapter, we have examined many of the concepts, management tools, and developments associated with these systems. The following are some of the major issues raised in this chapter:

1. Lean systems is a corporatewide approach that works to continuously identify, control, and eliminate all sources of waste both within the firm and across the supply chain. This requires that variance at all levels of the firm be eliminated.
2. The lean approach has seven major objectives: produce only what customers want, at the rate that customers want it, with only the features that customers want, with perfect quality, with minimum lead times, without wasting resources, and with methods that support people's development.
3. Workers implementing lean systems use many tools to reduce variance and waste. These tools work together synergistically, and are highly consistent with quality improvement tools.
4. In order to be most successful, firms should expand lean thinking and the lean culture across functions within the firm and with partners across the supply chain.
5. The lean approach is not universally applicable. It is less successful in turbulent business environments, and it is not conducive to radical innovation.

KEY TERMS

DISCUSSION QUESTIONS

1. While Taichi Ohno was impressed by certain aspects of the Ford Production System, he was bothered by other aspects. These included: large, special-purpose equipment, a focused specialized workforce, and an ever-driving emphasis on cost efficiency. Why are these aspects inconsistent with lean?
2. Figure 8-4 illustrates the analogy of a boat hitting rocks as the water level falls. Why is water a good analogy for inventory? Is the sequence in which rocks are encountered a good way to prioritize inventory reduction activities? How might this prioritization scheme differ from one used in an accounting department?
3. Why is achievement of the following goals critical to the success of lean systems?
   a. Setup time and cost reduction.
   b. A relatively stable shop load.
   c. Employee empowerment.
   d. Statistical quality control.

   Give an example of how each area contributes to the success of a lean system.
4. You work in the marketing department of a firm that sells mountain bicycles and related gear. Its manufacturing division has decided to wholeheartedly adopt the lean systems philosophy. Will this affect your ability to delight your customers? Make a list of the potential pluses and minuses of this lean systems decision.
5. Discuss how lean systems might apply to a fast-food hamburger stand. How will it have to be modified to deal with daily demand variation?
6. Using the discussion of Lean Design, consider the design of an iPod competitor. Give examples of each of the following design wastes:
   - Complexity
   - Precision
   - Immaturity
   - Danger
   - High skill
7. What would happen if you tried to introduce a new strategy based on radical innovation into a facility where the organization has adopted wholeheartedly the lean culture?
8. How would a restaurant use the 5-S program? How would an operating room use this program?
9. Why should you *not* include setup times when calculating the TAKT times?
10. What is the relationship between bottlenecks and TAKT time?
11. One lean systems' consultant has stated that "without standardization, there can be no improvement." Why?
12. Can lean systems enhance a worker's quality of life? Discuss how it might or might not.
13. Where would you most successfully apply lean systems principles, during the introductory or growth stages of the product life cycle?
14. Can a supply chain ever be too lean? What would happen to the supply chain if an unexpected disruption/interruption were to occur? How might you as a supply chain manager reduce the effects of such an unexpected disruption, while staying consistent with the lean approach?
15. Imagine that your customer base is located in North America and your suppliers are located in China. Is it possible to implement lean supply chain management under such conditions? What are the challenges now facing the firm?

CASE

Good Guy Hospital $upply

Good Guy Hospital $upply (GGH$) was founded in the 1960s to serve the hospital and nursing home industry. Since then, its sales have grown an average of 26 percent per year, through both geographical expansion and increased existing-market penetration. Key to GGH$'s success is service. It prides itself that it is able to fill 99.4 percent of all requests within 24 hours, and many requests actually are delivered more quickly. Recently, GGH$'s quality service coordinator developed a plan to improve service levels. The new system uses a just-in-time approach to the medical supply needs of GGH$'s clients. GGH$'s clients had been using personal computers in their hospital medical supply stockrooms to place GGH$ orders. While these clients could still purchase from other supply houses, the GGH$ order entry system made it much easier for the clerical staff to place an order with GGH$. The new JIT plan, however, eliminates supplies going through GGH$'s clients' medical supply stockrooms. Now the medical facility's staff and GGH$ will determine the type and desired level of supplies at each stocking point. GGH$ plans to place supplies at each of these stocking points; and a GGH$ sales representative will tour the medical facility, identify items that have been used, and immediately restock them using inventory in the sales representative's van. Using bar coded stock and a mobile sales register, GGH$ will give the hospital a detailed invoice for the items consumed each day. These reports will be designed to support each facility's medical cost control system.

GGH$'s quality service coordinator argues that the increased distribution costs of this proposed system will be offset by increased product and service pricing and by the increased share of each hospital's business, and GGH$ will become the vendor of choice for all items covered by its system. She argues that the hospitals will find this system attractive because it will greatly reduce their costs for stocking, ordering, and distributing medical supplies within the medical facility.

Questions

1. Is Good Guy's plan an appropriate application of JIT? Why, or why not?
2. Identify each of the stakeholders in this situation. What will each give up and get if the proposed system is accepted by GGH$'s clients?

CASE

Purchasing at Midwestern State University

Jane Polski, the newly hired director of university purchasing, took one final look at the report from her purchasing manager, removed her glasses, and rubbed the bridge of her nose. Surely, she thought, things could not be that bad. According to the report, which she had commissioned, the centralized ordering process at Midwestern State University was simply "out of control." Various academic departments that placed orders with through the purchasing system had complained that orders were often lost. Furthermore, the amount of time that it took for an order to be placed was difficult to predict. For example, the chemistry department had placed an order for two identical mass spectrometers, separated by three weeks. The first one took two weeks to arrive; seven months later the second order was still unfilled. Orders were often incorrectly entered. When this occurred, if the ordering department did not want to accept the incorrect order and if the item could not be returned (something that often happened because the items ordered were unique), the purchasing department was obligated to assume responsibility for the ordering error. A separate budget category had been set up for this problem (last year, it accounted for over 10 percent of total costs). Once a year, the purchasing department sold off all the mis-ordered items—often at a significant loss. Finally, university personnel complained that, when they called the purchasing department to identify the status of an order, no one seemed to know how to locate it.

This was bad, and Jane knew that she had to do something—that was one reason that she was hired—to significantly improve operations within the purchasing department. Midwestern University had grown tremendously in the number of programs it offered. It had been decided some 40 years ago to centralize purchasing activities in one department (previously, each unit managed its own purchases). The reason for this decision was to reduce costs and improve operating and acquisition efficiencies. The current department was staffed by some 40 buyers, planners, and clerks. Most of these people had little or no prior professional purchasing experience. Furthermore, many had little more than a high school education. Most of them saw their jobs as consisting mainly of simply placing orders. With the growth in technology and the rapid changes taking place in academic research, placing orders efficiently was becoming more difficult. Systems that had worked before were not working well now.

Jane had commissioned a series of purchasing team meetings aimed at identifying areas of possible improvement. As she reviewed the report, she noted the following issues uncovered by the team:

- The department had more than 6,000 different forms. Many of the forms were developed by individual buyers for their own uses.
- The forms were difficult to complete since critical terms were often undefined and were thus interpreted in different ways.
- The department lacked a standard approach to processing orders. Workers often felt that they had many "exceptional" items to purchase that required special processing. These exceptions were not well documented.
- Except for notification of when the orders were filled, there was little contact with the customers once the request for an order was submitted.
- Department performance was evaluated in terms of utilization and cost—what percentage of the staff time was devoted to receiving and processing orders.
- Every buyer processed orders differently. For example, one buyer tended to place all orders on the last day of the week, while another worked on each order to completion as soon as it arrived.
- Orders were typically worked on in the order received without any consideration of urgency or importance.

There were other issues, but Jane knew that she had enough to start devising a plan for change. The question was, where to start?

Questions

Jane is considering the application of lean services to this department. To help her, she needs the following questions addressed:

1. What should the desired outcome (objective) for this department be? How does the purchasing department create value?
2. Purchasing personnel feel that since Midwestern State University is a public, rather than private, institution, they really do not deal with customers. What is your assessment of this view? Why?
3. What measures should be used to evaluate the performance of this department?
4. Evaluate the suitability of lean services to this department.
5. What lean tools and procedures would you suggest Jane introduce into this department? Why?

SELECTED REFERENCES & INTERNET SITES

Bhote, K. R. *Strategic Supply Management: A Blue Print for Revitalizing the Manufacturer-Supplier Partnership.* New York: American Management Association, 1989.

Bicheno, J., and M. Holweg. *The Lean Toolbox.* 4th ed. Buckingham, UK: PICSIE Books, 2009.

Dennis, P. *Lean Production Simplified.* New York: Productivity Press, 2002.

Ford, H. *Today and Tomorrow.* Cambridge, MA: Productivity Press, 1989.

Goldratt, E. M., and J. Cox. *The Goal: A Process of Ongoing Improvement.* Great Barrington, MA: North River Press, 2004.

Grieco, P. L.; M. W. Gozzo; and J. W. Claunch. *Just-in-Time Purchasing: In Pursuit of Excellence.* Plantsville, CT: PT Publications, 1988.

Huthwaite, B. *The Lean Design Solution.* Mackinac Island, MI: Institute for Lean Design, 2004.

Imai, M. *Gemba Kaizen.* New York: McGraw-Hill, 1997.

Imai, M. *Kaizen: The Key to Japan's Competitive Success.* New York: Random House, 1986.

Little, J. D. C. "A Proof for the Queuing Formula: $L = \lambda W$," *Operations Research* 9 (1961), pp. 383–87.

Melnyk, S. A., and L. Fredendall. *Lean Systems Tools and Procedures.* Burr Ridge, IL: Primis On-Line Custom Publishing, 2006.

Monden, Y. *Toyota Production System.* Norcross, GA: Industrial Engineering and Management Press, 1983.

Nakajima, S. *TPM: Introduction to TPM, Total Productive Maintenance.* Cambridge, MA: Productivity Press, 1988.

Shingo, S. *A Revolution in Manufacturing: The SMED System.* Cambridge, MA: Productivity Press, 1985.

Sugimori, Y. K.; F. C. Kusunoki; and S. Uchikawa. "Toyota Production System and Kanban System—Materialization of Just-in-Time and Respect-for-Human System." *International Journal of Production Research* 15, no. 6 (1977), pp. 553–64.

Suzaki, K. *The New Manufacturing Challenge: Techniques for Continuous Improvement.* New York: Free Press, 1987.

Womack, J. P., and D. T. Jones. *Lean Thinking: Banish Waste and Create Wealth in Your Corporation.* New York: Simon and Schuster, 1996.

Womack, J. P.; D. T. Jones; and D. Roos. *The Machine That Changed the World.* New York: Rawson Associates, 1990.

PART 3

INTEGRATING RELATIONSHIPS ACROSS THE SUPPLY CHAIN

		relationships	sustainability	global
9	Customer Service Management	X		
10	Sourcing and Supply Management	X	X	X
11	Logistics Management	X	X	X

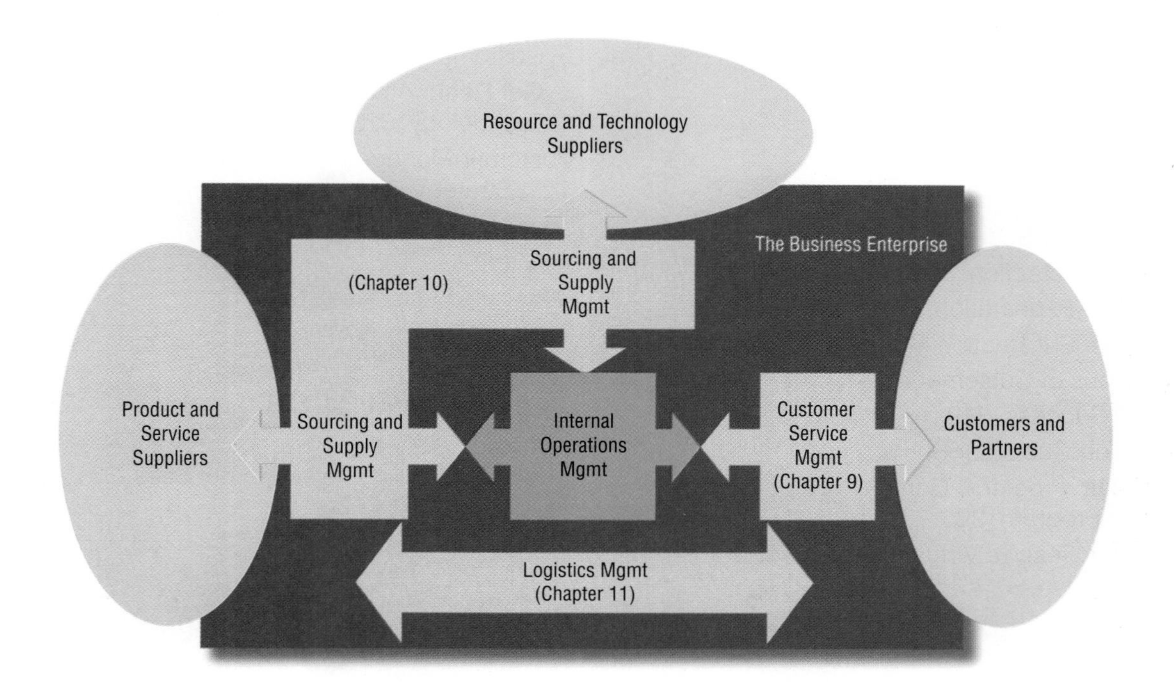

How do operations managers make the most of their relationships with other functions and organizations? Operations management activities take place both inside and outside organizations. Each of the chapters in Part 3 describes how to manage flows of information, materials, and associated organizational relationships to reach their greatest potentials. **Chapter 9** defines customer service and explains how operations and order fulfillment activities relate to meeting customer needs. **Chapter 10** similarly describes the importance of identifying, selecting, assessing, and managing suppliers who provide key inputs to the organization. **Chapter 11** shows how logistical decisions create the physical and informational networks that tie these supply chain partners together. Collectively, these three chapters explain how operational relationships in the supply chain can be improved for the benefit of all partners.

9 Customer Service Management

CHAPTER OUTLINE

LEARNING OBJECTIVES *After studying this chapter, you should be able to:*

LO9-1 Describe how operations management helps establish and fulfill different levels of organizational commitment to customers.

LO9-2 Define the elements of basic service and explain how they are measured.

LO9-3 Describe a model of customer satisfaction.

LO9-4 Explain how a commitment to customer success is the highest level of customer management.

LO9-5 Describe the technological and relational aspects of customer relationship management.

LO9-6 Describe a strategy for segmenting customers and for developing tailored relationships with them.

How Unilever Aligned Its Supply Chain and Business Strategies

With more than $50 billion in sales spread across the Americas, Europe, Asia, and Africa, Unilever is a truly global enterprise. The corporation has a presence in 150 countries around the world with some 179,000 employees, and offers a product portfolio that fills grocery stores with well-known brands in categories like spreads (I Can't Believe It's Not Butter), sauces (Ragu), dressings (Hellmann's and Wish-Bone), beverages (Lipton teas), ice cream (Good Humor and Breyers), frozen food (Bertolli dinners) and personal care products (Dove, Suave, and Axe).

Leading consumer products companies like Unilever are breaking away from the constraints of past retailer-manufacturer relationships. Customer business development has become the focus, as Unilever looks to collaborate with each key customer to increase sales. The old "customer service" approach was mainly about establishing information system links to improve the efficiency of operational transactions. The new customer business development model combines a range of sales growth initiatives jointly pursued by Unilever and each of its major retail customers—to the benefit of both parties.

To launch this new approach, Unilever surveyed all its customers in order to develop a complete understanding of their future requirements and anticipated trends. The survey topics touched upon ordering and inventory management practices, outsourcing, distribution models, service differentiation, order profiles and frequency trends, collaborative planning technologies, and product customization needs.

The survey made it clear that retailer performance expectations were rising. The vast majority favored 24- to 48-hour order lead times. Nearly half of all retailers expected to use scan-based trading, and all major chains required data synchronization, but these services were only the minimum requirements. Nearly two-thirds of respondents expected significant order or product customization, including more demand for special packs and mixed pallets. Almost 80 percent of retailers preferred that their suppliers should increase ownership of inventory.

These findings put more pressure on Unilever to examine sales data in detail so that specific channel and customer demands could be more accurately planned. In addition to their current emphasis on achieving on-time, in-full deliveries, Unilever decided that it needed strategic supply chain initiatives to improve its retail mix, consumer insights, and innovation opportunities. This more strategic approach helps Unilever to leverage the scale and breadth of its product portfolio.

Source: Adapted from Sean Monahan and Robert Nardone, "How Unilever Aligned Its Supply Chain and Business Strategies," *Supply Chain Management Review,* November 1, 2007. © 2007 Reed Business Information, a division of Reed Elsevier, Inc. All rights reserved.

In Chapters 1 and 2 we argued that customers are the focal point in design and management of operations across the supply chain. To survive and prosper in today's dynamic and demanding economy, every company needs to excel in attracting customers and keeping them. Recall also that most companies deal with several types of customers including internal customers, intermediate customers, and final customers, or consumers. In the situation described above, Unilever's focus was on retailers (intermediate customers) who serve Unilever's final consumers.

The Unilever story makes it clear that customer relationships are not solely the responsibility of marketing executives. Operations managers are responsible for the design and execution of the processes that provide customers with products and services they desire. We refer to this responsibility as **customer service management**. It requires an intense focus on understanding customers' desires and requirements, and translating this understanding into specific operational capabilities and processes. These efforts include the design of sales and order fulfillment processes. However, they extend far beyond order fulfillment to collaboration, information gathering, and customer relationship management.

customer service management The design and execution of the processes that provide customers with products and services they desire.

relationships

As the concept of supply chain management has evolved over the past two decades, so too has thinking about the nature of customer relationships. The use of the term *relationship* implies at least two participants, in this case a customer and a supplier. Just as suppliers must manage relationships with their customers, customers also have programs in place for managing relations with their suppliers. This chapter discusses general aspects of relationship management, as well as the specifics of how suppliers manage customer relationships. Chapter 10 discusses customers' efforts in managing relationships with their suppliers.

Figure 9-1 depicts a hierarchy of organizational commitment to customer service. Historically, operations managers tended to concentrate on providing excellent basic service. Today, excellent service is considered to be the foundation of customer service management. In addition, operations managers now think more holistically, in terms of customer satisfaction and success. Customer satisfaction requires a higher-level commitment than basic service in that it explicitly addresses expectations customers have regarding the organization's performance. A commitment to customer success focuses on leveraging the organization's operations capabilities to help customers meet their critical objectives.

LO9-1 Describe how operations management helps establish and fulfill different levels of organizational commitment to customers.

In the following pages we will describe each of these approaches and their implications for operations management. Keep in mind throughout this discussion that customer management is customer specific. That is, not all customers need or want the same thing from a supplier. Thus, a supplier's operational capabilities must have the flexibility to meet

FIGURE 9-1 Hierarchy of Commitment to Customers

the requirements of different customers. In fact, research has shown that customer specific knowledge is vital in developing operational supply chain strategies.[1]

Prepare

What are the elements of basic service and how is basic service performance measured?

Organize

Basic Service
- Product Availability
- Lead-Time Performance
- Service Reliability
- The Perfect Order
- Limitations of Basic Service

BASIC SERVICE

Most operations managers agree that service is important, yet they often find it difficult to explain exactly what "customer service" means. While common expressions include "easy to do business with" and "responsive to customers," it is more meaningful to think of service as providing six basic "rights" to customers:

- The *right* amount
- The *right* product
- The *right* place
- The *right* time
- The *right* condition
- The *right* information

Traditionally, it has been common to think of a company's **basic service** program in terms of product availability, lead-time performance, and service reliability.

basic service A supplier's ability to provide product availability, lead-time performance, and service reliability.

Product Availability

Product availability is the capacity to have inventory present when and where it is desired by a customer. To make products consistently available, managers have to make good decisions concerning safety stock and service level policies (as discussed in Chapter 7). From the standpoint of providing basic service, product availability is usually measured in terms of stockouts and fill rates.

product availability The capacity to have inventory present when and where it is desired by a customer.

Recall from Chapter 7 that a *stockout* refers to the situation when a firm has depleted inventory of an item that is supposed to be in stock. For example, a study was cited that revealed that at any point in time during a week, the average supermarket is out of stock of approximately 8 percent of the items that are supposed to be on its shelves. It is important to note, however, that a stockout does not necessarily result in failure to fulfill customer demand. A stockout only leads to a service failure when a customer actually attempts to order the product. Nevertheless, the aggregation of stockouts across products and over time is an indicator of how well a firm is positioned to provide basic service commitments. While this measure does not consider that some products may be more critical than others, it provides a good starting point for assessing product availability.

Store shelves empty of stock.

The most common way to report levels of product availability is in terms of fill rates. A **fill rate** measures the impact of stockouts over time or over multiple orders from customers. There are many ways that fill rates can be estimated; the most common measures being *unit fill rate, line fill rate,* and *order fill rate.*

fill rate A measure of the impact of stockouts over time or over multiple orders from customers.

The **unit fill rate** is the percentage of the total quantity of units ordered by customers that are actually delivered. It is calculated using the following equation:

unit fill rate The percentage of total quantity of units ordered by customers that are actually delivered.

(9.1a) Unit fill rate = Total units delivered / Total units ordered

The **line fill rate** is a more stringent measure of fill rate performance. It measures service performance as the percentage of purchase order lines that are filled in total. Thus,

line fill rate A measure of service performance as the percentage of purchase order lines that are filled in total.

[1]Alice H. W. Yeung, Victor H. Y. Lo, Andy C. L. Yeung, and T. C. Edwin Cheng, "Specific Customer Knowledge and Operational Performance in Apparel Manufacturing," *International Journal of Production Economics* 114, no. 2 (August 1, 2008), p. 520.

LO9-2 Define the elements of basic service and explain how they are measured.

even if most of the units of a specific item can be provided, the inability to provide all of them is considered to be a failure. Line fill rate is calculated using the following equation:

(9.1b) Line fill rate = Number of order lines delivered complete / Total order lines

order fill rate (orders shipped complete) A measure of the percentage of orders that are shipped complete with all items ordered by a customer.

Finally, **order fill rate (orders shipped complete)** is the most stringent measure of a firm's performance relative to product availability; it measures the percentage of orders that are shipped complete with all items ordered by a customer. An order that is missing only one unit of one item on a purchase order is considered to be incomplete. Order fill rate is measured as follows:

(9.1c) Order fill rate = Total complete orders delivered / Total orders

In practice, there are many variations to these fill rate measures that operations managers use to assess service. Fill rate performance can be used to differentiate the level of service offered on different products, keeping in mind that different customers may have different requirements. For example, if a customer needs 20 parts to repair a machine and receives only 19 of them, the failure to deliver a complete order means that the machine cannot be repaired. In situations where some of the items are not critical to a customer, receiving 19 of the 20 may be acceptable. The customer may be willing to accept a back order or reorder the product at a later time.

EXAMPLE 9-1

Table 9-1 presents a summary of customer order information that a company might collect to examine its fill rate performance.

Unit fill rate = Total units delivered/Total units ordered
= 19,500/ 20,000 = 97.5%

Line fill rate = Number of order lines delivered complete/Total order lines
= 4,800/5,000 = 96%

Order fill rate = Total complete orders delivered/Total orders
= 910/1,000 = 91%

TABLE 9-1 Summary Order Data

Orders Received	Total Units Ordered	Total Order Lines	Total Units Delivered	Total Complete Order Lines Delivered	Total Complete Orders Delivered
1,000	20,000	5,000	19,500	4,800	910

Lead-Time Performance

lead time The amount of time that passes between the beginning and ending of a set of activities.

order-to-delivery (OTD) lead time The time that passes from the instant the customer places an order until the instant that the customer receives the product.

Operations managers use the term **lead time** to describe the amount of time that passes between the beginning and ending of a set of activities. Value tends to be enhanced when lead time and lead-time variability are reduced. Of critical importance to customers is the **order-to-delivery (OTD) lead time**, which is the time that passes from the instant the customer placed an order until the instant that the customer receives the product. Many different time-consuming activities may constitute OTD lead time, including:

1. *Product design lead time* is the time interval needed to conceptualize, design, and test a new product.
2. *Order lead time* is the time required to place an order for a product plus the time to schedule the order so that operations can begin working on it.

3. *Procurement lead time* is the time associated with obtaining (through purchases) the inputs required for processing the order.
4. *Production lead time* begins at the moment the production or service system begins working on an order. It ends when the completed order is transferred to the distribution system for delivery.
5. *Delivery lead time* measures the time consumed by the distribution system, including warehousing and transportation. It ends the moment that product reaches the customer.

For some businesses, only certain lead-time elements apply. Customers who get a haircut, for example, only experience order and production lead time. On the other hand, customers who purchase highly customized goods will probably experience all five elements of lead time. From the customer's point of view, the elements of lead time that comprise the OTD lead time depend on the market orientation of the product. As discussed in Chapter 4, any product has one of four market orientations:

- Engineer to order (ETO)
- Make to order (MTO)
- Assemble to order (ATO)
- Make to stock (MTS)

These four categories describe how a firm processes customer orders as well as who (the supplier or the customer) bears the cost of lead time. Figure 9-2 illustrates differences in lead time according to market orientation.

Lead times are critical to creating value for customers. With ETO products there is a strong incentive to reduce lead times because shorter total OTD lead times are often very attractive to customers. For example, an airline buying new aircraft from Boeing historically has experienced total lead time measured in years, or at least many months. Airlines most likely would find a reduction in total lead time from Boeing to a matter of a few months to be a very attractive offering.

While a reduction in lead time may be desirable, lead-time reliability is generally more important to customers. The reason that reliability is particularly important can best be understood by thinking of our discussion of safety stocks in Chapter 7. Variation in OTD lead time is a major reason that customers must plan for safety stocks. If suppliers can be counted on to always deliver with the same lead-time performance, customers can significantly reduce the amount of safety stock they keep on hand. The same principle applies for service products. If a customer can depend on a service provider to be on time, then the customer can reduce any resources that would be needed for workarounds or contingency plans.

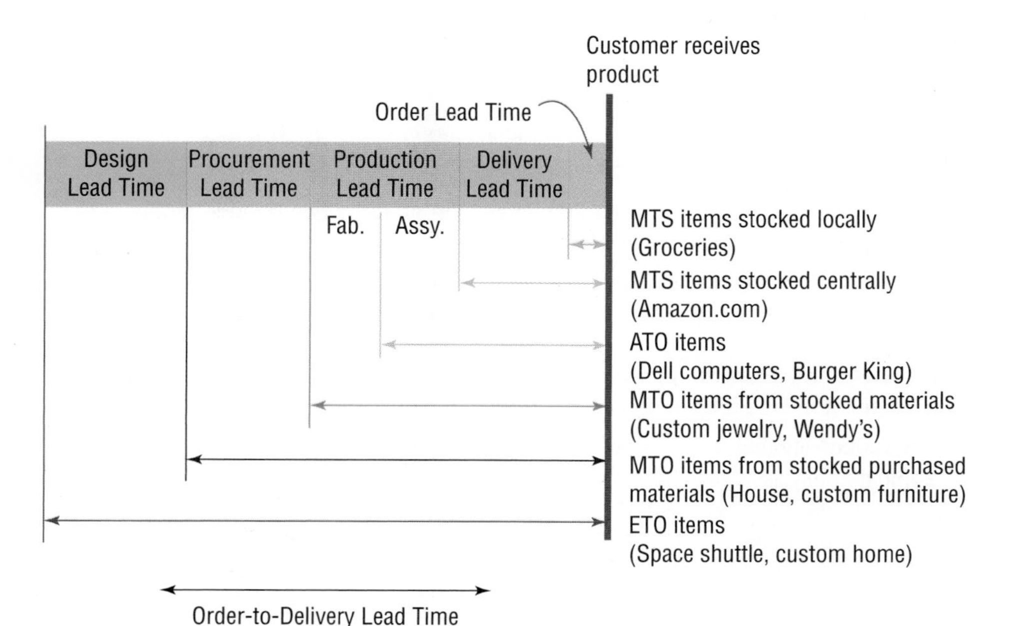

FIGURE 9-2 Market Orientation and Order-to-Delivery Lead Time

LO9-2 Define the elements of basic service and explain how they are measured.

service reliability A firm's ability to perform all order-related activities error-free. It also encompasses a firm's ability to provide customers with critical information regarding inventory and order status.

Service Reliability

Service reliability involves many specific attributes of customer order fulfillment. Overall, it refers to a firm's ability to perform all order-related activities error-free. It also encompasses a firm's ability to provide customers with critical information regarding inventory and order status. Attributes of reliability mean that orders arrive damage-free; invoices are correct and error-free; shipments are made to the correct locations; and the exact amount of product ordered is included in the shipment. While all aspects of reliability are difficult to enumerate, the point is that customers demand that suppliers handle details routinely and correctly.

Increasingly, customers indicate that advance notification of problems such as incomplete orders is more critical than the complete order itself. Customers hate surprises! More often than not, customers can adjust to an incomplete or late delivery, if they have advance notification. While this is particularly true in business-to-business relationships, it is equally important in dealing with consumers. Imagine the situation where a consumer takes time off work to stay at home, expecting a new appliance to be delivered and installed. If the appliance does not arrive, the consumer has not only been inconvenienced, but has also possibly lost a day's wages.

The Perfect Order

The ultimate in providing basic service is to do everything right and to do it right the first time. In the past, most operations managers used several independent measures to evaluate service performance. If each of these separate measures was acceptable relative to some standard, then overall service performance was considered acceptable.

Recently, however, operations executives across the supply chain have begun to focus attention on zero-defect performance across all elements in the OTD cycle. They realized that, even if performance meets a standard on each independent measure, a substantial number of customers may have some type of order-related failure.

perfect order The notion that an order should be delivered without failure in any attribute.

The notion of the **perfect order** is that an order should be delivered without failure in any attribute. In other words, total order cycle performance must be executed with zero defects. This means that availability and operational performance must be perfectly executed and that all support activities must be completed exactly as promised to the customer. Typical perfect order failures include shipping the wrong products, the wrong quantities, late delivery, missing or incorrect information, damaged items, and incorrect documentation. While it may not be possible to commit to zero defects as a basic service strategy offered across the board to all customers, such high-level performance may be an option on a selective basis.

EXAMPLE 9-2

Suppose a company determines that its service performance on four attributes of service is:

97 percent of orders are shipped complete (as the customer originally requested).
97 percent of orders are delivered on time (at the customer's requested date and time).
97 percent of orders are delivered damage-free.
97 percent of orders have correct documentation (including invoicing).

The probability that any order will be *perfect* with respect to these four attributes is approximately 88.5 percent ($.97 \times .97 \times .97 \times .97$). This means that 11.5 percent of all orders will have some kind of problem, even though performance on any given metric appears to be good.

Limitations of Basic Service

student activity

Using any Web browser or your library's electronic databases, enter the term *perfect order.* Look for articles that discuss the perfect order measure. Find and summarize an article that discusses specific companies and their ability to provide perfect orders to their customers.

Implementing a policy involves specifying the level of basic service commitment to customers in terms of availability, lead time performance, and reliability. The fundamental question is, "How much basic service should the operational system provide?" Managers usually answer this by considering order winners, qualifiers, and losers as discussed in Chapter 2. They attempt to provide high performance levels on those service attributes they perceive as the order winners, and performance that is at least as good as their competitors' for order qualifiers and order losers. In many industries, minimum and average service performance levels are generally well known by both suppliers and customers. Operations and supply chain executives frequently speak of basic service commitments in terms of "doing as well as competition" or "beating our major competitors' performance." For example, in the consumer packaged goods industries, it is common to hear major manufacturers and retailers talk in terms of 97–98 percent item fill rates and order-to-delivery lead times of three to five days. Suppliers who are unable to perform within these service parameters suffer significant competitive disadvantages.

A company's competitive strategy guides this decision. A firm which competes primarily on low price most likely will commit to lower levels of service due to the high costs of a high-level commitment. Firms desiring to differentiate themselves based on service are willing to spend more to do so. Yet even firms with a high level of basic service commitment generally do not seek to provide zero-defect service for all customers, because associated cost and resource requirements are too high. Instead, they seek to accommodate customers as well as or better than competitors.

It is important to realize that just because a firm outperforms its competitors on service, this does not necessarily mean that its customers are *satisfied.* For example, how many of us are truly satisfied with the performance of airlines, even the better ones? Customer satisfaction must be assessed from the customer's viewpoint, using measures that are external to the firm. The traditional approach to establishing a basic service platform is critical, but greater competitive advantage comes by ensuring that customers are, in fact, satisfied.

CUSTOMER SATISFACTION

Prepare

What is customer satisfaction and what model describes customer satisfaction development?

Organize

Customer Satisfaction
- Customer Expectations
- Customer Satisfaction Model
- Limitations of Customer Satisfaction

In building a customer satisfaction program, the first question that must be answered is, "What does it mean to say that a customer is satisfied?" The simplest and most widely accepted method of defining **customer satisfaction** is meeting or exceeding customer expectations. If a customer perceives that a supplier's performance meets or exceeds her expectations, the customer is satisfied. Conversely, if perceived performance is less than what the customer expected, the customer is dissatisfied. A number of companies have adopted this framework for customer satisfaction, and an often-heard phrase within many organizations is: "We strive to meet or exceed our customers' expectations."

While this framework for customer satisfaction is relatively straightforward, its implications for building customer relationships are not. To build upon this platform it is necessary to answer certain questions: What do customers expect? How do they form these expectations? Why do many companies fail to satisfy customers? If a company satisfies its customers, is that sufficient? The following sections provide some answers to these critical questions.

customer satisfaction
Meeting or exceeding customer expectations.

Customer Expectations

When customers transact business with a supplier, they have numerous expectations concerning the supplier's performance. Many of these expectations revolve around the supplier's basic service platform including availability, lead time, and service reliability performance, and they may have formal monitoring programs in place addressing each of these dimensions. However, research on service expectations and service quality has identified a larger set of categories of customer expectations, each of which has implications for supply chain operations management.[2] Customers usually have expectations regarding each of the following:

- *Reliability:* Suppliers will perform all activities as promised, including dimensions of basic service as well as special requests.
- *Responsiveness:* Suppliers will provide prompt service that goes beyond mere delivery to include issues related to quick handling of inquiries and resolution of problems.
- *Access:* Suppliers will provide easy contact for order placement, obtaining information regarding inventory, order status, and so on.
- *Communication:* Suppliers will proactively keep customers informed, rather than waiting for customer inquiries concerning order status, particularly if problems with delivery or availability arise.
- *Credibility:* Suppliers' communications will be believable and honest.
- *Security:* Suppliers will work to limit customers' feelings of risk or of doubt in doing business with them. This includes risks associated with resources customers commit based on orders placed, as well as risks associated with their need for confidentiality.
- *Courtesy:* Suppliers will be polite, friendly, and respectful. This can be a challenge considering that customers may have contact with numerous individuals in the organization (sales representatives, inventory managers, other operations executives, customer service personnel, truck drivers, etc.). Failure by one individual may destroy the best efforts of all the others.
- *Competence:* Suppliers will be competent in their execution of every interaction.
- *Tangibles:* Suppliers will maintain a level of physical appearance of facilities, equipment, and personnel. Consider, for example, the shock if a UPS delivery driver was not dressed in the well-known brown uniform.
- *Knowing the customer:* While suppliers may think in terms of groups of customers and market segments, customers think of themselves as individuals. Each customer expects a supplier to understand and adapt to his or her specific requirements.

In a business-to-business setting, customer expectations are particularly complex because a customer is a business organization made up of numerous functions and individuals. Different personnel in a customer organization may prioritize the criteria of performance differently, or they may have different levels of expectation for the criteria. For example, some personnel may be most concerned with responsiveness and rapid handling of an inquiry regarding order status, others may be more concerned with order completeness or meeting a delivery appointment. Meeting customer expectations requires an understanding of how expectations are formed and the reasons many companies fail to meet those expectations.

Customer Satisfaction Model

LO9-3 Describe a model of customer satisfaction.

Figure 9-3 provides a framework for understanding the process by which customers form their expectations of supplier performance. It also suggests that there frequently exists a number of gaps that a supplier must overcome as it seeks to satisfy its customers.

Customers' expectations regarding priorities and performance are influenced by several factors. The first is their defined requirements. These requirements come from

[2]This discussion and Figure 9-3 are based on: A. Parasuraman, V. Zeithaml, and L. L. Berry, *A Conceptual Model of Service Quality and Its Implications for Future Research,* Report No. 84–106 (Cambridge, MA: Marketing Science Institute, 1984).

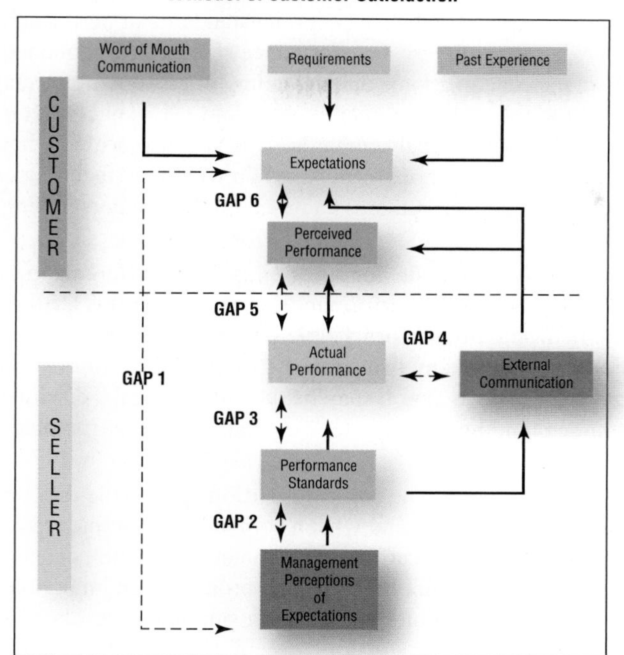

FIGURE 9-3 A Model of Customer Satisfaction

a customer's specific strategies and performance goals. Interestingly, however, customer expectations are frequently not the same as their stated requirements or needs. Previous supplier performance also influences their expectations. A supplier which consistently delivers on time will most likely be expected to deliver on time in the future. Similarly, a supplier with a poor record of performance will be expected to perform poorly in the future. Also, a customer's experience with one supplier may influence his expectations of other suppliers. For example, when Federal Express began delivering small packages on a next-day basis, many customers began to expect the same performance from other suppliers.

Word-of-mouth also shapes expectations. Customers frequently tell each other about their experiences with specific suppliers. At trade and professional association meetings, the subject of suppliers' performance capabilities is a common topic of discussion among companies. For consumer products, consumers get word-of-mouth inputs from acquaintances, product comparison publications, online user blogs, and so on, which influences their expectations.

Perhaps the most important factor influencing customer expectations is the communication coming from the supplier itself. Promises and commitments made by sales personnel or customer service representatives, statements contained in marketing and promotional messages, even the printed policies and procedures of an organization serve to influence customers' expectations. Suppliers can, to a major extent, proactively manage customer expectations through their communications. Unfortunately, companies often set themselves up for failure by overpromising in an attempt to influence customer expectations.

Figure 9-3 also provides a framework for understanding what an organization must do to deliver customer satisfaction. The failure of firms to satisfy their customers can often be traced to one or more of the gaps identified in the framework.

- *Gap 1: Knowledge Gap.* The first and the most fundamental gap that may exist is the gap between customers' real expectations and managers' perceptions of those expectations. The **knowledge gap** reflects management's lack of knowledge or understanding of customers. Reasons for this lack of understanding often include a lack of marketing research or intimacy with important customers.

knowledge gap The gap between customers' real expectations and managers' perceptions of those expectations.

- *Gap 2: Standards Gap.* Even if a supplier fully understands a customer's expectations it still might fail to establish appropriate standards of performance. The **standards gap** exists when internal performance standards do not adequately or accurately reflect the organization's understanding of customer expectations. Sometimes it is difficult to translate customer expectations ("I want courteous service" for example) into specific operational standards. This gap also occurs when operations managers develop their service platform based on what they feel they can deliver or what their competitors deliver, rather than based on their understanding of what customers expect.

standards gap The gap that exists when internal performance standards do not adequately or accurately reflect customer expectations.

- *Gap 3: Performance Gap.* The **performance gap** is the difference between the operational standard and actual performance. If the standard is a fill rate of 98 percent and the firm actually performs at 97 percent, a performance gap exists. It should be pointed out that many firms focus their efforts to improve satisfaction by eliminating the performance gap. It may be, however, that the dissatisfaction exists due to a poor understanding of customer expectations in the first place (the knowledge gap).

performance gap The difference between standard and actual performance.

- *Gap 4: Communications Gap.* The **communications gap** is the difference between a company's actual performance and what a company communicates about its performance. The role of communications in customer satisfaction cannot be overemphasized (this is especially important when the product is an intangible service). As discussed previously, overcommitment, or promising higher levels of performance than can actually be provided, is a major cause of customer dissatisfaction.

communications gap The difference between a company's actual performance and what a company communicates about its performance.

- *Gap 5: Perception Gap.* The **perception gap** exists when customers perceive performance to be lower (or higher) than what is actually delivered. In operations, managers often lament that "we're only as good as the last order." Even though performance over a long time period may have been very good, a late or incomplete or otherwise subpar delivery may still result in a customer's expression of extreme dissatisfaction.

perception gap The gap that exists when customers perceive performance to be different than actually provided.

- *Gap 6: Satisfaction Gap.* The **satisfaction gap** is the difference between perceived performance and the customer's expectation regarding performance.

satisfaction gap The difference between perceived performance and the customer's expectation regarding performance.

Any of the first five gaps leads to gap 6, customer dissatisfaction. The key to delivering satisfaction is to ensure that these gaps are identified and eliminated. This model is a useful tool for companies whose customers have expressed dissatisfaction. It can guide research to determine which gaps exist, and to prescribe actions needed to eliminate them.

For example, a major agricultural chemical company learned that many of its distributors were so dissatisfied that they were recommending other suppliers' products to farmers. Using the model to structure its research, the company learned that it had a significant communications gap. Operations personnel consistently underestimated delivery times when talking to salespeople and to customers. Therefore, both internal salespeople and customers expected delivery much sooner than what actually occurred. As a solution, operations managers trained personnel to better estimate delivery times. Over the next 12 months customer satisfaction improved dramatically.

Limitations of Customer Satisfaction

Due to its explicit focus on customers, an emphasis on customer satisfaction represents a step beyond a basic service platform in an organization's efforts to build relationships with its customers. A firm that satisfies customer expectations better than its competitors will probably gain competitive advantage in the marketplace. Nevertheless, an emphasis only on customer satisfaction has limitations, too.

The first limitation is that many executives make a fundamental (yet understandable) mistake in assuming that customers who are satisfied are also "happy" with the suppliers' performance. That may or may not be the actual situation. Remember that satisfaction is the customer's perception of actual performance in relation to expectation of performance.

Satisfied customers are not necessarily loyal customers. Even though their expectations are being met, satisfied customers may choose to do business with a competitor because they expect a competitor to perform at a higher level, or at least as well as the organization in question. Research has frequently shown that many customers who report being satisfied are still likely to do business with competitors.

Another limitation to a focus on customer satisfaction is that firms frequently forget that satisfaction is an individual customer phenomenon. The "standards gap" frequently exists in an organization because standards are established based on the presumption that all customers have the same expectations. There is a tendency to aggregate expectations across customers and to neglect their differences. What satisfies one customer may not satisfy another, much less all, customers. When a single standard is used, some customers' expectations are exceeded while others are underserved.

student activity

Think of a time that you were dissatisfied with a service provider. Which of your expectations were not met? How did you form these expectations? Which gap do you believe resulted in your dissatisfaction?

Despite these limitations, a customer satisfaction platform does represent a forward step in a firm's efforts to manage relationships with its customers. Firms that primarily focus on industry and competitor standards of basic service performance are much less likely to find that their customers are very satisfied or highly satisfied with their performance. Simply stated, the only way to know if customers are really satisfied is to ask them.

CUSTOMER SUCCESS

Prepare

What is customer success? Describe the technological and relational aspects of customer relationship management.

Organize

Customer Success
- Achieving Customer Success
- Customer Relationship Management

There is yet another step that can be taken in the attempt to gain competitive advantage through customer service management. A firm's ability to grow and expand market share depends on its ability to attract and hold the industry's most successful customers. Thus, a supplier should develop its performance capabilities to enhance the success of those customers. A focus on **customer success** shifts the emphasis from customers' expectations to customers' "real" requirements. Recall that customer requirements, while helping form expectations, are not the same as expectations. Requirements are frequently downgraded into expectations due to perceptions of previous performance, word-of-mouth, or by communications from the firm itself. This explains why simply meeting expectations may not result in "happy" customers. For example, a customer may be satisfied with an average 98 percent fill rate. However, for the customer to be successful in executing its strategy, a 100 percent fill rate on certain key products may be necessary.

customer success Helping customers to meet their real business requirements.

Achieving Customer Success

Explain how a commitment to customer success is the highest level of customer management.

A customer success program involves a thorough understanding of individual customer requirements and a commitment to focus on long-term business relationships that have high potential for growth and profitability. Such commitment most likely cannot be made to all potential customers. A supplier must work intensively with a customer to understand the customer's requirements, internal processes, competitive environment, and what it takes for the customer to be successful in its own competitive arena. Further, the supplier organization must understand how it can utilize its own capabilities to enhance customer performance.

This level of understanding requires a supplier to consider how its customers deal with *their customers.* Ideally, the supplier develops a comprehensive understanding of competition and strategy for each level of customers within its supply chain. Then it can develop programs that ensure that its immediate customers are successful in meeting the requirements of customers further down the supply chain.

relationships

GET REAL

Procter & Gamble's New Service Program

At the 2011 Council of Supply Chain Management Professionals annual conference, Deirdre Wilson, associate director, customer service operations for Procter & Gamble (P&G), presented a new service measurement approach now firmly established at P&G. The core concept in this measurement scheme is: Service as Measured by Customer (SAMBC). With SAMBC, Procter & Gamble now measures its customer service in terms of how well it performs against the individual metrics of each customer included in the new program. SAMBC is defined as: *The percent of customers for which P&G is meeting or exceeding all customer-unique expectations.*

SAMBC is built on the reality that different customers have different requirements and levels of importance for certain dimensions of performance. Wilson showed a chart highlighting differences in the core metrics of 10 major retail customers (with names removed). Even universally embraced metrics such as fill rate and on-time delivery are calculated differently by various retailers, and there is a wide variety of expectations. For example, some customers want 98 percent on-time delivery, while others are satisfied with 94 percent.

SAMBC obviously requires a very collaborative approach with customers, as they may find it difficult to immediately define the metrics and levels of performance that they require. In their discussions with retailers, P&G many times found that retailers define metrics differently than P&G does. Also important, once customer-specific metrics are defined, they must be applied back through the supply chain all the way to individual manufacturing sites. Plant managers need to be aware of how they are performing, not just at an aggregate level, but at a customer-specific level, for each of perhaps dozens of key customers. Applying this approach has a major impact on supply chain performance management, as well as on supply chain planning and execution.

Adapted from: Dan Gilmore, *Supply Chain Digest,* November 3, 2011, http://www.scdigest.com/.

For example, in the electronics industry one supplier of component parts adopted the slogan, "We take pride in helping customers compete." This statement implies that the supplier attempts to do more than provide basic service and meet customer expectations. This supplier attempts to understand the real requirements of its customers so it can develop products and operational capabilities that help its customers succeed in their own competitive environments. Managers disseminated their slogan throughout the company, from the reception area to the manufacturing plants. A senior executive of the company summarized the benefits of this customer orientation in stating, "If they are more successful due to our ability to provide them with better products, more timely delivery, lower total costs, or whatever, then they will gain market share and grow. Of course, when they grow, we grow!"[3]

The Get Real box concerning Procter & Gamble's new service approach provides a clear example of focusing on the requirements of individual business customers. This commitment by P&G demonstrates their desire to help key retail customers by meeting the requirements critical for their success.

To achieve customer success, a supplier may need to reinvent the way a product is produced, distributed, or sold. It often requires suppliers and customers to collaborate in ways that create new relationships, processes, and other avenues for success. For example, the Get Real story about Tesco shows how a major retail company understood the unique

[3]This example and quote are adapted from Stanley E. Fawcett and M. Bixby Cooper, "Customer Service, Satisfaction, and Success," *Innovations in Competitive Manufacturing,* Paul M. Swamidass (ed.) (Norwell, MA: Kluwer Academic Publishers, 2000), p. 43.

GET REAL

Tesco's Virtual Store

To compete against Korean supermarket retailer E-Mart's dominant retail store presence, Tesco Homeplus (their local Korean brand) took the bold move of not trying to match E-Mart's number of physical store locations. As the number two grocery retailer in the Korean market, Tesco's research showed that Koreans are among the most hard-working people in the world, and grocery shopping is a dreaded task for many of them. Based on the research, Homeplus developed the concept of a virtual store in a space where masses of people were already located (subways) at a time when they had nothing else to do (waiting for the next train) and using an ordering mechanism that most consumers carry with them at all times (smartphones).

The implementation was simple but incredibly effective. Photos of the Homeplus grocery shelves were blown up into huge wall-sized posters that covered the subway walls, with all of the typical products consumers would be looking for when grocery shopping. Each product has a price and QR code attached; each shopper simply snaps a picture with his/her mobile camera to arrange for home delivery. The idea allows busy commuters to scan their groceries on their way to work in the morning and, as long as their order is placed before 1:00 p.m., their items will be delivered home that same evening. This creates even greater speed and convenience for the whole shopping experience. All of this occurs without a single Tesco staff member needed on site.

In the first three months, Homeplus online sales increased 130 percent. Homeplus became number one in the Korean online market and a very close second in the offline market. The concept has been so popular that Tesco is expanding it to other markets, including its home country, the United Kingdom.

A shopper using the Homeplus virtual display

needs of a segment of its customers in South Korea, and developed a totally new approach to online retailing which made the entire shopping experience more convenient for those consumers. Companies that are adopting a customer success focus have also been leaders in implementing customer relationship management programs (discussed next) as a tool for accomplishing customer success.

relationships

Table 9-2 presents a selected set of companies (10 of the 25 total) ranked by *BusinessWeek* magazine as outstanding in aspects of customer service management as we have described it. It also includes some of their actions in recent years. Notice that these actions start with improving basic service, some are oriented toward satisfaction, and still others reflect a focus on customer success.

Customer Relationship Management

LO9-5 Describe the technological and relational aspects of customer relationship management.

Customer relationship management (CRM) is a relatively new term in supply chain management; it does not yet have a standard definition across different businesses. For many, CRM is equated with computer software and information technology that is

customer relationship management (CRM) A software and information technology based approach used to collect and analyze customer data from numerous sources for the purpose of developing strategically appropriate relationships with customers.

TABLE 9-2 Examples of Actions for Customer Service Management

Company/Industry	Actions
Amazon.com (Online/Catalog Retail)	Some 30 percent of sales come from outside retailers who sell goods on Amazon. Amazon rolled out new services for these retailers, including aid in setting up shop or managing order fulfillment.
Lexus (Auto)	Lexus awards cash to dealers—as much as $50,000 to dealers with the best new service ideas.
The Ritz-Carlton (Hotel)	To lure corporate event planners worried about spending on high-end meetings, Ritz will donate 10 percent of meeting fees to charity.
Publix Super Market (Supermarket)	To ensure consumers always find what they come looking for, Publix adopted "automated replenishment" for fresh items. Scanners indicate when inventory levels are low and software automatically orders replenishment
Hewlett-Packard (Consumer Electronics)	In 2008, HP opened eight new customer service centers and gave experienced agents access to Instant Care, a tool that allows tech support reps to remotely control a customer's desktop.
Key Bank (Banking)	Key Bank unveiled new online tools that give entrepreneurs many of the cash management services long reserved for large companies.
Cadillac (Auto)	Despite General Motors' cash crunch, Cadillac has not scaled back on guaranteeing loaner cars to customers while their cars are in the shop.
Amica (Insurance)	Investing in new technology to speed claims processing, Amica also invests heavily in staff, which has a turnover rate of less than 7 percent.
JetBlue Airways (Airlines)	JetBlue created the industry's first Customer Bill of Rights, which includes compensation for problems caused by the carrier, and introduced free e-mail and instant messaging on some flights.
Charles Schwab (Brokerage)	A new direct-dial feature lets clients call back a Schwab rep directly rather than navigate the automated system a second time.

Source: Adapted from "Customer Service Champs," *BusinessWeek,* March 2, 2009, pp. 32–33. See the article for the entire list and ranking of 25 companies.

used to manage and analyze data from numerous sources within an organization (sales calls, call centers, actual purchases, etc.) in order to gain greater insight into customers' buying behaviors. To others, CRM includes not only technology, but also all forms of information and communication that help suppliers develop better relationships with customers.

The objective of customer relationship management is to develop a customer-centered organization that utilizes every opportunity to delight customers, foster their loyalty, and build long-term, mutually beneficial relationships. CRM involves the science of first gathering and analyzing data that describe individual customer needs and purchasing habits and, second, developing the operational capability to meet those individual needs more completely. In this way, CRM systems can ensure rapid response to customer requirements, achieving the goal of better serving customers at lower cost and in less lead time. The Get Real box concerning Amazon describes how CRM technology can be used to benefit both a company and its customers.

CRM is not only based on technology. It involves developing personal and organizational relationships as well. For example, it is becoming increasingly common for suppliers to have their own personnel maintain an office very near, or even inside, the facilities of key customers. In this way, the supplier gains critical knowledge of the customer's needs and plans, and can anticipate the customer's actions with a high degree of certainty.

Companies may include numerous other activities in a CRM approach, including the actions described in Table 9-2. Many companies also establish customer councils to provide customers with an opportunity to provide feedback on proposed products and plans. A full discussion of CRM technology and processes is beyond the scope of this text. In fact there are entire textbooks devoted to the topic. Our purpose here is to establish that customer–supplier relationships can involve many layers of cross-functional interaction. However, it is usually not desirable (or possible) for all relationships to involve the intensity of a customer success commitment. In the next section we discuss different types of relationships that suppliers and customers might develop.

GET REAL

Amazon's Automated CRM Technology

Amazon.com has been one of the leaders in automating CRM functionality, to gather information and communicate with customers. For example, Amazon customers frequently receive e-mail messages from Amazon informing them of new books written by authors of books that they previously purchased. In addition, every time repeat customers log on to Amazon.com, they get tips on other products they might like based on their previous purchases. Also, when a customer selects a particular title from Amazon's Web site, the customer is informed of book titles that other customers have ordered in conjunction with the title selected.

All of these actions certainly benefit Amazon by increasing sales revenue. However, most customers also appreciate this ability on the part of Amazon, as it adds significantly to their reading enjoyment. This service provided by Amazon is made possible by its online interface and its massive data storage and computational capabilities. By recording customers' searches and selections, Amazon is able to develop customer profiles that give a clear picture of each customer's interests and purchasing habits.

Prepare

What strategy can be used for segmenting customers and developing tailored relationships?

Organize

Customer Management and Relationship Strategy

LO9-6 Describe a strategy for segmenting customers and for developing tailored relationships with them.

CUSTOMER MANAGEMENT AND RELATIONSHIP STRATEGY

A basic principle of supply chain management is that companies must segment customers based on their needs and adapt supply chain operations to serve those segments. In many instances a segment may consist of only one customer. For example, Procter & Gamble has a highly publicized relationship with Walmart that includes many specialized operational characteristics. Many P&G employees live and work in Bentonville, Arkansas, the headquarters of Walmart. P&G is extensively involved in managing inventories for Walmart, determining when Walmart distribution centers should be replenished with P&G products. In addition they have collaborated on numerous initiatives to reduce cost across the two organizations.

Earlier, it was stated that committing at levels beyond basic service and satisfaction to the level of customer success is extremely time consuming and resource intensive. The P&G Get Real box earlier demonstrates that the company collaborates with customers other than Walmart, but certainly not with every customer, and none to the extent that it does with Walmart. Clearly, no company can implement such approaches with every potential customer. In fact, many customers may not desire such relationships with all (or any) suppliers. From a strategic point of view, then, a company must determine which level of commitment and relationship is appropriate for each customer segment.

Procter & Gamble relationships with Walmart—P&G products in Walmart.

One approach for determining levels of commitment makes use of the Pareto principle introduced in Chapter 7. Just as some products are more critical than others, so too are some customers more critical. It is not uncommon for a company to find that the vast majority of its revenue comes from a small percentage of its customers. The same is true for a company's profit. Finally, it is also often true that the customers who account for a large portion of revenue are not necessarily the most profitable customers with whom to do business. The combination of these facts leads to the diagram presented in Figure 9-4.

Typically, only a small number of customers are both high revenue generators and also highly profitable. These customers are naturally the most deserving of a customer success relationship, as depicted in the upper right-hand corner of Figure 9-4. On the other hand, suppliers should carefully

FIGURE 9-4 Selection of Appropriate Customer Relationships

Revenue \ Profit	Low	High
High	High basic service or customer satisfaction	Commitment to customer success
Low	Review reason for doing business	High basic service or customer satisfaction

question whether they should continue serving customers that provide both low revenue and low profit (the lower left-hand corner of Figure 9-4). In many instances there may be good reasons to continue. For example, they may be new customers or may be small but rapidly growing companies. In some instances it may simply be a wiser decision to stop doing business with them.

Customers who occupy the other two areas of Figure 9-4 are candidates for a level of commitment that emphasizes a high degree of basic service or satisfaction. The choice between service and satisfaction often depends on the supplier's potential to influence the customer to increase the quantity it buys, or its potential to serve the customer more efficiently, thereby raising profitability. Recall that in the opening vignette for the chapter, Unilever found that many customers desired much shorter lead times, and some desired the ability to significantly modify orders. Supplier ability to provide these types of operational modifications can significantly influence customer buying preferences.

Customers can be segmented and analyzed in many different ways that are suggestive of strategic actions. The important point to remember is that commitment at the level of customer success should be reserved for a few customers; for others an emphasis on basic service or satisfaction is appropriate. Like all other operational activities, managing customer relationships consumes scarce resources. Therefore, it is important to spend these resources in ways that provide the greatest returns with the lowest risks.

student activity

The text references the close relationship between P&G and Walmart. Conduct a literature search on the Web to learn more about P&G's relationships with major retail customers. See what else you can learn about Walmart's relationships with suppliers other than P&G.

CHAPTER SUMMARY

In this chapter we have explored the evolution of customer management in supply chain operations. Over the past two decades the focus has shifted from provision of basic service to customer satisfaction and customer success. The major issues discussed in the chapter are:

1. Traditionally, it has been common to think of a company's basic service program in terms of product availability, lead-time performance, and service reliability.
2. Of critical importance to customers of an organization is the order-to-delivery lead time (OTD), which is the lead time that passes from the instant the customer recognizes need for product until the instant that product is received. The components of OTD differ depending upon a product's market orientation.
3. Customer satisfaction is achieved when customers perceive that a company's performance meets or exceeds the customers' expectations.
4. A customer success program focuses on a customer's strategic objectives and involves a thorough understanding of individual customer requirements.
5. Customer relationship management involves the science of first gathering and analyzing data that describe individual customer needs and purchasing habits and, second, building systems that enable the organization to meet those individual needs more completely.
6. There are several different types of relationships and levels of commitment that may exist between suppliers and customers. Excellent companies tailor their customer relationships and associated operational capabilities to maximize revenue and profit, while minimizing risk.

KEY TERMS

basic service 311
communications gap 318
customer service management 310
customer relationship management (CRM) 322
customer satisfaction 315
customer success 319
fill rate 311
knowledge gap 317
lead time 312
line fill rate 311
order fill rate (orders shipped complete) 312
order-to-delivery (OTD) lead time 312
perception gap 318
perfect order 314
performance gap 318
product availability 311
satisfaction gap 318
service reliability 314
standards gap 318
unit fill rate 311

DISCUSSION QUESTIONS

1. Explain the critical differences between basic service, customer satisfaction, and customer success.
2. Consider some of your recent shopping experiences and discuss instances in which a store was out of stock of items you were planning to purchase. What did you do as a result of the stockout?
3. Consider products you consume. Identify purchases you have made from firms with the following market orientations:
   a. Make to stock
   b. Make to order
   c. Assemble to order
   d. Engineer to order

   In each case, describe the components and your estimate of order-to-delivery lead time that you as the customer experienced.
4. Which market orientation would you consider for a standard product that has low, infrequent demand? What are the trade-offs you would consider in making this decision?
5. How can a company use the gap model of customer satisfaction to improve its operations management processes?
6. Why don't companies attempt to offer a commitment at the level of customer success with all of their customers?
7. What aspects of operations management can contribute to customer success?
8. The chapter offers one approach to customer management and relationship strategy based on sales volume and profitability. Can you think of other criteria that might be used to determine the most appropriate form of relationship?

SOLVED PROBLEM

The accompanying table presents order fulfillment data for a company. Compute the unit, line, and order fill rates.

Orders Received	Total Units Ordered	Total Order Lines	Total Units Delivered	Total Complete Order Lines Delivered	Total Complete Orders Delivered
8,000	40,000	20,000	37,500	18,250	7,150

Solution:

Unit fill rate = 37,500/40,000 = 93.75%

Line fill rate = 18,250/20,000 = 91.25%

Order fill rate = 7,150/8,000 = 89.375%

PROBLEMS

1. Aldo Inc. was reviewing its quarterly performance in providing service to customers. An analysis of order and shipping data was prepared and is shown in the table below. How well did Aldo perform in unit, line, and order fill rate?

Orders Received	Total Units Ordered	Total Order Lines	Total Units Delivered	Total Complete Order Lines Delivered	Total Complete Orders Delivered
450	15,000	3,000	14,250	2,700	360

2. The following quarter, Aldo's senior executive was interested in knowing whether performance had improved. The following table presents order and shipping data collected for the next quarter. How would you answer the senior executive?

Orders Received	Total Units Ordered	Total Order Lines	Total Units Delivered	Total Complete Order Lines Delivered	Total Complete Orders Delivered
500	18,000	3,200	17,200	2,950	425

3. Suppose a firm, in discussions with customers, learns that customers identify eight factors that they evaluate for every order they receive from suppliers. The firm then finds that its performance is 95 percent on six of these factors and 92 percent on the other two factors. What is the firm's probable perfect order performance?

4. In problem 3, suppose performance on two of the factors that had been 95 percent falls to 90 percent. What is the impact on perfect order performance?
5. ABBA Inc. collected the following data concerning orders and shipments during the most recent year.

Orders Received	Total Units Ordered	Total Order Lines	Total Units Delivered	Total Complete Order Lines Delivered	Total Complete Orders Delivered
25,000	5,000,000	150,000	4,800,000	146,500	24,150

   How well did ABBA perform in providing product to its customers?
6. In addition to the information concerning product availability, ABBA collected the following data concerning service performance:

   Late delivery—6 percent

   Damage—1 percent

   Incorrect documentation—4 percent

   Assuming these are the critical attributes for perfect orders, how well did ABBA perform?
7. Jones Company found the following results when analyzing its delivery performance.

Total Orders	Total Units Ordered	Total Order Lines	Total Units Delivered	Order Lines Delivered Complete	Complete Orders Delivered
1,245	22,350	5,830	18,750	4,824	898

   How would you assess Jones Company's performance in product availability?
8. Jones Company also found the following information about delivery to customers. Late deliveries were made for 8 percent of the orders. Early arrivals, which are unacceptable to customers, occurred for 2 percent of the orders. The company also experienced a 1.5 percent damage rate during delivery. It also had incorrect information on 3 percent of the invoices billed to customers. Based on this information, what was the approximate perfect order performance at Jones Company?

CASE

Tiler Industries

Harry Chamberlain, vice president of Tiler Industries, closed the phone call by saying, "Well thanks, Jim. We appreciate the call even though it was bad news. We're sorry we didn't get the contract for the SRW installation from Phoenix, but we understand. And, we'll do better next time." Most of the executive committee members heard the news as they filed in for the division's weekly status meeting. In the few minutes before the meeting started, Harry started to organize his thoughts, concerns, and ideas as to where to go from here with the loss of a major sale to a long-standing customer.

As the meeting convened, he said, "Well, as most of you have just heard we didn't get the contract for this year's SRW installation at Phoenix Engineering. That would have been a $12 million project plus ongoing service and parts business. That call was from Jim Gray, their head of purchasing. He said our price was okay. But their new cross-functional commodity team was unanimous on many benefits, some tangible and some intangible, and supply chain approaches that were provided in the proposal from Eastern Star Electronics. We took a bad hit on this one. The real harm is the long-term impact by Eastern Star with a customer who has been very loyal to us over the years."

Tiler Industries is a manufacturer of industrial tools and machinery with headquarters in Wisconsin. It also has operations in Europe and South America and makes nine specialty lines of equipment. The SRW equipment line is used by customers for precision shaping, forming, and assembly of fluid dynamics components that are subsequently sold to original equipment manufacturers of such items as diesel engines, electrical generation equipment, jet engines, turbines, and marine motors. It involves precise measuring, cutting, and forming processes. Tiler has traditionally been number two in the industry, behind Acton Tools, the dominant price leader. Acton and Tiler have led the industry for many years.

The Executive Committee Meeting

"We lost the job to Eastern Star, and it wasn't on price. Eastern Star came at us from out of nowhere and we were caught without warning," Harry said.

Bill Mathews, sales and marketing head, spoke up: "Eastern Star is starting to become a major player now. We just came back from the Milan Machine Tool Show last week, and they were there in a big way. That's the third time I've seen their displays at major trade shows this year. Each time they have new and innovative features in their equipment. It makes ours look weak in comparison. Our products show only minor modifications and small efficiency changes, but theirs have technical leaps. They have a new laser module component that looks quite good. None of the U.S. firms are close to that technology. And you can't beat Eastern Star's output quality."

Sally Morgan, finance director, said, "Our quality is good. In fact, it's great. All of our benchmark warranty and survey studies against Acton Tools show we are comparable or better. And they are still the industry leader."

Harry asked Phil Chung, director of research, "OK, just what makes this latest equipment from Eastern Star better than our SRW?"

Phil replied, "Well, this is the first trade show the company ever sent me to. And it was a real eye-opener for me. As Bill Mathews said, Eastern Star has a real state-of-the-art line. At first look, it does just what our machine does. And it doesn't really perform any better in comparison to the SRW or Acton's units. But the real advantage is that Eastern also sells a module that a company like Phoenix can attach to components that go onto the OEM's generator, turbine, or motor. A technician can then come along with a diagnostic reader and determine if those units are performing properly. If there is a problem, fine-tuning adjustments can be made. This just isn't possible with our SRW line."

He continued, "They also spend a lot of time talking about the supply chain. They look a lot at the end users of turbines and diesel engines. And, they talk to their customers about issues like lead times and delivery. Eastern can promise a customer like Phoenix that they'll be able to install a big system similar to our SRW in two months. We couldn't possibly do that since it would take us almost that long just to get the components we need to start making the SRW. The best we could do would probably be in the neighborhood of four months."

Bill Mathews said, "Phil's right. We don't really know much about Phoenix's customers. What's happening with cars, boat engines, and power generation equipment? One time a couple of years ago I went with Phoenix's people to visit Ford and Cummins Engine. I thought that was a big deal."

Harry brought the conversation back into focus. "Seems like we're playing by the old rules of the ballgame, and this is an entirely different one. Eastern pretty well blindsided us while we were happy trying to make sure we were at least as good as Acton. This is a good lesson for us. We need an across-the-board approach to figure out what to do. Maybe we ought to get some people here from Phoenix to talk over these issues. It might not hurt to get someone from Detroit Diesel or a power generation company. What do you think about getting some people from a couple of our key suppliers to meet with us? What we end up doing may change this company, more than just our products and marketing. There are some issues that may fundamentally change how we do business."

As the meeting ended, Harry's thoughts returned to Jim Gray's comment about the tangible and intangible benefits. He wondered what all of this would mean for the organization, structure, planning, and operations of the company. He had an uneasy feeling that some fundamental changes were in order.

Questions

1. What do you think are the intangible benefits Eastern Star provides to customers? What is the role of operations management in providing these benefits?
2. What changes in organization and/or planning would help Tiler respond to the challenges raised by Eastern Star?

Source: Adapted from a case prepared by Joseph L. Cavinato, Department of Business Logistics, The Pennsylvania State University.

CASE

Johnson Snacks

Murray Griffin, manager of distribution for Johnson Snacks, was faced with a difficult task. Harold L. Carter, the new CEO, had circulated a letter from Johnson Snacks' only mass merchandise customer, Discount 2 You, complaining of poor operating performance. Among the problems cited by Discount 2 You were: (1) frequent stockouts (2) poor basic service responsiveness and (3) high prices for Johnson Snacks' products. The letter suggested that if Johnson Snacks were to remain a supplier to Discount 2 You, it would need to eliminate stockouts by: (1) providing direct store delivery four times per week (instead of three) (2) installing an automated order inquiry system to increase basic service responsiveness ($300,000 investment) and (3) decreasing product prices by 5 percent. While the previous CEO would most certainly have begun implementing the suggested changes, Harold Carter was different. He requested that Murray prepare a detailed analysis of profitability by customer segment. This was something that Murray had never previously attempted, and it was needed first thing in the morning.

Johnson Snacks is a small manufacturer of salty snacks in the southeastern United States. The company was founded in 1922 and following an unsuccessful attempt at national expansion has remained primarily a local operation. The company currently manufactures and distributes several varieties of potato chips to three different types of retail accounts: grocery, drug, and mass merchandise. The largest percentage of business is concentrated in the grocery segment, with 250 retail customer locations accounting for 2,100,000 annual unit sales and more than 74 percent of annual revenue. The drug segment comprises 140 customer locations which account for 365,000 annual unit sales and more than 14 percent of annual revenue. In the mass merchandise segment, Johnson Snacks has one customer with six locations that account for 400,000 annual unit sales and almost 12 percent of annual revenue. All distribution is store-direct, with delivery drivers handling returns of outdated product and all shelf placement and merchandising.

Recently, the company has actively sought growth in the mass merchandise segment because of the perceived profit potential. However, while the company is acutely aware of overall business profitability, there had never been an analysis on a customer segment basis.

Murray began by gathering data about the service to the customers. All deliveries were store-direct with two deliveries per week to grocery stores, one delivery per week to drugstores, and three deliveries per week to mass merchandiser stores. The cost of delivery to each store was dependent on the type of vehicle used. Standard route trucks were used for drugstores and grocery stores, while extended vehicles were used to accommodate the volume at mass merchandisers. Jonson's selling prices for each unit were different for grocery ($1.70), drug ($1.90), and mass merchandise ($1.40) customers. Murray was also aware that Discount 2 You required Johnson Snacks to cover the suggested retail price (generally about $3.00 per unit regardless of channel) with a sticker bearing its reduced price at the store. Murray knew that many costs could be directly related to the specific type of customer. There were, of course, other costs that Johnson incurred but could not be related to a specific customer segment. Murray's analysis of the costs and expenses revealed the following:

Cost and expenses directly associated with:

Grocery stores:	$3,230,000
Drugstores:	$ 652,000
Discount 2 You:	$ 542,000

As Murray sat in his office compiling this information to complete the analysis of profitability, he received several unsolicited offers for assistance. Bill Smith, manager of marketing, urged him not to bother with the analysis, saying:

> *Discount 2 You is clearly our single most important customer. Look at the sales per store. We should immediately implement the suggested changes.*

Steve Brown, director of manufacturing, disagreed. He felt the additional manufacturing cost required to meet Discount 2 You requirements was too high:

> *We should let Discount 2 You know what we really think about their special requirements. Stickers, of all things! What business do they think we are in?*

The sales force had a different opinion. Jake Williams, sales manager, felt the grocery segment was most important:

> *Just look at that volume! How could they be anything but our best customers?*

Questions

1. Using the framework in Figure 9-4, how would you categorize each of the three customer segments?
2. How should Johnson Snacks respond to the letter from Discount 2 You?

SELECTED READINGS & INTERNET SITES

Customer Relationship Management Association
www.crmassociation.org

Supply Chain Brain
www.supplychainbrain.com/content/home/ Anderson, D. L.; F. F. Britt; and D. J. Favre. "The Best of Supply Chain Management Review: The Seven Principles of Supply Chain Management." *Supply Chain Management Review* 11, no. 3 (April 2007), p. 57.

Bensaou, M. "Portfolios of Buyer–Supplier Relationships." *Sloan Management Review,* Summer 1999, pp. 35–44.

Chauhan, S. S., and J-M Proth. "Analysis of a Supply Chain Partnership with Revenue Sharing." *International Journal of Production Economics* 97, no.1 (July 2005), p. 44.

Fawcett, S. E., and M. B. Cooper. "Customer Service, Satisfaction, and Success." In *Innovations in Competitive Manufacturing,* ed. P. M. Swamidass. Norwell, MA: Kluwer Academic Publishers, 2000, pp. 35–44.

Fawcett, S. E.; J. A. Ogden; G. M. Magnan; and M. B. Cooper. "Organizational Commitment and Governance for Supply Chain Success." *International Journal of Physical Distribution & Logistics Management* 36, no. 1 (2006), p. 22.

Hart, C. W. "Beating the Market with Customer Satisfaction." *Harvard Business Review,* March 2007, p. 30.

Parsons, A. L. "What Determines Buyer–Seller Relationship Quality? An Investigation from the Buyer's Perspective." *Journal of Supply Chain Management* 38, no. 2 (Spring 2002), pp. 4–12.

Stading, G., and N. Alta. "Delineating the 'Ease of Doing Business' Construct within the Supplier–Customer Interface." *Journal of Supply Chain Management* 43, no. 2 (Spring 2007), p. 29.

10 Sourcing and Supply Management

CHAPTER OUTLINE

LEARNING OBJECTIVES *After studying this chapter, you should be able to:*

LO10-1 Define supply management and understand its impact on a firm's performance.

LO10-2 Understand how factors such as cost, risk, and globalization affect supply management decisions.

LO10-3 Analyze and make insourcing/outsourcing decisions.

LO10-4 Explain the steps in a strategic sourcing process.

LO10-5 Describe the components in a sourcing strategy.

LO10-6 Assess and select suppliers using competitive bidding, online reverse auctions, and negotiation.

LO10-7 Understand ways to manage ongoing supplier relationships.

IKEA Partners with its Suppliers

Selling over 7,000 items, one-third of which are new each year, IKEA, the Swedish retailer, depends upon its suppliers for success. Starting with a single store in 1958, IKEA is now an iconic global brand offering trendy, environmentally friendly products at low prices. Its network of 1,300 suppliers in 53 countries enables IKEA to quickly customize and deliver products to global markets.

Supply managers at IKEA form the bridge from the retail shelves to suppliers' manufacturing operations. They have reduced the number of direct suppliers and increased the use of single sourcing to build long-term, collaborative supplier partnerships that lead to innovative and low-cost ways to bring new products to market. For instance, IKEA's supply managers asked a ski manufacturer, an expert in bending wood, to produce armchairs, and a grocery cart manufacturer to produce parts for durable sofas. They worked with a supplier of low-price coffee mugs to offer colors that have the least costly pigments.

IKEA also emphasizes sustainability in its dealings with suppliers. The "IWAY" code of conduct communicates IKEA's expectations on the prevention of child labor, the environment, and responsible forestry management. Suppliers, in turn, must use these same expectations upstream in the supply chain when working with their suppliers.

Adapted from K. Capell, A. Sains, C. Lindblad, A.T. Palmer, J. Bush, D. Roberts, and K. Hall, "IKEA," *BusinessWeek,* November 14, 2005, pp. 96–106, and www.ikea-group.ikea.com.

Suppliers provide a wide range of resources to firms. Consider the case of IKEA. Upstream suppliers work with IKEA's designers to create innovative products at affordable prices using sustainable business practices. Downstream, logistics suppliers move products from suppliers' plants, through the distribution channel to IKEA stores. Clearly, IKEA depends upon many different types of suppliers. Thus, sourcing and supply management are important for its success.

supply management The identification, acquisition, and management of inputs and supplier relationships.

sourcing The identification, evaluation, and selection of suppliers.

Supply management is the identification, acquisition, and management of inputs and supplier relationships that a firm needs to attain its strategic objectives. Supply management is also called *purchasing* or *procurement*. **Sourcing**, which is the identification, evaluation, and selection of suppliers, is an important part of supply management. This chapter discusses the role that supply management plays in the operations of a firm and its supply chain. We examine how managers decide what to purchase and what to make internally, whom to purchase from, how to get the best value, and how to manage suppliers after the contract is signed.

Prepare

How does supply management affect a firm's performance?

Organize

Supply Management's Impact on Firm and Supply Chain Performance
- Ensure Timely Availability of Resources
- Reduce Total Costs
- Enhance Quality
- Access Technology and Innovation
- Foster Sustainability

SUPPLY MANAGEMENT'S IMPACT ON FIRM AND SUPPLY CHAIN PERFORMANCE

Supply management is critical to an organization's success. Organizations buy raw materials, parts, and components that go into the products they make. They also buy indirect materials such as office supplies, and a wide range of different services.

In many industries, purchased goods and services account for a large percentage of a product's cost. For example, 75–80 percent of the cost of a car made by Honda of America comes from purchased parts and components. The costs of parts for Apple's iPad are over 30 times larger than the cost to assemble it. Corporate purchases go beyond raw materials and parts. As firms focus on their core competencies, suppliers take on noncore business functions such as accounting, information systems, maintenance, inventory management, office support services, human resources management, and engineering design.

LO10-1 Define supply management and understand its impact on a firm's performance.

Effective supply management enables a firm to meet its strategic objectives and improve performance. Its goals are to:

- Ensure timely availability of resources.
- Reduce total costs.
- Enhance quality.
- Access technology and innovation.
- Foster sustainability.

Ensure Timely Availability of Resources

Ensuring that the right purchases are available at the right time to support new product launches, production, and shipments is an important supply management goal. Late supplier deliveries or poor supplier quality can halt operations, causing deliveries to customers to be late. Think about the problems that would occur if the right materials were not available for a surgery or if the security team for a concert failed to show up. In the automotive industry, stopping an assembly line costs thousands of dollars per minute in idle time. Deliveries that are too early also cause problems, as they increase inventory costs, waste resources, and reduce flexibility for the buyer.

supply risk The probability of an unplanned event that negatively affects a firm's ability to serve its customers.

Supply managers gather information and carefully evaluate suppliers' capabilities to assess **supply risk**, the probability of an unplanned event in acquisition, delivery, and use that negatively affects a firm's ability to serve its customers. In 2011, the earthquake and tsunami in Japan and floods in Thailand disrupted the computer and automotive industries.

Besides supply delays and disruptions, supply risks include thefts of intellectual property, price increases, product safety problems, or circumstances that harm the firm's reputation. For example, the Fisher-Price division of Mattel recalled millions of toys made by its suppliers in China because of health concerns associated with lead paint. The standards for lead paint are more stringent in the United States than in China. Lean manufacturing, just-in-time deliveries, reliance on a single supplier for each component, and global sourcing tend to increase supply risks.

In the past, natural disasters, strikes, and theft were the key sources of supply risk. Today, deliberate tampering with goods, information, packaging, or shipping containers is also a concern. Since 9/11, the U.S. Bureau of Customs and Border Protection requires increased supply chain security. Global sourcing heightens risks because countries around the world have very different levels of security and protection of intellectual property.

global

Reduce Total Costs

LO10-2 Understand how factors such as cost, risk, and globalization affect supply management decisions.

Because purchases often are a firm's largest expense, effective supply management reduces costs and improves cash flows. By collaborating with suppliers, creative ways to reduce costs emerge. For example, Nissan suppliers integrated the dashboard and other interior parts into a single module that is installed by supplier employees at Nissan's assembly plant. This reduced costs by up to 30 percent compared to traditional assembly methods.

The true cost of using a product can be much greater than its purchase price. Think about purchasing a used car. The car that is the lowest price may need more repairs, be less reliable, have lower fuel economy, and may not last as long. Similarly, selecting a supplier based solely on purchase price can be a bad business decision. The supplier with the lowest price may not have the capabilities to meet the buyer's quality or delivery requirements, ultimately resulting in delays and higher costs.

The **total cost of ownership (TCO)** considers all the costs incurred before, during, and after the purchase of a good or service. These include sourcing costs, purchase price, transportation, handling, inspection, quality, rework, maintenance, and disposal as shown in Table 10-1. Returning to the used car example, think about the costs that happen before, during, and after your purchase. Your costs increase as you take more time and drive to various locations to look at cars, hire a mechanic to inspect potential cars, and make repairs after the purchase.

total cost of ownership (TCO) **All of the costs incurred before, during, and after a purchase.**

Consider the total costs of ownership associated with global sourcing. For example, for a firm located in the United States, sourcing in Vietnam will have a lower purchase price than from a U.S. supplier. However, purchasing from a low-cost country such as Vietnam creates problems such as:

- Long lead times.
- Higher transportation costs.

global

TABLE 10-1 Total Cost of Ownership

When the Costs Occur	Type of Costs
Before the transaction	Time spent and costs of searching for, visiting, evaluating, and certifying suppliers.
During the transaction	Purchase price and costs of ordering, transporting, expediting, receiving, inspecting, and follow-up.
After the transaction	Costs of inventory, supply risk, production downtime, defects in finished goods, warranty, safety recalls, replacements, repairs, lost sales, liability, and damaged reputation.

Source: Adapted from L. Ellram, "Total Cost of Ownership," *International Journal of Physical Distribution and Logistics Management* 25, no. 8/9 (1995), pp. 4–24.

- Higher inventory costs because of higher safety stock and in-transit inventory.
- Lack of flexibility to make changes in quantity or specifications because of the long transportation pipeline.
- Costs of travel and communication.
- Complexity, delays, and costs from customs clearance, duties, and border security.
- Potential quality problems because of differing standards and difficulty in monitoring.
- Cost of poor quality because the entire transportation pipeline from the supplier could be filled with poor-quality materials.

Until recently, the trend has been to outsource the production of such products as clothing, toys, televisions, refrigerators, and electronics to low-wage countries (most often China). Rising wages in these locations, higher transportation costs, and the need to respond faster to customers have managers focusing on the total costs of ownership. Consequently, American products that were once outsourced to Asia are being brought back to the United States or "nearshore" to Central America, the Caribbean, and Mexico. For example, Kirstie Kelly Couture moved production of moderately priced wedding dresses from China to Nashville, Tennessee, after evaluating the total cost of ownership. (See the nearby Get Real box.) Products are manufactured in China increasingly to serve its growing middle class.

GET REAL

Rethinking Offshoring in Fashion

Kirstie Kelly Couture is a Los Angeles-based designer that produces one-of-a-kind wedding gowns that sell for $10,000 a copy. The company funds high-end operations by teaming up with Disney to produce more moderately priced gowns that go for about $3,800 per gown, under the Disney Fairy Tale Weddings Collection label. In 2007, Kelly looked to reduce costs by offshoring 80 percent of that line's production to China (the high-end gowns were always produced by hand in Los Angeles). However, the lower labor costs did not offset the other unanticipated costs—high shipping costs, day-long flights for plant visits, language barriers, and overall lack of quality control.

In late 2008, Kelly moved 40 percent of Disney dress production to a factory in Nashville, Tennessee. With only a four-hour flight to this plant, Kelly notes that she can better monitor everything from sewing to fittings. Because 85 percent of her revenues come from U.S. customers, Kelly estimates that the savings on shipping alone will cut the overall cost of production by 29 percent per dress. Not included are savings from faster turnaround, shorter lead times, and reduced inventories.

"Disney Bridal Dresses Designed by Kirstie Kelly," www.disneybridal.com, accessed February 22, 2009.

Supply managers have to consider all of the relevant costs when making purchases. Although some costs such as purchase price and transportation costs are easy to evaluate, other costs such as defects in finished goods, warranty, safety recalls, replacements, repairs, lost sales, liability, and customer satisfaction are difficult to accurately estimate in advance.

Enhance Quality

A product's quality depends in large part upon the quality of all of its inputs. For example, if you have a question about your credit card, the service provided by the customer service representative, an employee of a supplier, impacts your impression of the credit card company. Similarly, the failure of low-cost parts, such as thermostats, can cause engines to overheat, increasing warranty costs and impacting a car manufacturer's reputation. In fact, Audi faced a supplier quality problem that proved to be very costly and reduced customer satisfaction. (See the Get Real box below.)

A supplier's quality is an order qualifier with a specified level of quality required to do business with the buyer. If a supplier's quality is poor, buyers will often look for a new supplier. Most large corporations require that their suppliers have extensive quality management systems such as ISO 9000 and statistical process control as discussed in Chapter 6. Many companies, such as Intel, expect suppliers to demonstrate continuous improvement in quality and use continuous improvement as a key performance indicator.

Access Technology and Innovation

Firms look to suppliers as sources of innovation and new technology to aid the design of new products and the improvement of existing ones. Very few firms have all the necessary expertise to develop needed innovations on their own. Example, Procter & Gamble acquires new product and packaging ideas from suppliers using a process called "Connect + Develop." Key ingredients for its Olay[R] Regenerist line of skin creams were developed by a French supplier. Suppliers often provide essential technical knowledge and expertise by being directly involved early in product development activities.

global

GET REAL

Supplier Quality Causes Problems for Audi

After spending years building a reputation for high quality and sophisticated technology, by 2002, Audi North America had a major problem on its hands. In cold weather, cars with its four-cylinder engines experienced failures and would not start. Customers had to have their cars towed to the repair shop. Audi estimated that the failure rate was up to 50 percent on cars produced from 2001–2003, affecting about 50,000 vehicles.

Audi's quality team found that the underlying cause was defective circuit boards from its only supplier of that part. Things went from bad to worse when, because of quality problems, the supplier could not keep up with demand for replacement parts. Because Audi did not have a second supplier, customers faced long waits to have their cars repaired.

The supplier quality team at Audi sent a team of experts to work closely with the circuit board supplier to improve its quality processes. In addition, to reduce supply risk, Audi added a second circuit board supplier. Although the experience was painful, Audi changed its supply management practices for the better. Overall reliability increased while warranty costs went down.

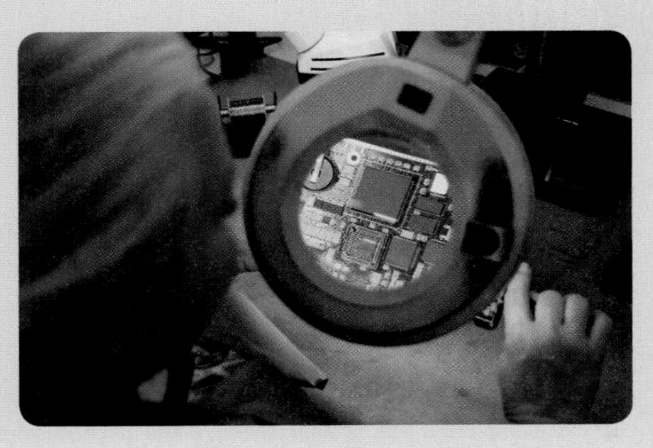

Foster Sustainability

sustainability Business practices designed to positively affect people, society, the planet, as well as profits.

Supply managers play important roles in fostering sustainability, which simultaneously addresses how decisions made within the firm and throughout the supply chain affect people, the planet, and company profits. Firms develop policies and procedures designed to improve sustainability. **Sustainability** has become increasingly important in recent years due to growing government regulations and social pressures. Chapter 16 discusses the broader idea of sustainability in a supply chain management context.

Sustainability typically addresses the following goals:

Goals:	Supply Management Example:
Support and provide value to the community	Provide jobs in the supplier's community
Increase social diversity	Hire minority owned suppliers
Encourage environmental responsibility	Require environmental compliance from suppliers
Display ethical behavior	Fair negotiations of contracts
Practice and promote financial responsibility	Accurate reporting of financial dealings with suppliers
Respect human rights	Hire suppliers who conform to child labor laws
Ensure a safe working environment	Hire suppliers who conform to safety standards

student activity

Review the most recent list of the 100 Best Corporate Citizens as ranked by *Corporate Responsibility Officer* (www.thecro.com). Select a company from the list, visit its Web site, and search for "supplier code of conduct." If you were a supplier, how would this code affect the way you do business? Why?

Sustainability can improve financial performance, lower total costs, increase quality, instill customer loyalty, and enhance reputation. Most large corporations have a code of conduct that communicates expectations for sustainability in their own organizations and across the supply chain. The Get Real box shows an example of how Walmart developed an index to measure sustainability

GET REAL

Walmart Measures Suppliers' Sustainability Performance

Walmart has three key sustainability goals: (1) to use 100% renewable energy, (2) to create zero waste, and (3) to sell products that sustain people and the environment. To attain these goals, Walmart must influence its supply base of over 100,000 suppliers worldwide to adopt or increase sustainable business practices. As a first step, in July 2009, Walmart introduced its Sustainable Product Index, which requires suppliers to complete a 15-question survey about energy and climate, material efficiency, natural resources, and people and community. Suppliers are categorized as below target, on target, or above target in each of these four areas. Walmart intends to reward suppliers who make significant progress toward aggressive sustainability goals. Ultimately, Walmart plans to communicate a sustainability score for each product to consumers.

http://walmartstores.com/Sustainability/9292.aspx

Caribou Coffee works with the Rainforest Alliance to guarantee that the environment and wildlife are protected; workers receive decent wages and enjoy improved working and living conditions; workers and their children have access to schools, medical care and clean drinking water; and coffee is harvested responsibly. The pursuit of the Rainforest Alliance certification was a way for farmers to aim for a premium price for their coffees, "green up" their practices, gain some production efficiencies, and feel a great sense of pride and accomplishment once certification was achieved.

performance in its supply base. In another example, coffee production in many parts of the world can occur in conditions that are very poor for workers and detrimental to the environment. Caribou Coffee is committed to sustainable sourcing[1] and works with suppliers to ensure that coffee beans are grown using sustainable farming practices. In fact, over 50 percent of the coffee purchased by Caribou Coffee is certified to be grown in conditions that ensure basic human rights of the farm workers such as receiving fair wages and reasonable living conditions. Farming methods also protect wildlife and the environment. In addition, by being fair trade-certified, farmers are guaranteed to receive a minimum price per pound.

Prepare
How do managers decide which activities should be done by suppliers?

Organize
Making an Insourcing/Outsourcing Decision

MAKING AN INSOURCING/OUTSOURCING DECISION

LO10-3 Analyze and make insourcing/outsourcing decisions.

After supply management goals are agreed upon, you must determine which resources and activities should be provided by the firm (**insourcing**) and which should be done by its suppliers (**outsourcing**). On a personal level, deciding whether to make dinner at home or get take-out is an example of an insourcing (cook) or outsourcing (take-out) decision. Strategically, organizations must focus on their current or future core competencies. Noncore activities are candidates for outsourcing to suppliers whose expertise and capabilities are a better fit with the activities. For example, Korean Air's core business is providing air transportation. In 2009, Korean Air renewed its 10-year contract with IBM to manage its data systems. Data systems are clearly important to Korean Air's business but not one of the company's core competencies. IBM's core competences include managing data systems.

insourcing Acquiring inputs from operational processes done within the firm.

outsourcing Acquiring inputs from operational processes done by suppliers.

Advances in information technology and globalization have enabled many processes such as manufacturing, customer care, logistics, supply management, information services, engineering, and human resource management to be outsourced. A **make or buy decision** considers insourcing or outsourcing the production of parts and components. The same type of analysis can be done when deciding whether to do a service with internal resources or to buy it from a supplier. When outsourcing to a different country, the term *offshoring* is sometimes used.

global

Outsourcing offers several advantages. The buyer avoids having to invest capital into production assets. The supplier often has economies of scale and lower labor and facilities costs. Other benefits include higher quality, increased flexibility, greater capacity, and better access to market information and technology.

make or buy decision The choice between making a product internally or purchasing it from a supplier.

[1]http://www.cariboucoffee.com/page/1/responsible-coffee-sourcing.jsp

However, outsourcing is not without risks. Suppliers may not perform well on quality and delivery, and total costs may increase. The buyer must manage suppliers, and suppliers' activities must be seamlessly integrated into the buyer's processes. Outsourcing of services can be especially challenging because intangible aspects are difficult to clearly define for suppliers.

Another concern is that outsourcing may give suppliers critical expertise and access to intellectual property. This is especially a concern when sourcing in low-cost countries. Suppliers then compete against the buyer or may transfer knowledge to other customers. Without having to invest in R&D and product development, suppliers can sell products at a lower price. Trying to stop theft of intellectual property using the legal system can be slow and costly, and the outcome is uncertain. To avoid having suppliers become competitors, some companies, such as Honda and Toyota, spend three months or more assessing and working on-site with their potential suppliers. Other firms, such as Ericsson, a global telecommunications equipment and services company, outsource only mature technology, protecting their competitive advantages.

Because of its complexity, insourcing/outsourcing analysis should be done by a cross-functional team. The team must consider quantitative and qualitative issues. The steps in making an insourcing/outsourcing decision are shown in Figure 10-1.

Step 1. Assess Fit with the Firm's Core Competencies. Evaluate the product's or process's relationship to the firm's current or future core competencies. Compare the savings from outsourcing to the risk of losing core competencies or intellectual property. To reduce risk, firms usually insource processes in their areas of core competencies, even if outsourcing is lower cost.

Step 2. Evaluate the Suitability for Outsourcing. Certain characteristics favor outsourcing. Mature products with standard processes and requirements are often outsourced. Known technology means that there are many capable suppliers and the intellectual property risk is low.

Step 3. Evaluate the Reasons for Outsourcing. If the product or process seems appropriate for outsourcing, compare the benefits of outsourcing to those of insourcing. For

FIGURE 10-1 Insourcing/Outsourcing Decision Process

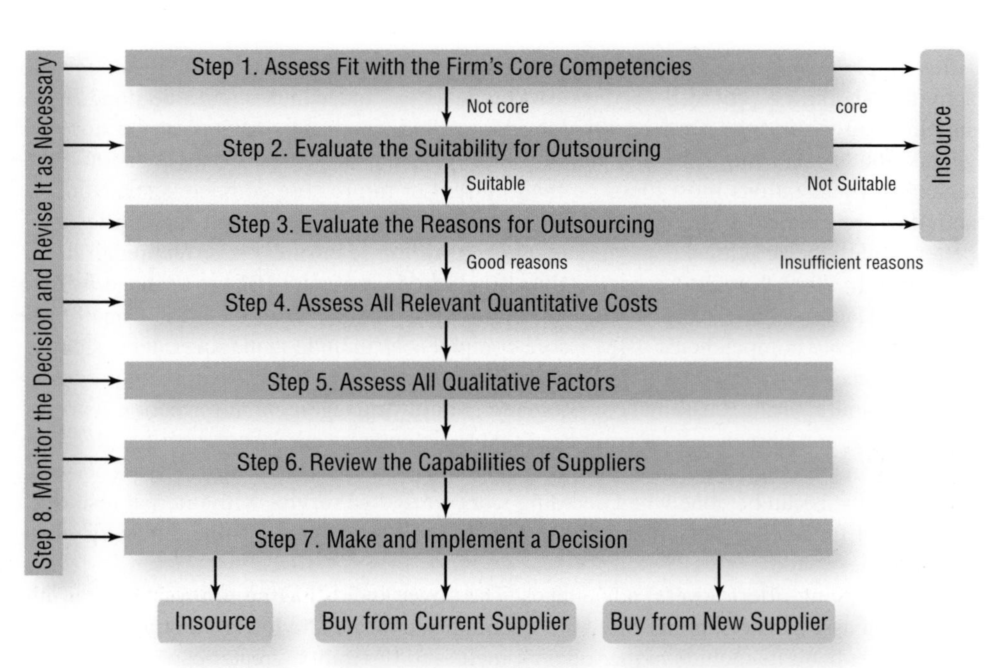

example, outsourcing might free up internal resources to produce other, more profitable products. However, costs will not be lower if freed-up resources sit idle.

Step 4. Assess All Relevant Quantitative Costs. If previous steps indicate that outsourcing makes sense, compare the costs to make the product internally against the total cost of purchasing it. Classify costs as either fixed or variable:

- **Fixed costs per contract**. These are the one-time costs incurred by the buying firm at the start of the contract or when beginning to make a product. For example, the firm may have to acquire tools to produce in-house or to pay reorganization costs to purchase the product.
- **Fixed costs per order**. The firm will incur costs each time it places a new order, for example, costs to inspect and refurbish tools for individual production runs.
- **Variable costs**. These are costs associated with each unit produced including labor, materials, asset depreciation, energy, or the purchase price.

fixed costs per contract Costs incurred at the start of production or the beginning of a new contract.

fixed costs per order Costs incurred each time an order is placed, regardless of the size of the order.

variable costs Costs that change in proportion to the quantity of units produced or service delivered.

Step 5. Assess All Qualitative Factors. It is not always possible to quantify all factors affecting the insourcing/outsourcing decision. Numerous qualitative factors are often important, including:

- Loss of control by releasing work to a supplier.
- Risk of dealing with a supplier.
- Importance assigned to a supplier's location and the convenience of site visits.
- Quality of the supplier's management team.
- Compatibility of organizational cultures and values.
- Supplier's willingness to remain flexible and accommodate changes.
- Supplier's labor–management climate.
- Supplier's warranty, repair, and support systems.
- Proprietary information and degree of secrecy required.

Step 6. Review the Capabilities of Suppliers. After assessing the costs and qualitative factors of insourcing and outsourcing, determine whether to use current or new suppliers. This requires a review of the technical, financial, manufacturing, and quality-related capabilities of suppliers as described later in this chapter.

Step 7. Make and Implement a Decision. After extensive study, make a decision based on the available information. If you decide to outsource, select a supplier and document the anticipated benefits of outsourcing. If you decide to insource, document the reasons for this decision. Then, negotiate the terms of the purchase contract or acquire assets to initiate internal production.

Step 8. Monitor the Decision and Revise It as Necessary. Insourcing/outsourcing analysis does not end with the start of production or a purchase. Compare the actual results of the decision against estimates and identify potential problems. This information may indicate a need for corrective action such as terminating or renegotiating the contract.

LO10-4 Explain the steps in a strategic sourcing process.

EXAMINING THE STRATEGIC SOURCING PROCESS

Prepare

What are the steps in a strategic sourcing process?

Organize

Examining the Strategic keep Sourcing Process

Analyze Spend and Supply Markets

If the decision is to outsource, suppliers must be identified, evaluated, selected, and managed. The processes that are used to identify, evaluate, and award business to suppliers must be linked with an organization's strategic objectives. A typical strategic sourcing process is shown in Figure 10-2. The following sections discuss each step of the strategic sourcing process.

FIGURE 10-2
Typical Strategic Sourcing Process
Source: Adapted from L. Smeltzer, J. Manship, and C. Rossetti, "An Analysis of the Integration of Strategic Sourcing and Negotiation Planning," *The Journal of Supply Chain Management* 39, no. 4 (2003), p. 18.

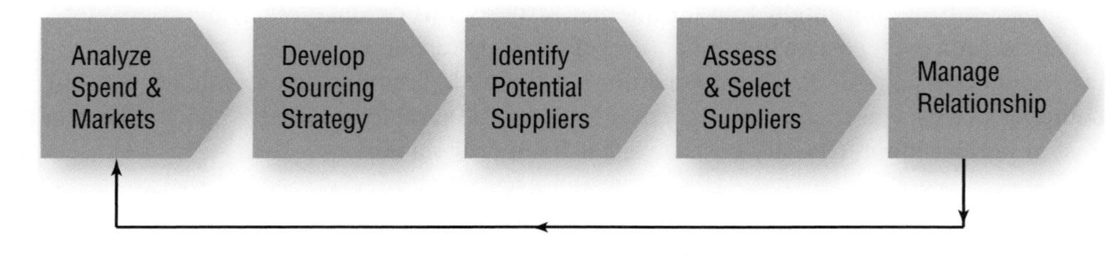

ANALYZE SPEND AND SUPPLY MARKETS

spend analysis A process that identifies what purchases are being made in an organization.

The first step of the strategic sourcing process is to understand what your firm is buying. Often different people within a firm purchase the same or similar products from different suppliers at different prices. **Spend analysis** is a process to understand what purchases are being made and at what price from which specific suppliers. A spend analysis at Boeing found that it was buying 200 different types of safety glasses when two or three different types would suffice. Based on a spend analysis, specifications can be standardized so purchases can be consolidated with fewer suppliers, reducing administrative costs, inventory costs, and often leading to lower prices.

When doing a spend analysis you should consider all purchases, even those that traditionally have not been made by supply managers. For example, purchases made in human resources management (worker benefits programs), in marketing and sales (advertising and printing), information technology (software), and in other functional areas should be included in spend analysis.

A market analysis gathers data on the market's structure including the number of suppliers, the number of buyers, and the nature of competition. This analysis provides information to assess the level of supply risk and to help develop an appropriate sourcing strategy, in coordination with other functions.

Prepare
How do you develop a sourcing strategy?

Organize
Develop a Sourcing Strategy
- Number of Suppliers
- Capabilities and Location
- Type of Supplier Relationship and Contract Length

DEVELOP A SOURCING STRATEGY

When managers reevaluate sourcing practices as the result of a spend analysis, or when something new needs to be purchased, they develop a sourcing strategy. To communicate details, such as what, when, and how many, to the supply management department, people use an internal company document referred to as a **purchase requisition**. The requisition should be clear, correct, and complete because this is used to develop the criteria used to select suppliers. Otherwise, purchases may not meet the users' needs. For example, the requisition for a cell phone cover would include a blueprint showing dimensions, acceptable tolerances, acceptable materials, and color.

A sourcing strategy is developed using information from the spend analysis and the market analysis. A classic framework developed by Kraljic in 1983 is still relevant today. It categorizes sourcing strategies based on supply risk and value of the total amount spent by the firm, and recommends a sourcing strategy (see Figure 10-3).

LO10-5 Describe the components in a sourcing strategy.

purchase requisition A document that communicates needs between the user and supply management.

Sourcing approaches and tactics vary by category:

- Strategic purchases represent a high spend level and are high risk. Typically these purchases are unique and core to the firm's performance. Tactics—Use one or two suppliers and build partnerships with them to foster collaboration and innovation.
- Bottleneck purchases are high risk and low spend, and typically are not core to the firm's performance, but lack of availability can cause delays. Tactics—Use at least two suppliers to assure supply, develop new suppliers, and explore using different materials.
- Leverage purchases are low risk but represent a high level of spend. They typically involve standard goods or services where many possible suppliers are available.

Value of Spend to Firm	Low Level of Supply Risk	High
High	**Leverage** Standardize purchases Use competition to select suppliers Consolidate purchases	**Strategic** Build collaborative partnerships Single or dual source Have executive champions in both companies
Low	**Noncritical** Increase efficiencies Electronic catalogs Purchasing cards Vendor managed inventory	**Bottleneck** Use multiple sources Find substitute materials Develop new suppliers

FIGURE 10-3
Sourcing Strategies
Source: P. Kraljic, "Purchasing Must Become Supply Management," *Harvard Business Review* 61, no. 5 (1983), p. 112.

Tactics—Standardize purchases across the company, use competition to select suppliers, and consolidate purchases with one or a few suppliers to get discounts.

- Noncritical items typically are a low percentage of overall spend and have little impact on performance. Tactics—Use electronic catalogs, vendor-managed inventory (discussed in Chapter 7), and corporate credit cards (called *purchasing cards*) to lower the transaction costs of purchasing. Using a purchasing card, the user directly purchases noncritical items without involving the supply management department.

The sourcing strategy determines which suppliers to use for which purchases. The strategy must support the corporate strategy as well as the other functional strategies within the firm. A sourcing strategy must consider:

- Number of suppliers to use.
- Capabilities and location of suppliers.
- Type of relationship and contract length.

Number of Suppliers

How many suppliers should a firm use? Making this decision is called **supply base optimization**. Using too few suppliers increases the risk of a supply disruption if a supplier goes out of business, is purchased by a competitor, or has a business disruption from a fire or natural disaster. Lack of competition means that prices may be higher, and sources of innovation are limited. Using too many suppliers increases complexity and administrative costs and makes communication and control difficult. Recently, firms have been reducing the number of suppliers. There are several ways that buyers reduce the number of suppliers. One approach is to standardize purchases and buy families of similar items from a single supplier. Another approach is to use modular designs as described in Chapter 4.Rather than purchasing many individual parts from many different suppliers, you can purchase a module from a single supplier, for example, automobile dashboards modules integrating the electronics such as the speedometer and fuel gauge and plastic parts assembled by first-tier suppliers.

supply base optimization The determination of the number of suppliers to use.

When considering a single type of purchase, you can choose either single or multiple sourcing. Single sourcing is the deliberate choice to use a single supplier for a specific purchase. Multiple sourcing involves purchasing a specific material or service from more than one supplier. Multiple sourcing may be too costly if there are high start-up costs, for example when specialized tooling must be purchased. Further, with multiple sourcing, suppliers may be unwilling to share information and ideas for fear these will be shared with their competitors.

Some purchases should be single sourced and others should be multiple sourced (Figure 10-3). In bottleneck situations, multiple sourcing decreases supply risk because backup suppliers are available. For strategic purchases, using single sourcing increases cooperation, and for leverage purchases single sourcing leads to quantity discounts and more consistency. Firms with multiple product lines, such as car manufacturers, can get the benefits of both approaches by single sourcing for each model but by using different suppliers for different models.

Capabilities and Location

An important part of a sourcing strategy is determining the capabilities and location of suppliers. Because of advances in transportation and communications it is possible to source from almost anywhere in the world. Consider the following questions when deciding upon a supplier location.

sustainability

- How important is it to use a close, local supplier? Close proximity makes it easy to communicate, collaborate, and keep delivery costs low. Quality, safety, and sustainability are other reasons that firms choose to source locally. For example, Chipotle Mexican Grill locally sources pork and vegetables as part of its commitment to sustainability. Purchasing locally helps the local economy and creates goodwill in the community.
- Is it important to source nationally/regionally? Countries sometimes have laws requiring a company to source in the same country in which it sells products, especially for large purchases such as airplane and construction projects. Other firms use suppliers within regions because of lower transportation costs, quicker response, and lower trade barriers because of agreements such as the North American Free Trade Agreement (NAFTA).
- Should the supplier have a global presence? This can be important so that the supplier can expand into the same regions as the firm. Many global companies such as Ford work with global first-tier suppliers.
- Is low cost the primary objective? Then low-cost countries can be considered. However, the analysis must consider the total cost of ownership, not just purchase price. Sourcing in low-cost countries can create challenges for logistics and sustainability.

Type of Supplier Relationship and Contract Length

relationships

What types of relationships should a firm have with its suppliers? Buyers and suppliers interact in different ways, depending on the circumstances. Sometimes, they simply receive and fill orders. Other times they work closely together and seamlessly integrate many activities from initial product or process design through routine deliveries of standing orders. The relationship's design should fit with the situation. Four types of relationships categorize the degree of interaction, information sharing, and collaboration between buyers and suppliers as shown in Figure 10-4:

1. Adversarial relationships.
2. Arm's-length relationships.
3. Relationships that acknowledge acceptance of mutual goals.
4. Full partnerships.

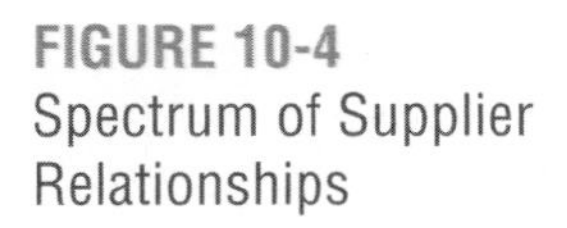

FIGURE 10-4
Spectrum of Supplier Relationships

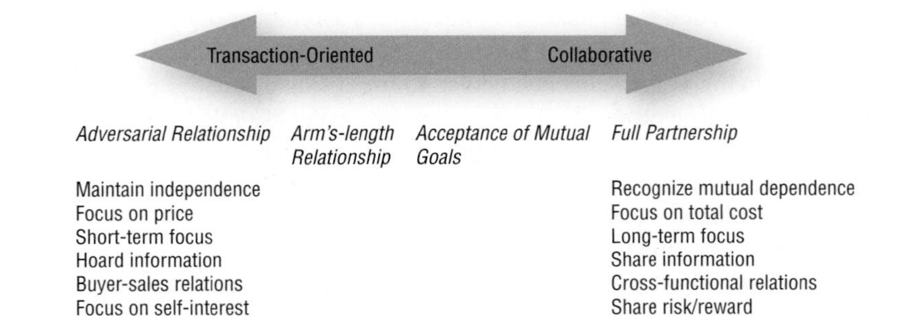

At one end of the spectrum, **adversarial relationships** represent a traditional way that buyers and suppliers have approached each other. These relationships are typified by distrust, limited communications, and short-term business transactions. Adversarial relationships can be serious obstacles to effective supply chain management. **Arm's-length relationships** tend to be limited to simple purchasing transactions, but they lack the high levels of distrust and antagonism often associated with adversarial relationships. For some supplier relationships, an arm's-length relationship is sufficient.

adversarial relationships Relationships characterized by distrust and limited communications.

arm's-length relationships Relationships limited to simple purchasing transactions.

In adversarial and arm's-length relationships, buyers attempt to minimize dependency through multiple sourcing. Suppliers also try to minimize dependency on any one buyer, to minimize the buyer's power in negotiations. Price is the focus in adversarial or arm's-length relationships. Suppliers try to obtain the highest possible price while buyers try to squeeze the supplier's profit margin to a minimum. Buyers and suppliers do not share information about cost, the market, competition, or their strategies. They view information as a resource to be used to gain power over the other party. Lack of trust, loyalty, and commitment typically limit relationships to the short term. Price competition and high stress levels make for high turnover in adversarial and arm's-length relationships.

Acceptance of mutual goals represents a major step toward collaboration, but it lacks the commitment of resources associated with full partnership. Also called strategic alliances, **full partnerships** have close working relations, trust, mutual respect, and highly integrated operations. Full partners acknowledge their interdependencies and work together to reduce total costs so both parties benefit. Partners frequently exchange schedules, information and specifications for new product designs, and cost data, along with other information. Many buyers allow suppliers direct access to their information systems, and vice versa. By working together, partners expect to create better solutions than they could create alone. In Brazil, Ford Motor Co.'s Camaçari assembly plant is an excellent example of buyer–supplier partnerships. (See the Get Real box below.)

acceptance of mutual goals A collaborative relationship that lacks the commitment of a full partnership.

full partnerships Relationships that have close working relations, trust, mutual respect, and highly integrated operations.

It takes a long time to build true partnerships; thus, long-term contracts are common. Partnerships foster long-term loyalty and mutual respect, ultimately leading to many of the advantages of vertical integration. Partners must trust each other. Trust is elusive, but it tends to grow when both the supplier and buyer benefit. Further, a partnership requires close, open, informal interactions, and frequent contact among members of several different

GET REAL

Supplier Partnerships at Ford Brazil

Rural Brazil has turned out to be a success story for the Ford Motor Co. Ten years ago Ford was struggling in Brazil, but its amazing turnaround is due in part to a state-of-the-art assembly plant with a twist. At Ford's Camaçari assembly plant, more than two dozen suppliers work side-by-side with Ford employees inside the complex. For example, Visteon Corp. workers connect the wiring in a dashboard module for a Ford EcoSport while in the manufacturing cell next to them Lear Corp. employees build seats for the same vehicle.

By working together, both Ford and its suppliers benefit. Inventories are minimized as subassemblies flow directly into the main Ford assembly line at the precise point and time they are needed. Suppliers have more flexibility and better understand Ford's needs. When quality problems occur they are fixed quickly through collaboration with Ford and supplier engineers.

functions in the respective firms (sales, engineering, operations, and so on). In many cases, this contact extends beyond the professional level and includes social interactions.

The Japanese keiretsu system used by Toyota and Honda provides an example of partnership relationships. Toyota and Honda have long-term relationships with their suppliers and work closely with them to improve the entire supply chain. Honda and Toyota spend an extensive amount of time understanding their suppliers' operations and organizations. They supervise suppliers and provide constant feedback. In addition, they improve suppliers' technical capabilities and work together to improve processes. Honda and Toyota encourage suppliers to collaborate with each other through supplier study groups.

Ultimately, the type of relationships developed with a given supplier should be consistent with the category it fits as shown in Figure 10-3. Most firms reserve partnerships for only the most critical suppliers who provide strategically important purchases. Arm's-length relationships are appropriate for bottleneck or noncritical items. However, a commitment to purchase more over a period of time reduces transaction costs, confirms supply availability, and reduces price uncertainty. For leverage purchases, annual contracts are often used. For strategic purchases, longer-term contracts lasting through the product's life are the norm.

Prepare

What approaches can you use to assess and select suppliers?

Organize

Identify Potential Suppliers
Assess and Select Suppliers
Competitive Bidding
Online Reverse Auctions
Negotiation

IDENTIFY POTENTIAL SUPPLIERS

Once you have a sourcing strategy, the next step is to identify potential suppliers. There are many ways to do this. A starting point is to consider the firm's current suppliers or those used in the past. Using current suppliers saves time, reduces sourcing costs, and is consistent with supply base optimization. To reduce the time and effort needed to find qualified suppliers, supply managers develop preferred supplier lists that are used when a new supplier is needed. Sources of information about potential new suppliers include the Internet, catalogs, trade directories, trade journals, and networking through trade associations.

ASSESS AND SELECT SUPPLIERS

LO10-6 Assess and select suppliers using competitive bidding, online reverse auctions, and negotiations.

As you know from experience, you need to spend much more time evaluating suppliers for some purchases than for others. For example, when buying milk, typically you make a quick decision based on the lowest price or a brand name that you trust. However, when buying a new car, you will spend much more time researching the car's performance, options, reliability, warranty, and financing packages, and will likely visit several dealers to take test drives before making your purchase.

Similarly, the evaluation and supplier selection processes differ for corporate purchases. How suppliers are assessed and selected depends upon the level of spend, nature of the purchase, and the type of relationship desired. Purchases that account for a large amount of spend, are strategically important, are from a new supplier, or need a full partnership require an extensive formal evaluation. To understand all aspects of the supplier's capabilities and organization, cross-functional teams typically do these evaluations. For smaller spend levels and noncritical purchases the supply manager typically makes the selection decision.

Competitive Bidding

competitive bidding A selection process in which suppliers submit bids to win the buyer's business.

After you have assessed suppliers, competitive bidding, online reverse auctions, or negotiation are used to select the suppliers. **Competitive bidding** is used when price is the most important factor, the specifications are known and clear, the spend level is large enough, and there are a number of equally qualified suppliers who are willing to compete. Mature, standard products are often sourced using competitive bidding. Competitive bidding is often required for puchases by local, state, and the federal governments. Competitive bidding is used when relationships are adversarial or arm's-length.

The first step in competitive bidding is for the supply manager to issue a **request for proposal (RFP)** or a **request for quotation (RFQ)** to potential suppliers. These describe the purchase requirements as clearly as possible in terms of technical specifications, quality, quantity, delivery requirements, packaging, shipping, and any other characteristics. The RFP or RFQ must be correct, because this is what the supplier uses to determine what to sell and at what price. Most companies use electronic RFPs and RFQs.

request for proposal (RFP) or request for quotation (RFQ) Documents that describe the purchase requirements as specifically as possible.

If the supplier wishes to do business with the firm, a salesperson submits a bid or quotation (usually electronically) that is then evaluated by the supply manager and a cross-functional team, if it is a major purchase. Each bid is carefully evaluated compared to the requirements in the RFP. For full partners, compatibility between the firm and supplier on strategy, goals, and culture is important. The team may elect to visit the supplier to evaluate the following aspects:

- Operations processes and systems.
- Quality processes and systems.
- Labor skills, training, and morale.
- Technological capabilities.
- Supply management processes.
- Logistics systems.
- Financial stability.
- Management capabilities and attitudes.

Suppliers have different strengths and weaknesses, making direct comparisons difficult. Tools for analyzing and comparing suppliers' capabilities range from simple methods such as categorical ratings and weighted-point models, to more comprehensive approaches such as the analytic hierarchy process (AHP) (see Chan, 2003 in the Selected Readings at the end of the chapter for more details) and mathematical programming models.

A **weighted-point model** links the supplier's performance rating to the firm's competitive priorities. Working with members from key functions, weight each performance category so the total sum of the weights equals 100 percent. The weights should reflect your company's priorities for the purchase. As business needs change, adjust the weights to reflect new priorities.

weighted-point model Establishes performance categories that are weighted according to importance.

After assigning weights, use the data gathered in the assessment to rate each supplier on each category using scales of 1 to 3 or 1 to 5, with the higher score indicating better performance. Multiply the rating for each category by the weight to get its score as shown in Table 10-2 on the next page. Based on this model, select Supplier B because its score is the highest. Although this method results in a numerical score, it is important to note that both the ratings and the weights are subjective based on managerial judgment. In practice, use judgment, not just the total score, to determine which suppliers to select. The weighted-point model also is used for ongoing supplier evaluations in supplier scorecards.

student activity

Assume that you will be selecting a new apartment. Develop a weighted-point model to assist in your decision-making process.

Online Reverse Auctions

Using the Internet, **online reverse auctions** allow suppliers to competitively bid for a buyer's business in real time. During a fixed time period, suppliers submit multiple bids and typically can see the bid prices submitted by other suppliers, creating competition. This is similar to e-Bay, but instead of an auction to sell an item—driving prices higher—reverse online auctions use bidding to drive prices lower. Procter & Gamble reportedly identified over $290 million in potential savings through online reverse auctions.

online reverse auctions Competitive bidding systems that allow suppliers to submit multiple bids within a fixed time.

Because of the emphasis on price, most successful online reverse auctions are used in situations similar to competitive bidding: when price is the most important factor, the specifications are known and clear, the spend level is large enough, and there are a number of

TABLE 10-2 Weighted-Point Model for Supplier Selection

		Supplier A		Supplier B		Supplier C	
Category	**Weight**	**Rating**	**Score**	**Rating**	**Score**	**Rating**	**Score**
Quality systems	40%	3	1.2	5	2.0	3	1.2
Delivery capability	40%	2	0.8	3	1.2	4	1.6
Price	20%	5	1.0	3	0.6	2	0.4
Weighted score	100%		3.0		3.8		3.2

*All scores on a five-point scale with 1 = poor, 5 = excellent.

equally qualified suppliers who are willing to compete. However, reverse auction software can weigh other factors as well. To ensure that suppliers competing in the auction are qualified, a preliminary supplier assessment is done prior to the auction. A more thorough supplier assessment is normally done on the winning supplier after completion of the auction.

A benefit of reverse auctions is that the selection decision can be made quickly. A drawback to reverse auctions is that sometimes the lowest bidder is not qualified and can have performance problems. The bidding process can also damage supplier relationships if suppliers feel they are not treated fairly.

Negotiation

negotiation A bargaining process involving a buyer and seller seeking to reach mutual agreement.

If one supplier is preferred or is the only one qualified, *negotiation* establishes the price and other details and terms of the contract. **Negotiation** is an exploratory bargaining process (planning, reviewing, analyzing, compromising) involving a buyer and seller seeking to reach mutual agreement on all aspects of a contract—including price, service, specifications, technical and quality requirements, and payment terms.

Normally, negotiation is the preferred method of supplier selection for strategic purchases that require full partnerships. Unlike the situation for competitive bidding and online reverse auctions, negotiation is a better choice when there is:

- A high degree of uncertainty in the requirements or the requirements may change because of a long lead time.
- Different combinations of requirements may be acceptable.
- A need for early supplier involvement in product development.
- A complex start-up or customized equipment is needed.

student activity

Find an example of a negotiation in a TV show or movie. Was the negotiation successful? Why, or why not? What went well in the negotiation and what would you change if you were doing this negotiation?

Unlike the typical Hollywood depiction of negotiation, ideally, both the buyer and the supplier should be able to meet their objectives. During the face-to-face meeting, problem solving creates solutions where both the buyer and the supplier benefit. The information sharing and give and take that occurs can build close, cooperative relationships. The outcome of a successful negotiation should be a contract and a good working relationship between the buyer and the suppler.

A successful negotiation starts well in advance of the actual face-to-face meeting. Planning is the most important stage in negotiation. For major negotiations, the supply manager facilitates a cross-functional team whose role is to gather and analyze information. During planning, a negotiation range is set for all of the important aspects of the negotiation, including price. The range must have a minimum, target, and maximum level, with room to move. The overlap of the buyer's and the supplier's ranges is where the give-and-take occurs. For example, if you are buying a used car, your target might be $10,000, and you would be willing to pay up to $12,000, but you suspect that the seller will not go below $9,000. Then, your negotiation range is $9,000 to $12,000. The seller's range is actually $10,000 to $13,000, so the actual area for negotiation is the overlap of $10,000 to $12,000.

MANAGE ONGOING SUPPLIER RELATIONSHIPS

Prepare

What are some ways to manage ongoing supplier relationships?

Organize

Manage Ongoing Supplier Relationships
- Information Sharing and Coordination with Suppliers
- Supplier Performance Monitoring and Improvement
- Supplier Relationship Management

The signing of a contract and a handshake is just the beginning of a buyer–supplier relationship. Buyers and suppliers must develop processes to share information and coordinate their activities. Buyers must monitor supplier performance and ensure that suppliers improve if necessary. Many firms take a holistic approach called *supplier relationship management.* Each of these aspects of managing the ongoing relationship is discussed in this section.

Information Sharing and Coordination with Suppliers

LO10-7 Understand ways to manage ongoing supplier relationships.

To signal to the supplier that goods or services are needed, a *purchase order (PO)* can be used. A purchase order (PO) is a legally binding document prepared by a buyer to describe all terms and conditions of a purchase. To reduce costs, and the time involved in receiving goods or services, POs are typically communicated electronically using the Internet or **electronic data interchange (EDI)**.

electronic data interchange (EDI) The structured secure electronic transmission of data between organizations.

The structured secure transmission of data between organizations by electronic means such as the Internet or direct company-to-company computer connections is EDI, as shown in Figure 10-5. The buyer and supplier share business documents needed for the purchase transaction, including purchase orders, invoices, and shipping notices, in formats based on agreed upon standards. The payment process requires matching of the PO, the supplier's invoice, and receiving documents that show what was actually sent. The documents can contain a variety of information types (text, graphics, specifications). Thus, EDI helps to integrate operations across the supply chain.

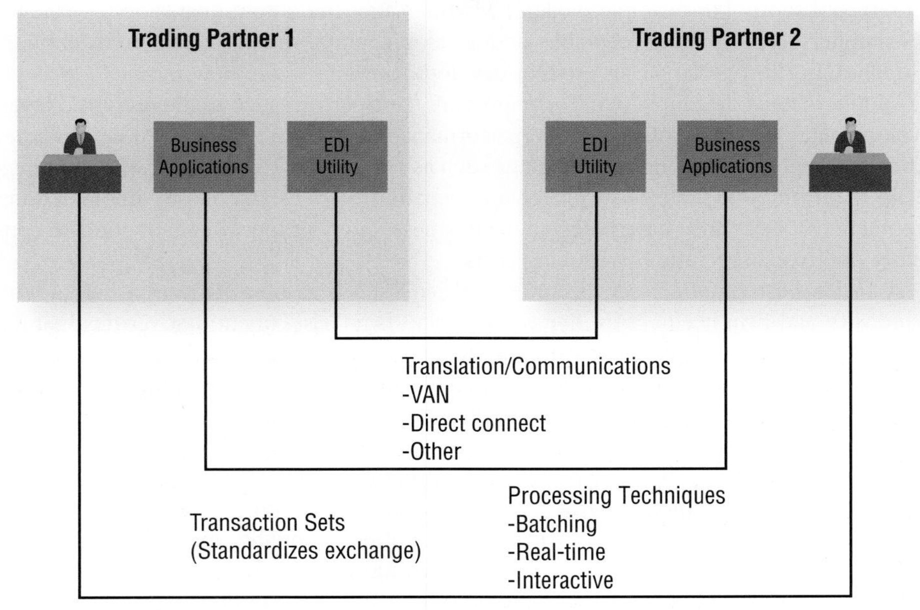

FIGURE 10-5 An EDI System

Buyers and suppliers must carefully coordinate forecasting, planning, and scheduling so goods and services arrive exactly when needed. Sharing sensitive information such as forecasts and customer demand underscores the importance of trust among supply chain members. Better information reduces the need for finished goods inventory. Chapter 12 explains collaborative planning, forecasting, and replenishment (CPFR), in which supply chain members collaborate to meet customer demand while reducing supply chain inventory and costs.

Firms integrate information systems with key suppliers. For example, many share planning and scheduling information using materials requirements planning (MRP—see Chapter 14). Buyers have supplier portals on their Web sites so suppliers can access the buyer's scheduling information. Current scheduling information helps suppliers to set priorities and to do a better job of operations planning. Representatives of the buyer and suppliers can share reactions to the schedules and discuss the impact of changes. These discussions educate each party about the other's capabilities, helping both to plan for the future. They allow the supplier and the buyer to cooperatively adjust production schedules to optimize throughput, to ultimately reduce costs and lead time, and to enhance quality.

As was described in Chapter 7, some firms, especially big-box retailers and grocery stores, use vendor-managed inventory (VMI) in which the supplier manages its customer's inventory. Walmart was a leader in adopting VMI, and many other retail firms now use this approach. The supplier regularly reviews the customer's inventory and restocks as needed. With VMI, suppliers understand what their customers are actually using and thus can plan their own operations more effectively, reducing excess inventory and waste in the supply chain.

Supplier Performance Monitoring and Improvement

sustainability

supplier scorecard Used to report a supplier's performance on key performance indicators (KPI).

For ongoing supplier relationships, it is important to set formal goals for suppliers and to measure performance against these goals on a regular basis. Supply managers identify the key performance indicators (KPI) in terms of quality, delivery, cost reduction, service, or other performance attributes that are important for their firms. Suppliers receive regular feedback, typically monthly or quarterly, in a **supplier scorecard**. Philips, an electronics company, rates its suppliers on five main performance areas: delivery, quality, cost, responsiveness/support, and innovation. Large companies post scorecards on their Web sites in supplier portals that suppliers can access using a secure login.

Supplier scorecards are used in several ways. Some firms categorize suppliers based on an overall score. For example, Federal Mogul, a first-tier automotive supplier, categorizes suppliers as preferred, acceptable, and developmental. Firms give preferred suppliers the opportunity to participate in product development and to win new business. Acceptable suppliers must develop a plan for improving their performance to the preferred level. Developmental suppliers must improve performance, or they are targeted to be replaced. Rather than replacing suppliers, companies such as Honda and Toyota work with suppliers to help them improve their performance and capabilities (for example, by implementing lean practices). Once they have received the business, buyers expect their suppliers to continually improve, especially by reducing costs.

supplier certification An assessment that verifies effective procedures related to the buyer's requirements.

A firm's best suppliers can become certified. The type of certification varies with the industry and firm needs. **Supplier certification** is an assessment that verifies that the supplier operates, maintains, improves, and documents effective procedures related to the buyer's requirements. Quality certification reduces the need for incoming quality inspections. When suppliers are certified, buyers do not have to do incoming inspection, a process called "dock to stock."

Some firms develop their own processes to certify suppliers. For example, suppliers who consistently demonstrate excellence in quality, reliability, delivery, cycle time, and productivity, and who provide evidence of an effective quality management system, become certified. Typically, a formal audit, including a site visit, is done as part of the certification process. To reduce certification costs and to provide objectivity, some companies rely upon certifications done by external organizations such as ISO certifications in quality (ISO 9000) and environment (ISO 14000). Chapter 6 describes ISO 9000 quality certifications.

Supplier Relationship Management (SRM)

Supplier relationship management (SRM) tries to do for supplier management what CRM (Chapter 9) does with customers. That is, SRM is a comprehensive system, facilitated by software, that manages the firm's interactions with its supply base. The goal of SRM is to streamline the processes and interactions that exist between the firm and its various suppliers so they are more efficient and transparent. SRM helps the firm identify critical suppliers and to improve how the firm works with these suppliers on such activities as reducing costs, introducing new products, creating cash (through inventory reduction and payment term management—how the firm pays its suppliers), mitigating supply and regulatory risks, and ensuring a secure supply of scarce materials. SRM deals with all stages of the supply management process (identifying suppliers, working with suppliers, placing orders, and postorder contract activities, which includes inventory management and warranty recoveries). SRM is widely used and can be found in media and entertainment, automotive, pharmaceutical and medical products, and health care industries.

supplier relationship management (SRM) A comprehensive system, facilitated by software, that works on managing the firm's interactions with its supply base.

CHAPTER SUMMARY

1. Effective supply management contributes to an organization's performance by reducing supply risk and ensuring availability, reducing costs, enhancing quality, ensuring timely delivery, increasing flexibility, accessing technology, and fostering sustainability.
2. The strategic decision to insource or outsource goods or services is based on a thorough analysis that considers both cost and qualitative factors.
3. Strategic sourcing is a process used to identify, evaluate, and award business to suppliers to meet a firm's strategic objectives.
4. A sourcing strategy is a plan for the number of suppliers, their capabilities and locations, and the types of buyer-supplier relationships.
5. Suppliers are selected using competitive bidding, online reverse auctions, or negotiations.
6. Managing the ongoing relationship with suppliers involves developing processes for information sharing and coordination and measuring supplier performance. Supplier relationship management is a systematic approach to managing all supply management processes.

KEY TERMS

adversarial relationships 345
acceptance of mutual goals 345
arm's-length relationships 345
competitive bidding 346
electronic data interchange (EDI) 349
fixed costs per contract 341
fixed costs per order 341
full partnerships 345
insourcing 339
make or buy decision 339
negotiation 348
online reverse auctions 347
outsourcing 339
purchase requisition 342
request for quotation (RFQ) 347
request for proposal (RFP) 347
sourcing 334
spend analysis 342
supplier certification 350

supplier relationship management (SRM) 351
supplier scorecard 350
supply base optimization 343
supply management 334
supply risk 334
sustainability 338
total cost of ownership (TCO) 335
weighted-point model 347
variable costs 341

DISCUSSION QUESTIONS

1. Can you think of an organization that has benefited by extending sustainability to its supply chain? What about one whose supply chain practices have hurt its reputation?
2. Consider the purchase of a new mobile phone. How would you determine the total cost of ownership? What are the costs that you might incur before the purchase, during the purchase, and after the purchase?
3. How would you do a spend analysis if you were the supply manager for a large state university?
4. The top management team at your company is considering outsourcing the supply management function. Do you support this idea? Why, or why not?
5. Consider Marriott or Hilton corporations, which have hotels around the world. What type of purchases should be local, national/regional, or global? Why?
6. For an organization that you are familiar with, provide an example of each of the four categories of purchases shown in Figure 10-3. What sourcing strategy would you use for each? Why?
7. Why don't companies seek full partnerships with all of their suppliers?
8. When evaluating a supplier's financial stability, what are some key indicators to consider? Why?
9. What are the costs and challenges involved with switching suppliers?

SOLVED PROBLEMS

Insourcing/Outsourcing Decision Process

A major corporation that develops and manufactures lawn care products such as fertilizer, herbicide, and seed is evaluating whether it should insource or outsource the landscaping and lawn care of its corporate headquarters located outside of Augusta, Georgia. Currently, the landscaping is outsourced, and the supplier's performance has been excellent. In the Augusta area, there are a number of landscaping companies that have the capabilities to do this job.

To maintain the corporate headquarters grounds, approximately 5,000 hours per year are needed. The annual fixed costs to insource are estimated to be $10,000 per year and the variable costs are $14/hour. Bids from 10 qualified landscaping companies range from a low of $78,000 to a high of $90,000 for a one-year contract. The current supplier's bid is $81,000/year.

Apply the insourcing/outsourcing decision process in Figure 10-1 to make a recommendation.

Solution:

Developing and producing lawn care products are core competencies of the company. However, *doing* landscaping and lawn care is not. There are many capable suppliers available, the process is standard, technology is known, and risk is low, suggesting that landscaping and lawn care are suitable for outsourcing. By outsourcing, the company can focus its internal resources on its core business rather than lawn maintenance.

The cost to insource is $80,000. Suppliers are able to provide this service at the same or a lower price.

$$\begin{aligned}\text{Total Cost} &= (\text{Variable Costs} \times \text{Volume} + \text{Fixed Costs}) \\ &= [(\$14/\text{hour} \times 5{,}000 \text{ hours/year}) + \$10{,}000] \\ &= \$80{,}000/\text{year}\end{aligned}$$

The current supplier's performance has been excellent. Based on the lack of fit with the company's core competencies, the good suitability for outsourcing, the cost analysis, and the current supplier's excellent performance, outsourcing is recommended. Further, it makes sense to continue to use the current supplier. Although other suppliers quoted a lower price, the cost of switching to a new, unproven supplier is likely to consume the small $3,000 cost savings.

Weighted-Point Model for Supplier Evaluation

Dazzling Lighting Inc. in Cincinnati, Ohio, is evaluating suppliers for its new line of lighting products to be sold to home builders. Three potential suppliers have been identified and evaluated by a cross-functional team. Using the data gathered from a supplier survey and site visits, the team applied a weighted-point model to be used in the supplier selection decision.

Overview of Suppliers

Supplier name:	EZ Lite	North-South Trading	Zhenjiang Lighting
Annual sales:	$200 million	$350 million	$100 million
Location:	Fremont, Ohio	Matamoros, Mexico	Zhenjiang, China
Defective parts per million (ppm):	75	130	120
Transportation time:	1 day	5 days	45 days
On-time delivery:	99%	92%	86%
Purchase price:	$4.50/unit	$3.00/unit	$2.15/unit

Supplier Evaluation Scores

		EZ Lite		**North-South Trading**		**Zhenjiang Lighting**	
Category	**Weight**	**Rating**	**Score**	**Rating**	**Score**	**Rating**	**Score**
Quality performance and systems	40%	4	1.6	3	1.2	3	1.2
Management capabilities and attitudes	30%	4	1.2	3	0.9	3	0.9
Delivery performance	20%	5	1.0	4	0.8	2	0.4
Purchase price	10%	1	0.1	4	0.4	5	0.5
Total Weighted Score			**3.9**		**3.3**		**3.0**

*All scores on a five-point scale with 1 = poor, 5 = excellent.

Solution:

EZ Lite received the highest overall weighted score. However, the final decision of which supplier to use should be based on judgment.

PROBLEMS

1. Your company has used competitive bidding to select a supplier for janitorial services. Three suppliers returned acceptable bids within the allotted time frame. Based on these ratings from the supplier assessment, which supplier appears to be the best? Why? How would the final selection decision be made?

Category	Weight	Supplier A	Supplier B	Supplier C
		Rating	Rating	Rating
Quality systems	40%	3	3	4
Financial stability	25%	2	3	1
Management experience	20%	2	3	3
Price	15%	4	4	5

*All scores on a five-point scale with 1 = poor, 5 = excellent.

2. As the buyer for the city of Perrysburg, you are evaluating a supplier for garbage cans to be used in the city's parks. Three suppliers returned acceptable bids within the allotted time frame. Based on these ratings from the supplier assessment, which supplier appears to be the best? Why? How would the final selection decision be made?

Category	Weight	Supplier A	Supplier B	Supplier C
		Rating	Rating	Rating
Design	10%	4	3	2
Delivery	30%	2	3	5
Warranty	20%	5	1	2
Price	40%	3	5	4

*All scores on a five-point scale with 1 = poor, 5 = excellent.

3. Simply Chocolate, a retailer selling gourmet candy, has decided to expand its market by adding online sales. The supply and marketing managers must select a company to develop a Web site. Based on an initial screening, the team has narrowed the list to four potential suppliers. Based on these ratings, which supplier appears to be the best? Why? How would the final selection decision be made?

Company	Weight*	WebTex	CoolWeb	Dazzling Designs	Major Marketing
		Rating	Rating	Rating	Rating
Number of sites developed	45%	3	1	4	5
Technical expertise	30%	3	3	5	4
Responsiveness	15%	4	5	3	1
Price	10%	4	5	3	1

*All scores on a five-point scale with 1 = poor, 5 = excellent.

4. The senior buyer at How Does Your Garden Grow Inc. needs to select a supplier for plastic patio chairs for a one-year contract. The chairs will be shipped to the company's distribution center in Toledo, Ohio. Three potential suppliers have been identified and the data were gathered. Develop a weighted-point model. Based on this model, which supplier should be selected? What other factors should be considered?

Company	ABC Molding	Perfection Plastics	I-Products
Annual sales	$ 9 million	$ 80 million	$ 30 million
Plant location	Erie, PA	Oakland, CA	St. Louis, MO
Purchase price per unit*	$9.50	$11.39	$11.25
Quality (defective parts per million)	300 ppm	60 ppm	160 ppm
Delivery (% on time)	99.5%	90%	94%
Transportation time	1 day	5 days	2 days

*Shipping is not included.

Supplier Assessment Scores

		ABC Molding		Perfection Plastics		I-Products	
Category	**Weight**	**Rating**	**Score**	**Rating**	**Score**	**Rating**	**Score**
Quality performance and systems	50%	2		5		3	
Management capabilities and attitudes*	10%	3		5		3	
Delivery performance	20%	5		1		3	
Purchase price	20%	5		2		2	

*All scores on a five-point scale with 1 = poor, 5 = excellent.

5. The supply manager at a dishwasher manufacturer is assessing whether the company should purchase the pump from a supplier or assemble the pump in-house. Forecasts suggest that 15,000 pumps are needed per year. The annual fixed costs to assemble the pumps are $120,000 per year. The variable costs per unit to assemble the pump are $25/unit. The pumps can be purchased for $30/unit. Does the cost analysis support insourcing or outsourcing pump assembly?
6. An online retailer must decide if it should insource or outsource its Web site maintenance. The company estimates that 4,000 hours per year will be needed to maintain its Web site. To insource maintenance requires $25,000 in fixed costs per year and $27/hour in variable costs. Quotes from suppliers show that Web site maintenance can be outsourced for $35 per hour. Does the cost analysis support insourcing or outsourcing Web site maintenance?
7. A furniture manufacturer is assessing whether it should make or buy the wooden frames for upholstered dining room chairs. The forecast is for 100,000 chairs to be produced per year. The fixed costs per year to make the frames are $150,000 and the variable costs are $5/frame. The supplier's bid is $8/frame. Does the cost analysis support insourcing or outsourcing the chair frames?
8. The Big Apple Pizza Company, a manufacturer and distributor of frozen food products, is introducing a new frozen Chicago-style pizza. The new sauce for this pizza is a unique, special recipe and it resulted in very positive taste test ratings in market research studies. The supply manager is trying to decide if the company should make or buy this sauce. The current forecast is for 120,000 total gallons of the sauce to be used over the estimated three-year life of the product. The first year, 30,000 gallons are forecast with 45,000 gallons each in years two and three.

   Currently, Big Apple purchases all of the sauce used in its products, ready-made, from a single source, Top Tomato. The supplier's production plant is located 320 miles from Big Apple's production plant, and weekly truckload deliveries are currently used. The company buys approximately 600,000 gallons of sauce per year from Top Tomato. The sauce supplier has provided high-quality, low-cost standard pizza sauces to Big Apple and other pizza makers for over five years. The current sauce supplier has quoted a delivered price of $2.85/gallon for the sauce if a three-year contract is used. Conformance to quality standards for Top Tomato's sauce has been 99 percent and on-time delivery has been 95 percent.

Big Apple's manufacturing manager has stated that a facility and sauce-making equipment are needed at an investment of $60,000 because the company does not make any sauces. The manufacturing manager stated that he had been considering laying off several workers because of lower demand for frozen pot pies, so he was in favor of making the sauce. The following direct costs have been estimated for making the sauce. Typically, overhead costs for Big Apple's production facility are allocated to products at a rate of 200 percent of direct labor.

Direct labor	$ 0.25/gallon
Direct materials	$ 2.00/gallon

Apply the eight steps for the insourcing/outsourcing decision. Should Big Apple Pizza make or buy the sauce? Why?

CASE

Strategic Sourcing at Best Banks

Karen Williams, the new director of supply management at Best Banks, was excited to be working at her new job. After gaining over 10 years of experience in various supply management positions at a first-tier automotive supplier, she was looking forward to being in a new industry.

Best Banks is a medium-sized bank with assets of over $1 billion. It is a community-focused financial services company with 35 branches in northwest and central Ohio. Providing competent and friendly service to its customers is critical while keeping the costs of banking affordable. Bank employees are encouraged to remember their customers and call each by name.

Historically, each branch manager did purchasing. However, within the last five years, the bank created a centralized supply management department that is responsible for the bank's major purchases. For instance, this group handled the sourcing when the bank upgraded its information system to make online banking easier for its customers.

Based on her experience in the automotive industry, Karen knew strategic sourcing could be a way to increase the value that supply management could bring to Best Banks. As a first step she conducted a spend analysis. After information systems (30 percent), the two top spend categories for the bank were temporary personnel (15 percent) and print advertising and promotional materials (8 percent).

Karen decided to explore each of these categories in more detail. She found that each of the branch locations selected and made its own decision for which temporary agency to use. In fact, over 20 different temporary personnel agencies were being used. The marketing department at the bank's headquarters made all of the sourcing decisions for advertising spend, and Karen was surprised to learn that the supply management department was not involved.

Questions

1. Using the framework in Figure 10-3, how would you categorize information technology, temporary personnel, and advertising as spend categories for the bank? Why?
2. What recommendations do you have with respect to sourcing temporary personnel? Why? What challenges is Karen likely to encounter?
3. Should the supply management department be involved in purchasing of the print advertising and promotional materials? Why, or why not? What should supply management's role be?

CASE

Trail Frames Chassis: Insourcing/Outsourcing Decision

Trail Frames Chassis (TFC) of Elkhart, Indiana, is a major manufacturer of chassis for the motor home and van markets. Two unemployed truck-manufacturing engineers founded TFC in 1976. Since then, the company has grown into one of the largest suppliers of chassis. In the past, TFC has produced only a pusher type of chassis, one that is powered by a diesel engine located in the rear. This design offers many advantages (e.g., no tunnel for the transmission, reduced engine noise, better handling). However, these chassis tend to be expensive, and they are used in motor homes that are very expensive ($150,000 and up). Recently, TFC entered into an agreement with Gulf Stream to produce low-end pusher-type chassis for motor homes priced under $100,000. These new designs offer some of the features of the higher-end pushers, but at a lower cost.

Today's market for motor homes and vans is increasingly made up of people in their late 40s to 60s. These older customers want a motor home that rides like a car, and they are willing to pay for innovations such as ABS (anti-lock breaking systems), assisted steering, and computer-balanced suspension. TFC is the technological leader in this market. TFC sells to large manufacturers such as Winnebago, Airstream, and Gulf Stream. In general, these companies order small quantities (5 to 10 in a batch), and many of the units in a batch are customized to a specific customer's requirements.

Achieving continued success in the motor home and van markets is difficult because of the rate of change taking place. TFC has become successful because of its ability to develop new product designs in a timely fashion. This ability stems from TFC's extensive experience with motor home users and TFC's knowledge of new technological advances. It is generally recognized that no one in the industry can match TFC's design and marketing knowledge base. Until recently, TFC could design and build a chassis in less than 30 days. However, the lead times have been growing. As a result of limited capital, TFC has found itself unable to keep up with demand. Management has identified the design department as the major bottleneck. While pondering this problem, the management team was approached by Computer-Images, a design house located in Grand Rapids, Michigan. Computer-Images has made an attractive offer to take over the design responsibilities for the low end of TFC's product line. Furthermore, Computer-Images has offered to work with TFC as a virtual corporation—one in which specifications would be generated by TFC and sent electronically to Computer-Images. The new drawings would then be designed and electronic copies sent back to TFC. Outsourcing the low-end work to Computer-Images would free up TFC's staff to focus on meeting the demand for medium to high-end chasses.

Based on the information provided in Table 10-3 on the next page, complete the insourcing/outsourcing analysis. Prepare a report for the company president with the findings and your recommendation. Only one option can be recommended.

TABLE 10-3 Information for the Analysis

	Computer-Image Proposal	TFC Make Option
Contract period	3 years (with option to cancel after first year with 45 days warning)	Not applicable
Cost per design	$225 per chassis	$490 per chassis (arrived at by summing direct labor computers and including corporate overhead)
Number of chassis per year	1,000 minimum to 2,500 maximum (1,250 expected) TFC must commit to 1,250 designs per year	2,000 chassis maximum (assuming stable growth in other chassis lines)
Setup costs (one time cost)	$300,000 (computer systems, training, establishing computer linkages)	$200,000 (to expand design capacity)
Lead times (sending specifications to receipt of new design	<2 working days	5 to 10 working days
Quality	All designs to be tested via computer simulation and to be certified feasible.	Feasibility of designs based on expertise of designers
Time until delivery of design 1	3 months	Immediately
Other terms and conditions	Understood that Computer-Images would be free to work with any other chassis builder. All designs generated by Computer-Images would remain the property of Computer-Images. Computer-Images insists on a training period of 6 months in which the designers of TFC would teach Computer-Images designers about the critical design tasks encountered in the motor home market.	To significantly expand design capacity would require a period of between 6 and 8 months.

SELECTED READINGS & INTERNET SITES

Federal-Mogul Corporation

www.federal-mogul.com

IKEA Group

www.ikea-group.ikea.com

Institute for Supply Management

www.ism.ws

Kirstie Kelly Couture

http://www.kirstiekelly.com/home.html

Philips

www.philips.com

Procter & Gamble

www.pgconnectdevelop.com

Walmart

www.walmart.com

Arruñada, B., and X. Vázquez. "When Your Contract Manufacturer Becomes Your Competitor." *Harvard Business Review* 84, no. 9 (2006), pp. 135–44.

Bartholomew, D. "Quality Takes a Beating." *Industry Week,* March 1, 2006, **www.industryweek.com/articles/quality_takes_a_beating_11444.aspx**.

Black, J. "In the Trial Run, Chipotle Heads to the Farm." *Washington Post,* March 28, 2008, p. F1, **www.washingtonpost.com/wp-dyn/content/article/2008/03/25/AR2008032500813.html**.

Burt, D.; D. Dobler; and S. Starling. *World Class Supply Management: The Key to Supply Chain Management,* 7th ed. New York: McGraw Hill, 2003.

Capell, K.; A. Sains; C. Lindblad; A.T. Palmer; J. Bush; D. Roberts; and K. Hall. "IKEA." *BusinessWeek,* November 14, 2005, pp. 96–106.

Chan, F. "Interactive Selection Model for the Supplier Selection Process: An Analytical Hierarchy Process Approach." *International Journal of Production Research* 41, no. 15 (2003), pp. 3549–79.

Duffy, R. "Reverse Auctions Step by Step." *Inside Supply Management* 16, no. 11 (2005), p. 36.

Ellram, L. "Total Cost of Ownership." *International Journal of Physical Distribution and Logistics Management* 25, no. 8/9 (1995), pp. 4–24.

Engardio, P. "The Future of Outsourcing: How It's Transforming Whole Industries and Changing the Way We Work." *BusinessWeek,* January 30, 2006.

Fair, D. C. "Total Recall: What Is Quality Worth to You." *Quality Digest,* June 26, 2006, **www.qualitydigest.com/inside/quality-insider-article/total-recall**.

Handfield, R., and S. Straight. "What Sourcing Channel Is Right for You?" *Supply Chain Management Review* 7, no. 4 (2003), pp. 62–69.

Hoffman, B. G. "Ford's Test Bed: Brazil's Camaçari Plant Is Model for the Future." *The Detroit News,* August 22, 2007, **www.detroitnews.com/apps/pbcs.dll/article?AID=/20070822/AUTO01/708220407/1148**

Holmes, S. "Cleaning Up Boeing." *BusinessWeek,* March 13, 2006, p. 68.

Institute for Supply Management Glossary of Key Purchasing and Supply Management Terms, **www.ism.ws**.

Kraljic, P. "Purchasing Must Become Supply Management." *Harvard Business Review* 61, no. 5. (1983), pp. 109–17.

"Korean Air Renews Strategic Outsourcing Contract with IBM for Ten Years." IBM Press Release, January 14, 2009, **www-03.ibm.com/press/us/en/pressrelease/26476.wss**.

Liker, J., and T. Choi. "Building Deep Supplier Relationships." *Harvard Business Review* 82, no. 12 (2004), pp. 104–13.

Petersen, K. J.; R. B. Handfield; and G. L. Ragatz. "Supplier Integration Into New Product Development: Coordinating, Product, Process, and Supply Chain Design." *Journal of Operations Management* 23, no. 3/4 (April 2005), pp. 371–88.

Poeter, D. "IHS iSuppli Breaks Down Cost of Parts in the New iPad." *PCMagazine,* March 17, 2012, **http://www.pcmag.com/article2/0,2817,2401725,00.asp.**

Pollock, L. "Mattel Puts Lead Probe Behind It." *The Wall Street Journal,* December 16, 2008, p. B3.

Roberts, J. "Responsible Business—Good Business." *Inside Supply Management,* May 2004, pp. 5–7.

Sandholm, T.; D. Levine; M. Concordia; P. Martyn; R. Hughes; J. Jacobs; and D. Begg. "Changing the Game in Strategic Sourcing at Procter & Gamble: Expressive Competition Enabled by Optimization." *Interfaces* 36, no. 1 (January–February 2006), pp. 55–68.

Sherman, L. "Rethinking Outsourcing in the Recession." *Forbes,* February 2, 2009, **www.forbes.com/2009/02/19/fashion-week-china-entrepreneurs-finance_manufacturing.html**.

Smeltzer, L.; J. Manship; and C. Rossetti. "An Analysis of the Integration of Strategic Sourcing and Negotiation Planning." *The Journal of Supply Chain Management* 39, no. 4 (2003), p. 18.

Smock, D. "Strategic Sourcing: It's Now Deeply Rooted in U.S. Buying." *Purchasing Metals Edition* 133, no. 14 (2004), p. 20.

"Wal-Mart Unveils 'Packaging Scorecard' to Suppliers," **http://walmartstores.com/FactsNews/NewsRoom/6039.aspx**.

Willis, B. "Central America Lures Sportswear Makers as Adidas Shifts Orders." *BloombergBusinessWeek,* December 20, 2011, **www.businessweek.com**.

Zsidisin, G., and Ellram, L. "An Agency Theory Investigation of Supply Risk Management." *Journal of Supply Chain Management* 39, no. 3 (2003), pp. 15–27.

11 Logistics Management

CHAPTER OUTLINE

LEARNING OBJECTIVES *After studying this chapter, you should be able to:*

LO11-1 Explain logistics and the major decisions made by logistics managers.

LO11-2 Estimate cost savings from consolidation.

LO11-3 Choose efficient transportation modes and carriers.

LO11-4 Make decisions regarding warehouses, distribution centers, and facility networks.

LO11-5 Explain the importance of packaging and materials handling.

LO11-6 Locate facilities using the center-of-gravity model.

LO11-7 Describe the benefits of integrated service providers.

Starbucks Transforms Its Supply Chain

In 2008, Starbucks was opening stores around the world at a rapid pace. The supply chain organization had to focus on keeping up with that expansion. "We had been growing so fast that we had not done a good enough job of getting the [supply chain] fundamentals in place," says Peter D. Gibbons, executive vice president of global supply chain operations. As a result, he says, "the costs of running the supply chain—the operating expenses—were rising very steeply."

To better balance cost and performance, Starbucks had to make significant changes to its operations. With production spread across a wide territory, transportation, distribution, and logistics made up the bulk of Starbucks' operating expenses because the company ships so many different products around the world. Getting that under control presented a challenge for the supply chain group. "Whether coffee from Africa or merchandise from China, [our task was to integrate] that together into one global logistics system, the combined physical movement of all incoming and outgoing goods," says Gibbons. "It's a big deal because there's so much spend there, and so much of our service depends on that. . . . With 70,000 to 80,000 deliveries per week plus all the inbound shipments from around the world, we want to manage these logistics in one system."

The creation of a single, global logistics system was important for Starbucks because of its far-flung supply chain. The company generally brings coffee beans from Latin America, Africa, and Asia to the United States and Europe in ocean containers. The beans are trucked to six storage sites at or near a roasting plant. After the beans are roasted and packaged, the finished product is trucked to regional distribution centers. Starbucks runs five regional distribution centers (DCs) in the United States; two are company-owned and the other three are operated by third-party logistics companies (3PLs). It also has distribution centers in Europe and in Asia, all of which are managed by 3PLs. Coffee, however, is only one of many products held at these warehouses. They also handle other items required by Starbucks' retail outlets—everything from furniture to cappuccino mix.

Depending on their location, the stores are supplied by either the large, regional DCs or by smaller warehouses called central distribution centers (CDCs). The CDCs carry dairy products, baked goods, and paper items like cups and napkins. They combine the coffee with these other items to make frequent deliveries via dedicated truck fleets to Starbucks' own retail stores and to retail outlets that sell Starbucks-branded products.

Because delivery costs and execution are intertwined, Gibbons and his team set about improving both. One of their first steps was to build a global map of Starbucks' transportation expenditures—no easy task, because it involved gathering all supply chain costs by region and by customer, Gibbons says. An analysis of those expenditures allowed Starbucks to winnow its transportation carriers, retaining only those that provided the best service.

In Gibbons' eyes, the transformation effort has been a success. "Today there's a lot of confidence in our supply chain to execute every day, to make 70,000 deliveries a week, to get new products to market, and to manage product transitions, new product introductions, and promotions," he says. "There's a lot of confidence that we now are focused on service and quality to provide what our stores need and what our other business customers need."

Source: Adapted from James A. Cooke, "From Bean to Cup: How Starbucks Transformed Its Supply Chain," *Supply Chain Quarterly,* Quarter 4, 2010.

Prepare

What is logistics and what are the major decisions made by logistics managers?

Organize

From the beginning of civilization it has been necessary to move, store, and handle products. Today, logistics is one of the most exciting and challenging operational areas because of its critical strategic consequences as demonstrated in the opening vignette about Starbucks. This chapter explains the strategic role of logistics in the supply chain, and it describes the basic operating principles that managers use to make logistics decisions.

THE ROLE OF LOGISTICS IN SUPPLY CHAIN MANAGEMENT

LO11-1 Explain logistics and the major decisions made by logistics managers.

logistics management Management of the movement and storage of materials at lowest cost while still meeting customers' requirements.

relationships

The Council of Supply Chain Management Professionals has defined **logistics management** as "that part of supply chain management that plans, implements, and controls the efficient, effective forward and reverse flow and storage of goods, services, and related information between the point of origin and the point of consumption in order to meet customers' requirements."[1] In short, it is concerned with moving and storing materials at lowest cost while still meeting customer requirements. While most consumers take logistics for granted, it is clear that no marketing, manufacturing, or other business activity can be completed without logistics.

Figure 11-1 illustrates the primary activities involved in accomplishing logistics management objectives: (1) inventory management; (2) order management; (3) transportation management; (4) warehousing; (5) packaging and materials handling; and (6) network design. By its very nature, logistics is an integrating activity. Logistics managers work closely with suppliers and procurement managers to ensure that the inbound flow of materials meets the firm's requirements for its own operations. Logistics managers also have responsibility for flows of information, products, and materials among a firm's different plants and facilities. Finally, logistics managers work with marketing and sales personnel, as well as with customers, to ensure that customer requirements are satisfied. Integrating these activities accomplishes the dual objectives of providing service to customers and efficiently managing costs.

Logistics Service Benefits

Many research studies have shown that logistical service is critical to industrial buyers' selection of suppliers. It is frequently ranked as the second most important criterion in

[1]See the organization's Web site at: www.cscmp.org.

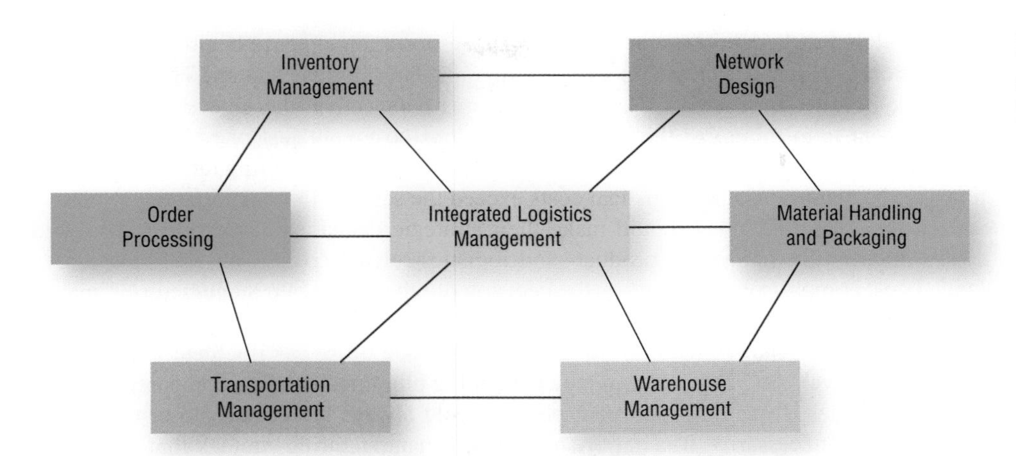

FIGURE 11-1 The Activities of Integrated Logistics Management

selection decisions (after cost).[2] This finding should not be surprising when you consider that failure by a supplier to deliver a needed component or material on time to a manufacturing plant could potentially result in a plant shutdown.

Recall from Chapter 9 that customer service benefits include *availability, lead-time performance,* and *service reliability.* Logistics plays a critical role in fulfilling all three of these service benefits. Logistics managers frequently are responsible for product availability, particularly for finished goods. They manage and determine the locations for storing inventories in most make-to-stock organizations. In addition, transportation to customers is a critical aspect of overall lead-time performance. Many aspects of service reliability are also the responsibility of logistics. For example, delivery must be made without damage to the exact location desired (no misshipments to the wrong location). Delivery should include all items ordered by the customer (no shortages or overages). Ultimately, logistics has primary responsibility for execution of perfect orders as described in Chapter 9.

Logistics Cost Minimization

Each of the six activities of integrated logistics involves significant expense. In many firms the total cost of logistics amounts to as much as 25–30 percent of each dollar of sales revenue. While these costs may be less significant in other firms, another way to think about the importance of logistics cost is that in 2010, the total cost of U.S. logistics was $1.3 trillion, approximately 8.3 percent of the U.S. Gross Domestic Product (GDP).[3]

The challenging (and most interesting) aspect of managing logistics rests in the fact that providing ever-higher service levels typically results in higher cost. Logistics managers deal with two critical types of trade-offs as they strive to minimize total logistics cost: cost-to-service trade-offs and cost-to-cost trade-offs.

The **cost-to-service trade-off** is relatively simple to describe. As service levels increase, typically so do costs. For example, to provide better product availability larger amounts of inventory may be necessary, resulting in higher carrying cost. Improved lead-time performance might be accomplished by using faster, more expensive transportation. Logistics managers must first determine what level of service performance customers require, and then provide that service most efficiently.

cost-to-service trade-off As service levels increase, typically so do costs.

A **cost-to-cost trade-off** occurs when increasing the cost of one logistics activity reduces the cost of another activity. For example, operating a large number of warehouses results in higher warehousing expenses. However, transportation expenses are reduced.

cost-to-cost trade-off Increasing the cost of one logistics activity reduces the cost of another.

---

[2] C. S. Katsikeas, N. G. Paparoidamis, and E. Katsikea, "Supply Source Selection Criteria: The Impact of Supplier Performance on Distributor Performance," *Industrial Marketing Management* 33, no. 8 (2004), pp. 755–64.

[3] R. Wilson, "22nd Annual State of Logistics Report," Council of Supply Chain Management Professionals, Oak Brook, IL, June 2011.

As the number of warehouses gets very large, transportation expense begins to rise again. (The rationale for this relationship will be explained later in this chapter.) There are many other such cost-to-cost trade-offs. From a systems perspective, the objective of logistics management is to minimize the total of all logistics costs, not just one element. It does little good to make a change that reduces transportation costs if resulting increases in warehousing, inventory, or other logistical costs exceed the savings in transportation.

total landed cost The sum of all product- and logistics-related costs.

global

Ultimately, companies should make their strategic decisions based on **total landed cost**, which is the sum of all product- and logistics-related costs. Consider how a total landed cost comparison would affect the decision of where to locate manufacturing plants. Many companies have "offshored" manufacturing (located manufacturing plants in far-off global locations). They're the ones most at risk as crude oil prices fluctuate wildly, labor costs rise in developing countries, and the U.S. dollar plummets in value compared to major Asian currencies. Does this mean that plants should always be located closer to product demands? Not necessarily. It is important to pick a manufacturing strategy that minimizes a product's total landed cost. The relevant costs in such a decision would include:

- Costs within each country of manufacture: raw materials, storage, labor, quality, overhead, obsolescence, packaging, risk of disruption, and exchange rates.
- Costs in transit from country of manufacture to country of sale: fuel, insurance, port charges, handling, security, banking, potential demurrage (detention), duties, and handling agency charges.
- Costs within the country of sale: local handling, transportation, taxes, safety stock, productivity implications, maintenance, and environmental impact.

It is also important to include costs related to lead times and lead time variability. These can differ significantly depending on the distances from the destination location. These costs can be summed to compare the total landed cost of manufacturing a product domestically and the total landed cost of manufacturing a product offshore (while taking exchange rates into account). Logistics managers use a similar total landed cost approach to evaluate all sorts of operational decisions affecting supply chain design and execution.

Inventory Management

Managing inventory is a fundamental concern of all managers involved in supply chain operations, but it is especially important to logistics managers. The details of inventory management were discussed in Chapter 7, and it is important to understand that inventory is linked to all logistics management decisions.

Critical inventory decisions include deciding how much inventory of each material item to hold, where in the system to hold each item, in what form (raw material, work in process, finished goods), and how often to replenish each item. A popular mantra in business today is, "information replaces inventory." Logistics managers seek ways to provide more accurate and timely information, thus reducing the need to hold inventories as a buffer against uncertain product demand, supply, or lead times.

The amount and location of inventories in a supply chain are also strongly influenced by logistics decisions. For example, the level of inventory in the system is dependent on the mode of transportation. Slower transportation modes mean that products are in transit for longer periods of time, thus creating a higher level of transit inventory and cost. Total system inventory is also a function of the location and number of warehouses in the system. All other things being equal, total inventories are less in centralized systems where all items are held in just a few large warehouses. Inventories are also lowered when firms offer lower levels of customer service; that is, lower levels of product availability to customers.

Logistics managers continually weigh the costs and benefits of holding different quantities of inventories at different locations in the logistics system. They also have a significant role in determining what management policies, procedures, and technological investments are needed to improve inventory management.

Order Processing

Specific customer requirements flow into a firm as customers' orders. They may arrive by mail, phone, fax, the Internet, or other form of technology. When received, they must be edited and entered into a company's information system. Failures and errors in order processing impact the cost of logistics, as well as the speed and accuracy of service provided to customers. Improving the speed of the order cycle can result in a competitive advantage for a firm, because many customers desire to do business with suppliers that are most responsive to their requirements. However, accuracy is every bit as important as speed. Errors made in order entry or in order filling, such as selecting the wrong items in the warehouse, result in delays and in significant extra cost, as corrections of the errors are required.

TRANSPORTATION MANAGEMENT

Every minute of every day trucks, trains, ships, airplanes, and pipelines are busy moving products from one place to another. The process of transportation never ends. This vital activity is the most visible part of the work of logistics. Because it impacts the cost of products and services we buy, transportation management receives considerable attention in most firms. After all, no business transaction can be complete until customers have actually received the goods they ordered. Transportation has taken on even more importance as companies have increased their global reach, both selling and sourcing products across the world. The increased distances and more complex geographical span lead to substantially increased lead times and the potential for many more problems related to transportation performance.

Prepare

What role does government play in transportation? How does consolidation reduce cost? How do managers choose among transportation carriers?

Organize

Transportation Management
- Government's Role in Transportation
- Transportation Economics
- Consolidation
- Transportation Modes
- Carrier Types
- Transportation Service Selection

Government's Role in Transportation

Because transportation is so vital to the overall economy, governments typically play a major role. All governments realize that a stable and efficient transportation system is vital to economic development. In some situations, governments actually own and provide transportation services. In others, governments regulate private industry, which provides transportation services. Governmental concern regarding transportation addresses both economic regulation and safety regulation.

Economic Regulation

Economic regulation is designed to ensure that transportation services are available to everyone at reasonable cost. Governments may actively control the entry, rates, and services provided by transportation carriers. In the early history of the United States, significant federal legislation and many governmental agencies existed to control who could form a transportation company, where they could operate, what services they would provide, and what rates they could charge. As a result, logistics managers had few operational choices and little influence on pricing and costs. While the vast majority of these regulations no longer exist in the United States at the federal level (having been repealed in the 1980s), some of the individual states still maintain such control within their borders. The deregulation at the federal level, however, opened up many opportunities for logistics managers to develop and negotiate new arrangements, terms, and conditions with carriers. In addition, competition increased dramatically. Rather than being clerks who simply place orders with carriers, today's logistics managers have become negotiators and purchasers of transportation services. Deregulation has also created opportunities for rethinking traditional practices and for introducing new logistical solutions aimed at reducing costs, improving customer service, and increasing transportation productivity.

economic regulation Government controls of the entry, rates, and services provided by transportation carriers.

Safety Regulation

safety (and social) regulation Regulation designed to ensure that transportation carriers conduct their activities in a safe and responsible manner.

While the economic regulation of transportation has lessened in the United States in recent years, **safety (and social) regulation** has increased significantly. This form of regulation is designed to ensure that transportation carriers conduct their activities in a safe and responsible manner. There is tremendous concern, for example, about the movement of hazardous goods, the number of hours that a truck driver can work without rest, and the congestion caused on the highways and in the cities due to transportation vehicles. Other regulations addressing larger environmental concerns already exist or are being considered. For example, a carbon-dioxide emissions cap-and-trade system exists in Europe and is being considered in the United States as well as other parts of the world.

sustainability

A full description of the regulations regarding these issues is far beyond our scope, but it is important to realize that numerous regulations exist and more can be expected in the future. Since 2001, another issue of concern has been the security of the transportation system. The concerns range from the potential to contaminate products (especially food) while it is in transport to the potential to use a transportation vehicle as a weapon of destruction. These concerns ultimately impact the efficiency of the transportation system.

Transportation Economics

LO11-2 Estimate cost savings from consolidation.

economy of scale The cost per unit of weight decreases as the size of the shipment increases.

There are two fundamental economic principles underlying the efficiency and the cost of transportation movements: transportation *economy of scale* and *economy of distance.* **Economy of scale** is described by the fact that the cost per unit of weight decreases as the size of the shipment increases. This relationship has frequently been expressed as, "the larger the load, the lower the cost per pound." Thus, it is less costly per pound to move 10,000 pounds of product a given distance than it is to move 5,000 pounds that same distance. This is true because the fixed costs associated with transportation (equipment and expenses at the origination and destination points) are spread over a larger weight (or quantity of items). Certainly, the total cost of the larger shipment will be greater, but the cost per pound is less. This principle also explains why larger-capacity transportation equipment is generally less costly to use (per unit of weight) than smaller-capacity equipment. Figure 11-2(A) graphically illustrates economies of scale.

economy of distance The cost per unit of distance decreases as the distance moved increases.

The second principle, **economy of distance**, refers to the principle that the cost per unit of distance decreases as the distance moved increases. The popular phrase here is, "the longer the haul, the lower the cost per mile." The rationale for this relationship is essentially the same as for the economy of scale. Longer distances traveled allow the fixed costs to be spread over a larger number of miles. Economy of distance is illustrated in Figure 11-2(B).

FIGURE 11-2 Economies of Scale and Distance

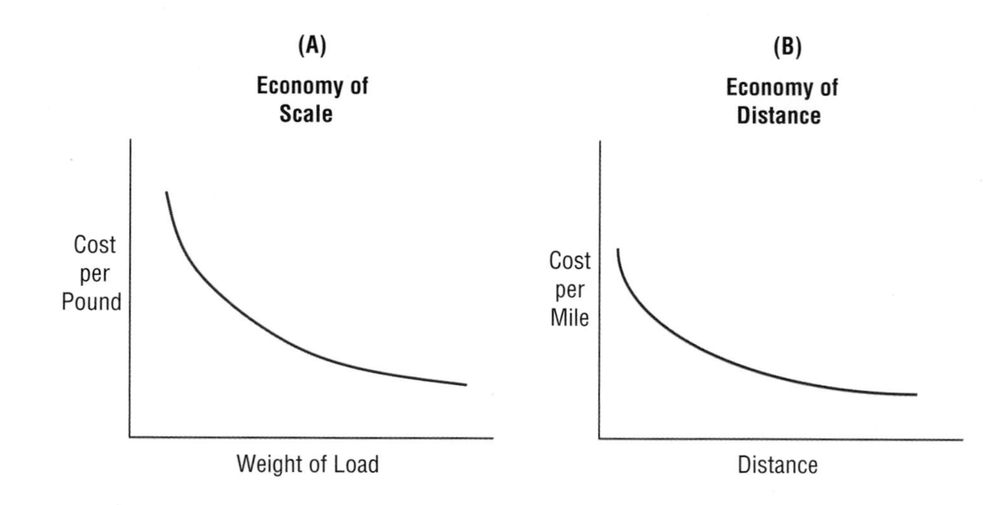

Consolidation

Given these economic principles, logistics managers often use consolidation strategies to improve transportation efficiency. **Consolidation** is the practice of combining small orders or shipments into one larger shipment to take advantage of the economies described above. There are three basic consolidation strategies that are widely practiced by logistics managers: market area consolidation, pooled delivery consolidation, and scheduled delivery consolidation.

consolidation Combining small orders or shipments into one larger shipment to take advantage of transportation economies.

Market area consolidation is achieved by combining several small shipments from one shipper that are going to the same market area into one shipment. Suppose, for example, that Kellogg's has several orders from different customers located in Alabama. Rather than put each order on a separate transportation vehicle, they combine shipments into a single load to be moved to the destination point.

market area consolidation Combining several small shipments from one shipper that are going to the same market area into one shipment.

Pooled delivery consolidation is similar to market area consolidation, except that it combines small shipments from *different shippers* that are going to the same market area. Generally, pooled delivery consolidation is handled by independent transportation companies such as UPS or FedEx (and many other transportation carriers). These firms merge the freight from numerous shippers into large shipments headed for the same market area. By doing so, each shipper can achieve some economy that would not be possible if the individual shipments were separately delivered.

pooled delivery consolidation Combines small shipments from *different shippers* that are going to the same market area.

Scheduled delivery consolidation refers to establishing specific times when deliveries will be made to customers. Customers then adjust their pattern of ordering to fit the schedule. For example, rather than delivering to a customer or a market area every day, which might result in daily small quantity orders, shipments to that customer or market might be scheduled for delivery only on Thursday. The result is larger quantity orders and less frequent shipment. While the economic advantage of this practice is easily understood, it is only possible to accomplish within the constraints of customers' requirements for delivery. It is quite possible that customers may decide to use a different supplier who does not limit their ordering practices. This represents one of the cost-to service trade-offs that logistics decision makers face.

scheduled delivery consolidation Establishing specific times when deliveries to customers will be made.

The cost reduction from consolidation comes from the transportation economies discussed previously. Example 11-1 demonstrates how these economies might work to justify consolidation. The cost savings represented by consolidation strategies are clearly quite considerable.

EXAMPLE 11-1

Spartan Company, located in Atlanta, has orders from three customers located in Lansing, Michigan. The weight of each individual shipment is 12,000 pounds. The transportation carrier quotes a freight rate of $15.75 per hundredweight (or cwt.) for individual direct shipments between the two cities, as is the normal practice in the transportation industry. Alternatively, the carrier's rate for a shipment that weighs more than 30,000 pounds is $10.50 per cwt. However, if the orders are combined into one shipment, the carrier will charge $300 for each stop it is required to make. Should Spartan consolidate the orders into one shipment?

SOLUTION

The total cost of one individual shipment is:

$15.75 × (12,000 pounds / 100 pounds) = $15.75 × 120 hundredweight = $1,890

Therefore, three separate shipments will total $1,890 × 3 = $5,670. A consolidated shipment of 36,000 pounds will cost:

$10.50 × (36,000 pounds / 100 pounds) = $10.50 × 360 hundredweight = $3,780.

Adding three stop-off charges of $300 each to the cost of the consolidated shipment brings the total cost of the consolidation to $4,680, providing a cost savings of $990 in the transportation bill.

LO11-3 Choose efficient transportation modes and carriers

transportation mode A form or method of transporting items.

Transportation Modes

A **transportation mode** is simply a form or method of transporting items. There are five basic transportation modes: rail, truck (motor carrier), water, air, and pipeline. The combined total expenditure for transportation in the United States in 2010 was over $769 billion[4] modes 2008 utilizing these Table 11-1 shows a breakdown of usage of the five modes in the United States in 2009 and forecasts for later years.

Transportation managers have to decide which mode of transportation to use for each order that must be delivered. Choosing which mode to use requires consideration of both the service characteristics and the cost of each mode. The service characteristics of the modes are typically compared on five dimensions:

- *Speed:* the elapsed time required to move from the point of origin to destination.
- *Availability:* the ability to service any possible location.
- *Dependability:* the variance in the expected delivery times.
- *Capability:* the ability to handle any type of product and/or size of load.
- *Frequency:* the number of scheduled movements that can be arranged by a shipper.

The modes also differ significantly in their cost characteristics and, therefore, the rates they charge to shippers. Because of the differences in capabilities and costs, logistics managers should choose the mode of transportation that best meets the needs of each order. Therefore they must understand the advantages and disadvantages of each mode. Table 11-2 summarizes the operating characteristics of the five transportation modes.

Truck

Given the combination of service characteristics, it is no wonder that truck is the major transportation mode in the United States. Virtually all consumer goods move at least partially, if not entirely, via truck. Trucks (also referred to as motor carriers) have been a major mode of transportation since the 1910s (unlike rail, which has been present since the 1800s). U.S. motor carriers have experienced rapid growth due to several factors; most important has been the impact of the very extensive system of highways and roads financed largely at public expense (both state and federal). This is in contrast to rail where corporations largely financed the rights-of-way. Trucks can offer door-to-door service anywhere. Also, motor carriers have relatively low fixed costs (because the government builds and maintains the roads) and relatively high variable costs (due to high labor content). Given this combination of characteristics, it's no wonder that truck carries the majority of the freight in the United States.

TABLE 11-1 Modal Share of U.S. Domestic Freight Volume (By Weight)

Mode	Mode Share (%)		
	2009	2015 (forecast)	2021 (forecast)
Truck	68.0%	69.8%	70.7%
Rail	13.6%	13.0%	12.5%
Rail intermodal	1.1%	1.3%	1.6%
Air	0.1%	0.1%	0.1%
Water	6.4%	6.2%	5.9%
Pipeline	10.9%	9.6%	9.2%

Source: *U. S. Freight Transportation Forecast to 2021,* American Trucking Association, Inc., 2010, p. 25.

[4]R. Wilson, "22nd Annual State of Logistics Report," Council of Supply Chain Management Professionals, Oak Brook, IL, June 2011.

TABLE 11-2 Characteristics of Transportation Modes

Operating Characteristics*	Truck	Rail	Water	Pipe	Air
Speed	2	3	4	5	1
Availability	1	2	4	5	3
Dependability	2	3	4	1	5
Capability	3	2	1	5	4
Frequency	2	4	5	1	3
Cost to shippers**	2	3	4	5	1
Typical uses	Medium and light manufacturing; Wholesale and retail distribution	Heavy bulk commodities	Bulk commodities; cement; agricultural products	Petroleum; natural gas; slurry	Small shipments; emergency shipments

* 1 = best, 5 = worst.
** 1 = highest cost, 5 = lowest cost.

The trucking industry can be broken into three distinct segments: (1) *truckload (TL),* (2) *less-than-truckload (LTL),* and (3) *specialty carriers.* **Truckload (TL)** carriers generally carry only full trailers of freight (i.e., with shipments in excess of 15,000 pounds). Since the loads are full, there is no need for consolidation. Trucks can be routed directly from the shipper to the consignee. Currently in the United States, this segment consists of a large number of relatively small carriers who are very competitive, although there are several large firms such as Schneider National and J. B. Hunt Transportation Services. **Less-than-truckload (LTL)** carriers usually move loads of less than 15,000 pounds. Unlike the TL carriers, the LTL carriers experience relatively higher fixed costs, which result from the need to stop at a terminal where load consolidation takes place (the cost of the terminals is part of the fixed costs). Also, LTL carriers typically pay higher marketing costs because they want to generate full loads. Because of these factors, the LTL segment is dominated by a small number of large carriers that you may often see on the highways (carriers such as FedEx Freight, YRC National, Con-Way Freight, and ABF Freight). Finally, **specialty carriers** include package haulers such as FedEx and United Parcel Service (UPS).

truckload (TL) Truckload carriers generally carry only full trailers of freight (i.e., with shipments in excess of 15,000 pounds).

less-than-truckload (LTL) Less-than-truckload carriers usually move loads of less than 15,000 pounds.

specialty carriers Specialty carriers include package haulers such as FedEx and United Parcel Service (UPS).

Rail

Historically, rail has been best suited to moving large shipments over long distances. Rail has high fixed costs, due to the costs of expensive equipment (e.g., railroad engines, railcars), rights-of-way (railroads must build and maintain their own tracks), switching yards, and terminals. In contrast, variable costs are relatively low. For example, a good deal of energy is expended in starting and stopping a train. Once a train is moving, relatively little energy is needed to keep it moving. Advances in diesel and electrical technology (used by the locomotives) have further reduced the variable costs.

Rail is well suited to the movement of bulky, low cost commodities such as coal, grain, and chemicals. However, rail transportation is relatively slow. And, because trains move according to fixed and rigid schedules, shipping flexibility is low.

Still, rail is currently experiencing a renaissance. Almost any product can be transported by rail. Therefore, rail is used by many companies that need to move large quantities very economically. Railroads have significantly improved operations in recent years, making rail a more attractive choice for shippers. In addition, railroad companies have formed alliances with carriers from other modes of transportation. The result has been an increase in the total amount of freight moving by rail.

Water

Of the five transportation modes, water is the oldest. In North America, this mode consists of two segments: domestic and deep-water transport. Domestic consists of the Great Lakes, all canals, and all navigable rivers. Deep-water transport consists of the oceans surrounding the United States.

The major advantage of water transportation is its ability to move extremely large shipments economically. One tow barge, for example, can carry the equivalent of over 800 truckloads of freight. The major disadvantages of water are speed and availability. Ships and barges are not fast carriers, and water transport simply doesn't serve that many locations. In addition, to load freight on a ship requires first getting the freight to a dock or loading area, usually by truck or rail. In general, water transport is an attractive way to move large tonnage at very low cost when speed is not critical.

Pipeline

Pipelines are appropriate for moving products that exist in a gaseous, liquid, or slurry form. Slurry is created when a solid product is suspended in a liquid. For example, crushing coal and then mixing it with water makes coal slurry. At the end of the pipeline, the slurry is taken out, the water is evaporated, and the product is made ready for use. Pipelines have been used to move natural gas, oil, chemicals, and even orange juice (in Florida).

Pipeline transportation offers users several advantages. First, it operates 24 hours a day, seven days a week, 52 weeks a year. It never stops, except for maintenance or cleaning. Second, pipeline transportation is typically not affected by the weather. A dense fog or ice storm that would immobilize airplanes, trucks, and trains would have no impact on product flows within a pipe. Of the five modes, pipe has the highest fixed costs and the lowest variable costs. The fixed costs are associated with getting rights-of-way combined with the construction and maintenance of pipelines, the control stations, and the pumping capabilities. The very low variable costs are due to the lack of labor required to move product within the pipe.

Air

Air transport is both the newest and the least utilized mode. The major advantage of air is clearly speed. Against this advantage (which is important under certain conditions), air offers some significant disadvantages. It is relatively limited in the sizes, shapes, amounts, and types of freight that it can carry. It may seem strange that air is rated worst on dependability. The reason for this is that, although the speed is extremely fast (a matter of hours), air transport is subject to frequent delays due to weather or maintenance issues. A delay of several hours on a six-hour shipment represents a significant difference from the expected delivery time.

Another major disadvantage is the relatively high cost of air for shipping products. In general, air is most appropriate for very high value, low-bulk items, or those that are extremely perishable. Air is basically used when speed is critical. Air transport is frequently used for moving Christmas presents, high fashion items, medical supplies and items (e.g., hearts for transplants), and fresh fish. It is also frequently used for products such as repair parts when the need for rapid delivery outweighs the high cost.

intermodal transportation A combination of two or more transportation modes to take advantage of the economies and service characteristics of each.

student activity

Search the Internet to find out which transport mode produces the least damage to products. Which one is the safest to operate? Which one consumes the least amount of energy? Which one is least subject to disruptions from events such as labor strikes or natural disasters?

Intermodal Transportation

Intermodal transportation combines two or more modes to take advantage of the economies and service characteristics of each. The most common form of intermodal transportation is commonly referred to as *piggyback service* and integrates truck and rail transportation. Piggyback service is more technically called either *trailer on flatcar (TOFC)* or *container on flatcar (COFC)*. In this arrangement, a trailer or a container is placed on a rail flatcar for the long distance movement between cities (say Chicago to Los Angeles). At the destination city, a truck picks up the trailer or container to complete the delivery. This arrangement allows for the service availability of truck combined with the cost efficiency of rail. It may surprise some people to know that one of the largest shippers utilizing piggyback service is United Parcel Service.

The popularity of piggyback service led to the development of many other intermodal formats. In fact, any two or more modes might be combined into an intermodal arrangement. The Get Real story concerning Tuesday Morning provides an interesting example of the advantages of intermodal transportation.

Carrier Types

Not only are there different transportation modes to choose from, logistics managers also have several types of carriers to choose from, especially in truck transportation. Many logistics managers make use of more than one type of carrier, depending on the specific situation they face.

Common carriers are transportation companies that provide service to the public. Common carriers publish their rates, although negotiation between shippers and common carriers regarding specific charges results in many discounts off the published rate schedules. **Contract carriers**, as the name implies, have specific contracts with a limited number of shippers. Many of the trucks you see on the highways may bear the name of a well-known manufacturer, but in fact are owned and operated by a contract carrier.

common carriers Transportation companies that provide service to the public.

contract carriers Carriers that have specific contracts with a limited number of shippers.

Private carriers are companies that own and operate transportation equipment to transport their own products. While private carriage was at one time a fairly popular option for many manufacturers and distributors, most have turned to common or contract

private carriers Companies that own and operate transportation equipment to transport their own products.

GET REAL

Tuesday Morning Shifts Modes

Tuesday Morning is a Dallas-based retailer specializing in upscale closeout merchandise with 865 stores across the U.S. Since Tuesday Morning's stores function on an event basis, a challenge is getting store merchandise from its origin through distribution channels and into their stores by a specified date and time for their more than 20 specialty sales events per year.

Tuesday Morning started looking for ways to save money while meeting its tight deadlines—and what the team came up with was a solution ahead of its time. They decided to use intermodal transport out of the West Coast ports where merchandise arrives from Asia to a single, national distribution center (DC) just outside of Dallas.

"We started to take a hard look at intermodal for our inbound needs," says Cheryl Bailey, Tuesday Morning's logistics manager for transportation. "We found that it gave us many options."

Tuesday Morning's outbound distribution to its network of 865 stores is unique among national retailers in that it has chosen to cover the nation with its one DC in Farmers Branch. One of its primary carriers was Averitt, which provides both TL and LTL services. And while Averitt understood that sometimes the deadlines for this link of the supply chain were tight, it felt intermodal services could meet the majority of time demands while earning major savings.

Given the cost savings, Tuesday Morning now looks at intermodal service as a viable transportation option in all lanes that exceed 500 miles. And Averitt, one of its main transportation partners, says it's fine with that. "Tuesday Morning is an excellent customer," says Averitt's Richards. "Intermodal is a piece of that, and it's going to grow a lot with them. In fact, I don't want to call them a customer or client—it's a true partnership. We share a lot of knowledge and we share a lot of ideas."

Source: Adapted from John D. Schulz, "Tuesday Morning Shifts Modes," ***Logistics Management*** **(February 2012), pp. 24–27.**

transportation specialists. They simply felt that transportation is not their core competency and that specialists can do the job more effectively and efficiently. Nevertheless there are still firms, such as Steelcase, who operate their own truck fleets in addition to using the services of other types of carriers in some situations.

Transportation Service Selection

Selecting a mode of transportation, or a particular carrier within a mode, is not a trivial problem. The decision involves several factors: the cost related to transportation itself, the cost of inventory while in transit, and the service requirements related to speed, availability, and so on. However, to illustrate the basic cost-to-cost trade-offs in the decision, we will assume that the service dimensions are negligible. When managers are faced with this decision, they usually seek to balance the inventory costs of products in-transit against the costs of moving these products. Faster delivery means less in-transit inventory, yet faster modes are usually more expensive. Other things being equal, managers typically pick the mode that offers the lowest total cost. Example 11-2 illustrates the calculation of the lowest total cost in making this decision.

The primary cost variables driving the transportation service decision are the value and weight of the items being shipped. Product value drives inventory costs, and product weight drives transportation cost. If the weight of the shipment were substantially greater, the transportation cost would be much higher. Thus, in Example 11-2 if the same decision were being made at a less-expensive watch manufacturer, ground might easily be the lowest cost choice. Because of this relationship between total transportation cost, product value, and weight, a shipping load's **value density** is usually a key determinant of the transportation mode used to move it. Value density is simply the ratio of a product's value to its weight. All other things being equal, faster, more expensive transportation is usually

value density The ratio of a product's value to its weight.

EXAMPLE 11-2

Consider the choice faced by a manufacturer of high-end wristwatches (such as Omega or Rolex) who must ship an assortment of 30 watches valued at $500 each from its manufacturing warehouse to a distributor located 1,000 miles away. The manufacturer is paid for the watches upon receipt at the distributor, so the manufacturer owns the in-transit inventory. Assume that the two most favorable transportation options include parcel 8-day ground service or air express 2-day air service. The basic question is: Does the inventory cost savings from faster shipping justify the additional cost of air versus ground shipping? Given the cost information shown below, the total cost for each transportation option would be calculated as follows:

Shipping weight = 10 pounds   Total Product value = $15,000

Parcel ground cost = $50.00   Air express cost = $90.00

Inventory holding cost rate = 20% of product value per year

(11.1) Total cost = In-transit inventory holding cost + Carrier cost

(11.2) In-transit inventory holding cost = # of days in-transit/365 × shipment value × annual inventory carrying cost percentage

Total cost for ground = [(8 days/365) × $15,000 × 0.20] + $50.00
= $65.74 + $50.00 = $115.74

Total cost for air = [(2 days/365) × $15,000 × 0.20] + $90.00
= $16.64 + $90.00 = $106.44

In this case, the inventory savings of a faster mode of transportation outweighs the additional carrier cost, so the transportation manager should use the air express service option.

TABLE 11-3 Freight Transportation Mode Greenhouse Gas Emissions

Mode	Grams/Ton-km
Air	1,000–1,800
Bulk vessel/barge	10–60
Container vessel	10–30
Rail	20–70
Long-haul truck	80–150
Light duty delivery truck	350–450

sustainability

justified for more value-dense items. Sometimes the ratio of a product's value to its volume (i.e., cubic space it fills) is also important. It depends on whether weight or volume is the driving factor affecting freight charges.

The analysis in Example 11-2 is based purely on inventory and carrier cost considerations. In many situations, of course, other factors would come into play. It may be that the customer is simply unwilling to wait eight days to receive shipment. Also, differences in delivery reliability, the potential for damage or loss, packaging requirements, or other factors might ultimately drive the transportation decision.

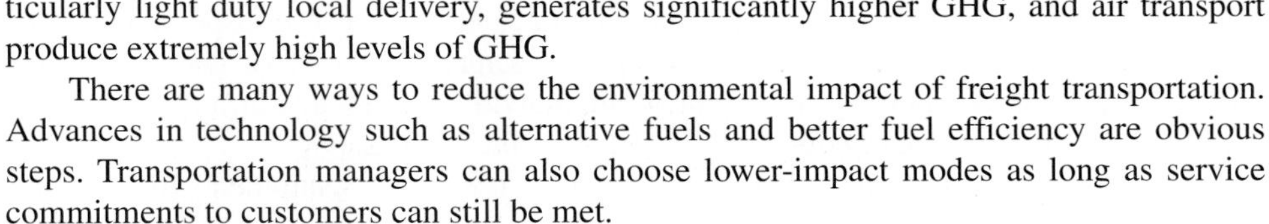

student activity

Rework the transportation cost analysis in Example 11-2 given all the same parameters, except that the 30 watches are now valued at only $50 each. Why is ground service now the best choice?

Increasingly, managers are considering the sustainability issues related to transportation decisions, including energy consumption and environmental impacts. For each of the transport modes, Table 11-3 shows estimates of the greenhouse gas emissions (GHG) per ton of freight transported per kilometer. Rail, pipe, and water are relatively low in GHG emissions, which reflect the fact that these modes specialize in carrying large quantities at relatively slow speeds, which generates significant economy of scale. Trucking, particularly light duty local delivery, generates significantly higher GHG, and air transport produce extremely high levels of GHG.

sustainability

There are many ways to reduce the environmental impact of freight transportation. Advances in technology such as alternative fuels and better fuel efficiency are obvious steps. Transportation managers can also choose lower-impact modes as long as service commitments to customers can still be met.

WAREHOUSE MANAGEMENT

Prepare

What are the functions of warehouses and distribution centers? What are their major activities?

Organize

Warehouse Management
- Primary Functions of Warehousing
- Warehouse Operations

Historically, a warehouse was simply a place to store inventory. While storage is an important function, warehouses today are often used for other important purposes, including creating final product configurations and assortments that are in accordance with customer requirements. In fact, in an ideal logistics system, storage is minimized as inventory moves continuously throughout the supply chain. Of course, some storage is typically justified on the basis of cost or service requirements, but to emphasize the difference between the storage activity and the strategic role of warehouses, many people today use the term **distribution center** rather than warehouse.

Primary Functions of Warehousing

Like all other areas of logistics management, warehousing tends to center on cost and customer service improvements. In terms of customer service, warehouses located near customers enable quicker product fulfillment than remote manufacturing plants or

distribution center Term used to describe the strategic role of warehouses in storage and creating assortments that meet customer requirements.

LO11-4 Make decisions regarding warehouses, distribution centers, and facility networks.

stocking locations do. In addition, warehouses offer the benefits of market presence. Having a warehouse visibly located in a given customer market frequently leads customers to believe that they will be better supported.

Warehouses are often the most cost-effective means to provide an assortment of products to geographically dispersed customers. They enable logistics managers to take advantage of the transportation economies associated with consolidation that we discussed earlier. In addition, warehouses are increasingly being used as transshipment points. At a **transshipment point**, products are received, sorted, sequenced, and selected into loads consistent with the customers' needs. Transshipment warehouses are most evident in grocery and retail businesses. Warehouses are also increasingly being used to do final product modification and light assembly, which will be discussed later in the chapter. The following activities describe some of the primary functions provided by warehouses.

transshipment point A facility where products are received, sorted, sequenced, and selected into loads consistent with the customers' needs.

Stockpiling

Stockpiling is the storage of inventories in warehouses to protect against seasonality either in supply or demand. For example, ketchup can only be produced during the times of the year when tomatoes are harvested, yet there is year-round demand for this product. Demand seasonality is evidenced in products such as lawn furniture, snow blowers, and toys. Stockpiled inventories cover demand when there is no production, or they store production when there is no demand.

stockpiling The storage of inventories in warehouses to protect against seasonality either in supply or demand.

Production Support

Today, manufacturers are increasingly asking suppliers to locate warehouses very near their major manufacturing plants. A **production support warehouse** is dedicated to storing parts and components needed to support a plant's operations. The cost of stopping a production line due to a lack of needed material can be very high (hundreds of thousands of dollars each day). Thus, it is sometimes worthwhile to dedicate a supporting warehouse, especially if supplier lead times would otherwise be very long, or if the usage of material is quite variable.

production support warehouse A warehouse dedicated to storing parts and components needed to support a plant's operations.

Break-Bulk, Warehouse Consolidation, and Cross-Docking

When suppliers use market area consolidation strategies to reduce transportation costs, they send large shipments to a warehouse in a local market area. That warehouse then conducts **break-bulk**, splitting the shipment into individual orders and arranging for local delivery to customers. Break-bulk is illustrated in Figure 11-3(A).

Warehouse consolidation occurs when a warehouse receives shipments from a number of sources and combines those shipments into one larger shipment going to a single location. This allows the customer to receive an assortment of products in a single shipment, thus reducing time and effort required for the customer. It also takes advantage of transportation economies by combining small shipments into a single large shipment. Figure 11-3(B) illustrates the warehouse consolidation activity.

Cross-docking combines break-bulk and consolidation activities. In cross-docking, large shipments from many sources are scheduled to arrive at the facility's receiving docks simultaneously. Meanwhile, several vehicles are positioned at the shipping docks, each bound for a different destination. As the incoming shipments are unloaded, they are broken into the quantities needed at each customer location and loaded into the appropriate outbound vehicles. Generally, customers have specified exactly how much of each product is required at each location and suppliers have presorted their shipments into these quantities. This approach simplifies the unloading and reloading process. Once the trucks have the loads of mixed products completed, they depart for their final destinations. Cross-docking provides tremendous efficiency in transportation, avoids the need for product storage, and provides a sizable service benefit to customers by providing one shipment containing their requirements for many different products. Many retailers, especially grocery and mass merchants, use cross-dock facilities extensively to replenish their stores. Figure 11-3(C) illustrates how cross-docking works.

break-bulk Splitting a large shipment into individual orders and arranging for local delivery to customers.

warehouse consolidation Combining shipments from a number of sources into one larger shipment going to a single location.

cross-docking Combines break-bulk and consolidation warehouse activities.

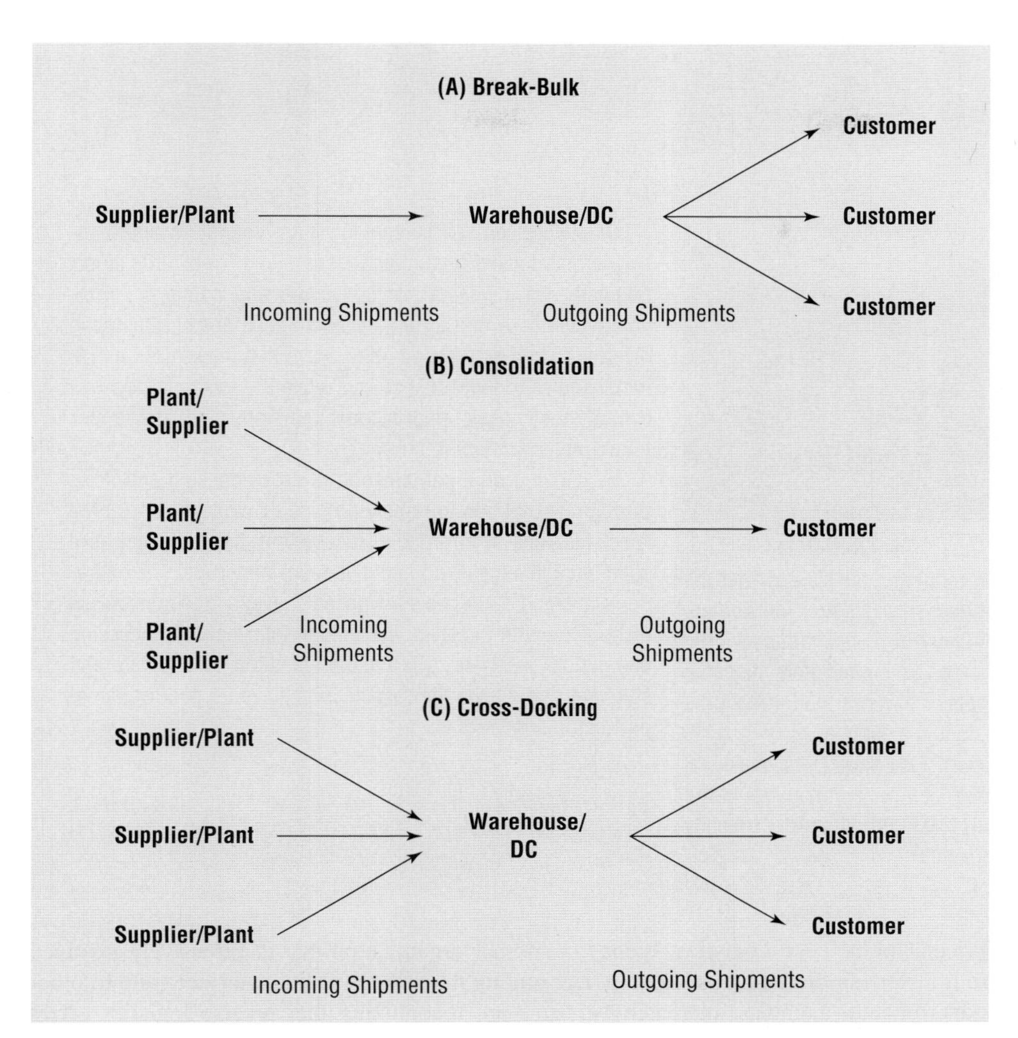

FIGURE 11-3 Break-Bulk, Consolidation, and Cross-Docking Warehouse Operations

Sometimes cross-docking is not practical because it requires precise scheduling of shipments from suppliers or trucks destined for customers. Even in these instances, however, warehouses provide important benefits by mixing or creating assortments**.** While this function is similar to cross-docking, the difference lies in the fact that incoming shipments do not have to be scheduled as precisely. They may be put into storage until all of the needed products are available. The nearby Get Real box describes how the fashion retailer Dots uses cross-docking to support its business strategy.

A U-Shaped Cross-Dock. Trailers with inbound shipments are staged at the outside walls of the cross-dock facility, while trailers bound for customer destinations are staged on the inside of the U-shaped facility. Inside the building, workers unload the inbound trailers and quickly fill the outbound equipment with an assortment of products.

Source: www2.isye.gatech.edu/~ jjb/wh/book/xdock/xdock.html.

Reverse Logistics Support

As products become more complex and as consumers become more environmentally conscious, the number of products that are returned and reclaimed is growing dramatically. The growth of leasing and online purchasing has also contributed to this growth (some online sellers process returns equaling as much as 50 percent of their sales). Sometimes this activity involves the handling of hazardous materials, or it requires special handling of damaged or defective products.

To cope with this increasing need, warehouses are being used as collection points for reverse logistics; that is, the logistics needed to send products or packaging materials back to disassembly, reclamation, or disposal sites. Frequently, returned products can be remanufactured or updated for resale. For example, many electronics manufacturers disassemble and/or remanufacture used equipment, which can then be sold at a discounted

GET REAL

Cross-Docking at Dots

There's no wasting time at Dots. This Ohio-based fashion retailer uses a unique sourcing model to quickly interpret the latest fashion trends into everyday-wear apparel for women. And because what's hot today may not be hot tomorrow, the retailer's distribution team needs to immediately dispatch these latest looks from its suppliers to more than 400 stores within a 26-state radius—and do it in a flash.

How do they make this happen? Lisa Akey, Dots' divisional vice president of distribution and lead project manager of the company's new, state-of-the-art, 193,000-square-foot facility in Glenwillow, Ohio, shares her secret:

Once received, 20 percent of Dots' volume is automatically cross-docked to shipping—sometimes in as little as six minutes—via a network of conveyors and conveyor sortation systems. Within 24 hours, another 70 percent has been diverted to two high-speed unit sorters that flow-through bulk merchandise to individual stores, while the remaining 10 percent of mostly basic, nonseasonal items goes into storage for future replenishment.

By banking on a combination of cross-docking and flow-through distribution to rapidly provide its customers with the latest fashions at affordable prices, Dots has emerged as a solid force in a highly competitive retail landscape. The operation is a blend of the most advanced conveyor and mechanical technology with the latest systems in information processing and control software. It is this combination of hardware and software that allows the retailer to achieve its goal of same-day distribution.

Source: Adapted from Maida Napolitano, "Cross Dock Fuels Growth at Dots," *Logistics Management* (February 2011), pp. 32–37.

price. The Defense Logistics Agency is another organization that is extensively involved in transferring or selling used equipment among the various military services and to other governmental agencies. Increasingly, firms are recognizing that reverse logistics offers opportunities for reducing costs, increasing profits, and differentiating themselves from the competition.

Value-Added Services

value-added services Any work that creates greater value for customers.

The demand for highly customized service has transformed modern distribution warehouses into facilities that specialize in performing **value-added services**. A value-added service is any work that creates greater value for customers. These services may change the physical features or configuration of products so they are presented to customers in a unique or customized manner. For example, companies frequently postpone final product configuration by completing packaging, labeling, and even light manufacturing in a warehouse facility. A well-known application of this occurs in food processing. Many food processors sell canned vegetables to different customers who want their own labels to be placed on the cans. Vegetables can be processed and canned in "brights" (cans without labels) at the processing plants. Once a specific customer order is received, the warehouse can complete labeling and finalize packaging. Other examples range from packaging pharmaceuticals to customizing appliances to installing software on electronics.

Warehouse Operations

Once the roles of a warehouse have been determined, the next step is to design and manage the operations. It is useful to think of this as an exercise in process design. In the case of a warehouse, the primary process activities involved are:

- *Receiving and unloading:* Inbound shipments must be received and unloaded from the transportation vehicles. Part of this activity may also involve checking the shipment for the correct quantities and for potential damage to products.

- *In-storage handling:* Once unloaded the goods must be moved to the desired destination within the facility, whether this is an actual storage location or a shipping area in the case of a cross-dock facility.
- *Storage:* Products are held, even if for only a few minutes, in a storage area.
- *Orderpicking:* The products are removed from storage and assembled into appropriate quantities and assortments to fill customer orders.
- *Staging:* The assembled orders are moved to an area in the warehouse in readiness for loading into a transportation vehicle bound for customer locations.
- *Shipping:* Shipping involves verifying that the assembled orders are correct and the actual loading of the transportation vehicles.

Designing and operating a warehouse is no different in concept than designing and managing any other process. Capacity must be determined, activities and flows must be managed, and potential bottlenecks and delays must be identified.

Companies have three options in choosing warehouse facilities: private warehouses, public warehouses, or contract warehouses. A private warehouse is owned and operated by the firm that owns the products. A private warehouse offers more control over the products, opportunities to integrate the warehouse operations with the other activities within the logistics system, and flexibility in operating policies and procedures. However, ownership requires that financial resources be committed to fixed physical assets.

A public warehouse is a firm that offers warehouse services to the public for a fee based on the amount of space used and the number of shipments into or out of the facility. Using public warehouses may be especially appropriate for a firm whose needs for warehouse capacity vary substantially throughout the year; for example, firms moving products into critical markets only at certain times of the year. Agricultural chemical companies make extensive use of public warehouses, storing herbicides and pesticides in markets only for the growing seasons.

Contract warehouse companies offer to build, own, and operate warehouse facilities for the benefit of clients who do not want to undertake those responsibilities themselves. In addition, contract warehouse operators typically offer expanded services in such areas as transportation, inventory control, order processing, customer service, and returns processing.

student activity

Contact a company that has a warehouse operation nearby (it may be that your college or university has a warehouse facility). Arrange for a tour of the warehouse. Ask the warehouse manager about the different functions the facility performs (consolidation, break-bulk, etc.) for the organization.

MATERIALS HANDLING AND PACKAGING

Prepare

Why are materials handling and packaging important?

Organize

Materials Handling and Packaging

At its core, logistics management is very much about materials handling. Both transportation and warehousing managers must plan the best ways to load, offload, move, sort, and select products. They also work closely with packaging engineers to design or select packaging materials that facilitate materials handling. Packaging and materials handling decisions affect value in many ways. First, materials handling costs can be substantial, and improved labor and equipment productivities can significantly improve profits. Second, materials handling is usually the number one cause of product damage and loss in logistics. Poor handling practices and improperly packaged items lead to scratched, dented, and broken products that no one wants to buy. Usually, the less a material is handled, the better.

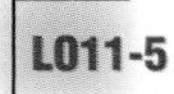

Explain the importance of packaging and materials handling.

Packaging protects the product while it is in the logistics system. Beyond this basic function, however, packaging can facilitate ease of handling in a number of ways. First, packaging schemes are often devised to create one large container out of several smaller units. For example, individual soft drinks are frequently packaged in six-packs. The six-packs may be grouped together into cases of four six-packs. Cases are then grouped together into one unit of many cases. This process, called **containerization or unitization**, greatly reduces overall handling cost.

containerization or unitization
Creating one large container out of several smaller units.

Packages also contain information about the products they contain (useful when sorting products and processing orders). Today, many new packaging and labeling approaches are improving the speed and ease with which products can be identified, selected, and routed. For example, many warehouses today use **automated storage and retrieval systems (AS/RS)**. These computer-controlled systems use robots to automatically select, find, retrieve, and convey product items from storage bins to loading docks. In order for these systems to work reliably, products need to be packaged in generic, unitized containers. Furthermore, labels need to be designed so that automated scanners are able to easily scan packaging information. The advantages of systems such as AS/RS include reduced labor requirements, reduced picking errors, more densely packed storage bays, and greater facility utilization (because racks can be built several stories high, much higher than human workers could safely operate).

automated storage and retrieval systems (AS/RS) Computer-controlled systems that use robots to automatically select, find, retrieve, and convey product items from storage bins to loading docks.

An AS/RS system. The photograph shows an aisle in a warehouse with an automated picking capability. The robot moves on a rail to the appropriate location, then automatically pulls products from their storage location.

www-lib.icu.ac.jp/ASRS/index-e.htm

Packaging and materials handling is a rapidly changing field in logistics management. There are numerous opportunities to improve logistics efficiencies through advanced technologies such as AS/RS, new data communication technologies, and computerized control. In addition, supply chain managers are integrating operations across corporate boundaries by standardizing packaging designs, instruction formats, and data protocols.

Radio frequency identification (RFID), discussed in Chapter 7, is another technology that has rapidly gained acceptance in packaging and materials handling. RFID places a coded electronic chip in or on a package that emits a signal identifying its contents as it moves through facilities or on transportation equipment. Walmart and other major retailers are requiring that their major suppliers place RFID tags on their cases to facilitate

GET REAL

General Dynamics Develops AS/RS for the Navy

General Dynamics Armament and Technical Products, a business unit of General Dynamics, was awarded a $4.8 million contract to develop a land-based demonstrator of technology for the automated storage and retrieval system, an automatic warehouse system designed to be used aboard ships. The automated storage and retrieval system (AS/RS) will accept a palletized load from a fork truck, automatically identify the load through radio frequency identification (RFID), verify load size and weight, and then securely stow the load within the hold of a ship. This next-generation, low-maintenance storage and retrieval technology will allow the automatic inventory and total visibility of all materiel within the hold, greatly improving shipboard efficiency and reducing the need for dedicated manpower. The AS/RS design will be adaptable to a wide variety of ships and hold configurations.

Source: Adapted from "General Dynamics Awarded $5 Million to Develop Automated Storage and Retrieval System for U.S. Navy," ***PR Newswire,*** **June 20, 2005.**

processing in distribution centers to reduce handling expense. The U.S. Department of Defense uses RFID to list the contents of containers so that they can be tracked as they are loaded on transportation equipment or moved through facilities. The Get Real box on General Dynamics provides an interesting and rather unique application of both AS/RS systems and RFID.

Finally, many firms are being forced to reexamine their approaches to packaging as a result of environmental initiatives. Packaging materials recycling and disposal has become a major concern, especially for companies that do business in Europe and other more environmentally stringent regions of the world.

sustainability

NETWORK DESIGN

Prepare

How do logistics managers make network design decisions?

Organize

Network Design
- Facility Location
- Number of Facilities
- Logistics Postponement

Perhaps no other set of decisions impacts supply chain operations more than network design. Network design determines the number and location of facilities. It also establishes the linkages among facilities through which information and material transportation flows occur in the network. For example, network designers decide which customers will be served by which facilities and which facilities share inventories. These network decisions clearly impact a firm's cost and ability to service customers.

Numerous factors influence location decisions. Some of the most important of these are:

- Labor (availability and cost)
- Proximity of suppliers
- Proximity of customers
- Construction costs
- Land costs
- Taxes
- Regulations
- Incentive packages
- Transportation infrastructure
- Quality of life for employees

Within each of these factors there are many specific items to evaluate. For example, regulations may be federal, state, and local. Building a facility at a specific place can require approval from each level of government. Even if a proposed facility meets all federal and state regulations, local officials could refuse to grant permission due to local zoning regulations.

Given the importance of location, sophisticated computer models have been developed to aid in decision making. In-depth discussion of those models is beyond the scope of this text, but we will briefly review a few fundamental location principles. First we examine issues related to choice of a location. Then we address issues related to determining the number of facilities needed.

Facility Location

LO11-6 Locate facilities using the center-of-gravity model.

There are several quantitative approaches that can help in facility location decisions. The **center-of-gravity method** provides an example of the distribution-related considerations involved in location. The center-of-gravity method attempts to find the lowest-cost location for a facility based on demand and distance.

center-of-gravity method Attempts to find the lowest-cost location for a facility based on demand and distance.

The first step in the center-of-gravity method is to position the demand locations on a map with X and Y coordinates. Figure 11-4 at the top of page 330 shows a plot for three locations (A, B, and C) which represent markets to be served. The coordinate system's scale and origin do not matter as long as the relative distances between the locations are correct. The next step is to determine the amount of demand at each location. Demand can

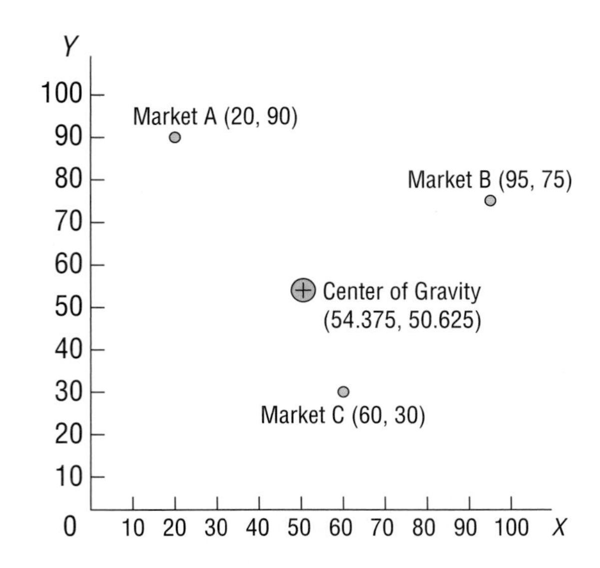

FIGURE 11-4 Coordinate Locations of Markets and Their Center of Gravity

be measured in a number of ways. Often it is estimated as a function of the population at each location. Other factors, such as historical weight of products shipped, number of shipments, or sales dollars are also used as measures of demand.

The center of gravity is then determined by solving for the X and Y coordinates as follows:

(11-3a) $$\text{X coordinate of center of gravity} = X^* = \frac{\sum_i D_i X_i}{\sum_i D_i}$$

(11-3b) $$\text{Y coordinate of center of gravity} = Y^* = \frac{\sum_i D_i Y_i}{\sum_i D_i}$$

where:

D_i = Demand at location i
X_i = X coordinate of location i
Y_i = Y coordinate of location i

EXAMPLE 11-3

Suppose, given the locations plotted in Figure 11-4, we determine the following information:

Location	X coordinate	Y coordinate	Weight shipped
A	20	90	200,000 lbs.
B	95	75	100,000 lbs.
C	60	30	500,000 lbs.

Solving for the center-of-gravity coordinates results in:

$$X^* = \frac{20(200{,}000) + 95(100{,}000) + 60(500{,}000)}{200{,}000 + 100{,}000 + 500{,}000} = \frac{43{,}500{,}000}{800{,}000} = 54.375$$

$$Y^* = \frac{90(200{,}000) + 75(100{,}000) + 30(500{,}000)}{200{,}000 + 100{,}000 + 500{,}000} = \frac{40{,}500{,}000}{800{,}000} = 50.625$$

The calculated center-of-gravity coordinates are plotted and represented by the "⊕" in Figure 11-4.

The center-of-gravity method involves certain assumptions. One of the most critical of these is the assumption of straight-line distances between all locations. In reality, roads or other transportation infrastructure are not straight lines. Another assumption is that amount of demand is a good proxy measure of transportation cost, which is not always true. In addition, there are no qualitative factors included in the determination of location using the center-of-gravity method. For example, there is no consideration of environmental regulations or other costs associated with a given location.

Despite these assumptions and limitations, the center-of-gravity method does give a reasonable first approximation of where a facility might be located. This methodology, with considerable enhancement, forms the core of several of the more sophisticated computerized location models.

Number of Facilities

The basic principles driving the number of facilities in the network can be looked at from the perspective of transportation consolidation, the impact of facilities on inventory requirements, and customer service considerations. All of these directly impact the number of facilities and their location in a network.

Transportation Cost

Earlier in the chapter we demonstrated the financial savings possible from transportation consolidation. Frequently, this consolidation is achieved by positioning facilities in local markets to receive large inbound shipments from remote locations; the shipments are then distributed locally. The local facilities could be storage warehouses, break-bulk terminals, or cross-dock facilities. As long as the cost of operating the facility and the cost of local market delivery are less than the cost of making direct, small quantity shipments from the remote location, a facility can be justified on a total cost basis.

A company serving a large geographic area would find it advantageous to add local facilities as long as this relationship holds true. As a general rule, total cost will initially decline as the number of facilities increases. However, a point will be reached where the total cost is minimized and then increases as the number of facilities goes up. This point is reached because continual expansion of the number of facilities not only increases total facility costs, it also eventually results in each facility beginning to receive smaller inbound shipments, resulting in the loss of the consolidation benefit. Thus, inbound transportation costs also begin to increase. As an illustration of this point, consider the maximum number of potential network locations that would exist when a firm decides to put a facility at each customer location. In this case, there is no consolidation and therefore the inbound transportation cost is the same as direct shipments to customers, with the added costs of all of the facilities in the network. Figure 11-5 illustrates this general relationship between transportation cost and the number of warehouse facilities.

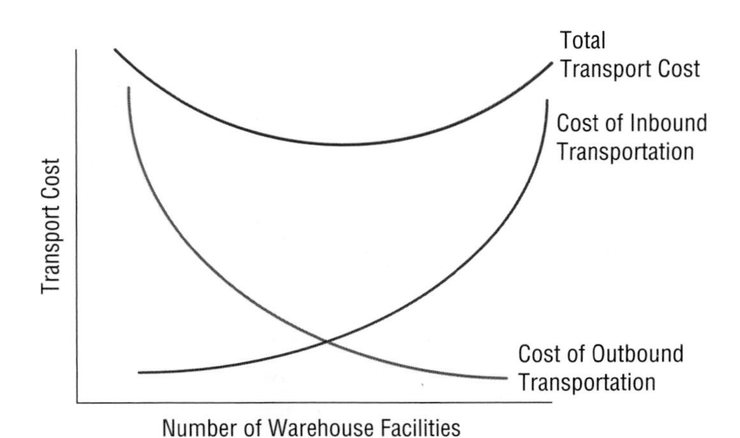

FIGURE 11-5 Transportation Cost Related to Number of Warehouse Locations

Inventory Cost

Recall that in Chapter 7, we discussed basic fundamentals of inventory management. A critical point to remember from that discussion is that if you expand your network from one warehouse to two warehouses, you don't just divide your inventory in half and split it between the two locations. The reason that this will not work is that each facility must maintain its own safety stock. In fact, the total amount of inventory a company must hold increases as the number of warehouse locations increases.

Total Network Cost

Total network cost can be derived by combining the cost curves for transportation and inventory, and adding the fact that facility costs also increase as the number of facilities increases. The result is depicted in Figure 11-6. Note in the figure that the "ideal" number of locations does not occur where inventory or facility costs are the lowest, which would be one facility. Neither does it occur where transportation cost is minimized, as that would require high inventory and facility costs.

Logistics Postponement

At the beginning of this chapter, we said that logisticians are concerned with both cost and service. The number of facility locations has a significant impact on the service provided to customers, particularly with respect to delivery speed. When customers require short lead times, the company must have a larger number of warehouses. For example, Grainger Distribution, a distributor of maintenance, repair, and operating supplies, has a network of over 400 warehouses throughout the United States, driven primarily by the fact that many customers have emergency needs for repair parts for major equipment. While maintaining such an extensive network is certainly not the lowest-cost alternative, it is profitable for Grainger because customers are willing to pay higher prices to receive delivery within a few hours.

logistics postponement Stock products in a single or only a few locations rather than spread inventory out across a large number of warehouses.

In contrast to Grainger's approach, the strategy of **logistics postponement** is to stock in a single or only a few locations rather than spread inventory out across a large number of warehouses. Logistics postponement is practiced by many firms, particularly those who manufacture high–value density products. In this situation, it would be very expensive to position inventory in a large number of locations in anticipation of a customer order arising in any given area. It may be substantially less expensive, for example, to maintain one central location of inventory and then to use a premium mode of transportation such as FedEx or UPS Air to deliver directly to customers. The savings in warehousing and inventory costs could make it more economical, even though the transportation cost may be high. Of

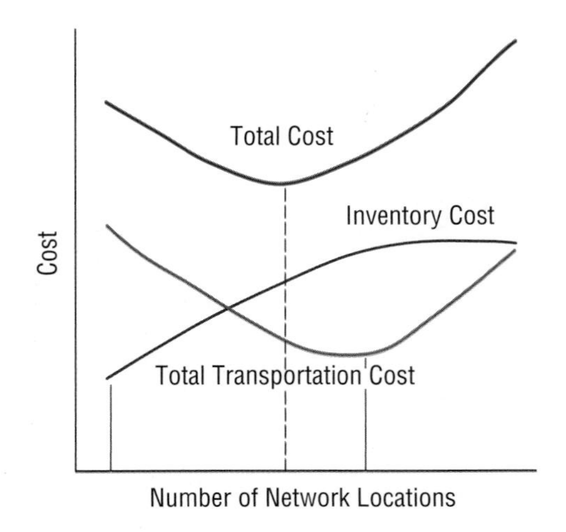

FIGURE 11-6 Total Network Cost

GET REAL

Kimberly-Clark Redesigns the Network

Kimberly-Clark, the Irving, Texas, based maker of Kleenex facial tissue, Huggies, Scott paper towels, and many other health and hygiene brands, began to address facility network questions when it started a project to update its supply chain. The primary goal was "customer-centric, to improve customer service," said Mark Jamison, vice president of customer service at Kimberly-Clark North America. "The second goal was to fashion a lower-cost network."

The company examined its network, which comprised 70 mill and plant distribution centers. "Each manufacturing location had multiple warehouses, and many were not located near major markets. So the intent was to streamline the distribution network," he said.

Kimberly-Clark has reduced those 70 facilities to nine regional megacenters that are located close to its key retail customers and markets. The change enables the company to reach 90 percent of the North American population within eight hours. The nine regional distribution centers are located at Chicago; Scranton, Pa.; Atlanta; Graniteville, S.C.; Dallas; Redlands, Calif.; Kansas City, Mo.; Conway, Ark.; and Seattle.

"As we have seen the cost of oil increase and its significant impact on distribution expenses, the decision to consolidate and streamline the network has become a real positive," Jamison said. "Our inventory is no longer scattered among many manufacturing and distribution centers."

Kimberly-Clark figures that in its first year the network restructuring saved 473,000 gallons of fuel and decreased the number of miles driven from distribution centers to customer locations by 2.8 million. Another initiative that Kimberly-Clark recently began will move some 22 co-packaging facilities into the regional distribution centers. Under the current system, the company has to move its product from the manufacturing and distribution plant to the co-packer and then ship it back to the distribution center for shipment. "This will eliminate moving the same product twice, and it eliminates the costs of shipping to the co-packer and the additional material-handling costs," Jamison said.

Source: B. DiBenedetto, *The Journal of Commerce Online*, June 17, 2008.

course, logistics postponement is only feasible if the transportation mode chosen can still meet customer requirements regarding delivery speed.

Imagine all of the cost trade-offs and customer service issues that you would have to consider when making structural changes such as logistics postponement. Such decisions should not be made from a short-term point of view. Network designers must consider changes in customers (e.g., the opening of a new market), changes in technology, changes in supply and demand, changes in competitive actions, changes in products (e.g., new or modified products), and changes in costs. Modifications to the logistics network often require substantial investments in information systems, land, facilities, training, and transportation infrastructure. Consequently, logistics network design is an area of strategic concern that often constrains many other operating decisions. The Get Real box about Kimberly-Clark illustrates the complexity of these decisions.

INTEGRATED SERVICE PROVIDERS

Prepare
What are integrated service providers?

Organize
Integrated Service Providers

More and more, firms are foregoing the costs of owning private transportation and warehousing in favor of purchasing logistical services from specialists. For example, in the transportation industry there are thousands of carriers who specialize in product movement between geographic locations. Over the years, a comprehensive network of common and contract carriers has emerged. In addition, a large number of service companies have traditionally provided public or contract warehouse services.

LO11-7 Describe the benefits of integrated service providers.

In recent years there has been a radical shift from single function to multifunctional specialists. Today, **integrated service providers (ISPs)** provide a range of logistics services. For example, United Parcel Service (UPS) stocks Nike shoes and warm-up suits at a Louisville warehouse and processes orders hourly. All related communication and administration activities are handled by a UPS call center, and UPS provides delivery to retail customers. Thus, Nike has effectively outsourced basic logistics services to UPS. The common name used throughout the industry to describe ISPs is **third-party logistics service providers (3PLs)**.

integrated service providers (ISPs) Companies that provide a range of logistics services.

third-party logistics service providers (3PLs) A common term used in the industry to describe ISPs.

The continuing globalization of business has put tremendous pressure on logistics executives. Lead times are considerably longer and more subject to variation. It is more difficult to determine shipment status and anticipate arrival times. In addition, there is a substantial increase in the volume and type of documentation required to deal with international logistics, much of which is country specific. As a result, few companies have the resources and capabilities to deal with these issues internally. Integrated service providers provide a potential solution to these problems for many organizations.

global

CHAPTER SUMMARY

This chapter describes the role of logistics in supply chain operations. We explored the following issues:

1. Logistics management provides for the flow and storage of information and products between: (1) the firm and its suppliers (inbound logistics); (2) the firm and its customers (outbound logistics); and (3) the various plants, divisions, and units of the firm (internal logistics).
2. The objective of logistics management is to provide customers with their required service benefits at the lowest total logistics cost.
3. A complete logistics management system comprises six major decision areas: (1) facility network design, (2) information and inventory management, (3) order management, (4) transportation management, (5) warehousing management, (6) and packaging and materials handling management.
4. Economies of scale and distance offer opportunities to lower cost through consolidation in transportation management. The transportation modes each have significant advantages and disadvantages, which makes the choice of transportation service a complex decision.
5. Warehouses perform several functions over and above storage. They also provide benefits through consolidation, break-bulk, cross-docking, and assortment activities.
6. Network design and facility location are extremely complex decisions involving a number of considerations. Quantitative techniques such as center-of-gravity can be used to approximate ideal locations. Determining the proper number of locations involves many cost trade-offs as well as a clear understanding of customers' service requirements. Integrated service providers are increasingly being utilized by companies due to their expertise in accomplishing logistics activities.

KEY TERMS

automated storage and retrieval systems (AS/RS) 378
break-bulk 374
center-of-gravity method 379
common carriers 371
consolidation 367
containerization or unitization 377
contract carriers 371
cost-to-cost trade-off 363
cost-to-service trade-off 363
cross-docking 374
distribution center 373
economic regulation 365
economy of distance 366
economy of scale 366
integrated service providers (ISPs) 384
intermodal transportation 370
less-than-truckload (LTL) 369
logistics management 362
logistics postponement 382
market area consolidation 367
pooled delivery consolidation 367
private carriers 371
production support warehouse 374
safety (and social) regulation 371
scheduled delivery consolidation 367
specialty carriers 369
stockpiling 374
third-party logistics service providers (3PLs) 384
total landed cost 364
transportation mode 368
transshipment point 374
truckload (TL) 369
value-added services 376
value density 372
warehouse consolidation 374

DISCUSSION QUESTIONS

1. What are the two types of trade-offs that are of concern to logistics managers? Provide examples of each type of trade-off, beyond those given in the text.
2. Why has the importance of logistics management been growing over the past few decades?
3. What is the role of government in transportation? Do you believe economic deregulation is positive or negative for the overall economy?
4. What is transportation consolidation? How do consolidation strategies take advantage of the basic economic characteristics of transportation?
5. Which mode of transportation would you use for the following products? Why?
   a. Steel.
   b. Oil from Alaska.
   c. Roses from Texas bound for New York.
   d. Cancelled checks moving from Hartford to Chicago.
   e. A contract that must be signed within 24 hours.
6. Why do you think so many firms are concerned about logistics issues when they move into new markets such as China and Russia?
7. Why is the use of warehouses for cross-docking and for transshipment much more attractive to retail and grocery firms, compared to their more traditional use as storage points?
8. What are the critical trade-offs involved in logistics postponement?
9. Based on the information contained within this chapter, what are the critical linkages between the logistics management system and other functions such as production and purchasing?
10. Think about the increasing importance of environmental concerns. What do you think the impacts of these changes will be on logistics management?

SOLVED PROBLEMS

1. Jones Nurseries has received orders from four different customers located in Alabama. Each order has a shipment weight of 6,000 pounds. In discussions with transportation carriers, the best rate Jones received was $28 per hundredweight for a 6,000-pound shipment. However, one carrier quoted a transportation cost of $20 per hundredweight for a consolidated shipment, with an additional charge of $200 for each stop on the delivery. Should Jones choose the consolidated shipment alternative?

Solution

The cost of four individual shipments is:
$4 \times (6{,}000 \text{ pounds}/100) \times \$28 = \$6{,}720$

The cost of a consolidated shipment is:
$(24{,}000 \text{ pounds}/100)(\$\ 20) + 4(\$200) = \$5{,}600$

Jones Nurseries should choose the consolidated shipment, which saves $1,120 in transportation expense.

2. Bill's glass store needs to ship an order of five chandeliers to a builder about 1,000 miles away. The chandeliers cost about $5,000 each, and Bill will be paid upon delivery. Bill plans to ship the order by truck at a cost of $250. The delivery will take five days. Bill uses a 20 percent annual inventory carrying charge with an operating schedule of 360 days per year. What will be the approximate total shipping and transit inventory cost of the shipment?

Solution

The cost of carrying the inventory while it is in transit is:
$5 \text{ days}/365 \text{ days } (\$25{,}000)\ (.20) = \$68.49$

Since the transportation cost is $250, the total cost is $318.49.

3. Johnson's Department Store has decided to build a warehouse to serve its store locations. It has three large stores, one each located in the cities of Sparta, Troy, and Athens. The map coordinates of these cities and the weight of shipments per month to each is shown in the following table:

City	X coordinate	Y coordinate	Weight/Month
Sparta	25	50	100 tons
Troy	75	10	200 tons
Athens	90	80	50 tons

Calculate the X and Y coordinates of the center-of-gravity for Johnson's Department Store.

Solution

$$X^* = \frac{25(100) + 75(200) + 90(50)}{100 + 200 + 50} = \frac{22{,}000}{350} = 62.86$$

$$Y^* = \frac{50(100) + 10(200) + 80(50)}{100 + 200 + 50} = \frac{11{,}000}{350} = 31.43$$

PROBLEMS

1. Richard's Sporting Goods needs to fill an online order for a gross (144) of hockey sticks. The manager is considering shipping the order by truck to the customer in Wisconsin, at a carrier charge of $75. The delivery will take five days and the order is paid on delivery (Richard's doesn't get paid until the sticks are received). The hockey sticks are valued at $50 for each stick and Richard's uses a 25 percent annual inventory carrying charge.
   a. What will be the total shipping and transit inventory cost of the shipment?
   b. If the shipment could be delivered in only 2 days at a cost of $100, should the manager do it? How much money would be saved or lost?
2. The following table provides shipping rates for packages using UPS next day air or ground service options. The rates vary according to both the weight of the package and the distance of the shipment (larger numbered zones are farther away). Note that the zone number also indicates the number of days required to deliver a package using ground service. For example, it would take three days and cost $7.40 to send a 10-pound package to zone 3 using ground service.
   a. Suppose you have a package weighing 15 pounds that needs to be shipped to zone 5. The value of the material is $10,000 and the annual inventory holding rate is 40 percent of the product value. Which transportation mode (air or ground) minimizes the total shipping and transit inventory cost?
   b. How high would the inventory holding rate have to be in order to justify next day air service?

Table of Shipping Rates

Next Day Service Weight	**Domestic Zones**						
	1	2	3	4	5	6	7
1 Lbs.	$ 16.25	$ 19.25	$ 22.75	$ 24.75	$ 27.00	$ 28.25	$ 29.00
2	$ 17.25	$ 20.75	$ 25.50	$ 27.75	$ 30.25	$ 31.25	$ 32.00
3	$ 19.00	$ 21.75	$ 28.25	$ 30.50	$ 33.50	$ 34.75	$ 35.50
4	$ 20.00	$ 22.75	$ 31.00	$ 33.50	$ 36.50	$ 37.75	$ 38.50
5	$ 21.25	$ 24.25	$ 33.50	$ 36.25	$ 39.50	$ 40.75	$ 41.75
6	$ 22.00	$ 25.25	$ 36.00	$ 39.00	$ 42.75	$ 44.00	$ 45.00
7	$ 22.75	$ 27.00	$ 38.50	$ 42.00	$ 46.00	$ 47.00	$ 48.25
8	$ 23.75	$ 28.25	$ 41.00	$ 44.75	$ 49.25	$ 50.25	$ 51.25
9	$ 24.50	$ 29.75	$ 43.75	$ 47.50	$ 52.50	$ 53.75	$ 54.50
10	$ 25.25	$ 31.00	$ 46.25	$ 50.25	$ 55.25	$ 56.75	$ 57.75
11	$ 26.25	$ 32.50	$ 48.75	$ 52.75	$ 58.00	$ 60.00	$ 60.75
12	$ 27.00	$ 33.50	$ 51.25	$ 55.50	$ 60.75	$ 63.00	$ 63.75
13	$ 27.75	$ 34.75	$ 53.75	$ 58.00	$ 63.25	$ 65.75	$ 66.50
14	$ 28.50	$ 36.00	$ 55.75	$ 60.50	$ 65.75	$ 68.50	$ 69.25
15	$ 29.50	$ 37.50	$ 58.00	$ 63.00	$ 68.25	$ 70.75	$ 72.00

Ground Service Weight	Domestic Zones Transit Time in Days						
	1	2	3	4	5	6	7
1 Lbs.	$ 4.75	$ 4.90	$ 5.25	$ 5.35	$ 5.65	$ 5.70	$ 5.85
2	$ 4.85	$ 5.15	$ 5.65	$ 5.80	$ 6.25	$ 6.40	$ 6.80
3	$ 5.00	$ 5.40	$ 6.00	$ 6.25	$ 6.70	$ 6.90	$ 7.55
4	$ 5.15	$ 5.60	$ 6.30	$ 6.60	$ 7.10	$ 7.30	$ 8.05
5	$ 5.40	$ 5.80	$ 6.60	$ 6.95	$ 7.40	$ 7.75	$ 8.55
6	$ 5.55	$ 6.00	$ 6.75	$ 7.20	$ 7.65	$ 8.05	$ 8.85
7	$ 5.75	$ 6.15	$ 6.90	$ 7.45	$ 7.95	$ 8.35	$ 9.25
8	$ 6.00	$ 6.35	$ 7.10	$ 7.60	$ 8.25	$ 8.75	$ 9.90
9	$ 6.20	$ 6.55	$ 7.25	$ 7.80	$ 8.45	$ 9.25	$ 10.55
10	$ 6.40	$ 6.70	$ 7.40	$ 8.00	$ 8.80	$ 9.90	$ 11.25
11	$ 6.60	$ 6.90	$ 7.55	$ 8.25	$ 9.20	$ 10.60	$ 12.05
12	$ 6.80	$ 7.10	$ 7.70	$ 8.45	$ 9.60	$ 11.35	$ 12.95
13	$ 7.00	$ 7.35	$ 7.85	$ 8.65	$ 10.05	$ 12.05	$ 13.80
14	$ 7.15	$ 7.55	$ 8.00	$ 8.85	$ 10.60	$ 12.75	$ 14.65
15	$ 7.35	$ 7.80	$ 8.15	$ 9.05	$ 11.15	$ 13.45	$ 15.55

3. Use the data in the table from the previous problem to answer this question. A transportation manager must ship orders of materials weighing three pounds each to destinations in each of the seven zones listed in the table. The daily inventory holding rate is $7.50 per day for all orders. The manager has decided to use next day air service for all shipments. Would you agree that this is the right course of action? Why, or why not?
4. Using the rate schedule in the table in problem 2, determine whether or not economies of scale (weight) and economies of distance exist. *Hint:* assume that distance from each zone to the next farthest zone is approximately constant across all zones.
5. You are shipping 200 diamonds to a customer located 2,000 miles away. The average value of the diamonds is $1,500. You can ship via air for $500 and the diamonds will arrive in two days or you can ship via a specialty ground carrier for $200 and the diamonds will arrive in six days. You figure your inventory carrying cost is 25 percent. Your customer will immediately transfer funds to your bank account on receipt of the shipment. What is your total cost if you use the ground carrier? The air carrier? What other considerations are involved besides the cost?
6. Suppose Jones Company has orders from three customers located in the same market area. One order has a total weight of 4,000 pounds, the second weighs 8,000 pounds, and the third weighs 14,000 pounds. The transportation carrier quotes a freight rate of $20.00 per hundredweight (or cwt.) for direct shipment to the customer for shipments weighing 1,000 to 4,999 pounds, $18.00 per cwt. for orders weighing 5,000 to 9,999 pounds, and $16.00 for shipments weighing between 10,000 and 15,000 pounds. Alternatively, the carrier's rate for shipments weighing more than 20,000 pounds is $13.50 per cwt. However, if the orders are combined into one shipment, the carrier will charge $200 for each stop it is required to make. Should Jones consolidate the three shipments?
7. Suppose you have three shipments to make. One shipment has a weight of 3,000 pounds, the second weighs 7,000 pounds, and the third weighs 14,000 pounds. The transportation rates are: $18/cwt. for shipments of 1,000–5,000 pounds, $16/cwt. for 5,000–10,000 pounds, and $14/cwt. for shipments over 10,000 pounds. For consolidated shipments, there is a charge of $200.00 per stop. How much will you save if you choose to consolidate the shipments rather than ship each individually?

8. A trucking company publishes the following rates:

Shipment Weight	Cost per 100 Pounds
Less than 500 lbs.	$20.00
500–999 lbs.	$18.00
1,000–4,999 lbs.	$15.50
5,000–9,999 lbs.	$14.00
10,000 lbs. or more	$13.00

Suppose you have 10 shipments to make, each of which weighs 800 pounds. The carrier offers to consolidate them into one shipment of 8,000 pounds but will charge an additional $300 (total) to do so. Should you agree to this offer?

9. Using the rates in problem 8, suppose you have eight shipments of 900 pounds each that the carrier will consolidate into one shipment, for an additional charge of $200 (total). Should you agree to this?

10. Dansville Cabinets is considering a new warehouse to serve its major markets. Find the center of gravity using the following information:

Market	X Coordinate	Y Coordinate	Demand
North	45	80	200 truckloads
East	85	45	100 truckloads
South	45	10	500 truckloads
West	10	45	50 truckloads

11. Determine the center-of gravity location for a company that wants to serve customers located in Chicago, Detroit, Indianapolis, and Cincinnati. To do this, you can find the X and Y coordinates by looking at the longitude and latitude for each city. Estimate demand for each city by simply looking up the population of each.

12. Atlas Corporation is considering a distribution center which will serve three primary market areas: Dallas, Texas; Atlanta, Georgia; and, St. Louis, Missouri. Atlas has determined that the latitude, longitude, and populations of the three metropolitan areas are:

Metropolitan Area	Approx. Latitude	Approx. Longitude	Approx. Population
Atlanta	33.75	−84.39	5.4 million
Dallas	32.80	−96.77	6.5 million
St. Louis	38.62	−90.20	2.8 million

Using the center-of-gravity method, determine the latitude and longitude of the best location for the distribution center. Use Google Maps or some other resource to plot the location. Then suggest other factors to recommend a location for the distribution center.

CASE

Spartan Plastics

Elise Lovejoy, the new logistics coordinator at Spartan Plastics, was looking at the stack of papers before her and at the two computer screens in front. It was Friday afternoon—the Friday before the long weekend—and she still had not come to resolution. She knew that first thing Tuesday morning she would have a meeting with Bob Barley, CEO and major owner of Spartan Plastics. The issue that they would be discussing: how to get the increasing shipping costs under control. With the forecasts for the upcoming year looking promising, shipping volumes were expected to increase by 10 to 25 percent. Consequently, the shipping costs had to be addressed because, simply put, they were too high.

Spartan Plastics—Background Information

Spartan Plastics was a medium-sized producer of high-quality, highly engineered plastic components. These components were typically found on the interior of most trucks and cars. They tended to come in variety of colors and finishes—everything from small door panels to panels that looked like wood. Typically, their critical major customers consisted of the Big Three (General Motors, Ford, and Chrysler) and were located in the Detroit-Toledo-Lansing area. During the last year, Spartan Plastics had shipped approximately 10,000 pounds of components per day to each assembly plant served.

Located in St. Louis, MO (where the company was known for its aggressive policy of recruiting minorities for its workforce and for its progressive supplier diversification program), Spartan Plastics employed 450 people: 200 direct assembly line employees, 150 engineers, and 100 others.

Originally begun in 1976, the company had grown quickly. However, management's primary focus was on engineering and product design. Management's mantra was simple and known to everyone: high-quality components, designed right, built right, sold at a fair price, and delivered on-time.

The Shipping Problem

Logistics and shipping, as a result, were traditionally not a high priority at Spartan Plastics. Until recently, shipping was seen as simply being a clerical task. Consequently, this responsibility was assigned to a shipping clerk who simply called a local shipping company. Unsurprisingly, shipping costs tended to be high.

In the past, Spartan Plastics had used an LTL carrier from its plant to each of the assembly plants. The carrier charged Spartan Plastics $0.05 per hundredweight per mile. What this policy meant was that to ship one day's worth of components to the Lansing plant, for example, it would cost Spartan Plastics $2,435 (over $600,000 per year).

With its customers becoming more cost sensitive, top management agreed that something had to be done. The first step was to increase the "professionalism" of the logistics and shipping department. One of the first actions triggered by this step was the hiring of Elise Lovejoy. Elise had previously worked as a manager in a shipping department of a local St. Louis company that was widely respected for its expertise in this area. Upon arriving at Spartan Plastics, Elise undertook an assessment. After three weeks, she agreed with top management—the shipping costs were simply too high; there were no controls on them.

Consequently, she approached several Midwestern logistics/shipping companies and asked them to submit proposals in response to her RFQ (request for quotes). After an initial screening review, she identified two proposals that seemed to be highly attractive.

Consolidated Shipping LLC (CS): The first proposal recommended a consolidated delivery approach. That is, CS would consolidate the three shipments into one 30,000-pound truckload. The carrier would then use a "milk-run" approach in which the truck would stop first at the Lansing assembly plant, then continue on to Detroit, and finish in Toledo. The carrier's charge for the milk-run approach would be based on distance only with a charge of $6.00 per truck mile, plus a stop-off charge of $250/stop, including the final stop in Toledo.

Amalgamated Integrated Services (AIS): The second proposal came from AIS, who could provide both transportation and cross-docking capability. AIS proposed to handle deliveries to the various automotive plants by consolidating the shipments into a full truckload in St. Louis. This full truckload would then travel from St. Louis to Ypsilanti, MI, where the shipment would then be broken down into cross-docked shipments for delivery to the appropriate assembly plants (again handled by AIS). AIS established a cost of $6.00 per mile to the cross-dock facility, and then a flat cost per delivery to each assembly plant from Ypsilanti of $500.

To help in evaluating these two proposals, Elise put together a mileage table for all of the relevant origin/destination points. She also knew that she would have to consider the cost implications of the alternatives. Yet, she felt that there were some potential qualitative and service considerations present as well.

Origin	Destination	Distance
St. Louis, MO	Lansing, MI	487 miles
St. Louis, MO	Detroit, MI	552 miles
St. Louis, MO	Toledo, OH	499 miles
Lansing, MI	Detroit, MI	88 miles
Detroit, MI	Toledo, OH	65 miles
St. Louis, MO	Ypsilanti, MI	521 miles

As Elise proceeded to turn off her computer and to put the various notes and calculations into her briefcase, she knew that on Tuesday, she would have to be ready with a comprehensive, well-reasoned analysis and set of recommendations.

Questions

1. What are the cost implications of each delivery option?
2. What are the qualitative and service characteristics of each delivery option?
3. Based on your analysis, what would you recommend to Bob?

CASE

Lear Corporation

Lear Corporation, headquartered in Southfield, Michigan, is one of the world's 10 largest independent automotive suppliers and the leading player in the $45 billion global auto interiors market. This market consists of such items as seating systems, interior carpets, safety restraining systems, and interior paneling. By most measures of performance, Lear is a very successful company. It has experienced a compound annual growth rate of 33 percent over a 13-year period.

One of the most successful plants within the Lear system is the Romulus I plant. This facility, located about 250 yards from the on- and off-ramps of I-275 (a major highway located in the Detroit area), was initially built to serve a GM plant that has now been shut down. The plant today provides seat assemblies for the Chrysler Warren Plant, which is located some 38 miles away. The Chrysler Warren Plant assembles the Dodge Ram and Dakota trucks.

All seats are assembled at Lear on a just-in-time basis. Lear has a five-hour window between the time that Lear's Romulus plant receives notice of the specific types of seats that it must deliver and the time that the seats are needed at Chrysler Warren. Thus, Lear must assemble, test, sequence (i.e., arrange them on the trucks so that the seats can be withdrawn in the exact order that they are needed), and deliver the seats within five hours. This plant has met these demands in a number of ways. First, the entire production line has been rethought. Operations have been extensively analyzed and simplified (thus reducing the need for highly skilled employees). All employees are cross-trained. The plant also is electronically linked to the Warren plant. The Romulus plant receives information about type of vehicles and their seating options as the trucks move through framing. This information ensures that the right types of seats are made in the right order. The material for seats comes off trailers parked near the assembly lines. These trailers bring material up from suppliers located in Mexico. All material is bundled (one bundle per seat) and sequenced by a daily schedule so that the material can be brought in as needed. When the seats are finished, they are temporarily stored on-site. This storage is used to consolidate loads and to ensure that the loads are correctly sequenced (i.e., the first seats needed are loaded last, the last seats are loaded first). When a load is completed, it is shipped by truck to the Warren plant.

How successful is the Romulus plant? In recent years the plant has turned its inventory in excess of 200 times each year.

Questions

1. What elements define value for the customers of the Romulus plant?
2. What is the role of logistics and logistics considerations in the success of the Romulus plant? In your answer, focus on such issues as information processing, warehousing, mode of transportation, and network design.

SELECTED READINGS & INTERNET SITES

The major professional association for logistics professionals is the Council of Supply Chain Management Professionals. Visit the Web site at **www.cscmp.org**

Many excellent up-to-date articles and case studies can be found at the following Web sites:

www.logisticsmgmt.com

www.scdigest.com

www.supplychainbrain.com

Bowersox, D. J.; D. J. Closs; M. B. Cooper; and J. C. Bowersox. *Supply Chain Logistics Management,* 4th edition. New York: McGraw-Hill, 2013.

Closs, David J.; Cheri Speier; and Nathan Meacham. "Sustainability to Support End-to-End Value Chains: The Role of Supply Chain Management." *Journal of the Academy of Marketing Science* 39, no. 1 (2011), pp. 101–16.

Closs, David, et al. "A Framework for Protecting Your Supply Chain." *Supply Chain Management Review* (March–April 2008).

Golicic, Susan; Courtney Boerstler; and Lisa Ellram. "Greening the Transportation in Your Supply Chain." *MIT Sloan Management Review* 51, no. 2 (2010), pp. 47–55.

Lynch, C. F. *Logistics Outsourcing: A Management Guide,* 2nd edition. Memphis: CFL Publishing, 2004.

Schulz, John D. "Trucking Game Changing Movement." *Supply Chain Management Review* (May–June 2010), pp. 56–66.

Stock, J.; T. Speh; and H. Shear. "Many Happy (product) Returns." *Harvard Business Review* 80, no. 7 (2002), p. 16.

PART 4

PLANNING FOR INTEGRATED OPERATIONS ACROSS THE SUPPLY CHAIN

		relationships	sustainability	global
12	Demand Planning: Forecasting and Demand Management	X		X
13	Sales and Operations Planning	X	X	X
14	Materials and Resource Requirements Planning	X		X

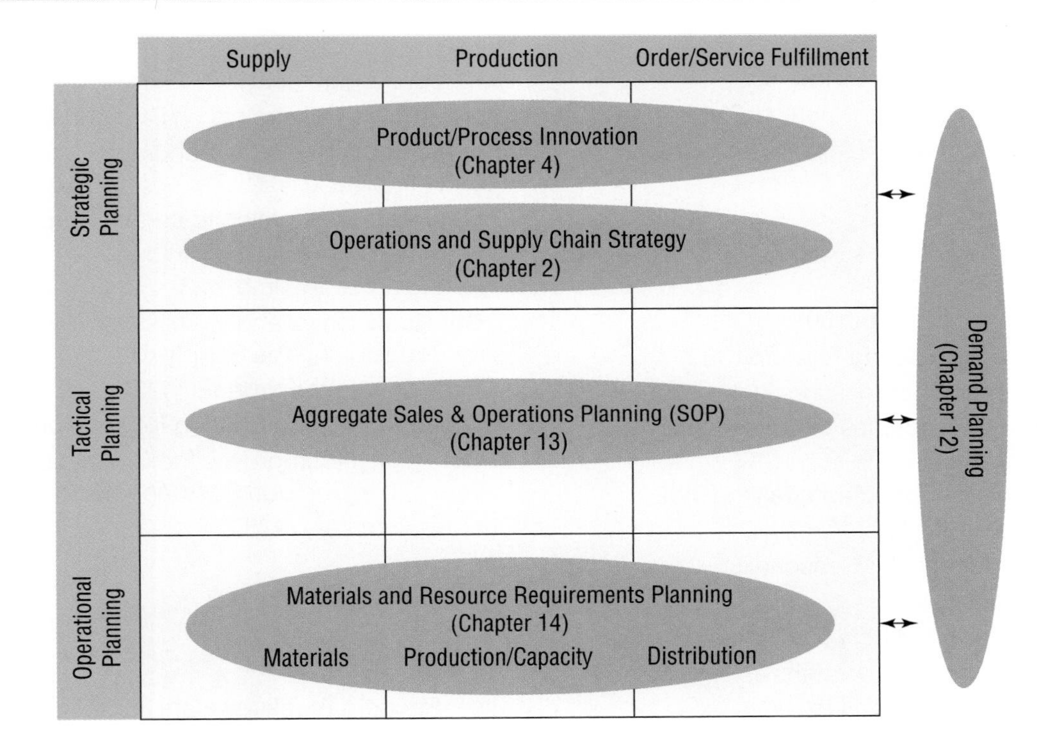

How do operations managers make sure that they have the right products at the right place at the right time?* Surely you have heard the adage, "If you fail to plan, you plan to fail." Part 4, *Planning for Integrated Operations Across the Supply Chain,* explains how operations managers develop resource plans and put them in place. As the figure above indicates, planning typically takes place at three levels: strategic (long term) planning, tactical (medium term) planning, and operational (short term) planning. At each level the primary goal is to ensure that capacity (the amount and types of resources available) is enough to satisfy demand. While this may sound simple, many planning processes at different levels must be coordinated, creating a hierarchy of decisions as shown in the figure above.

Because strategic planning decisions were covered in Part 2, this part of the book addresses tactical and operational planning. **Chapter 12** explains processes used to forecast and to manage (influence) customer demand. This topic comes first because demand planning is the starting point for all the other types of planning. **Chapter 13** describes tactical planning, used to identify customer demands for aggregate product families, and to establish the inventory and capacity plans needed to satisfy these overall demands. **Chapter 14** discusses planning processes for the short term, addressing the most detailed levels of inventory and resources. These chapters will introduce you to several collaborative planning processes such as CPFR and S&OP. These types of processes help ensure that all the needed inputs from customers, suppliers, and internal operational functions are integrated to create effective and efficient plans for all supply chain partners.

12 Demand Planning: Forecasting and Demand Management

CHAPTER OUTLINE

LEARNING OBJECTIVES *After studying this chapter, you should be able to:*

LO12-1 Explain the role of demand planning in operations management, in the firm, and in the supply chain.

LO12-2 Differentiate between demand planning, demand forecasting, and demand management activities.

LO12-3 Describe various qualitative and quantitative demand forecasting procedures.

LO12-4 Develop forecasts using moving average, exponential smoothing, and linear regression models.

LO12-5 Evaluate and select forecasting models using various measures of accuracy and bias.

LO12-6 Explain how certain improvements to both product design and operations across the supply chain can make demand planning easier.

Demand Forecasting Excellence Gives Longaberger an Advantage

The Longaberger Company (www.longaberger.com) is known primarily for its high-quality baskets—still handmade—just like when the company was born in 1918. In recent years Longaberger has experienced phenomenal growth; quite a feat considering the challenges of competing in the home decorating industry. Demand planning in general, and sales forecasting in particular, are usually quite tough for a fast-growing company with a complex set of continually changing product lines. Since these are "fashion" items subject to changing trends and customer tastes, it is often difficult to judge which products will be fast sellers and which will be slow. Moreover, keeping track of pricing changes and promotional programs can be a complex planning task.

Forecasting processes at Longaberger must consider many different factors, including the growth strategy of the company, seasonal and holiday demand patterns, and both regular and irregular promotional events. The forecasting approach used at Longaberger addresses these factors by integrating three sources of information: historical sales trends and seasonal patterns; economic data quantifying market, sales, and environmental conditions; and the qualitative judgmental expertise of managers.

For Longaberger, the key to forecasting success has not been to simply pick the "right" statistical analysis method, but rather to develop an integrated system of techniques that helps managers accurately plan for future demand. Forecasts generated by the system drive all kinds of production, procurement, and capacity management plans. Ultimately, the accuracy and insights provided by the demand planning system have been instrumental in helping the Longaberger Company to give customers the products they want, when they want them.

Prepare

What is demand planning and how does it drive other operations management planning activities?

Organize

DEMAND PLANNING: AN OVERVIEW

Almost all operational planning activities start with some estimate of what customers' demands will be. In order to develop demand estimates, every company has to forecast both the quantity and timing of demands, and many companies can also influence or "manage" customers' demand patterns through product pricing and through other means. These two activities, demand forecasting and demand management, are collectively known as *demand planning.*

Demand planning is the combined process of forecasting and managing customer demands to create a planned pattern of demand that meets the firm's operational and financial goals. **Demand forecasting** is a decision process in which managers predict demand patterns, whereas **demand management** is a proactive approach in which managers attempt to influence patterns of demand. Usually, demand management involves the use of pricing and promotional activities.

LO12-1 Explain the role of demand planning in operations management, in the firm, and in the supply chain.

demand planning The combined process of forecasting and managing customer demands to create a planned pattern of demand that meets the firm's operational and financial goals.

demand forecasting A decision process in which managers predict demand patterns.

demand management A proactive approach in which managers attempt to influence the pattern of demand.

By doing a good job of demand planning, operations managers can more effectively plan for the amount of productive capacity and other resources their business will need, both in the short term and in the long term. Demand planning also helps operations managers know what customers they should serve and at what levels of service. Demand planning is especially difficult when products have highly varying and uncertain demand patterns. Precisely because it is so difficult, companies like Longaberger have built competitive advantages as a result of their superior abilities.

The Role That Demand Planning Plays in Operations Management

Demand planning drives almost all other activities in operations management. For many tangible products, making products to order is not an option. The lead time required is longer than customers are willing to wait. For example, you probably would not be willing to wait for a company to build a toaster oven from scratch for you. Consequently, managers have to anticipate demand and plan what materials and resources they will need well in advance of actual orders. In order to make these production plans, managers need to make good predictions of the quantities of products that will be demanded at a given time and place. Accurate planning information has many benefits, and there are severe costs to being wrong. The costs of making forecasts that are too high include money lost in holding inventory that is never sold, lost capacity that is spent making products that no one wants to buy, lost wages spent paying workers who are not needed, and so on. These costs are borne by firms throughout the supply chain, but they are also passed on to customers in the form of higher prices. Similarly, costs of making forecasts that are too low include lost sales and lowered product availability for customers.

Planning Activities

LO12-2 Differentiate between demand planning, demand forecasting, and demand management activities.

Figure 12-1 illustrates how demand forecasting and demand management activities relate to one another, and to other operational planning activities. Forecasting activities integrate information gathered from the market, from internal operations, and from the larger business environment to make predictions about future demand. This information includes past demand, past forecasts and their associated errors, business and economic metrics, and the judgments of experts. In addition, the forecasting system uses demand management plans that specify the firm's pricing strategies and promotional plans. By combining all of these factors, the forecasting system creates new forecasts of future demand. The demand management system in turn uses these forecasts as inputs for future demand management planning. In addition, the forecasts and demand management plans are passed on to materials and capacity planning and scheduling systems. These systems are used to manage resources and operating processes.

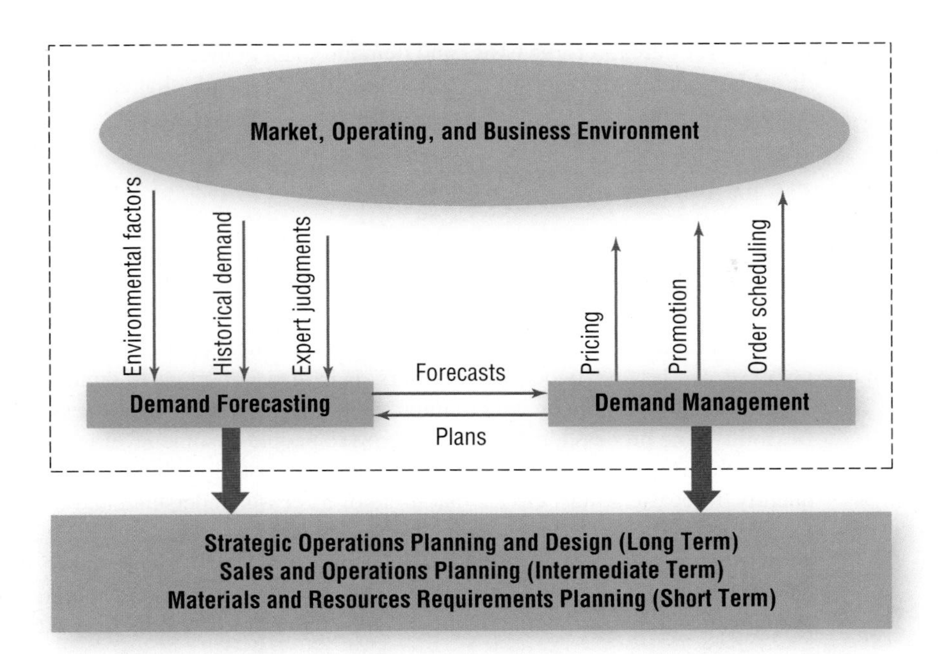

FIGURE 12-1 Elements of Demand Planning

Table 12-1 describes the types of demand planning that support various levels of operational planning across the supply chain.[1] In this chapter we will explore different

TABLE 12-1 Demand Planning for Different Time Horizons

Time Horizon/Type of Planning	Demand Planning Units	Uses of Forecasts and Demand Management Plans	Types of Decisions Involved
Long term/strategic: 1–5 years Discussed in Chapters 2 and 4	Total dollar or unit sales for a business unit across the sales network	–Supply chain network design –Technology investments –Capacity planning (investments or divestments)	–Find new sources of supply –Build or sell a plant –Contract for transportation services –Open or close new service location
Intermediate term/ tactical: 6–18 months Discussed in Chapter 13	Total dollar or unit sales for a product family in a region	–Sales and operational planning –Product portfolio planning	–Aggregate production plans –Employee hiring and firing –Planned overtime work –Subcontracting –New product launches
Short term/operational materials and resources: 1–12 weeks Discussed in Chapter 14	Dollar or unit sales for a given item or service at a given location	–Inventory planning –Purchasing plans –Labor scheduling	–Daily production schedule –Daily work schedule –Purchase orders

[1]We will discuss different levels of operational planning in more detail in Chapter 13, "Sales and Operations Planning."

Prepare

How do operations managers design an effective forecasting process? What different types of forecasting models exist?

Organize

Demand Forecasting
- Components of Demand
- Designing a Forecasting Process
- Judgment-Based Forecasting
- Statistical Model-Based Forecasting
- Estimating Trends
- Causal Models
- Adjusting Forecasts for Seasonality
- Simulation Models

methods for demand forecasting and demand management. In addition, we describe sources of uncertainty in demand planning and what can be done to reduce them.

DEMAND FORECASTING

In this section, we discuss the objectives and techniques of demand forecasting. It is important to think of forecasting as a process, rather than simply as a technique or a model. The process should be sophisticated enough to achieve acceptable levels of forecast accuracy, but simple enough so that steps involved can be understood by the users. It is also important to continually improve the forecasting process to improve its accuracy, user-friendliness, and flexibility. The process almost always involves people at some level who may lack sophisticated knowledge of statistics and forecasting techniques. Consequently, forecasters must ensure that users of forecasts understand and accept the underlying logic of the system. Then users will have the confidence and knowledge to use forecasting processes intelligently. As is suggested in the Get Real box about the 1948 presidential election, faulty forecasts can create skepticism among users, and possibly even embarrassment for the forecasters.

Components of Demand

Most forecasting techniques seek to uncover patterns in demand and to extrapolate them to the future. Figure 12-2 shows common demand patterns. These patterns suggest that some systematic forces are influencing the data. The forecasting objective is to uncover and describe the processes generating these time series patterns. A demand pattern is typically made up of different component processes that work together.

stable pattern A consistent horizontal stream of demands.

seasonality and cycles Regular demand patterns of repeating highs and lows.

A **stable pattern** is a consistent horizontal stream of demands. Mature consumer products, for example shampoo or milk, often exhibit this type of pattern.

Seasonality and cycles are regular patterns of repeating highs and lows. Seasonality may be daily, weekly, monthly, or even longer. For example, restaurants experience seasonal

GET REAL

The *Tribune*'s Famous Fallacious Forecast

Forecasting problems are not new, and not unique to any given area of business. In 1948, the *Chicago Tribune* tried to scoop its competitors by conducting a telephone survey in order to predict the outcome of the presidential election. Based on those results, the paper's editors ran an election day special proclaiming "Dewey Wins." When a final count reviewed that Democrat Harry S. Truman had defeated Republican Thomas Dewey, the misfortunes experienced by the *Chicago Tribune* taught the world two lessons. The first is the danger of basing forecasts on inaccurate information sources. The survey's sampling plan ignored the bias introduced by telephone polling—more Republicans than Democrats owned telephones. The second and more important lesson was that it is always important to consider the consequences of forecast errors. Since perfect forecasts don't exist, one should always consider the cost of being wrong.

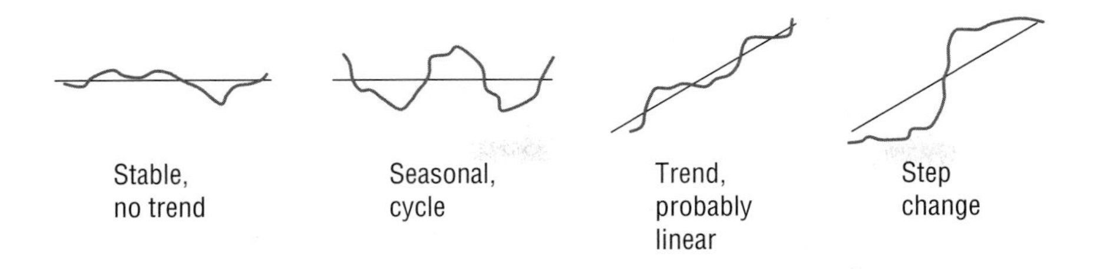

FIGURE 12-2
Patterns in Demand

patterns during the day with peaks for breakfast, lunch, and dinner. Banks typically experience a monthly seasonal pattern with peaks coinciding with company pay periods. Economic, political, demographic, and technological factors influence these patterns.

A **trend** identifies the general sloping tendency of demand, either upward or downward, in a linear or nonlinear fashion. New products in the growth phase of the life cycle typically exhibit an upward, nonlinear trend.

A **shift or step change** in demand is a one-time change, usually due to some external influence on demand such as a major product promotional campaign.

Autocorrelation describes the relationship of current demand with past demand. If values of demand at any given time are highly correlated with demand values from the recent past, then we say that the demand is highly *autocorrelated.*

Forecast error is simply the "unexplained" component of demand that seems to be random in nature. If the straight line in each panel of Figure 12-2 represents the forecast and the curved line represents the actual demand, then the differences between these lines are the forecast errors.

A good forecasting process acquires and analyzes information inputs in ways that address all of the relevant components of demand, while not overreacting to random changes in demand. If successful in this way, then the forecasting process will produce smaller errors.

trend The general sloping tendency of demand, either upward or downward, in a linear or nonlinear fashion.

shift or step change A one-time change in demand, usually due to some external influence on demand.

autocorrelation The correlation of current demand values with past demand values.

forecast error The difference between a forecast and the actual demand.

Designing a Forecasting Process

A forecasting process attempts to understand the various components of demand so that it can convert data inputs into reliable predictions of future events. As Figure 12-3 on the next page illustrates, the forecasting process often combines statistical data with judgments from knowledgeable sources. The sources of data and judgment may include information systems and experts both inside and outside the company. For example, suppliers and product distributors often can provide excellent information regarding overall market and sales trends. The primary goal in designing a forecasting process is to generate forecasts that are usable, timely, and accurate. The following five steps can help managers achieve this goal.

1. *Identify the users and decision-making processes that the forecast will support.* The forecasting process needs to be designed with the following users' characteristics and needs in mind:

   Time horizon. The forecasting process should suit the period of time over which the user's current actions will affect future business performance. Most important is the lead time required to implement decisions influenced by the forecast. For example, if a production system requires an eight-week lead time, then a product demand forecast should cover a period of no less than eight weeks.

   Level of detail. Forecasts can be generated for an individual product, for an entire product family, or even for an entire business or industry. Similarly, forecasted demand could be for a location, a country, a region, or worldwide. Levels of detail and time horizon characteristics are usually related (as shown in Table 12-1). It is important for forecasters to understand the levels of product and geographic detail that are needed by users of the forecasts.

   Accuracy versus cost. Greater accuracy usually requires greater effort and greater forecast system sophistication. It is important to weigh the costs created by forecast errors against the costs of achieving greater accuracy.

FIGURE 12-3 The Forecasting Process

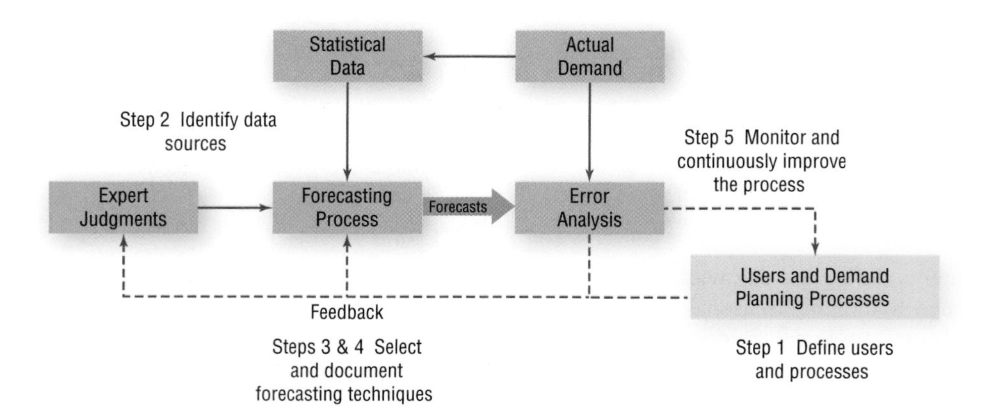

Fit with existing business processes. In order for it to be useful, the forecasting process must be integrated into other business processes. For example, as much as possible the data for forecasts should come from collection processes that already exist. Also, the logic used to generate forecasts must be easily understood by the users. People are not likely to trust forecasting approaches that they don't understand.

2. *Identify likely sources of the best data inputs.* Today's information-rich environment typically provides numerous sources of information, including all kinds of experts, corporate records (past sales, promotion programs), the Internet, the government (for information on the state of the economy), suppliers, and sellers of sales and customer databases. It is important to identify the potential drivers of demand (marketing personnel are good at this) and then find data that best represent those drivers. For example, consumer confidence and feelings of personal wealth are drivers of purchases of luxury items (such as diamonds). Governments usually report disposable income and consumer confidence numbers that can be used as leading indicators of luxury purchases.
3. *Select forecasting techniques that will most effectively transform data into timely, accurate forecasts over the appropriate planning horizon.* In short-term planning for stable demand environments, forecasters can usually create suitable forecasts using only simple statistical models based on historical demand. More volatile and longer-term planning situations usually require multiple inputs including judgments, historical data, and leading indicator data. In this case, forecasting approaches also need to be more flexible or adaptive. Forecasters have access to many simple to use software programs that automate most of the tedious calculations and data management aspects of collecting and combining inputs from various sources. Some programs enable the user to quickly evaluate many different forecasting models in order to select the best forecast according to user-input criteria.
4. *Document and apply the proposed technique to the data gathered for the appropriate business process.* The entire set of assumptions and steps included in the forecasting process should be well understood by all people involved. This enables the users to identify those conditions under which the forecasts are most and least applicable.
5. *Monitor the performance of the forecasting process for continuous improvement.* Forecasters should carefully track and study the accuracy of the forecasts and work with users to refine the forecasting process. Periodic reviews of the basic assumptions that underlie the forecasts help to keep the process on target for future forecasts.

In the following sections we briefly discuss some broad categories of forecasting techniques: judgment-based techniques that gather and use subjective inputs, statistical model-based techniques that use quantitative data, and techniques for assessing forecast error and providing feedback to the forecasting system.

Judgment-Based Forecasting

LO12-3 Describe various qualitative and quantitative demand forecasting procedures.

Judgment-based forecasts are built upon the estimates and opinions of people, most often experts who have related sales or operational experience. Judgment techniques seek to incorporate factors of demand that are difficult to capture in statistical models. This approach is useful when there is a lack of quantitative historical information; for example, when a new product is about to be launched. It is also useful when information about the past may not support good decisions for the future (underlying demand-generating processes have changed). For example, historical sales patterns could not forecast the drop in demand for trucks and SUVs when gasoline prices rose dramatically in 2008. The following judgment-based forecasting techniques are among the most common approaches.

Grassroots Forecasting

Grassroots forecasting is a technique that seeks inputs from people who are in close contact with customers and products. A marketing study, for example, might ask sales representatives for their sales estimates and comments on current market conditions in their respective sales areas. The Get Real box on the next page shows how Texas Instruments and Sport Obermeyer use grassroots forecasting. A major limitation of this technique is that "experts" may unconsciously base their forecasts on their most recent experiences, rather than the entire set of experiences. They also may adjust their forecasts because of other motivations. For example, a sales representative who is rewarded for exceeding sales goals is likely to understate future sales forecasts.

grassroots forecasting A technique that seeks inputs from people who are in close contact with customers and products.

Executive Judgment

While grassroots approaches are most useful for developing short-term forecasts for individual products, executives using their **executive judgment** are usually better equipped to make judgments regarding long-term sales or business patterns. High-level business managers have experience and access to sources of information upon which to base their judgments.

executive judgment Forecasting techniques that use input from high-level experienced managers.

Historical Analogy

The **historical analogy** approach to forecasting uses data and experience from similar products to forecast the demand for a new product. For example, when color television sets were first introduced, managers used sales patterns for black-and-white television sets to predict the life cycle stages for the new TVs. Economists use historical analogy extensively when forecasting business cycles and related developments.

historical analogy A forecasting technique that uses data and experience from similar products to forecast the demand for a new product.

Marketing Research

Marketing research bases forecasts on the purchasing patterns and attitudes of current or potential customers. Marketers have developed a wide range of tools for evaluating the purchasing patterns and attitudes of current or potential buyers of a product, including consumer surveys, interviews, and focus groups. A panel of knowledgeable people (often potential customers) can be convened to develop a forecast by engaging in an open dialogue over a relatively short period of time. This technique assumes that no single group or person is likely to have access to all of the key inputs in a demand-forecasting process.

marketing research A forecasting technique that bases forecasts on the purchasing patterns and attitudes of current or potential customers.

Delphi Method

The **Delphi method** develops forecasts by asking a panel of experts to individually respond to a series of questions. The forecaster compiles and analyzes the respondents' inputs and shares the data with the group. Once everyone has seen the collective responses, they are given the chance to revise their responses or to ask new questions. This question-answer-feedback process is repeated until a consensus is achieved that reflects input from all of the experts while preventing any single individual from dominating the process.

Delphi method Forecasts developed by asking a panel of experts to individually and repeatedly respond to a series of questions.

GET REAL

Two Examples of Grassroots Forecasting

Companies in two vastly different industries provide innovative approaches for gathering forecasts from employees on the operations front lines.

Managers at Texas Instruments developed an artificial "stock" market to solve the problem of extracting forecasts from sales representatives. The company issues securities to sales reps that represent different levels of product sales. Then, the sales reps can trade the securities so that they "invest" in securities representing their best guess of what actual product sales will be. At the end of the sales period, the value of the securities depends on the actual product sales. For example, if you sell pocket calculators and you expect next year's sales to be 800,000 units, you would try to buy securities denominated "800,000." You would want to unload any securities you have that are denominated "700,000" or "950,000" or other values, because you don't expect them to pay off. In this artificial market, if the "800,000" security ends up trading at the highest price, then forecasting managers use that number as the firm's best estimate of next year's calculator volume.

Sport Obermeyer, a designer and producer of ski apparel, uses an innovative grassroots approach to develop forecasts of sales for the items they offer each new season. The company invites retail store managers and sales associates from around the country to come "shop" at a simulated store located at headquarters containing all the new items. Each sales associate rates the desirability of each item using a seven-point scale. The ratings are then tabulated, and the items are ranked based on the average ratings. Managers then create sales forecasts by allocating the total sales estimate for a given category of items to the individual items in that category using a graduated scale based on past sales. For example, they know from experience that the top 10 most highly rated items in a category will account for a certain percentage of sales, the next 10 will account for a lower percentage of sales, and so on.

By using such approaches, companies like Texas Instruments and Sport Obermeyer are able to gather unbiased judgments from employees who interact with customers directly.

Statistical Model-Based Forecasting

LO12-4 Develop forecasts using moving average, exponential smoothing, and linear regression models.

Statistical model-based forecasting techniques transform numerical data into forecasts using one of three methods:

1. Time series analyses, which extrapolate forecasts from past demand data.
2. Causal studies, which look for causal relationships between leading variables and forecasted variables.
3. Simulation models, which try to represent past phenomena in mathematical relationships and then evaluate data to project future outcomes.

Table 12-2 provides a comparison of the requirements needed to implement the different techniques.

Time Series Analysis Models

time series analysis models
Forecasting models that compute forecasts using historical data arranged in the order of occurrence.

Time series analysis models compute forecasts using historical data arranged in the order of occurrence. Forecasting models that are based only on a series of past demands assume that a demand pattern of the past will continue in the future. Thus, if some new event changes the underlying drivers of demand, then these models will not work well. Forecasts are generated by summing weighted values of past demands, and the weighting schemes range from very simple to very complex. The type of weighting used depends upon the demand pattern. For example, with a stable demand pattern, the simplest time

TABLE 12-2 Comparing Different Statistical Forecasting Methods

Forecasting Method	Amount of Historical Data	Data Pattern	Forecast Horizon	Preparation Time	Personnel Background
Time series: Moving average and exponential smoothing based methods	10 to 15 observations to set the parameters	Stable, trend and seasonality	Short	Short	Little to moderate sophistication
Time series: Regression	10 to 20; for seasonality at least 5 per season	Trend and seasonality	Short to medium	Short	Moderate sophistication
Causal modeling	10 observations per each independent variable	Complex patterns	Short, medium, or long	Long development time, short time for implementation	Considerable sophistication
Simulation models and focused forecasting	50 or more observations	Distributions of demand-creating processes must be approximated	Medium or long	Long	High sophistication

series forecasting model is a **naïve model**, which simply assumes that tomorrow's demand will be the same as today's. For example, if on a given day a restaurant served 55 customers, managers might expect to serve 55 customers on the following day as well. While this simple approach is sometimes effective, it ignores the trend, seasonal, or other components of the historical time series, and it creates highly erratic forecasts if these components or random variations are present. For this reason, most time series models use multiple values of past demands. For example, a restaurant manager might want to use a weighted average of daily demand over a week as a better forecast of tomorrow's demand. The following sections discuss two simple time series models, *moving average* and *simple exponential smoothing,* that are used when demand patterns are stable.

naïve model A simple forecasting approach that assumes that recent history is a good predictor of the near future.

Moving Average Models

One way to create forecasts that reflect changes in demand while dampening or smoothing out erratic movements is to forecast future demand as a simple average of past demand values. This model is used when the demand pattern is relatively stable, without trend or seasonality. A **moving average** forecasting model computes a forecast as the average of demands over a number of immediate past periods (n), as shown in equation (12.1).

moving average A forecasting model that computes a forecast as the average of demands over a number of immediate past periods.

(12.1)
$$F_{t+1} = \frac{d_t + d_{t-1} + d_{t-2} + \ldots + d_{t-n}}{n}$$

where:

F_{t+1} is the forecast for the next period
d_t is the demand from the most recent period
n is the number of periods used to compute the moving average

To use the moving average forecasting model, the forecaster must decide upon the number of past periods (n) to use. Increasing the number of periods (n) reduces the impact of random or atypical demands in isolated time periods, but it also reduces the sensitivity of the moving average to actual shifts in demand. Figure 12-4 compares the forecasts that

EXAMPLE 12-1

Suppose the manager of an ice cream store is trying to forecast the pounds of ice cream that they will sell based on what they have sold in the past four days. Recent actual sales numbers are:

Day	Sales (in lbs)
Sunday	137.1
Monday	123.6
Tuesday	134.9
Wednesday	160.0
Thursday	140.4

A four-day moving average forecast of Friday's demand would be computed as follows:

$$F_{\text{Friday}} = \frac{123.6 + 134.9 + 160.0 + 140.4}{4} = 139.7 \text{ lbs}$$

Suppose that the actual sales on Friday turns out to be 135.0 lbs. Then, the forecast for Saturday would be:

$$F_{\text{Saturday}} = \frac{134.9 + 160.0 + 140.4 + 135.0}{4} = 142.5 \text{ lbs}$$

would be created over time using moving average models with different values of *n*. Note that a smaller value of *n* produces forecasts that are more sensitive to changes in demand, while larger values tend to smooth out demand changes.

weighted moving average
A forecasting model that assigns a different weight to each period's demand according to its importance.

An adjustment to the moving average model that is sometimes used for stable demand patterns is a **weighted moving average** model. This model assigns a different weight to each period's demand according to its importance, for example, giving more recent periods

FIGURE 12-4
Comparing Moving Average Forecasting Models

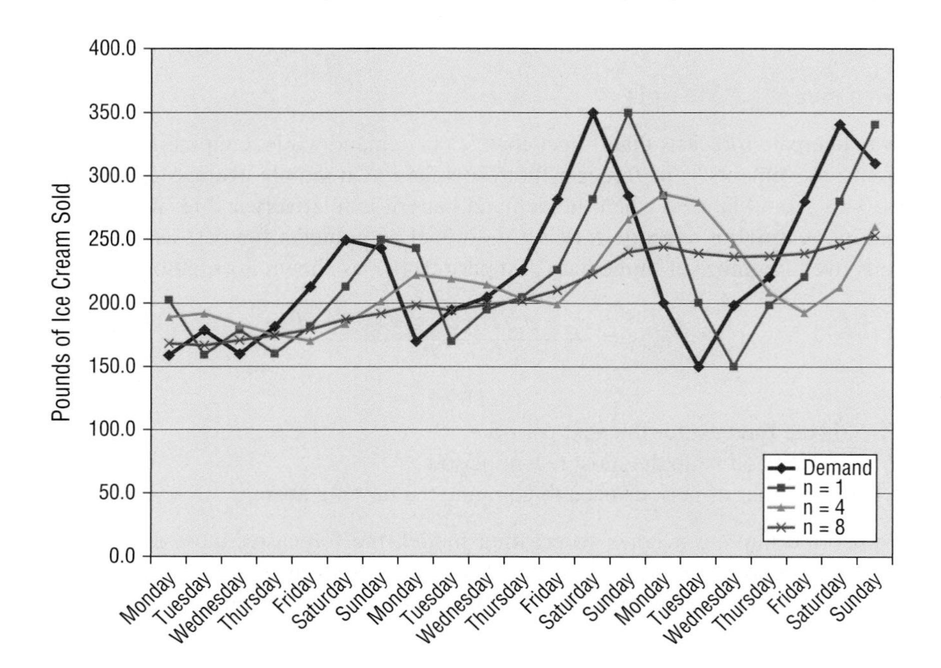

more importance than the earlier periods. Typically, more weight is given to more recent demand, because this is thought to capture market effects that are more relevant to the current demand situation.

The equation for a weighted moving average model is

(12.2) $$F_{t+1} = a_t d_t + a_{t-1} d_{t-1} + a_{t-2} d_{t-2} + \ldots + a_{t-n} d_{t-n}$$

where:

a_t is the weight given to the demand value in period t (the sum of all a_t should equal 1)

EXAMPLE 12-2

Continuing the ice cream store example from Example 12-1, let's assume the following weights:

Day	Weight
4 days ago	0.1
3 days ago	0.2
2 days ago	0.2
Yesterday	0.5

Total	1.0

Using the weighted moving average model, the forecasts for Friday and Saturday are

$$F_{Friday} = (.1)\ 123.6 + (.2)\ 134.9 + (.2)160.0 + (.5)\ 140.4 = 141.5 \text{ lbs}$$

$$F_{Saturday} = (.1)\ 134.9 + (.2)\ 160.0 + (.2)140.4 + (.5)\ 135.0 = 141.1 \text{ lbs}$$

Notice that Saturday's forecast is lower than Friday's forecast, yet in Example 12-1 Saturday's forecast was higher than Friday's forecast. This difference in results is because the weighted moving average puts more emphasis on recent demand, and demand has decreased in the last couple of days.

Exponential Smoothing

Another time series model used for stable demand patterns assigns weights to a moving average calculation in a systematic way; it is known as **exponential smoothing**. In this approach, an exponentially smaller weight is applied to each demand that occurred farther back in time. Each weight is a certain percentage smaller than the weight assigned to demand data for the previous period. The exponential smoothing model is shown in equation (12.3).

exponential smoothing A moving average approach that applies exponentially decreasing weights to each demand that occurred farther back in time.

(12.3) $$F_{t+1} = \alpha\, d_t + (1 - \alpha)\, F_t$$

where α is a constant between 0 and 1, called the **smoothing coefficient**. The forecast for a given period is a linear combination of the most recent subsequent period's result, d_{t-1}, and the forecast for that period, F_{t-1}. For example, suppose that a manager uses a forecasting model with a smoothing coefficient to $\alpha = 0.1$. This model will create a new forecast by adding one-tenth of last period's demand plus nine-tenths of last period's forecast.

smoothing coefficient A parameter indicating the weight given to the most recent demand.

By rearranging the terms, equation (12.3) can be rewritten as:

(12.4) $$F_{t+1} = F_t + \alpha\, (d_t - F_t)$$

In equation (12.4), the term $d_t - F_t$, is the *forecast error* (recall that we defined this earlier in the chapter). This new way of looking at the exponential smoothing model states that the new forecast is equal to the prior forecast, plus an adjustment to account for the forecast error from the last period. For example, if last period's forecast was too high, then the forecast error will be negative, and the new forecast will be adjusted downward. Later in this chapter, we show other ways that forecast errors can be monitored and used to improve the forecasting process.

EXAMPLE 12-3

Returning to our ice cream example, let's say that actual sales for a given day totaled 115 pounds, while the forecast for that day was 110 pounds. With a smoothing constant of 0.10, the next day's forecast is

$$F_{t+1} = 110 + (0.1)(115 - 110) = 110.5 \text{ lbs.}$$

Note that the new forecast is slightly higher than the previous forecast, owing to the fact that our last forecast was 5 pounds too low. But the new forecast is only *slightly* higher. This is because we aren't putting much weight (only 0.1) on the most recent demand data. Using an $\alpha = 0.9$ would produce a forecast of 114.5, a value much closer to the recent actual demand. Thus, the higher the value of the smoothing coefficient, the greater the weight placed on most recent actual demand value. Figure 12-5 shows the increasing sensitivity of forecasts when alpha is increased.

Moving forward one day, now let's say that the actual sales for period $t + 1$ was 107 pounds. The forecast for the next day would be:

$$F_{t+2} = 110.5 + (0.1)(107 - 110.5) = 110.2$$

By using the exponential smoothing equation again and again from one period to the next, each new forecast is implicitly built upon many past actual demands, each of which receives less and less weight as one goes back in time. This is because each past forecast (F_t in the equation) is itself a function of prior demands. In this way, the exponential smoothing approach is really just a sophisticated form of the weighted moving average model.

Figures 12-4 and 12-5 illustrate the fact that even the most sensitive simple exponential smoothing and moving average models are still only reactive; they do not *anticipate* the effects of a trend, or any seasonal or cyclical variations in demand. When such variations are present, the forecast will lag the actual demand time series. The forecaster can reduce the lag effect by increasing the value of α or reducing the n, but this also increases the risk of adding unwanted variability to forecasts as they overreact to random variations in demand. As a remedy to this problem, there are a number of enhancements that can be made to exponential smoothing models that make them more anticipative of trends and seasonal effects, and more reactive to major shifts in demand patterns.

Estimating Trends

Exponential Smoothing with Trend Effects

Early users of the exponential smoothing model soon started to augment the simple model to accommodate trend and other components of demand in a more predictive way. The following equations show how to change each period's forecast to include an adjustment for a known trend:

(12.5) $$FIT_{t+1} = F_{t+1} + T_{t+1}$$

(12.6) $$F_{t+1} = FIT_t + \alpha (d_t - FIT_t)$$

(12.7) $$T_{t+1} = T_t + \beta (F_{t+1} - FIT_t)$$

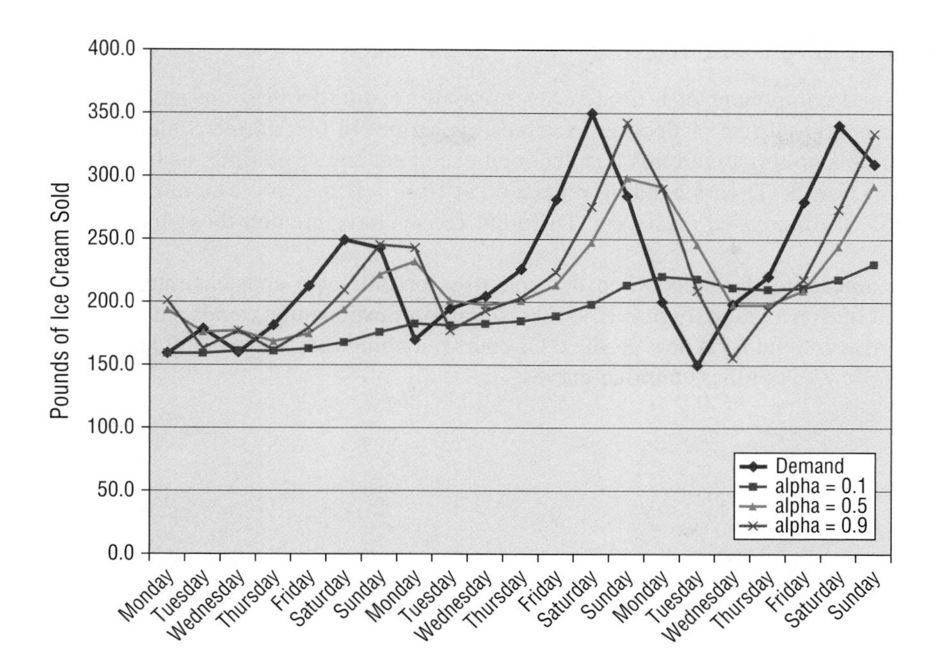

FIGURE 12-5
Comparing Exponential Smoothing Models

where:

FIT_t = the forecast including trend for period t
F_t = the "base" forecast for period t from the simple exponential smoothing model
T_t = the forecast of the trend component of demand for period t
α = the base smoothing coefficient
β = the trend smoothing coefficient

Equation (12.5) is simply the sum of the forecasts for the base and trend components of demand respectively. Equations (12.6) and (12.7) are used together to compute the new smoothed forecasts for the base and trend components.

EXAMPLE 12-4

As an example of using the exponential smoothing model with trend effects, assume that the forecast for the last period is $FIT_t = 250$ units, and recent experience suggests a likely sales increase of 10 units each period. Actual sales for the last period reached 270 units. Assuming a smoothing coefficient of $\alpha = 0.20$ and a trend smoothing coefficient of $\beta = 0.10$, the forecast for the next period is given by

$$F_{t+1} = FIT_t + \alpha(d_t - FIT_t) = 250 + 0.20\,(270 - 250) = 254$$

$$T_{t+1} = T_t + \beta(F_{t+1} - FIT_t) = 10 + 0.10\,(254 - 250) = 10 + 0.4 = 10.4$$

$$FIT_{t+1} = F_{t+1} + T_{t+1} = 254 + 10.4 = 264.4$$

If the demand in period $t + 1$ turned out to be 260, then the forecast for period $t + 2$ would be

$$F_{t+2} = 264.4 + 0.20\,(260 - 264.4) = 263.52$$

$$T_{t+2} = 10.4 + 0.10\,(263.52 - 264.4) = 10.4 - 0.088 = 10.31$$

$$FIT_{t+2} = 263.52 + 10.31 = 273.8$$

Determining Trend Factors

The trend component of a time series normally results from some market force that causes a general rise or decline in values over time. In the United States, the number of people smoking cigarettes has declined each year for some time, as has the number of 1980 Ford LTD cars needing replacement front left fenders. The number of people over 65 has increased each year. Different causes have created these long-term trend effects.

A linear trend results when demand rises or falls at a constant rate, describing a straight line on a graph. Figure 12-6 shows graphs of exponential trends and the traditional sales growth trend for a new product. Of course, nothing dictates that any long-term trend must follow any of these familiar curves.

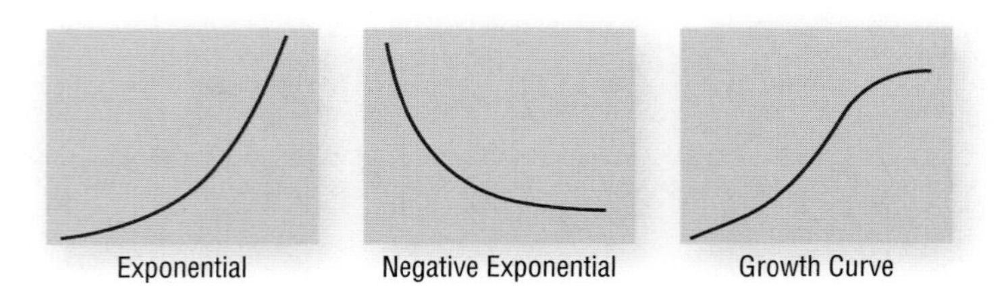

FIGURE 12-6 Common Nonlinear Trends

To estimate a trend, the forecaster should begin by graphing the data. Many times forecasters can make a good approximation of a trend by simply hand-drawing a line through the data. You will recall that the equation for a line is

$$d_t = a + b * t \tag{12.8}$$

where:

d_t = demand value for period t
t = number of periods from the origin
a = y-axis intercept of the line
b = slope of the line.

Simple Linear Regression: Time Series

regression analysis A mathematical approach for fitting an equation to a set of data.

Regression analysis is the most commonly used method for estimating relationships between leading indicators and demand. Simple linear regression is a technique that finds "optimal" values for the parameters a and b shown in equation (12.8), that is, parameters that will most closely equate the independent variable, t, and the dependent variable, d_t over a set of values. More specifically, simple linear regression computes values of a and b that minimize the expression

$$\sum_{t=1}^{t=n} (d_t - F_t)^2 \tag{12.9}$$

where:

d_t = actual demand value for period t
F_t = forecasted demand from the regression equation for period t

Recall that $d_t - F_t$ is the forecast error. Linear regression seeks to minimize the sum of the squared errors between the actual values of demand and the values of demand predicted by the straight line. For this reason, it is also known as least-squares regression. The linear regression formulas for values of a and b are

(12.10)
$$b = \frac{\sum_{t=1}^{t=n} td_t - n\bar{t} * \bar{d}_t}{\sum_{t=1}^{t=n} t^2 - n\bar{t}^2}$$

(12.11)
$$a = \bar{d}_t - b\bar{t}$$

where:

$\bar{t}$ = of all t values
$\bar{d}_t$ = of all d_t values
n = number of data points

Equations (12.10) and (12.11) use past demand values to compute the parameters a and b for the regression model. Most spreadsheet programs have functions that will automatically calculate regression parameters given a set of values for t and d_t.

EXAMPLE 12-5

Table 12-3 on the next page illustrates the calculations needed to specify a linear regression model using example data.

Using the linear regression formulae, the slope and the intercept are

$$b = [17{,}785.1 - (16)(8.5)(127)]/[1{,}496 - (16)(8.5)^2] = 1.5 \text{ per period}$$

$$a = (127) - (1.5)(8.5) = 114.2$$

The trend for the data given in our example is 1.5 units per period. The forecaster could use this trend value as the starting trend value in an exponential smoothing forecasting model. Alternatively, the forecaster might choose to use the regression model itself to make forecasts. Combining our parameter estimates, we get the following as the linear formula for the forecasted demand in each period:

$$F_t = a + bt = 114.2 + 1.5{*}t$$

The forecasts for the next few periods are then

$$F_{17} = 114.2 + 1.5{*}17 = 139.8$$

$$F_{18} = 114.2 + 1.5{*}18 = 141.8$$

$$F_{19} = 114.2 + 1.5{*}19 = 142.8$$

Adjusting Forecasts for Seasonality

Seasonal variations in demand can be estimated by applying a **seasonal index** to adjust forecast values for each seasonal time period. Remember, a "season" can occur daily, weekly, monthly, or in larger periods. The seasonal index is computed by dividing each period's actual demand by an estimate of the average (or base) demand across all periods in a complete seasonal cycle; that is, the average demand that would be expected if no seasonality existed. For example, if there are four periods in a complete seasonal cycle, then one would compute the average demand across the four periods in the cycle. Alternatively, the average demand can be estimated using a time series regression model, because it creates estimates of average demand all across the time horizon. Using the regression approach to estimate average demand is better if there is a trend in the demand. In either case, it is usually wise to compute and compare seasonal indexes over several seasonal cycles to ensure that the indexes are stable.

seasonal index An adjustment factor applied to forecasts to account for seasonal changes or cycles in demand.

TABLE 12-3 Example Linear Regression Calculation

	Period	Actual demand		
	t	d_t	$t * d_t$	t^2
	1	117.8	117.8	1
	2	117.1	234.2	4
	3	123.7	371.1	9
	4	117.1	468.4	16
	5	118.3	591.5	25
	6	129.2	775.2	36
	7	121	847	49
	8	127.9	1023.2	64
	9	123	1107	81
	10	129.8	1298	100
	11	125.9	1384.9	121
	12	129	1548	144
	13	136.6	1775.8	169
	14	130.8	1831.2	196
	15	141.8	2127	225
	16	142.8	2284.8	256
Total			**17785.1**	**1496**
Average	**8.5**	**127.0**		

EXAMPLE 12-6

Table 12-4 illustrates the procedure using data from the ice cream sales example. The actual daily sales for three weeks are divided by the forecasts from a simple regression model to obtain a seasonal index for each day. The regression model provides *deseasonalized* estimates of average demand; that is, estimates of demand that account for trend but remove seasonal influences. A daily seasonal index is estimated by averaging the values over all three weeks. For example, the seasonal index for Monday is the average across all three Mondays included in the data = (0.93 + 0.90 + 0.84)/3 = 0.89. As one might expect for ice cream sales, the indexes indicate that sales are above average (index > 1) on the weekends and below average (index < 1) on other days in the week.

Suppose that instead of using the regression estimates as the base for calculating the seasonal indexes, we used the average demand in each week as the base. Using this approach the seasonal indexes for week 1 would be

Average demand for week 1 = (123.6 + 135.0 + 160.0 + 140.4 + 187.9 + 195.0 + 171.8)/7 = 159.10

Seasonal indexes using demands for week 1:

Monday SI = 123.6 / 159.1 = 0.78

Tuesday SI = 135.0 / 159.1 = 0.85

Wednesday SI = 160.0 / 159.1 = 1.01

Thursday SI = 140.4 / 159.1 = 0.88

Friday SI = 187.9 / 159.1 = 1.18

Saturday SI = 195.0 / 159.1 = 1.23

Sunday SI = 171.8 / 159.1 = 1.08

TABLE 12-4 Calculating Seasonal Indexes Using Regression Estimates as the Base

		Actual Demand (a)	Average Demand Estimate (from regression) (b)	Seasonal Index SI = a/b	Three Week Average Indexes
Week 1	Monday	123.6	132.9	0.93	Average SI for Mondays = 0.89
	Tuesday	135.0	137.0	0.98	Average SI for Tuesdays = 0.90
	Wednesday	160.0	141.1	1.13	Average SI for Wednesdays = 0.93
	Thursday	140.4	145.2	0.97	Average SI for Thursdays = 0.90
	Friday	187.9	149.3	1.26	Average SI for Fridays = 1.16
	Saturday	195.0	153.4	1.27	Average SI for Saturdays = 1.17
	Sunday	171.8	157.5	1.09	Average SI for Sundays = 1.10
Week 2	Monday	145.9	161.5	0.90	
	Tuesday	130.0	165.6	0.78	
	Wednesday	145.0	169.7	0.85	
	Thursday	147.2	173.8	0.85	
	Friday	214.2	177.9	1.20	
	Saturday	190.0	182.0	1.04	
	Sunday	202.1	186.1	1.09	
Week 3	Monday	159.0	190.1	0.84	
	Tuesday	178.7	194.2	0.92	
	Wednesday	160.0	198.3	0.81	
	Thursday	181.5	202.4	0.90	
	Friday	212.8	206.5	1.03	
	Saturday	249.4	210.6	1.18	
	Sunday	242.9	214.7	1.13	

Performing the same calculations for weeks 2 and 3, we can fill out Table 12-5 (on the next page).

Note that the seasonal indexes in Tables 12-4 and 12-5 are not exactly the same, but they are fairly close. Using the average demand each cycle as the base for calculating the seasonal index can be thought of as a looser approximation method than the regression approach. In practice, however, either approach can be effective.

(continued)

(continued)

TABLE 12-5 Calculating Seasonal Indexes Using Average Demand per Cycle as the Base

		Actual Demand (a)	Average Demand for Week (b)	Seasonal Index SI = a/b	Three Week Average Indexes
	Monday	123.6		0.78	Average SI for Mondays = 0.82
Week 1	Tuesday	135.0		0.85	Average SI for Tuesdays = 0.84
	Wednesday	160.0		1.01	Average SI for Wednesdays = 0.89
Week 1	Thursday	140.4	159.1	0.88	Average SI for Thursdays = 0.89
	Friday	187.9		1.18	Average SI for Fridays = 1.18
	Saturday	195.0		1.23	Average SI for Saturdays = 1.21
	Sunday	171.8		1.08	Average SI for Sundays = 1.17
	Monday	145.9		0.87	
	Tuesday	130.0		0.77	
	Wednesday	145.0		0.86	
Week 2	Thursday	147.2	167.8	0.88	
	Friday	214.2		1.28	
	Saturday	190.0		1.13	
	Sunday	202.1		1.20	
	Monday	159.0		0.80	
	Tuesday	178.7		0.90	
	Wednesday	160.0		0.81	
Week 3	Thursday	181.5	197.8	0.92	
	Friday	212.8		1.08	
	Saturday	249.4		1.26	
	Sunday	242.9		1.23	

TABLE 12-6 Seasonal Adjustments for Forecasts

		Forecasted Base Demand (from regression) (a)	Seasonal Index (b)	Adjusted Forecast a × b
	Monday	218.7	0.89	194.6
	Tuesday	222.8	0.90	200.5
	Wednesday	226.9	0.93	211.0
Week 4	Thursday	231.0	0.90	207.9
	Friday	235.1	1.16	272.7
	Saturday	239.2	1.17	279.9
	Sunday	243.3	1.10	267.6
	Monday	247.4	0.89	220.2
	Tuesday	251.4	0.90	226.3
	Wednesday	255.5	0.93	237.6

		Forecasted Base Demand (from regression) (a)	Seasonal Index (b)	Adjusted Forecast $a \times b$
Week 5	Thursday	259.6	0.90	233.6
	Friday	263.7	1.16	305.9
	Saturday	267.8	1.17	313.3
	Sunday	271.9	1.10	299.1

The next step is to use the average seasonal indexes to adjust the future forecasts. For example, regression based forecasts (the average demands) for the next two weeks (weeks 4 and 5) would be adjusted as shown in Table 12-6. We could use a method other than regression for generating the base demand; it is up to the forecaster to decide what method best approximates trends or other demand patterns that exist before seasonal impacts.

Figure 12-7 shows the forecasts for weeks 3, 4, and 5 of the time series. Compare this to the forecasts shown in Figure 12-5. The seasonally adjusted forecasts clearly do a better job of matching seasonal shifts in the demand pattern, where the forecasts shown back in Figure 12-5 lag the shifts by at least one period.

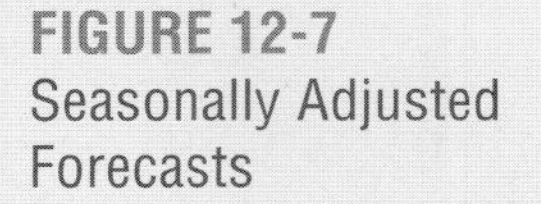

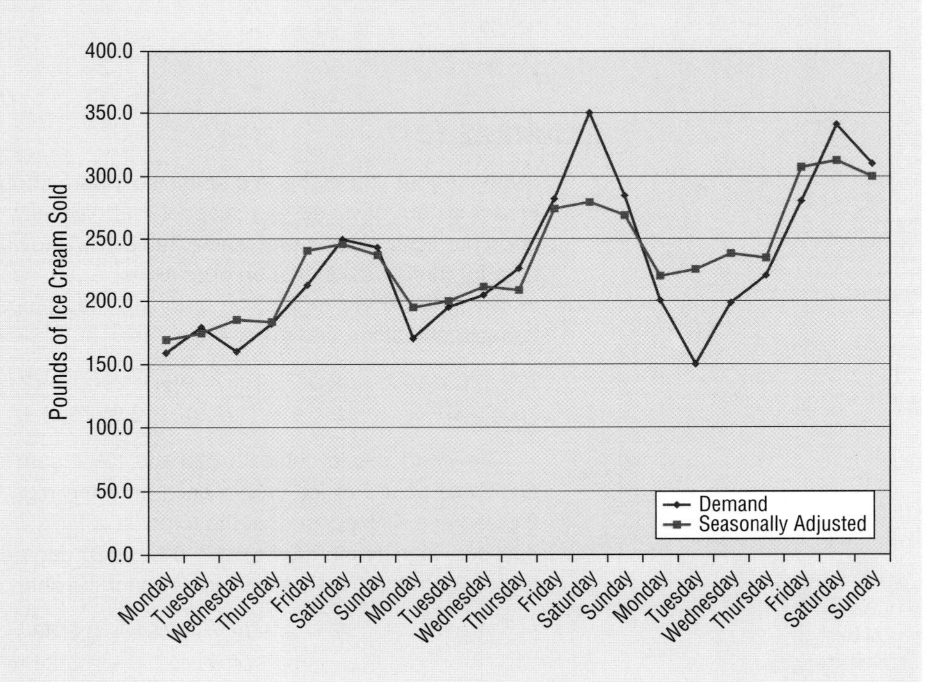

FIGURE 12-7
Seasonally Adjusted Forecasts

Causal Models

Where time series models use only past demand values as indicators of future demand, causal models use other independent, observed data to predict demand. These models concentrate on external factors that are thought to *cause* demand. For example, the amount of household disposable income in an economy might be a good leading indicator of the sales of luxury items, such as sailboats.

As mentioned earlier, regression analysis is the most commonly used method for estimating relationships between leading indicators and demand. In fact, the technique can be extended to include multiple indicators in a multiple regression analysis. In this approach, a forecaster would gather past data describing demand and multiple independent indicators considered important as predictors of demand. The regression analysis computes the coefficients (indicator weights), forming an equation that best describes the past relationships between the predictors and the actual demand data. The resulting equation is then used to forecast future values of demand, based on observed values of the leading indicators. For example, we might see the following multiple regression equation used to forecast sailboats sales:

$$\text{Sales forecast} = \text{B} + b_d(\text{D}) + b_a(\text{A}) + b_f(\text{F}) + b_s(\text{S})$$

where:

B = Base sales (computed y-intercept)
D = Disposable personal income
A = Advertising expenditures
F = Fuel prices
S = Sales from prior year

Each of the indicator weights (values of b) is computed by a regression method. Each value of b represents the incremental contribution of the corresponding leading indicator to the sales forecast.

Simple Linear Regression: Causal Modeling

Let's look at an example of causal modeling with one leading indicator using simple linear regresssion.

EXAMPLE 12-7

Suppose that you manage a small ice cream shop. People tend to like to buy ice cream on hot days, so you suspect that each day's high temperature might be a good predictor of ice cream sales. Table 12-7 provides daily sales and temperature data for three weeks of shop operations.

Using the linear regression formulae with temperature as the leading indicator variable, the slope and the intercept are

$$b = [283240.2 - (21)(76.0)(174.9)]/[122900 - (21)(76.0)^2] = 2.6 \text{ per degree F}$$
$$a = (174.9) - (2.6)(76.0) = -21.1$$

The trend results indicate that the ice cream shop should expect to sell an additional pound of ice cream each time the high temperature for a day rises by 2.6 degrees F. Suppose that the forecast is for a warming trend over the next three days with high temperatures of 82, 84, and 87 degrees, respectively. Using the causal regression model, the forecasted sales for the shop would be given as follows:

$$F_t = a + bt = -21.1 + 2.6{*}82 = 190.5 \text{ pounds}$$
$$F_{t+1} = a + bt = -21.1 + 2.6{*}84 = 195.6 \text{ pounds}$$
$$F_{t+2} = a + bt = -21.1 + 2.6{*}87 = 203.4 \text{ pounds}$$

simulation models Sophisticated mathematical programs that offer forecasters the ability to evaluate different business scenarios that might yield different demand outcomes.

focused forecasting A combination of common sense inputs from frontline personnel and a computer simulation process.

Simulation Models

Simulation models are sophisticated mathematical programs that offer forecasters the ability to evaluate different business scenarios that might yield different demand outcomes. This evaluation helps forecasters to better understand how different variables and drivers of demand relate to one another.

Bernie Smith first proposed a relatively simple simulation-based approach known as **focused forecasting** in the early 1980s. Focused forecasting combines commonsense

TABLE 12-7 Ice Cream Shop Sales and Daily High Temperatures

		High Temperature (degrees F)	Sales (lbs)		
		t	d_t	$t * d_t$	t^2
Week 1	Monday	70	123.6	8652.0	4900.0
	Tuesday	78	135.0	10530.5	6084.0
	Wednesday	75	160.0	12000.0	5625.0
	Thursday	60	140.4	8424.0	3600.0
	Friday	66	187.9	12401.4	4356.0
	Saturday	75	195.0	14625.0	5625.0
	Sunday	82	171.8	14087.6	6724.0
Week 2	Monday	75	145.9	10942.5	5625.0
	Tuesday	60	130.0	7800.0	3600.0
	Wednesday	63	145.0	9135.0	3969.0
	Thursday	64	147.2	9420.8	4096.0
	Friday	75	214.2	16065.0	5625.0
	Saturday	81	190.0	15390.0	6561.0
	Sunday	83	202.1	16774.3	6889.0
Week 3	Monday	78	159.0	12402.0	6084.0
	Tuesday	85	178.7	15189.5	7225.0
	Wednesday	85	160.0	13600.0	7225.0
	Thursday	82	181.5	14883.0	6724.0
	Friday	85	212.8	18088.0	7225.0
	Saturday	87	249.4	21697.8	7569.0
	Sunday	87	242.9	21132.3	7569.0
	Total			**283240.2**	**122900.0**
	Average	**76.0**	**174.9**		

inputs from frontline personnel (such as sales managers) with a computer simulation process.[2] The focused forecasting process asks managers to suggest rules of thumb that should be followed when developing forecasts. For example, one rule might be, "we will probably sell 10 percent more product this month than we did in the same month last year." These types of rules are embedded in a simulation model, and their usefulness is then tested by estimating how effective they collectively would have been in predicting demand data from the past. The forecaster then makes new forecasts using the combination of rules that would have provided the best forecasts for the past demands. Managers from different functional areas adjust the forecasts as they see fit. This approach has delivered better results than exponential smoothing or other time series-based models have given. However, the focused forecasting approach requires more preparation and user involvement.

student activity

Interview one or two small business managers. Ask them to describe their demand forecasting processes.

[2]B.T. Smith, *Focused Forecasting: Techniques for Inventory Control* (Boston, MA: CBI, 1984).

Prepare

How do you know if the forecasting process is working well?

Organize

Assessing the Performance of the Forecasting Process
- Tracking Forecast Error Acceptability
- Situational Drivers of Forecast Accuracy

ASSESSING THE PERFORMANCE OF THE FORECASTING PROCESS

The primary measure of forecasting performance is forecast error. As we noted earlier, forecast error is defined as the actual demand value minus the forecasted demand value for a given time period. Thus, a positive forecast error indicates an overly pessimistic forecast; a negative value indicates an overly optimistic forecast. Forecast errors can be examined to determine two primary aspects of forecast performance over time: *forecast accuracy* and *forecast bias.* **Forecast accuracy** measures how closely the forecast aligns with the observations over time. Every error, whether the forecast was too high or too low, reduces accuracy. **Forecast bias**, on the other hand, is simply the average error. Forecast bias indicates the tendency of a forecasting technique to continually overpredict or underpredict demand.

LO12-5 Evaluate and select forecasting models using various measures of accuracy and bias.

Forecast bias is the average forecast error over a number of periods:

$$\text{Bias} = \text{Mean Forecast Error (MFE)} = \frac{\sum_{t=1}^{n}(d_t - F_t)}{n} \tag{12.12}$$

forecast bias The tendency of a forecasting technique to continually overpredict or underpredict demand. Also called *mean forecast error.*

forecast accuracy The measurement of how closely the forecast aligns with the observations over time.

A positive forecast bias indicates that over time forecasts tend to be too low; a negative bias indicates that forecasts tend to be too high.

Forecast bias makes intuitive sense, and it is simple to calculate. However, it does not always allow easy comparisons across products when the average demands are different. Suppose that your company sells two different products, gadgets and widgets, at the rates of about 1,000 per month and 10 per month, respectively. Now suppose that the bias for each of the products over the past few months using both metrics is equal to 5. This means that on average, the forecasts for each of these two products were below demand by about five units each month. Does this mean that both forecasting models are performing equally well? Certainly not! A bias of 5 units on 1,000 units of sales is outstanding performance, whereas a bias of 5 units on 10 units of sales is relatively poor performance.

For comparability's sake, forecasters often compute average error (bias) on a percentage basis. This metric is known as **mean percent error (MPE)** and is calculated as

mean percent error (MPE) Average error represented as a percentage of demand.

$$\text{Mean percent error (MPE)} = \frac{\sum_{t=1}^{n}\frac{d_t - F_t}{d_t} * 100}{n} \tag{12.13}$$

Remember that both average forecast error and mean percent error are good indicators of bias, but they do not necessarily provide good indications of forecast *accuracy.* A measure of forecast accuracy seeks to indicate the overall errors, regardless of the direction of the errors. Forecasts that are too low or too high are both undesirable. The simplest measure of forecast accuracy is known as **mean absolute deviation** (or the mean absolute error). This measure provides the average size of forecast errors, irrespective of their directions. It is computed as

mean absolute deviation (MAD) The average size of forecast errors, irrespective of their directions. Also called *mean absolute error.*

$$\text{Mean Absolute Deviation (MAD)} = \frac{\sum_{t=1}^{n}|d_t - F_t|}{n} \tag{12.14}$$

EXAMPLE 12-8

Table 12-8 shows the calculation of bias (MFE) and MAD for two different forecasting models. While the bias for model 2 is slightly higher than that of model 1, model 2 is preferred to model 1 because its MAD is far smaller (9.3 as compared to 50). A forecasting manager can use this approach to test many different model parameters, and then select the model that yields the lowest errors.

TABLE 12-8 Computing Bias (MFE) and MAD

Period	Actual Demand	Forecast Model 1	Forecast Error	Absolute Error	Forecast Model 2	Forecast Error	Absolute Error
1	100	150	−50	50	104	−4	4
2	100	50	50	50	93	7	7
3	100	150	−50	50	88	12	12
4	100	50	50	50	102	−2	2
5	100	150	−50	50	90	10	10
6	100	50	50	50	107	−7	7
7	100	150	−50	50	89	11	11
8	100	50	50	50	83	17	17
9	100	150	−50	50	110	−10	10
10	100	50	50	50	113	−13	13
		Average	0	50		2.1	9.3
			MFE	MAD		MFE	MAD

We should note that for normally distributed forecast errors, 1 MAD equals 0.80 standard deviations (or 1.25 MAD equals 1 standard deviation). We will return to this point later.

For purposes of comparability across products, forecasters sometimes adjust the MAD to create a related metric, the **mean absolute percentage error (MAPE)**. The MAPE indicates how large errors are relative to the actual demand quantities. Computationally, the MAPE is determined as follows:

mean absolute percentage error (MAPE) The MAD represented as a percentage of demand.

(12.15)

$$\text{Mean absolute percent error (MAPE)} = \frac{\sum_{t=1}^{n} \frac{|d_t - F_t|}{d_t} * 100}{n}$$

Though intuitively appealing, measures like MAD and MAPE are sometimes inadequate as measures of forecast accuracy in that they do not recognize that forecasts that are really far off the mark may be more harmful to the user than forecasts that miss the actual demand by a small amount. To deal with this issue of sensitivity to the magnitude of the errors, researchers developed the **mean squared error (MSE)**.

mean squared error (MSE) A more sensitive measure of forecast errors that approximates the error variance.

(12.16)

$$\text{Mean squared error (MSE)} = \frac{\sum_{t=1}^{n} (d_t - F_t)^2}{n - 1}$$

Because of the squared term, the MSE gives exponentially more weight to larger and larger errors. The MSE equation looks like the formula for the variance of the forecast errors. However, there are some important differences. The variance of errors would use the actual forecast errors and the mean of the forecast errors.

(12.17) $$\text{Forecast error variance} = \frac{\sum_{t=1}^{n}(e_t - \bar{e})^2}{n-1}$$

where:

e_t is the forecast error for period t
$\bar{e}$ is the mean forecast error

At the same time, the MSE usually does give a decent *approximation* of the variance of forecast errors. Thus, the square root of MSE provides a good approximation of the standard deviation. For this reason, forecasters often track the **root mean squared error (RMSE)**, or

root mean squared error (RMSE) Gives an approximation of the forecast error standard deviation.

(12.18) $$\text{Root mean squared error (RMSE)} = \sqrt{MSE}$$

EXAMPLE 12-9

To compare the measures of forecast accuracy, let's apply them to the data presented in Table 12-9. Here, we calculate the MAD to be 6.7 and the RMSE to be 8.3. As was mentioned earlier, the MAD value is typically 80 percent of the value of the standard deviation of error. Dividing the MAD by 0.80 yields 8.4. Thus, both the adjusted MAD and RMSE provide good rough approximations to the actual standard deviation of forecast errors, which in this case is 8.2.

TABLE 12-9 Assessing Forecast Accuracy: A Comparison of MAD, RMSE, and Standard Deviation

Period	Actual	Forecast	Forecast Error (Actual − Forecast)	Absolute Error |Actual − Forecast|	Error Squared
1	345	340	5	5	25
2	328	341	−13	13	156
3	335	339	−4	4	18
4	330	339	−9	9	78
5	334	338	−4	4	16
6	340	338	2	2	6
7	338	338	0	0	0
8	328	338	−10	10	96
9	345	337	8	8	67
10	350	338	12	12	153
			8.2	6.7	8.3
			STD DEV	MAD	RMSE

Tracking Forecast Error Acceptability

Forecasters generally use forecasting metrics such as MAD and MSE to quickly and continuously evaluate forecasting models, sometimes for thousands of different products at a time. In this environment, metrics are often used to identify exceptional cases that require

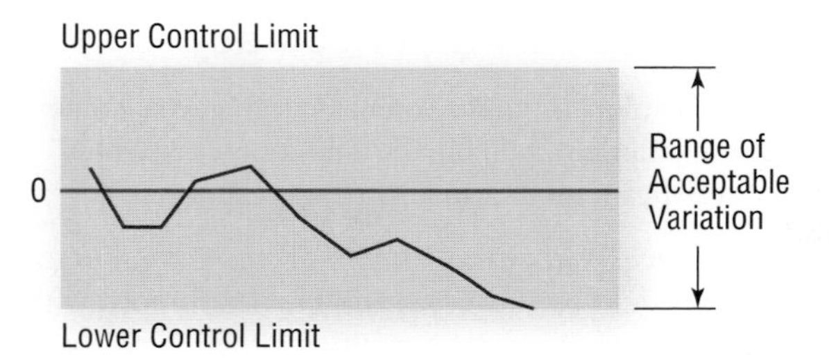

FIGURE 12-8 Tracking Signal Control Chart

adjustments to model parameters. Managers need a simple test for determining when the forecast error is unacceptable. One way to test the forecast error is to develop a control chart in which forecast errors are plotted and compared to expected upper and lower control limits.[3] Such a control chart is illustrated in Figure 12-8. Several statistical tests can be done to determine with some level of confidence whether or not forecast errors are exhibiting new and unacceptable patterns. In lieu of these rather sophisticated tests, managers often opt for a simpler metric known as the **tracking signal**. The tracking signal records the ratio of a running total of forecast error to MAD. Mathematically, this signal is expressed as

tracking signal The ratio of a running total of forecast error to MAD that indicates when the pattern of forecast error is changing significantly.

(12.19)
$$\text{Tracking signal} = \frac{\sum_{t=1}^{n} (d_t - F_t)}{MAD_{t=1 \rightarrow n}}$$

The tracking signal is essentially a comparison of forecast bias (sum of errors, rather than MFE) to forecast accuracy (MAD) over *n* periods. By tracking this metric over successive periods of time, managers can observe whether undesirable trends or highly biased errors are occurring. For example, managers might program a computer to compute the tracking signal each month using the most recent six months of data. If the tracking signal exceeds some control limit value, say +/−3, then the computer would send an alert to the forecaster. Tracking signal control limits are typically set somewhere between +/−3 and +/−8. A smaller limit gives a more sensitive indicator, and would probably be used for high volume or high revenue items.

Once a tracking signal control limit is exceeded, forecasters take action by changing the forecasting approach or model parameters. In **adaptive forecasting**, the smoothing coefficients in exponential smoothing models are automatically adjusted as a function of the tracking signal (a larger tracking signal creates a larger smoothing coefficient). Such automatic correction for unpredictable data can simplify the life of the manager, but when a particular demand forecast routinely misstates actual results, it warrants some sort of management intervention. For example, when the tracking signal frequently exceeds control limits, this suggests that something in the underlying process that drives demand has fundamentally changed, and needs to be investigated. This investigation should include some assessment of the real effects of poor forecasts on organization operations. For example, consistently low forecasts may suggest that the popularity of the product has grown. Managers may also decide to raise the safety stock level to keep more inventory as a buffer against the continuing uncertainty.

adaptive forecasting A technique that automatically adjusts forecast model parameters in accordance with changes in the tracking signal.

Past patterns of forecast errors can give managers hints about the processes that generate both demand and errors. This knowledge can help managers to focus resources to develop sales plans and to eliminate the causes of undesirable errors. Hence, forecasters should review the model and parameters of a forecasting tool that fails to capture actual demand accurately.

[3]The logic and steps for building such a control chart are presented in the Chapter 3 Supplement.

Situational Drivers of Forecast Accuracy

All forecasters want to develop accurate forecasts. However, some demand forecasting situations create greater challenges than others. The following "rules" give an indication of how situational characteristics tend to affect forecast accuracy:

Rule 1: Short-term forecasts are usually more accurate than long-term forecasts. It is almost always easier to predict what will happen tomorrow than it is to predict what will happen next week, or next year (think about predicting the weather, for example). As the time horizon for forecasting increases, more and more potentially unknown factors can affect demand.

Rule 2: Forecasts of aggregated demand are usually more accurate than forecasts of demand at detailed levels. Aggregate forecasts benefit from a cancellation of errors that exist in item-level forecasts. For example, suppose you are tasked with forecasting demand for products A1 and A2. If your forecasts are unbiased, each forecast has a 50 percent chance of being either too high or too low. However, the chance that forecasts for both products are simultaneously too high (or simultaneously too low) is less than 50 percent (it is only 25 percent if the product demands are independent). Considering a larger number of products, there is a good chance that forecasts for some products will be too high and forecasts for other products will be too low. Thus, when the individual product forecasts are combined, the aggregate forecast is overall more accurate, because some of the negative errors are cancelled out by some of the positive errors. This same logic applies when you attempt to forecast aggregate demand directly (as opposed to summing up individual forecasts). The random forces that affect demand for individual products tend to be inconsistent across all products. The effects cancel one another. Thus, aggregate demand is more stable and predictable. This aggregation benefit also applies to geographic aggregation. For a single product, an overall global demand forecast is typically more accurate than forecasts of demand in any specific geographic region.

global

Rule 3: Forecasts developed using multiple information sources are usually more accurate than forecasts developed from a single source. Many different market forces may drive demand for a given good or service. It is difficult for any single source of information (historical demand data, executive judgments, sales force estimates, and so on) to comprehend all of these forces. In addition, any single source is potentially biased. Consequently, a forecast created by combining information from multiple different sources is likely to reflect a more complete and unbiased picture of actual demand patterns. It is unlikely that all sources will be "wrong" in the same direction.

DEMAND MANAGEMENT

Prepare

How can businesses shape the quantity and timing of demand to meet their needs?

Organize

Demand Management

Forecasting is essentially a reactive approach that considers fluctuations in demand to be mostly outside the firm's control. Rather than simply forecasting and reacting to changes in demand, however, business executives would prefer to influence the timing, pattern, and certainty of demand to whatever extent they can. They do this through demand management activities that adjust product characteristics including price, promotion, and availability. The purpose is to influence product demand to achieve sales objectives, and to accommodate the supply chain resources and capacities that the firm has in place.

Demand management is especially important when customers' demands fluctuate in an unpredictable way. These fluctuations cause operational inefficiencies all across the supply chain, including:

1. Extra resources to expand and contract capacity to meet varying demand.
2. Backlogging (delivering later than originally promised) certain orders to smooth out demand fluctuations.
3. Customer dissatisfaction with the system's inability to meet all demands.
4. Buffering the system through the use of safety stocks (excess inventories), safety lead time (lead times with a cushion), or safety capacity (excess resources).

relationships

To be effective, demand management requires coordination of many sources of demand information. Different people working throughout the organization and the supply chain may each see only parts of the overall demand picture. Demand management planning often crosses organizational boundaries in the supply chain. It requires sales, marketing, supply management, and operations personnel, as well as suppliers and intermediate customers, to work together in planning strategies for developing and fulfilling orders. Sales and marketing personnel need to be aware of the costs and constraints of operations in order to make good pricing and product availability decisions. Furthermore, operations managers must understand customer requirements regarding acceptable lead times, as well as priorities associated with different customer orders.[4]

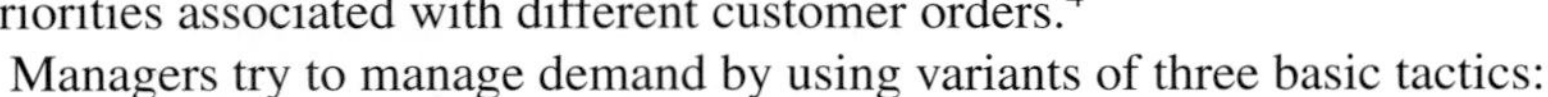

Managers try to manage demand by using variants of three basic tactics:

1. *Influence the timing or quantity of demand through pricing changes, promotions, or sales incentives.* These moves are usually intended to increase demand during the low periods and to reduce or postpone demand during the peak periods. For example, automobile manufacturers sometimes offer promotional packages including zero percent financing or rebates to stimulate purchases. Many service operations such as hotels, airlines, and theaters use these approaches because their services cannot be inventoried.
2. *Manage the timing of order fulfillment.* In some situations, it is possible to negotiate with customers regarding when they will take delivery of their products. Information systems can be used to inform customers of the availability of certain products, including the expected delivery date. Different customers might be quoted different delivery dates depending on their importance to the business. In some services, customers are encouraged to choose when they will order, based on expected lead times. For example, amusement parks such as Disney World use this tactic when they place signs at points in a waiting line telling you how long you can expect to wait from that point.
3. *Substitute by encouraging customers to shift their orders from one product to another, or from one provider to another.* Suppose you are ordering a new computer, but the model with the features you desire is not readily available. You might be willing to take a near substitute, or perhaps an upgraded model if you can get it immediately, or at a lower price. Dell, a computer manufacturer, is famous for "selling what they have." Their information systems enable sales representatives to know exactly which products are immediately available, and marketing managers price products dynamically to move those items that are in stock.

Characteristics of the product, customers' lead-time expectations, and the operations environment all influence how the above tactics are employed in a demand management process. However, in every case the ultimate goal of demand management is to match demand and operational capacity in order to attain the business's competitive objectives.

Prepare

How do operational aspects of the supply chain hinder or enable effective demand planning? What can operations managers do about it?

Organize

Improving the Constraints on Demand Planning
- Improving Information Accuracy and Timeliness
- Reducing Lead Time
- Redesigning the Product
- Collaborating and Sharing Information

IMPROVING THE CONSTRAINTS ON DEMAND PLANNING

Many business firms today are redesigning operations across their supply chains to facilitate more effective demand planning and order fulfillment. Improvement initiatives are aimed at changing information sharing systems, manufacturing and service processes, supply chain relationships, and even the product design itself, so that the company can reduce both the magnitude and impact of forecast errors on its operations.

---

[4]Chapter 13, "Sales and Operations Planning," discusses in detail the coordination of demand management with operational constraints.

GET REAL

Destination Maternity Corporation, Customer Quickstep

Destination Maternity Corporation (originally known as Mothers Work, Inc.) is a leading designer, manufacturer, and marketer of maternity fashion in the United States, with over 900 locations nationwide. Destination was founded by President and Chief Creative Officer Rebecca Matthias in 1982 in the front closet of her Philadelphia home, with the investment of $10,000 of her own savings. A civil engineer and pregnant with her first child, Ms. Matthias was unable to find clothing appropriate to her role in the business world.

Since the time of its initial public offering in March 1993, Destination has increased its store base by over 1300 percent, and grown financially to more than 10 times its original size. A critical success factor has been the company's ability to gather extensive point-of-sale information at each store. Managers developed an information system with the following capabilities:

- Capture all customer information and create a buying history.
- Run individual mailing lists by due date.
- Receive alerts about any operational errors that may have occurred the previous day.
- Review all orders on the way to their stores.
- Make customer-unique price tickets.
- Send and receive digital photos.
- Provide sales trend information

The system also provides such features as custom profiles for each store, daily inventory replenishment, and daily updated selling information for each style.

Complementing the information system are the company's fast-turn, in-house design, and quick response material sourcing processes (shown below left). By coupling current and accurate information with a very responsive supply chain, Destination has been able to avoid lost sales while maximizing in-store inventory turns and sales per square foot. Destination provides an excellent example of how improving the constraints that otherwise limit the effectiveness of the demand planning system can yield big operational and financial benefits.

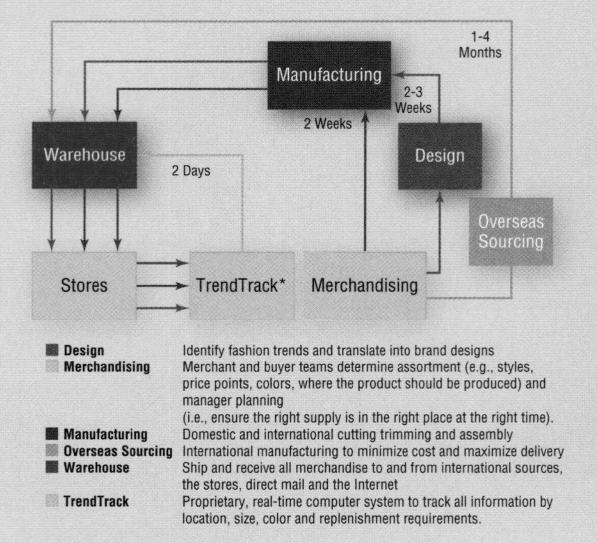

Source: Information taken from http://Motherswork.com/.

Improving Information Accuracy and Timeliness

LO12-6 Explain how certain improvements to both product design and operations across the supply chain can make demand planning easier.

The fashion-driven clothing industry vividly demonstrates the important role of information in demand planning. Predicting the sales of a new line of merchandise is difficult. Once the firm launches a product line, it needs quick information about the market's response to the new goods. Information systems that rapidly collect and distribute accurate sales information are important in the fashion industry and in many other industries as well. Quick sales data collection is important because current data is more relevant for forecasting future sales. Initial forecasts made at product launch can be hugely improved by incorporating early sales data. In addition, rapid access to customer sales information, coupled with an operations system capable of rapid response, decreases a firm's reliance

Calyx and Corolla Delivers Freshness by Redesigning the Supply Chain

Calyx and Corolla is a company that sells flowers from growers located around the world to customers located around the world. The company promotes itself as "the flower lover's flower company™" as it competes primarily through "freshness." On the company's homepage (www.calyxandcorolla.com), Calyx and Corolla tells its customers that their flowers will last 5 to 10 days longer than most others. How are they able to deliver on this promise? Most traditional florists must deal with a very long supply chain. Growers grow the flowers. Distributors buy them and sell them to regional sellers, who in turn sell them to local florists. At each stage, the flowers are produced or purchased based on the party's forecast of demand.

A typical flower can last about 19 days, once it has been cut. The traditional supply chain consumes about 10 to 11 days of this time. The founders of Calyx and Corolla redesigned the supply chain to reduce lead time by working directly with the growers. Orders received from customers (in response to printed catalogs or the Internet) are placed by Calyx and Corolla directly with the growers, who then cut, package, and ship the flowers directly to the customer via FedEx. Consequently, flowers delivered this way spend three days or less in the supply chain. The benefit for the customer is that they arrive at their destination fresher, and they also last longer. The benefit for Calyx and Corolla is that they only need to forecast demand for three to four days into the future in order to arrange for sufficient product and transportation capacities. Their competitors have to forecast demand for several weeks into the future.

on forecasting, because the firm doesn't have to forecast as far into the future. The Get Real box describing Destination Maternity Corporation provides a good example of the impacts of information accuracy and timeliness.

Reducing Lead Time

As we noted earlier in the chapter, it is a basic fact of forecasting that the longer the time period over which you have to forecast, the greater the forecast error. A forecast of demand for two years from now is far less accurate than a forecast of demand for next month. In most cases, the number of periods that managers have to forecast into the future is determined by the order-to-delivery (OTD) lead time provided by the supply chain; that is, the time required to source, make, and deliver the product. Thus, reducing lead time improves forecast accuracy, because shorter lead times require shorter-term forecasts.

Speeding up or eliminating process steps that are redundant, unnecessary, or poorly executed reduces lead time. Opportunities for improvement usually extend beyond the firm throughout the supply chain. The Get Real box above about Calyx and Corolla gives an example of extreme lead-time reduction facilitated by the company's redesign of the supply chain. If lead times are reduced sufficiently, operations managers can move from a build-to-stock (build-to-forecast) process to a build-to-order process where little forecasting is required.

Redesigning the Product

For a firm offering a wide range of products, forecasting is especially challenging. Consider the problems faced by Hewlett-Packard when it comes to inkjet printers, which are consumed around the world (described in the Get Real box on the next page). Ultimately, HP responded by developing *postponable products*. A **postponable product** is one that can be configured to its final form quickly and inexpensively once actual customer demand is known. In this operations system, only components, not finished goods, are stocked near sources of demand. The components are then assembled into finished product configurations once the actual demand materializes.

postponable product A product designed so that it can be configured to its final form quickly and inexpensively once actual customer demand is known.

GET REAL

HP Improves the Constraints on Forecasting through Postponement

While the "guts" of an inkjet printer are basically the same regardless of where they are sold, instruction manuals, power supplies, and cables have to be made different to accommodate differences in language and electrical grids in various countries. Initially, HP forecasted each country's demand for inkjet printers and then stocked all printer variants according to the forecasts. However, forecasts were never accurate enough to make this approach work—inventories were high, expediting was common, and customer service was low.

To solve this problem, HP decided to produce and stock only the generic inkjet printer bases, along with separate power supplies, cables, and instruction manuals, in regional warehouses around the world. The warehouses act as both storage locations and as light assembly plants. Once an order is received for an inkjet printer for Germany, for example, the order is sent to the nearest regional warehouse. There, a generic printer base is withdrawn from stock and paired with the appropriate power supply, cable, and instruction manual. The entire system is then tested and packed in country-specific packaging. HP has found that this approach has reduced total landed cost (manufacturing, shipping, and inventory) by 25 percent. In addition, they reduced total inventories by 50 percent while simultaneously increasing customer order fill rates significantly.

"Smartek" chips stacked and ready for final assembly in HP printers in manufacturing plant.

The postponable product approach largely eliminates the need for large and complex forecasting systems, as only the demands for the relatively few individual components are forecasted, not the demands for the many different end-item configurations. The keys to this approach are redesign of the product, and redistribution of production resources so that the products can be easily configured close to the source of demand. Electronics firms such as HP often use this approach. So do private-brand producers of grocery products (e.g., canned beans, corn, peas). The grocery producers stock unlabeled cans, then they print the labels and make cartons for specific brands only after actual orders are received.

Collaborating and Sharing Information

The need for forecasting partially arises from a lack of information sharing across stages of the supply chain. Suppliers make assumptions about the actions of their customers, and vice versa. Many firms today use both formal and informal approaches to share planning information with their suppliers and customers, including forecasts of product demand and planned product promotions, as well as production plans and capacity limitations. The planning partners then make commitments to a collaboratively established overall sales and production plan, taking into account the demands and constraints of the various organizations involved. This approach reduces the risks associated with forecast errors; it reduces the inventories that supply chain players typically hold to guard against such risks; and it improves customer service levels by reducing lead times.

collaborative planning, forecasting, and replenishment (CPFR)
A method by which supply chain partners periodically share forecasts, demand plans, and resource plans in order to reduce uncertainty and risk in meeting customer demand.

One systematic process for improving collaboration and information sharing in the supply chain is known as **collaborative planning, forecasting and replenishment** (CPFR). It began as a 1995 initiative led by Walmart. Since then, many companies have adopted various versions of the approach. The CPFR process requires buyers and sellers to collaboratively develop their demand plans and then to collaboratively adjust and execute those plans, with the goal of meeting customer demand with minimal inventories, lead times, and transaction costs.

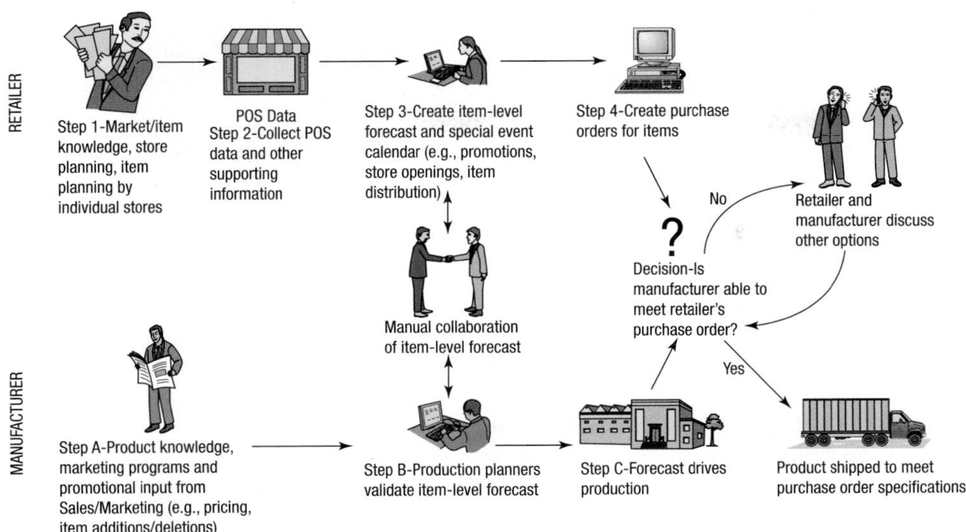

FIGURE 12-9
The CPFR Approach

To engage in CPFR, supply chain partners must first come to an understanding of their relationships and the roles they will play. Included in this mutual understanding are definitions of the accounts and operational processes involved and jointly developed business goals. Figure 12-9 illustrates one common version of the CPFR process, which typically consists of four collaborative activities:

- *Market planning.* The partners collaboratively discuss such issues as the introduction of new products, store openings/closings, changing inventory policies, and product promotions.
- *Demand and resource planning.* Customer demand and shipping requirements are forecasted.
- *Execution.* Orders are placed, delivered, received, and paid for. This includes preparation of shipments and recording of sales. Since logistics/distribution is critical, third-party logistics providers may be included in the CPFR effort.
- *Analysis.* Execution is monitored and key performance metrics are collected with the goal of identifying opportunities for future improvement.

CHAPTER SUMMARY

Demand planning is a process that every firm must develop in order to deal with variability and uncertainty of product demand. This chapter discussed two fundamental elements of demand planning, demand forecasting and demand management. The following points and issues were raised:

1. The choice of a forecasting process depends on conditions in the operating environment, including the time horizon for management decisions, the level of detail that the user of the forecast needs to support decisions, the number of products for which the process must generate forecasts, the decision makers' emphasis on control or planning needs, the constancy of forecasted events, and the firm's current methods for developing forecasts.
2. Forecasting methods fall into two categories: judgment-based and statistical model-based methods. Judgment-based approaches gather inputs through grassroots methods, executive judgment, focused forecasting, historical analogy, market research,

and the Delphi method. These techniques are appropriate in those situations where past data are either unavailable or no longer appropriate. They are also appropriate for forecasting technological innovations (another use of forecasting). Statistical model-based forecasting approaches try to extend the past by decomposing historical time series data and other causal factors, into seasonal, trend, and other components to reveal the residual effects of unique, current forces on demand. Operations managers may develop naïve forecasts or employ much more sophisticated methods.

3. Both accuracy and bias should be considered in the evaluation of forecasting errors. Mean forecast error (MFE) and mean percentage error (MPE) are good at measuring bias, while metrics such as mean absolute deviation (MAD), mean squared error (MSE), root mean squared error (RMSE), and mean absolute percentage error (MAPE) are used to monitor forecast accuracy. Managers often set up tracking signals for forecasting systems so that they can be notified when forecast errors become unusually large. This type of monitoring of forecasting performance leads to continuous updating and improvement of forecasting models.
4. Demand management involves varying the price, promotion, or availability of the product or service in order to increase, decrease, or shift the pattern of expected demand.
5. By improving supply chain constraints, operations managers can make the system more responsive to actual demand and less sensitive to forecast error. This can be done by improving information systems, reducing lead times (by changing the underlying processes and systems), redesigning the product to facilitate product postponement, and by sharing information and collaborating with other supply chain partners.

KEY TERMS

adaptive forecasting 419
autocorrelation 399
collaborative planning, forecasting, and replenishment (CPFR) 424
Delphi method 401
demand forecasting 396
demand management 396
demand planning 396
executive judgment 401
exponential smoothing 405
focused forecasting 414
forecast accuracy 416
forecast bias 416
forecast error 399
grassroots forecasting 401
historical analogy 401
marketing research 401
mean absolute deviation (MAD) 416
mean absolute percentage error (MAPE) 417
mean percent error (MPE) 416
mean squared error (MSE) 417
moving average 403
naïve model 403
postponable product 423
regression analysis 408
root mean squared error (RMSE) 418
seasonal index 409
seasonality and cycles 398
shift or step change 399
simulation models 414
smoothing coefficient 405
stable pattern 398
time series analysis models 402
tracking signal 419
trend 399
weighted moving average 404

DISCUSSION QUESTIONS

1. Think of four instances in your life when you confronted sellers' demand management practices. As a value-conscious customer, do you think that each of the four sellers served you well?
2. Your boss wants you to explain the term *exponential smoothing*. How do you reply?
3. Someone in your organization suspects a causal relationship between statistics on corrugated board shipments reported in *BusinessWeek* and your company's shipments using the boxes. How would you test this assertion? If you were to verify the relationship, how could you use it in your business?
4. In what way is an exponential smoothing model really a moving average model?
5. Your boss has less training than you have in business statistics. She asks you to explain the logic of the least squares regression method for determining a trend line. What would you tell her?
6. Your firm is considering reducing staff, and your forecasting department has been mentioned as a prime candidate for this treatment. Outline a brief memo to defend the value of your department's services to the firm. How could you quantify your claims?
7. Assume that you are the regional operations manager responsible for 27 Burger Queen restaurants. What types of demand forecast models do you think you would need for your short-term planning? What decisions would each forecast support? Identify the users of each forecast.
8. As the regional manager of 27 Burger Queens, you are thinking about expanding the number of outlets in your area. What types of forecasts would you want to create in order to support your decision?
9. What arguments would you use in order to justify tightening the limits used on a tracking signal control chart? How about for loosening the limits?
10. Describe the likely effects of the following business trends on demand forecasting processes:
    a. Fast-to-market product design.
    b. Division of many markets into isolated niches.
    c. The Internet.
    d. More powerful and cheaper computers and forecasting software packages.

    How would you modify your firm's demand management or demand forecasting processes in response to these trends?

SOLVED PROBLEMS

1. Vinod Malhotra is trying to decide how many wait staff he will need to support his restaurant operations for the next month. First he needs to identify a suitable forecasting model to estimate next month's demand. He is considering three alternative models:

   Model 1: Four-month moving average
   Model 2: Four-month weighted moving average with weights = .1, .2, .3, .4.
   Model 3: Exponential smoothing with $\alpha = 0.7$

   Based on past performance, which model should Vinod use?

Solution:

To evaluate the three competing forecasting models, we need to compare the errors that would have been produced if they had been used in the past. The table below shows the forecasts created by each model using eight months of past demand.

Month	Actual Demand	Model 1 Forecast	Error	Abs Error	Model 2 Forecast	Error	Abs Error	Model 3 Forecast	Error	Abs Error
1	1940									
2	2250									
3	2301									
4	2630									
5	2264	2280.3	−16.3	16.3	2386.3	−122.3	122.3	2630.0	−366.0	366.
6	2736	2361.3	374.8	374.8	2379.8	356.2	356.2	2373.8	362.2	362.
7	2503	2482.8	20.3	20.3	2529.7	−26.7	26.7	2627.3	−124.3	124.
8	2422	2533.3	−111.3	111.3	2537.8	−115.8	115.8	2540.3	−118.3	118

In order to complete the table, forecasts will be needed for each month. As an example, the calculations are shown below for forecasting demand for month 8:

Model 1: $F_8 = (2630 + 2264 + 2736 + 2503) / 4 = 2533.3$

Model 2: $F_8 = (0.1)\ 2630 + (0.2)\ 2264 + (0.3)\ 2736 + (0.4)\ 2503 = 2537.8$

Model 3: $F_8 = (0.7)\ 2503 + (1 - 0.7)\ 2627.3 = 2540.3$

Calculations of Bias and MAD:

Model 1: Bias $= (-16.3 + 374.8 + 20.3 - 111.3) / 4 = 66.9$;
MAD $= (16.3 + 374.8 + 20.3 + 111.3) / 4 = 130.6$

Model 2: Bias $= (-122.3 + 356.2 - 26.7 - 115.8) / 4 = 22.9$;
MAD $= (122.3 + 356.2 + 26.7 + 115.8) / 4 = 155.3$

Model 3: Bias $= (-366.0 + 362.2 - 124.3 - 118.3) / 4 = -61.6$;
MAD $= (366.0 + 362.2 + 124.3 + 118.3) / 4 = 242.7$

Conclusion: Vinod would probably be advised to use model 2, the weighted moving average model, as it has provided the lowest amount of bias in the past. Though the MAD for this model is slightly worse than that for model 1, the bias is significantly better. Vinod might want to try some other model parameters to see if he can develop an even more accurate model.

2. Suppose that an electronics company has the monthly sales shown below. They want to develop forecasts using a time series regression model, a trend enhanced exponential smoothing model using $\alpha = 0.30$ and $\partial = 0.40$, and then seasonally adjust these two models using the regression forecasts as the base for calculating the seasonal indexes. Finally, they want to determine which forecasting model fits the data better, and use this model to predict sales for the next six months.

Month	1	2	3	4	5	6	7	8	9	10	11	12
Sales ($1,000,000)	16	20	35	18	24	33	21	23	51	35	36	64

Solution:

The parameters for the regression model are calculated in Table 12-10.

TABLE 12-10 Regression Parameter Calculations

	Month	Sales		
	t	d_t	$t * d_t$	t^2
	1	16	16	1
	2	20	40	4
	3	35	105	9
	4	18	72	16
	5	24	120	25
	6	33	198	36
	7	21	147	49
	8	23	184	64
	9	51	459	81
	10	35	350	100
	11	36	396	121
	12	64	768	144
Total			2855	650
Average	6.5	31.3		

Using the linear regression formulae, the slope and the intercept are

$$b = [2{,}855.1 - (12)(6.5)(31.3)]/[650 - (12)(6.5)^2] = 2.9 \text{ per period}$$
$$a = (31.3) - (2.9)(6.5) = 12.6$$

Regression-based estimates for each time period are calculated as

$$\text{Month 1 forecast} = 12.6 + 2.9(1) = 15.5$$
$$\text{Month 2 forecast} = 12.6 + 2.9(2) = 18.4$$

Table 12-11 (next page) shows the regression forecast values for all 12 months.

The trend enhanced exponential smoothing model forecasts are calculated as follows. Since no starting values are provided, we choose the actual sales in month 1 as the initial base demand value and the slope from the regression model as the initial trend value. The forecasts are

$$\text{Month 1 forecast} = F_{t+1} + T_{t+1} = 16 + 2.9 = 18.9$$

Month 2:

$$\text{Base forecast} = FIT_t + \alpha(d_t - FIT_t) = 18.9 + 0.3(16 - 18.9) = 18.0$$
$$\text{Trend forecast} = T_t + \beta(F_{t+1} + FIT_t) = 2.9 + 0.4(18.0 - 18.9) = 2.5$$
$$\text{Month 2 forecast} = F_{t+1} + T_{t+1} = 18.0 + 2.5 = 20.5$$

Table 12-11 shows the trend enhanced exponential smoothing forecast values for all 12 months.

To seasonally adjust these forecasts we need to first estimate the seasonal indexes. As shown in Table 12-11, this is done by simply dividing the sales in each month by the base sales provided by the regression forecast. By examining the indexes, it is clear that a quarterly demand pattern exists, with most sales occurring in the third month of each quarter. We average the seasonal indexes across the four quarters represented in the data, and then use these values to adjust the regression and trend enhanced forecasts, as shown in Table 12-11.

TABLE 12-11 Forecasts for the Solved Problem

Month	Sales (a)	Regression Forecasts (b)	Trend enhanced ES Forecasts (c)	Seasonal Indexes = a / b	Average Seasonal Indexes (d)	Season Adjusted Regression Forecasts d × b	Season Adjusted Trend Enhanced ES Forecasts d × c
1	16	15.5	18.9	1.03	SI for first month = (1.03 + 0.75 + 0.64 + 0.85)/4 = 0.82	0.82(15.5) = 12.7	0.82(18.9) = 15.4
2	20	18.4	20.5	1.09		0.86(18.4) = 15.8	0.86(20.5) = 17.6
3	35	21.3	22.8	1.65	SI for second month = (1.09 + 0.89 + 0.65 + 0.81)/4 = 0.86	1.36(21.3) = 28.9	1.36(22.8) = 31.0
4	18	24.1	30.4	0.75		19.7	24.8
5	24	27.0	29.1	0.89		23.2	25.0
6	33	29.9	29.4	1.10	SI for third month = (1.65 + 1.10 + 1.32 + 1.36)/4 = 1.36	40.6	39.9
7	21	32.8	32.7	0.64		26.7	26.7
8	23	35.6	30.1	0.65		30.6	25.8
9	51	38.5	27.9	1.32		52.3	37.9
10	35	41.4	37.6	0.85		33.8	30.7
11	36	44.3	39.3	0.81		38.0	33.7
12	64	47.1	40.4	1.36		64.0	54.8

Now we can compare the forecasts provided by both seasonally adjusted models. Table 12-12 compares the Bias, MAD, MAPE, and MSE for each of the forecast models.

TABLE 12-12 Comparison of Forecasting Errors

		Seasonally Adjusted Regression				Seasonally Adjusted Trend Enhanced ES			
Month	Sales	Forecast	Forecast Error	Absolute Error	% Absolute Error	Forecast	Forecast Error	Absolute Error	% Absolute Error
1	16	12.7	3.3	3.3	21%	15.4	0.6	0.6	4%
2	20	15.8	4.2	4.2	21%	17.6	2.4	2.4	12%
3	35	28.9	6.1	6.1	17%	31.0	4.0	4.0	11%
4	18	19.7	−1.7	1.7	9%	24.8	−6.8	6.8	38%
5	24	23.2	0.8	0.8	3%	25.0	−1.0	1.0	4%
6	33	40.6	−7.6	7.6	23%	39.9	−6.9	6.9	21%
7	21	26.7	−5.7	5.7	27%	26.7	−5.7	5.7	27%
8	23	30.6	−7.6	7.6	33%	25.8	−2.8	2.8	12%
9	51	52.3	−1.3	1.3	3%	37.9	13.1	13.1	26%
10	35	33.8	1.2	1.2	4%	30.7	4.3	4.3	12%
11	36	38.0	−2.0	2.0	6%	33.7	2.3	2.3	6%
12	64	64.0	0.0	0.0	0%	54.8	9.2	9.2	14%
		Average	**Bias = − 0.9**	**MAD = 3.5**	**MAPE = 14%**		**Bias = 1.1**	**MAD = 4.9**	**MAPE = 16%**

It is clear that the seasonally enhanced regression-based forecasting model outperforms the trend enhanced model, as it has better scores on all bias and accuracy metrics.

Using the seasonally enhanced regression model, the forecasts for the next six months would be

Month 13 forecast = [12.6 + 2.9(13)] (0.82) = 41.2
Month 14 forecast = [12.6 + 2.9(14)] (0.86) = 45.8
Month 15 forecast = [12.6 + 2.9(15)] (1.36) = 76.3
Month 16 forecast = [12.6 + 2.9(16)] (0.82) = 48.4
Month 17 forecast = [12.6 + 2.9(17)] (0.86) = 53.2
Month 18 forecast = [12.6 + 2.9(18)] (1.36) = 88.1

PROBLEMS

1. Assume you are forecasting with an exponential smoothing model using $\alpha = 0.6$. How much weight is placed on the most recent actual demand? How much weight is given to the demand one time period older than the most recent data? How much weight is given to data from two periods in the past?
2. Given the series of demand data below

Period:	1	2	3	4	5	6	7	8	9	10
Demand:	40	33	56	43	23	45	38	40	29	40

   a. Calculate the forecasts for periods 7 through 11 using moving average models with $n = 2$, $n = 4$, and $n = 6$.
   b. Calculate the bias and MAD for each set of forecasts. Which moving average model is best?
3. If last period's forecast was 27 and the demand was 30, what was the forecast error? What would be the forecast for the next period using an exponential smoothing model with alpha = .5?
4. Use the Excel spreadsheet that accompanies this chapter to evaluate different forecasting models using the ice cream sales data. Try the following parameters for the moving average and simple exponential smoothing models: $n = 1, 4, 8$; alpha = 0.1, 0.5, 0.9. Which parameters yield the best forecasting model for the periods under evaluation?
5. You have become concerned about the amount of copier paper used in your office after repeatedly running out of supplies. Your assistant keeps track of the number of reams (packages of 500 sheets) for 24 weeks:

Week	1	2	3	4	5	6	7	8	9	10	11	12
Reams of paper	232	263	271	248	235	261	207	243	237	293	243	260
Week	13	14	15	16	17	18	19	20	21	22	23	24
Reams of paper	253	270	230	253	238	272	222	243	289	238	262	234

   a. Compare the effectiveness of two-week, four-week, and six-week moving averages. Which should you use to forecast copier paper use during the next week?
   b. Compare the performance of the simple exponential smoothing model with smoothing constants of 0.01, 0.05, and 0.25. Assume a forecast for week 1 of 230 reams. Which constant worked best?
6. Assume that you are the production manager for Fast Current Kayaks of Washington State. One of the products that you make and sell is the "Fast Current" sea touring

kayak paddle. You are responsible for ensuring that there is enough production capacity to meet demands (given the very high markup on the paddles).

Year	Quarter	Demand	Year	Quarter	Demand
Year 1	Q1	18	Year 5	Q1	42
	Q2	19		Q2	38
	Q3	18		Q3	59
	Q4	17		Q4	58
Year 2	Q1	19	Year 6	Q1	60
	Q2	21		Q2	61
	Q3	18		Q3	62
	Q4	19		Q4	62
Year 3	Q1	20	Year 7	Q1	64
	Q2	24		Q2	65
	Q3	28		Q3	66
	Q4	32		Q4	68
Year 4	Q1	30	Year 8	Q1	69
	Q2	31		Q2	68
	Q3	34		Q3	67
	Q4	40		Q4	68

a. Given the data shown above, beginning in quarter 1 of year 2, use a moving average based on four quarters to predict the demand in each quarter.
b. Using the same data, forecast demand using exponential smoothing. You are given an initial forecast for year 1, quarter 1 of 17. When generating your forecasts, assume that the smoothing coefficient is 0.10.
c. Which of the forecasting procedures performed the best? Why? *Hint:* Plot the demand data to better understand what is going on.

7. Using $\alpha = 0.5$ and the following data, compute exponential smoothing forecasts for periods 2 through 8.

Period:	1	2	3	4	5	6	7
Forecast:	10						
Actual demand:	12	15	11	13	11	11	10

8. The owner of an online video rental service has recorded the following rentals each week:

Week:	1	2	3	4	5	6	7	8
Rentals:	1202	1503	1444	1254	1609	1499	1689	1555

a. Use a three-week moving average to forecast sales for each of the weeks 4 through 9.
b. Use a four-week moving average to forecast sales for each of the weeks 5 through 9.
c. Compare the forecasts created by these two methods using mean absolute deviation. Which forecasting method would you recommend?

9. A ski repair shop at a resort in Colorado sells replacement poles each season. The shop needs to develop a forecast of next season's sales so that they can place an order for poles with their supplier well in advance of the beginning of the season. Sales data for the past five years are shown below. Compare the forecasts given by the following models.

Year:	1	2	3	4	5
Sales (units):	375	395	360	400	380

Develop forecasts using:

a. A five-year moving average.

b. A weighted moving average model with weights of 0.1, 0.1, 0.2, 0.3, and 0.3 for years 1 through 5 respectively.

c. An exponential smoothing model with year 1 forecast of 380 and $\alpha = 0.2$.

10. The following data show the number of laptop computers sold each month at a retail store:

Month	Unit Sales
January	200
February	230
March	225
April	240
May	210
June	180
July	160
August	310
September	320
October	270
November	250
December	300

a. Assuming the estimated trend from May to June was -4 and the forecast for June was 190, use trend-adjusted exponential smoothing with $\alpha = 0.3$ and $\beta = 0.2$ to forecast sales for each of the seven following months: July, August, September, October, November, December, and January.

b. Use regression for the data from January to June to create a forecast for each month from July to the following January.

c. Compare the two sets of forecasts generated in parts a and b. Which forecast model produces a better MFE? MAD?

11. Use the data from problem 10:

a. Using the average demand for the year as the base, compute a seasonal index for each month.

b. Use regression to estimate the deseasonalized demand in each of the given months. Using these base values, compute a seasonal index for each month.

c. Are the seasonal indexes computed in parts a and b the same or different? Why?

d. Using the regression model and the seasonal indexes you computed in part b, compute a seasonally adjusted forecast for January, February, March, April, and May of the next year.

12. Monthly usage data for pallets used in a distribution center are as follows:

Year	**1**	**2**	**3**	**4**
January	1484	1482	1792	1902
February	1394	1400	1586	1722
March	1552	1548	1770	1876
April	1796	1864	2110	2218
May	2060	2198	2408	2548
June	2214	2446	2652	2844
July	2330	2580	2606	2972
August	2432	2698	2872	3110
September	2416	2682	2946	3208

October	2262	2592	2906	3200
November	1942	2132	2340	2806
December	1566	1802	2046	2418

a. Calculate the monthly usage index for each month.
b. Use simple linear regression to forecast total usage of pallets for year 5.
c. Forecast the seasonally adjusted usage for pallets for each month in year 5.

13. Given the data shown below, use $\alpha = .2$ and $\beta = .4$ to create a trend enhanced smoothing based forecast for period 7. Assume that $FIT_1 = 22$ and $T_1 = 7.83$.

Period:	1	2	3	4	5	6
Demand:	19	33	37	49	52	60

14. Repeat problem 13 using $\alpha = .4$ and $\beta = .8$. Which model gives a better approximation of the demand pattern for periods 1 through 6?
15. Calculate the slope and intercept for the data in problem 13 using simple linear regression. You may want to use an Excel spreadsheet to check your answer.
16. Wamaco Corporation uses the same simple exponential smoothing forecasting model for all of its products. The model has yielded the following weekly forecasts:

Week:	1	2	3	4	5	6
Product 1 forecast:	12	10.6	10.9	12.4	13.5	12.5
Product 1 sales:	10	11	13	14	12	10
Product 2 forecast:	102	100.6	103	104.4	104.8	108.4
Product 2 sales:	100	104	105	105	110	106

a. What value of α is Wamaco Corp using in its forecasting model?
b. Calculate the forecast for period 7 for product 1 and product 2.
c. Using the first six periods of data, calculate the Bias (MFE), MAD, MPE, and MAPE. Does the forecasting model provide about the same bias and accuracy for both products? What would you recommend?

17. Many supply managers use a monthly reported survey result known as the purchasing managers' index (PMI) as a leading indicator to forecast future sales for their businesses. Suppose that the PMI and your business sales data for the last 10 months are the following:

Month:	1	2	3	4	5	6	7	8	9	10
PMI:	42.1	43.0	41.0	38.2	40.2	44.1	45.8	49.0	48.7	52.0
Sales (1000s):	121	123	125	120	118	118	122	127	135	136

a. Construct a causal regression model using PMI as the causal variable. How well does your model fit the data?
b. Suppose that the PMI is truly a *leading* indicator. That is, the PMI value in one period influences sales in the following period. Construct a new regression model using this information. Is the new model better or worse than the model you made for part a?
c. Pick the best model from parts a and b, and create a forecast for sales given PMI = 47.3.

18. Assume that the following demands vary according a four-period seasonal cycle:

Month:	1	2	3	4	5	6	7	8
Demand:	20	30	40	20	50	70	95	50

a. Compute the seasonal indexes using the average demand in each cycle as the base.
b. Compute the seasonal indexes using regression estimates as the base.
c. How do the answers for parts a and b differ? How would you explain the difference?

19. Use the Excel spreadsheet that accompanies this supplement to evaluate different forecasting models using the ice cream sales data.
    a. Which model, time series regression, causal regression using temperature, or trend enhanced exponential smoothing, gives better forecast accuracy? Report all bias and accuracy metrics.
    b. What combination of parameters for the trend enhanced smoothing model gives the best results?
    c. Calculate seasonally adjusted forecasts, first using the average demand as the base, then using the time series regression forecasts as the base, then using the causal regression forecasts as the base. Which model is better? Why?
20. Suppose that you have become concerned about the amount of copier paper used in your office after repeatedly running out of supplies. Your assistant keeps track of the number of reams (packages of 500 sheets) for 24 weeks, as follows:

Week:	1	2	3	4	5	6	7	8	9	10	11	12
Reams of paper:	232	263	271	248	235	261	207	243	237	293	243	260
Week:	13	14	15	16	17	18	19	20	21	22	23	24
Reams of paper:	253	270	230	253	238	272	222	243	289	238	262	234

    a. Evaluate alternative forecasting models. Is a simple model or a trend or seasonally enhanced model better?
    b. How could you use this information to solve the paper shortage problem?

CASE

Rachel's Breakfast Café

Rachel Kirkpatrick thought to herself, "What a waste," as she threw away three bags full of unsold items and spoiled ingredients. "I have to get better at estimating how much food to order and prepare."

Rachel owned and operated a small café that specialized in fresh baked quiches, breakfast casseroles, and breads, as well as ready-made country style breakfasts. The café was open six days a week, and closed on Sundays. Rachel had run her shop for over a year now, and business seemed to be taking off. While she had made a number of operating improvements related to the consistency and quality of her products, she still struggled between two extremes of the same problem. On some days Rachel did not have enough ingredients on hand to satisfy the day's customers. In this case some of the people who expected to get one of her famous quiches were disappointed. Other days Rachel had far too much food on hand. On days like today, Rachel found herself throwing away food because she had vastly overestimated the number of customers she would have.

While it was difficult for Rachel to know exactly how many customers she served each day, she was able to accurately track the total dollar value of sales. It seemed to her that her business was growing, but she had not taken the time to see whether the increasing demand was a true trend or just her perception. Based on this perception, Rachel had been placing larger orders with her suppliers of milk, eggs, cheese, and other ingredients each week. Each day Rachel placed orders for supplies online at a nearby grocer's Web site, and he delivered each order five days later.

As Rachel considered how to improve her forecasts for needed items, she thought about possible factors that caused demand to be greater or smaller each day at her café. Fridays and Saturdays were usually busier than other days. Beyond the weekend effect, she noted that the weather had an impact. On rainy days people were less likely to go out for breakfast. Rachel wondered how she could use this information to improve her business.

Over the next four weeks Rachel collected the data shown in the following table. The "5 day forecast" column shows the probability of rain (percentage) for the area around Rachel's café, as predicted by the local weather service five days into the future. For example, the table shows a forecasted 10 percent probability of rain on the first Monday in the table; this was the forecast released by the weather service on the Wednesday five days earlier. Since it currently took Rachel five days to receive orders for her supplies, she knew that she would need to have the weather forecast at least this far in advance in order for it to be of use to her. At the same time, she also knew that shorter term forecasts are usually more accurate. So, she also decided to also track the "2 day forecast," that is, forecasts made two days in advance.

Day	Probability of Rain (%) 5 day forecast	Probability of Rain (%) 2 day forecast	Total Sales
Monday	10	40	5520
Tuesday	20	30	4320
Wednesday	30	10	4212
Thursday	50	40	4987
Friday	80	80	5545
Saturday	90	90	6023
Monday	60	30	4590
Tuesday	70	30	4733
Wednesday	90	30	4923
Thursday	100	50	4687
Friday	100	100	5988
Saturday	20	70	6132
Monday	10	10	5324
Tuesday	10	10	4526
Wednesday	10	10	5232
Thursday	50	50	5684
Friday	20	70	5911
Saturday	60	60	6328
Monday	20	20	4932
Tuesday	15	15	5235
Wednesday	20	50	5862
Thursday	20	20	4862
Friday	10	80	6100
Saturday	60	70	6255

Questions

1. Develop forecasts using regressions of sales on each of the series of rain forecasts respectively. Calculate the MFE (bias), MAD, and MAPE for the two forecasting models. Which rain forecast seems to be better at predicting Rachel's daily sales, the five-day forecast or the two-day forecast?
2. How can Rachel make use of the rain forecasts to improve her forecasts of total sales each day? What other changes to her business would she need to make in order to capitalize on this information?
3. How are order lead time and forecasting accuracy related to each other in this case?
4. Plot and visually inspect the sales data. What other suggestions would you give Rachel for improving her sales forecasts? What type of time series model would be appropriate? Why?

CASE

C&F Apparel, Inc.

Bill Smith, director of business planning for C&F Apparel, chewed on a pencil as he looked out the window of his fourth-story office. These bad forecasts are killing us, he thought. Forecast errors for the Fall season's sales had ranged from 50 to 200 percent of demand. As a consequence, C&F had discounted their apparel heavily, with average markdowns of 30 percent. In addition, they had written off some 15 percent of inventory as obsolete.

C&F Apparel was a medium-sized designer and producer of sports apparel and active wear, including pants, shirts, sweaters, and some accessories. Though it did not own any retail stores, it sold through most of the larger retail outlets throughout North America. The clothes sold by C&F were considered by most consumers to be durable and reasonably priced. While its fashions were not cutting edge, C&F managed to keep up with trends and changing designs from season to season. Each selling season lasted about 15 weeks.

Developing good forecasts and maintaining product availability were constant challenges for C&F. To keep costs low, the company sourced most of its products from material and assembly plants located in the Pacific rim countries including China, Vietnam, and Thailand. The lead time to have new designs made and shipped from these countries was typically two to three months, so it was important for initial sales estimates to be as accurate as possible. Bill Smith and his marketing team took it upon themselves to develop forecasts each season. They used sales from the previous year's season, along with their judgments regarding upcoming changes in economic conditions and consumer tastes. While the aggregate sales forecasts developed by Bill and his team were sometimes fairly accurate, forecasts for specific items were all over the map. Bill knew that their forecasting process was not as totally consistent from season to season as it could be, but he felt that flexibility was needed to cope with changing conditions.

Bill had recently heard about "fast fashion" apparel makers like Zara, a Spanish company that designs, produces, and sells expensive, top-of-the-line apparel. An article describing Zara's forecasting and fulfillment policies intrigued him. Zara had price markdowns that were much lower than industry averages, and their sales per square foot were 20–30 percent higher. The article attributed better performance to several factors. First, Zara was known for developing long-term purchase contracts, mostly with domestic suppliers. Their supply lead times were typically two to three weeks. Second, Zara used store manager inputs and sales information from its own retail stores to rapidly update its sales forecasts throughout each sales season. The company was known to invite store managers to corporate headquarters at the beginning of each season so that they could evaluate the new product lines. Finally, Zara had focused product teams responsible for developing the forecasting process for each product category.

Bill wondered if these approaches might work at C&F.

Questions

1. What are the advantages and disadvantages of Zara's methods?
2. Would these methods work at a company like C&F?
3. What advice would you give to Bill Smith?

SELECTED READINGS & INTERNET SITES

Institute of Business Forecasting and Planning

www.ibf.org

Armstrong, J. S. (ed). *Principles of Forecasting: A Handbook for Researchers and Practitioners.* New York: Kluwer Academic Publishers, 2001.

Crosby, J. V. *Cycles, Trends, and Turning Points: Practical Marketing & Sales Forecasting Techniques.* Lincolnwood, IL: NTC Business Books, 2000.

Ghemawat, P., and J. N. Nueno. "ZARA: Fast Fashion." *Harvard Business Review,* April 1, 2003.

Gilliland, M. "Is Forecasting a Waste of Time?" *Supply Chain Management Review* 6, no. 4 (July/August 2002), pp. 16–23.

Kahn, K. B. "An Exploratory Investigation of New Product Forecasting Practices." *Journal of Product Innovation Management* 19, no. 2 (March 2002), pp. 133–43.

Makridakis, S., and S. C. Wheelwright. *Forecasting Methods for Management,* 5th ed. New York: John Wiley & Sons, 1989.

Robb, D. J., and E. A. Silver. "Using Composite Moving Averages to Forecast Sales." *Journal of the Operational Research Society* 53, no. 11 (November 2002), pp. 1281–85.

Woolsey, R. E. D., and H. F. Swanson. *Operations Research for Immediate Application: A Quick and Dirty Manual.* New York: Harper & Row, 1975.

13 Sales and Operations Planning

CHAPTER OUTLINE

LEARNING OBJECTIVES *After studying this chapter, you should be able to:*

LO13-1 Describe the role and the process of sales and operations planning.

LO13-2 Define the contents of an aggregate plan.

LO13-3 Explain the relevant costs in developing an aggregate plan.

LO13-4 Contrast different types of aggregate production strategies.

LO13-5 Develop alternative aggregate production plans.

LO13-6 Explain the differences in aggregate planning in services versus manufacturing industries.

Sunsweet Growers Implements Advanced S&OP

In most supply chains, the key constraint lies either on the supply side or the demand side. But for dried-fruit producer Sunsweet Growers, both supply and demand are determined by factors beyond the company's control. The company's Yuba City plant operates throughout the year, but harvest takes place only during September and October. The fruit is dried and stored immediately after harvest, and then processed and shipped throughout the year. Demand, however, is highly seasonal, with peak times occurring during the Christmas holiday period, resulting in costly overtime and difficulty in maintaining its 98 percent customer fill rate. The wide variety of products requires sophisticated scheduling and planning. For example, the fruit is packaged in clear bags, stand-up pouch bags, cartons, bulk cases, and cans. Containers range in size from one ounce to 50 pounds and are labeled in 20 languages, and there are 20 different sizes and grades of prunes to be processed and packaged.

Sunsweet recognized that sales and operations planning (S&OP) is key to running an optimized supply chain. Implementation of an S&OP process has provided all groups within the organization a better understanding of how to work together to reduce cost and improve order lead time. Sunsweet is now able to develop a more accurate forecast and has seen major improvements in delivery performance and cost management. The company has reduced the number of production lines, reduced changeovers, and reduced overtime from 30 percent to 10 percent.

By implementing a successful S&OP program, Sunsweet benefits from increased visibility into its supply chain and is better able to align all areas within the organization to make better business decisions. Participants in the process can now understand sales and marketing expectations and how they relate to realistic manufacturing scheduling and production. As a result, they can make better collaborative decisions on issues that affect the supply chain performance of the entire organization.

Source: Adapted from H. Upton and H. Singh, "Balanced S&OP: Sunsweet Growers' Story," *Supply Chain Management Review* 11, no. 2 (2007), p. 51.

This chapter discusses a fundamental challenge that every organization faces, balancing supply with demand. It is often difficult to supply the exact quantity of products and services at the exact time customers demand them. Compounding the problem, in many organizations sales and marketing executives often do not discuss their plans with their counterparts in supply chain operations functions. Likewise, operations executives frequently do not tell sales and marketing personnel about supply constraints and capacity plans. The inevitable result is a mismatch between the organization's sales plan and its operations plan. For example, countless stories are told about companies who were not prepared for the amount of demand created by highly discounted promotions, resulting in product shortages and dissatisfied customers.

sales and operations planning (S&OP) A process to develop tactical plans by integrating customer-focused marketing plans for new and existing products with the operational management of the supply chain.

Sunsweet Growers found the solution to this problem in a process called **sales and operations planning (S&OP)**. S&OP is a process to develop tactical plans by integrating customer-focused marketing plans for new and existing products with the operational management of the supply chain.

This chapter discusses S&OP by building on the inventory and demand planning principles discussed in Chapters 7 and 12. It describes the process of sales and operations planning, and then focuses on procedures for developing an aggregate production plan. The chapter closes with a discussion of the application of these processes in service industries.

Prepare

What is the role and the process of sales and operations planning?

Organize

Sales and Operations Planning
- S&OP Benefits
- The S&OP Process

SALES AND OPERATIONS PLANNING

In the hierarchy of supply chain planning activities described at the beginning of Chapter 12, S&OP is considered to be intermediate-range planning; that is, it focuses on a time period ranging from 3 to 18 months. Typically, it is broken into time increments that are weekly, monthly, or quarterly, depending on the specific needs of a company. Planning occurs at the aggregated, product-family level, though it may include some detailed planning for critical items and special events such as new product launches. The process brings together all of the plans for the business (sales, marketing, new products, logistics, manufacturing, supply, and financial) into one integrated set of plans. While the implementation of S&OP often varies from company to company, there are certain common features present in nearly all S&OP processes.

relationships

Figure 13-1 provides an overview of S&OP. Typically, sales and marketing executives bring to the S&OP meetings their ideal or unconstrained sales plans based on their analysis of existing customer orders, plus plans for new product introductions, promotions, expected competitive actions, and the like. Operations executives bring plans and knowledge concerning capacity constraints, inventory policies, suppliers' capabilities, materials

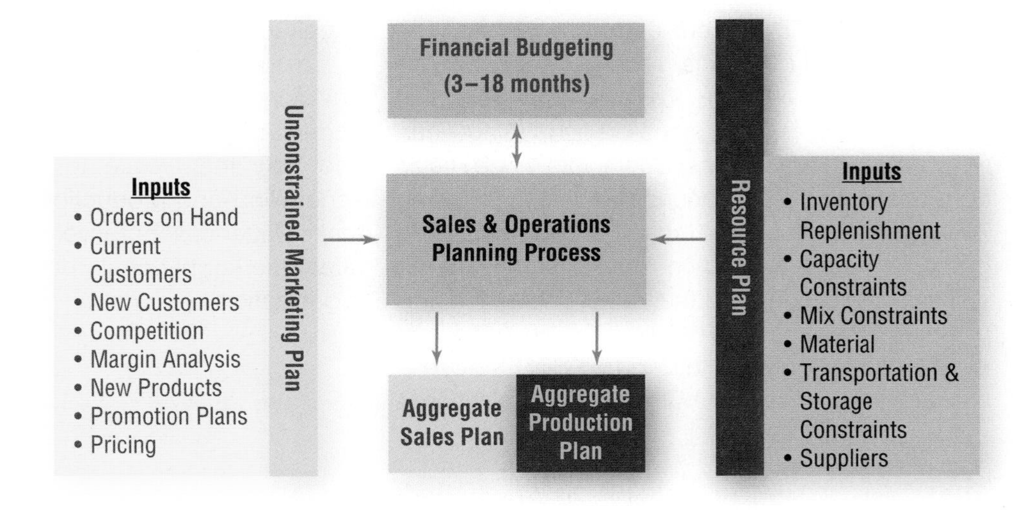

FIGURE 13-1 Overview of Sales and Operations Planning

availability, and transportation and storage capabilities. Financial managers bring budgets that define goals for managing inventories, cash flows, and other capital expenditures.

In S&OP, the parties involved try to resolve potential conflicts among the objectives of three primary functional groups: sales, operations, and finance. (See Tables 13-1 and 13-2.) For example, sales personnel might want to offer many different variations of a product to attract more customers. However, operations and financial planners might prefer to limit product offerings in order to maximize production runs, avoid costly changeovers, and focus on the most profitable customers. In addition, the company may not have the capacity either internally or in the supply base to meet all of sales' objectives.

LO13-1 Describe the role and the process of sales and operations planning.

Similarly, finance and operations managers might disagree over scheduling decisions. Operations managers typically want to minimize costs and maximize equipment uptime and product quality, whereas finance managers typically focus more on working capital and profitability. How these competing concerns are resolved has major implications for how the firm positions itself competitively. S&OP forces the different functional managers to explicitly consider each other's concerns, and to create a unified and balanced plan that fits with the firm's overall strategic objectives.

S&OP Benefits

Organizations that have effective S&OP processes have experienced both "hard" (quantifiable) and "soft" (qualitative) benefits. The hard benefits include:

- Improved forecast accuracy. Detailed discussions between executives representing all of the key functions results in a consensus forecast that is usually more accurate.
- Higher customer service with lower finished goods inventory levels due to better forecasts and coordination of supply with demand.
- More stable supply rates, resulting in higher productivity (for purchasing, suppliers, and operations).
- Faster and more controlled new product introduction.

In addition, the soft benefits include:

- Enhanced teamwork at both the executive and operating levels.
- Better decisions with less effort and time.

TABLE 13-1 Sales and Operations: Balancing Objectives

Sales	Operations
Aggregate forecasts	Detailed forecasts
Many product variations	Few product variations
Rapid response	Long production runs
High service	Stable production schedules
Maximize revenue	Maximize output/minimize costs

TABLE 13-2 Finance and Operations: Balancing Objectives

Finance	Operations
Maximize financial returns	Minimize costs
Reduce financial risk	Reduce variance
High returns on investment	Maintain uptime
Focus on customers with highest contribution margins	Focus on grouping orders together to enhance operational efficiency or to reduce setups

- Better alignment of operational, marketing, and financial plans.
- Greater accountability for results.
- A window into the future to see potential problems soon enough to prevent them from becoming real problems.

The Get Real box below about Heinz provides an example of the conflicting objectives that exist between functions, and the benefits of developing an S&OP process.

The S&OP Process

relationships

While there is no specific set of steps that must be followed, Figure 13-2 summarizes a typical S&OP process. The S&OP team first reviews prior plans and results so that lessons learned can be applied to the new planning period. The supply and demand functional reviews produce a consensus forecast that guides the initial functional plans. In reality, planning is usually an iterative process, where the S&OP team develops a consensus forecast and then each functional area develops its initial plans. The S&OP team then meets again (as indicated by the red lines in the diagram), to work out problems or potential inconsistencies. For example, when the sales team is exposed to an initial aggregate production plan with its costs and constraints, they may consider alternative sales strategies and tactics that impact the sales forecast and result in a more efficient production plan. Likewise, the operations team, once exposed to the sales plan, may be able to adjust the production plan to meet the sales objectives.

GET REAL

One-Number Forecasting at Heinz

Heinz North America (HNA) is well-known for such brands as Heinz Ketchup, Pickles, Vinegar, and Relish as well as sauces such as 57 Sauce, Home-Style Gravy, and Classico Pasta Sauces. It also has frozen brands including Smart Ones Frozen Meals and Desserts, Boston Market Meals and Sides, Ore-Ida Potatoes, Bagel Bites, and TGIF Appetizers.

Until 2002, the responsibility for forecasting resided with marketing/brand management, which posed both benefits and challenges. In this approach each brand manager led initiatives to grow their businesses. However, challenges included the presence of different motives underlying different forecasts. Brand management teams tended to be optimistic in forecasting, while sales management was conservative because of sales quotas. Finance typically added more optimism to the forecast, while production planning often applied a bit of conservatism in their desire to maintain low inventories. The functional groups' estimates differed from each other because of their different assumptions and motivations. When shipments did not materialize as forecasted, everyone had their own explanation of why they missed the forecast.

Recently, Heinz required the forecasting department to begin reporting to the VP of supply chain, who was tasked with responsibility to provide the essential link between the front end (marketing/sales) and the back end (supply chain and operations) using the same forecast. Now, one forecast drives both the front-end business planning and the supply chain through constant communication and consensus meetings.

The one-number forecast enabled the entire organization to plan based on the same assumptions, risks, and upsides. In addition, it encouraged productive conversations around true planning for the first time. For instance, budgeting became less confusing because the same volume forecast drove plans of marketing, sales, production, inventory, transit/warehousing, manufacturing/co-packing, and, ultimately financials. When spending increased or decreased, appropriate volume was either added or removed from the forecast. When large events at certain accounts shifted in execution timing, the associated volume also was moved. When promotions changed at the account level, deployment plans changed accordingly.

With this approach, potential issues surrounding supplies/suppliers and capacity at factories and warehouses surfaced much earlier than before. Most importantly, everyone was held accountable for the inputs and assumptions for the final forecast.

Source: Adapted from S. Park, "One-Number Forecasting: Heinz's Experience and Learning," *The Journal of Business Forecasting* 27, no. 1 (2008), pp. 29–32.

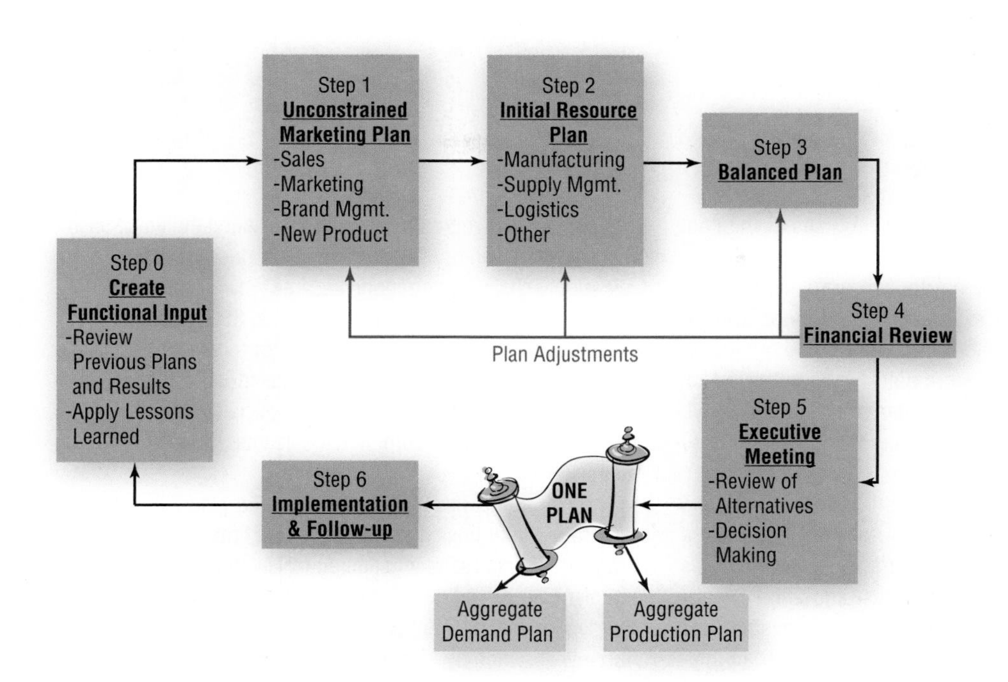

FIGURE 13-2
The S&OP Process

S&OP is a dynamic process, not a one-time event. It would be extremely rare for a company to establish an aggregate production plan at the beginning of a year and simply follow it blindly for the next six or twelve months. Most firms that have incorporated S&OP as a part of their overall management process hold monthly, or at least quarterly, review meetings. Operations personnel and marketing/sales personnel review performance to date and bring new information to the process. For example, two months into the year, sales and marketing personnel have some actual demand data, more information concerning future orders from customers, and possibly revised forecasts of sales for the remainder of the year. Likewise, based on events that occur, sales plans for new products or promotions may be revised.

LO13-2 Describe the contents of an aggregate plan.

Similarly, conditions in operations may change. Unexpected machine breakdowns, employee strikes, and other events can drastically change the aggregate production plan. Many companies incorporate **rolling planning horizons**, meaning that they replan each period (month or quarter), for a given number of periods into the future. This approach updates the S&OP sales plan and aggregate production plan as conditions change.

rolling planning horizons Replan each period (month or quarter), for a given number of periods into the future.

Working collaboratively with customers and suppliers is one of the main ingredients of a successful S&OP program. Bringing customers into the process through CPFR initiatives (discussed in Chapter 12) provides much deeper insight into demand. Sharing aggregate production plans with key suppliers allows them to be better positioned to meet the requirements for materials, components, and supplies. Leveraging the capabilities and influence of customers and suppliers expands the scope of potential improvements for the organization and for the entire supply chain. The Get Real story about Lowe's and Whirlpool on the next page describes how those firms worked together to develop an integrated planning process that has resulted in better financial results for both companies.

Ultimately, the output of the S&OP process is a balance in the demand plan and the **aggregate production plan**. The aggregate production plan specifies the production rates, inventory, employment levels, backlogs, possible subcontracting, and other resources needed to meet the demand plan. Aggregate planning is typically accomplished at the level of a product line or product family rather than the individual product or SKU, thus the term *aggregate*. Techniques and methods for modifying demand were discussed in detail in Chapter 12, "Demand Planning: Forecasting and Demand Management." The remainder of this chapter is devoted to techniques for modifying supply to meet demand through development of the aggregate production plan.

aggregate production plan Specifies the production rates, inventory, employment levels, backlogs, possible subcontracting, and other resources needed to meet the sales plan.

Whirlpool and Lowe's Integrate Their Planning

Historically, interactions between Lowe's and Whirlpool addressed only immediate merchandising and sales issues. Limited communications between the two firms led to problems from time to time. For example, when Whirlpool introduced a new line of products, both Lowe's and Whirlpool wanted to get the line into the store quickly. When the launch date was set, the merchandising leader from Lowe's asked, "When did you know you were going to bring this line to the market?" The answer was, "We've known for months." Because Whirlpool had not shared this information, the two companies had to negotiate the split for tens of thousands of dollars of liquidation costs required for Lowe's to sell out its inventory of the existing line. A little trust and shared information would have saved both companies aggravation and money. Today, Lowe's and Whirlpool are working in an integrated planning process.

The effort began with a focus on collaborative demand planning. After developing a collaborative demand planning process, Lowe's' and Whirlpool moved more towards supply planning. Lowe's' initial focus was on recognizing the capabilities and limitations of Whirlpool's manufacturing divisions. Both companies worked to develop an understanding of each other's target inventory levels and new product planning. Next, their supply chain organizations became actively involved with the sales and merchandising organizations. Structured demand and supply reviews created a single set of forecasts and sales plans for both companies. They focused collaboration on promotions, product launches, and special-event planning, creating an integrated promotional calendar for each product category.

The two companies developed a shared planning process built around joint business objectives that emerged from each company's internal sales and operational planning process. This joint planning helped Lowe's and Whirlpool to realize improvements in several key metrics. Unit sales growth increased over a three-year period by 12 percent, while overall inventory costs went down by 5 percent.

Source: Based on L. Smith, J. C. Andraski, and S. E. Fawcett, "Integrated Business Planning: A Roadmap to Linking S&OP and CPFR.," *The Journal of Business Forecasting* 29, no. 4 (2010), pp. 4, 7, 9–13.

Prepare

What is an aggregate plan? What are the costs involved in the different aggregate production strategies?

Organize

Aggregate Production Planning
 Relevant Aggregate Planning Costs
 Aggregate Production Strategies

AGGREGATE PRODUCTION PLANNING

The overall goal of aggregate production planning (also called *aggregate capacity planning*) is to set targets for inventory and various sources of capacity so that supply will match demand over the intermediate time frame in the most efficient way possible. The aggregate plan also takes into account other constraints formed by the company's strategy and the often conflicting wishes of each of the functional areas. Though it is called *production* planning, this type of planning is equally important in service businesses as well as in manufacturing. In either case, evaluating the merits of various plans requires the evaluation of a large number of cost trade-offs.

Relevant Aggregate Planning Costs

LO13-3 Explain the relevant costs in developing an aggregate plan.

To do aggregate planning, several different types of costs must be identified and quantified, including the following:

- *Inventory holding cost.* As discussed in Chapter 7, maintaining inventory involves a number of expenses related to the cost of capital invested in inventory, insurance, storage, obsolescence, and taxes.
- *Regular production cost.* The regular production cost includes the average labor cost to produce an aggregate unit and any benefits that are a part of the pay package.
- *Overtime cost.* In many instances, overtime may be scheduled for the labor force to gain additional output. Overtime costs are generally stated as some percentage of regular production cost.

- *Hiring cost.* This cost includes the cost of advertising for new workers, interviewing them, processing their applications, and then training them. In addition, new workers may not be as productive as veteran workers and this should be factored into the cost as well. In many instances, temporary workers may be hired for a short time period. Hiring and firing costs for temporary workers may be less than for permanent workers.
- *Firing/layoff cost.* When the workforce level is decreased, there are costs associated with either firing or laying off the workers. Separation costs can include unemployment compensation or lump sum separation payments. Some union contracts require that workers receive a portion of their normal pay for a period of time after they have been laid off.
- *Backorder/lost sales cost.* A firm may plan to either backorder a demand or lose the sales for that demand. In the backorder case, there will likely be an explicit penalty for late delivery, but there is also a good chance that there is a customer ill-will cost that is harder to quantify. In the case of lost sales, there is the direct loss of profit and the additional ill-will cost of not being able to meet demand.
- *Subcontracting cost.* A company may choose to subcontract (outsource) production to another firm for a period of time. Associated costs are generally stated on a per-unit basis. An additional cost is sometimes added above the contracted price because of the lack of control over quality and delivery, although this portion is difficult to estimate.

Some of these costs may be difficult to precisely measure, and estimates may be required. In some cases, where a cost is extremely difficult to determine, some firms choose to leave the costs out. They compare scenarios based on multiple criteria, making a judgment about the level of the removed factor as opposed to the cost impact of that factor. This is particularly true for the cost of backorders and possible lost sales.

In addition to these costs, there are other constraints on production plans. For example, company policy may limit the number of layoffs allowed in any one period. Subcontracting might be limited by corporate fiat due to the lack of control over quality. Limits on the level of working capital might limit the amount of inventory allowed. Companies often limit the degree to which backorders and lost sales can be included in a plan. The belief is that these can damage the company's image in the eyes of its customers. However, some companies might find meeting peak demand to be cost-prohibitive during very high demand periods, in which case backorders may be necessary.

Certain functional area requirements may create additional constraints in the production planning process. For example, marketing may want a minimum service level that can be expressed as a minimum inventory level for each period. This minimum inventory may be needed to provide protection against uncertain demands and to provide a proper mix of finished goods to meet customer demands. Similarly, human resource managers may limit the amount of overtime allowed, as the strain of working long hours may lead to safety and labor problems, lost productivity, or turnover. Thus, along with minimizing costs, aggregate planning must address other goals in a sustainable way.

sustainability

LO13-4 Contrast different types of aggregate production strategies.

Aggregate Production Strategies

Solving aggregate planning problems involves formulating alternative production strategies for meeting demand and determining the cost and feasibility of those alternatives. There are two "pure" strategies that form extreme alternatives of aggregate plans. In a **level production strategy**, the firm produces at a constant rate over the year, building inventory in periods of low demand and depleting the inventory in periods of high demand. In a **chase strategy**, the production rate is changed in each period to match the amount of expected demand. In reality, most firms typically use a mixed or hybrid strategy somewhere between these generic strategies, but these generic options are worth discussing to better understand the trade-offs involved for developing a good aggregate plan.

level production strategy The firm produces at a constant rate over the year.

chase strategy The production rate is changed in each period to match the amount of expected demand.

As we mentioned earlier, aggregate planning is not limited to manufacturing firms. All organizations face a problem of matching their productive capacity to the pattern of demand. Consider the demand pattern of a hypothetical retailer illustrated in Figure 13-3. Retailers often attempt to manage demand to obtain somewhat more stable patterns; consider early bird specials and attempts to encourage early Christmas shopping, for example. However, at least some level of variation in demands is usually unavoidable. Retailers are likely to adopt a plan that is closer to a chase strategy.

Level Production Strategy

A level production strategy is used when the costs of ramping production up and down are high and inventory costs are relatively low. If a firm's processes require highly skilled workers that are hard to find, it is more likely to use a level strategy. For example, a shop that employs highly skilled machinists is likely to avoid hiring and firing them, especially if they are hard to find, or if they are protected by a strong union. Similarly, if the constraining resources are machines that cannot easily be scaled up or down (such as in a paper mill), the firm will likely pursue a level strategy.

The level production strategy provides a constant rate of output over the entire planning time period, and requires no overtime, no changes in the workforce level, and no subcontracting. The disadvantage of this is that it can cause inventory levels to be quite high following low-demand seasons. It generally results in the highest investment in inventory, high inventory carrying cost, and risk of inventory obsolescence, and it requires storage space capacity. However, it requires the least overall investment in plant and equipment because an average production rate can be maintained throughout the year.

Chase Strategy

A chase strategy is generally used by firms that have high per-unit inventory holding cost rates relative to their cost of changing the production rate. They may use part-time seasonal workers who can be hired during peak-demand periods and laid off during low-demand seasons. Firms that require little in the way of labor skills or training, or those producing goods that are perishable or quickly become obsolete, are candidates for some form of a chase strategy.

Most service businesses use a chase strategy because they don't have the option of building inventory of their product. Retailers who have very high peak-demand periods, such as the Christmas season, make extensive use of temporary workers. Many firms in high-technology industries follow a chase strategy because product changes occur so rapidly that inventory held over any substantial amount of time can easily be rendered obsolete.

A chase strategy can be executed by adjusting labor, subcontracting, or some mixture of the two. One approach is to hire and fire or lay off workers as needed. This, of course, involves the associated costs of hiring and terminating employees. It also might require higher investment in production plant/equipment, as enough capacity is needed to produce

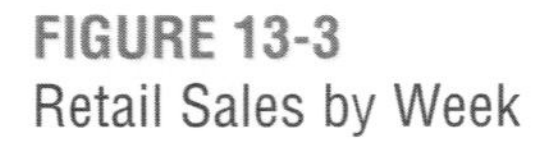
FIGURE 13-3
Retail Sales by Week

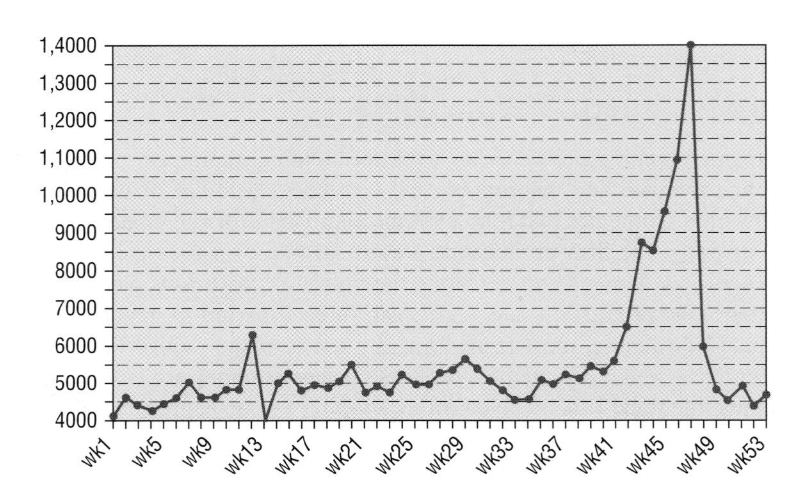

GET REAL

Canon Struggles to Shrink Level of Digital Camera Inventory

The global economy's dizzying downturn brought an abrupt end to the digital camera boom. In the middle of the 2008 Christmas shopping season, digital camera makers cut prices deeply in a desperate effort to reduce their excess inventories. This was a dramatic reversal of fortunes for the industry. The global digital camera market expanded briskly for several years, with annual sales of about 126 million units in 2007, up 26 percent from the previous year. Digital camera makers had already manufactured products for the 2008 Christmas shopping season, based on projections that sales would continue growing at the same torrid pace as in the past several years. As a result, the industry found itself saddled with mountains of oversupply.

"The biggest waste for a manufacturer is inventory," said Canon Executive Vice President Toshizo Tanaka. "We need to cut down on unnecessary spending as much as possible in the current tough environment." Even Canon's efficient and flexible supply chain management system failed to adjust production quickly enough to match the rapid collapse of final demand, allowing excessive output to build up.

Canon's sharp output reduction did not come without strain. Contract workers at the company's digital camera manufacturing unit in Oita Prefecture were laid off. Canon buys digital cameras from a contract manufacturer, which was forced to shed about 1,100 jobs when its order was slashed.

Source: Excerpted and adapted from "Canon Struggles to Shrink Level of Digital Camera Inventory," *Nikkei Weekly*, Yoshiki Tanaka and Masamichi Hoshi, staff writers, January 5, 2009.

at the required rate in the highest-demand period. Consider the hypothetical retailer discussed earlier who must have enough checkout lanes and equipment available to meet demand in the heaviest weeks, although much of this equipment is hardly used during the majority of the year. There are also ethical concerns involved in frequent changes to workforce size. In reality, most companies try to avoid continual hiring, firing, or layoff as much as possible given the impact of these practices on workers and their families and communities.

sustainability

Managers can also use overtime to vary the production rate. Because workers generally earn premium wages for overtime work, the manufacturing cost per unit increases when this option is used. There is also a practical limit to the amount of overtime for employees. If too much overtime is used, worker burnout, safety risks, and/or quality problems can result.

A firm can use subcontracting to supplement output while maintaining a level workforce or production rate inside its own walls. Subcontractors are sometimes paid an amount that is higher than the per-unit cost of making the product internally. However, subcontracting allows firms to maintain less overhead and investment in fixed assets. There is some loss of control when subcontractors are used, with an increased possibility of problems related to product quality. One way firms manage this risk is by maintaining the production of the high-value products or components requiring the latest product or process technology, and subcontracting the lower-value, more mature products or components.

Hybrid Strategies

Most firms implement a **mixed or hybrid strategy**. Such a strategy includes some elements of both level and chase strategies. For example, a company might use inventory to help smooth production during part of a season, and then workforce changes, including

mixed or hybrid strategy A strategy that includes some elements of level production and some elements of chase production strategies.

overtime and temporary workers, to supplement production during another part of the season. These mixed strategies tend to keep costs lower than pure strategies.

Regardless of the chosen strategy, aggregate production plans need to be revisited when circumstances change. The Get Real box about Canon on the previous page shows how the unexpected downturn of the economy in 2008 affected that company's production plans.

Prepare

How do operations managers develop alternative aggregate production plans?

Organize

Creating an Aggregate Production Plan
- Level Production Plan
- Chase Plans
- Hybrid Plans
- Comparing Aggregate Production Plans

LO13-5 Develop alternative aggregate production plans.

CREATING AN AGGREGATE PRODUCTION PLAN

Suppose you have been given responsibility for developing the six-month aggregate production plan at Soda Galore, a manufacturer of soft drinks. Your company makes three types of soft drinks: regular, diet, and super-caffeinated. Fortunately, all three types are made using the same production process, and the costs related to switching between the three types are so minimal that they can be ignored. Thus, you can treat your problem as an aggregate planning exercise where the planning unit is cases of soft drinks, regardless of what types of drinks they are.

The S&OP team has developed a forecast of demand for the first six months of the year as shown in Table 13-3. The S&OP team has also provided you with the cost data shown in Table 13-4.

The material cost of a case of soda is the same regardless of whether it is produced in regular time or overtime. Also assume that Soda Galore always plans to hold 5,000 cases

TABLE 13-3 Monthly Demand at Soda Galore

Month	Demand Forecast
January	24,000 cases
February	32,000 cases
March	32,000 cases
April	48,000 cases
May	60,000 cases
June	44,000 cases
Total Demand	240,000 cases
Average Monthly Demand	**40,000 cases**

TABLE 13-4 Soda Galore Planning Data

Current workforce	8 workers
Average monthly output per worker	4,000 cases per month
Inventory holding cost	$.30 per case per month
Regular wage rate	$20.00 per hour
Regular production hours/month	160 hours
Overtime wage rate	$30.00 per hour
Hiring cost	$1,000 per worker
Subcontracting cost	$1.15 per case
Firing/layoff cost	$1,500 per worker
Beginning inventory	5,000 (all safety stock)

of safety stock to meet unanticipated customer demand. Table 13-4 shows that at the beginning of January the only inventory on hand is safety stock.

Before comparing alternative aggregate production plans, it is necessary to convert some of the given data into common values for planning purposes. In this instance it is simplest to convert the labor costs into a cost per case. A worker earns $3,200 per month in regular wages (160 hours × $20.00/hour). This equates to a labor cost of $.80/case, since the monthly output per worker is 4,000 cases of soda ($3,200/4,000 cases). The overtime wage rate of $30.00 per hour is 1.5 times the regular wage rate; therefore a case of soda produced using overtime has a labor cost of $1.20 per case.

You have been asked to evaluate the cost of a level plan, a chase plan, and a hybrid plan in order to make a recommendation to the S&OP team.

Level Production Plan

A level production plan sets production at the average rate of demand, after adjusting for beginning inventory and desired ending inventory.

(13.1)
$$P = (\Sigma D_i + EI - BI)/N$$

where:

P = level production rate
D_i = demand in period i
EI = desired level of ending inventory
BI = beginning inventory
N = number of planning periods

EXAMPLE 13-1

The level production rate for the Soda Galore plan is

$$P = (24{,}000 + 32{,}000 + 32{,}000 + 48{,}000 + 60{,}000 + 44{,}000 + 5{,}000 - 5{,}000)/6$$
$$= 40{,}000 \text{ cases}$$

In this case, the level production rate is equal to the average demand (40,000 cases) because the beginning and ending inventory levels are equal. In months when demand is less than average, the excess product produced will be stored in inventory. When demand is more than the monthly average, the inventory will be depleted to fill customer orders.

Next, you need to determine the number of workers needed to produce the required quantity each month. Because the average worker produces 4,000 cases in a month and the average demand is 40,000 cases, you will need a total of 10 production employees. Given that the current workforce is eight workers, you will need to hire two employees, resulting in hiring cost of $2,000.

Table 13-5 (see next page) shows the impacts of the level production plan on hiring and inventories. No firing, overtime, or subcontracting is required in the level plan.

Assuming that the inventory holding cost is incurred based on the number of cases of soda in inventory at the end of a month, the total inventory holding cost for the level production plan at Sodas Galore is 130,000 cases ($.30/case) = $39,000. The total production cost is 240,000 cases ($.80/case) = $192,000.

Total Level Plan Cost = Regular Production Cost + Inventory Cost + Hiring/Firing Cost
= $192,000 + $39,000 + $2,000
= $233,000

TABLE 13-5 Soda Galore Level Production Plan

Beginning inventory = 5,000; Beginning workers = 8							
Month	Demand	Regular Production	Overtime or Subcontract Production	Ending Inventory*	Workers Required (4,000 cases/ worker)	Hire	Fire/ Lay Off
Jan.	24,000	40,000	0	21,000	10	2	0
Feb.	32,000	40,000	0	29,000	10	0	0
March	32,000	40,000	0	37,000	10	0	0
April	48,000	40,000	0	29,000	10	0	0
May	60,000	40,000	0	9,000	10	0	0
June	44,000	40,000	0	5,000	10	0	0
Total	**240,000**	**240,000**	**0**	**130,000**		**2**	**0**

*Ending inventory in any month = Ending inventory in previous month + Current month production − Demand. For example, January ending inventory = 5,000 + 40,000 − 24,000 = 21,000.

student activity

Verify the ending inventory levels in Table 13-5 for the months after January.

Chase Plans

In a chase plan, the objective is to match production in each period to the demand in that period, thus avoiding the need to hold inventory. There are actually three options to accomplish this objective:

1. Produce all units internally by hiring workers in high-demand months and firing/laying off workers in low-demand months.
2. Produce internally the quantity required to meet demand in the lowest-demand month and use overtime production to meet demand in other months.
3. Produce internally the quantity required to meet demand in the lowest-demand month and use subcontracting to meet demand in other months.

EXAMPLE 13-2

Table 13-6 provides the data necessary to determine the total cost of option 1 at Soda Galore, adjusting the size of the workforce to the amount of demand each month.

TABLE 13-6 Chase Plan: Adjust Workforce Size

Beginning inventory = 5,000; Beginning workers = 8							
Month	Demand	Regular Production	Overtime or Subcontract Production	Ending Inventory	Workers Required (4,000 cases/ worker)	Hire	Fire/ Lay Off
Jan.	24,000	24,000	0	5,000	6	0	2
Feb.	32,000	32,000	0	5,000	8	2	0
March	32,000	32,000	0	5,000	8	0	0
April	48,000	48,000	0	5,000	12	4	0
May	60,000	60,000	0	5,000	15	3	0
June	44,000	44,000	0	5,000	11	0	4
Total	**240,000**	**240,000**	**0**	**30,000**		**9**	**6**

The total cost of adjusting the workforce size to accomplish the chase plan is

Total Cost = Regular Production Cost + Inventory Cost + Hiring/Firing Cost
= 240,000 cases ($.80) + 30,000 cases ($.30) + 9 hire ($1,000) + 6 fire/layoff ($1,500)
= $192,000 + $9,000 + $9,000 + $9,000
= $219,000

Notice that no inventory other than that required to meet current demand is created or used during the chase plan. The only carrying cost is due to the safety stock requirement.

To evaluate options 2 and 3 for the chase plan, we need to estimate the costs of maintaining a workforce large enough to meet the minimum monthly demand and supplementing output with either overtime or subcontracted labor in months when demand is greater than the minimum. These options are described in Example 13-3.

EXAMPLE 13-3

Table 13-7 below describes the options for supplementing capacity with either overtime or subcontract labor.

For this plan, it is assumed that the workforce is stable at six workers, which means that you must also include the cost of initially laying off or firing two workers (since the initial assumption was that eight workers are employed).

The total cost of a chase plan using overtime is

Total Cost = Regular Production Cost + Overtime Cost + Inventory Cost + Hiring/Firing Cost
= 144,000 cases ($.80) + 96,000 cases ($1.20) + 30,000 cases ($.30) + 2 fire ($1,500)
= $115,200 + $115,200 + $9,000 + $3,000 = $242,400

The total cost of a chase plan using a subcontractor to supplement regular production is

Total Cost = Regular Production Cost + Subcontract Cost + Inventory Cost + Hiring/Firing Cost
= 144,000 cases ($.80) + 96,000 cases ($1.15) + 30,000 cases ($.30) + 2 fire ($1,500)
= $115,200 + $110,400 + $9,000 + $3,000 = $237,600

TABLE 13-7 Chase Plan: Overtime or Subcontract

Beginning inventory = 5,000; Beginning workers = 8

Month	Demand	Regular Production	Overtime or Subcontract Production	Ending Inventory	Workers Required (4,000 cases/ worker)	Hire	Fire/ Lay Off
Jan.	24,000	24,000	0	5,000	6	0	2
Feb.	32,000	24,000	8,000	5,000	6	0	0
March	32,000	24,000	8,000	5,000	6	0	0
April	48,000	24,000	24,000	5,000	6	0	0
May	60,000	24,000	36,000	5,000	6	0	0
June	44,000	24,000	20,000	5,000	6	0	0
Total	**240,000**	**144,000**	**96,000**	**30,000**		**0**	**2**

Hybrid Plans

Usually, the actual production plan combines some aspects of level production and building inventory with aspects of chase, or varying the production rate during each period to match production and demand. A company may face some of the constraints mentioned earlier, or simply may have policies related to the use of personnel.

EXAMPLE 13-4

Suppose Sodas Galore has an established policy of maintaining a stable workforce. It is believed that constantly adjusting workforce size is not practical, and there is a desire to keep morale high among the permanent employees by allowing them the opportunity to earn some overtime pay. After much internal discussion, the company decides to maintain a permanent workforce of eight production workers. Therefore, in periods of relatively low demand, the company will allow inventory to build. In periods of higher demand, the inventory will be used to satisfy as much demand as possible and overtime or subcontract production will be used to satisfy remaining demand. The costs associated with this hybrid plan are presented in Table 13-8.

TABLE 13-8 Sodas Galore: A Hybrid Solution

Beginning inventory = 5,000; Beginning workers = 8

Month	Demand	Regular Production	Overtime or Subcontract Production	Ending Inventory	Workers Required (4,000 cases/ worker)	Hire	Fire/ Lay Off
Jan.	24,000	32,000	0	13,000	8	0	0
Feb.	32,000	32,000	0	13,000	8	0	0
March	32,000	32,000	0	13,000	8	0	0
April	48,000	32,000	8,000	5,000	8	0	0
May	60,000	32,000	28,000	5,000	8	0	0
June	44,000	32,000	12,000	5,000	8	0	0
Total	**240,000**	**192,000**	**48,000**	**54,000**		**0**	**0**

The total cost of this hybrid aggregate plan is

Total Cost = Regular Production Cost + Overtime Cost + Inventory Cost
= (192,000 cases)($.80/case) + (48,000 cases)($1.20/case) + 54,000 cases ($.30)
= $153,600 regular production + $57,600 overtime production + $16,200
= $227,400

Comparing Aggregate Production Plans

Table 13-9 compares the costs related to the five alternative aggregate plans for Sodas Galore. Given the various planning assumptions used in this exercise, the plan that results in the lowest total cost is the chase plan with monthly hiring and firing.

In evaluating these plans, we should consider the assumptions we have made. For example, we have assumed that newly hired workers are just as productive as experienced workers. For that matter, it was also assumed that workers are in fact available. Worker availability can be a serious issue for a firm which has a reputation of frequently hiring,

TABLE 13-9 Comparison of Five Plans at Sodas Galore

Aggregate Plan	Reg. Prod. Cost	Overtime Cost	Subcontr. Cost	Inventory Cost	Hire Cost	Fire/Lay Off Cost	Total Cost
Level	$192,000	0	0	$39,000	$2,000		**$233,000**
Chase—Hire/Layoff	$192,000	0	0	$ 9000	$9,000	$9,000	**$219,000**
Chase—Overtime	$115,200	$115,200	0	$ 9000	0	$3,000	**$242,400**
Chase—Subcontract	$115,200	0	$110,400	$ 9000	0	$3,000	**$237,600**
Hybrid	$153,600	$ 57,600	0	$16,200	0	0	**$227,400**

then laying off employees. The overtime example assumes that the existing workforce is capable of working enough overtime hours to meet the total demand. There are often limitations to the amount of overtime. Moreover, workers may become less productive the longer they work. We also assumed that the operation has a make-to-stock (MTS) orientation. Since make-to order (MTO) and assemble to-order (ATO) operations do not build finished goods inventory ahead of demand, they follow something closer to a chase strategy.

There are, of course many other possible hybrid solutions to the Soda Galore planning situation. It is likely that a hybrid solution exists that is less costly than the pure chase plan. Sometimes operations may employ more workers than they actually need in low demand periods just to avoid other hidden costs or risks associated with hiring/firing, overtime, and/or subcontracting (such as labor strikes, quality problems, and so on). A manager could easily set up a spreadsheet on a personal computer in order to quickly evaluate many different scenarios. If used interactively, this methodology can be effective at generating a solution that all major functions can agree on, and the interactive process allows managers to see the effect of the changes as they are made, which can uncover unrealistic cost assumptions and unworkable situations. This is especially important when all of the constraints haven't been identified up front. Dialogue between managers and eventual agreement on a good production plan could actually be better than an optimal one that is forced on everyone.

Sophisticated modeling techniques such as linear programming, integer programming, and others can be applied to the aggregate production planning process. These techniques require precise specification of assumptions, constraints, costs, and objectives in a mathematical format. For those who are interested in the more sophisticated models, the supplement to this text demonstrates an optimal solution using linear programming and spreadsheet modeling.

AGGREGATE PLANNING FOR SERVICE INDUSTRIES

Prepare

How does aggregate planning differ in service industries?

Organize

Aggregate Planning for Service Industries
- Yield Management
- An Example of a Service Aggregate Plan

As mentioned earlier, S&OP and aggregate planning are just as critical in service industries as in manufacturing. In some ways such planning is even more critical because there is no ability to build inventory in anticipation of demand. When supply and demand do not match, the impact is almost always on human resources.

Yield Management

Because of the inability to inventory demand, service companies often make extensive use of the demand management tactics discussed in Chapter 12. Consider, for example, how airlines and hotels change prices almost constantly in an attempt to fill flights or rooms.

GET REAL

Yield Management in the Hotel Industry

Yield management (also called *revenue management*) provides a means to maximize revenue from a perishable product. How is a hotel "perishable"? Well, a year's worth of room inventory (i.e., total rooms × 365 days) dwindles with each passing day, and potential revenue for the year goes with it. Yield management practices help you preserve all the gains you can in terms of revenue versus expenses.

In principle, yield management tactics are fairly straightforward. In practice, they require you to be diligent, shrewd, and always on top of your game as a hotelier. Gone are the days of simply offering a rate discount to convention attendees in order to lengthen their stay beyond convention days. Today's hotelier must know the tendencies of each demand segment and how to satisfy those tendencies in a way that maximizes profit.

A profitable yield management strategy involves exploiting the best (and diminishing the least-efficient) aspects of a hotel's daily operation. Wholesale cost-cutting rarely proves effective because there aren't many viable areas, depending on a hotel's brand and service level, in which to make cuts: you can't close down one day a week to save on energy and maintenance, you can't shut down the pool just because only a handful of guests are there to swim, and you can't leave the front desk unmanned to save the cost of a shift.

Instead, leveraging some routine costs can be useful in bolstering hotel revenue. For example, costs associated with a hotel's breakfast buffet, including food preparation and waste disposal, will exist whether the hotel is fully or sparsely occupied on any given day; that is, the table could be all laid out but with too few guests to partake of what's offered. A "free breakfast" offering during slow periods can encourage more guests to stay at your hotel, improving overall revenue with only a marginal effect on food and beverage costs. Likewise, complimentary phone and Internet use are swiftly becoming the norm for negotiated corporate rates. Such value-added amenities can prove an essential lure in capturing demand.

Source: Excerpted from S. Sampson, "Yield Management in 2009: How to Keep Your Hotel Up and Running in a Downturn," *Hospitality Trends,* March 10, 2009. Copyright (c) 2009 Shannon Sampson. Reprinted with permission.

yield management A process that adjusts prices as demand for a service occurs (or does not occur).

These companies use a process called **yield management**, which adjusts prices as demand occurs (or does not occur) for a service (such as seats on a specific scheduled flight or hotel rooms for a specific night).

The purpose of yield management is to shape demand in a way that yields greater revenues or profits. For example, in Michigan, there is a wonderful vacation spot known as Mackinac Island, home of the Grand Hotel. As you might expect, demand for hotel rooms on the island is greatest during the summer. Consequently, room rates fall in September and remain low until the end of May. Airlines routinely practice yield management by adjusting prices and travel restrictions to maximize revenues on each flight. Their computer systems periodically compare the expected revenue of offering a seat on a flight at the normal fare against the expected revenue from offering it at a discount. As the date of the flight approaches, the airline increases the tickets' prices.

Yield management can involve very sophisticated mathematical models that simulate customer behaviors under different scenarios. Complex computer programs have been developed in those industries to continuously analyze demand versus available capacity and make the price adjustments. Effective yield management requires extensive analysis of past demand so that typical demand patterns and trends are clear. It also requires continuous tracking of actual demand for the service. The Get Real box above on yield management in the hotel industry provides more insight into this practice.

An Example of a Service Aggregate Plan

LO13-6 Explain the differences in aggregate planning in services versus manufacturing industries.

Ultimately, most service businesses have to develop aggregate plans based on human resource requirements. The process is not greatly different from that already discussed, except that there is no inventory to be considered. Instead, demand for services is often stated in terms of the amount of service labor required rather than the amount of product required.

EXAMPLE 13-5

Suppose Nile Inc., an Internet retailer, needs to develop an aggregate plan for its warehouse operation. Demand in the warehouse is stated in terms of the number of labor hours required each quarter to pick, pack, and ship customers' orders. Because the business is seasonal, demand is expected to be as follows:

Quarter 1: 15,000 labor hours
Quarter 2: 12,000 labor hours
Quarter 3: 10,000 labor hours
Quarter 4: 18,000 labor hours

Full-time employees work 500 hours per quarter, and their total compensation (including benefits) is $10.00 per hour. A worker can work overtime, up to a maximum of 100 hours per quarter, for $15.00 per hour. If, however, a full-time employee is not busy for 500 hours, the employee is still paid for those hours.

Part-time workers can be hired as needed, as long as each works no more than 400 hours per quarter (there is no minimum requirement of hours for a part-time employee). Part-time workers earn $8.00 per hour. The company currently employs 20 workers. Hiring and firing cost for a part-time employee is $1,000 for each hire or fire.

In this case, a level plan would require maintaining a stable workforce, meaning that the number of full-time employees must be able to fulfill the maximum demand. The level plan is shown in Table 13-10 on the next page. Because the maximum number of hours a full-time employee can work is 600 hours per quarter (regular 500 hours plus 100 overtime hours), the level number of workers required is 18,000 hours maximum/600 = 30 workers. Keep in mind that these 30 workers will have 15,000 hours of regular time pay each month regardless of the number of hours actually worked. A total of 10 workers must be hired immediately to meet the first quarter demand.

Cost of Level Plan = Regular Pay + Overtime Pay + Hiring Cost
= (60,000 hours) ($10.00/hour) + (3,000 hours) ($15.00/hour) + 10($1,000)
= $655,000

There are several possible variations on a chase plan for Nile Inc. We will evaluate a pure chase plan. In this instance, the permanent workforce will only be large enough to meet the minimum demand requirement of 10,000 hours, working the regular hours (500 hours). Thus, the permanent workforce is 20 workers. This results in a maximum of 2,000 hours of overtime available. The permanent workforce will always work the maximum possible before part-time workers are used. Finally, since you can't hire part of a person, when part-timers are hired, you must incur the full hiring cost even though the person may not work the maximum of 400 hours that part-timers are allowed to work. Table 13-11 shows the results of this plan.

Cost of Plan = Regular Pay + Overtime Pay + Part-Time pay + Hire/Fire Costs
= (40,000 hours)($10.00) + (6,000 hours)($15.00) + (9,000)($8.00) + (31 hire/fire)($1,000)
= $593,000

TABLE 13-10 Level Plan for Nile Inc.

Quarter	Demand (hours)	Regular Hours Paid	Overtime Hours Paid	Number of Hires
1	15,000	15,000	0	10
2	12,000	15,000	0	0
3	10,000	15,000	0	0
4	18,000	15,000	3,000	0
Total		**60,000**	**3,000**	**10**

TABLE 13-11 Chase Plan for Nile Inc.

Quarter	Demand	Regular Hours Paid	Overtime Hours Paid	Part-Time Hours	Part-Time Workers Needed	Hire	Fire
1	15,000	10,000	2,000	3,000	7.5 = 8	8	0
2	12,000	10,000	2,000	0	0	0	8
3	10,000	10,000	0	0	0	0	0
4	18,000	10,000	2,000	6,000	15	15	0
Total		**40,000**	**6,000**	**9,000**		**23**	**8**

student activity

Rework the Nile Inc. chase plan assuming that the permanent workforce is 17 workers. How does your answer differ from the chase plan illustrated in Table 13-11?

As in the planning for Soda Galore, there are again many alternatives that might be considered for Nile Inc., depending upon assumptions concerning how the labor force might actually be utilized. For example, the chase plan would be different if Nile Inc. decided that the permanent workforce only needs to be large enough to meet minimum demand by working maximum hours (in this case 600 total hours). Thus, the permanent workforce would only consist of 10,000 hours/600 = 16.67, or rounded up, 17 workers. All other aspects of the plan would be different from those shown.

CHAPTER SUMMARY

This chapter has dealt with the sales and operations planning process, with specific emphasis on aggregate production planning. The major issues discussed in the chapter were as follows:

1. All firms experience difficulty in balancing supply and demand.
2. Sales and operations planning is a cross-functional process that brings representatives from sales, marketing, manufacturing, purchasing, and logistics together to develop plans for most efficiently and effectively meeting expected customer demand.
3. The sales and operations planning process results in two plans: a sales plan attempts to influence demand to match supply, and an aggregate production plan (APP) attempts to match supply to demand.

4. Sales and operations planning should be a dynamic process conducted frequently during the year to update plans as new information becomes available.
5. The relevant costs in aggregate production planning are inventory holding cost, regular production cost, overtime cost, temporary workforce cost, firing/layoff cost, backorder/lost sales cost, and subcontracting cost.
6. The three basic aggregate production strategies are level production, chase, and mixed strategies. The alternatives should be compared to determine which one provides the lowest total cost.
7. Service industries have aggregate planning approaches similar to manufacturing. The major difference is that there is no inventory to consider.

KEY TERMS

aggregate production plan 443
chase strategy 445
level production strategy 445
mixed or hybrid strategy 447
rolling planning horizons 443
sales and operations planning (S&OP) 440
yield management 454

DISCUSSION QUESTIONS

1. What is the value of the S&OP process to an organization? Why should it be a dynamic process rather than a one-time annual event?
2. Explain in your own words the typical differences in objectives for production managers and sales managers.
3. Do you think chase strategies might be more appropriate in some industries than in others? Give some examples and explain why.
4. What are the key cost advantages of a level production strategy over a chase strategy? Of a chase strategy over a level production strategy?
5. Suppose your firm is using a level production planning approach to manage a seasonal demand. Your production manager is evaluated on lowest production cost but the logistics manager is evaluated on the amount of inventory the firm holds. Explain the issues.
6. Explain why the following is not necessarily a true statement: "If a company is chasing demand, then it is overinvesting in balance sheet assets because inventories will be high."
7. If most aggregate production planning problems include assumptions and ignore many needs of the company that are difficult to quantify, then what is the benefit of the process?

SOLVED PROBLEM

Neal Industries manufactures blue jeans for the teen market. The S&OP team has agreed upon a demand forecast for the following year, as shown below. Given the planning information, determine the cost of a level production plan and a plan to chase demand by adjusting the size of the workforce each month. The company begins with 1,000,000 jeans in safety stock and desires to maintain this level consistently (and end with this level).

Quarter	Demand
1	6,000,000
2	9,000,000
3	15,000,000
4	10,000,000

Current workforce	400 workers
Average output per worker	20,000 jeans per quarter
Inventory holding cost	$.10/pair per quarter
Regular wage rate	$16.00 per hour
Regular production hours	500 hours per quarter
Hiring cost	$300 per worker
Firing/layoff cost	$200 per worker
Beginning inventory	1,000,0000

Solution

The total demand for the year is 40,000,000 jeans. Therefore, the average demand per quarter is 10,000,000 jeans, and 10,000,000 jeans is the level production rate.

The average worker produces 20,000 jeans per quarter. Therefore the current workforce can produce 8,000,000 jeans per quarter. To produce 10,000,000 per quarter using a level production plan will require the addition of 100 workers (2,000,000 jeans/20,000 jeans per worker).

An average worker earns $8,000 per quarter (500 hours × $16.00 per hour) and produces 20,000 jeans. Therefore, the regular production (labor) cost is $0.40 per unit.

Beginning Workers = 400 Beginning Inventory = 1,000,000						
Quarter	**Demand**	**Production**	**Ending Inventory**	**Workers Required**	**Hire**	**Fire**
1	6,000,000	10,000,000	5,000,000	500	100	0
2	9,000,000	10,000,000	6,000,000	500	0	0
3	15,000,000	10,000,000	1,000,000	500	0	0
4	10,000,000	10,000,000	1,000,000	500	0	0
Total	40,000,000	40,000,000	13,000,000		100	0

The total cost of the level production plan for Neal Industries is
$0.40/unit (40,000,000 jeans) + $0.10/unit (13,000,000 jeans) + 100 hires ($300)
= $16,000,000 + $1,300,000 + $30,000 = $17,330,000.

A plan to chase demand has the following results:

Quarter	Demand	Production	Ending Inventory	Workers Required	Hire	Fire/ Lay Off
1	6,000,000	6,000,000	1,000,000	300		100
2	9,000,000	9,000,000	1,000,000	450	150	0
3	15,000,000	15,000,000	1,000,000	750	300	0
4	10,000,000	10,000,000	1,000,000	500		250
Total	40,000,000	40,000,000	4,000,000		450	350

The total cost of this plan is
\$0.40/unit (40,000,000 jeans) + \$0.10/unit (4,000,000 jeans) + 450 hires (\$300) + 350 fires (200) = \$16,000,000 + \$400,000 + \$135,000 + \$70,000 = \$16,605,000

The level production plan costs \$725,000 more than this chase plan.

PROBLEMS

1. For the Soda Galore problem discussed in the chapter, assume that employees negotiate an increase in the regular production wage rate to \$24.00 per hour and \$36.00 per hour for overtime. Rework all aspects of the problem using the new wage rates.
2. Using the existing data in the solved problem (Neal Industries), assume that the overtime production wage rate is \$24.00 per hour. Compute the cost of a chase plan using a stable workforce of 300 workers.
3. The Johnson Company manufactures expensive medical diagnostic equipment. It plans to meet all of its projected demand (given below for the next year by quarter). The firm plans to use a constant production rate of 300 units/quarter. Production costs are \$20,000 per unit and holding costs are \$2,000 per quarter per unit.

Quarter	**1**	**2**	**3**	**4**
Demand	200	300	400	300

   What is the cost of this production plan?
4. The current aggregate demand requirements for a firm are shown below for the next six months:

Month	**May**	**June**	**July**	**Aug**	**Sept**	**Oct**
Demand	120	100	100	100	130	150

   The firm always plans to meet all demand. The firm currently has 120 workers capable of producing 120 units in a month (1 unit/worker). The workforce can be increased (at a cost of \$500 per worker) or decreased (at a cost of \$1,000 per worker). Inventory holding cost is \$100 per unit per month. The firm currently has 40 units of inventory on hand, and it would like to have 40 units available at the end of each month. Regular production cost is \$3,000 per unit.

   a. What should the aggregate plan be if the inventory holding cost is to be minimized?
   b. What is the cost of this plan?
5. A firm must plan production for the next six months. Each unit costs \$250 to produce and it has an inventory holding cost of \$10 per unit per month based on ending inventory levels. The cost to hire a worker is \$100, and the cost to fire a worker is \$200 per worker. Each worker produces 10 units per month. There are 20 persons on the payroll at the beginning of the first month. The company currently has 100 units of inventory in stock, and it wants to hold these as safety stock.

Month	**1**	**2**	**3**	**4**	**5**	**6**
Demand	300	300	300	300	400	500

   a. From the information given above, what level production rate will meet demand for the next six months?

b. At that production rate, what is the maximum end-of-period inventory experienced at some time during the six months? What would be the cost of a level production plan?

c. From the information given above, what is the total cost of a chase (hire and fire only) production plan?

6. JokersRWild makes playing cards in several different styles, but a "standard" deck of cards is used for planning purposes. The average worker at JokersRWild can make 10,000 sets of decks of cards per month at a cost of $1.00 per deck during regular production and $1.30 during overtime. The company currently employs 25 workers. Experience shows that it costs $500 to hire a worker and $500 to fire a worker. Inventory carrying cost is $.25 per deck per month. Given the following demand estimate, develop a six-month production plan based on level production, chase using overtime (no workers will be fired and inventory increases if necessary), and chase by changing workforce level. The beginning inventory is 50,000, and at least that amount is desired each month.

Month	**January**	**February**	**March**	**April**	**May**	**June**
Demand	200,000	150,000	200,000	400,000	550,000	250,000

7. Trexoid Inc. makes a popular video game console. Demand varies each month, with highest demand coming in the last quarter of the year. Regular production costs are $120 per unit and inventory carrying cost is $5 per unit per quarter. Overtime production cost is $150 per unit. Assume that the 10 current Trexoid employees can produce 50,000 units per quarter in regular production and can work enough overtime hours to produce the amount required if a chase plan is employed. On the other hand, hiring cost is $5,000 per employee and firing cost is $10,000 per employee. Trexoid currently has zero inventory on hand, and they would like to have zero inventories at the end of the year. Forecasted demand is as follows:

Quarter 1	30,000 units
Quarter 2	20,000 units
Quarter 3	70,000 units
Quarter 4	120,000 units

What do you suggest to Trexoid management?

8. Appliances Inc. is preparing an aggregate production plan for washers for the next four months. The company's expected monthly demand is given below in the chart. The company will have 500 washers in inventory at the beginning of the month and desires to maintain at least that number at the end of each month. Below is other critical data:

Production cost per unit = $300
Inventory carrying cost per month per unit = $50 (based on ending month inventory)
Hiring cost per worker = $1,000
Firing cost per worker = $2,000
Beginning number of workers = 10

Each worker can produce 100 units per month.

Level Plan						
Month	**Demand**	**Regular Production**	**Ending Inventory**	**Workers Required**	**Hire**	**Fire**
1	4,000					
2	6,000					
3	3,000					
4	7,000					
Total	20,000					

Chase Plan						
Month	Demand	Regular Production	Ending Inventory	Workers Required	Hire	Fire
1	4,000					
2	6,000					
3	3,000					
4	7,000					
Total	20,000					

Complete the tables and determine the cost of the two plans.

9. Togo makes riding lawn mowers and tractors. The company's expected quarterly demand is given below in the chart. The company will have 300 mowers in inventory at the beginning of the month and desires to maintain at least that number at the end of each month. Below is other critical data:

   Production cost per unit = $200
   Inventory carrying cost per month per unit = $60 (based on ending month inventory)
   Hiring cost per worker = $500
   Firing cost per worker = $750
   Beginning number of workers = 40
   Each worker can produce 100 units per quarter.

Level Plan						
Quarter	Demand	Regular Production	Ending Inventory	Workers Required	Hire	Fire
1	5,000					
2	9,000					
3	7,000					
4	9,000					
Total	30,000					

Chase Plan						
Quarter	Demand	Regular Production	Ending Inventory	Workers Required	Hire	Fire
1	5,000					
2	9,000					
3	7,000					
4	9,000					
Total	30,000					

Complete the tables and calculate the cost of the two plans.

10. Jones Inc. is preparing an aggregate production plan for next year. The company expects demand to be 1,000 units in quarter 1; 2,000 units in quarter 2; 4,000 units in quarter 3; and 3,000 units in quarter 4. The company will have 100 units in inventory at the beginning of the year and desires to maintain at least that number at the end of each quarter as safety stock. Other information:

    Regular production labor cost = $100 per unit
    Overtime production cost per unit = $150
    Inventory carrying cost = $25/unit/quarter based on quarter-ending inventory

Hiring cost = $2,000 per worker
Firing/layoff cost = $3,000 per worker
Beginning number of workers = 15
Each worker can produce 100 units per quarter.

a. What is the total cost of a level plan?
b. What is the total cost of a chase plan utilizing hiring and firing?
c. Suppose Jones management is reluctant to constantly change the workforce by hiring and firing. The company decides to hire seven additional workers at the beginning of the year. The company will build inventory in low-demand months and use it in high-demand months. In addition, if necessary, overtime will be used to meet demand requirements if there is not sufficient inventory available. What is the total cost of this plan?

11. Dale's Dance Studio currently has three full-time instructors who are each paid $2,500 per month. A dance instructor can only work a maximum of 100 hours per month because instruction normally takes place at night. They do receive $2,500 even if they do not work 100 hours, however. Part-time instructors can be hired at a cost of $40 per hour. Dale's has forecasted that demand for the next six months will be as follows:

Month	1	2	3	4	5	6
Hours	380	280	450	420	520	390

Should Dale hire more full-time instructors or rely on part-time instructors to meet demand?

12. Dave's Stove-Top Popcorn currently has three full-time employees who are each paid $1,500 per month. An employee can only work a maximum of 100 hours per month because production normally takes place at night. They do receive $1,500 even if they do not work 100 hours, however. Part-time employees can be hired at a cost of $25 per hour. Dave's Stove-Top Popcorn has forecasted that demand for the next six months will be as follows:

Month	1	2	3	4	5	6
Hours	380	280	450	420	520	390

a. What is the total cost if Dave relies on part-time employees to meet additional demand?
b. What is the total cost if Dave hires one more full-time employee to meet additional demand?

CASE

Med-Chem Products: Hospital Division

The following case is based on the experiences of one of the co-authors with an actual company and its management.

Fiona Richey knew that she had been given the opportunity of a lifetime. She had just been hired to be an internal troubleshooter and consultant by the Hospital Division of Med-Chem Products. This was quite a feat. After all, she had graduated about four years ago with an undergraduate degree in Operations Management and Logistics from a large midwestern university. During that time, she had developed a reputation for being a good team player, creative thinker, and someone who got things done quickly (and correctly). That was one of the major reasons that Med-Chem had hired her. Originally, she had been working for a supplier to Med-Chem. About six months ago, she had been approached by one of the managers of Med-Chem, with a very attractive job offer.

Even though she had been at Med-Chem for only four weeks, she had begun to get a feel for the division, its products, its operating plans and procedures, and its problems. During this time, she had not been given any major projects. Rather, she was told to get to know people and to look around. As a result, she was ready and eager when Todd Hall, the division director, called her and gave her the first real assignment, and what an assignment. At this time, over coffee, Todd told Fiona that he had been concerned about the current planning system that was in place. He seemed to be finding out about problems after they occurred. The marketing and operations groups within the division always seemed to be making after-the-fact corrections to the plans that they each had generated. More important, no one in the division seemed to feel any responsibility for the plans. Whenever things went wrong, everyone took the position of blaming everyone else. What Todd wanted Fiona to do was two-fold: he wanted her to review the current system and to prepare a critique of it. In addition, he wanted her to recommend changes. Fiona knew that she had to do well on this project.

The Hospital Division of Med-Chem

Med-Chem was a Fortune 100 drug and chemical manufacturer, headquartered in Germany and with divisions and plants located worldwide. The Hospital Division was a division of this company. In the United States, it was headquartered in Atlanta, Georgia. This division manufactured a line of pharmaceuticals and testing equipment for use in hospitals, emergency rooms, nursing homes, and so on. Within this division, there were two major groups: marketing and operations.

Marketing was responsible for three major activities: sales, distribution, and forecasting. Of these three, forecasting was considered to be the most important. The products offered by this division were essentially make-to-stock. As a result, it was important that the right amounts be in stock at any point in time. As the marketing people had told Fiona, forecasting was a nightmare task. First, Med-Chem had a very broad product line, consisting of some 5,000 items. In addition, not all of the products were equally important. The group had adopted the product model developed by the Boston Consulting Group when describing the products. According to this model, the various products could be assigned to one of four categories. The first category was that of a *star.* A star product was one that was seen as being important. A product could be important because of a high contribution margin, unique position in the marketplace, or because it helped to enhance the reputation of the division (for being a leader in this product). These were products that management always wanted to ensure were delivered at or near 100 percent of actual demand. About 10 percent of the products fell into this category. Next came the *cash cows.* These products, about 35 percent of the current catalog, were highly stable, highly predictable in nature. They generated a very good revenue stream. Management never wanted to stock out of these items. The third group was the *question marks* (25 percent). In general, these were new products or ones that had not yet established their value in the marketplace. The final category, *dogs,* were products that were considered low performers. Typically, such product lines were old, were positioned in segments where the competition was severe, had very low contribution margins, or were not unique (i.e., there were a number of equally effective generic substitutes available). Many dogs were kept because marketing felt that they helped to round out Med-Chem's product offerings. For all four groups, marketing rarely informed operations of large orders by major customers or its attempts to stimulate ordering through special promotions or discounts. Marketing was allowed to change the forecasts at any point, up to and including the point that the products were scheduled to be shipped.

Operations was responsible for building the products required by marketing. At present, operations viewed this as a major problem because of marketing's constant modifications to the forecasts and the lack of any data concerning actual sales occurring in the marketplace. After talking with some of the plant managers, Fiona knew that their primary objective was to minimize the total production cost, including the cost of holding inventory. With the frequent production changes dictated by changes in the forecasts, operations found themselves expediting orders and undertaking dramatic production changes. If left alone, Fiona knew that operations would schedule operations to reduce cost.

Med-Chem's Current Planning System

The current system had been in place for as long as anyone could remember. This system did not differentiate between the performance of marketing and the performance of operations. Everyone agreed that all the information needed by management to reduce the problems existed but no one really knew how to proceed. As Todd told Fiona before she left, there had to be a better way of planning at Med-Chem.

Questions

1. Describe the current system in use as it applies to the operations personnel and marketing personnel. To what extent does this system help or hinder Med-Chem's ability to achieve its objectives? Why?
2. For marketing and operations, what are the critical activities that they must do well for Med-Chem to be successful in the marketplace?
3. What general recommendations would you make to Todd regarding the current situation?

CASE

Fitch and Hughes, P.C.

Fitch and Hughes, P.C., is a small law firm specializing in family law, wills, estates, and trusts. The firm, begun in 1980 by Jason Fitch and George Hughes, currently has three attorneys who are shareholders, and three associate attorneys. The firm is managed by George Hughes since the retirement of his cofounder of the firm, Jason Fitch. In early December, Hughes was thinking about the firm's workload for the first half of next year.

Given the current client load and projections for the next six months, Hughes estimated the number of billable hours for the firm is as follows:

Month	Hours
Jan.	1,100
Feb.	1,150
Mar.	1,450
Apr.	1,450
May	1,250
June	1,200

The three attorneys who are shareholders each receive a monthly salary of $10,500, while the associate attorneys are paid $7,000 each month. The three shareholders, of course, also receive additional compensation at the end of each year when the firm's profits are distributed to them based on their proportionate shareholdings.

Under normal circumstances, each of the six attorneys can bill a total of 175 hours per month. When any attorney bills more than 175 hours, he or she receives additional compensation of $80 per hour for associate attorneys or $120 per hour for the shareholders. The four shareholders have agreed that no attorney can bill more than 225 hours per month. In the interest of fairness, they also have decided that any "overtime" work required would be divided equally among all attorneys. This arrangement would allow each attorney the opportunity to increase income while preventing a few from benefiting excessively over the others.

While Jason Fitch does not really want to work any longer, he has agreed that he would be willing to help out in extreme situations at a rate of $150 per hour, as long as he is guaranteed a minimum of 30 hours during any single month. The firm could, of course, hire an additional associate attorney at the same salary as the current associates. If an additional attorney is hired, Hughes wants to do so by the beginning of the year so that the new attorney is familiarized with the firm as soon as possible. He is strongly opposed to letting any attorney go during the six-month period.

Questions

1. Determine the cost of a plan which uses only overtime and the services of Jason Fitch.
2. Suppose clients pay the same hourly rate regardless of which attorney bills the hours, and Hughes is interested in determining the lowest-cost plan for the firm. What should Hughes do, given the current policies of the firm?
3. What other considerations might influence the plan that Hughes develops?

SELECTED READINGS & INTERNET SITES

More case studies on sales and operations planning can be found at the following Web sites:

www.scmr.com
www.supplychainbrain.com

Bower, P. "How the S&OP Process Creates Value in the Supply Chain." *The Journal of Business Forecasting* 25, no. 2 (Summer 2006), pp. 20–32.

Fisher, M. L.; J. H. Hammond; W. Obermeyer; and A. Raman. "Making Supply Meet Demand in an Uncertain World." *Harvard Business Review* 72, no. 3 (May–June 1994), pp. 83–93.

Lapide, L. "S&OP: The Linchpin Planning Process." *Supply Chain Management Review* 15, no. 6 (2011), pp. 4–5.

Muzumdar, M., and J. Fontanella. "The Secrets to S&OP Success." *Supply Chain Management Review* 10, no. 2 (April 2006), pp. 34–41.

Smith, L., J. C. Andraski, and S. E. Fawcett. "Integrated Business Planning: A Roadmap to Linking S&OP and CPFR." *The Journal of Business Forecasting* 29, no. 4 (2010), pp. 4, 7, 9–13.

Smith, M. "Sales and Operations Planning: Making BPM Work." *Business Performance Management Magazine,* March 2008, pp. 4–6, 8, 10.

Spiegel, R. "Tallying the Benefits of S&OP." *Supply Chain Management Review* 15, no. 3 (2011), pp. 54–56.

14 Materials and Resource Requirements Planning

CHAPTER OUTLINE

LEARNING OBJECTIVES *After studying this chapter, you should be able to:*

LO14-1 Explain the materials requirements planning (MRP) process and when it should be used.

LO14-2 Conduct MRP planning for items at multiple levels in the BOM.

LO14-3 Explain how distribution requirements planning (DRP) is used.

LO14-4 Conduct capacity requirements planning (CRP) using an infinite loading approach.

LO14-5 Describe how materials requirements and resource planning functions work together within an enterprise resource planning (ERP) system.

LO14-6 Explain how advanced planning systems and scheduling (APS) systems improve the requirements and resource planning process.

Putting the Fire into Fire Engine Production

Spartan Motors of Charlotte, Michigan, has a unique product mix. Most of its production is devoted to chassis for RVs, armored vehicles for the U.S. military, and fire engines. The chassis for fire engines are highly customized because most towns, cities, and villages have their own unique requirements. On-time delivery is a critical requirement for success, with quality being a close second. Managing the operations for fire engine chassis is very challenging because of the high customization and the fact that chassis consist of thousands of components. To manage these challenges, managers at Spartan Motors depend upon materials requirements planning (MRP) to develop their production schedules. The computerized MRP system and associated planning processes help them identify which components are needed, how many are needed, and when they are needed. They also use MRP to place orders with suppliers for components such as seats, steering columns, engines, transmissions, wheels, and tires. MRP can easily adjust production and supply schedules when customers make changes. Planning of such a complex set of requirements would be impossible to do manually. The MRP system at Spartan Motors (and many other companies as well) gives them the ability to deliver customized products quickly, using relatively low levels of inventory.

In a supply chain, managers make plans at many levels to ensure the right materials and resources are available to make and deliver the products that customers want at the right price. For example, Spartan Motors relies upon its MRP process to make sure it has the right parts at the right time, while keeping inventory costs low. Chapter 13 described the sales and operations planning process and explained how to develop aggregate production plans. This chapter explains how aggregate production plans are translated into operational level production and distribution plans for individual products. Specifically we discuss three requirements planning processes: materials requirements planning (MRP), distribution requirements planning (DRP), and capacity requirements planning (CRP).

- MRP calculates when and how much of raw materials, parts, and subassemblies are needed for production.
- DRP plans when and how to supply finished goods at the right time to the right places in the distribution system.
- CRP determines if sufficient resources (labor, equipment, space, suppliers) are available when needed for production.

These planning processes share information with customers and suppliers for their own planning processes. It can be difficult to coordinate planning across the supply chain. Consider a company such as Conair, which makes a wide variety of health and beauty products such as hair dryers. Many different retailers sell Conair's products, including Bed Bath & Beyond, Best Buy, Walmart, Kohl's, Amazon.com, and Conair's own online store. Conair combines information gathered from all its retailers and uses it to develop production plans. To assemble its products, Conair purchases parts and subassemblies from many different suppliers, which purchase from other companies that are their suppliers. All this complexity makes supply chain coordination and planning a very important and challenging process.

independent demand Demand that is created by customers.

dependent demand Demand that depends upon decisions made by internal operations managers.

Planning processes differ for independent demand and for dependent demand. You will recall from Chapter 7 that **independent demand** is created by customers; it includes the demand for finished products (for example hair dryers) and replacement parts. **Dependent demand** is *dependent* on decisions made by internal operations managers, and is usually derived from demand for other items. After managers decide how many finished products to make in a given period, they calculate the dependent demand quantities for materials and resources needed to make those products. The hair dryer's heating element and fan are examples of dependent demand items; their demand depends on the production schedule set for hair dryers. When used for dependent demand, inventory management approaches such as reorder point and periodic review (discussed in Chapter 7) can lead to high inventory costs and poor customer service. These approaches are more appropriate for independent demand items.

Consider an example. When you order a large pepperoni pizza for delivery, this creates independent demand for the pizza shop. A pizza ordered by one customer is independent of an order placed by another. The shop's manager does not know exactly how many pepperoni pizzas will be ordered on any day, but she can develop and use a forecast to decide how many pizzas she will plan to produce. From this production plan, the manager calculates dependent demand for the dough, sauce, pepperoni, cheese, and a pizza box. She also can determine how many cooks, ovens, delivery drivers, and other resources will be required. In this way, dependent demands for materials and resources are calculated directly from actual orders and forecasts.

The following sections explore dependent demand operational planning processes. In a supply chain, the DRP process is downstream from the manufacturer, closer to the end consumer (see Figure 14-1), and can be an input into the MRP process. However, to illustrate the planning logic that is similar in both MRP and DRP, we will start with a discussion of MRP and then describe DRP, followed by an explanation of CRP.

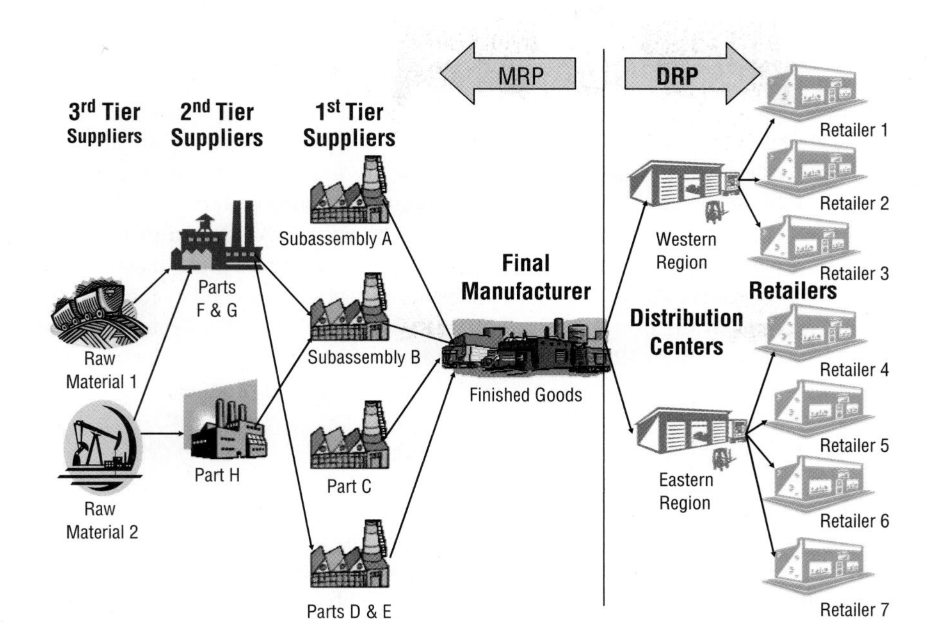

FIGURE 14-1 MRP and DRP in the Supply Chain

MATERIALS REQUIREMENTS PLANNING (MRP)

Prepare

What is the materials requirements planning (MRP) process and when should it be used?

Organize

Materials Requirements Planning (MRP)

A primary function of **materials requirements planning (MRP)** is to match supply with demand, so the right quantities of raw materials, parts, and subassemblies are available when needed for production. It determines how much and when to produce using a time-phased schedule that is based on lead time. The time-phased schedule typically considers both actual orders and forecasts and is considered a *push* system. The MRP schedule pushes work from one workstation to the next without considering if the downstream station is ready for the work. Thus, MRP differs from kanban (pull) scheduling described in Chapter 8. In kanban (pull) scheduling, production is triggered only when it is needed by the next workstation in the process. In practice, firms often use a combination of MRP for planning and kanban (pull) scheduling to trigger production on the shop floor.

materials requirements planning (MRP) A planning system used to ensure the right quantities of materials are available when needed.

MRP is used widely, especially in manufacturing; it is a standard function found in enterprise resource planning (ERP) software. According to one study, 80 percent of high-performing manufacturing plants have implemented MRP.[1] Operations that assemble complex, discrete products in batches are especially good candidates for MRP. For example, MRP works well for computers, appliances, furniture, and motor homes. Operations that make large volumes of less complex products, for example soft drinks or laundry detergent, or those that make-to-order unique products, can also use MRP, but the benefits may be less. Services such as hotels and hospitals use MRP for planning as described in the Get Real box, "MRP in Services."

LO14-1 Explain the materials requirements planning (MRP) process and when it should be used.

The next section describes the detailed planning steps for MRP and discusses MRP inputs, the detailed calculation process, and MRP outputs in turn. As an example, we will use a BBQ grill gift set (see Figure 14-2) as a product to illustrate the MRP process. The gift set consists of a tote bag, a fork, a spatula, and tongs.

[1] D. Bartholomew, "9 Lives and Counting," *Industry Week,* May 2006, p. 44.

Prepare

What are the inputs needed for MRP?

Organize

MRP Inputs
- Master Production Schedule (MPS)
- Bill of Materials (BOM)
- Inventory Records

MRP INPUTS

Accurate input information is essential for MRP performance. Operations managers must coordinate activities closely within the organization and with other firms in the supply chain to ensure that forecasts, product information, inventory data, and lead-time estimates are current and correct. If the inputs are wrong, the outputs of MRP will be wrong. As shown in Figure 14-3 on page 472, MRP uses three key information inputs—the master production schedule (MPS), the bill of materials (BOM), and inventory records. Together, the information contained in MPS, the BOM, and inventory records files enables the MRP process to determine the quantity and timing of requirements for all components needed to make related products.

Master Production Schedule (MPS)

master production schedule (MPS) The quantities of each finished product to be completed each period.

time bucket The individual time period for planning.

global

planning horizon The entire time period covered by the MPS.

cumulative lead time The longest lead-time path in the BOM.

available to promise The part of planned production that is not committed to a customer.

The **master production schedule (MPS)** shows the quantities of end items to be completed in each time period (hour, day, week) into the future. The time period used for planning is called a **time bucket**. The MPS shows how many of each individual end item must be completed each period. The MPS is developed from the aggregate production plan and aggregate sales plan, which are the outputs from the sales and operations planning process (Chapter 13). For example, the aggregate production plan for Conair might show the total number of all hair dryers to be produced each month for the next year. The MPS would indicate how many hair dryers of each type must be completed each week for the next quarter. In making this plan, managers would consider forecasted demands, actual customer orders, orders generated through DRP, demand for replacement parts, interplant transfers, lead times, and current inventory levels.

The entire time period covered by MPS is the **planning horizon** and must be at least as long as the longest lead-time path in the overall assembly of the product, called the **cumulative lead time**. This ensures that there is enough time to plan, order, receive materials, and make the end items. Global sourcing has increased the lead times for some items (think about purchasing furniture parts from Vietnam), requiring plans that extend even further into the future. The size of time buckets depends on the overall planning horizon and the dynamics of the market. Most companies plan in weekly buckets, though a company like Dell plans in terms of hours.[2]

An MPS for the BBQ grill gift set is shown in Figure 14-4 on page 472. To develop the MPS, the first step is to calculate the projected end item on-hand inventory at the beginning of each time bucket. Projected on-hand inventory is the previous period's on-hand inventory minus *either* the actual customer orders *or* the forecast orders. The largest quantity of either customer orders or the forecast is used. When the projected on-hand inventory in any time period is negative, more end items are needed. Look at Figure 14-4. In week 1, the actual customer orders of 40 exceeds the forecast of 35. So, the number of additional items needed is the beginning on-hand inventory of 10 minus the customer orders of 40; this equals negative 30. If we order 30 BBQ gift sets to be built in week 1, this will leave 0 projected on-hand inventory for week 2.

Some part of the production planned in the MPS may be committed to specific customers that have placed firm orders. The remaining planned production is **available to promise** to other customers as orders arise. The number of items that are available to promise are communicated to sales and marketing personnel so that they can arrange

[2]Research shows that using smaller time buckets improves performance. Steele et al., "Comparisons between Drum-Buffer-Rope and Materials Requirements Planning: A Case Study," *International Journal of Production Research* 43, no. 15 (2005), pp. 3181–3208.

GET REAL

MRP in Services

Although less widely used than in manufacturing, MRP can be applied to services. Hotel chains use MRP for renovation planning. For example, if a hotel chain plans to renovate 1,000 rooms, a planner can calculate the number of dressers, beds, chairs, and mirrors needed, and work with suppliers to understand how long it takes for each to be delivered, and when they should be ordered. The goal is to have all of the right materials arrive at the right time so renovations can be completed on time.

To increase operating room efficiency, many hospitals purchase preassembled surgical kits from suppliers. These kits contain almost everything that a surgeon needs to complete a specific surgical procedure. Medical suppliers, who sell surgical kits to many different hospitals, use MRP to plan and assemble surgical kits for their customers. Surgical kits are a good candidate for MRP because of the complexity created by a high variety of different kits that are assembled from a wide variety of items.

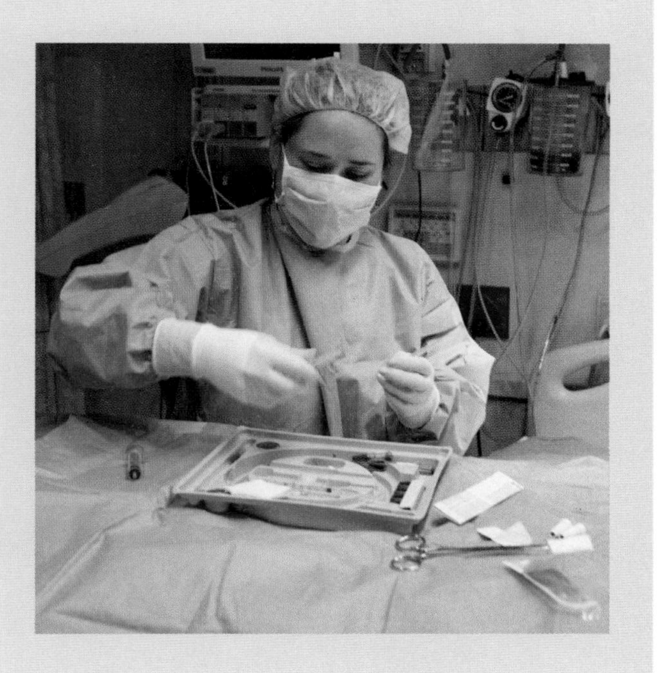

feasible delivery times and quantities for customers that wish to place new orders. For example, Figure 14-4 shows that in week 4, there are 15 units available to promise because only 25 of the 40 units in the MPS have been committed to actual customer orders.

FIGURE 14-2
BBQ Grill Gift Set

FIGURE 14-3 Overview of the Materials Requirements Planning (MRP) Process

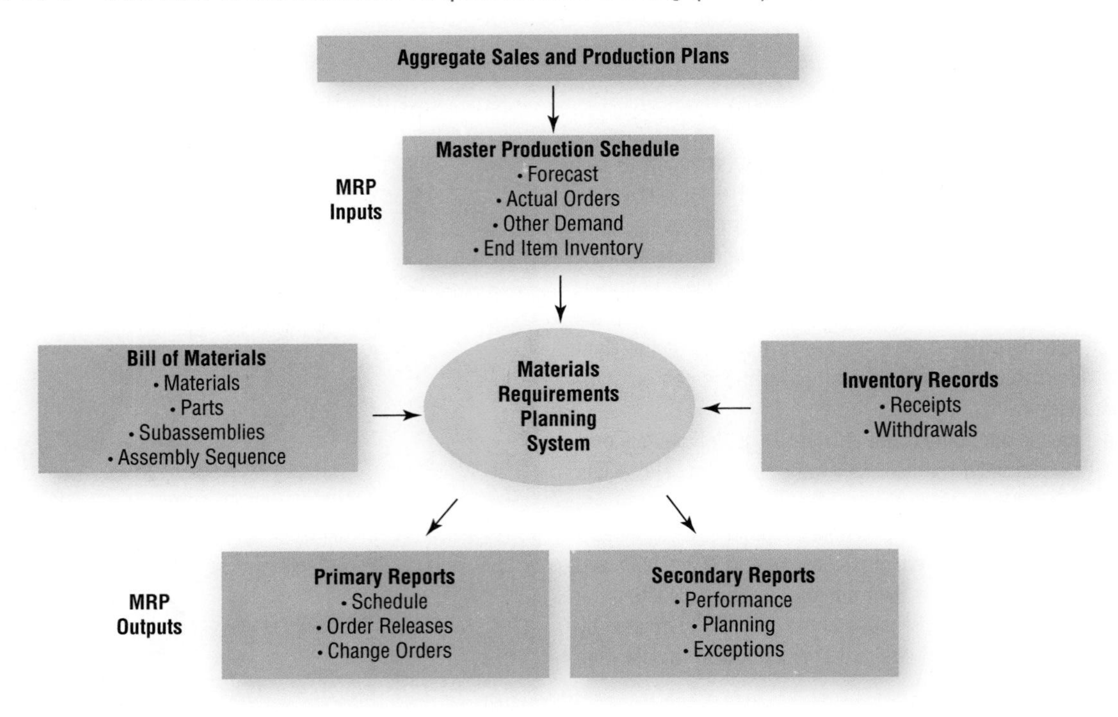

FIGURE 14-4 MPS for the BBQ Grill Gift Set

	Part Name: BBQ grill gift set							
	April				May			
MPS Beginning inventory = 10	**Week 1**	**Week 2**	**Week 3**	**Week 4**	**Week 5**	**Week 6**	**Week 7**	**Week 8**
Forecast	35	20	25	40	50	40	30	30
Actual customer orders	40	30	30	25	25	20	10	0
Projected on-hand inventory	0	0	0	0	0	0	0	0
Available to promise	0	0	0	15	25	20	20	30
MPS	30	30	30	40	50	40	30	30

rough-cut capacity planning An estimation of the availability of the critical resources needed to support the MPS.

The MPS does not consider whether the critical resources needed to complete the end items according to schedule are available during the planning horizon covered by the MPS. Recall that the aggregate production plan considers resources, but it does so using larger time buckets than the ones used in the MPS. Critical resources might include space, labor, equipment, suppliers, and even money. **Rough-cut capacity planning** estimates the availability of the critical resources needed by the MPS. If the resources are not available, then the MPS or the resource levels must change. For example, you could change the MPS by increasing the delivery time for some customers, acquiring critical resources, or diverting resources from other products. Some planning software systems calculate "capable to promise," which considers capacity when determining if new customer orders can be met.

Bill of Materials (BOM)

The **bill of materials (BOM)** is a detailed description of an "end item" along with a list of all of its raw materials, parts, and subassemblies. The BOM is essentially a "recipe" for the product; it shows the number of each type of component that is required to make *one unit* of the end item. The BOM also shows the sequence of assembly. The BOM is created when a new product is developed. Product engineering managers are responsible for making updates to the BOM.

bill of materials (BOM) A detailed description of an "end item" and list of all of its raw materials, parts, and subassemblies.

The BOM is shown as an indented list, a parts list (see Figure 14-5), or as a product structure diagram, also called a *product structure tree* (see Figure 14-6 next page). In our example, the BBQ grill gift set is the end item, shown as level 0 in the BOM. Each set consists of four "level 1" inputs: a tote bag, a fork, a spatula, and tongs. The dependent

FIGURE 14-5 Indented Bill of Materials (BOM) and Parts List

Indented Bill of Materials	Parts List
Boxed BBQ grill gift set	Boxed BBQ grill gift set
* Tote bag (1)	Tote bag (1)
* Fork (1)	Fork (1)
** Metal fork (1)	Spatula (1)
*** Steel sheet (1)	Tongs (1)
** Handle A (1)	
*** Wood block (1)	Fork
** Rivet (2)	Metal fork (1)
** Leather tie	Handle A (1)
* Spatula (1)	Rivet (2)
** Metal spatula (1)	Leather tie
*** Steel sheet (1)	
** Handle A (1)	Spatula
*** Wood block (1)	Metal spatula (1)
** Rivet (2)	Handle A (1)
** Leather tie	Rivet (2)
* Tongs (1)	Leather tie
** Metal tong (1)	
*** Steel sheet (1)	Tongs
** Handle B (2)	Metal tong (1)
*** Wood block (2)	Handle B (2)
** Rivet (8)	Rivet (8)
	Metal fork
	Steel sheet (1)
	Handle A
	Wood block (1)
	Metal spatula
	Steel sheet (1)
	Metal tong
	Steel sheet (1)
	Handle B
	Wood block (2)

LO14-2 Conduct MRP planning for items of multiple levels in the BOM.

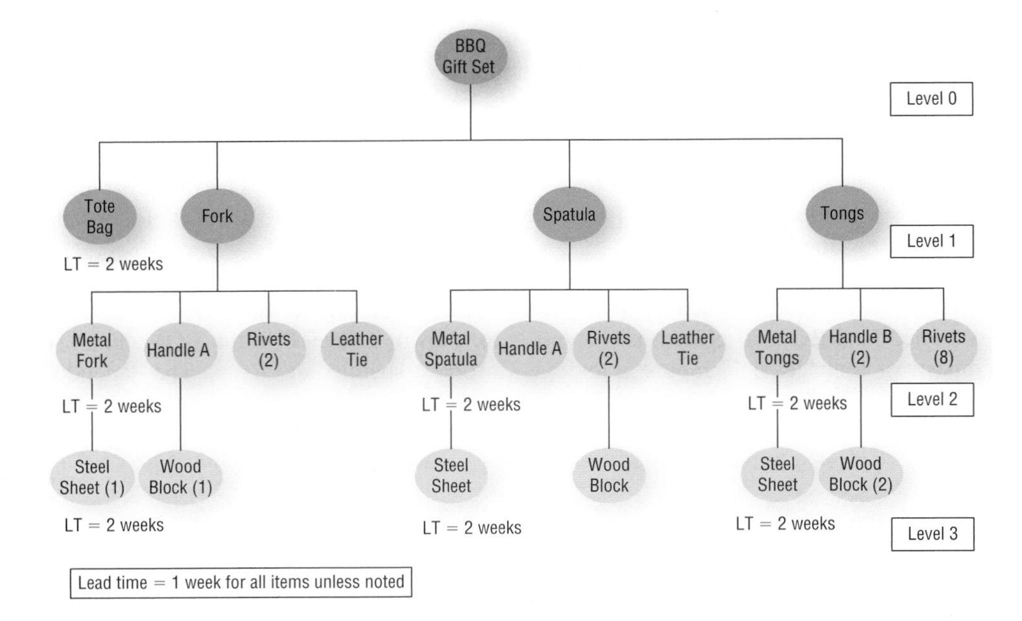

FIGURE 14-6 Product Structure Bill of Materials (BOM)

demand for the level 1 items is driven by the needs of the level 0 item. Similarly, the demand for the level 2 items is driven by the needs of the level 1 items, and so on. The BBQ grill gift set (level 0) can be thought of as the "parent" of the tote bag, fork, spatula, and tongs. These items are components, or "children," of the gift set.

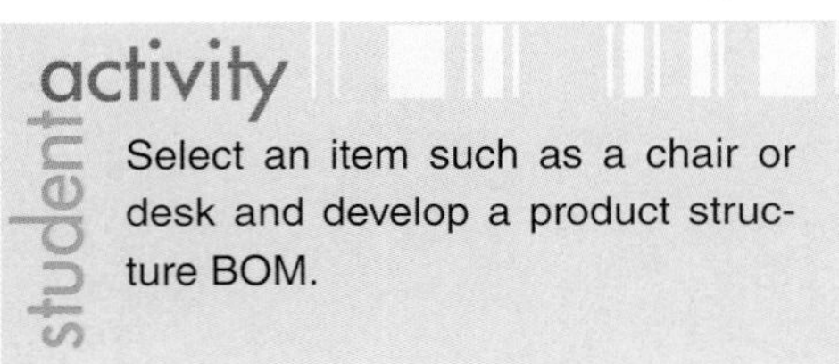

The trends toward modular products and toward purchasing subassemblies from suppliers rather than making them in-house reduce the number of levels in a product's BOM, making it flatter. For example, the tote bag is purchased as a finished item from a supplier. For this reason, its children (raw materials, parts, and subassemblies) are not shown in the company's BOM. These raw materials, parts, and subassemblies are shown on the supplier's BOM for the tote bag.

Inventory Records

inventory status file A file that contains detailed inventory and procurement records.

Inventory records are contained in an **inventory status file**. Each inventory record includes:

- The item number.
- Description of the item.
- The lead time to order and receive the item from a supplier or to produce it internally.
- The preferred order quantity (lot size).
- Safety stock quantity.
- Other information such as cost or process descriptions.
- Quantity of on-hand inventory.
- Amount of inventory committed to a use.
- **Scheduled receipts** (the quantity that has been ordered but not yet received).

scheduled receipts The quantity that has been ordered but not yet received.

One of the key managerial decisions in MRP is the order quantity, or production lot size. Operations managers consider carrying costs, ordering costs, product costs, and stockout costs when deciding upon the appropriate lot-sizing strategy. For purchased items, suppliers typically set the lot sizes. Consider the choices at your local grocery store for purchasing milk—typically one gallon, one quart, or a single serving. Some of the typical lot-sizing strategies are:

lot-for-lot (L4L) An order for the exact amount needed.

- **Lot-for-lot (L4L)**. An order is placed for exactly the amount that is needed in each period. L4L minimizes carrying costs, but maximizes setup or ordering costs.

- **Fixed order quantity (FOQ).** The same amount is ordered each time. For example, the economic order quantity EOQ (discussed in Chapter 7) might be used. A slight variation of FOQ is *multiples of FOQ,* where purchased items may only be available in a fixed order quantity such as a carton of 10 items. So if 14 items were needed, the order quantity would be two cartons of 10 (20 items) rather than 14.
- **Periodic order quantity (POQ).** An amount that covers the requirements for a fixed number of future periods is ordered. For example, enough is ordered to cover two periods worth of net requirements each time an order is placed.

fixed order quantity (FOQ) An order for the same amount each time.

periodic order quantity (POQ) An order for an amount that covers a fixed period of time.

Use of fixed order quantities, multiple fixed order quantities, and periodic order quantities can create "lumpy" orders rather than a smooth continuous flow of materials. These lot-sizing rules can minimize ordering or setup costs for the firm. However, spikes in orders become accentuated and more dramatic as orders flow upstream in the supply chain to direct suppliers, and then to their suppliers, contributing to the bullwhip effect. When this effect occurs, inventory can fluctuate dramatically, going from excesses to stockouts. Coordination and information sharing among supply chain members helps to reduce this effect and its associated costs.

relationships

MRP PROCESS

Prepare

What steps are involved in MRP planning?

Organize

MRP Process

MRP calculations are done using computer software. However, managers need to know the mechanics in order to make good decisions using MRP outputs. Let's work through the MRP process using the BBQ grill gift set as an example. The planning process always starts with the level 0 items in the BOM and then continues down each successive level. The planning logic determines when items are needed and then works backward to determine when to place orders. As we go step-by-step through the process we will define the key items that are shown in an MRP record (see Figure 14-7 on the next page).

Gross requirements are the total amount of an end item (finished good, subassembly, or part) that is required by *all* of its parents during each period. This must include end items that are used as replacement parts, interplant transfers, or service items. Start with the MPS for the BBQ grill gift set. The production schedule for the MPS creates the gross requirements in the MRP record for each week, as shown in Figure 14-8 on the next page.

gross requirements The total amount of an end item that is required.

As discussed earlier, *scheduled receipts* are the total quantity of items from orders placed in the past and due to be delivered by the beginning of the period in which the quantity is shown. The scheduled receipts of 30 BBQ grill gift sets in week 1 (see Figure 14-9 on page 477) were ordered one week ago. Note that the *order* is not shown on the current record form, just the *delivery.* The order placement was on last week's version of the record form, because the lead time for the gift sets is one week.

The next step in the process is to determine how many additional units, if any, are needed to meet the week's gross requirements. This calculation is called **requirements explosion**, and it determines the *net requirements* (see Figure 14-10 on page 477). **Net requirements** are the minimum quantity required in the period based on gross requirements minus the sum of scheduled receipts and available inventory at the end of the last period which is the inventory available at the start of the current period. When safety stock is needed, the net requirements are calculated based on the gross requirements plus safety stock minus the sum of scheduled receipts and available inventory at the end of the last period (starting inventory of current period). Of course, if the total of available inventory plus scheduled receipts is greater than the gross requirements, then the net requirements is zero. Available inventory is the inventory quantity that is available *at the end* of a period.

requirements explosion The determination of how many additional units are needed.

net requirements The minimum amount needed in the period.

(14.1) Available inventory = Available inventory at the start of the period + scheduled receipts + planned order receipts − gross requirements

The next step is to calculate the planned order receipts for each week. The quantity that is planned to arrive at the *beginning* of a period is the **planned order receipt**. These arrivals come from orders that are planned to be placed at the designated time in the future.

planned order receipt The amount that is planned to arrive at the beginning of a period.

FIGURE 14-7 Example of an MRP Record

MRP Record Lead time = On-hand inventory = Safety stock = Order quantity:	Part Name: Week 1	Week 2	Week 3	Week 4	Week 5	Week 6	Week 7	Week 8
Gross requirements								
Scheduled receipts								
Available inventory								
Net requirements								
Planned order receipts								
Planned order releases								

FIGURE 14-8 Gross Requirements for the BBQ Grill Gift Set

Part Name: BBQ grill gift sets

	April				May			
MPS Beginning inventory = 10	Week 1	Week 2	Week 3	Week 4	Week 5	Week 6	Week 7	Week 8
Forecast	35	20	25	40	50	40	30	30
Actual customer orders	40	30	30	25	25	20	10	0
Completed end items	(30)	30	30	40	50	40	30	30

Part Name: BBQ grill gift sets

MRP Record Lead time = 1 week On-hand inventory = 0 Safety stock = 0 Order quantity: L4L	Week 1	Week 2	Week 3	Week 4	Week 5	Week 6	Week 7	Week 8
Gross Requirements	(30)	30	30	40	50	40	30	30

In this example, because we use a L4L policy the planned order receipts exactly equal the net requirements as shown in Figure 14-11 on the next page.

planned order release The amount of an item that is planned to be ordered in a period.

The last step is to determine *when* to place the order. A **planned order release** is the quantity of an item that is planned to be ordered in the period. Because of the rolling time horizon of MRP records, when an order is placed (released), it shifts from being a *planned* receipt to being a *scheduled* receipt. To determine the planned order release for each period, count backward from the planned order receipt using the lead time. In the example, the planned order releases are scheduled one week before the planned order receipts, as shown in Figure 14-12 on page 478.

FIGURE 14-9 Scheduled Receipts for the BBQ Grill Gift Set

Part Name: BBQ grill gift sets								
MRP Record **Lead time = 1 week** **On-hand inventory = 0** **Safety stock = 0** **Order quantity: L4L**	**Week 1**	**Week 2**	**Week 3**	**Week 4**	**Week 5**	**Week 6**	**Week 7**	**Week 8**
Gross Requirements	30	30	30	40	50	40	30	30
Scheduled Receipts	(30)							

Ordered last week.

FIGURE 14-10 Net Requirements for the BBQ Grill Gift Set

Part Name: BBQ grill gift sets								
MRP Record **Lead time = 1 week** **On-hand inventory = 0** **Safety stock = 0** **Order quantity: L4L**	**Week 1**	**Week 2**	**Week 3**	**Week 4**	**Week 5**	**Week 6**	**Week 7**	**Week 8**
Gross requirements	30	30	30	40	50	40	30	30
Scheduled receipts	30							
Available inventory								
Net requirements		30	30	40	50	40	30	30

FIGURE 14-11 Planned Order Receipts for the BBQ Grill Gift Set

Part Name: BBQ grill gift set								
MRP Record **Lead time = 1 week** **On-hand inventory = 0** **Safety stock = 0** **Order quantity: L4L**	**Week 1**	**Week 2**	**Week 3**	**Week 4**	**Week 5**	**Week 6**	**Week 7**	**Week 8**
Gross requirements	30	30	30	40	50	40	30	30
Scheduled receipts	30							
Available inventory								
Net requirements		(30)	30	40	50	40	30	30
Planned order receipts		(30)	30	40	50	40	30	30

After the planned order releases for the BBQ grill gift sets are known, the planning process continues through the BOM for each component, level by level. Look back at Figures 14-5 and 14-6, which show the BOM for the BBQ grill gift set. The next step

FIGURE 14-12 Planned Order Releases for the BBQ Grill Gift Set

MRP Record Lead time = 1 week On-hand inventory = 0 Safety stock = 0 Order quantity: L4L	Week 1	Week 2	Week 3	Week 4	Week 5	Week 6	Week 7	Week 8
Part Name: BBQ grill gift set								
Gross requirements	30	30	30	40	50	40	30	30
Scheduled receipts	30							
Available inventory								
Net requirements		30	30	40	50	40	30	30
Planned order receipts		(30)	30	40	50	40	30	30
Planned order releases	(30)	30	40	50	40	30	30	

Place order one week before needed because lead time = 1 week.

would be to develop MRP records for the level 1 items: the tote bag, the fork, the spatula, and the tongs. Once the MRP records for the level 1 items are complete, then MRP records are developed for the level 2 items: the metal fork, the metal spatula, the metal tongs, handles A and B, the rivets, and the leather tie. Similarly, after the level 2 records are complete, MRP records for level 3 items are calculated. This process, called an MRP "explosion," continues until the planning is complete for all levels of the BOM.

Let's walk through the calculation steps for the tote bag. Then we'll show the MRP records for the fork and spatula and develop the gross requirements for handle A, which has the fork and spatula as parents. Tote bags are purchased in cartons of 100 bags each from a supplier in China , and the lead time is two weeks with shipment by air. Because of the risk of delays, one carton (100 bags) is held as safety stock. If the available inventory drops below the safety stock level of 100, the MRP process calculates the net requirements needed to bring the inventory level back up to a minimum of 100.

First determine the tote bag's gross requirements by asking who its parents are. Because the tote bag is only used in the BBQ grill gift set and no replacement bags are purchased, the gross requirements come *only* from the planned order releases for the BBQ grill gift set. Note in Figure 14-13 that the numbers in the gross requirements line for tote bags are identical to the numbers in the planned order releases line for the BBQ grill gift set. If tote bags were used in multiple products, the planned order releases for *all* of its parents would be combined to determine its gross requirements.

Next, calculate the net requirements and associated orders. The scheduled receipt of 100 in week 1 covers the gross requirements for the first three weeks, so the first net requirement occurs in week 4. In week 4, the net requirement is 50 bags. Schedule a planned order release of 100 bags, which is the lowest order quantity possible. Because of the two-week lead time, the order must be released in week 2 so that it can be received in week 4. This same logic is used to complete the rest of the record, as shown in Figure 14-13.

Continue with the MRP records for the fork and spatula (see Figure 14-14 on page 480). The gross requirements for each come from the planned order releases from the

FIGURE 14-13 MRP Requirements for Tote Bags

Part Name: BBQ grill gift set								
MRP Record **Lead time = 1 week** **On-hand inventory = 0** **Safety stock = 0** **Order quantity: L4L**	**Week 1**	**Week 2**	**Week 3**	**Week 4**	**Week 5**	**Week 6**	**Week 7**	**Week 8**
Gross requirements	30	30	30	40	50	40	30	30
Scheduled receipts	30							
Available inventory								
Net requirements		30	30	40	50	40	30	30
Planned order receipts		30	30	40	50	40	30	30
Planned order releases	(30)	30	40	50	40	30	30	

Part Name: Tote bag								
MRP Record **Lead time = 2 weeks** **On-hand inventory = 100** **Safety stock = 100** **Order quantity:** **Multi = 100**	**Week 1**	**Week 2**	**Week 3**	**Week 4**	**Week 5**	**Week 6**	**Week 7**	**Week 8**
Gross requirements	(30)	30	40	50	40	30	30	
Scheduled receipts	100							
Available inventory 100	170	140	100	150	110	180	150	
Net requirements				50		20		
Planned order receipts				(100)		(100)		
Planned order releases		(100)		(100)				

BBQ grill gift set. Let's develop the MRP record for one level 2 item: handle A, as shown in Figure 14-15 on page 481. The gross requirements for handle A come from the planned order releases from its parents (fork and spatula). The BOM (Figures 14-5 and 14-6) shows that one handle each is needed for the fork and the spatula. There are no other sources of demand for handle A. Notice that there is beginning on-hand inventory of 60 units. When needed, handle A is always produced in fixed order quantity (FOQ) lot sizes of 100.

To complete the entire materials requirements plan, MRP calculations would be done for all of the remaining level 2 items and then all of the level 3 items in the BOM. Some organizations use MRP for planning the higher-level items in the BOM, but use kanban (pull) systems to replenish lower-level items.

FIGURE 14-14 MRP Records for the Fork and the Spatula

Part Name: Fork								
MRP Record **Lead time = 1 week** **On-hand inventory = 0** **Safety stock = 0** **Order quantity: L4L**	**Week 1**	**Week 2**	**Week 3**	**Week 4**	**Week 5**	**Week 6**	**Week 7**	**Week 8**
Gross requirements	30	30	40	50	40	30	30	
Scheduled receipts	30							
Available inventory								
Net requirements		30	40	50	40	30	30	
Planned order receipts		30	40	50	40	30	30	
Planned order releases	30	40	50	40	30	30		

Part Name: Spatula								
MRP Record **Lead time = 1 week** **On-hand inventory = 0** **Safety stock = 0** **Order quantity: L4L**	**Week 1**	**Week 2**	**Week 3**	**Week 4**	**Week 5**	**Week 6**	**Week 7**	**Week 8**
Gross requirements	30	30	40	50	40	30	30	
Scheduled receipts	30							
Available inventory								
Net requirements		30	40	50	40	30	30	
Planned order receipts		30	40	50	40	30	30	
Planned order releases	30	40	50	40	30	30		

Prepare

What are the outputs from MRP and how do managers use them?

Organize

MRP Outputs and Use

MRP OUTPUTS AND USE

MRP outputs include primary and secondary reports. The primary reports are schedules of the planned order releases that trigger purchases and production of items in the proper time frame. Secondary reports provide cost, inventory, and schedule attainment information that helps managers judge how well the operation is performing. If a major difference between actual performance and the MRP plan occurs, then an exception report is generated.

Once set, numerous changes made to the MPS can cause **nervousness** throughout the system. Significant MPS changes can modify the timing and quantities of orders for raw materials, parts, and subassemblies, making suppliers' planning very difficult. As a result, users may not trust the MRP plan.

nervousness Inconsistencies in the plan caused by changes to the MPS.

FIGURE 14-15 MRP Record for Handle A

MRP Record Lead time = 2 weeks On-hand = 60 Safety stock = 0 Order quantity: FOQ = 100	Week 1	Week 2	Week 3	Week 4	Week 5	Week 6	Week 7	Week 8
Part Name: Handle A								
Gross requirements	60	80	100	80	60	60		
Scheduled receipts		100						
Available inventory 60	0	20	20	40	80	20		
Net requirements			80	60	20			
Planned order receipts			100	100	100			
Planned order releases	100	100	100					

60 = 30 forks + 30 spatulas

MRP assumes that parts produced or received from suppliers are defect free and are delivered as scheduled. This is especially important if a L4L lot-sizing strategy is used. Thus, quality management is critical within the firm and by its suppliers. If quality and delivery performance are not perfect, then safety stock or increased lead times are required. These increase cost and decrease the effectiveness of the planning process.

DISTRIBUTION REQUIREMENTS PLANNING (DRP)

Prepare

How is distribution requirements planning (DRP) used?

Organize

Distribution Requirements Planning (DRP)

Distribution requirements planning (DRP) calculates the positioning and replenishment of *finished goods inventories* throughout the distribution network using logic similar to MRP. DRP is typically a module in enterprise resource planning system software. Distribution networks can be very complex, with multiple levels of distribution centers and thousands of retailers (think about Conair, for example). Thus, planning and coordination across the supply chain can be difficult. The output of DRP is used for input into operations and logistics planning processes.

distribution requirements planning (DRP) Determination of replenishment and positioning of finished goods in the distribution network.

Similar to MRP, inventory replenishment decisions are based on a time-phased schedule considering forecasts and actual orders. The DRP process starts by combining forecasts and firm orders, ideally at each customer or the contact point as close as possible to the customer, such as the retailer or regional distribution center. Forecasts and actual orders at the customer or contact points are added to create the independent demand for the finished goods, and planned order receipts are determined for each of these locations for the planning horizon. Looking back at Figure 14-1, forecasts and actual orders create the planned order releases for Retailers 1, 2, and 3. These planned order releases are combined to form gross requirements for the Western Region distribution center, while those for Retailers 4, 5, 6, and 7 form the gross requirements for the Eastern Region distribution center.

LO14-3 Explain how distribution requirements planning (DRP) is used.

As with MRP, the planning horizon must extend far enough into the future so that replenishment orders can be scheduled in plenty of time to make the required shipments.

For each future week at each customer location, the gross requirements estimate is compared with the amount of inventory projected to be on-hand at that location. If the projected inventory available is less than the estimated gross requirements, a replenishment order is planned for the net requirements.

The next step is to compare the schedule of gross requirements at each distribution center against its projected on-hand inventory for each week into the future. This comparison creates net requirements and planned orders, and these orders are consolidated to make gross requirements for the next upstream source of supply, while considering required lead times. The process continues to consolidate requirements and orders across all stages in the distribution network up to the production plant that makes the finished goods. The result is a week-by-week plan of demands placed on the plant that ultimately reflects the forecasted independent demands taking place at each of the customer locations. At this point, MPS and MRP processes take over.

Prepare

How do managers perform capacity requirements planning (CRP)?

Organize

Understanding Capacity Requirements Planning (CRP)

UNDERSTANDING CAPACITY REQUIREMENTS PLANNING (CRP)

DRP and MRP focus on material feasibility—can we get the right amount of material at the right time? To meet customer needs, an operation also needs sufficient capacity of key resources. A load is the amount of work given to a worker, machine, work center, or facility during a specific period of time. To make sure a plan is feasible, the load is compared to the capacity, which is the output that can be done during a period of time.

Though rough-cut capacity planning suggests an MPS is feasible, after development of an MRP plan, a more detailed assessment of capacity is needed to ensure this is still the case. MRP does not compare the planned orders to the available capacity in the supply chain. Most MRP plans assume **infinite loading**; that is, an infinite amount of capacity is available, which is not realistic. **Capacity requirements planning (CRP)** determines if all the work centers involved have the capacity to implement the MRP plan. The CRP process uses planned order releases and scheduled receipts to estimate work center loads. A **load profile** compares weekly loads needs against a profile of actual capacity.

infinite loading The assumption that there is an infinite amount of capacity available.

capacity requirements planning (CRP) An estimate of the capacity needed at work centers.

load profile A comparison of production needs to actual capacity.

LO14-4 Conduct capacity requirements planning (CRP) using an infinite loading approach.

Figure 14-16 shows available capacity and a load profile for the spatula. The planned order releases are from the spatula's MRP record (Figure 14-14). The CRP table in Figure 14-16 estimates the number of production hours needed to make the spatulas, based on a machine rate of 30 minutes per spatula. The available machine capacity is 20 hours per week. The table and load graph show that process will be overloaded in week 3, when the load of 25 hours exceeds the available capacity of 20 hours. The load exactly equals capacity in weeks 2 and 4. Underloading occurs in weeks 1, 5, and 6.

Having too much or too little capacity can be problematic. When underloading occurs, the extra capacity could be used to build anticipation inventory, but this increases costs. If underloading is an ongoing problem, the firm should find new business or develop new products to use the capacity or reduce the capacity. If there is not enough capacity to meet the production requirements, the use of overtime or outsourcing some operations are options, but costs increase. Alternatively, you can increase delivery lead times or create a backlog of orders, but this may reduce customer satisfaction and sales. If capacity is available earlier, goods can be made in advance and held in inventory until needed. Because of the differences between the load and available capacity for the spatula, managers must decide to change capacity or to change the MPS. One alternative would be to produce 10 of the units needed in week 3 in week 1, when capacity is available, and hold these units in inventory. A cross-functional team including operations, sales, marketing, finance, supply, and engineering should decide upon the best approach to manage capacity to meet the company's objectives.

FIGURE 14-16 Capacity Requirements for Spatulas

Part Name: Spatula								
Processing Time = 30 minutes per unit	**Week 1**	**Week 2**	**Week 3**	**Week 4**	**Week 5**	**Week 6**	**Week 7**	**Week 8**
Planned order releases	30	40	50	40	30	30		
Processing load (hours)	15	20	25	20	15	15		
Available capacity (hours)	20	20	20	20	20	20		

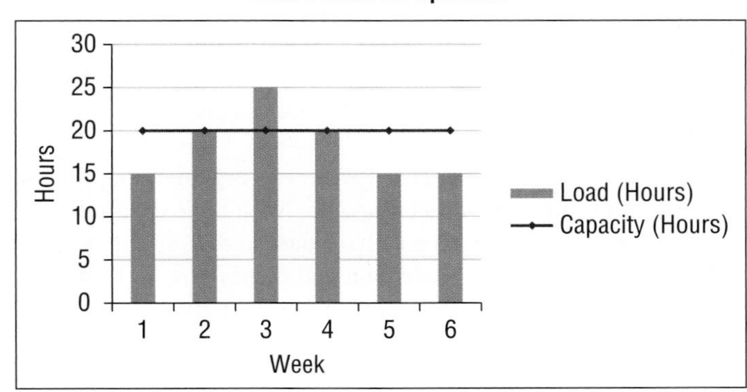

ADVANCES IN PLANNING SYSTEMS

Prepare

How does an enterprise resource planning (ERP) system facilitate planning?

Organize

Advances in Planning Systems
- Enterprise Resource Planning (ERP)
- Advanced Planning and Scheduling (APS)

The logic of requirements and resources planning has been around for a long time. The army's ordering system used in World War II was essentially a manual MRP system. In the past few decades, however, the benefits of DRP, MRP, and CRP processes have become more fully realized because of the dramatic increase in computer power and the availability of low-cost MRP software. Today, the planning for very complex operations can be done using fairly low-cost requirements planning software systems.

Over the years, requirements planning systems have evolved. Initially, the focus of MRP was on manufacturing planning and scheduling. However, managers soon recognized that the output from MRP would be useful for planning in other functions such as accounting, purchasing, marketing, sales, finance, distribution, and engineering. MRP evolved into manufacturing *resource* planning, or MRP II, which considers a wider range of cross-functional issues. MRP II also has the capability to simulate the impacts of different plans. This was a precursor of the enterprise resource planning (ERP) systems that have been adopted by many firms. Three recent advances in requirements and resources planning systems are being implemented today: (1) enterprise resource planning (ERP) systems, (2) advanced planning and scheduling (APS) systems, and (3) extended planning across the supply chain.

Enterprise Resource Planning (ERP)

enterprise resource planning (ERP) system Software that consolidates all of the business planning systems and data throughout an organization.

Rather than existing as independent, stand-alone systems, DRP, MRP, and CRP are usually embedded as integral parts of an **enterprise resource planning (ERP)** system. An ERP

LO14-5 Describe how materials requirements and resource planning functions work together within an enterprise resource planning (ERP) system.

system consolidates all of the business planning systems and related data throughout a company, so the planning processes across all business functions can be integrated and consistently applied. The goal of ERP systems is to allow business processes to function seamlessly and in unison. The improved coordination of planning from ERP takes MRP II to an even higher level. Companies such as SAP and Oracle are the leading providers of ERP software.

A typical ERP includes the functionality of many requirements and resource planning systems, including sales, billing, accounting, finance, human resource management, and project management, along with the supply chain planning systems discussed in this chapter. Before ERP, these different planning functions were done using "legacy" software systems that were developed and used within each function, such as accounting, operations, and human resources, but were not linked or compatible with one another. As a result, data needed by other legacy systems (say operations data were needed by accounting) had to be manually transformed via spreadsheets or databases, thus wasting time and creating errors. By allowing all business data to be in one ERP system, planning and coordination across business functions is easier, time is saved, and errors are reduced. All types of companies can gain benefits from an ERP system. An ERP system helped Red Door Spas to reduce costs, improve customer service, and make better business decisions, as discussed in the Get Real box.

Although they were initially focused within an organization, ERP systems and add-on software are being used to integrate companies with their customers and suppliers. In the same ways that ERP helps companies share data and planning across internal functions, expanded ERP helps a company share data and planning with its suppliers and customers. However, ERP systems are not without drawbacks. ERP software is written to meet the needs of many different companies. Thus, companies either need to modify their business processes to fit the software or spend a lot of time and money customizing the software to fit their particular needs. This requires high cost and long implementation times, complexity of the software, and lack of flexibility. Mergers and acquisitions can be especially challenging, for example. When companies have different ERP systems, data must be combined into a single system and processes must be standardized.

GET REAL

ERP Improves Performance at Elizabeth Arden Red Door Spas

ERP systems are not just for manufacturing. Elizabeth Arden Red Door Spas has 30 locations designed to provide the ultimate in pampering through salon and spa services. The management team was planning to add locations both within the United States and internationally. However, its human resource, finance, and logistics systems were not integrated, making decision making difficult. In 2006, to give its business performance a makeover, Red Door Spas replaced its legacy business systems with an ERP system by SAP. The system made it easier to track orders. Inventory at its salons and distribution center dropped, reducing costs. Employees could spend more time with customers and less time on administrative tasks. More importantly, the ERP system provided more consistent data that could be used for making better business decisions.

Advanced Planning and Scheduling (APS)

LO14-6 Explain how advanced planning systems and scheduling (APS) systems improve the requirements and resource planning process.

Conventional requirements planning systems were sequential and iterative in nature, and today many still are. In this chapter, we have described a process in which DRP outputs feed the MPS, which feeds MRP, which feeds CRP. Problems identified in the CRP process must be remedied by a revision to the MPS, and the process repeats until a feasible solution is found. This approach, which emerged in the past because of the lack of computer power and connectivity across legacy data systems, is fundamentally inefficient.

Imagine a planning process that simultaneously considers materials requirements along with resource capacity constraints. In this process a plan could be developed that optimizes all related costs, for example, inventory, labor, capital, and other costs. This level of joint optimization is the goal of **advanced planning and scheduling (APS) systems** that are often included in ERP systems. APS systems use the same fundamental explosion logic of MRP. However, they integrate materials and capacity planning into one system. APS is possible because of vast improvements in computing power coupled with the development of sophisticated mathematical algorithms that help to solve very complex scheduling problems. The result is better plans that are generated much faster.

advance planning and scheduling (APS) systems Systems that integrate materials and capacity planning into one system.

Requirements and resource planning systems have achieved a high level of acceptance because of the important advantages that they offer to a firm. As multiple firms work together to adopt and share compatible planning systems, the supply chain can experience significant benefits. Planning systems that are extended across supply chain partners provide greater visibility into the current status and into plans for the future. By anticipating supply and demand conditions into the future, APS systems help managers to identify and avoid problems, and quickly evaluate alternatives. Supply chain partners can jointly plan their operations using what-if analyses. They evaluate different scenarios of changes in customer demand and material delays. This analysis helps supply chain partners to identify options and create contingency plans.

Supply chain partners who work to coordinate and share planning systems typically see tremendous reductions in order fulfillment lead times, large improvements in information accuracy, reductions in inventory, and lower costs. APICS—The Association for Operations Management—is an excellent source of information on the latest trends and directions in materials and resources planning across the supply chain.

CHAPTER SUMMARY

This chapter defined dependent demand and described materials and resources planning processes.

1. Dependent demand is for raw materials, parts, and subassemblies needed to make end items.
2. Inputs to MRP include the master production schedule (MPS) for the end items, the bill of materials (BOM), which shows what components are needed, and inventory records.
3. The key steps in the MRP process include calculating the gross requirements, determining net requirements, establishing the timing for planned order receipts, and offsetting to determine planned order releases.
4. MRP outputs include primary reports used for operations planning and secondary reports used for performance measurement and process improvement.
5. Distribution requirements planning (DRP) uses the logic of MRP to determine the positioning and replenishment of finished goods inventories (independent demand) within a distribution network.

6. Plans developed by MRP may not be feasible unless there is adequate capacity available within the supply chain. With basic MRP, an additional step, capacity requirements planning (CRP), is used to determine if the plan developed by MRP is feasible.
7. Advances in computer technology are streamlining the planning process by combining materials and capacity planning into advanced planning and scheduling (APS) systems that are part of ERP systems.

KEY TERMS

advanced planning and scheduling (APS) systems 485
available to promise 471
bill of materials (BOM) 473
capacity requirements planning (CRP) 482
cumulative lead time 470
dependent demand 468
distribution requirements planning (DRP) 481
enterprise resource planning (ERP) systems 483
fixed order quantity (FOQ) 475
gross requirements 475
independent demand 468
infinite loading 482
inventory status file 474
load profile 482
lot-for-lot (L4L) 474
master production schedule (MPS) 470
materials requirements planning (MRP) 469
nervousness 480
net requirements 475
periodic order quantity (POQ) 475
planned order receipt 475
planned order release 476
planning horizon 470
requirements explosion 475
rough-cut capacity planning 472
scheduled receipts 474
time bucket 470

DISCUSSION QUESTIONS

1. Why are spare parts and service parts considered to be independent demand, not dependent demand?
2. Why is collaboration within an organization and the supply chain important when using DRP and MRP?
3. The planning process involves a rolling time horizon. What does this mean to a planner?
4. What is the relationship between cumulative lead time and changes in the MPS? Why?
5. What types of companies are likely to benefit the most from using MRP? Why?
6. What problems can MRP create for suppliers as you go upstream in the supply chain? Why?
7. As an organization increases its level of outsourcing, what will be the impact on its bill of materials? Why?
8. How do L4L, FOQ, and POQ ordering policies impact setup/ordering costs and inventory costs? Why?
9. What impact will a supplier's quality and delivery problems have on a company using MRP? Why?
10. In what ways are DRP and MRP similar and how are they different?
11. How have advances in computer technology changed the planning process? Why? What changes do you expect in the future?

SOLVED PROBLEMS

The Comfort Chair Company makes furniture that is used in waiting rooms for doctors' offices. Its most popular model is an upholstered chair that comes in two colors of fabric, blue and burgundy. The BOM, provided as a product structure diagram, is shown in Figure 14-17. All of the components are the same for the blue and burgundy chairs, with the exception of the fabric.

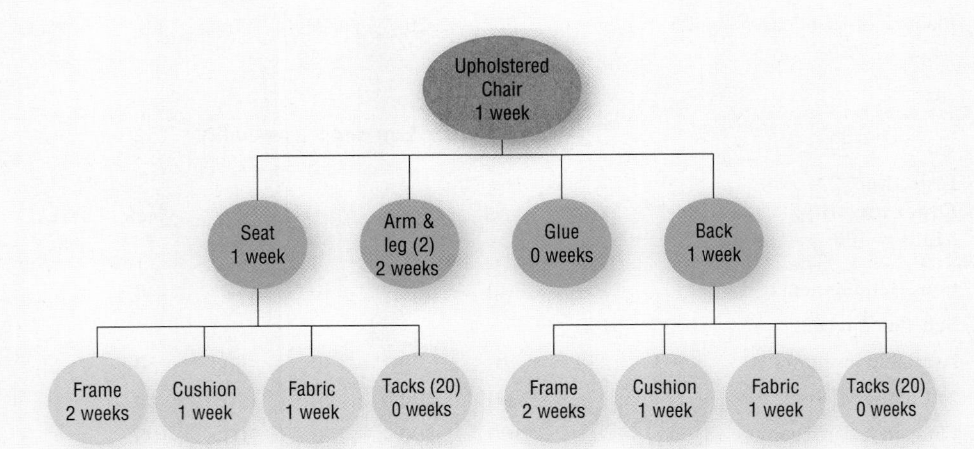

FIGURE 14-17 BOM for the Upholstered Chair

1. What is the cumulative lead time for the chair, and why is this important?

   Solution:

   The cumulative lead time is four weeks. The longest path is one week (upholstered chair) plus one week (seat or back) plus two weeks (frame). Thus, the planning horizon for the MPS must be at least four weeks to provide enough time to produce the chairs.

2. Given the MRP for the blue and the burgundy chairs, complete the MRP for the arm and leg assembly. Assume that the gross requirements for the arm and leg assembly depend only upon the blue and burgundy chairs.

Part Name: Blue upholstered chair								
Lead time: 1 week **Order quantity: L4L**	**Week 1**	**Week 2**	**Week 3**	**Week 4**	**Week 5**	**Week 6**	**Week 7**	**Week 8**
Gross requirements			50	50	50	50	50	50
Scheduled receipts								
Available inventory								
Net requirements			50	50	50	50	50	50
Planned order receipts			50	50	50	50	50	50
Planned order releases		50	50	50	50	50	50	

Part Name: Burgundy upholstered chair								
Lead time: 1 week **Order quantity: L4L**	**Week 1**	**Week 2**	**Week 3**	**Week 4**	**Week 5**	**Week 6**	**Week 7**	**Week 8**
Gross requirements		25		20	20	20	20	20
Scheduled receipts								
Available inventory								
Net requirements		25		20	20	20	20	20
Planned order receipts		25		20	20	20	20	20
Planned order releases	25		20	20	20	20	20	

Part Name: Arm and leg assembly								
Lead time: 2 weeks **Order quantity: Multi = 100**	**Week 1**	**Week 2**	**Week 3**	**Week 4**	**Week 5**	**Week 6**	**Week 7**	**Week 8**
Gross requirements	50	100	140	140	140	140	140	
Scheduled receipts	100	100						
Available inventory 0	50	50	10	70	30	90	50	
Net requirements			90	130	70	110	50	
Planned order receipts			100	200	100	200	100	
Planned order releases	100	200	100	200	100			

Solution:

The gross requirements for the arm and leg assembly come from both the blue and the burgundy chairs. Because each chair requires two arm and leg assemblies, planned order release quantities from the upholstered chairs must be doubled.

3. If it takes 45 minutes to assemble each upholstered chair, and there is one worker in the assembly department who works 40 hours per week, can the MPS for week 4 be met for both the blue and burgundy chairs? Why, or why not?

Solution:

The time required for each chair is 45 minutes/60 minutes = .75 hours. The requirements to complete 50 blue chairs and 20 burgundy chairs in week 4 is 70 chairs × .75 hours = 52.5 hours. This exceeds the available capacity with one worker.

4. The Organic Juice Co. produces a line of fresh, natural organic juices. Given the MPS and BOM for one type of juice, Passion Swirl, complete the MRP schedules for the components: orange juice, passion fruit juice, and mango juice. There are 128 fluid ounces per gallon.

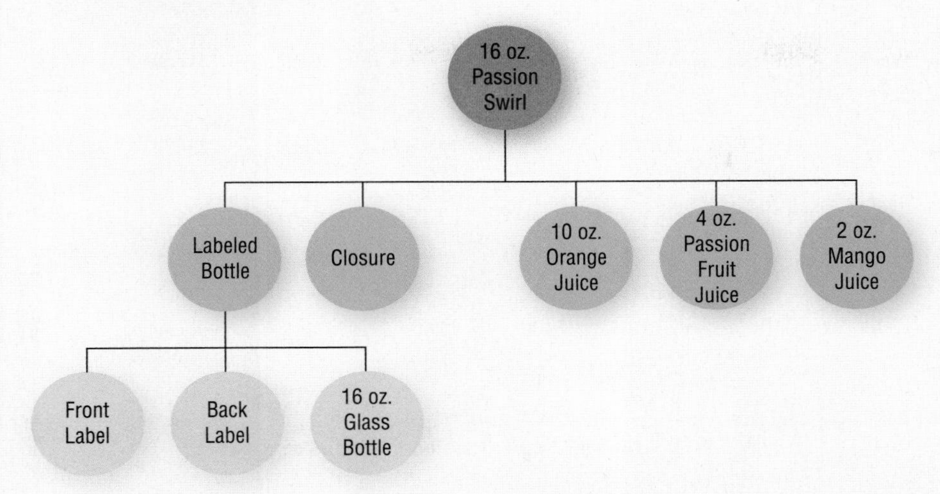

MPS

Item	Week 1	Week 2	Week 3	Week 4	Week 5	Week 6	Week 7	Week 8
Passion Swirl Number of 16 oz. bottles	2,000	2,000	2,500	2,500	2,500	3,000	3,000	3,000

Item	Orange Juice	Passion Fruit Juice	Mango Juice
Lot size rule	Multiples FOQ = 120 gallons	Multiples FOQ = 50 gallons	Multiples FOQ = 50 gallons
Safety stock	50 gallons	10 gallon	10 gallons
Beginning inventory	80 gallons	10 gallons	40 gallons
Lead time	2 weeks	3 weeks	2 weeks

Solution:

MRP can be used to determine the schedule for continuous products as is the case in this example. To determine the gross requirements, take the MPS quantity for a period and multiply it by the number of ounces that are in the product. In week 1, 2,000 16-ounce bottles of Passion Swirl are needed. Because there are 10 ounces of orange juice in each bottle of Passion Swirl, the total number of bottles, 2,000, is multiplied by 10 ounces to get the gross requirements of 20,000 ounces. The order quantity for each of the juices is in gallons, so the total number of ounces required must be divided by the number of ounces in a gallon (128 ounces/gallon) to get the gross requirements in gallons as shown in the MRP records. Repeat for the remaining periods. Use a similar approach for passion fruit juice and mango juice.

After the gross requirements are determined, complete the MRP schedule using the same approach as for discrete products. In this example, for orange juice, 50 gallons of safety stock are required. This means that the inventory level should always be 50 or more gallons. Take a look at week 3 to see how the net requirements are calculated when safety stock is used. The gross requirements of 195.3 gallons plus the safety stock of 50 gallons make up the total requirements of 254.3 gallons in week 3. At the beginning of week 3 there are 127.4 gallons available in inventory. The net requirements in week 3 are 117.9 gallons (254.3–127.4 gallons).

MRP Record **Material Name: Orange Juice**

Lead time = 2 weeks
On-hand = 80 gallons
Safety stock = 50 gallons

Order quantity: Multiples FOQ = 120 gallons	**Week 1**	**Week 2**	**Week 3**	**Week 4**	**Week 5**	**Week 6**	**Week 7**	**Week 8**
Gross requirements (gallons)	156.3	156.3	195.3	195.3	195.3	234.4	234.4	234.4
Scheduled receipts	240	120						
Available inventory 80 gallons	163.7	127.4	52.1	96.8	141.5	147.1	152.7	158.3
Net requirements			117.9	193.2	148.5	142.9	137.3	131.7
Planned order receipts			120	240	240	240	240	240
Planned order releases	120	240	240	2400	240	240		

MRP Record **Material Name: Passion Fruit Juice**

Lead time = 3 weeks
On-hand = 10 gallons
Safety stock = 10 gallon

Order quantity: Multiples FOQ = 50 gallons	**Week 1**	**Week 2**	**Week 3**	**Week 4**	**Week 5**	**Week 6**	**Week 7**	**Week 8**
Gross requirements (gallons)	62.5	62.5	78.1	78.1	78.1	93.8	93.8	93.8
Scheduled receipts	100	50	100					
Available inventory 10 gallons	47.5	35	56.9	28.8	50.7	56.9	13.1	19.3
Net requirements				31.2	59.3	53.1	46.9	90.7
Planned order receipts				50	100	100	50	100
Planned order releases	50	100	100	50	100			

MRP Record **Material Name: Mango Juice**

Lead time = 2 weeks
On-hand = 40 gallons
Safety stock = 10 gallons

Order quantity: Multiples FOQ = 50 gallons	**Week 1**	**Week 2**	**Week 3**	**Week 4**	**Week 5**	**Week 6**	**Week 7**	**Week 8**
Gross requirements (gallons)	31.3	31.3	39.1	39.1	39.1	46.9	46.9	46.9
Scheduled receipts	50							
Available inventory 40 gallons	58.7	27.4	38.3	49.2	10.1	13.2	16.3	19.4
Net requirements			21.7	10.8		46.8	43.7	40.6
Planned order receipts			50	50		50	50	50
Planned order releases	50	50		50	50	50		

PROBLEMS

1. Using the BOM shown below, how many of part E will be needed if 20 units of end item A are needed? How many part Cs will be needed?

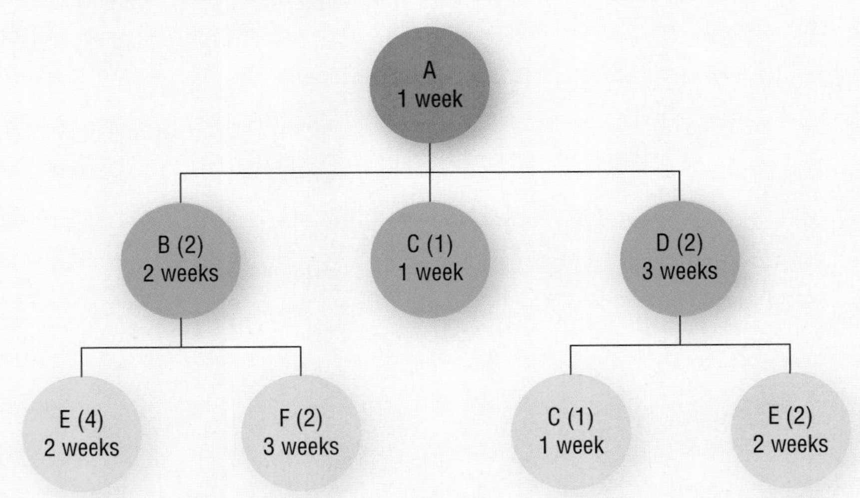

2. Based on the BOM in problem 1, what is the cumulative lead time for end item A? How will this information be used?
3. Develop an indented BOM for the product structure tree in problem 1.
4. Based on the BOM shown below, how many units of part F will be needed if 15 units of end item A are needed? If the company decided to purchase part D from suppliers, how would the BOM change? Assuming part D is purchased, how many units of part F are needed to make 15 units of end item A?

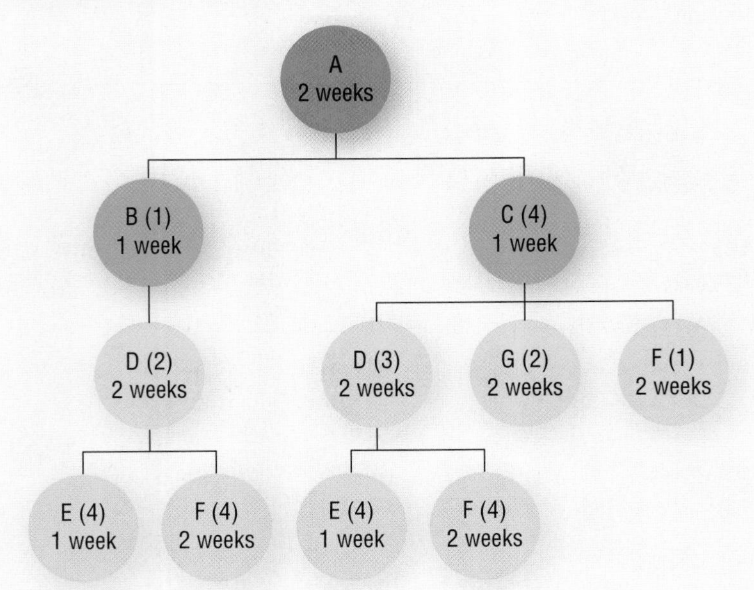

5. Based on the BOM in problem 4, what is the cumulative lead time for end item A?
6. Develop an indented BOM for the product structure tree shown in problem 4.
7. Based on the BOM shown below, how many of part D will be needed if 100 units of end item A are needed? How many of part F?

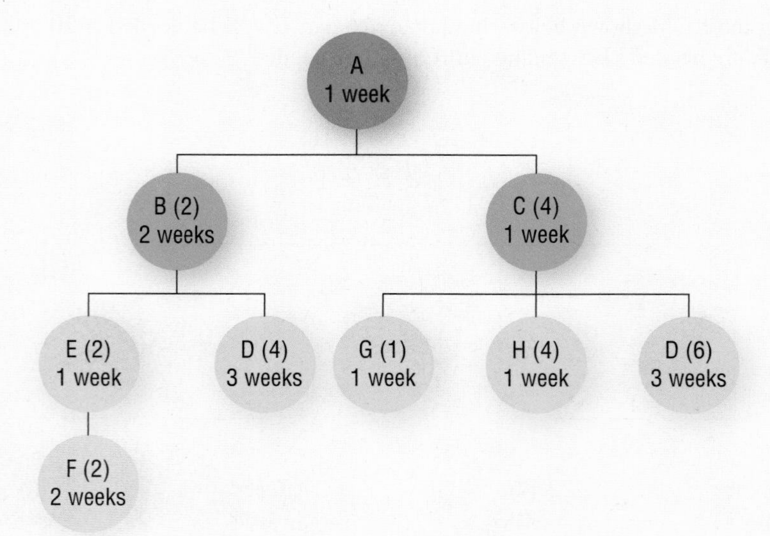

8. Using the information in problem 7, develop an indented BOM.
9. How many of part J will be needed if 40 units of end item A are needed? Managers have decided to outsource part G. Revise the BOM for end item A, assuming that item G is now purchased from a supplier. How many of part J will now be needed if 40 units of end item A are needed?

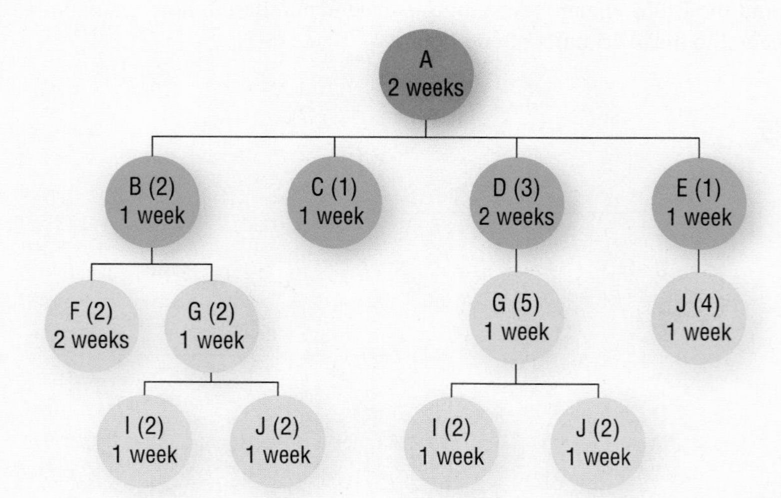

10. Draw a product structure tree for the BOM for the square patio planter. If there are plans to make eight patio planters, how many bolt and nut sets will be needed?

Patio Planter
* Planter box assembly
** Base assembly (1)
*** Base (1)
*** Rolling casters (4)
*** Bolt and nut set (4)
** Side assembly
*** Side panels (4)
*** Corner Braces (8)
** Bolt and nut sets (4)
* Top (1)
* Bolt and nut sets (4)

11. Complete the MRP record for a bicycle frame using a L4L lot-sizing strategy. Considering the lead time, where should scheduled receipts be shown? Repeat using a fixed order quantity of 100 frames. Again, show scheduled receipts. Compare and contrast the results. What are the benefits and drawbacks to each approach?

MRP Record **Lead time = 2 weeks** **On-hand = 0** **Safety stock = 0** **Order quantity: L4L**	**Part Name: Bicycle frame** **Week 1**	**Week 2**	**Week 3**	**Week 4**	**Week 5**	**Week 6**	**Week 7**	**Week 8**
Gross requirements	70	50	80	80	70	60	80	80
Scheduled receipts								
Available inventory								
Net requirements								
Planned order receipts								
Planned order releases								

MRP Record **Lead time = 2 weeks** **On-hand = 0** **Safety stock = 0** **Order quantity:** **FOQ = 100**	**Part Name: Bicycle frame** **Week 1**	**Week 2**	**Week 3**	**Week 4**	**Week 5**	**Week 6**	**Week 7**	**Week 8**
Gross requirements	70	50	80	80	70	60	80	80
Scheduled receipts								
Available inventory								
Net requirements								
Planned order receipts								
Planned order releases								

12. Complete the MRP record for a bicycle seat.

MRP Record				**Part Name: Seat**				
Lead time = 1 week **On-hand = 40** **Safety stock = 20** **Order quantity** **FOQ = 100**	**Week 1**	**Week 2**	**Week 3**	**Week 4**	**Week 5**	**Week 6**	**Week 7**	**Week 8**
Gross requirements	70	50	80	80	70	60	80	80
Scheduled receipts								
Available inventory								
Net requirements								
Planned order receipts								
Planned order releases								

13. Given the BOM and the MPS for end item A, complete the MRP schedule for items A, C, D, and E.

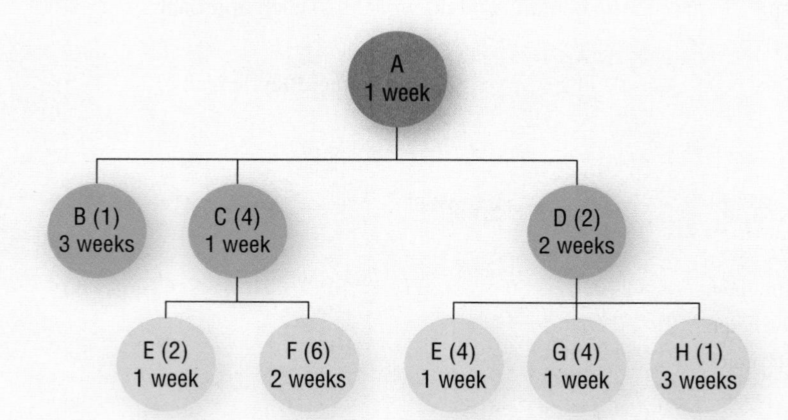

MPS

Item	**1**	**2**	**3**	**4**	**5**	**6**	**7**	**8**
A	60	20	50	120	100	50	80	40

Item	**A**	**C**	**D**	**E**
Lot size rule	L4L	L4L	L4L	Multiples FOQ = 500
Safety stock	0	0	0	100
Beginning inventory	0	0	0	300

14. Given the BOM and MPS for end items A and B, complete the MRP schedules for items A, B, C, D, and E.

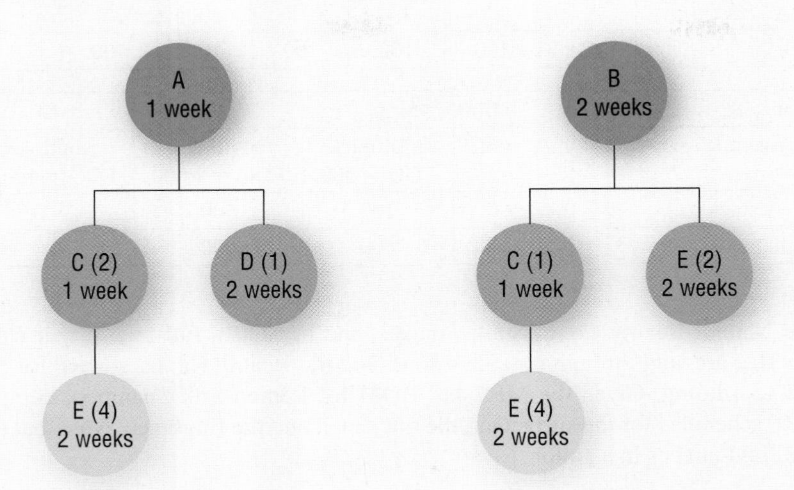

MPS

Item	1	2	3	4	5	6	7	8
A			200	200		200	200	
B				150			150	150

Item	A	B	C	D	E
Lot size rule	L4L	L4L	FOQ = 500	FOQ = 1,000	L4L
Safety stock	0	0	0	200	50
Beginning inventory	0	0	50	500	1,000

15. Given the BOM and MPS for end items A and B, complete the MRP schedules for items A, B, C, F, and G.

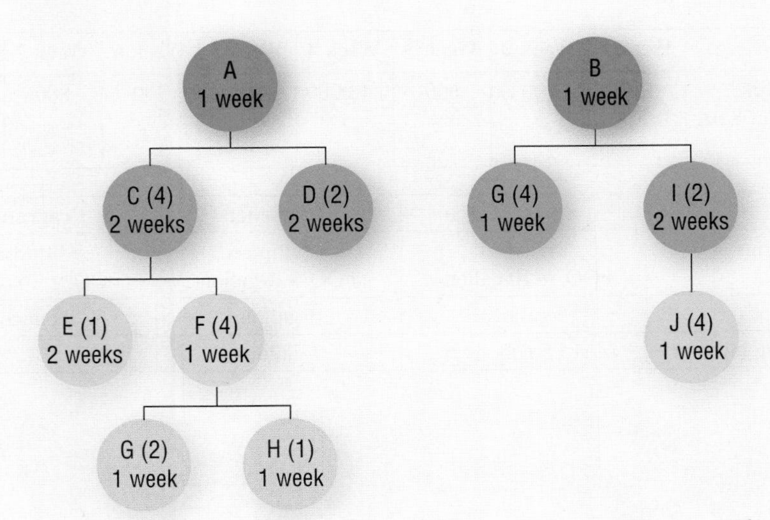

MPS

Item	1	2	3	4	5	6	7	8
A			200	250		300		
B		100	100	100	100	100	100	

Item	A	B	C	F	G
Lot size rule	L4L	L4L	Multiples FOQ = 500	Multiples FOQ = 1,000	Multiples FOQ = 1,000
Safety stock	0	0	100	500	500
Beginning inventory	0	0	400	500	800

16. The Natural Beauty Co. develops, makes, and markets a full line of hair care products that are sold through upscale salons. Natural Beauty Co. uses MRP for planning and scheduling. Given the MPS and BOM for Lemon Silk Shampoo, complete the MRP schedules for the surfactant, the thickener, and the fragrance. Note that there are 128 fluid ounces in a gallon.

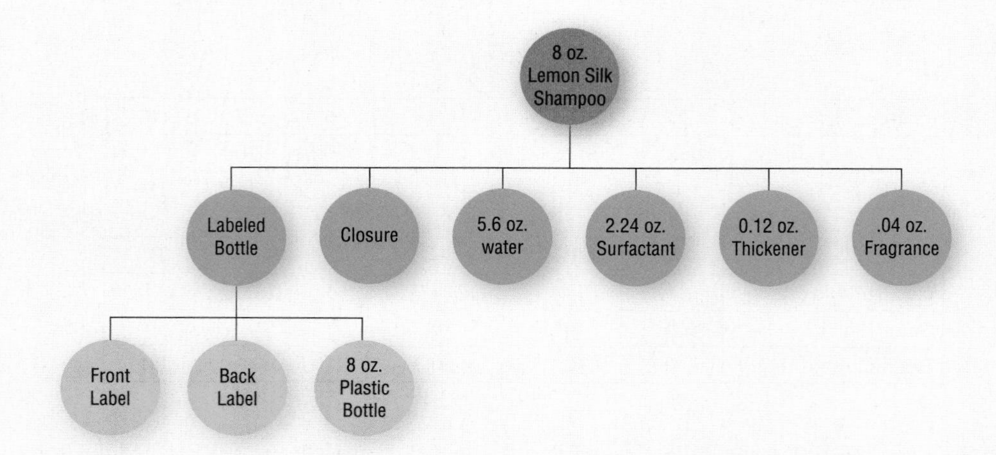

MPS

Item	Week 1	Week 2	Week 3	Week 4	Week 5	Week 6	Week 7	Week 8
Lemon Silk Number of 8 oz. bottles	500	500	600	1,000	800	700	800	1,000

Item	Surfactant	Thickener	Fragrance
Lot size rule	Multiples FOQ = 10 gallons	Multiples FOQ = 1 gallon	Multiples FOQ = 16 ounces
Safety stock	5 gallons	1 gallon	8 ounces
Beginning inventory	15.5 gallons	3 gallons	0

17. The computer keyboard assembly area has five employees who work 40 hours each week. Use this information to develop a load profile. What recommendations do you have?

Part Name: Computer keyboard								
Processing time = 9 minutes	**Week 1**	**Week 2**	**Week 3**	**Week 4**	**Week 5**	**Week 6**	**Week 7**	**Week 8**
Planned order releases	1,000	1,200	900	1,300	1,400	1,000	800	1,100
Processing load (hours)								
Available capacity (hours)								

18. Calculate the processing load and develop the load profile for the computer assembly process. As the planner, what concerns do you have (if any)? What changes might you consider?

Part Name: Computer								
Processing time = 2 hours	**Week 1**	**Week 2**	**Week 3**	**Week 4**	**Week 5**	**Week 6**	**Week 7**	**Week 8**
Planned order releases	60	50	40	35	70	55	45	60
Processing load (hours)								
Available capacity (hours)	120	120	120	120	120	120	120	120

19. Calculate the processing load and available capacity, and develop the load profile for the stereo speaker subassembly. Two employees work the assembly process for 40 hours each. As the planner, what concerns do you have and what changes would you make (if any)?

Part Name: Stereo speaker								
Processing time = 20 minutes	**Week 1**	**Week 2**	**Week 3**	**Week 4**	**Week 5**	**Week 6**	**Week 7**	**Week 8**
Planned order releases	210	180	220	260	200	180	230	190
Processing load (hours)								
Available capacity (hours)								

20. Calculate the processing load and available capacity and develop the load profile for a dishwasher. Eight employees work the assembly process for 40 hours per week each. As the planner, what concerns do you have and what changes would you make (if any)?

Part Name: Dishwasher								
Processing time = 30 minutes	**Week 1**	**Week 2**	**Week 3**	**Week 4**	**Week 5**	**Week 6**	**Week 7**	**Week 8**
Planned order releases	600	625	640	600	620	690	645	620
Processing load (hours)								
Available capacity (hours)								

CASE

QP Industries—The Challenges of Integration

Adam Rodriguez, the vice president of supply chain management for QP Industries, sat in his office, contemplating what he had to tell the executive leadership team at tomorrow's meeting. During the last two years, lead times for transmitting orders between QP Industries' six strategic business units (SBUs) were getting longer and longer; while the number of incorrect orders, inventory levels, and stockouts were dramatically increasing. Six weeks ago, the CEO of QP Industries, Ellen Higgins, had asked Adam to form a task force to identify the underlying problems and to develop a plan to solve them.

QP Industries—Corporate Background

QP Industries develops and makes gears and related engineered components, mostly used as replacement parts in heavy equipment. With sales of over $7 billion per year, QP serves the aerospace, automotive, recreational vehicle, medical, military, off-road, and power generation markets. QP is organized into six SBUs serving each of these markets.

Since its founding, QP Industries has grown by expanding on its core strengths—innovative designs, high-quality engineering, and a strict, almost fanatical adherence to quality standards and delivery schedules. The company prides itself on being the most responsive in the industry and offers "the 12-hour guarantee." For most of its product line, QP promises to pick or produce if necessary, and ship products within 12 hours of receiving customer orders.

Six years ago, QP's executive leadership team sought to grow sales by expanding beyond North America. They targeted Vietnam, India, Indonesia, Brazil, Argentina, China, and South Africa as desirable markets, and rapidly expanded primarily through acquisitions. During this time, QP Industries acquired over 30 different companies, many of which were leaders in their regional markets. With some 50,000 different stock keeping units (SKUs), there was a concern that the acquisitions caused unnecessary duplication of part numbers and SKUs. Subsequently, a corporate initiative identified and eliminated redundant or unnecessary SKUs (resulting in a 37 percent reduction in SKUs).

The 12-Hour Guarantee Problem

While expansion had given QP Industries 15 major distribution centers and a sales presence in 20 countries, increasingly QP was failing to meet its 12-hour guarantee. The standard was to have 95 percent of orders meet the 12-hour guarantee. Two years ago, only 83 percent of orders were shipped within 12 hours. Last year this rate had fallen to 71 percent, and year-to-date performance suggests that the downward trend will continue.

To address this problem, Adam formed a task force consisting of the supply chain directors for each division. Over a very intensive six-week period, the task force visited customers (especially key accounts), distribution centers, and manufacturing facilities. The task force made several key conclusions.

- QP Industries was using at least 22 different MRP systems and four different DRP systems.
- Many of the acquired companies were still using legacy sales and billing systems, each with its own unique database.
- The different systems had difficulty in "talking" to each other. Often, communications were delayed and errors created as orders generated by one system were manually entered into the other system.
- Each group believed that it needed to maintain its own MRP/DRP system because its unique features were necessary.
- In many cases, the bills of materials were inaccurate, because engineering changes introduced by newly acquired companies had not been incorporated into the bills.

The Task Force's Recommendations

After consulting with some of the major MRP/ERP software providers (SAP, QAD, Oracle, and JDA), the task force recommended that the current systems be consolidated into one corporate-wide ERP system and that all databases be consolidated into one database. In conjunction with this transition, core/critical processes were to be standardized and consolidated. It was estimated that this project would cost QP Industries around $25 million, but costs could run as high as $480 million (using 6.9% of total revenue as a proxy for the total cost of ownership). Implementation might take anywhere from 14 to 24 months. As Adam prepared for the meeting, he could not help wondering if these recommendations were sufficient and how they would be received by the executive team.

Questions

1. What are the benefits from implementing a single, companywide ERP system?
2. What challenges are likely to be encountered during implementation?
3. What additional recommendations would you make to Adam?

CASE

The Casual Furniture Company

The Casual Furniture Company (CFC) makes a variety of bookshelves for homes and businesses. The shelves come in various heights, widths, materials, and finishes. Effective requirements planning is essential for CFC's performance, and it uses MRP for planning.

The MPS and MRP records are shown for one of CFC's products, part number 4X3-01, a four-foot-high and three-foot wide standard depth oak bookshelf. The BOM as a product structure diagram is shown in Figure 14-18.

CFC uses one-week time buckets and a planning horizon of eight weeks. The MPS for the 4X3-01 Bookshelf is shown in Figure 14-19.

The final assembly area is set up to respond very quickly to demand so that product can be built to order when necessary, as long as the MRP system has ensured that all of the required components are ready. This short lead time, and the lack of any lot-sizing requirement, indicates that there is very little setup required to get ready to make this product. In fact, switching from one product to another in assembly is limited to the type of wood being used, and this has little effect on setups. Thus, the lead time for the final assembly is assumed to be zero. The component lot size is shown in Figure 14-20.

The cabinets are built in the cabinet assembly department and the shelves, backs, sides, and ends are made in the cutting department. Two associates work in the cutting department making the available capacity of 80 hours per week without overtime. The processing time for each component in the cutting department is shown in Figure 14-21.

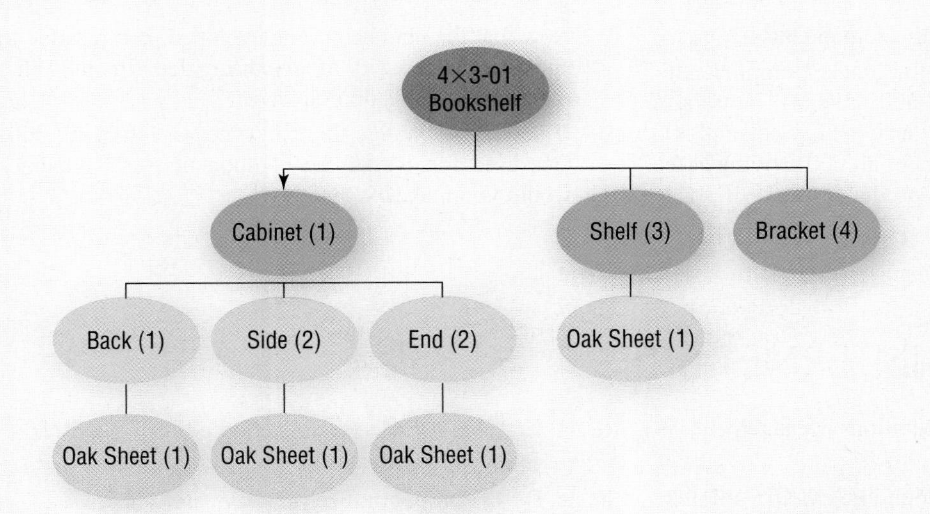

FIGURE 14-18 Bookshelf 4 × 3-01 BOM

FIGURE 14-19 MPS Bookshelf 4 × 3-01

Part Name: Bookshelf 4 × 3-01								
	Week 1	**Week 2**	**Week 3**	**Week 4**	**Week 5**	**Week 6**	**Week 7**	**Week 8**
MPS	70	70	80	90	60	80	80	70

FIGURE 14-20 Component Lot Size and Inventory Information

Item	Bookshelf 4 × 3-01	Cabinet	Back	Side	End	Shelf	Bracket	Oak Sheet
Lot size rule	L4L	L4L	L4L	L4L	L4L	FOQ = 500	FOQ = 600	FOQ = 1,000
Lead time	0	2 weeks	1 week	1 week	1 week	1 week	300	2 weeks
Available inventory	0	120	100	200	200	300	0	500
Safety stock	0	0	0	0	0	0	0	30

FIGURE 14-21 Cutting Department Processing Time

Component	Processing Time (minutes/part)
Back	10 minutes
Side	8 minutes
End	5 minutes
Shelf	7 minutes

Questions

1. Develop the MRP for all of the components.
2. During week 1 of the plan the bracket supplier notifies CFC that the order for 600 units will not arrive as planned. Instead, 300 will arrive this week and 300 will arrive next week, instead of all 600 arriving at the same time. Will this affect production and, if so, to what extent?
3. Now that the plan has been developed, is it feasible to consider the capacity of the cutting department? What recommendations do you have?
4. If you could change the lead times or lot-sizing policies used for any of the components, what changes would you make? Why?

SELECTED READINGS & INTERNET SITES

APICS—The Association for Operations Management **www.apics.org**

Bartholomew, D. "9 Lives and Counting." *Industry Week,* May 2006, p. 44.

Cox III, J. F., and J. Blackstone. *APICS Dictionary,* 12th ed. Chicago: APICS—The Association for Operations Management, 2008.

Jonsson, P., and S. Mattsson. "Inventory Management Practices and their Implications on Perceived Planning Performance." *International Journal of Production Economics* 46, no. 7 (2008), pp. 1787–1812.

Lee, H.; V. Padmanabhan; and S. Whang. "The Bullwhip Effect in Supply Chains." *Sloan Management Review* 38, no. 3 (1997), pp. 93–102.

Mabert, V. "The Early Road to Materials Requirements Planning." *Journal of Operations Management* 25, no. 2 (2007), pp. 346–56.

Plossl, G. *Orlicky's Materials Requirements Planning,* 2nd ed. New York: McGraw-Hill, 1995.

Rettig, C. "The Trouble with Enterprise Software." *MIT Sloan Management Review* 49, no. 1 (2007), pp. 21–27.

Steele, D.; P. Philipoom; M. Malhotra; and T. Fry. "Comparisons between Drum-Buffer-Rope and Materials Requirements Planning: A Case Study." *International Journal of Production Research* 43, no. 15 (2005), pp. 3181–3208.

Taylor, D. A. "A Master Plan for Software Selection." *Supply Chain Management Review* 8, no.1 (2004), pp. 20–27.

Vollman, T. E.; W. L. Berry; D. C. Wybark; and F. R. Jacobs. *Manufacturing Planning and Control Systems for Supply Chain Management,* 5th ed. New York: McGraw-Hill, 2004.

Wallace, T. F. *MRPII: Making It Happen,* 2nd ed. Essex Junction, VT: Oliver Wight Publishing, 1990.

Willcox, B. *Study Notes for Detailed Scheduling and Planning.* Chicago: APICS, 2004.

PART 5

MANAGING CHANGE IN SUPPLY CHAIN OPERATIONS

		relationships	sustainability	global
15	Project Management Supplement: Advanced Methods for Project Scheduling	X	X	X
16	Sustainable Operations Management—Preparing for the Future	X	X	X

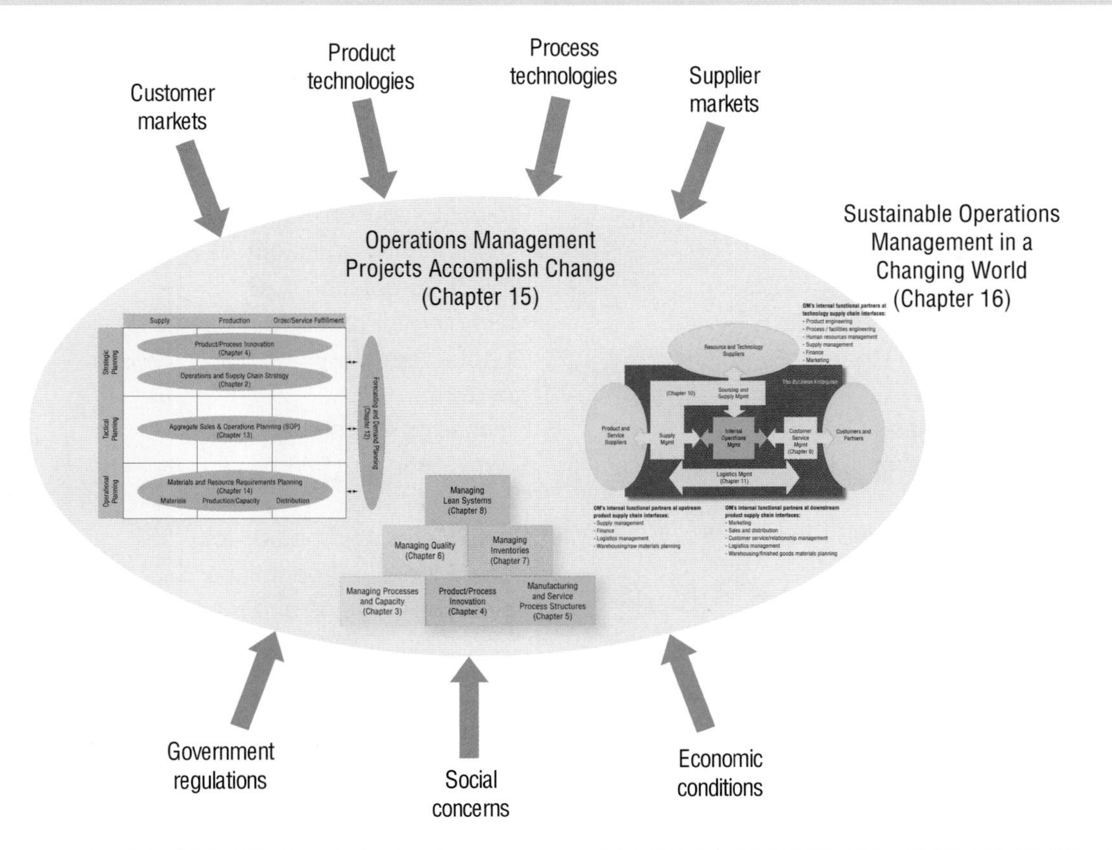

How do operations managers manage change and prepare for future challenges? Because social and economic conditions, government regulations, customer and supplier markets, and technologies are always changing, operations managers must continually plan, implement, and control changes to their operating processes. Part 5, *Managing Change in Supply Chain Operations,* explains how operations managers accomplish change in their organizations.

Chapter 15 and the accompanying supplement describe how projects serve as a means for managing change. A project is a one-time or infrequently occurring set of activities that creates outputs within prespecified time and cost schedules. Chapter 15 describes the factors that make projects successful, and it lays out a series of steps that operations managers use to plan and control them.

Chapter 16 concludes this book by discussing the "sustainable perspective" as an approach for managing the important challenges that loom on the horizon for operations managers. The chapter describes how operations managers are seeking to develop successful outcomes for people and the planet, while maintaining profits in a rapidly changing world.

15 Project Management

CHAPTER OUTLINE

LEARNING OBJECTIVES *After studying this chapter, you should be able to:*

LO15-1 Explain the difference between projects and other more routine operational processes.

LO15-2 Manage the social and technical factors that are critical for project success.

LO15-3 Choose the best type of project organizational structure for a given set of objectives.

LO15-4 Develop a comprehensive project plan, evaluating trade-offs, uncertainties, and risks.

LO15-5 Fashion criteria to guide project selection and management of a portfolio of projects.

Pixar Wins with Project Management

Pixar Animation Studios combines creative and technical artistry to create original stories in the medium of computer animation. Pixar has created some of the most successful and beloved animated films of all time, including: *Toy Story* (and its sequels), *A Bug's Life, Monsters Inc., Finding Nemo, The Incredibles, Cars, Ratatouille, Wall-E, Up!* and *Brave.* Its movies have won more than 18 Academy Awards® and have grossed billions of dollars at the worldwide box office.

What makes Pixar so successful? Project management certainly plays an important role. Pixar's approach for managing movie projects is quite different from the traditional Hollywood model. In the traditional approach, an ad hoc collection of actors, producers, and technicians come together around a film, and then disband once it is finished. Highly talented people agree to terms, do their jobs, and then move on to their respective next projects. This model allows for flexibility, but it inspires minimum loyalty among project team members, and it requires a substantial period for team members to learn and accept their respective roles.

Turn that model on its head and you get the Pixar version: a tight-knit company of long-term collaborators who stick together, learn from one another, and strive to improve with every production. Project team members are professionals who have traded one-time contracts for long-term affiliations with Pixar. They contribute to multiple projects that take place over time, taking the lessons learned from one project and immediately applying them to the next. In addition, the company has created a work environment that keeps employees motivated.

Pixar also excels in the technical aspects of project management. It puts a high priority on project management skills in its new hires, and offers courses on project management in its own Pixar University. The company is widely known as having the latest, most sophisticated project management software and movie production technologies.

By excelling in the management of both the social and technical aspects of project management, Pixar is able to put together enthusiastic project teams that are both creative and productive.

Prepare

How are projects different from other operational processes? What can project managers do to make their projects more successful?

Organize

Projects and Project Management
How Projects Succeed
Stages in the Life of a Project

PROJECTS AND PROJECT MANAGEMENT

This chapter discusses a special form of operational process known as a project.[1] You will recall from Chapter 5 that a project is one of the five basic types of processes found in operations management.

A **project** is a one-time or infrequently occurring set of activities that creates outputs within prespecified time and cost schedules, while *project management* is the combination of planning, directing, and controlling resources (people, equipment, information, material) in a project to meet technical objectives within budget and schedule constraints.

Using these definitions, projects sound a lot like other operational processes discussed in this book, so why do we need a chapter dedicated to project management? There are several specific characteristics of projects that make them particularly challenging to manage:

LO15-1 Explain the difference between projects and other more routine operational processes.

project A one-time or infrequently occurring set of activities that creates outputs within prespecified time and cost schedules.

relationships

- Every project is unique, having a planned beginning and end. Most business organizations are designed to efficiently manage repetitive, ongoing activities. Projects are not routine; they are used to manage change. Therefore, they require different management techniques.
- Most projects are multidisciplinary, involving many functional specialists who contribute to the overall project goals. The tasks that these specialists perform are interdependent, and because the project is a one-time set of activities, these interdependencies aren't always clearly understood. Imagine, for example, all of the complex relationships between tasks required to design an entirely new car using cutting-edge technologies.
- Projects are often staffed with people who are temporarily taken from functional groups (such as finance, operations, marketing, engineering, supply management) that perform routine operations. Along with expertise, these people have their own functional points of view, and they may feel more loyalty to their functional homes than to the project.
- Projects often compete with routine operations or with other projects for resources and personnel. For this reason, projects often involve a good deal of conflict among project team members.

Because a project is usually a one-time event, it does not usually have the same degree of certainty or repeatability that routine operations do. So it is up to the project manager and her team to anticipate and plan ways to deal with all of the issues mentioned above. Although many operations management concepts may be applied to projects, there are special tools for planning, coordinating, and controlling project activities. This chapter describes these tools and discusses factors that drive project success.

student activity

Note from the following list that business projects can be long or short, big or small. Can you add to this list some types of projects in which you have participated? Think about the last event, class, party or other "project" in which you participated. Write down the steps that were taken to plan for and execute the event.

Example projects:

Developing and launching a new product.
Merging two companies.
Constructing a new building.
Installing new equipment.
Planning and holding a company picnic.
Developing and launching a marketing campaign.
Holding an online auction or bidding event.
Starting up or closing a manufacturing plant.

[1]Portions of this chapter were adapted from K. A. Brown, "Project Management," in S. A. Melnyk and M. L. Swink (eds.), *Value Driven Operations Management: An Integrated Modular Approach* (New York: McGraw Hill/Irwin, 2002).

How Projects Succeed

LO15-2 Manage the social and technical factors that are critical for project success.

A "successful" project meets the following objectives:

1. Completed within budget.
2. Completed on time.
3. Deliverables meet the expectations of customers, project team members, and other stakeholders.

Meeting "deliverables" objectives includes completion of the specific work outputs of the project, as well as achieving goals such as learning new lessons from the project, executing activities with minimal environmental impact, and other considerations.

sustainability

As Figure 15-1 indicates, these outcomes usually conflict with one another. A general maxim in project management is, "faster, better, or cheaper; you can have two, but not three." This means that once a project has been planned and resources have been allocated, changes to the budget, schedule, and deliverables require tradeoffs. For example, if management wants to reduce the project budget and speed up the schedule, then they must reduce either the quality or the scope of deliverables for the project. On the other hand, by changing the technologies used to execute the project, or by changing how project activities are defined, project managers can sometimes achieve improvements in all three areas.

student activity

Think about all the activities involved in building a home. Can you identify a new technology that has enabled this type of project to be completed faster, better, and cheaper? On December 17, 2002, Shelby County Habitat for Humanity built a house in 3 hours, 26 minutes, and 34 seconds—breaking the previous record of 3 hours, 44 minutes, and 59 seconds. Go to any Internet search site and type "World's Fastest House." You will find a short video that shows the project through a time-lapse sequence. Imagine the project management work needed to set up and execute such an event!

In practice, there are many **technological factors** that make projects more or less successful. Think of technologies as including all "ways of doing things." Hard technologies including equipment, facilities, computers, and communications systems help project team members to execute tasks more quickly, more cheaply, and with better quality. In addition, soft technologies including decision support and planning software, information systems, organizational structure, and measures and reward systems can be very important contributors to success. Sometimes operations managers tend to focus on these technical factors. However, research has shown that **social factors** are often of equal or even greater importance to the success of projects. Social factors include

technological factors Systems, equipment, and processes that define how project work is done.

social factors Project team culture, norms of behavior, values, enthusiasm, experience, authority, and influence of team members.

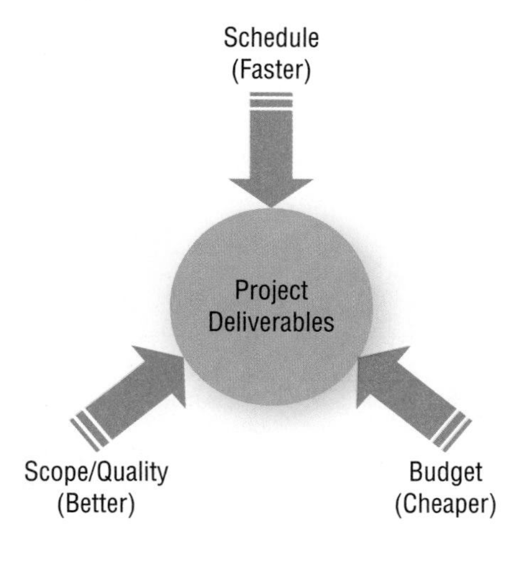

FIGURE 15-1 Three Primary Objectives in Project Management

In building thousands of homes, Habitat for Humanity has refined project management to a science.

the project team culture, norms of behavior, values, enthusiasm, experience, authority, and influence of team members. Project managers need to pay close attention to both the technical and the social aspects of their projects. The following list contains factors that are generally acknowledged to be important contributors to project success:

- A vision of project objectives that is clearly communicated and widely understood.
- A committed, talented, and well-connected project leader.
- Sufficient resources and top management support for the project.
- Disciplined procedures coupled with flexible project team members.
- Team members who have a "winning" spirit.

Stages in the Life of a Project

Figure 15-2 shows the stages in the life of a typical project, along with the level of resources typically required in each stage. Early project definition and planning activities may involve only a few people relative to the large number of personnel and other resources required in the execution of the project. However, the definition and planning stages are critical, because they define how the execution and completion stages will be done.

relationships

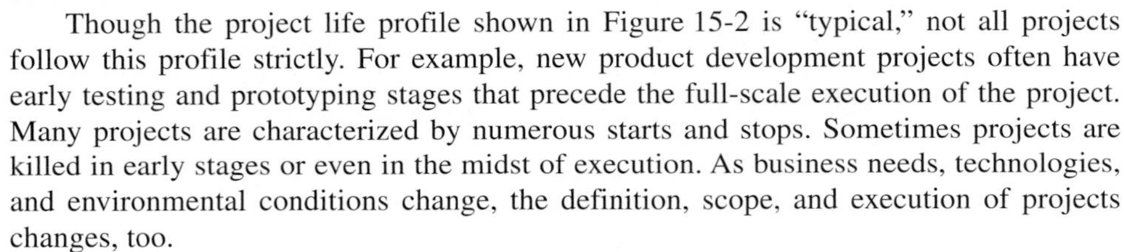

Though the project life profile shown in Figure 15-2 is "typical," not all projects follow this profile strictly. For example, new product development projects often have early testing and prototyping stages that precede the full-scale execution of the project. Many projects are characterized by numerous starts and stops. Sometimes projects are killed in early stages or even in the midst of execution. As business needs, technologies, and environmental conditions change, the definition, scope, and execution of projects changes, too.

Because many of the project success factors discussed above are established in the early planning stages of a project, a project manager usually has the greatest influence on the success of the project in the planning stage. Once a project has been defined and planned, many of the potential outcomes of the project have been set. Once a project is under way, it is often difficult to make major changes. For this reason, most of this chapter focuses on project definition and planning activities.

FIGURE 15-2 Stages in a Project's Life

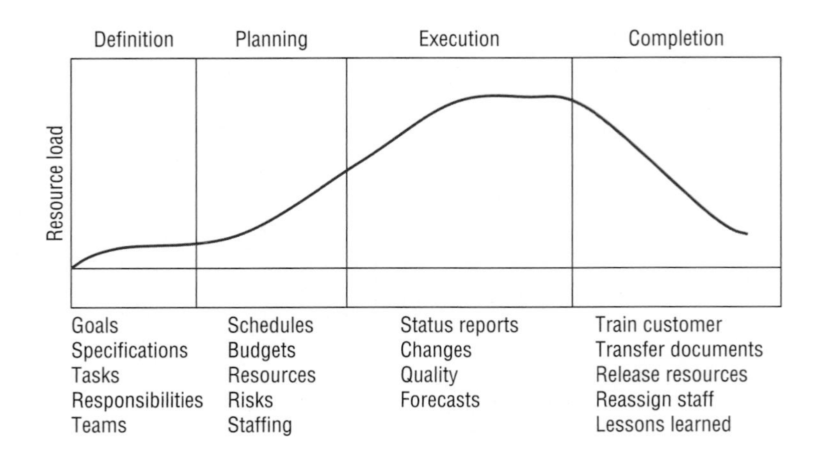

PROJECT DEFINITION

Prepare

What are the critical choices that define a project? What organizational options are right for a given set of project objectives?

Organize

Project definition starts with the initial idea for the project. The definition is refined as the business case for the project is developed and evaluated and eventually selected and funded. In the early stages of project definition, it is very important to clarify who are the clients or customers for the project, and what they care most about. Too often, project personnel assume they know what the customer wants. Even when they do ask the customer, they may not dig deep enough to uncover unexpressed needs that are at the heart of a customer's requirements.

A useful approach is to define a project using a concise project objective statement that includes the following contents:

- *Scope and major deliverables*—desired results, milestones, documents, products.
- *Schedule*—start and end dates.
- *Resources required*—dollars, person-months, special needs (equipment, skills, etc.).

A good **project objective statement** contains all of these issues in specific, concise, clear, measurable terms. Consider the following example: "we will put a man on the moon and return him safely to earth by the end of the decade, at a cost of less than $10B."[2] Defining a project in this way has several advantages. First, stating things clearly and concisely creates a strong vision and challenge for the project team members. Second, it establishes a baseline for detailed activities needed to achieve this overall objective, and those that should not be included. This list of activities should be reviewed with the customer to ensure that the expected deliverables can be achieved. For example, suppose your company is hired to produce a movie from a given screenplay within six months and at a cost of no more than $30 million. Does this include hiring of the actors? Promotion of the movie? In order to avoid surprises, your team must work with customers in determining all the deliverables associated with this objective statement.

project objective statement The identification of project deliverables, schedule, and resources in specific, concise, clear, measurable terms.

LO15-3 Choose the best type of project organizational structure for a given set of objectives.

Organizing the Project: Pure, Functional, and Matrix Projects

Most of the time, projects are planned and executed within an established organization. However, the project manager must organize the specific project team to maximize its potential for success. Projects typically fall along a spectrum of organizational forms, anchored by three specific types: functional project, pure project, and matrix project.

A **functional project** is housed and controlled within a single functional department during each project stage. Imagine, for example, a product development project in which the marketing function makes all of its promotional plans and inputs, then the engineering department creates all of the product designs, then the operations department establishes all of the process plans needed to deliver the product. At each stage of the project, a different function controls the activities and the budget for the project. Once the activities by one function are completed, the project is handed off to the next function.

functional project A project that is housed and controlled within a single functional department during each project stage.

A **pure (autonomous) project** is housed outside the normal functional departments in the business. The project team is made up of functional representatives that are fully dedicated to the project for the duration of the project's life. A pure project has a single project manager who is responsible for the budget, schedule, and all project activities. Consider, for example, a product development effort in which marketing, engineering, and operations personnel are all colocated and work together to simultaneously develop product promotional plans, product designs, and product process designs.

pure (autonomous) project A project that is housed outside normal functional departments and all stages are managed by a single leader.

[2]This is a paraphrase of a famous statement by John F. Kennedy in his 1960 inaugural address as President of the United States.

Table 15-1 lists the advantages and disadvantages of each of the project types. Efficiency is the primary advantage of a functional project approach because the project does not disrupt the existing organizational structure. A disadvantage is that project team members often have other job responsibilities, so the project may not receive top priority. This approach is appropriate for projects where the majority of work is in one specific function, little cross-functional integration is needed, and project leadership can be handled via the normal chain of command. The functional approach is mainly useful for incremental, fairly routine projects.

On the other hand, if various project activities requiring different functional expertise are interdependent, then a pure project can be much more effective. A pure project structure allows team members from each function to work together to solve problems faster and better. A major disadvantage to a pure project is its cost. Personnel dedicate 100 percent of their time to the project, though they may not always be needed at this level. Also, colocation and reorganization costs can be high. The pure project approach is best when:

- Speed is crucial.
- The project includes complex or uncertain tasks.
- Resource cost is not a tight constraint.
- Innovation is needed.

TABLE 15-1 Advantages and Disadvantages of Three Project Organizational Structures

Functional Project	Matrix Project	Pure Project
Advantages	***Advantages***	***Advantages***
• Functional manager controls both budget and activities • A team member can work on several projects • The functional area is the team member's home after the project is completed • Technical expertise is maintained within the functional area (critical mass of specialized knowledge)	• Enhanced interfunctional communications • Pinpointed responsibility • Duplication of resources is minimized • Functional home for team members • Policies of the parent organization are followed	• The project manager has full authority over the project • Team members report to one boss • Shortened communication lines • Team pride, motivation, and commitment are high
Disadvantages	***Disadvantages***	***Disadvantages***
• Aspects of the project that are not directly related to the functional area get short-changed • Needs of the client are secondary and are responded to slowly (no one involved in details is ultimately responsible for the final results) • Motivation of team members is often weak	• Project team members have multiple bosses • Success depends on project manager's negotiating skills	• Duplication of resources • Organizational goals and policies are ignored • Difficult to transfer technology / learning • Team members have no functional area "home"

- Managers want to shield the project from organizational influences.
- A high degree of team commitment is needed.

The **matrix project** approach is probably the most commonly used organizational structure because it balances the advantages and disadvantages of the functional and pure project types. A matrix project utilizes people from different functional areas who are "loaned" to the project from time to time. A full-time project manager plans the project's tasks and schedules, while functional managers determine which people and technologies are used. This approach is appropriate when organizations cannot afford to tie up critical resources on a single project, and when efficient use of resources (cost) is important. From a team member's perspective, the matrix approach can be quite stressful. He or she must balance the requirements of working on several projects at once and working for several managers at the same time. Because of the conflicts that are inherent in the matrix project structure, the stature of the project manager within the organization is critical to the project's success. A "heavyweight" project manager gets the resources and priorities that the project needs by virtue of his ability to influence the functional managers who control the resources. Matrix projects with weak project managers are not likely to succeed.

matrix project A project in which a full-time project manager works together with functional managers to control budgets and to supervise functional workers who are loaned to the project from time to time.

Selecting a Project Manager

Project managers need to have both technical and social skills. Good project managers typically have many of the following traits:

- A leader, an enthusiastic influencer of people.
- A clear and sometimes forceful communicator.
- A good time manager who is self-motivated.
- A high tolerance for ambiguity and stress.
- Politically astute and well-connected with the customer and with important people in the organization.
- Capable of understanding critical technical details of the project, including issues from different disciplines and functional areas.
- Has high ethical standards.

A project manager has to be both a generalist and a specialist. Good project managers can identify the most important schedule, technical, and resource-related details while not losing sight of the overall goals of the project and how they fit into the overall business strategy. They can speak the various "languages" of executives, technical personnel, and customers.

How does a person become an excellent project manager? Experience is the best teacher. However, because projects occur irregularly in many organizations, project management is sometimes referred to as the "accidental profession." Training, disciplined work on areas of weakness, and a wide variety of experiences in different functional areas of the firm are helpful in giving the project manager a broader view, along with the opportunity to build relationships across the organization. Informal relationships with key resource managers are invaluable to project managers. Training programs offered by companies and by societies such as the Project Management Institute can also be helpful (www.pmi.org).

Selecting a project manager for a given project can be tricky. Many times the "perfect" person isn't available or doesn't exist. Good project managers are a rare commodity. Usually the stature of the project manager should match the priority and importance of the project. Major projects should be led by top executives, whereas small projects provide a good training ground for junior managers. Sometimes it is useful to match the personal characteristics of the manager with those of the project. For example, the development of a new technology is best led by someone with an advanced technical background, coupled with a strong understanding of business strategy. It is important to create a profile of all of the technical and social factors that might be important for a given project so that a manager who best fits the profile can be identified.

Organizing Project Teams

What makes a good project team? The following list provides some of the best practices identified in research for creating high-performance project teams.

- Break the overall project group into teams, each with less than 10 members.
- Make sure that team members are committed; use volunteers if possible.
- To the extent possible, ensure that team members serve on the project from beginning to end.
- Try to get team members assigned full-time to the project, and have them report to only one boss.
- Design teams such that all relevant functional areas and needed skills are represented on the team; this includes interpersonal skills and roles as well as technical skills.
- Help the team members understand the importance of their team, and pick team leaders who foster cooperation and trust.
- Colocate team members within conversational distance of each other.

Though there is a wealth of research on this topic, it is still difficult to guarantee team success, even if all the "known" best practices are followed. Through preproject training, team members learn about the different roles they might play on the team. Training helps team members to learn how to handle conflict. Importantly, they can recognize their need to evolve quickly as a team member to become productive. By setting early milestones and deliverables, the project manager can encourage the team to coalesce into a productive working unit.

Globally Dispersed Project Teams

Throughout this book we have discussed the increasing roles of outsourcing and low-cost country suppliers. Due to these trends, project teams increasingly involve members in different companies and in different locations around the world. For example, a software development project initiated by a U.S. company might involve programmers and design personnel in India and other parts of the world. Managing such globally dispersed project teams involves unique challenges. Cultural, organizational, and technological barriers must often be overcome in order meet project goals.

In addition to the obvious challenges associated with team members who speak different languages, one of the biggest cultural barriers involves a reluctance of personnel in one company or location to share information or ask for help from personnel in other companies or locations. Often, this reluctance stems either from an unwillingness to trust project partners, or from the "not invented here" syndrome, which discounts the value of ideas that are not homegrown. The project manager must try to instill in the project team members a longer-term perspective that shifts the focus away from short-term gains and win-lose thinking that can impede project progress.

At the same time, it is imperative that the team at the center of the project does not force its culture and perspectives on its project partners. The value of collaboration in projects comes from diversity in culture, perspectives, and skills, not from similarities. Training programs can help members of all companies involved to appreciate their differences, especially when constituents represent different national cultures, languages, and work norms. In addition, a focus and priority placed on project goals and customer satisfaction can help personnel overcome barriers due to cultural differences.

Organizational boundaries sometimes stifle globally dispersed projects. Even if partners trust each other and are culturally compatible, stiff hierarchies and long lines of communication can prevent the collaboration from being as effective as it could be. Companies sometimes have strict guidelines regarding who can talk to whom in order to ensure that secrets are kept and that organizational hierarchies are respected. The consequence is that project details may be lost, leading to mistakes, incorrect assumptions, and project delays. Project managers need to ensure that team members establish appropriate working contacts in all functional areas across the respective organizational structures.

Finally, physical and temporal boundaries can pose difficulties in managing globally dispersed projects. The ability to use **24/7 project operations** (where groups in one time zone work while groups in other time zones sleep) is one of the potential benefits that entices firms to pick project partners located in distant locations. However, project managers need to develop the systems for effectively passing work back and forth. Information technologies have come a long way in establishing systems to enable secure and accurate knowledge transfer. In addition, video conferencing and other communication technologies offer some of the benefits of face-to-face communications. Managers of globally dispersed projects need to make sure that different information systems talk to each other and that everyone on the team knows where to go to get questions answered.

24/7 project operations Globally dispersed projects where groups in one time zone work while groups in other time zones sleep.

Establishing a Project Charter

An excellent way to summarize the project definition and organizational design is by means of a **project charter**. A project charter can be thought of as a contract that signals the authority to launch a project. Many examples of project charters can be found through an Internet search of the term "project charter." A good charter includes several key elements. First, it concisely defines the purpose of the project and establishes its role and priority in the overall project portfolio. It describes the customers, project team members, and other key stakeholders in the project, along with their roles. Finally, it presents the budget, high-level schedule, and major deliverables for the project. A charter serves an important role in establishing the initial plan for the project. As the project unfolds and new opportunities or problems arise, proposed changes to the project must be compared with the project scope as specified in the original charter. Without this sort of initial anchoring documentation, it is easy for a project to turn into something that was never originally intended. Also, by reading and signing the charter, team members understand their roles in achieving the project goals.

project charter A document that establishes the initial plan for a project, including its purpose and priority, its customers and project team members, and its budget, schedule, and major deliverables.

student activity

Find examples of project charters on the Internet. How many of them have all of the important elements we have identified?

PROJECT PLANNING

Prepare

What steps are included in the process of making a complete project plan? How can the plan be communicated?

Organize

Project Planning
- Budgeting for Time and Cost
- Detailed Scheduling Using the Critical Path Method
- Analyzing Resources and Trade-Offs
- Making Time-Cost-Scope Trade-Offs
- Planning for Uncertainty

Once the major elements of a project are defined and approved, the project management team can begin detailed planning by developing a **work breakdown structure (WBS)**. As shown in Figure 15-3, the WBS is a hierarchical listing of project activities. This particular project is designed to install a new supply chain planning system software program. The project includes steps needed to tailor the design of the software to the specific company's needs, to make adjustments to data that will be used in the system, to train the users and prepare user manuals, and to solve problems once the system is initiated (system rollout). While this is a fairly small project, a larger WBS hierarchy might include many levels, including tasks and subtasks, that are ultimately broken down to the lowest-level tasks, known as *work packages.*

Small projects may include only two or three levels in a WBS, whereas larger projects typically require many more levels of detail. The Get Real boxes in the chapter give an idea of the scope of work involved in huge projects such as staging the Olympics (see page 513) and expanding an airport (page 519). A work package defined at the lowest level of the WBS should have a measurable outcome that is assignable to a single individual or group. Responsibility for each work package

work breakdown structure (WBS) A hierarchical listing of project activities.

FIGURE 15-3 Work Breakdown Structure for a Planning System Installation Project

WBS Level	Project Tasks
0–Project	Planning System Installation
1–Task	System Design
2–Work Package	Select system modules
2–Work Package	Set system protocols
1–Task	Prepare Data
2–Work Package	Gather legacy system data
2–Work Package	Translate data
1–Task	Training
2–Work Package	Design training program
2–Work Package	Hold training sessions
1–Task	Prepare Documentation
1–Task	System Rollout
2–Work Package	Populate system data
2–Work Package	Test system
2–Work Package	Debug system
2–Work Package	Pilot test
2–Work Package	Hold "go live" meeting

LO15-4 Develop a comprehensive project plan, evaluating trade-offs, uncertainties, and risks.

should be unambiguous, and metrics should be clear. Here are some of the best practices for developing a WBS:

- Involve all project leaders in developing the WBS. This will instill ownership and provide creativity.
- Each work package should include a noun and a verb to imply action (e.g., "Meet with customers" rather than "Customers").
- As a rule of thumb, low-level tasks should be designed to be between 8 and 80 work hours in duration.[3]
- Include a risk analysis (discussed later in the chapter) at the WBS stage.
- Include any and all activities that consume resources, including project planning and management activities.
- Think hierarchically (top-down) or in a pure brainstorming mode. A hierarchical approach starts with major tasks and then identifies all subtasks related to each major category. A brainstorming approach allows for a rapid-fire listing of all activities that come to mind.
- Don't worry about the sequencing or time-phasing of activities. Scheduling comes later.
- A flexible and effective way to capture activities is to write them on sticky notes and paste them onto a wall. Then the notes can be reorganized to create the WBS hierarchy.
- For complex projects, it may be helpful to have two separate teams develop WBSs independently. Then bring the teams together and compare results.

student activity

Develop a WBS for a small project such as painting your parents' house. You might start by writing down each task on a sticky note. Then arrange the notes on a wall in a hierarchical (top-down) fashion. How can you ensure that you have not forgotten any tasks?

Budgeting for Time and Cost

The WBS can be used to estimate, allocate, and ultimately monitor resources for each of the work packages and major tasks in the project. The business case typically includes a preliminary budget based on rough cost estimates. The detailed WBS provides the framework for developing both time and cost estimates and for monitoring the progress of the project once activities begin. Usually time estimates are needed first, in order to then

[3]E. Verzuh, *The Fast Forward MBA in Project Management* (New York: Wiley, 1999).

GET REAL

Managing an "Olympic"-Sized Project

Imagine the work needed to develop a WBS for the Olympic Games. The host country must construct secure accommodations for 17,000 athletes and judges from 205 countries. In the case of the 2008 Summer Olympics in Beijing, China, 31 individual venues were needed. Of those 31 venues, 12 were permanent structures constructed specifically for the games, another 10 were renovated existing structures, and 9 were temporary sites. Each of these locations required electrical, water, and waste disposal systems to support them.

The management and planning that goes into the Olympics does not stop when all of the buildings have been completed, nor does it only start again when the athletes take the field. Indeed, Chinese PC-maker Lenovo spent an entire year leading up to the games providing and testing IT systems to support both the competition and the media associated with the events. Lenovo provided 20,000 pieces of computing equipment to help run 56 Olympic venues. To further complicate the project, several of the venues—especially the National Aquatics Center, also known as the "Water Cube"—had to have IT infrastructure that could handle 90 percent indoor humidity.

If testing all of the equipment was not difficult enough, the 580 engineers sent to run and troubleshoot the system also required training and work scheduling. Projects with this kind of multilayered complexity demand strong project management skills.

The 2012 Games in London, England, promised to be no less complex. Managing even a single part of a complicated system like the Olympic Games—regardless of whether it is construction, information technology, food delivery, or waste disposal—absolutely requires disciplined project management.

The "Water Cube" National Aquatics Center in Beijing.

calculate the costs of needed workers, equipment, and so on. Time estimates can be based on similar projects when many have been completed. For example, in the construction industry an experienced estimator can forecast the time and the cost required to construct a building just by knowing the type of construction and the number of square feet of floor space. For really new projects, estimating is more difficult, and it is usually beneficial to have a team of people to develop estimates together.

Once the time and cost estimates have been produced, the planning team makes initial adjustments based on overall budget and schedule constraints. Figure 15-4 shows a cost-allocated WBS for the planning system project introduced in Figure 15-3. The costs for project tasks are usually initially estimated by work package managers, and then added up to compute the costs for the major tasks and for the project as a whole. Then, adjustments and reallocations are made if the costs do not meet budget limitations or expectations. There may be some negotiations between project managers and customers, or between managers of major tasks in the project in order to arrive at an overall resource allocation that is reasonable and achievable. Managers typically use a combination of cost data from past similar projects and detailed resource analyses to make their cost estimates.

Detailed Scheduling Using the Critical Path Method

Once the overall budget and time estimates for tasks have been established, a detailed schedule can be created. A useful way to plan and communicate schedules is the **critical path method (CPM)**. The Get Real box next page describes the historical origins of this method.

critical path method (CPM)
A project planning technique that identifies in graphic form the activities that are most important and should receive focused attention.

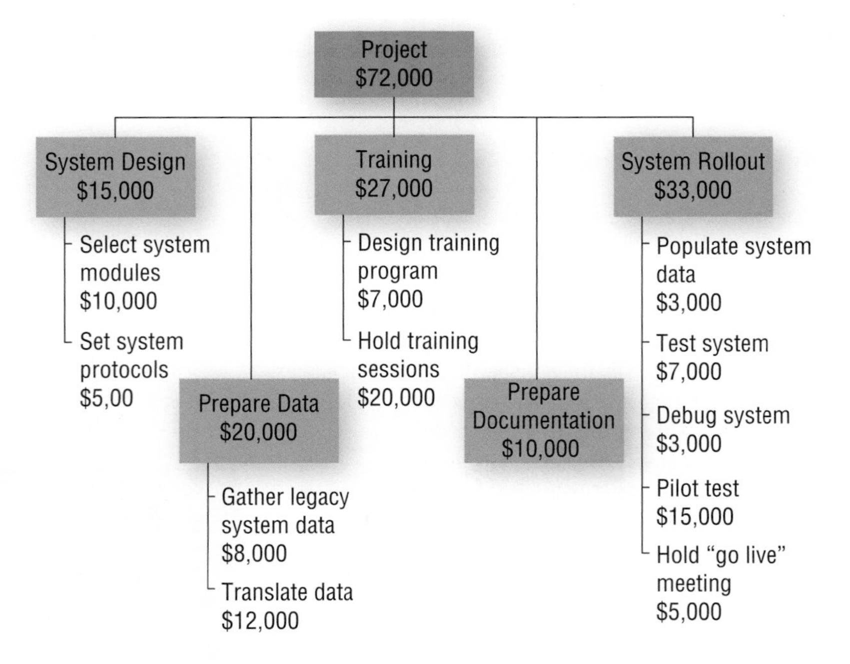

FIGURE 15-4 WBS for a Planning System Installation Project with Allocated Budget

Critical path scheduling techniques display a project in graphic form in a way that identifies the activities that are most important and should receive focused attention. Critical path scheduling is based on several key assumptions:

1. The project tasks have well-defined beginnings and endings.
2. The tasks are independent; the duration of one task is not dependent on the duration of another.
3. A required sequence of the tasks can be established.

For small projects, a formal schedule may be unnecessary; a simple check list may be sufficient. For larger projects, however, a special set of scheduling tools can clarify planning and help ensure that tasks are completed in the proper sequence. One such tool is a

GET REAL

The History of CPM and PERT

The critical path method (CPM) and its close relative, the project evaluation and review technique (PERT), were developed in the 1950s and 1960s at DuPont Corporation and at the U.S. Navy. Both techniques use network diagramming to graphically display and analyze projects, with a few differences. Managers at DuPont were scheduling fairly predicable facilities cleaning operations, so they developed the CPM with a focus on making time-cost trade-offs using fixed task time estimates. Naval officers were scheduling highly uncertain activities associated with the development of the Polaris missile system, so they developed PERT with a focus on managing uncertainties in the project by using probabilistic time estimates. The CPM approach typically uses "activity-on-node" notation, like we are using in this chapter. The PERT approach uses "activity-on-arc" diagramming, where each project task is represented by an arc or arrow. The advantage of activity-on-arc diagramming is that arrows can have different lengths representing the different lengths of task durations; this gives a more visual representation of the lengths of various paths in the project network. The disadvantage is that these networks are more difficult to draw, and some task interrelationships are difficult to represent.

Both DuPont and U.S. Navy operations gained large improvements in project outcomes through the use of these techniques. These early methods have been refined and computerized to provide the tools that thousands of managers use today.

TABLE 15-2 Task Information for the Planning System Implementation Project

Task	Task Label	Estimated Duration (days)	Immediate Predecessors
Start	Str	0	None
Select system modules	SSM	9	Str
Prepare data	PDat	5	Str
Populate system data	PSD	5	PDat, SSM
Test system	TS	6	PSD
Debug system	DS	4	TS
Pilot test	PT	3	DS, PDoc, HTS
Hold "Go Live" meeting	HGL	1	PT
Set system protocols	SSP	3	SSM
Prepare documentation	PDoc	14	SSM
Design training program	DTP	2	SSM
Hold training sessions	HTS	1	DTP

network diagram. A network diagram is constructed using the task definitions, estimated lengths, and precedence relationships (the definition of what has to come first, second, and so on).

network diagram A graphical display of project tasks and their interrelationships.

Table 15-2 shows project information for the planning system installation project. Figure 15-5 shows a network diagram for the planning system installation project. Each circle (or *node*) represents a task, and the arrows connecting the tasks show the precedence relationships among them. A parallel relationship between two tasks means that they can be performed simultaneously. For example, when building a house, one crew can landscape the yard at the same time that another crew installs the light fixtures indoors. On the other hand, sequential activities depend on each other—pouring the concrete for the foundation of a house cannot be done until the site excavation is completed.

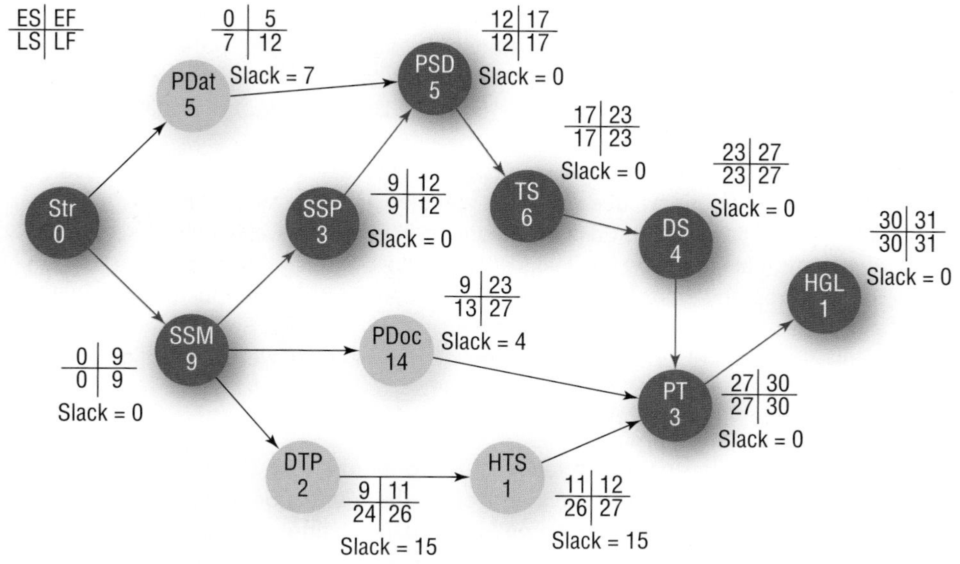

Red nodes are critical path (zero slack) activities.

FIGURE 15-5 Network Diagram for the Planning System Installation Project

critical path The longest path of activities reaching from the beginning node to the end node in a project.

earliest start date and earliest finish date The earliest dates that an activity can be planned to start and finish given the requirements of its predecessors.

latest start date and latest finish date The latest dates that an activity can be planned to start and finish given the requirements of its successors.

task slack The amount of time that a task duration can be increased without affecting the length of the project.

EXAMPLE 15-1

Let's use the information given in Figure 15-5 to understand how to use the critical path method. The **critical path** is defined as the longest path (or paths, if two or more paths tie for longest path) from the beginning node to the end node in the project. The longest path is deemed *critical* because, assuming all tasks are executed according to plan, the longest path of activities will determine the final completion date for the project. Thus, if one of the tasks on the critical path is late, then the entire project will be late.

The nodes and arrows colored in red in Figure 15-5 form the longest path in the network and, therefore, constitute the critical path. The critical path indicates that the current estimated project length is 31 days (add up the durations along the critical path).

The data given next to each of the nodes in the diagram indicate the **earliest start date** and **earliest finish date** for each task, and the **latest start date** and **latest finish date** for each task. The earliest start date for a task is simply the next period after the completion of the latest of the task's predecessors. For example, the earliest date that the "Populate System Data" task can start is on the day that the "Set System Protocols" task is completed, because that task must finish at the same time or later than the "Prepare Data" task. Earliest starts for tasks can be computed by adding up the durations of tasks along the network paths from left to right. This is known as a *forward pass* analysis. The longest path leading up to a given task determines that path's earliest possible start date. The earliest possible completion date for any task is simply its earliest start date plus the expected duration of the task.

Task slack (also called *float*) is the amount of time (working days) that a task duration can be increased without affecting the length of the project. Notice that the task slack for each of the activities on the critical path is zero. An increase in the duration of any of these activities lengthens the overall project. Therefore, a project manager must pay special attention to these tasks to ensure that they take no longer than their planned durations. There is no freedom in the schedule that allows any of the activities on the critical path to be completed late without delaying the overall project. On the other hand, the tasks not on the critical path all have slack. For example, the "Prepare Data" task has seven days of slack. Why seven days? Notice that the length of the start to finish path containing the "Prepare Data" task is 24 days long. This means that the "Prepare Data" could be lengthened by seven days (31 days – 24 days) and the project would still finish in 31 days. Looking at it another way, we could postpone the start of the "Prepare Data" task by as much as seven working days. As long as the task itself takes no more than the planned five days, the following task, "Populate System Data," could still be started on its planned date.

Both the "Design Training Program" and "Hold Training Sessions" tasks have 15 days of slack. This is because the path that they are on is 15 days shorter than the critical path. However, this does not mean that both tasks have 15 days of slack *independently.* Instead, these two tasks *share* a total of 15 days of slack. If the "Design Training Program" starts late or takes longer than planned, then the slack available at the subsequent task, "Hold Training Sessions," is reduced. Some of the slack can be used at either of the noncritical tasks and not affect the overall project duration.

Such sequential and parallel relationships are indicated in Figure 15-5 as well. For example, the start of "Debug System" must follow the completion of "Test System." However, the start of "Prepare Documentation" is not dependent on the start or completion of "Set System Protocols," so parts of these two tasks could be done simultaneously. It is important for every project to have a single starting point and a single ending point. The "Start" activity at the left end of the project consumes zero days because it is simply a node that indicates the proposed start date of the project.

The latest start date and latest finish date for any task are computed by adding the task slack to the earliest start and earliest completion dates possible for the task. Another way to compute the latest start and completion dates for all the tasks in the project network is to make a *backward pass* analysis. The backward pass is done by starting with the project completion date (defined by the critical path), and then subtracting the task times from right to left along the paths in the network.

We can summarize all of these network relationships in the following equations, which make up the critical path algorithm:

- *Forward pass:* Calculating the earliest start and finish dates.

  Earliest start date for a task = Maximum (latest) earliest finish date for all predecessors of that task (Earliest start date for tasks at the beginning of the network = 0)

  Earliest finish date for a task = Earliest start + Task duration

  Project completion date = Maximum (latest) earliest finish date for all tasks
- *Backward pass:* Calculating the latest start and completion dates.

  Latest finish date for a task = Minimum (earliest) latest start date for all followers of that task

  Latest start date for a task = Latest finish date − Task duration
- *Calculating task slack:*

  Task slack = Latest start date − Earliest start date, or latest finish date − Earliest finish date

Practice using these equations to verify the numbers shown in Figure 15-5. Another detailed example of how to use these equations is provided in the solved problem at the end of the chapter.

The information detailing the critical activities, earliest and latest starts and completions, and task slack helps project managers know where to focus their attention, and how much flexibility they have in scheduling noncritical tasks. Frequently re-analyzing a project in this way as tasks are completed helps project managers more effectively allocate resources. For example, if a critical task is completed late, then a manager might decide to move resources from a noncritical activity to other activities on the critical path in order to get the project back on schedule.

Figure 15-6 shows how the planning system implementation project network diagram looks when it is created using Microsoft Project, a widely used project management software program. In Figure 15-6, each box (or *node*) represents an activity. Each box contains the task slack, the earliest start and earliest complete dates, and the estimated duration of the task. Note that a tool such as this can automatically calculate calendar dates, accounting

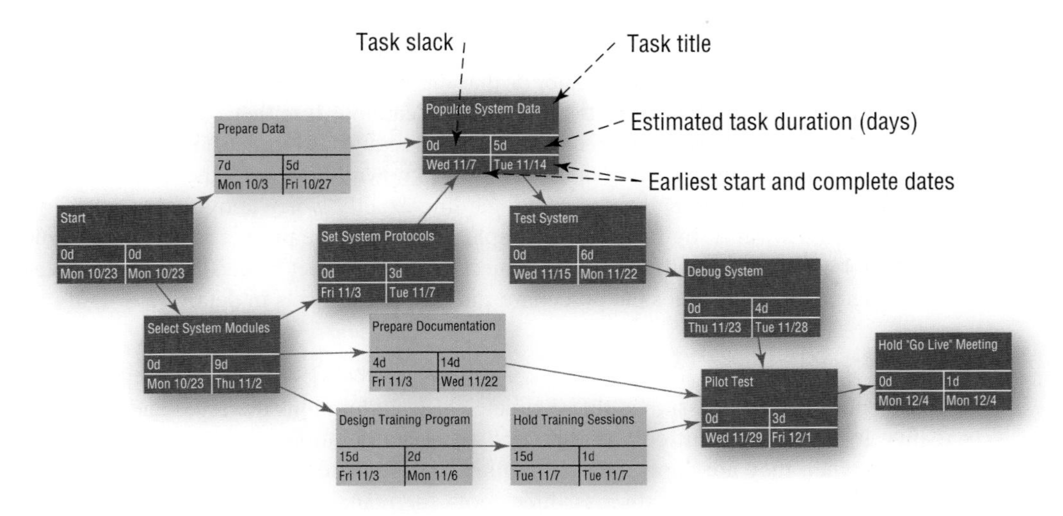

FIGURE 15-6 MS Project CPM Network for the Planning System Installation Project

for weekends and holidays. Figure 15-6 shows that, assuming no work is done on weekends, the estimated completion date is Monday, December 4. Since many project managers use software programs like this one to manage project information, we will use this format for the rest of the examples in this chapter.

Analyzing Resources and Trade-Offs

Once an initial project schedule is created, project managers review the resource requirements implied by the schedule to see if they are compatible with project constraints and goals. If a specific resource for a critical path activity is not available during the scheduled time period, the delay affects the entire project. For example, suppose that the "Populate System Data" task in Figure 15-6 is assigned to the marketing department, yet they will not have personnel available to work on this task until Friday, November 10. The project will be completed two days late, assuming nothing else changes. As another example, suppose that the person who is given the task of "Select System Modules" is also given the task of "Prepare Data." Because "Select System Modules" is a critical activity, the person will do that task first, taking nine days. Unfortunately, this means that the "Prepare Data" task will be completed late (because it has only seven days of slack). The start of "Populate System Data" will be postponed by two days, and again the project will be completed two days late, assuming nothing else changes.

Initial estimates of task durations are often made assuming certain resource availabilities, without a clear understanding of the schedule. Parallel activities can create overlapping and conflicting resource requirements at certain points in time. For this reason, managers need to evaluate the scheduled requirements and find solutions for resource conflicts. Important resources could include people (skill types), materials, technology (equipment), and capital (cash). Some useful questions to ask are:

- Are resources available in the windows of time identified by the schedule?
- Is the same resource required on parallel paths?
- Is a resource frequently used only a little at a time (e.g., part-time need for an electrician at multiple stages)?
- Should resources be dedicated full-time or part-time?

Making Time-Cost-Scope Trade-Offs

Remember the "faster-better-cheaper" trade-off discussed earlier in the chapter? If resource conflicts exist in the schedule, or if the current plan exceeds the budget or schedule requirements, changes to the plan may be required. Suppose that the current plan exceeds the available budget for the project. A simple change would be to reduce the scope of activities and eliminate some of the deliverables for the project. If that is not an option, the project managers often make trade-offs between budget (cost) and schedule (time). Suppose that current project activities are running late, or that the client has moved up the due date so that the current plan no longer meets the required deadline. In either case, more money could be spent to hasten project activities to meet the required completion date. In project management terminology, speeding up an activity is known as *crashing* the activity. When many activities are *crashable,* the decision regarding exactly which activities to crash can be complicated. However, by following a simple set of rules the project manager can usually find the lowest cost way to speed up a project in order to meet its deadline. The supplement for this chapter illustrates the procedure for crashing projects in detail.

Planning for Uncertainty

Up to this point we have assumed that estimates of task durations are fixed and accurate. In reality, it can be very difficult to accurately estimate durations, especially when tasks are new or when they are dependent on circumstances outside the control of the project team. In this section we will discuss three tools for managing uncertainty in projects: probabilistic estimates, buffering, and risk analysis.

GET REAL

Project Management Software Helps Get the Job Done

Hartsfield-Jackson Atlanta International Airport, one of the busiest air terminals in the world, was in the midst of a 15-year development and expansion program. One of the key projects of this comprehensive program was the addition of a fifth runway to meet expanding demand at this major hub. Building a nearly two-mile runway in a major metropolitan area like Atlanta required not just constructing the runway itself, but also rerouting through a newly constructed tunnel under the tarmac.

The project encompassed some 15,000 interdependent schedule items and 23 subprojects, including working with important government and local constituencies to prevent delays, raw material delivery, and subcontractor schedules. Getting the project done on time, despite the massive complexity of the task, was particularly important because each week of delay was estimated to cost the airline industry $5 million in revenue, and each day of delay carried a $5 million penalty for the bidding company.

Project managers used a software program to manage this massively complex task. The software allowed users to plan the project in great detail, see how delays in one subproject might impact the entire project, and run scenarios to attempt to work around delays. The software also helped manage payment to contractors by having them check off their progress as they completed each task. This documentation made it easy to check whether contractors had made all the progress they claimed on schedule.

The result of this close and efficient project supervision aided by project management software was extremely positive. Despite the complexity of the task both from a political and engineering standpoint, the runway was completed 11 days early and $102 million under budget.

Probabilistic Task Duration Estimates

One method for analyzing the impacts of uncertainty on projects is to use **probabilistic task duration estimates**, which include a range of possible task durations for each task, rather than relying on a single point estimate. "Best case," "worst case," and "most likely case" durations are estimated for each task in the project. By making some assumptions about the statistical properties of these estimates, project analysts can create distributions of possible outcomes for each project task, and ultimately for the project as a whole. Instead of simply expecting the project to be completed on a certain date, the project manager can use this new statistical information to estimate the probability that the project will be completed on or before a given date. If the probability of completion by a given deadline is unacceptably low, then the manager can using project crashing, buffering, or other techniques to improve the project's chances of on-time completion. The calculations for probabilistic task duration estimations are illustrated in the supplement to this chapter.

probabilistic task duration estimates A tool for conveying uncertainty that includes a range of possible task durations for each task, rather than relying on a single point estimate.

Buffering the Project

When managers are asked to submit estimates of task durations for project planning, they sometimes build in extra time (a buffer) "just to be safe." For example, if a manager expects that a task may take four days, he might tell his boss five days (have you ever done this?). However, because these buffers are hidden from the project manager, they often are wasted in terms of helping complete projects on time. A more useful approach is to design buffers into the project plan, making them plain for everyone on the project to see and utilize.

EXAMPLE 15-2

Consider the revised planning system installation project plan shown in Figure 15-7. In this example, the project will most likely take 31 days, yet the due date for delivery of the survey is 35 days. This leaves four days for buffering. As the figure suggests, it is usually a good idea to place explicit buffers in the following parts of the network:

- Immediately after high uncertainty tasks.
- Where noncritical tasks merge with the critical path.
- Where scarce resources are needed.
- At the end of the project.

Project buffers are a means for hedging against unforeseen problems in the project execution. By making buffers visible and by managing them closely, the project team can have a better idea of where uncertainties lie and how the project is doing relative to its schedule.[4]

FIGURE 15-7 Revised Planning System Installation Project Plan Including Buffers (Due date for the project: December 8)

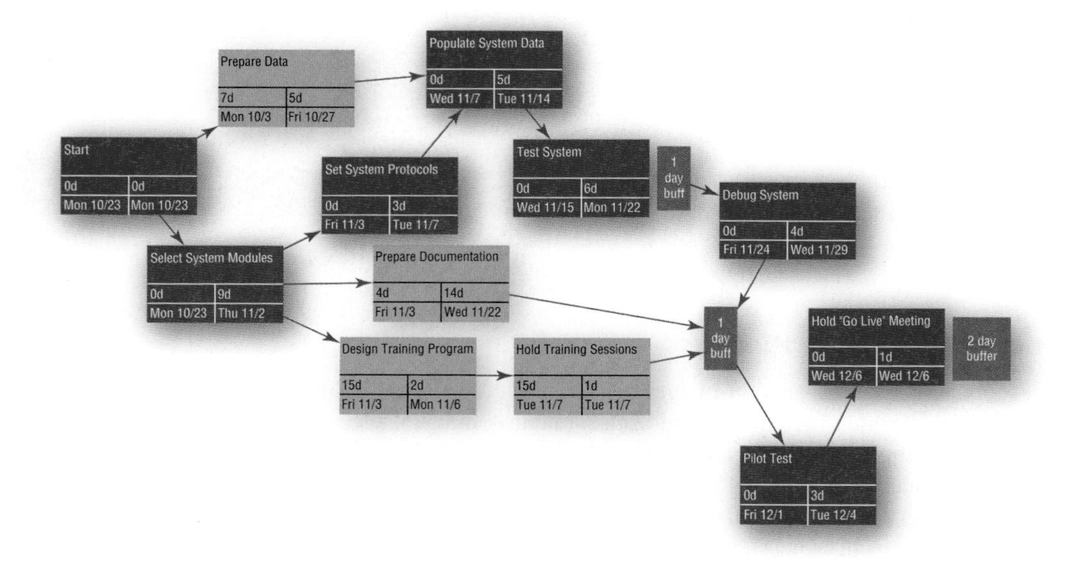

project buffer A time period set aside to provide slack along activity paths that are critical or highly variable.

A **project buffer** is simply a designated time period that provides some slack along paths that are critical or highly variable.

Risk Analysis

Risk analysis is an important thing to do early on in project definition, at the development of the WBS, and after a detailed schedule is created. Project managers should always consider "Murphy's Law: What can go wrong, will go wrong!" There are numerous tools available for assessing project risk. A simple risk analysis technique[5] involves several steps:

Step 1: Hold a team brainstorming session to identify the possible risks associated with technologies, resources of all kinds, markets and customers, and competitors.

[4]Eli Goldratt discusses the technical and behavioral issues associated with buffering projects in his book, *The Critical Chain* (Great Barrington, MA: North River Press, 1997).

[5]This technique is an application of the FMEA approach discussed in Chapter 4, "Product / Process Innovation."

TABLE 15-3 Risk Analysis for Shooting of Winter Scenes in a Movie

Risk	Outcome/Impact	Likelihood	Strategies/ Responses	Cost*	Triggers
No snow for winter scenes	• Delay filming • Incomplete story-line.	• 50% in October (current schedule) • 20% in December	1. Film winter scenes in December 2. Move location 3. Rent snow making machines	$10,000 to change schedule $100,000 move cost $20,000 rental charge	• Schedule delay of 1 week • Weather fore-cast showing <20% chance of snow

*Note that costs do not necessarily have to be indicated in monetary terms.

Step 2: Establish the probability that each risk event will occur.

Step 3: Establish the potential impacts of each risk event on the budget, schedule, and deliverables of the project.

Step 4: Determine plans for dealing with the risk events that are of highest probability and impact. Risk mitigation plans could include:

- Preventive measures
- Contingency plans
- Emergency funds
- Time buffers

Step 5: Select the risk mitigation plans that give the best prevention or protection against risk for the minimum investment required.

The final steps of this analysis can be communicated as a risk table. An example of a risk table is shown in Table 15-3. In addition to the steps above, the risk planning team should establish a signal or metric that determines the circumstances under which a contingency or risk mitigation plan should be invoked. These "triggers" establish concrete decision points for the project team. For example, the team might decide that they would rent snowmaking machines once filming had been delayed by one week. Risk assessment is typically one of the most important, and most neglected, activities in project management.

PROJECT EXECUTION

Prepare

How does a project manager motivate and communicate project progress clearly and concisely?

Organize

Project Execution

When to Kill a Project

Project execution is the phase in which the project work is actually done. At this point, the project manager plays the important roles of encouraging, monitoring, and controlling performance. For small projects, performance monitoring can be fairly informal; the project manager can frequently speak with each of the project team members. In larger projects, however, it is important to determine the levels of reporting frequency and formality that project managers will require. This is often a question of balance. Managers don't want project team members to be so busy preparing status reports that they never get any work done. On the other hand, more frequent reports give managers a more up-to-date picture of the project's status.

One way to achieve balance is for project managers to give most of their attention to critical path activities, and less to others, unless they are particularly risky. For example, a large project might require weekly reports from owners of critical path activities, and only monthly reports from owners of noncritical activities. It is also especially important to get regular status updates early on in the project. Research shows that early budget and schedule performance are strong predictors of the ultimate completed project performance.

FIGURE 15-8 MS Project Bar Chart for the Planning System Installation Project

ID	Task Name	Duration
1.	Start	0d
2.	Prepare Data	5d
3.	Populate System Data	5d
4.	Test System	6d
5.	Debug System	6d
6.	Prepare Documentation	14d
7.	Design Training Program	2d
8.	Hold Training Sessions	1d
9.	Pilot Test	3d
10.	Hold "Go Live" Meeting	1d
11.	Select System Modules	9d
12.	Select System Protocols	3d

Oct 22 10/22 | Oct 29 10/29 | Nov 5 11/5 | Nov 12 11/12 | Nov 19 11/19 | Nov 26 11/26

10/23

Gantt chart A bar chart that shows the timing, relationships, and percentage completion for activities in a project.

Status reports should contain updates on budget, schedule, and the quality of output. Though many more sophisticated reporting formats exist, a common and simple way to communicate schedule status is through use of a bar chart (also known as a **Gantt chart**) showing percentage completion for each activity. Figure 15-8 displays an example of an MS Project bar chart. Note that the dark line through the center of any task bar indicates the percentage that the task is complete. For example, task 2, "Prepare Data," is 50 percent complete. "Select System Protocols" (task 12) has been completed entirely. "Populate System Data" awaits the completion of "Prepare Data" before it can start.

In addition to monitoring the budget, schedule, and quality/scope conditions of an ongoing project, it is often important to monitor other key indicators of project progress and success. Sometimes project managers routinely estimate the financial returns of a project using metrics like net present value and return on investment. It is also important to frequently answer questions like:

sustainability

- Is our customer happy?
- Are the project sponsors/leaders still committed?
- Are we overcoming technical hurdles and avoiding risks?
- How is the project team's morale?
- Do we have issues that are not being resolved?
- Is the project receiving the resources that it needs?
- Are we being socially responsible (safe and environmentally friendly)?

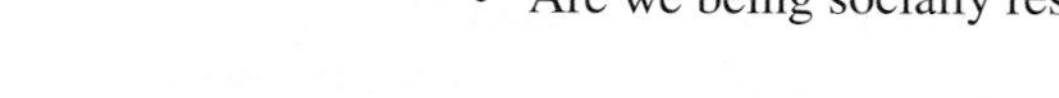

When to Kill a Project

Sometimes the best way to execute a project is to actually "execute" it, that is, to kill it. This can be a very difficult decision and process. Consequently, unhealthy projects are often allowed to persist for too long. Projects are often aggressive efforts that involve lots of uncertainty, and conditions that initially made the project attractive can quickly change. For this reason, it is important for project sponsors and managers to periodically gage the progress of a project from a strategic perspective. If a project is no longer expected to meet its objectives, it should be killed quickly to avoid wasted resources. There are many reasons to kill a project, including:

- *Consistent budget or schedule overruns.* This can be an indication that resource needs and costs were severely underestimated at the beginning of the project. Or perhaps conditions have changed so that inexpensive resources are no longer available. At some point rising costs may exceed the value of the project.

- *Failure to create value.* Projects sometimes involve technical hurdles that just cannot be surmounted at a reasonable cost. On the other hand, the project may be meeting its objectives, but those objectives are no longer valuable. For example, suppose that a competitor introduces a new product that makes your new product project obsolete. Customers and clients may also change their minds about a project based on changing needs and market trends.
- *Changing priorities.* Organizations change their priorities over time, and these changes may make a current project less attractive. For example, if a company falls on hard times financially, it may need to scrap projects that do not provide immediate benefits. In another case, a new project idea may come along that is actually more important or gives a better return than the current project. In this case it would be prudent to kill the current project and shift the resources to the new opportunity.
- *Wrong resources.* Perhaps the project idea still has merit, but the organization does not currently have the skills or talent needed to bring the project to a successful conclusion. Sometimes political forces come into play that stifle a project's progress. As some point it may be better to kill the current project and start again when proper resources and a unified commitment become available.

PROJECT COMPLETION

Prepare

What are the critical issues to consider as a project nears completion?

Organize

Project Completion

Project completion occurs when all project deliverables have been completed to the satisfaction of the client, sponsor, and other decision makers with acceptance authority. Project managers should make sure that project team members stay motivated at this stage, as it is easy for them to experience burnout, or to start turning their attention to other projects prematurely. It is usually a good idea to hold reviews of all activities, with checklists and other reports to make sure that no final deliverables are missed.

Immediately after project completion is also the best time to evaluate the key successes and failures of the project. This activity is commonly known as a **postproject review** (also called a *postmortem*). Ideally, an independent team should review the project and develop a detailed report of lessons learned. This team is not to second-guess or place blame, but to identify both effective and ineffective practices that can be compared against other project reviews. This will help ensure that the good practices are repeated and that the weaker practices are corrected in future projects. In addition, the postproject review can be the time to recognize the contributions of project team members and to highlight the success of the project to executives throughout the organization. Points to be addressed in a postproject review include:

postproject review An effort to capture the lessons learned from the project experience and to recognize the contributions of project team members.

- How well were deliverables met in terms of scope, quality, and dealing with changes throughout the project?
- How well was the project budget met? Where were the important variances?
- Was the project on time? What were the constraining resources?
- Have all remaining project tasks been completed? Have results been communicated to all important stakeholders?
- Is the customer happy? How has this project affected our relationships with customers?
- Are the project team members satisfied? What specific morale issues need to be addressed? In what ways were employees' skills and knowledge enhanced?
- What problems were solved on this project? What new market or technical knowledge needs to be documented and used in future projects?
- What was learned regarding new management approaches or use of new project management technologies (organizational approach, software, information systems, and so on).

MANAGING A PORTFOLIO OF PROJECTS

Prepare
How can projects be selected and managed in a way that advances the organization's strategies?

Organize
Managing a Portfolio of Projects

Large organizations typically have many projects going on at the same time, at many locations across the supply chain. A business development unit, for example, could be developing several new products simultaneously. Supply chain managers typically have many process improvement and relationship management projects going on, potentially involving product suppliers, customers, consultants, and technology vendors. It is important for managers to view such a mix of projects as a portfolio of efforts that are used to execute the organization's overall strategy. Each project's unique contribution to the overall goals of the business unit should be clearly established.

LO15-5 Fashion criteria to guide project selection and management of a portfolio of projects.

Too often in businesses, projects are not managed strategically. Team members on various projects often do not understand how projects relate to one another and to the business strategy. There are many reasons for this. A primary cause is that often the criteria used to select projects are not consistent with higher-level business goals. For example, projects are often selected using financial criteria alone. Figure 15-9 shows a mix of projects positioned according to their probability of success (risk) and value if successful (contribution). If these were the only important criteria, then we would select only projects that are in the upper right-hand quadrant of the figure.

There are other, more strategic, reasons to select and include projects in the portfolio. Projects can be viewed as opportunities to learn new things, to build technical capabilities, to develop new partnerships, and to identify the strengths and weaknesses of people in the organization. Projects can also be designed to build upon previous successes or failures in order to move the organization toward long-term strategic goals.

In general, managers should evaluate potential new projects by considering three categories of factors:

1. The project's fit with overall organizational strategy and existing portfolio of projects.
2. Financial returns or other benefits associated with the project.
3. The feasibility of the project, including availability of required resources.

business case A well-developed justification of the financial and strategic reasons for pursuing a project.

Project selection should be based on a **business case**, a well-developed justification including both financial and strategic reasons for the project. A comprehensive business case includes:

- Financial and market analyses identifying required resources, costs, and benefits of the project.
- Description of assumptions, risks, and how risks will be managed.
- Importance of the project to the organization's strategic mission.

Small projects may not require such a formal analysis, but some evaluation of benefits, costs, and risks should always precede the start of a project.

FIGURE 15-9
Estimating the Value of a Portfolio of Projects

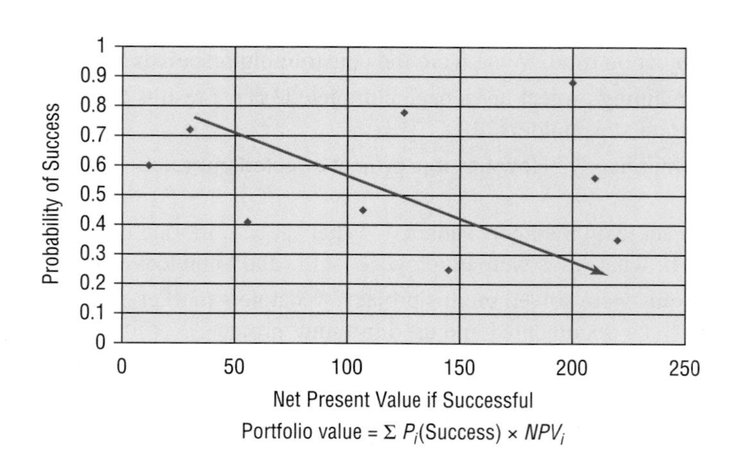

Portfolio value = $\Sigma P_i(\text{Success}) \times NPV_i$

CHAPTER SUMMARY

A project is a one-time or infrequently occurring set of activities that creates outputs within prespecified time and cost schedules. Project management is the combination of planning, directing, and controlling resources (people, equipment, information, material) in a project to meet technical objectives within budget and schedule constraints. To make projects successful, project managers should keep the following facts in mind:

- Most projects are important processes for managing change. Such projects are often challenging because most organizations are not configured for projects; they are configured for routine operations and processes.
- A large part of the project manager's ability to influence the success of a project comes in the definition and planning stages that occur before project execution. In defining the project objectives and in assigning resources, project managers should remember that both social and technical factors contribute to a project's success.
- Projects can be organized and executed in three different ways: pure (autonomous) project, functional project, and matrix project. Each of these organizational structures offers advantages and disadvantages that should be matched to the requirements of the project at hand.
- Project managers need to be aware of tools and techniques for budgeting, scheduling, and controlling projects. These include the work breakdown structure, critical path method, time-cost trade-offs, probabilistic methods, and risk analysis.
- Large organizations typically must manage a portfolio of projects at the same time. Selection and prioritization of projects should be seen as ways to strategically manage change and generate new capabilities for the organization.

KEY TERMS

DISCUSSION QUESTIONS

1. What are some of the assumptions underlying the critical path method (CPM)? Can you think of situations in which the CPM assumptions would not be valid?
2. Think of the last project in which you participated that did not go as well as planned (e.g., this could be a team assignment for a class). Were the causes of failure mainly social or technical in nature? Explain.
3. At what point in the life of a project does the project manager have the greatest ability to influence the success of the project? Name three things you would try to get executive sponsors of a project to agree to before you accepted the job as project manager.
4. Suppose that you are the leader of a project aimed to quickly develop and explore radical new business opportunities that exploit the company's strengths in supply chain management. What types of personnel would you want on your team? How would you organize the project?
5. What strengths do you possess that would make you an excellent project manager? In what areas do you need to improve?

SOLVED PROBLEM

Bill and Judy are planning their upcoming wedding. They have laid out the following tasks and estimated durations:

Task	Task Label	Estimated Duration (days)	Immediate Predecessors
Book the wedding site and date	A	2	None
Purchase rings and gifts	B	5	None
Hire a caterer	C	2	A
Select wedding party	D	7	A
Hire a videographer	E	2	A
Select dresses and tuxedos	F	10	D
Alter dresses and tuxedos	G	15	F
Hold rehearsal	H	1	B, E, G
Hold wedding	I	1	C, H

What is the earliest date that Bill and Judy can get married? What activities are critical, and how much can the noncritical activities be late or postponed? To answer these questions, we will need to take the following steps:

1. Draw the network diagram.
2. Identify the critical path.
3. Compute the project length along with earliest and latest start and completion times for each task.

Using the information provided in the preceding table draw the network diagram starting from left to right. The following diagram shows the paths and durations in an activity-on-node format.

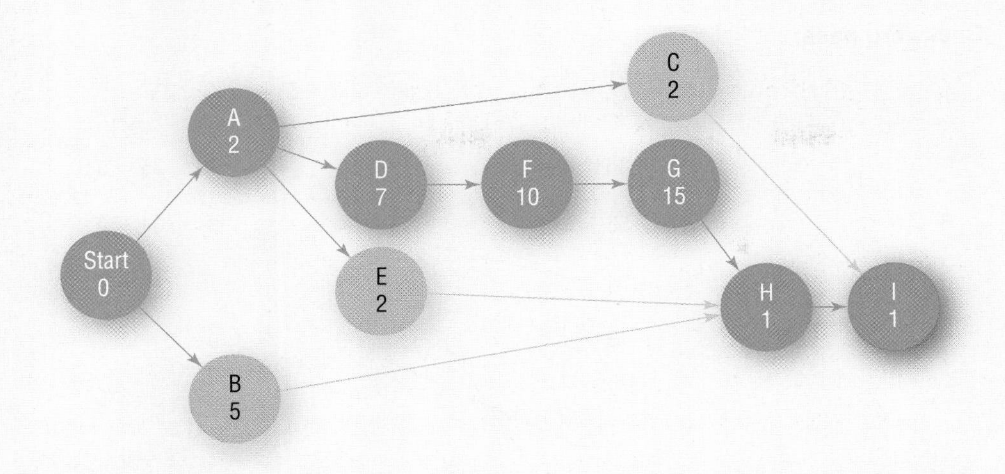

Solution:

By adding up the path lengths, we see that the critical (longest) path is A-D-F-G-H-I, with a length of 36 days. Bill and Judy could get married in as little as 36 days if all tasks go as planned.

Using the critical path algorithm, we can compute the earliest start, earliest completion, latest start, and latest completion dates for all the tasks as shown in Table 15-4.

The slack values given in Table 15-4 indicate how much the noncritical tasks can be late or postponed. For example, task B can be postponed as much as 29 days without making the project late.

TABLE 15-4 Forward and Backward Pass Calculations

Forward pass:

Task	Immediate Predecessors	Earliest Start (ES)	Earliest Completion (EC) = ES + Task Duration
A	None	0	2
B	None	0	5
C	A	2	4
D	A	2	9
E	A	2	4
F	D	9	19
G	F	19	34
H	B, E, G	34	35
I	C, H	35	36

Backward pass:

Task	Immediate Successors	Latest Completion (LC)	Latest Start (LS) = LC − Task Duration	Slack = LS − ES
I	None	36 (proj length)	35	35 − 35 = 0
H	I	35	34	34 − 34 = 0
G	H	34	19	19 − 19 = 0
F	G	19	9	9 − 9 = 0
E	H	34	32	32 − 2 = 30
D	F	9	2	2 − 2 = 0
C	I	35	33	33 − 2 = 31
B	H	34	29	29 − 0 = 29
A	C, D, E	2	0	0 − 0 = 0

PROBLEMS

1. Suppose that you have been given the task of organizing a graduation open house party for your younger brother who is graduating from high school. Write an objective statement and develop a WBS for the project, with at least three levels of detail. Write a few sentences describing how the elements in the WBS support the project objective statement.
2. Somewhere in the United States, committee members in a voting precinct have decided to conduct a vote recount following an election. They have developed a preliminary WBS and have asked you to critique it. What are the weaknesses of this WBS?

Vote Recount Project

Task	Subtask	Work Package
1. Personnel	1.1 Establish criteria for selection	1.1.1 Screen criteria for redundancy
	1.2 Bipartisan	
	1.3 Select Democratic Party Representatives	1.3.1 Contact Party 1.3.2 Ask for nominees 1.3.3 Select nominees
	1.4 Contact Republican Party	
	1.5 Training	

2. Process	2.1 Local and state requirements/history	2.1.1 Examine local historical practices 2.1.2 Determine state legal requirements
	2.2 Procedures	2.2.1 Benchmark procedures in other states 2.2.2 Select best procedures 2.2.3 Make modifications to best procedures selected 2.2.4 Document procedures 2.2.5 Test procedures 2.2.6 Modify procedures as needed
	2.3 Maintain objectivity	
3. Facilities	3.1 Nice work environment	
	3.2 Search for available space	3.2.1 Contact real estate agents 3.2.2 Contact government agencies 3.2.3 Scan real estate Web sites 3.2.4 Contact failed dot-coms
	3.3 Prepare rental agreement	3.3.1 Install utilities
	3.4 Contract for support services	3.4.1 Janitorial service
4. Budget	4.1 Determine budget needs	4.1.1 Prepare formal budget proposal 4.1.2 Request budget allocation from county
5. Media and Public Relations		

3. Answer these questions for the following simple set of project tasks. Task times are shown in hours.

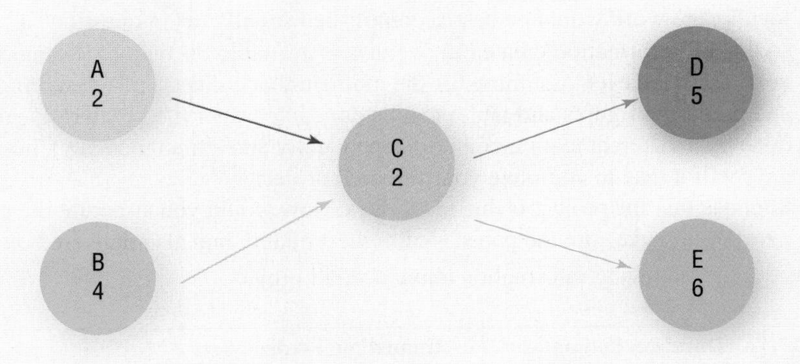

a. What is the expected time that all five tasks will be completed?
b. What is the earliest start for task C?
c. What is the latest start for task A?

4. Answer the following questions for the following network. Times shown are in days.

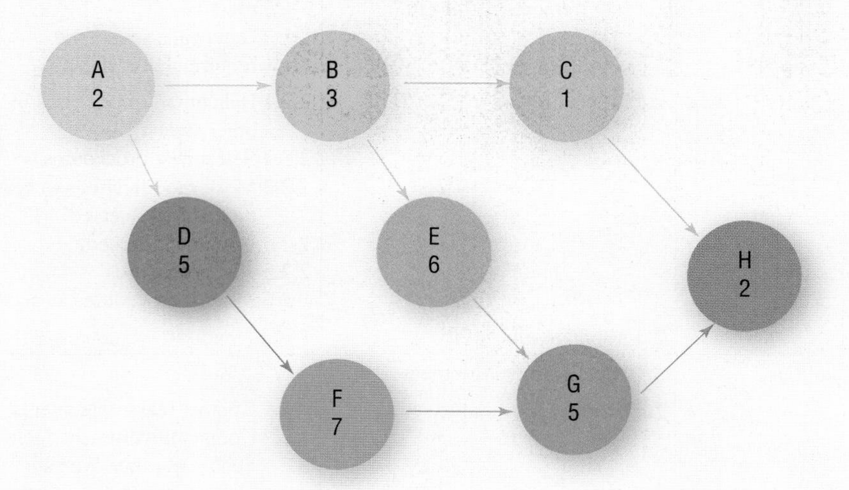

   a. What is the length of the critical path?
   b. What are the earliest start and latest start for E?
   c. What is the latest start for B?
   d. If all other tasks are completed in their expected durations, will the project length be affected if task B actually takes five days instead of the expected three?

5. Suppose that you and two other students are working on a team research project for a course you are all taking. To complete the project, you expect that the three of you will need to work together on reviewing related literature for about five days. Then, you will divide the work into three parts: collecting financial data (2 days), writing the text of the paper (5 days), and preparing the figures and tables (2 days). Then the team will work together in assembling and editing the paper (2 days).
   a. Assuming that none of the work can be done in parallel (i.e., collecting data must precede writing, which must precede preparing figures and tables), how many days will it take to complete your research project?
   b. Ideally, the work would be best accomplished serially (as in question "a" above) so that all information created in one task is available for the processing of the next task. However, assuming for the moment that collecting data, writing text, and preparing figures and tables can be done in parallel (i.e., each task can be done by a different team member independently and simultaneously), how many days will it take to complete your research project?
   c. Suppose that the project is due in 14 days. How would you structure the project in order to make sure the paper is of highest quality and also delivered on time?

6. Consider the following information about a small project:

Task	Duration Estimates	Immediate Predecessors
A	2 days	None
B	5 days	A
C	1 day	B
D	2 days	A
E	3 days	B & D
F	12 days	E & C

   a. Draw a network diagram.
   b. Identify the critical path, earliest start and finish, and slack for each task.
   c. Which of these activities should the project manager track most closely?
   d. What would happen if a new estimate for task D increases its expected duration from two days to six days? Would the project take longer? Would anything else change?

7. Consider the following table of precedence relationships for a portion of a house-building project:

Task	Duration Estimates	Immediate Predecessor(s)
Prepare Site	4 days	None
Install Rough Plumbing	3 days	Prepare Site
Pour Concrete Foundation	2 days	Install Rough Plumbing
Concrete Curing Time	3 days	Pour Concrete Foundation
Preassemble Wall Frames	8 days	None
Erect Wall Frames	4 days	Preassemble WF, Cure Concrete
Install Roof	2 days	Erect Wall Frames
Install Wiring	3 days	Install Roof
Install Exterior Siding	4 days	Install Roof
Install Insulation	2 days	Install Exterior Siding
Hang Drywall	3 days	Install Insulation, Install Wiring
Windows	1 day	Hang Dry Wall
Paint Interior	6 days	Install Windows
Paint Exterior	5 days	Install Exterior Siding
Level Yard	2 days	Cure Concrete
Landscape Yard	4 days	Level Yard

a. Draw a network diagram for this project and identify the critical path.
b. What assumptions may have been made in the development of the time estimates?
c. What will happen to the project if the materials needed for the frame preassembly are not available until the second day of the project? What if the materials were delayed until the tenth day?
d. Do you see any potential resource conflicts in this schedule? Will there be any incompatible tasks occurring simultaneously?

8. Based on the precedence table below, draw a network diagram for this project. Identify the critical path, earliest start and finish, and slack for each task.

Activity	Duration (Days)	Immediate Predecessor
A	2	none
B	3	none
C	4	none
D	5	A
E	3	B
F	7	C
G	2	D, E
H	4	F
I	3	F
J	1	H
K	3	I
L	1	G, J, K

9. Given the following project network:

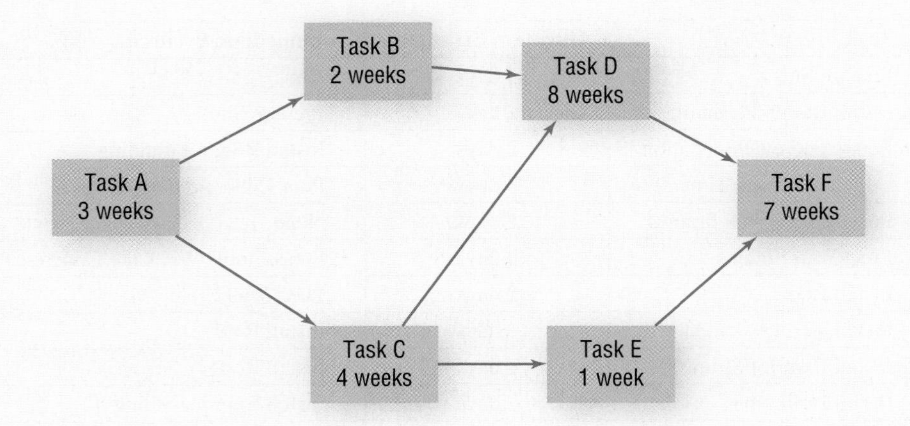

   a. Identify the critical path and earliest start and finish for each task.
   b. Calculate slack for every project activity.
   c. Draw this network as a Gantt chart.

10. Given the network in problem 9, enter project data into a project management software program such as MS Project. Print a network and a bar chart (Gantt) view. Interpret the results.

CASE

Derek's European Tour

Derek had a busy summer ahead of him. It was February 1, and Derek was planning out a summer full of activities that include a backpacking tour of Europe, doing some work for his father, and completing an online summer course offered by his university. Derek was in the midst of the spring semester of his senior year at State University, and he looked forward to taking a once-in-a-lifetime trip to Europe before starting a job in August that year. He had already secured a position as a drummer for a musical group on Holland America Cruise Lines. The job required him to report for training on August 1.

After completing his spring semester and going through graduation ceremonies on May 15, Derek planned to visit most of the larger countries in Western Europe, and also to attend a couple of key events while there. His tentative plan was to spend a week in Spain, two weeks in the UK, two weeks in Italy, a week in France, a week in Benelux (Belgium, Netherlands, Luxembourg), and two weeks in the area of Germany, Switzerland, and Austria. In addition to travel, Derek had two passions in his life, jazz and tennis. It was his dream to attend all three days of the largest jazz event on the planet, the North Sea Jazz Festival, to be held in Rotterdam on July 13–15. He also wanted to spend at least a couple of days watching matches at Wimbledon, the most prestigious tennis tournament in the world. This year's tournament was scheduled for June 22 through July 6 in Wimbledon, England.

Derek also had some work to do this summer. He had promised that he would help his father, a professor, by preparing figures and tables for a new textbook that he was writing. His father expected that the work would take Derek about four weeks to complete, given that he did the work on his laptop computer while traveling. Derek preferred to complete the work in one four-week period, rather than starting and stopping the work multiple times over the summer. His father did not care when Derek did the work, as long as it was completed before he started his new job on August 1.

Derek also had one last course to take in order to finish his degree (even though he attended graduation ceremonies in the spring). He had to complete the course this summer in order to be eligible to start his job in the fall. Fortunately, his university offered an online course on ecology that would fulfill the general education requirement he needed. The course was self-paced and only required the completion of four online examinations. Derek expected that this course would take about four weeks, and he very much wanted to complete the course before attending the North Sea Jazz Festival, so that he could give full attention to networking with many of the jazz legends who would be playing there. He could start the course any time after June 1. But he felt that it would be quite difficult to take the course at the same time that he did the work for his father.

As he considered all the things he had planned for the summer, Derek started to wonder if it was all even feasible. He also began to think of all the things he needed to do to prepare for the trip. He had been told that he needed to apply for a passport at least 12 weeks before leaving the country. He wanted to book his airline flights at least eight weeks in advance in order to get low fares. And he estimated that it would take at least three weeks for him to procure and pack all the things he needed for his trip. Fortunately, his planning was made simpler by the fact that he could fly into and out of Europe from just about any country, and while in Europe he would simply buy a Eurail pass that enabled him to travel to all his planned destinations by train.

Questions

1. Draw a network diagram that gives a workable plan for Derek's trip and work.
2. Can Derek achieve all the things he wants to do this summer? What is the first thing he needs to do? In what order should he visit the various countries he wants to see?
3. When should Derek start doing the work for his father? When should he take the class?
4. What things might happen that put Derek's plans at risk? How can he mitigate or respond to these risks?

CASE

Monolith Productions*

The summit meeting at Monolith Productions started promptly on August 20 at 10:45 a.m. The president of the company, Hugo Monolith III, called the meeting of his vice presidents to order. "Ladies and gentlemen, thank you for meeting here on such short notice. A most important contract has been won by our company. Monolith has been signed to produce a new made-for-TV version of Charles Dickens's *A Christmas Carol.* The movie will be broadcast during prime time on Christmas Eve on the nationwide BAA Network.

"We are in complete control of the project. We will write a screenplay version of the story (with the BAA having final approval), produce the film, and support BAA's promotion of the film. We also have the rights to release a picture book based on the film. Steven Playhill will be the director, Bill Quinn will handle the promotion, and Kim Yoshikawa will be in charge of production and release of the picture book. It is now my privilege to introduce one of the most popular film producers of our time, Steven Playhill. Steven?"

The introduction of Playhill brought further applause. It was acknowledged by a slight, bearded man in rumpled casual clothing who walked to the front of the conference room and started to speak. "Thank you. I would like to explain the production process. We are targeting the completion of the film for December 17. The film is to be shown on the evening of December 24, but BAA wants one week in case last-minute rescheduling during Christmas week is necessary. The first task is to write a screenplay. The screenplay, with revisions, should take about four weeks to complete. The next step is to cast the leading roles according to the screenplay. Casting for the project should take about two weeks. Casting can occur while the screenplay is being written. Interior scenes requiring only the primary characters can be shot at a studio using soundstages. I expect we can comfortably complete the interior scenes in about four to five weeks. Exterior shots, depicting the streets of 19th-century London, will be shot in Boston. We are already committed to at least seven weeks of soundstage and equipment rental. Because of the long scheduling lead time, we signed a guaranteed rental agreement to assure their availability for our project.

"The shooting in Boston will probably take about three weeks. However, we want good amounts of fog and some snow available, so we cannot begin Boston shooting before November."

Playhill considered the other activities needed for the movie. "Let's see . . . well, some props would have to be constructed. I'd say that should take a week, but it can

* Revised with permission from V. A. Mabert and M. J. Showalter, *Cases in Operations Management* (Plano, TX: BPI, 1984).

be done while the screenplay is being written and prior to renting shooting sites. After each stage of filming is completed, we will need at least one week to edit the film that was shot. We'll need an additional week at each stage for shooting any retakes. Has anyone requested a preview?"

Mr. Monolith spoke up. "BAA always requires its films to be previewed. Why?"

"Because we should allow another week for staging the preview here in Burbank and processing any reedits they request. That should produce us a made-for-TV film. Again, this all has to be completed by December 17. Any questions? Thank you."

Playhill took his seat and Quinn began to discuss the promotion of the film. "BAA has requested two forms of promotion. They would like us to produce a 60-second and a 30-second commercial including actual film footage. The 60-second spot must include scenes from both interior and location shooting. The 30-second spot should contain only close-ups of the primary characters. They want to run these commercials from December 3 through December 24. I have set aside one week to complete this task, although an abbreviated schedule could be used. Using the abbreviated plan, the commercials can be completed in as little as three days, but the production staff size would have to expand, probably increasing the commercial cost."

"John, does that mean the film must be completed by December 3?"

"No, it means we'll take some action shots during the editing stage, produce copies, and expect those shots to appear in the film," Quinn replied.

"For the second phase of promotion, BAA will air several talk shows, including Jay Tenno and David Postman. They would like two or three of the stars of the movie to make the rounds of these shows after shooting is complete. They will appear, discuss the film, and introduce a film clip. The film clip accompanying a star has to spotlight that star. Arranging these talk shows (i.e., booking the appearance, completing the film clips, filming the shows) will require two weeks and must be completed by December 10. The shows will air during the two weeks leading up to the movie premier."

Kim Yoshikawa discussed the development of the book. "Ladies and gentlemen, this portion of the project is not exactly a 'picture book.' What we plan to do is develop a novella from the screenplay. Basically, we're editing Dickens into an action novel. Then we will combine this prose with color photos taken from the film. Similar products have been quite successful. Because we have total control over this part of the project, we are its sole benefactor and collect all revenues. We anticipate maximum sales if the book is finished and shipping begins during the week of November 26. A delay of one week would cost us about half our revenues due to missed holiday sales."

"Kim, are you saying now that the film has to be done by the third week of November?" asked Monolith.

"No, all that must be completed is the filming. Like the commercial, we can then take stills from the footage. Once we have the photos, it will take one week to put the photos in the book and print copies."

"What about the prose portion of the book, Kim?"

"The book has to be written from the original screenplay. Although some changes may occur during shooting, such changes should not affect the book significantly. The 'prose-ifying' of the screenplay should take about one week. We need another three weeks to choose an appropriate layout and composition for the book, which can also be shortened by one week for the same cost. Then it's all done except photos and printing. Are there any questions?"

Mr. Monolith rose to wrap up the meeting. "Ladies and gentlemen, we have one week to schedule and budget this project. We plan to let the people who made presentations here begin their work one week from today."

Questions

1. What analytical tools can be used to schedule the project? Is any tool more advantageous than others?
2. Using the most conservative estimates (longest times) for the timing of projects, can the movie be completed on time? Can the book be released on time to capture all holiday sales?
3. Which activities would you try to shorten? Why?
4. What are the most likely risks that threaten the completion of this project? As project manager, which activities should receive your greatest attention?

SELECTED READINGS & INTERNET SITES

Project Management Institute
www.pmi.org

Goldratt, E. *The Critical Chain.* Great Barrington, MA: North River Press, 1997.

Gray, C. F., and E. W. Larson. *Project Management,* 4th ed. New York: McGraw-Hill/Irwin, 2007.

Meredith, J. R., and Mantell, S. J. *Project Management,* 6th ed. Hoboken, NJ: John Wiley & Sons, 2006.

Project Management Journal, Project Management Institute.

Swink, M. "Product Development—Faster, On Time." *Research-Technology Management,* July–August 2002, pp. 50–58.

Swink, M.; S. Talluri; and T. Pandejpong. "Faster, Better, Cheaper: A Study of NPD Project Efficiency and Performance Tradeoffs." *Journal of Operations Management* 24, no. 5 (2006), pp. 542–62.

Verzuh, E. *The Fast Forward MBA in Project Management,* 3rd ed. Hoboken, NJ: John Wiley & Sons, 2008.

15 Chapter Supplement: Advanced Methods for Project Scheduling

CHAPTER SUPPLEMENT OUTLINE

LEARNING OBJECTIVES *After studying this supplement, you should be able to:*

LO15S-1 Make time and cost trade-offs in projects.

LO15S-2 Schedule projects using probabilistic task time estimates.

This supplement illustrates two of the more quantitative techniques for scheduling project tasks and resources. First, the reasoning for making time and cost trade-offs in projects is presented. This approach, called **crashing** a project, is useful when project managers need to speed up projects that are behind schedule or when deadlines have been changed. The second technique, **probabilistic scheduling**, is useful when the durations of project tasks are uncertain. Such uncertainty is common in "really new" projects, or in projects involving tasks that are subject to many factors outside the direct control of the project team (e.g., weather, competitor actions, regulators, and so on). Probabilistic scheduling uses statistics to model the uncertainty in the project and to estimate the likelihood of various project outcomes.

crashing Adding resources to efficiently speed up a project.

probabilistic scheduling The use of statistics to model the uncertainty in the project and to estimate the likelihood of various project outcomes.

To illustrate the techniques we will use the example project from Chapter 15. Figure 15S-1 shows the original network diagram for the supply chain planning system implementation project.

PROJECT CRASHING: MAKING TIME-COST TRADE-OFFS

Prepare
How does a manager determine the best places to spend more resources in order to speed a project up most efficiently?

Organize
Project Crashing: Making Time-Cost Trade-Offs

Revisions to a project schedule are often necessary due to many possible factors. Initial project activities may have taken longer than originally planned, project deadlines may have been changed, or critical resources may have become unavailable. Any of these causes can make the original plan no longer feasible or desirable, so the project manager needs to decide how to shift resources in ways that achieve project objectives in the most efficient way possible.

A common decision for managers to make is how best to spend more money (resources) to speed up the project. The following steps provide a process for making such a decision:

1. List the crash costs for each task in the project.
2. Choose the task or combination of tasks on the critical path that has the lowest crash cost, and reduce that task's duration by one period.
3. Update the lengths of all affected paths in the network. Identify any paths that have become critical.
4. Repeat this process until the plan meets the required deadline, or until the cost of reducing the project length exceeds the benefit.

LO15S-1 Make time and cost trade-offs in projects.

FIGURE 15S-1 Network Diagram for Planning System Implementation Project

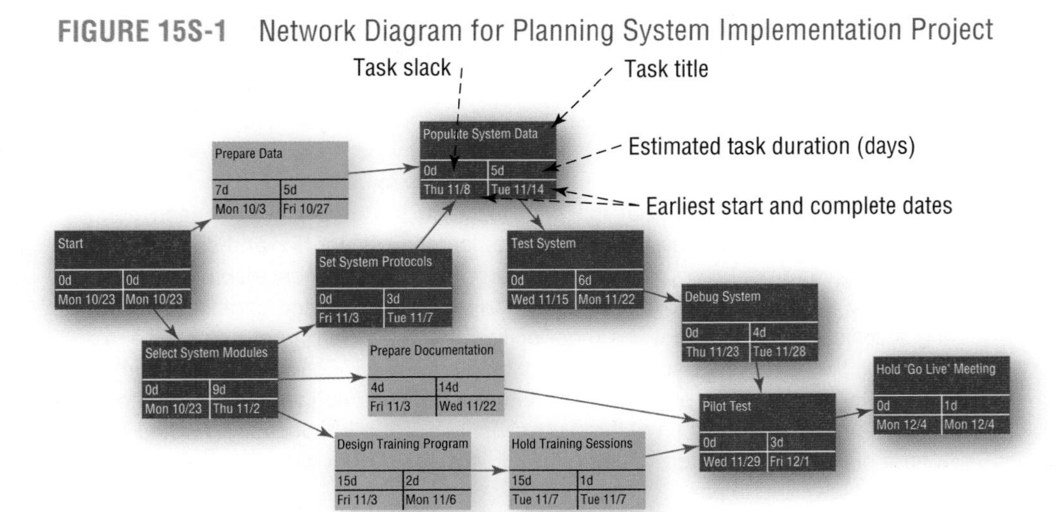

EXAMPLE 15S-1

Let's apply this decision process to the planning system installation project introduced in Chapter 15. Suppose that the client wants this project completed one week early (five working days). The current plan indicates that it will take 31 days to finish the project. What is the least expensive way to reduce the project length by five days?

Step 1. Assume that we have investigated the possibilities and created the crash cost information shown in Table 15S-1. The **crash cost** per day data are estimates of the additional costs (adding workers, overtime pay, etc.) required to speed up each task by one day. Note that several activities cannot be crashed, and all activities have some lower duration limit.

crash cost Estimated cost to reduce a project task by one time unit (e.g., a day or a week).

Steps 2 and 3. Start by examining the critical path tasks. Because "Set System Protocols" can be reduced by one day for a cost of $500, it offers the cheapest alternative. Note that reducing "Prepare Data" for a cost of $200 does not affect the project length because this task is not on the critical path. Planning to spend $500 to reduce "Set System Protocols" will change the planned project completion to 30 days. This change also reduces the slack in the noncritical tasks by one day each. This reduction is not enough to cause any of the noncritical tasks to become critical.

Repeating Steps 2 and 3. The best next step would be to reduce the "Set System Protocols" task by an additional day, as it remains the cheapest option on the critical path. Now the "Set System Protocols" task is planned to be done at its fastest (minimum) duration of one day, and the project will complete in 29 days.

Repeating Steps 2 and 3. The next cheapest crash option is "Test System." Crashing this task from six days to five days costs $600. This brings the critical path length down to 28 days. Note that by reducing the project a total of three days so far, we have reduced the slack in noncritical activities by the same amount.

Repeating Steps 2 and 3. The next cheapest crash option is still "Test System." Crashing this task from five days to four days costs $600. This brings the critical path to 27 days. Note that the path containing the "Prepare Documentation" is also 27 days long. In reducing the critical path by four days, the "Prepare Documentation" has now become critical! Any further efforts to crash the project must address both critical paths.

Repeating Steps 2 and 3. Consider the options for reducing the project further. We could reduce the "Test System" task by one more day at a cost of $600, but doing this would still leave the path with "Prepare Documentation" at 27 days long. To reduce the project by one day, we would need to reduce *both* activities "Test System" and "Prepare Documentation" by one day each, at a total cost of $1,000 ($600 + $400). However, a better option would be to crash the "Pilot Test" task by one day at a cost of $900. Because "Pilot Test" is on all paths leading to the completion of the project, we can reduce the overall project by reducing this one activity.

Now we have a plan to reduce the project length by a total of five days. The plan is summarized in Table 15S-2 and the crashed project network is shown in Figure 15S-2. If we wanted to crash the project further, we would have to crash both "Test System" and "Prepare Documentation" by one day each, because the "Pilot Test" task has already been reduced to its minimum duration.

You may have noticed that the cost to crash the project length each additional day increases as the planned project length gets shorter and shorter. This increasing incremental crash cost phenomenon is true in almost all projects. Consequently, it is important to continuously compare the costs and benefits of crashing a project to ensure that the most economical plans are made. Suppose, for example, that our client decided that he would only be willing to pay a maximum of $2,000 to complete the project earlier. Our crash schedule in Table 15S-2 shows that a project time reduction of three days would be justified, because it would cost a total of $1,600. However, to crash the project any further would cost more than the client is willing to pay.

TABLE 15S-1 Crash Schedule for Planning System Installation Project

Task	Current Planned Duration	Minimum Duration	Crash Cost per Day
*Select System Modules	9	6	$1200
Prepare Data	5	4	$ 200
*Set System Protocols	3	1	$ 500
*Populate System Data	5	3	$ 700
Prepare Documentation	14	10	$ 400
Design Training Program	2	2	_____
Hold Training Sessions	1	1	_____
*Test System	6	3	$ 600
*Debug System	4	2	$ 800
*Pilot Test	3	2	$ 900
*Hold "Go Live" Meeting	1	1	_____

*Task is on the critical path

TABLE 15S-2 Summary of Crash Plan for the Planning System Installation Project

	Activity to Crash	Crash Cost	Critical Path Length	Notes:
0			31 days	No tasks crashed
1	Set System Protocols	$ 500	30 days	Cheapest task on critical path
2	Set System Protocols	$ 500	29 days	Cannot crash this task any further
3	Test System	$ 600	28 days	Cheapest task on critical path
4	Test System	$ 600	27 days	Prepare Documentation becomes on a critical path
5	Pilot Test	$ 900	26 days	Crashing this task reduces both critical paths. Planned deadline met.
	Total Cost:	$3100		

FIGURE 15S-2 Planning System Installation Project Crashed to 26 Days

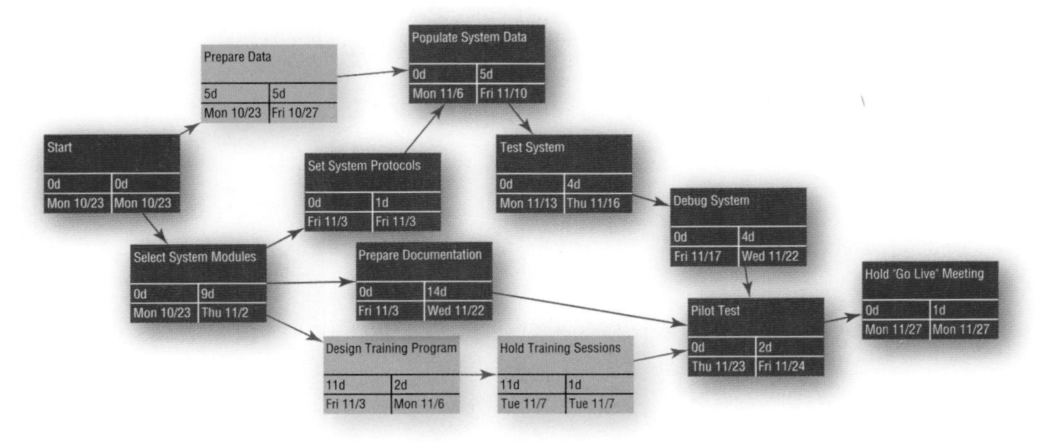

Prepare

How does a manager incorporate uncertainty into project planning?

Organize

Scheduling a Project with Probabilistic Task Duration Estimates

SCHEDULING A PROJECT WITH PROBABILISTIC TASK DURATION ESTIMATES

Sometimes it is difficult to accurately estimate the durations of project tasks. In these situations, it can be helpful to analyze the impacts of uncertainty on the project by developing a range of possible task durations for each task, rather than relying on a single point estimate. Using this approach, managers estimate the **best-case duration**, **worst-case duration**, and **most likely case duration** for each task in the project. The best-case duration is the manager's estimate of the time the task will take assuming everything goes exactly as planned. For example, the weather is perfect, no one on the project team gets sick, no technical problems arise, and so on. The worst-case duration is the expected time should all possible delays be realized, that is, if every imaginable thing goes wrong. The most likely duration is the manager's estimate of the most probable task time. By making some assumptions about the statistical properties of these estimates, project analysts can create distributions of possible outcomes for each project task, and ultimately for the project as a whole.

best-case duration Estimate of the task time given everything goes as planned.

worst-case duration Estimate of the task time given all possible delays are realized.

most likely case duration Estimate of the most probable task time.

LO15S-2 Schedule projects using probabilistic task time estimates.

Table 15S-3 recasts the original planning system installation project data using ranges of task time estimates. Some of the ranges are symmetrically distributed around the most likely duration, whereas others are skewed to the left or right. The distribution of durations for a task is often a result of resource uncertainties and dependencies. For example, suppose that we are dependent on an outside consultant for help with the task "Select System Modules." The duration estimates suggest that if all goes well and the consultant is available when we need her, the task may be finished in as little as seven working days. However, if the consultant is as much as a week late in becoming available, it might take up to 15 days to select the system modules. Using this kind of reasoning, managers can create ranges of task durations and, using some simple formulas and rules of thumb, assign probabilities to various outcomes.

TABLE 15S-3 Probabilistic Time Estimates for the Planning System Installation Project

Task	Best-Case Duration	Most Likely Duration	Worst-Case Duration
*Select System Modules	7	9	15
Prepare Data	4	5	10
*Set System Protocols	2	3	5
*Populate System Data	3	5	7
Prepare Documentation	10	14	16
Design Training Program	2	2	3
Hold Training Sessions	1	1	2
*Test System	4	6	8
*Debug System	2	4	6
*Pilot Test	2	3	4
*Hold "Go Live" Meeting	1	1	1

*Task is on the critical path

Here's how the probabilistic analysis works.

1. Compute the expected duration and standard deviation for each task using the following formulas:

(15S.1) $$t_i = (w + 4 * m + b) / 6$$

(15S.2) $$\sigma_i = (w - b) / 6$$

where:

w = worst-case duration
m = most likely duration
b = best-case duration

2. Compute the expected duration and standard deviation for each path.

(15S.3) $$t_{path} = \Sigma\, t_i$$

(15S.4) $$\sigma_{path} = \sqrt{(\Sigma\, \sigma_i^2)}$$

3. Use these estimates and the standard normal curve to evaluate probabilities for given completion dates.

EXAMPLE 15S-2

We know from the prior analysis that the planning system installation project is most likely to be completed in about 31 days. Suppose that the client has determined that the project absolutely must be finished within 33 days. Given the range estimates in Table 15S-3, what is the probability that the project will be finished on time? We can follow the three steps above to answer this question.

Step 1. Table 15S-4 on the next page shows the expected durations and standard deviations computed using the formulas above. For example, the results for "Select System Modules" are:

$$t_i = (15 + 4 * 9 + 7) / 6 = 9.67 \text{ days}$$
$$\sigma_i = (15 - 7) / 6 = 1.33 \text{ days}$$

Note that the expected duration for a given task might be longer or shorter than the most likely time, depending on the range of duration estimates. The expected time gives the "50/50" estimate of task duration. That is, the actual duration of the task has a 50 percent chance of being longer or shorter than the expected time.

Step 2. This step involves adding up the expected times for various paths in the project to identify the *expected* longest path. The expected length and standard deviation for the most likely critical path is

$$t_{path} = 9.67 + 3.17 + 5 + 6 + 4 + 3 + 1 = 31.84 \text{ days}$$
$$\sigma_{path} = \text{square root } (1.33^2 + 0.5^2 + 0.67^2 + 0.67^2 + 0.67^2 + 0.33^2 + 0^2) = 1.86 \text{ days}$$

This result indicates that there is a 50 percent chance that the project will last longer than 31.84 days, and a 50 percent chance that the project will be completed before 31.84 days. This assumes, of course, that the project length is determined by this one path. There is a possibility that one of the noncritical paths could in fact become critical, if those tasks are at their worst-case conditions, and the critical path tasks are at their best-case conditions. For now we will concentrate only on the expected critical path.

Step 3. To estimate the probability that the project will take 33 days or less to finish, we use the information from a standard normal table (given in Appendix A). We can assume that the length of a path in the network will vary normally around its mean (expected) value. The *z*-score for our expected critical path is

(15S.5) $$z = (\text{target completion time} - t_{path}) / \sigma_{path}$$
$$= (33 - 31.84) / 1.86 = .624$$

(continued)

From the partial z-table shown in Table 15S-5, a value of .624 corresponds to a probability of approximately .73, or 73 percent. Figure 15S-3 illustrates this probability upon a standard normal curve. The result indicates that there is about a 73 percent chance that the project duration will last no more than 33 days, given our estimates of best-case, worst case, and most likely scenarios. If this probability is unacceptable to us or our client, then we would want to investigate the potential for crashing critical activities to the point that an acceptable probability of completion on time is achieved.

TABLE 15S-4
Expected Duration and Standard Deviations for Planning System Installation Project

Task	Best-Case Duration	Most Likely Duration	Worst-Case Duration	Expected Duration	Standard Deviation
*Select System Modules	7	9	15	9.67	1.33
Prepare Data	4	5	10	5.67	1
*Set System Protocols	2	3	5	3.17	0.5
*Populate System Data	3	5	7	5	0.67
Prepare Documentation	10	14	16	13.67	1
Design Training Program	2	2	3	2.17	0.17
Hold Training Sessions	1	1	2	1.17	0.17
*Test System	4	6	8	6	0.67
*Debug System	2	4	6	4	0.67
*Pilot Test	2	3	4	3	0.33
*Hold "Go Live" Meeting	1	1	1	1	0

*Task is on the critical path

TABLE 15S-5
Standard Normal Table

z	F(z)	1-F(z)	z	F(z)	1-F(z)
0.0	0.5000	0.5000	1.9	0.9713	0.0287
0.1	0.5398	0.4602	2.0	0.9772	0.0228
0.2	0.5793	0.4207	2.1	0.9821	0.0179
0.3	0.6179	0.3821	2.2	0.9861	0.0139
0.4	0.6554	0.3446	2.3	0.9893	0.0107
0.5	0.6915	0.3085	2.4	0.9918	0.0082
0.6	0.7257	0.2743	2.5	0.9938	0.0062
0.7	0.7580	0.2420	2.6	0.9953	0.0047
0.8	0.7881	0.2119	2.7	0.9965	0.0035
0.9	0.8159	0.1841	2.8	0.9974	0.0026
1.0	0.8413	0.1587	2.9	0.9981	0.0019
1.1	0.8643	0.1357	3.0	0.9987	0.0013
1.2	0.8849	0.1151	3.1	0.9990	0.0010
1.3	0.9032	0.0968	3.2	0.9993	0.0007
1.4	0.9192	0.0808	3.3	0.9995	0.0005
1.5	0.9332	0.0668	3.4	0.9997	0.0003
1.6	0.9452	0.0548	3.5	0.9998	0.0002
1.7	0.9554	0.0446	3.6	0.9998	0.0002
1.8	0.9641	0.0359	3.7	0.9999	0.0001

F(z) is the standard normal cumulative probability from the left tail of the distribution to the value of z.

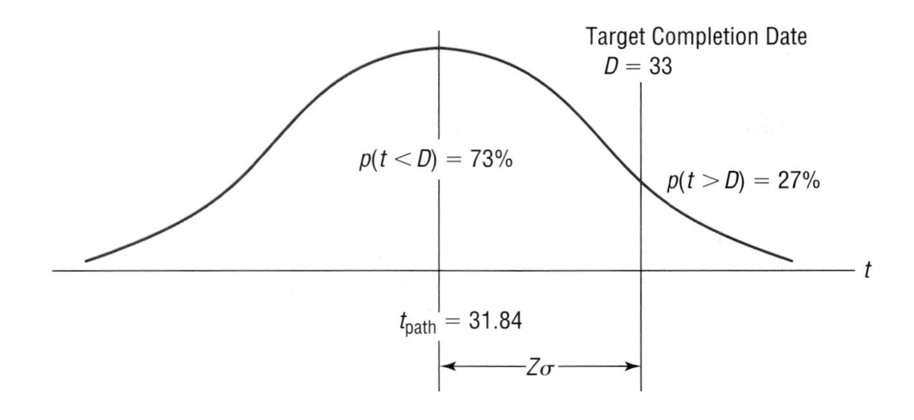

FIGURE 15S-3
Probability that the Planning System Installation Project Will Take 33 or Fewer Days

In this example we have assumed that the expected critical path will define the project length. If the critical path is much longer than other paths, then this is likely to be the case. As noted previously, however, each path in a project has some probability that it will actually turn out to be the longest path. What project managers really want to know is, what is the probability that *all* paths will be completed by a given target deadline. This is usually difficult to estimate directly because paths in projects are usually not independent (several paths share certain tasks in common). Instead, project managers often use simulation tools to automatically simulate thousands or millions of scenarios that randomly vary different task lengths according to their best, worst, and most likely case parameters. This type of analysis provides an overall distribution of project length. If the distribution is normal, then managers can use the z-table in the same way as before to estimate project completion probabilities.

SUPPLEMENT SUMMARY

This supplement provides brief explanations and examples of two quantitative means for analyzing projects and rearranging resources in order to achieve desired completion time goals. While much more sophisticated methods exist, these approaches are useful in many situations. Importantly, the logic underlying these methods helps the project manager to understand the nature of trade-offs between resources, time, and risk.

KEY TERMS

best-case duration 540
crashing 537
crash cost 538
most likely case duration 540
probabilistic scheduling 537
worst-case duration 540

DISCUSSION QUESTIONS

1. When does it make economical sense to *crash* project activities? How do you know when to stop?
2. Why does it never make sense to crash activities that are not on the critical path?

3. Suppose that your project has two activity paths of about the same length, but one path is made up of more uncertain activities while the other path is fairly routine. How would you manage the activities on these two paths differently?
4. What project factors would make you more or less comfortable with a lower probability that the project will be completed on time?

SOLVED PROBLEMS

Suppose that one of your professors has hired you as part of a team of students for a summer research project, for a total payment of $2,000. The preliminary project plan is shown in the network diagram shown in Figure 15S-4. Based on an hourly pay rate agreed upon by you and your teammates, you have estimated the cost for each activity as shown in Table 15S-6. It is possible to speed up certain activities. However, to do so you will have to add more teammates and work on weekends. Table 15S-6 also shows the costs for making these changes.

FIGURE 15S-4 Network Diagram for Research Project

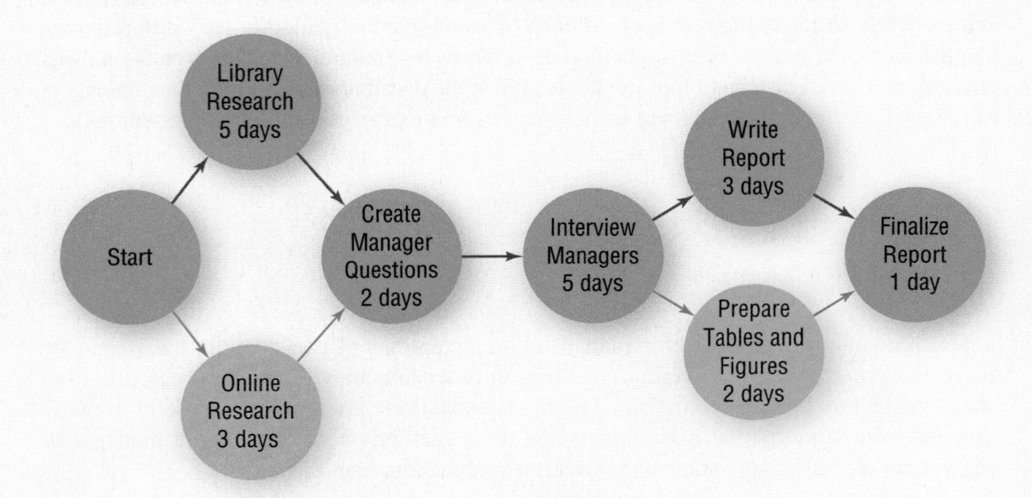

TABLE 15S-6 Crash Costs for Research Project

Activity	Planned Duration	Cost	Minimum Possible Duration	Crash Cost per Day
Library Research	5	$300	4	$250
Online Research	3	$100	2	$100
Create Manager Questions	2	$200	1	$400
Interview Managers	5	$300	5	-
Write Report	3	$200	1	$150
Prepare Tables and Figures	2	$100	1	$150
Finalize Report	1	$100	1	-

Part A. The critical path of the project (shown in red) indicates that the project will take 16 working days to complete. However, your professor needs the report in no longer than 13 working days. Come up with the lowest cost way to meet the 13-day goal.

Solution:

As currently planned, the project will cost $1,300 (netting your team a $700 profit) and will be completed in 16 working days. Your challenge is to complete the project in 13 days without spending all of your profit.

1. The cheapest critical path activity to crash initially is "Write Report," for a cost of $150. If we crash this activity by one day, then the critical path becomes 15 days long.
2. Now the cheapest way to reduce the project is to reduce "Library Research" by one day at a cost of $250. This brings the project length to 14 days. The alternative would be to crash both "Write Report" and "Prepare Tables and Figures" by one day each, but that total cost would be $300. We could also crash "Create Manager Questions" by one day, but that would cost $400.
3. Because "Library Research" is now at its shortest duration (four days), the cheapest way to reduce the project by a final day is to crash both "Write Report" and "Prepare Tables and Figures" by one day each, for a total cost of $300.

Figure 15S-5 shows the crashed project with a 13-day duration. The total crash costs are $150 + $250 + $300 = $600, which leaves $100 in unspent profit.

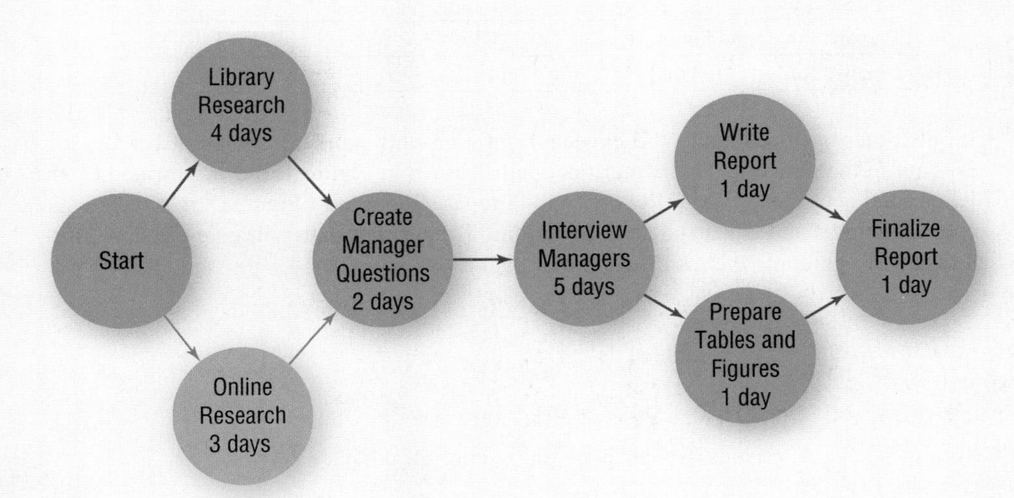

FIGURE 15S-5
Network Diagram for Crashed Research Project

Part B. Your professor has reviewed your crash plan and is not convinced that you will complete the project on time. He asks you to develop a probabilistic analysis of the project. As a start, you and your team have used the current duration estimates as most likely times, and added the best-case and worst-case time estimates as shown in Table 15S-7 on the next page. Use this information to provide your professor with your estimated probability that you will finish the project in 13 days or less.

Solution:

The first step is to calculate the expected duration and standard deviation for each activity. For example, the calculations for the "Library Research" activity are

$$t_i = (w + 4 * m + b) / 6$$
$$= (3 + 4 * 4 + 6) / 6 = 4.17$$
$$\sigma_i = (w - b) / 6$$
$$= (6 - 3) / 6 = 0.50$$

TABLE 15S-7 Probabilistic Time Estimates for Research Project

Activity	Best-Case Duration	Most Likely Duration	Worst-Case Duration
Library Research	3	4	6
Online Research	2	3	4
Create Manager Questions	2	2	3
Interview Managers	4	5	8
Write Report	1	1	2
Prepare Tables and Figures	1	1	2
Finalize Report	1	1	1

Using the same calculations, the expected durations and standard deviations for the other activities are shown below:

	Expected Duration	Standard Deviation
Library Research	4.17	0.50
Online Research	3.00	0.33
Create Manager Questions	2.17	0.17
Interview Managers	5.33	0.67
Write Report	1.17	0.17
Prepare Tables and Figures	1.17	0.17
Finalize Report	1	0

The next step is to compute the expected duration and standard deviation for the longest path in the network. The two critical paths shown in Figure 15S-5 are formed by the two parallel activities, "Write Report" and "Prepare Tables and Figures," that have equal expected lengths and equal standard deviations. Thus, either path will give the same overall result. We compute the results for either path as

$$t_{\text{path}} = \Sigma t_i = 4.17 + 2.17 + 5.33 + 1.17 + 1 = 13.84 \text{ days}$$

$$\sigma_{\text{path}} = \sqrt{(\Sigma \sigma_i^2)} = \text{square root } (0.50^2 + 0.17^2 + 0.67^2 + 0.17^2 + 0^2) = 0.87 \text{ days}$$

Given these characteristics, we calculate the z-score for the path as

$$z = (\text{target completion time} - t_{\text{path}}) / \sigma_{\text{path}} = (13 - 13.84) / 0.87 = -0.97$$

The negative sign indicates that there is a less than 50 percent chance that the path will be completed in less than or equal to 13 days. From the standard normal table (z-table), the probability associated with positive value of this z-score is approximately 0.83. Because our z-score is negative, this means that the probability of completing the path in 13 days or less is given by $1 - 0.83 = 0.17$, or 17 percent. Because there are two paths in the project with this low probability of success, the team should probably consider crashing another activity in order to increase the odds of completing the project on time.

PROBLEMS

1. Bill needs to schedule a meeting for tomorrow afternoon, but he also has a tee time for golf at 10:00 a.m. Bill usually finishes a round of golf in 4.25 hours. If the course is empty and he doesn't spend too much time looking for lost balls, he can finish in 3.25 hours. However, if the course is crowded, there are rain delays, and/or he hits many bad shots, a round can take as much as 5.5 hours.
   a. What is the expected time that Bill will complete his round of golf tomorrow?
   b. If Bill schedules a meeting to begin at 3:30 p.m. tomorrow and it takes 30 minutes for him to get from the golf course to his office, what is the probability that he will make it to the meeting on time?
2. In problem 1 we assumed that it would take Bill 30 minutes to get from the golf course to his office. Assume now that this is the most likely time, but traffic and other factors could make the commute time as little as 25 minutes or as much as 45 minutes. What is the probability that Bill will make it to his meeting on time if you take this variability into account?
3. Consider the supply chain planning implementation project depicted in Figure 15S-1. Suppose that the client has offered a $4,000 bonus to us if we can complete the project seven working days early. Based upon the crash cost information provided in Table 15S-1, would you accept the client's proposal? By how many days could you profitably shorten the project?
4. Annie is planning a large surprise party for her sister Gwendolyn. She has developed the plan below, including estimates of the time (in hours) and cost necessary to perform each of the activities required at the currently planned pace and at the crashed pace.

Activity	Predecessor	Current Planned Duration (hours)	Minimum Crash Duration (hours)	Current Planned Cost	Total Cost if Crashed
A. Create Guest List	—	8	4	$200	$310
B. Send Invitations	A	2	1	$125	$150
C. Buy Decorations	A	8	6	$300	$370
D. Plan Menu	A	3	2	$150	$210
E. Purchase Food	D	4	2	$475	$550
F. Prepare Food	E	5	3	$225	$475

   a. Annie is most interested in reducing the time associated with creating the guest list. What is the crash cost per hour for that activity?
   b. Annie will save $40 for every hour she can reduce from her plan. Annie has decided to crash her project and use the money she saves to purchase a larger gift for Gwendolyn. Which activity should she crash first?
   c. Annie has now crashed activity A by four hours at a cost of $110. What other activity could she crash to further reduce the project?
   d. Annie has now crashed activity A by four hours at a cost of $110 and activity E by two hours at a cost of $75. What other activity could she crash to further reduce the project?
   e. How much money did Annie save by crashing the project?
   f. What is the duration of the fully crashed project?

5. Given the data in Table 15S-3, what is the probability that the project will be completed in 32 days or less? What is the probability that the project will take longer than 32 days?
6. Jude and Pat Strohsal have a crack in their water line and need to replace it. This will require digging up the water line, replacing it, filling the hole, leveling the soil, and reseeding the grass. The Strohsals' plumber suggests that, because they will have the water line dug up, they also should replace the foot valve. Following are the plumber's estimates of the time (in hours) necessary to perform each of the activities required.

Activity	Description	Predecessor	Optimistic (Best Case)	Most Likely	Pessimistic (Worst Case)
A	Digging	-	2	3	4
B	Replace line	A	1	1.5	2
C	Replace foot valve	B	.5	1	1.5
D	Fill hole	C	1.5	2	5.5
E	Level soil	D	.5	1	1.5
F	Reseed lawn	E	.4	.5	.6

a. If the plumber and his crew begin working at 7:00 a.m., what time are they expected to finish?
b. The plumber has scheduled another small job at 6:00 p.m. If it takes 1/2 hour to drive from the Strohsals' to the other job, what is the probability the plumber will be able to make the 6:00 p.m. appointment on time?
c. Jude Strohsal can't bear to see her lawn all dug up, so she has decided to visit her mother on the day the work is to be done. Jude wants to return home at 6:45 p.m. What is the probability the work will be complete when she arrives home?

7. Consider the following software development plan.

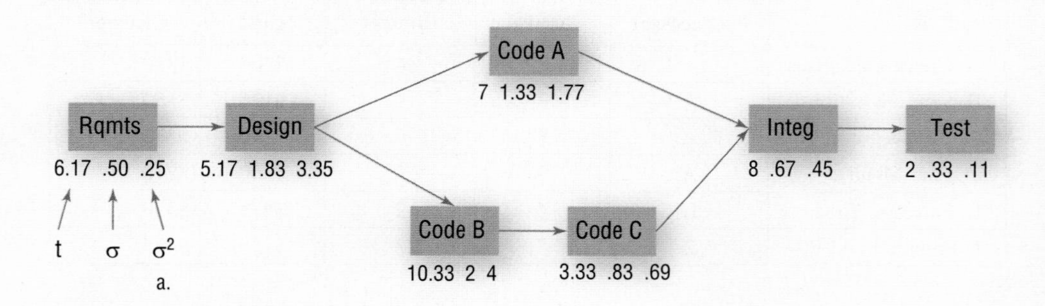

a. The client has asked for an estimated completion date. What would you tell her?
b. The client would like to have the completed software in 37 weeks. What is the likelihood that the *critical path* will be completed in that time frame?
c. The client has just asked if it would be possible to have the completed software in 36 weeks. What is the likelihood the *project* will be completed in that time frame?
d. The client wants to know if it would be possible to complete the project in 33 weeks. What is the probability of meeting the client's demand?
e. You are concerned about the accuracy of your calculations because the paths are not independent. What is the likelihood that all of the coding activities will be completed on time?

SELECTED READINGS & INTERNET SITES

Project Management Institute
www.pmi.org

Gray, C. F., and E. W. Larson. *Project Management,* 4th ed. New York: McGraw-Hill/Irwin, 2007.

Meredith, J. R., and Mantell, S. J. *Project Management,* 6th ed. Hoboken, NJ: John Wiley & Sons, 2006.

Project Management Journal, Project Management Institute.

16 Sustainable Operations Management—Preparing for the Future

CHAPTER OUTLINE

LEARNING OBJECTIVES

After studying this chapter, you should be able to:

LO16-1 Explain what it means to have "sustainable" operations.

LO16-2 Describe the "triple bottom line," and how this view of sustainability affects operational decisions across the supply chain.

LO16-3 Explain the reasons why operations managers are increasingly focusing on the environmental impacts of their activities.

LO16-4 Evaluate products using life cycle waste composition assessment.

LO16-5 Discuss the approaches used by operations managers to ensure social responsibility while improving performance in the "people" aspect of sustainability.

LO16-6 Understand the challenges operations managers face as they seek to develop and maintain a sustainable competitive advantage.

Paul Polman Transforms Unilever

Most people know Unilever, an Anglo-Dutch multinational consumer goods company whose products include food, beverages, cleaning agents, and personal care products. It is the world's third-largest consumer goods company (just after Procter & Gamble and Nestlé). Over 200 billion times a day someone in the world uses a Unilever product.

Despite Unilever's past successes, Paul Polman, the current CEO, is not satisfied with the status quo. He wants to transform Unilever from a financial and market powerhouse to a company that also positively contributes to society and the environment. At the heart of this new focus is the Unilever Sustainable Living Plan.[1] The Plan identifies seven strategic supply chain goals that Unilever wants to reach by the year 2020:

- *Health and Hygiene:* Help more than a billion people to improve their hygiene habits and bring safe drinking water to 500 million people.
- *Nutrition:* Double the proportion of the product portfolio that meets the highest nutritional standards, thus helping people to achieve a healthier diet.
- *Greenhouse Gases:* Halve the greenhouse gas impact of products across their life cycles (from sourcing to product use and disposal).
- *Water:* Halve the water usage associated with consumers uses of its products, especially in developing countries, where Unilever expects much of its future growth to be.
- *Waste:* Halve the waste associated with the disposal of its products.
- *Sustainable Sourcing:* Increase the amount of agricultural raw materials sourced sustainably from 10 percent today to 100 percent.
- *Better Livelihoods:* Link into the supply chain more than 500,000 small farmers and small-scale distributors so that they can benefit by working with Unilever.

Will Polman's plan to so embrace sustainability also be a successful business strategy? Time will tell. Where some might see a great deal of risk in the approach, Polman mostly sees opportunity, especially as he looks to developing countries to be not only a key source of future demand, but also future supply.

[1] A. Ignatius, "Unilever CEO Paul Polman: Captain Planet," *Harvard Business Review,* June 2012, pp. 112–18.

This chapter discusses how operations managers manage their operations with a long-term focus on sustainability. We have offered dozens of examples of sustainability issues throughout this book. In this chapter, we illustrate some of the major issues, tools, and techniques for managing sustainably. For a number of reasons, sustainability has become more and more important to companies like Unilever. Instead of seeking only profits, managers today are developing sustainable strategic visions that seek to balance three objectives: profit, people, and the planet.

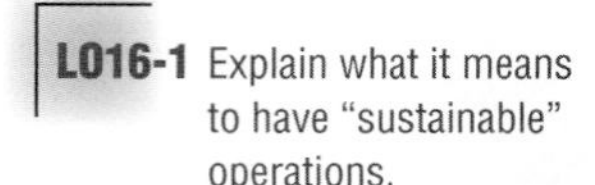

LO16-1 Explain what it means to have "sustainable" operations.

THE TRIPLE BOTTOM LINE

triple bottom line An approach to corporate performance measurement that addresses a firm's total impact, measured in terms of profit, people (social responsibility), and the planet (environmental responsibility). Also referred to the as the TBL, the 3BL, or the 3Ps.

The **triple bottom line** (3BL) approach (first discussed in Chapter 2 of this book) seeks to reduce the potentially negative impacts of a firm's processes and products on the environment (planet) and society (people). Put in a more positive light, the sustainability approach strives to improve the quality of life for people, in terms of health, fairness, and opportunity, especially for people who are disadvantaged or who live in developing countries.

global

For companies (such as Unilever) that are based in the developed world where markets are already saturated with products and services, sustainability not only seems to be the right thing to do, it also addresses the needs of markets in developing countries that represent most future business opportunities. At the same time, a shift toward sustainability is not without business risks. Sometimes sustainability initiatives involve costs that customers may not be willing to pay. Sometimes the immediate and direct benefits to customers are difficult to identify. Financial markets are notoriously focused on short-term results, and this can be at odds with the long-term focus that sustainability requires.

The primary message of this chapter is that operations managers need to develop systems that simultaneously reduce our demands on the limited (and shrinking) resources of this planet, play positive roles in providing safe and fair opportunities for people, and continuously create profits by providing critical customers with compelling reasons to buy products. Too much focus on any one of these Ps (planet, people, profit), to the exclusion of the other two, creates an unsustainable strategy. Consequently, sustainability must be tightly integrated into the thinking and actions of operations managers (especially those who work in a global environment).

Figure 16-1 illustrates the triple bottom line (3BL) approach and the topics addressed in this chapter. Other terms used to describe this approach include: corporate social responsibility (CSR), sustainability, ethical business practices, social/environmental responsibility, and

FIGURE 16-1
The Triple Bottom Line and Its Implications

LO16-2 Describe the "triple bottom line," and how this view of sustainability affects operational decisions across the supply chain.

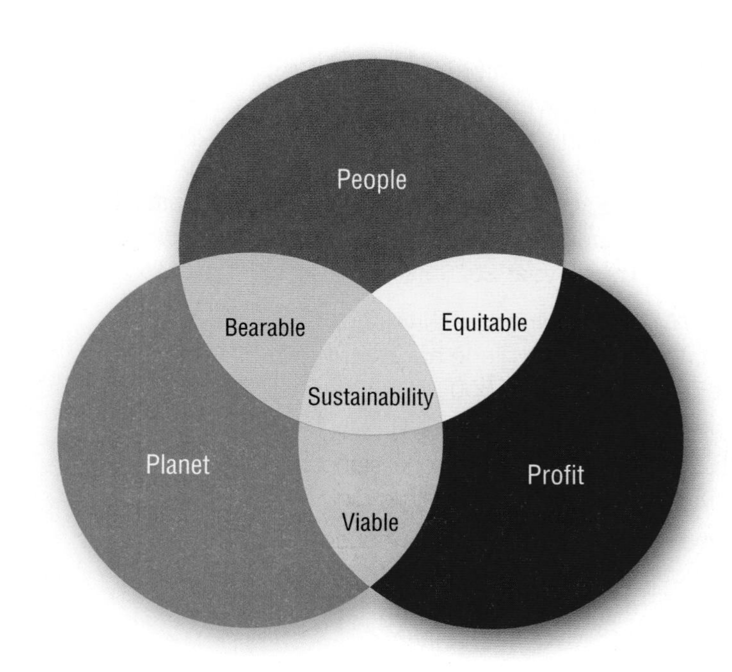

GET REAL

Disney Sustainability

Walt Disney is the world's largest media and entertainment company. Recently, it decided to become a leader in environmental sustainability. To this end, Disney has taken the following steps:

- ***Cutting Emissions:*** Disney plans to cut carbon emissions by half, reduce electricity consumption by 10 percent, reduce fuel use, halve the garbage at its parks and resorts, and ultimately achieve net zero direct greenhouse gas emissions and landfill waste. Consequently, Walt Disney World has been designated as Florida Green Lodging Certified.
- ***Recycling and More:*** The Disney Harvest Program distributes nearly 50,000 pounds of food to the Second Harvest Food Bank every month (taken from food that has been prepared but not served at Disney's various restaurants and convention centers). All used cooking oil at Walt Disney Resort is recycled into biofuel and other products that are used by local companies. Food scraps are recycled into compost, which is used locally as fertilizer. The Walt Disney Healthy Cleaning Policy has the goal of minimizing the environmental impact of its cleaning products. The majority of props, vases, and containers used by the Disney floral team for events are made from reusable glass and plastics. Finally, every day, 10 million gallons of wastewater are reclaimed and used in irrigation systems and other similar applications.
- ***Preserving the Wildlife:*** When building Walt Disney World Resort in Orlando, the company set aside more than one-third of the land for a wildlife conservation habitat. This habitat forms the basis for Disney's Animal Kingdom Theme Park, which is used to educate guests on the importance of conservation and preserving the future.

Ultimately, these and other initiatives are part of Walt Disney's long-term environmental goals of:

1. Zero waste.
2. Zero net direct greenhouse gas emissions from fuels.
3. Reduce indirect greenhouse gas emissions from electricity consumption.
4. Net positive impact on ecosystems.
5. Minimize water use.
6. Minimize product footprint.
7. Inform, empower, and activate positive action for the environment.

environmental social stewardship. Critical to the 3BL approach, as shown in Figure 16-1, are the intersections of the three sometimes competing objectives. In the next sections of this chapter we examine each of the three Ps and the potential trade-offs among them.

THE FIRST P—ENVIRONMENTAL SUSTAINABILITY

Environmental sustainability involves more than simply reducing air or water pollution. The United Nations Brundtland Commission defines **sustainability** as being able to meet "the needs of the present without compromising the ability of future generations to meet their own needs." With world population growth and increasing economic development, there is greater demand for all types of raw materials that are in short supply, including metals, petroleum, and natural gas. The more we use, the less there will be for future generations. Companies like Unilever, Dell, Steelcase, Phillips, Wal-Mart, Coca-Cola, Ford, Toyota, Disney (see Get Real box on this page), and the Inter-Continental Hotels

sustainability the ability to meet "the needs of the present without compromising the ability of future generations to meet their own needs."

student activity

Look up the listing of Global 100 most sustainable corporations in the world at www.global100.org. Review how the rankings were generated. Using Pareto analysis, determine in which geographic regions (Europe, United Kingdom, Africa, Middle East, Far East, Australia, South America, North America) most of the 100 firms could be found. Why do you think this is the case?

include environmental sustainability as a core aspect of strategic and operational planning.

The awareness of, and emphasis on, environmental sustainability has grown tremendously in recent years, due to several factors:

LO16-3 Explain the reasons why operations managers are increasingly focusing on the environmental impacts of their activities.

Customer Expectations: Customers (especially in economically developed markets) are now demanding products that are environmentally sustainable. Consider the following statistics:

- 54 percent of shoppers indicate that they consider elements of sustainability (sourcing, manufacturing, packaging, product use, and disposal) when they select products and stores.[2]
- 80 percent of consumers are likely to switch brands to ones that support a cause when the brands are equal in quality and price.[3]
- Approximately 75 percent of consumers say that they have bought products from a socially or environmentally responsible company, up from 47 percent a few years ago.[4]

The Economics of Environmental Sustainability: Instead of viewing environmental protection as a drag on business performance, managers are increasingly noting that environmental sustainability can lead to cost savings and other benefits. For example, Walmart, Ikea, Wawa, Google, and eBay are switching to solar power because it is renewable, and after the initial investment, the actual cost to produce electricity is inexpensive. Investments in commercial solar products are frequently

eBay's Solar Power System
Courtesy of SolarCity

[2] http://www.greenbiz.com/sites/default/files/document/US_CP_GMADeloitteGreenShopperStudy_2009.pdf (accessed July 11, 2012).
[3] http://www.coneinc.com/files/2010-Cone-Cause-Evolution-Study.pdf (accessed July 11, 2012).
[4] http://www.tillerllc.com/pdf/TillerGreenSurvey2009.pdf (accessed July 12, 2012).

seeing payback periods of between four and five years (which equates to an annual rate of return in excess of 20 percent).

Diminishing Natural Resources: Consumers, governments, and firms are becoming increasingly aware of our world's limited resources. Most people are aware that petroleum resources are finite. Some estimates indicate that, with no other changes, global petroleum resources will be exhausted by 2056.[5] The United Nations Environmental Program recently reported that, if nothing changes, the world would demand 140 billion tons of minerals, ores, fossil fuels, and biomass every year by 2050—amounts that far exceed what the earth can provide.[6] Producing your smartphone or LCD television may not be possible in the future unless something is done to preserve or replace scarce resources. Industrial materials such as platinum, indium, zinc, gallium, tantalum, and antium are important for these uses, and are expected to run out in the next 10 to 20 years. Further, as demand increases for nonrenewable materials, prices increase and become more volatile, making budgeting very difficult. For example, indium sold for about $60 per kilogram in January 2003; by August 2006, the price was over $1,000 per kilogram.

Water, the most basic of all resources, is also becoming scarce. While salt water is plentiful, there is only a limited amount of easily accessible fresh water, most of which is found in the Great Lakes in North America. Safe drinking water is becoming scarce, especially in developing countries.

Increased Business Demand for Scarce Resources: Further complicating matters is the increasing demand for resources from developing countries such as China, Vietnam, India, and various countries from Africa. This demand is not only for the resources needed to build products such as LCD televisions, but also for resources needed to build infrastructure such as roads, power generation, airports, and ports. For example, consider China's demand for steel. Over the past decade, China's average 15 percent annual growth in demand for steel means that China now accounts for over 40 percent of the global demand for steel.[7] Similar situations exist for concrete and the rare minerals.

New Initiatives/Programs: Programs and initiatives launched by governments, nongovernmental organizations (NGOs) such as the ISO, and professional societies are raising expectations on firms for environmental sustainability. Table 16-1 on the next page identifies some of these programs.

Global Climate Change: Finally, there is growing evidence that the world is experiencing global climate change, potentially caused by increased concentrations of carbon dioxide and other greenhouse gases produced by the burning of fossil fuel for heating, production, and transportation. The problem is worsened by deforestation, which reduces the earth's capacity to remove carbon from the atmosphere. Global climate change contributes to problems such as extreme weather (e.g., hot summers, droughts, violent storms, wildfires) and rising sea levels. Heat waves increase fatalities and illnesses. Rising sea levels may displace millions, and droughts can contribute to famines, especially in developing countries. These and other factors compel operations managers to take actions to become more environmentally responsible.

student activity

Examine one of the programs presented in Table 16-1, or find one of your own. What is the goal of the program? How will this program affect operations management and the supply chain? What are the advantages and shortcomings in the program? What did you learn?

[5] http://www.ncpa.org/pdfs/bg159.pdf (accessed July 11, 2012).

[6] C. Barnatt, "Resource Depletion," *ExplainingtheFuture.com* (February 18, 2012), www.explainingthefuture.com/resource_depletion.html (accessed July 9, 2012).

[7] L. Hook, "China's Steel Appetite Set to Wane," *Financial Times* (www.ft.com), http://www.ft.com/cms/s/0/2712469a-6377-11e1-9686-00144feabdc0.html (accessed July 12, 2012).

TABLE 16-1 Examples of Environmental Initiatives/Programs

Program/Initiative	*Source*	*Summary*
Kyoto Protocol	United Nations	Initially adopted on December 11, 1997, 37 countries committed to the reduction of four greenhouse gases. The accord introduced emissions trading, clean development mechanisms, and joint implementation to allow the countries to meet their limitations.
Responsible Care	Chemical industry	Global, voluntary initiative developed by the chemical industry (currently operating in 52 countries) to improve health, safety, and environmental effects.
Renewable Fuel Standard Program	EPA (USA)	Regulations designed to ensure that transportation fuel sold in the United States contains a minimum volume of renewable fuel.
Greenhouse Gas Reporting Program	EPA (USA)	Implemented in 2008, requires the mandatory reporting of greenhouse gases emitted by U.S. firms.
ISO 14000 (http://www.iso.org/iso/iso_14000_essentials)	ISO	A set of environmental management standards intended to help firms minimize their operations' impact on the environment.
Electronic Product Environmental Assessment Tool (EPEAT) (www.epeat.net)	Green Electronics Council	A method for evaluating the environmental impact of computers and other electronic equipment. Certifies that electronic products are recyclable and designed to maximize energy efficiency and minimize environmental harm. EPEAT rating is becoming a requirement for purchases by the U.S. government, state and city governments.
Cradle to Cradle Standard (www.mbdc.com/c2c/)	McDonough Braungart Design Chemistry	A set of standards intended to ensure that products are designed to make use of renewable resources and that the resulting products can be easily disassembled and the outputs converted back into inputs for future production (rather than being returned to the ground).
LEED Certification (Leadership in Energy and Environmental Design) (www.usgbc.org/LEED/)	U.S. Green Building Council (USGBC)	LEED is intended to provide building owners and operators a concise framework for identifying and implementing practical and measurable green building design, construction, operations, and maintenance solutions. Certification at three levels.

Implications for Operations Management: a Broader View of Waste

Chapter 8 describes how lean systems reduce wastes within the operating system. Environmental sustainability expands the concept of waste to include waste generated across a product's life cycle. For example, the waste created by the customer in using the product and the disposal waste produced at the end of the product's life are both considered in life cycle assessment (LCA).

Life cycle assessment is a tool that helps managers to assess the full impact of waste by quantifying its costs in five product stages: extraction, production, packaging/transportation, usage, and disposal.

life cycle assessment A tool for quantifying the various costs generated by waste in extraction, production, packaging/transportation, usage, and disposal.

- *Extraction* considers all the costs of getting the inputs that are used by the operations management system. Suppliers' harvesting, mining, or production processes may differ. For example, some processes may use more water or produce higher scrap levels. Prices paid do not necessarily reflect these differences because of differences in regulations, costs, and practices in different countries. The cost of inbound shipping of materials is also considered.
- *Production* considers the costs incurred by the firm that produces the finished good or service. These are the costs typically considered by most lean systems.
- *Packaging/transportation* includes wasted material and energy for packaging, which can sometimes be more damaging than the product itself (consider bottled water). Transportation can also contribute mightily to the overall waste picture in terms of energy consumption and CO_2 emissions.
- *Usage* consists of waste-related costs in use, including maintenance, repair, and operation (for example, CO_2 emissions). This element of waste is strongly influenced by the habits of the person using the product. For example, a person who performs regular maintenance on the product may generate a lower level of pollution compared to someone who does not.
- *Disposal and/or recycling* costs are incurred at the end of a product's life. These costs are difficult to estimate, for several reasons. First, disposal costs for a product sold today will occur in the future, sometimes in the distant future. Emerging technologies may radically change the limitations of recyclability today. Second, remanufacturing and recycling may make it difficult to determine when a product will finally have to be disposed of. Third, recycling often means *downcycling.* That is, recycling often results in lower-grade outputs—products that cannot be used in the same way that the original product was used. For example, recycled paper is usually not as bright as original paper; it is thus a lower grade of paper that can be used in fewer applications.

Life cycle assessment captures these various forms of waste using a common unit of measure. This unit can be monetary (dollars or euros), a measure of energy (barrels of oil or kilowatt-hours), or a simple rating of environmental impact. Gathering the data for such an analysis is not a trivial undertaking. However, products such as Herman Miller's Mirra chair (see Get Real box on the next page) are now being designed and built with the goal of minimizing life cycle costs.

When performing life cycle assessment, it is important to recognize that not all waste is equal. Every form of waste creates its own set of problems and issues. Wastes can be classified into five categories: (1) material choice (e.g., lead creates more environmental problems than steel), (2) energy usage, (3) solid residuals, (4) liquid residuals, and (5) gaseous residuals. Good materials choices use materials that are not toxic, are amply available, and can be recycled.

These five types of wastes can be assessed across the five life cycle stages to create a 5 × 5 *Environmentally Responsible Process/Material Matrix,* as shown in Figure 16-2. Ideally, a monetary cost of waste should be entered in each cell, but this is usually difficult to do. Alternatively, analysts can enter a value ranging from 0 (no impact, no effect—the

GET REAL

Herman Miller Designs a "Green" Chair

The Mirra chair is the result of a four-year design process by Herman Miller. From the outset, this chair was designed from the ground up to meet the Design for the Environment (DfE) criteria set down by Herman Miller. The chair is comfortable (it automatically shapes itself to every user), attractive, and easy to recycle (since it is designed using only a few components, each of which can be easily disassembled and recycled). The chair is also a sales hit, proving that you can be green (environmentally responsible) while earning green (money).

The Mirra Chair by Herman Miller

FIGURE 16-2
The Environmentally Responsible Process/Material Matrix

LO16-4 Evaluate products using life cycle waste composition assessment.

Life stage	*Material Choice*	*Energy Choice*	*Solid Residues*	*Liquid Residues*	*Gaseous Residues*
Resource Extraction					
Product Manufacture					
Product/ Packaging/ Transportation					
Product Use					
Reburbishment Recycling & Disposal					

desired state) to 4 (dangerous/extremely high environmental impact) into each cell, resulting in a total waste assessment score ranging from 0 to 100.

Using this approach, operations managers can quickly assess various production and material options and identify issues affecting environmental sustainability. In practice, the values are provided by users who draw on their experiences. In contrast, a full-blown LCA can be very expensive and time consuming because it requires data that most firms do not regularly collect.

carbon footprinting An analysis that evaluates environmental impact by calculating the greenhouse gas emissions caused directly and indirectly by a product.

A similar approach is **carbon footprinting**. Rather than creating a monetary value for environmental issues, the carbon footprint is the total set of GHG (greenhouse gas) emissions caused directly and indirectly by a product. This footprint can be evaluated across any of the five phases of the life cycle.

GET REAL

Paper or Plastic?

Many times we are asked, "paper or plastic?" when checking out at the grocery store. Which choice is more environmentally friendly? It turns out that answering this question for even a "simple" project such as grocery bags is not that simple after all. The following table summarizes some of the key findings of different life cycle assessments for these two options. Several studies indicate that plastic seems to be the overall better choice, because over its life cycle it consumes less energy, less fossil fuel, and less fresh water, and it produces less solid waste and lower greenhouse gas emissions. However, the *best* choice is to use neither type of bag, but instead to use reusable cloth bags or plastic crates. Unfortunately, many of us (at least in the United States) are not willing to give up the convenience of "disposable" bags.

Life Stage	Paper Bags	Plastic Bags
Extraction	Paper comes from trees, a renewable resource if obtained from sustainably managed forests.	Plastic bags come from polyethylene, a nonrenewable petroleum by-product.
Manufacturing	Paper bag production generates 70% more air and 50% more water pollution and consumes 20 times more fresh water.	It takes only one-fourth the energy to produce a plastic bag that it does to produce a paper bag.
Transportation	It takes seven trucks to transport the same number of bags that are in a single truck full of plastic bags	A plastic bag weighs about 10% of the weight of a paper bag, therefore requiring less energy to transport.
Usage	A paper bag can hold almost twice as many items as a plastic bag can, so fewer bags are needed.	Plastic bags usually cost one-third to one-fourth the cost of paper bags.
Disposal/Recycling	Paper bags are biodegradable, but few landfills allow the air and water to reach the product (due to potential air and groundwater pollution). About 10% of paper bags currently get recycled.	Plastic bags take less space in landfills, but stray bags are found almost everywhere. They especially pose threats to marine life. About 1% of plastic bags currently get recycled, even though recycling consumes less energy and produces about half the pollutants of paper bags.

Identifying and Eliminating Environmental Wastes

student activity

Did you know that there are numerous "calculators" for determining the carbon footprint? Go to the Internet and look up some of these calculators. A good starting point is http://www.carbonfootprint.com/calculator.aspx. Use this calculator to assess the impact of a flight, or your drive to the store (by car or motorcycle). Compare different methods of going to the store. What did you learn? Another calculator found at http://www.nature.org/greenliving/carboncalculator/index.htm allows you to estimate your carbon footprint from household, travel, eating, and recycling activities.

A guiding principle of environmental sustainability is that it is better to prevent the creation of waste than to minimize its effects. Waste is a symptom of deficiencies in product designs, operational processes, and packaging. Root causes must be identified and appropriate corrective actions introduced aimed at preventing waste. Chapter 3 describes a process for identifying and improving wasteful processes.

In many cases, organizations are unaware of how well or poorly they are doing in terms of environmental sustainability. The reason—their supporting cost accounting/information systems often do not record the needed data, such as energy consumption and waste disposal. These data are often hidden as they are incorporated into overhead costs. Along with direct costs, environmental sustainability typically affects indirect costs of storage, sorting, recording, information system management, and procedures for documenting, controlling, and dealing with environmental problems. Consequently, justifying sustainability improvement projects involves identifying, quantifying, and reporting these indirect costs. It is commonly believed that every dollar saved in direct sustainability costs creates many more dollars' worth of indirect savings.

ISO 14000—The Standard for Environmental Management Systems

ISO 14000 An international standard for environmental management.

environmental management system (EMS) The formal system responsible for the planning, documentation, and management of an organization's environmental program. It covers areas such as systems, software, and information databases.

As is the case for quality, there is an international standard for environment management: **ISO 14000**. Most firms are interested in ISO 14001:2004 and ISO 14004:2004, standards that deal with the **environmental management system (EMS)**. The EMS is responsible for:

- Identifying and controlling the environmental impact of a firm's activities, products, or services.
- Improving corporate environmental performance on a continuous basis.
- Implementing a systematic approach for setting environmental objectives and targets and for demonstrating that these targets have been achieved.

ISO 14001:2004 provides the requirements for an EMS, while ISO 14004:2004 gives general EMS guidelines. Being certified according to ISO 14001:2004 standards, while consistent with the goal of environmental sustainability, does not necessarily ensure sustainability performance. These standards simply ensure that the firm has a formal EMS—a necessary step toward improved environmental performance.

ISO 14000 standards are global in nature and significantly affect international trade. They lower trade barriers due to differences in environmental requirements. For more information on the overall ISO 14000 standards, see www.iso.org, the Web site for the International Organization for Standardization, the organization responsible for this certification standard.

Challenges of Being Environmentally Sustainable

In spite of its importance, it is not easy to be environmentally responsible. The trade-offs among choices are not always clear. For example, an "obvious" improvement in environmental sustainability might be to replace cardboard packing cases with returnable packaging. However, one must also consider the environmental impact of shipping empty containers back to the supplier. No matter how "green" you try to make a product, there will still be some form of environmental impact. Consider the following:

- PepsiCo undertook an initiative to ensure that Aquafina's bottles (even the caps and labels) are 100 percent recyclable, only to find that 80 percent of water bottles are not recycled.
- GE's new CFLs (compact fluorescent lights) use 75 percent less energy than a traditional incandescent light. However, CFL bulbs contain a hazardous substance, mercury, which poses a potential health concern if bulbs are broken or disposed of in traditional landfills. Is this health risk worth the energy savings?
- Patagonia, the outdoor-apparel company, decided to minimize the environmental impact of its fibers. It found that the most harmful fiber was cotton (not petroleum-based synthetics), because of the pesticides used. So it switched to organic cotton, only to find that to grow this type of cotton requires a great deal of water. A single pair of jeans, for example, requires 1,200 gallons of water.

Environmental sustainability requires managers to consider the complex interactions of product design and operations across the entire supply chain, and throughout a product's life cycle.

GET REAL

Starbucks and "Fairtrade"[8]

Fairtrade is an organized social movement that seeks to help producers in developing countries, thus making for better trading conditions and promoting sustainability. Through Fairtrade efforts, farmers are paid a price for their products that allows them to invest in better equipment, buy better food for their families, and send their children to school (rather than keeping them working on the farm to support the family). Many of the farmers affected grow commodity products such as coffee.

Starbucks Corporation is an international coffee company and coffeehouse chain. It is currently the world's largest coffeehouse company. In 2000, the company introduced a line of fair trade products. Since then, this practice has evolved into a corporate-wide system aimed at ethical sourcing. To this end, it has worked with Conservation International to develop coffee-buying guidelines, the ***Coffee and Farmer Equity (C.A.F.E.) Practices.*** This comprehensive set of guidelines focuses attention on four areas:

- Product quality
- Economic accountability
- Social responsibility (measures evaluated by third-party verifiers to ensure safe, fair, and humane working conditions and adequate living conditions; covers minimum wage, child labor, and forced labor requirements)
- Environmental leadership

In 2011, Starbucks bought over 428 million pounds of coffee, of which 367 million pounds were from C.A.F.E. Practices–approved suppliers. The company paid an average price of $2.38 per pound in 2011, up from $1.56 per pound in 2010. According to Conservation International, this premium has enabled farmers to keep their children in school and to preserve remaining forests on their land, while achieving higher performance. This program spans some 20 countries and affects over one million workers each year. It is affecting practices on 102,000 hectares each year (a hectare is about 2.47 acres). Starbucks has paid an additional $16 million in Fairtrade premiums to those producer organizations for social and economic investments at the community and organizational levels.

[8]http://www.starbucks.com/responsibility/sourcing/coffee (accessed July 20, 2012).

THE SECOND P—PEOPLE

LO16-5 Discuss the approaches used by operations managers to ensure social responsibility while improving performance sustainability.

The second element of the triple bottom line focuses attention on people, specifically human rights, health and safety, and quality of life in communities. Think of all the people groups that a typical business directly affects: (1) customers, (2) workers, (3) suppliers, and (4) investors. In addition, businesses can indirectly affect the larger community and society as a whole. Each of these stakeholder groups has its own needs and priorities (see Table 16-2).

As the examples in Table 16-2 illustrate, operations managers need to consider the needs and demands of many stakeholders when they make choices about sources, process designs, labor policies, and so on. Media stories often point out potential inequities, or even oppressive conditions that operations managers and their suppliers might create, either knowingly or unknowingly. For example, in recent years the media have brought attention to the exploitation of workers and small businesses in developing countries. As a result, more and more operations managers are participating in established **Fairtrade** practices. The Get Real box "Starbucks and 'Fairtrade'" shows how such practices affect the ways that Starbucks buys coffee.

Fairtrade An organized social movement that seeks to help producers in developing countries, thus making for better trading conditions and promoting sustainability.

The seven foundations of Unilever's new strategic initiative, as described at the start of this chapter, are interlinked with people. Unilever strives to improve the lives of its consumers through better nutrition, reduced waste, reduced greenhouse gases, access to fresh water, and better health and hygiene. Further, Unilever has developed a supplier code to require that its suppliers comply with all labor laws, do not use forced or child labor, and provide safe and healthy working conditions. Suppliers are required to apply this code with their own suppliers.

TABLE 16-2 People: Four Key Stakeholders and Their Expectations

Customers	Workers	Suppliers	Investors
Good "value" for their money Products that are safe Privacy and protection of personal information Honesty in marketing and sales communications Integrity in fulfilling contracts and obligations Quick response to questions System transparency	Fair labor practices and a "living wage" that affords a reasonable standard of living. Safe working and living environment (both for themselves and the community) Equal opportunities for advancement Support for social and economic developments (e.g., schools, arts, parks, charities)	Working with firms that share similar values Opportunities for supplier development and improvement Opportunities to grow—shared success Consistent application of rewards and punishments Receiving a "fair" payment for goods and services provided	Providing competitive returns on investments Having a sustainable business model so that investors can expect consistent returns over time Integrity in reporting operating and financial conditions Reduction of unreasonable risks and uncertainties (due to poor practices on the part of the firm and its operations management system)

student activity

Many companies are currently implementing versions of the triple bottom line (e.g., IKEA, Hewlett-Packard, GE, Citigroup, FedEx Kinko's, PepsiCo, Anheuser-Busch, Dow Chemical, Weyerhaeuser Company). Select two companies (do a search on the Internet). Review their triple bottom line reports. What did you learn? What new practices were introduced? How did the pursuit of the triple bottom line affect financial performance?

Unfortunately, the supply chains in some industries, including electronics, textiles, cocoa, and coffee, involve developing countries that are plagued by human rights and health and safety violations. Human rights issues include excessive overtime, low wages, unsafe working conditions, and even forced child labor. For example, in 2012, an audit supported by Nestlé found violations of its labor code of conduct, including the use of child labor by suppliers in the Ivory Coast, which is the world's largest producer of cocoa. Stating that eliminating child labor in its supply chain is its number one priority, Nestlé is collaborating with the Fair Labor Association to train and certify suppliers, increase monitoring, and work with the Ivory Coast's government.

Human rights and health and safety problems in the supply chain are complex challenges that are typically driven by underlying economic, social, and political issues. Companies try to combat these problems in a number of different ways. Most large companies have detailed codes of conduct for themselves and their direct suppliers. Many have extensive training programs for their own employees and their suppliers and use external agencies to regularly audit suppliers. Companies also work closely with nongovernmental organizations (NGOs) and industry associations to help address some of the broader economic, social, and political issues. Some companies such as Nike evaluate how their own business practices, such as short deadlines, poor forecasting, and last-minute changes, contribute to problems such as excessive overtime.

An important part of the people aspect of the triple bottom line is supporting the communities in which companies operate. By supporting the local community, companies contribute to the health and wellness of their employees as well as their quality of life. For example, Marathon Petroleum is a major supporter of United Way as a way to improve health and human services. Walmart provides volunteers and financial support to over

GET REAL

Zappos Culture Sows Spirit[9]

Zappos.com is considered one of the leading online success stories. It has developed a loyal following of customers by selling them something that many consider hard to sell online: shoes. Their Web site describes each shoe in great detail. Another important feature is their liberal return policy (you have one year in which to return the shoes, and Zappos pays shipping both ways).

Critical to Zappos's success is their highly regarded customer service group. An extremely high level of customer service is a direct result of the Zappos culture. All new corporate employees receive four weeks of customer loyalty training—answering phones in the call center—before starting their jobs. After training, they are offered $2,000 to leave the company—no questions asked. This "quit now" bonus is designed to ensure that employees stay at Zappos for the right reasons. About 97 percent decline the offer.

Zappos.com annually publishes a "Culture Book" in which employees describe what the company culture means to them. Among the company's 10 core values are: "Create fun and a little weirdness," "Be adventurous, creative and open-minded," and "Build a positive team and family spirit." CEO Tony Hsieh views company culture as the number one priority. A great culture translates into a great service, and great service is what Zappos is all about. Culture matters because it means attracting great people, motivating them to continue giving their best or retaining them, and giving customers an experience that brings them back to Zappos. So far, it is working.

[9]C. Gergen and G. Vanourek, "Zappos Culture Sows Spirit," *The Washington Times,* July 16, 2008, http://www.washingtontimes.com/news/2008/jul/16/zappos-culture-sows-spirit/print/, (accessed February 26, 2009).

100,000 community-based organizations and charities. Delta Airlines is a strong supporter of the arts and helps to fund museums, orchestras, and music festivals.

For the second P to be successfully addressed, people-focused initiatives must first be ingrained in the organization's corporate culture; they must be part of the widely accepted way of doing things within the company. Second, initiatives must recognize and adapt to differences in the ways that people in different countries deal with issues. Country cultures, norms, and values can vary drastically, leading to different expectations and requirements for social responsibility.

Organizational Culture

Organizations affect how their members see issues, deal with problems, and identify what is important. People are influenced by organizational goals, structure, training, coworkers' attitudes, successes and failures, and a host of other aspects of organizational life. Operational programs such as those we have discussed in this book can have large impacts on organizational culture, and a given set of goals may be more or less appropriate for different cultures. For example, the organizational culture that evolves over time in a lean system emphasizes waste and variance reduction, along with process standardization and discipline. Such an approach may seem stifling to employees who wish to be rewarded for radical innovations. Operational initiatives can greatly affect the culture and work life of employees. Operations managers must often address conflicts between changing organizational goals and existing cultural norms. In fact, preexisting cultural norms often form serious impediments to organizational change. This is why in environments of rapid change, operations managers have to be so attuned to the strengths and weaknesses of their organization's culture. These strengths and weaknesses are often difficult to identify. As one manager put it, "organizational culture is what the employees do when the boss is not around."

While culture can be difficult to change, it can also be a key source of competitive advantage. For example, consider the success of Apple. Many people believe that the reason that Apple has been successful is because it has developed a culture of innovation. Similarly, much of Zappos's success is attributed to its culture; see "Get Real: Zappos Culture Sows Spirit."

relationships

Organizational culture is an increasingly important issue as operations managers seek to integrate partners in the supply chain. Culture affects supply chain–related issues like trust and compliance. In general, the people in an organization work most comfortably with others whom they perceive to be like them. They tend to have less trust when dealing with people who are perceived to have different goals or motivations. For this reason, operations manager have to carefully consider differences in the organizational cultures of potential partners before they enter into long-term collaborative agreements.

Consider the failure of the Daimler-Benz/Chrysler merger. On paper, this should have worked. Daimler-Benz was strong in product areas where Chrysler was weak (luxury vehicles). Conversely, Chrysler was strong in areas where Daimler-Benz was weak (SUVs, minivans, low-end cars). Yet the merger failed at least in part because of a clash in cultures. Daimler-Benz had a formal, status-conscious, highly structured culture. Chrysler was highly informal and goal-oriented—anything that got the desired outcomes achieved was acceptable. Managers were not successful in meshing the two cultures. As a result, many of the best people within Chrysler left the company. They could not tolerate working in an environment where they were told that what they did in the past was no longer acceptable.

Organizational culture plays a critical role in achieving sustainability goals. People within the organization must embrace and support the organization's view of sustainability in order for goals to be met. This is not always easy. There is disagreement and controversy surrounding some sustainability issues (global warming, for example). Leadership plays an important role in defining the culture and related sustainability goals. For example, Herman Miller of Zeeland, Michigan (a furniture company; see earlier Get Real box) has had extensive success with sustainability. One of the founders of Herman Miller was a minister who believed strongly in corporate stewardship and responsibility. In large part, the company's commitment to sustainability stems from the values and corporate culture created by this founding leader.

National Culture

global

Throughout this book we have maintained that globalization is a primary change driver in operations management. Most supply chains are now global and involve interactions among multiple national cultures. Supply chains often source from suppliers and provide products and services to customers located all around the world. Therefore, it is important to recognize that people from different nations or regions often differ from each other in a number of important ways:

- Different ways of looking at things.
- Different ways of dressing.
- Different ways of expressing personality and what constitutes goodness or success.
- Different ways of interacting with each other.
- Different skills.

These differences in national culture can have major effects on operations management. Processes that work in one country may not necessarily work in another. For example, when designing supply chains for North America, managers typically assume that all the people involved can read and write. This assumption is not always valid in some parts of the world (read about dabbawallahs in the Get Real box on the next page). Thus, labor practices that are sustainable in one region might not be sustainable in another.

Culture also affects how people deal with problems. In an American/British/Canadian setting, problems are usually identified explicitly. In a Japanese setting, people are likely to deal with problems less directly. Dave Barry, a famous American humorist, describes a situation that he encountered on a trip to Japan. When he requested that he be booked on a flight between two cities, the clerk asked if he would rather take the train. Barry rejected this option; he wanted to fly. The clerk then pointed out that there were numerous options

GET REAL

Dabbawallahs—Managing the Lunchtime Food Supply Chain in Bombay, India

Five thousand people, 150,000 lunch boxes per day, almost zero errors—that is the bottom line for Bombay's dabbawallas. In the large cities of India, business managers want hot, homemade lunches, not cafeteria-bought meals. Given the crowded conditions of Bombay, this would seem to be a difficult, if not impossible, task—except for dabbawallahs. Dabbawallahs (translated, the term means "box people") are a group of individuals responsible for picking up the meals from the homes, bringing them to the offices, picking up the dishes and then returning them home. They must do this every day; they must do it fast; and, they must do it without error (for a mistake means that someone goes hungry). What makes this supply chain and service unique is that nearly all dabbawallas are illiterate. To provide this service, they have developed a system that relies on simple color-coding and a few other codes readily understood by the people involved. The results are amazing; only one delivery in a million goes wrong. That is good performance anywhere.

http://trak.in/tags/business/2009/02/08/mumbai-dabbawallahs-inspire-their-us-counterparts/.

available for going between the two cities. Dave insisted that he wanted to fly. To this, the clerk replied that it would be difficult to accommodate this request. After a great deal of discussion (that greatly frustrated both parties), the clerk finally stated that there were no direct flights between the two specific cities (a source of embarrassment for the clerk). The problem was that each person was operating in a manner appropriate to their culture, but their notions of what was appropriate did not mesh. To the Japanese clerk, it was impolite to tell Dave Barry that there was no direct flight. To Dave Barry, it was important to know whether or not he could fly between the two cities.

The challenge for operations managers is to understand and anticipate differences in national cultures that have the potential to make operational processes less effective and to lower the quality of work life for employees. Conversely, it is also important for managers to build upon the strengths of different cultures as they relate to the demands of different operational processes. The meshing of cultures continues to be a very important issue as supply chains become more and more interconnected and global.

To successfully bring about changes related to sustainability, operations managers must be prepared to invest not only in new systems, processes, tools, and technology, but also in changing culture when possible, and adapting to it when necessary.

THE THIRD P—PROFIT AND LONG-TERM COMPETITIVE ADVANTAGE

LO16-6 Understand the challenges operations managers face as they seek to develop and maintain a sustainable competitive advantage.

The third P, profit, is the one that operations managers and their businesses have typically prioritized in the past, at least in "for-profit" organizations. Advocates of sustainability sometimes argue for less emphasis on profit. However, it is important to recognize that profit (or funding for nonprofit organizations) is equally important for the long-term sustainability of an enterprise, and maintaining profits can be difficult in rapidly changing conditions. Ultimately, an organization's business model must change if the firm is to survive and to maintain its competitive advantage in the marketplace. If a firm is able to successfully change its business model over time, we can say that it has developed a *sustainable competitive advantage.* Developing and maintaining such an advantage is not easy. One indication comes from the *Fortune 500.* Every year since 1955, *Fortune* magazine (http://money.cnn.com/magazines/fortune/) has published a list of the largest 500 publicly traded companies. Consider the following statistics:

- It took 20 years to replace one-third of the Fortune 500 companies listed in 1960; starting in 1998, it only took four years to replace one-third of the Fortune 500.[10]
- According to Peter Senge, MIT professor, the average life of a Fortune 500 firm is only 30 years.[11]
- Jim Collins, the author of *Built to Last,* noted that only 71 companies of the original 1955 Fortune 500 still exist.[12]

In preparing for the future, operations managers have to anticipate and manage for changes in the elements of their business models. Recall from Chapter 2 that these elements include the critical customers, the value proposition, and the organization's operational capabilities. Over time, an organization might begin to serve new critical customers (due to the introduction of new products and services, or movement into new geographic markets, for example). Alternatively, the expectations of an organization's existing critical customers might change, for a number of reasons:

- Changes in Economic Conditions: During the recession that began in 2008, many firms found that cost had become an order winner (where previously it was an order qualifier).
- Changes in Competitors' Actions: Suppose that a competitor offers a new feature to your customer, and now that customer expects you to do the same.
- Changes in Income Levels: As income levels increase, customers can afford more, and they expect more (this is common in rapidly developing countries).
- Changes in Educational Levels: As customers' educations increase, they are exposed to, and may develop tastes for, new and different things and experiences.

All value propositions are fundamentally dynamic. They must be revised in response to customer changes, competitor moves, and economic shifts. Such changes often call for supporting changes in operational capabilities. As noted in Chapter 2, a firm's capabilities stem from its resources, assets, and processes, and its investments in new management practices (e.g., the next "lean" systems), new supply chain relationships, and new technological advances. Technology especially is important because it enables the firm to develop and implement new business models that would not have been possible otherwise.

Today, environmental and social concerns are increasingly important drivers of new operational practices and technologies. These investments can affect a firm's profit in two fundamental ways. First, a firm's efforts to be more environmentally and socially sustainable can improve its value proposition and associated sales revenues, because customers place importance on these aspects and are willing to pay more for them. Think of paying a higher price for "organic" foods, for example. Second, more sustainable practices can either lower or raise the costs of providing a good or service. For example, minimizing transportation of products might simultaneously lower both cost and carbon emissions—a "win-win." In other cases, however, a firm might have to choose between a high-cost, highly sustainable option and lower cost, less sustainable one. The value proposition, and its effect on profit, should not get lost in a firm's efforts to become more sustainable.

---

[10]Commission of the European Communities, *Green Paper: Entrepreneurship in Europe* 9 (2003), *at* http://eur-lex.europa.eu/LexUriServ/site/en/com/2003/com2003_0027en01.pdf.

[11]Toby Elwin, "The Cost of Culture, a 50% Turnover of the Fortune 500," 2010, *at* http://www.tobyelwin.com/the-cost-of-culture-a-50-turnover-of-the-fortune-500/.

[12]Ibid.

MEASURING AND REPORTING SUSTAINABILITY THROUGH THE TRIPLE BOTTOM LINE

LO16-2 Describe the "triple bottom line," and how this view of sustainability affects operational decisions across the supply chain.

For an organization to pursue its mission sustainably, it needs to measure its progress in each of the three Ps. Comprehensive measures of sustainability are being developed. For example, Walmart is developing a sustainability index that consumers can use to assess products and the firms that produce them. As a first step, it has surveyed its first-tier suppliers on energy and climate, material efficiency, nature and resources, and people and community. Walmart is now working with a consortium to develop a database of information on product life cycles. The ultimate goal is to develop a simple, easy-to-understand tool for customers.

More broadly, many organizations have launched initiatives seeking to make the sustainability performance of businesses and products more visible, either to better inform potential investors, or to put pressure on firms to raise their levels of sustainability. For example, the Dow Jones Sustainability Index evaluates and rates applying firms by administering a survey questionnaire and by scanning media reports. Figure 16-3 shows the breakdown of criteria assessed by the Dow Jones index. Economic criteria include issues such as the degree to which the firm protects the privacy and security of its customers (e.g., against fraud or identity theft). Social issues include how well the firm provides access to its products for underprivileged customers (e.g., in developing countries). A unique aspect of the Dow Jones Sustainability Index is that many of the criteria are tailored to specific industry contexts.

To provide a sense of the breadth of issues addressed under sustainability, Table 16-3 shows the criteria used by three other organizations to evaluate sustainability performance.

LO16-6 Understand the challenges operations managers face as they seek to develop and maintain a sustainable competitive advantage.

- The Global Reporting Initiative (GRI) is a nonprofit organization founded in the United States in 1997 by the Coalition of Environmentally Responsible Economies (CERES) and the United Nations Environment Program (UNEP). The GRI produces a sustainability reporting framework to enable greater organizational transparency, with the goal of developing a standard practice for reporting which allows stakeholders to compare sustainability-related data.
- The Global 100 Most Sustainable Companies is an annual project initiated by Corporate Knights Inc., a company that promotes clean capitalism. Inclusion in the Global 100 is limited to a select group of the top 100 large-cap companies in the world.

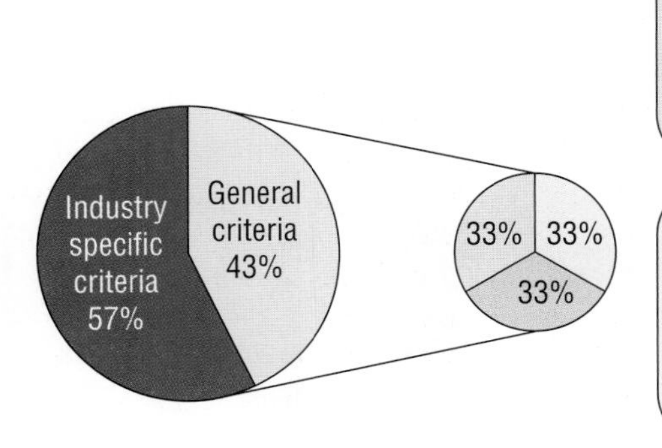

FIGURE 16-3 Criteria for the Dow Jones Sustainability Index.

Source: http://www.sustainability-indexes.com/sustainability-assessment/corporate-sustainability-assessment.jsp

TABLE 16-3 Examples of Sustainability Criteria Used by Rating Organizations

Global Reporting Initiative	Global 100 Sustainable Companies	Ethical Consumer
Economic • Market presence • Indirect economic impacts	• % Taxes paid	
Environmental • Materials • Energy • Water • Biodiversity • Emissions, effluents, and waste • Products and services • Compliance • Transport	• Energy productivity • Greenhouse gas (GHG) productivity • Water productivity • Waste productivity • Innovation capacity	Environment • Environmental reporting • Nuclear power • Climate change • Pollution & toxics • Habitats & resources
Labor Practices and Decent Work • Employment • Labor/management relations • Occupational health and safety • Training and education • Diversity and equal opportunity • Equal remuneration for women and men Human Rights • Investment and procurement practices • Nondiscrimination • Freedom of association and collective bargaining • Child labor • Forced and compulsory labor • Security practices • Indigenous rights • Assessment • Remediation	• Safety productivity • Employee turnover • Leadership diversity • Clean capitalism paylink • CEO to average employee pay	People • Human rights • Workers' rights • Supply chain management • Irresponsible marketing • Arms & military supply Animals • Animal testing • Factory farming • Animal rights & cruelty
Society • Local communities • Public policy • Compliance Product Responsibility • Customer health and safety • Product and service labeling • Marketing communications • Customer privacy • Compliance		Politics • Antisocial Finance • Boycott calls • Genetic engineering • Political activity Sustainability • Company ethos • Product sustainability (organic, fair trade, energy efficient, vegan & vegetarian products)
https://www.globalreporting.org/	http://www.global100.org/	http://www.ethicalconsumer.org/

- The Ethical Consumer is but one example of many watchdog groups who seek to make global businesses more sustainable through consumer pressure. Such organizations research and report on what they deem to be good and bad company behaviors.

Operations managers need to be aware of these kinds of independent assessments. They can have a large impact on a business's financial success as a growing number of investors and consumers pay attention to them. In many cases, groups create "scorecards," "buyers' guides," or "stamps of approval" in order to signal sustainability practices to consumers, and they can organize boycotts and other grassroots movements. Such programs are increasing the visibility and quantification of issues associated with sustainability. In doing so, they are forcing organizations not only to measure and report different aspects of sustainability, but also to take actions aimed at improving their performance.

CHAPTER SUMMARY

Operations management must be dynamic in dealing with a changing world. Further, to be sustainable, operations management must address issues that go beyond standard accounting and financial objectives. These are the primary messages of this chapter:

1. Both today and in the increasingly competitive environment of the future, operations managers must be concerned with sustainability. We defined sustainability in terms of the triple bottom line: planet, people, and profit.
2. Environmental sustainability, the first P, is becoming increasingly critical as resources become more scarce, population and demand for these resources are increasing, and products and processes are creating environmental problems (such as global warming). Tools like life cycle assessment and standards such as ISO 14001 can help guide operations managers' decisions.
3. The people aspect of sustainability focuses on issues such as human rights, health and safety, and quality of life in the community. Each organization should consider at least four key stakeholders: customers, workers, suppliers, and investors.
4. In addressing the people aspect of sustainability, operations managers need to stay mindful of the need to manage and adapt to differences in both corporate and national cultures.
5. In order to sustain profits, the third P, operations managers need to continually improve or change the firm's business model, ensuring that it continues to offer critical customers a value proposition that is both attractive and supportable by the organization's capabilities. Maintaining the fit between customers, value propositions, and capabilities is difficult over time, because these elements are always changing.
6. Organizations and agencies are growing in their influence and power in making the sustainability practices of a given firm visible to the public. Operations managers need to be cognizant of the criteria that these organizations are using, and the ways in which their businesses are being perceived.

KEY TERMS

carbon footprinting 558
environmental management system 560
Fairtrade 561
ISO 14000 560
life cycle assessment 557
sustainability 553
triple bottom line 552

DISCUSSION QUESTIONS

1. Review the new strategic direction for Unilever, as presented at the beginning of this chapter. What are the economic rationales for these seven key strategic imperatives? What are the risks? To what extent are these initiatives driven by concerns of environmental as compared to business sustainability?
2. Why does the concept of "cradle to grave" no longer make business and environmental sense?
3. What would the business model look like if we were to compete primarily on environmental sustainability?
4. In a recent study by MIT, it was found that the Toyota Prius, a hybrid, was less environmentally responsible than a Hummer SUV. How could this be? You might want to consider using the AT&T Environmental Assessment Matrix in addressing this question.
5. What are some operations/supply chain management strategies that can be used to deal with the challenges of diminishing natural resources?
6. Why is it that some managers are not willing to more aggressively pursue environmental sustainability even when presented with compelling reasons for its need? (*Hint:* Think about issues such as level of resources available, risk of failure, and how the managers are measured and rewarded.)
7. The triple bottom line can be viewed as a three-legged stool in that each element must be present or, if one or more elements are removed, then the entire structure collapses. To what extent do you agree with this approach? Why is it important that each element be present?
8. Do you think companies should invest in community-based programs such as support for the arts? Why or why not?
9. One common approach that companies use to protect human rights is a supplier code of conduct. How can you increase the effectiveness of a code of conduct?
10. The American South and the American Midwest experience natural disasters on a regular basis (hurricanes such Hurricane Katrina in the American South and tornados in the American Midwest). Whenever such a disaster takes place, organizations such as the American Red Cross must respond. Part of this response is to set up a supply chain structure. Identify and discuss several of the factors that can influence the design and deployment of such a supply chain. How can technology be used to improve and enhance the operation of this supply chain?

CASE

EuroConstellation Electronics

"Welcome everyone. Robert, please turn on the television." Vice President of Global Procurement, Stefan Schrettle, started the meeting with these words. The components sourcing and procurement team had been hurriedly assembled at Schrettle's request. Robert Schmidt walked to the control center of the rather cramped conference room and clicked the icons needed to project the BBC World News onto the screen at the front of the room. The face of a well-known anchorperson for the BBC filled the screen. While he talked, pictures of factory workers appeared.

The BBC had been repeatedly airing a special report focused on the working conditions at a large electronics supplier located in Mongolia, MongTronics. MongTronics had rapidly become one of the leading suppliers of electronic toys, subassemblies, and components to consumer goods manufacturers around the world, including EuroConstellation Electronics, the company that Robert worked for. The BBC was reporting that a worker at the MongTronics facility had committed suicide a day earlier by throwing himself off the roof of the seven-story dormitory where workers were housed. Alarmingly, this was the ninth suicide at the factory in the past 12 months. A BBC correspondent was raising questions about the working conditions at MongTronics. Though the facilities were toured regularly by MongTronics' major customers, little was actually known about the policies and work practices employed at the company. The correspondent was interviewing the general manager at the MongTronics plant. He had a concerned look on his face as he explained that worker safety and quality of life were important priorities for the company. The camera quickly cut to video of workers installing large nets around the dormitory walls to catch workers who might contemplate similar forms of suicide in the future.

After a few more minutes, Schrettle walked over to the control panel, turned off the projector, and raised the lights. He stated, "This is a serious situation, and we need to decide what, if anything, we can and should do about it. I'm putting Robert in charge of a task force to develop immediate responses to this situation, as well as a longer-term sourcing strategy for the parts we buy at MongTronics." As Mr. Schrettle spoke, the hairs on the back of Robert's neck stood up. He knew that this was an important assignment, and his first real opportunity to demonstrate his leadership skills. Since joining the company almost a year earlier, Robert had mostly been learning the ropes, as he participated in some sourcing trips to China and other locations in Eastern Asia.

Later that afternoon, Robert considered the facts that he had about the business that EuroConstellation did with MongTronics. EuroConstellation designed and assembled many different kinds of remote-controlled toys and equipment, including small robots, toy vehicles, and also monitoring and control systems for industrial equipment. Numbers from their ERP system showed that they had spent 25 million euros on purchases from MongTronics in the last year. MongTronics was their largest supplier, and this amount accounted for almost 30 percent of EuroConstellation's total materials purchasing spend. The items that EuroConstellation purchased included completely finished and packaged electronic toys (such as radio-controlled airplanes and cars), as well as a large number of subassemblies and components that were assembled into finished products by EuroConstellation's own factories. Low labor costs were the most attractive part of doing business with MongTronics. On average, Robert figured that his company was able to purchase items at about half the unit cost that they would pay from suppliers in Europe and the United States. Even after taking transportation and inventory costs into account, he figured that the Mongolian source still offered about a 30 percent cost advantage. On the other hand, labor costs were rising in the country; some analysts estimated that labor costs there would match those of low-cost Eastern European locations within five years.

As he dug into Internet and newspaper articles about MongTronics and the surrounding areas of Mongolia, Robert noted that most of the articles were quite positive regarding the economic benefits that the company had brought to a previously depressed region of the country. Before the growth of MongTronics, the population in the area had very low standards of living, at least from a Western perspective. Most people lived by subsistence farming or by raising horses. Many still lived as nomads in temporary shelters. Few individuals were educated beyond very basic levels. MongTronics had provided relatively high paying and stable employment for the people. In addition, it had built living quarters, a hospital, and schools for employees and their children.

Representatives from EuroConstellation had toured the MongTronics facility as recently as six months earlier. As Robert read the trip report written by the visiting team he noted that facilities were clean, processes seemed to be disciplined, and the workers seemed to be fairly satisfied with their conditions. In fact, the team had noted that the factory was a fine example of a lean operation.

Several questions floated around in Robert's head. How bad could this BBC report be for EuroConstellation? Was there a need for them to respond? How would continuing to do business with MongTronics affect them financially? Were there ethical issues to be considered too?

Questions

1. What are the possible ramifications of the BBC story for EuroConstellation's business prospects?
2. What is the socially responsible thing to do regarding future business with MongTronics?
3. Outline an action plan that Robert can give to his task force. What further information do they need? What actions, if any, should be taken immediately?

CASE

The Problem with Plastics

"Lucy, I thought that you told me and the planning committee that this move to recycle storage plastics was going to save us money. But, look here. I just got the bill for last month's disposal of our plastic. We wound up paying $3,000, rather than being paid for the value of the recycled material. This is the third month in a row that this has happened. I want to know what is going on and I want to know by Friday. If you can't solve the problem, we are going to simply throw out the plastic with the garbage, the way we used to do. It was less hassle for us and we would recover the space now being used for the recycling bins. Again, I want recommendations by Friday."

With those words, Fred Morgenstern, plant manager for the Novi plant of Voiture Automotive Supplies, turned around and walked out the door. Lucy Po, the environmental, health, and safety (EHS) manager for this facility, sat in her office considering what had just happened. What a way to start the week. It was Monday and she knew that she had five days to get to the heart of the problem. It was her initial analysis that had led to the decision to sell the various plastics to a recycler. It should have been a winner, but she must have missed something. In her mind, she reviewed the chain of events that led up the meeting with Fred this morning.

The Novi plant, located in a suburb of Detroit, used over 40,000 square meters of 40 different plastics for storage. These various plastics were used to cover the parts during storage and in transportation. Once used, they were collected and thrown out. With landfills in Michigan becoming scarcer (especially in the Detroit area), landfill costs were increasing. Lucy could have recommended that the Novi plant truck the plastics out to Mount Pleasant, where landfill space was still available. But that seemed to attack the symptom of the problem, not the root cause.

As she looked around for options, she was approached by R-CYCL, a new start-up recently founded by a husband and wife team. The purpose of the start-up was to provide employment for chronically unemployed people in Detroit. Their proposal was simple but attractive. R-CYCL would pick up the plastic and pay the Novi plant a recovery price, provided that the plastics were properly sorted. If the plastics were not properly sorted, then the personnel at R-CYCL would sort the plastic and charge the plant for the labor required. This charge would be deducted from any recovery prices.

There was the problem. The Novi plant used 40 different types of plastic. It seemed that every time a new part was designed, the engineers would specify a new storage plastic. Whenever a new plastic covering was introduced, a number of things happened: a new item master had to be developed and entered into the system; inventory storage locations had to be identified (the Novi facility generally used a fixed inventory location system); and operators had to be trained on the material. Because of the high usage of plastic, the purchasing department had been aggressive in looking for the lowest-priced suppliers. They were currently buying much of the required materials from low-cost Chinese suppliers. Lucy was told that purchasing was generally happy with these suppliers, though on-time delivery was an issue (causing an increase in safety stock).

When it came time to recycle the plastic, the processes in place clearly described what was supposed to happen. The operator was to take the plastic to the recycling storage area, where 40 large bins were located next to the operation and parts storage areas. The operator was to review the code and then to put the plastic into the appropriate bin. Once a week, R-CYCL would empty the bins and recycle the material. Lucy remembered how plant management had almost rejected the recycling plan because of the space requirements to locate 40 storage bins. Facility management had argued that this space would have been better used for production.

That was the theory. The practice was different. Though each plastic item was stamped with a code, the material differences between the plastics were slight. Sometimes the codes got covered by grease or paint. Because the operators often could not read the codes (or they did not care), they often stuffed the plastic into the first bin available. Operators could be "written up" if they persistently failed to put plastics in the wrong bin, but it was difficult to know when, or how often, this happened. When bins were nearly full, items often fell out onto the floor. This created problems for housekeeping, and plastic on the floor had contributed to several workplace injuries (thus increasing worker's compensation charges). In two cases the injuries resulted in fines being assessed against the plant. Lucy could see why Fred wanted to return to the old system. She had to recommend a better, more sustainable, approach. She also knew that the Novi plant was R-CYCL's biggest customer; if the plant stopped recycling plastic it would effectively put this start-up out of business.

The Proposal: After reviewing the facts, Lucy spoke to the engineers to get an idea of what types of plastic film they could consider at least minimally acceptable. With this information, she worked with purchasing to ask several suppliers for proposed solutions within 48 hours. Only one supplier responded—FilmTech.

FilmTech was located in Lapeer, Michigan (about 50 miles from the Novi plant). The company proposed to replace all 40 plastics with one plastic that could meet all of the technical requirements. Lucy wondered whether the engineers at the plant would accept the one substitute plastic material. An even larger problem with the proposal was that the new film, while recyclable, was higher quality and cost almost twice as much as the average material provided by the Chinese suppliers. Lucy figured that such a cost differential might make the FilmTech proposal a loser right away.

Questions

1. Review FilmTech's proposal from a triple bottom line perspective. What opportunities and costs are exposed that Lucy may have overlooked? How would these hidden costs affect the economic analysis being developed by Lucy?
2. What else can Lucy do to reduce the cost of buying and using FilmTech's plastic?
3. What else can Lucy do make these operations truly sustainable?

CASE

The HyperCar

From his solar-powered digs down the road from the ski slopes of Aspen, Amory Lovins is gearing up to take on the giants of the global auto industry. Mr. Lovins has a degree from Oxford University, a MacArthur Foundation "genius" grant, and a reputation as an environmental consultant that fetches him as much as $20,000 a day. At the age of 53, he has written or co-written 27 books and cofounded an environmental think tank that has spun off three for-profit businesses. But his pet project these days involves a new level of risk and ambition: Hypercar Inc., a fledging car company with a plan to build a superefficient sport-utility vehicle that he is convinced will revolutionize the industry. All he needs is about a quarter of a billion dollars to get the thing out of the lab and onto the street.

His dream is an earth-friendly SUV that would get the equivalent of 99 MPG of gas and emit nothing but drinkable water. It would be powered not by an internal-combustion engine, but by a fuel cell that cleanly converts hydrogen into electricity.

But that would be only the start for the Hypercar. Mr. Lovins's machine would be made not out of steel, but of lightweight carbon fiber—the kind used to make fighter planes, tennis rackets and skis. And it would be driven by two joysticks instead of a steering wheel—one result of its sophisticated electronic brain, which would do everything from linking the car to online entertainment programs to suggesting when it's time to take the car into the shop.

At least that's the theory. No one has yet figured out how to build a carbon-fiber car economically. No one has put a fleet of fuel-cell–powered cars on the road. No one has built a production car steered by joysticks. And none of the established industry players is willing to fork over the piles of money the Hypercar needs for a real rollout. None of which seems to bother Mr. Lovins in the least.

BP Amoco PLC has invested about $500,000 in Hypercar. Its hope is that Mr. Lovins's project will spur the world's established auto makers to move boldly to produce cleaner vehicles. BP sees the radical Hypercar as a way to apply "a bit of competitive pressure" to prod the big auto makers to produce even more efficient designs, says Chris Mottershead, BP's London-based technology vice president for lower carbon growth.

Mr. Lovins hatched the idea for a superefficient automobile about a decade ago, and spent the next several years trying to convince auto makers that they could make money by building it. General Motors Corp., for one, didn't bite. "I have a lot of strange friends, and Amory is on the outer limit," says Donald Runkle, former head of GM's advanced-technology labs. He invited Mr. Lovins to talk to his engineers, but GM concluded that building the kind of car Mr. Lovins envisioned didn't make much business sense. "Those puppies cost a lot of dough," explains Mr. Runkle, now an executive vice president of Delphi Automotive Systems Corp., the big auto supplier.

On a recent morning, Mr. Lovins stood in a conference room at the Mirage hotel and casino in Las Vegas. He had flown in to give a slideshow about the Hypercar at a conference dealing with how the Internet will affect the auto industry. More empty seats than people greeted his presentation. But afterward, he thought he had hit the jackpot when he got a few minutes to make his pitch to a software executive sporting a green golf sweater and very deep corporate pockets.

The executive was Barry McNealy, brother of Sun Microsystems Inc. Chairman Scott McNealy. Sun is working with some of the world's biggest auto makers in a race to design software that will link cars to the Internet, and Barry McNealy, who is in charge of Sun's dealings with its automotive customers, had convened an annual meeting of his staff at the conference where Mr. Lovins had just spoken. He tried to convince Mr. McNealy that the Hypercar would be the perfect test vehicle for Sun's software. That way, he told Mr. McNealy, "you get there first."

Mr. McNealy was polite. "I love what you guys are doing," he told Mr. Lovins. He added that his brother might be interested in hearing more about the Hypercar if Mr. Lovins pitched it as a possible office on wheels, an idea Sun believes could catch on with consumers. But Mr. McNealy stopped far short of writing a check. "Your ability to get to market remains to be seen," he noted, and in the auto industry, "the barriers to entry for a niche player are very high."

That week, Mr. Crumm, the CEO for the Hypercar and retired GM executive, received three representatives of Terra Trust, an environmentally focused Swiss investment fund. Terra had pledged to invest $1.5 million of the $5 million Hypercar has raised so far. But Terra has come up $100,000 short because of managerial problems that the representatives blame on their predecessors.

Over coffee and cookies, Mr. Crumm and his staff gave the Terra people an overview of their Hypercar plans. The group cut to the chase. "You can have all these fancy plans, but you could be nowhere near assembly," said Urs Lustenberger, a young lawyer who serves on Terra's new management team.

He was particularly impressed by the Hypercar model's high-tech tires, which are designed both to increase fuel economy by reducing rolling resistance and to run safely for short distances when flat. Like almost all components on the Hypercar except its carbon-fiber body, the tires would be made by an outside supplier. The idea is that by depending heavily on suppliers, Hypercar won't have to do as much manufacturing itself.

The Hypercar staff was itching to raise about $60 million that they figure they need to build 20 or so test Hypercars that actually run. They need those test cars before they can move to full-scale production, which itself could cost around another $140 million, the company estimates. But the Terra representatives apologized that their fund doesn't have the kind of money Hypercar needs.

The week before Christmas, the Hypercar team convened a three-day summit in Basalt. Because of the problems with raising money, some of the young staffers suggested scaling back the company's do-or-die production goal. Messrs. Lovins and Crumm agreed that the company will start trying to license its technology to other auto makers in two years, regardless of whether it's ever able to build a fleet of Hypercars. Mr. Crumm had been "pushing for the brass ring," he acknowledged a few days later. But the company found that to raise the funds needed, it must offer a short-term way for investors to reap a profit. "There are some investors who want to harvest the technology and unload," Mr. Crumm says.

It is now three years later and you have been approached by Amory Lovins for advice (address your report to him). As you prepare your recommendations, assume that the Hypercar is technically feasible (that is, it can and will work within the next two years). You should also assume that the purchase price for this car would be within $2000 of a comparable, conventional car.

Questions

1. What is the overall business feasibility of the Hypercar (use any models and frameworks that are appropriate)?
2. To what extent are the conditions "right" for the successful introduction and launch of this car?
3. What are the major obstacles to the successful introduction and launch of this new approach to designing and building cars?
4. What should Lovins do next with the Hypercar concept?

Source: Adapted from "One Quest to Build a Truly 'Clean' Car Has Gathered Steam," by Jeffrey Ball, Staff Reporter of *The Wall Street Journal.*

SELECTED READINGS & INTERNET SITES

"Nestlé Sets Out Actions to Address Child Labour in Response to Fair Labour Association Report on the Company's Cocoa Supply Chain." June 29, 2012, http://www.nestle.com/Media/NewsAndFeatures/Pages/fla-report-cocoa.aspx.

http://www.delta.com/about_delta/global_good/arts_culture/index.jsp

http://www.marathonpetroleum.com/Corporate_Citizenship/Philanthropy/

http://www.walmartstores.com/communitygiving/

http://www.walmartstores.com/Sustainability/9292.aspx

Elkington, J. "Towards the Sustainable Corporation: Win-Win-Win Business Strategies for Sustainable Development." *California Management Review* 36, no. 2 (1994), pp. 90–100.

Hayes, R.; G. Pisano;, D. Upton;, and S. Wheelwright. *Operations, Strategy, and Technology: Pursuing the Competitive Advantage.* Danvers, MA: John Wiley and Sons, 2005.

Keegan, P.; J. Dawsey; and B. Feldman. "The Trouble with Green Product Ratings." *Fortune* 164, no. 2 (2011), pp. 130–34.

Lee, H. L. "The Triple-A Supply Chain." *Harvard Business Review* 82, no. 10 (2004.), pp. 102–12.

McDonough, W., and M. Braungart. *Cradle to Cradle: Remaking the Way We Make Things.* New York: North Point Press, 2002.

Murrary, S. "Textiles Industry: How to Be the Solution, Not the Problem." *The Financial Times,* June 19, 2012. http://www.ft.com/intl/cms/s/0/d609cf9e-a434-11e1-84b1-00144feabdc0.html#axzz20dJYCDo3.

Schein, E. *Organizational Culture and Leadership.* Fort Worth, TX: Harcourt College Publishers, 1993.

Appendix A

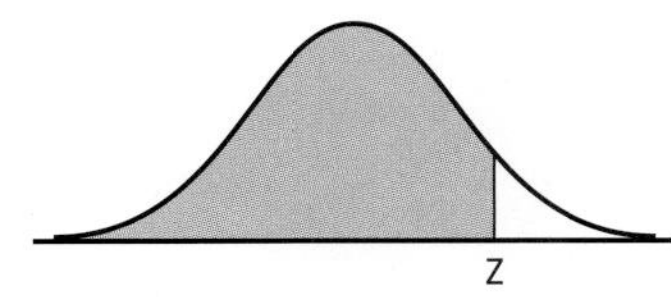

Table of Cumulative Probability of the Normal Distribution (one-tail)

Z	0.00	0.01	0.02	0.03	0.04	0.05	0.06	0.07	0.08	0.09
0.0	0.5000	0.5040	0.5080	0.5120	0.5160	0.5199	0.5239	0.5279	0.5319	0.5359
0.1	0.5398	0.5438	0.5478	0.5517	0.5557	0.5596	0.5636	0.5675	0.5714	0.5753
0.2	0.5793	0.5832	0.5871	0.5910	0.5948	0.5987	0.6026	0.6064	0.6103	0.6141
0.3	0.6179	0.6217	0.6255	0.6293	0.6331	0.6368	0.6406	0.6443	0.6480	0.6517
0.4	0.6554	0.6591	0.6628	0.6664	0.6700	0.6736	0.6772	0.6808	0.6844	0.6879
0.5	0.6915	0.6950	0.6985	0.7019	0.7054	0.7088	0.7123	0.7157	0.7190	0.7224
0.6	0.7257	0.7291	0.7324	0.7357	0.7389	0.7422	0.7454	0.7486	0.7517	0.7549
0.7	0.7580	0.7611	0.7642	0.7673	0.7704	0.7734	0.7764	0.7794	0.7823	0.7852
0.8	0.7881	0.7910	0.7939	0.7967	0.7995	0.8023	0.8051	0.8078	0.8106	0.8133
0.9	0.8159	0.8186	0.8212	0.8238	0.8264	0.8289	0.8315	0.8340	0.8365	0.8389
1.0	0.8413	0.8438	0.8461	0.8485	0.8508	0.8531	0.8554	0.8577	0.8599	0.8621
1.1	0.8643	0.8665	0.8686	0.8708	0.8729	0.8749	0.8770	0.8790	0.8810	0.8830
1.2	0.8849	0.8869	0.8888	0.8907	0.8925	0.8944	0.8962	0.8980	0.8997	0.9015
1.3	0.9032	0.9049	0.9066	0.9082	0.9099	0.9115	0.9131	0.9147	0.9162	0.9177
1.4	0.9192	0.9207	0.9222	0.9236	0.9251	0.9265	0.9279	0.9292	0.9306	0.9319
1.5	0.9332	0.9345	0.9357	0.9370	0.9382	0.9394	0.9406	0.9418	0.9429	0.9441
1.6	0.9452	0.9463	0.9474	0.9484	0.9495	0.9505	0.9515	0.9525	0.9535	0.9545
1.7	0.9554	0.9564	0.9573	0.9582	0.9591	0.9599	0.9608	0.9616	0.9625	0.9633
1.8	0.9641	0.9649	0.9656	0.9664	0.9671	0.9678	0.9686	0.9693	0.9699	0.9706
1.9	0.9713	0.9719	0.9726	0.9732	0.9738	0.9744	0.9750	0.9756	0.9761	0.9767
2.0	0.9772	0.9778	0.9783	0.9788	0.9793	0.9798	0.9803	0.9808	0.9812	0.9817
2.1	0.9821	0.9826	0.9830	0.9834	0.9838	0.9842	0.9846	0.9850	0.9854	0.9857
2.2	0.9861	0.9864	0.9868	0.9871	0.9875	0.9878	0.9881	0.9884	0.9887	0.9890
2.3	0.9893	0.9896	0.9898	0.9901	0.9904	0.9906	0.9909	0.9911	0.9913	0.9916
2.4	0.9918	0.9920	0.9922	0.9925	0.9927	0.9929	0.9931	0.9932	0.9934	0.9936
2.5	0.9938	0.9940	0.9941	0.9943	0.9945	0.9946	0.9948	0.9949	0.9951	0.9952
2.6	0.9953	0.9955	0.9956	0.9957	0.9959	0.9960	0.9961	0.9962	0.9963	0.9964
2.7	0.9965	0.9966	0.9967	0.9968	0.9969	0.9970	0.9971	0.9972	0.9973	0.9974
2.8	0.9974	0.9975	0.9976	0.9977	0.9977	0.9978	0.9979	0.9979	0.9980	0.9981
2.9	0.9981	0.9982	0.9982	0.9983	0.9984	0.9984	0.9985	0.9985	0.9986	0.9986
3.0	0.9987	0.9987	0.9987	0.9988	0.9988	0.9989	0.9989	0.9989	0.9990	0.9990

B Appendix

ANSWERS TO SELECTED PROBLEMS

Chapter 2

1. a. 16.67%.
   b. 2.09 times.
   c. 34.78%.
   d. $23,000,000.

Chapter 3

7. a. 70 minutes.
   b. The desired waiting time is 30 minutes; yet, the actual expected waiting time is 70 minutes, which is greater than the desired 30 minutes. To bring the actual and promised waiting times into agreement, we can do the following:
      - Reduce the processing time for jobs from 6 to less than 2.6 minutes.
      - Reduce either of the coefficients of variation.
      - Reduce the utilization from 70 to 50 percent by increasing the staffing levels in the health center.

9. a. 2.86, rounded to 3.
   b. 42.
   c. 70.
   d. If we were to set the resources to the levels indicated in the preceding calculations, then we should not have any bottlenecks. However, in reviewing the numbers, where the potential bottleneck emerges can be identified based on how sensitive the calculations are to violations in the assumptions. With that perspective, we can see if we were to have 3 cash registers, we are assuming that each order will have 4 people on the order. If this assumption is violated (e.g., we have a number of checks where there are less than 4 people per check), then this becomes the bottleneck.

11. a. 32 jobs per day.
    b. 10 days.
    c. 6.25 days.
    d. Process A (less labor).
    e. Process B (15 minutes per job compared to 24 minutes per job under Process A).

13. a. If we have an inventory of $200 and daily sales of $400, then the flow rate of 1 day could not be supported.
    b. To keep the flow times constant, we have to increase the inventory.

Chapter 3S

3. a.

Process Flow Chart

Page ____ of ____

Overall Description of Process Charted:

Date Charted: ____________________ Charted by: ______________________________

Check appropriate box: Current Process: (x) Proposed Process: ( )

Dist FT Meters	Time (avg.)	Symbol	Pers Invol.	Value Code V/W/N/?[1]	Description of Activity (indicate outcome)
		O ➡ □ D ∇		?	Transport in the raw materials
		O ⇒ □ D ▼		N	Store the raw materials
		O ⇒ ■ D ∇		?	Inspect the material
		O ⇒ □ D ▼		N	Put the raw materials in storage
		O ➡ □ D ∇		W	Move the materials to the area where mixed
	60 min	● ⇒ □ D ∇		V	Mix the items, place in pans
50 yds.		O ➡ □ D ∇			Move to shipping area
		O ⇒ □ D ∇			Put into inventory
		● ⇒ □ D ∇		V	Order, rearrange the number of bagels, match to an order
		O ➡ □ D ∇			Move to trucks
		O ⇒ □ ◗ ∇			Wait to be loaded into trucks
	20 min	● ⇒ □ D ∇			Place into trucks
	40 min	O ➡ □ D ∇			Transport (while allowing bagels to rise)
		O ⇒ □ ◗ ∇			Wait to be unloaded
		● ⇒ □ D ∇			Unload trucks
		O ➡ □ D ∇			Move to work areas
	40 min	● ⇒ □ D ∇		V	Mix, cook
		O ➡ □ D ∇			Move to cooling area
		● ⇒ □ D ∇		N	Allow bagels to cool
		O ➡ □ D ∇			Move to retail area displays
		O ⇒ □ D ▼		V	Sit in displays and wait to be sold
		6 8 1 2 4			

b. Value-adding activities are indicated in the preceding chart.

[1] The value code indicates the extent to which the activity is value-adding (V), waste-creating (W), not value-adding but necessary (N), or unknown (?).

Chapter 5

1. a. 50 seconds.
   b. 82.8%.
   c. 72 units per hour.
   d. 45 seconds per unit.
   e. The time at workstation 4 needs to be reduced by 5 seconds so that it does not exceed the TAKT time of 45 seconds.
3. a.

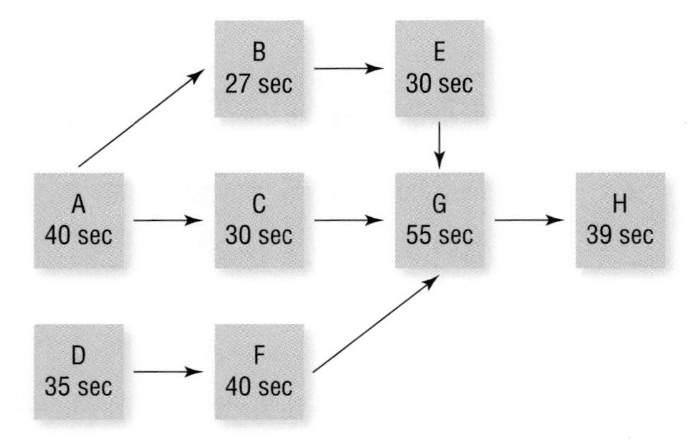

   b. 96 seconds per unit.
   c. 3.08, round up to 4 workstations.
   d.

Workstation	Tasks in Order	Workstation Time (Seconds)	Idle Time (Seconds)
1	A, D	75	21
2	F, C	70	26
3	B, E	57	39
4	G, H	94	2

   e. 77.1%.
9. V = 2,667 claims.
   Use the newer, more automated process because the total cost will be lower because the volume of 3,500 claims per year exceeds the indifference point.

Chapter 6S

1.

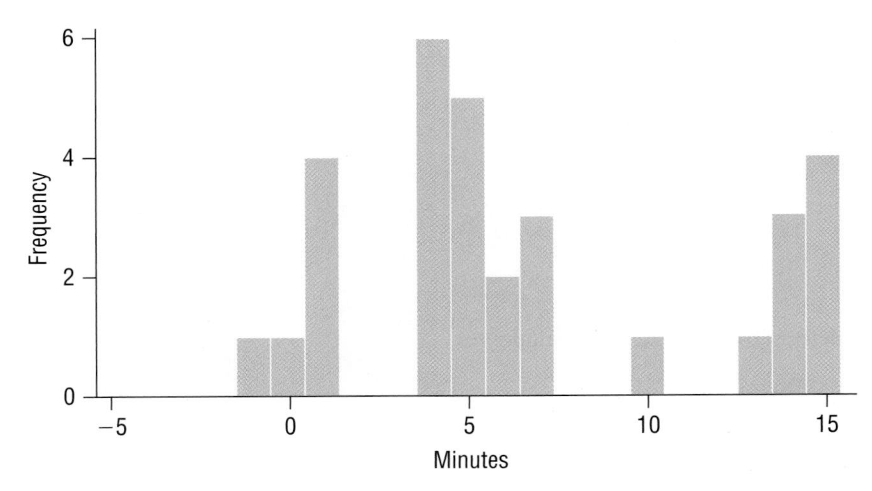

2. Histogram

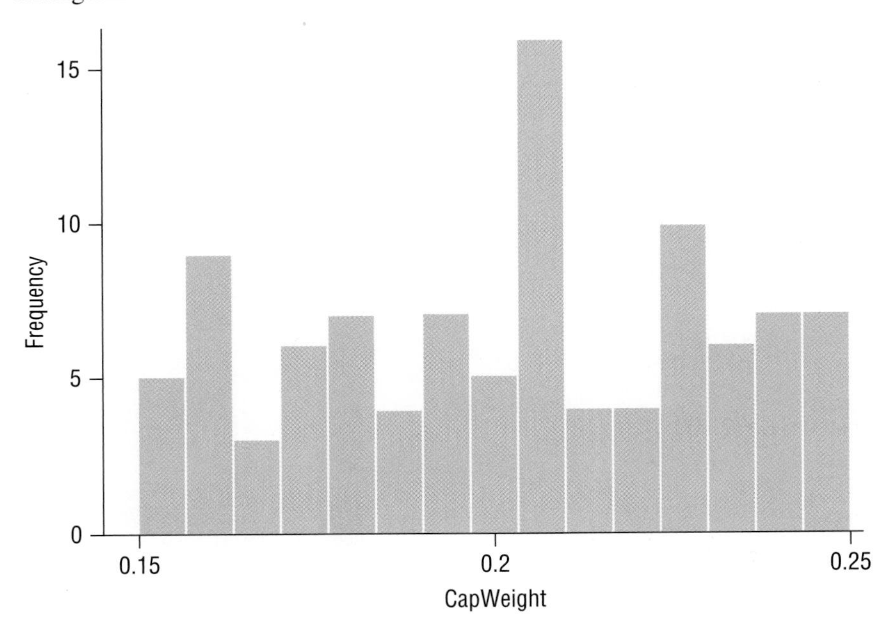

3. C_p = S/P = 1/.6 = 1.67
   C_{pk} = 1.64

13.

Data Points	*x*-bar Chart	*R*-bar Chart
Central line	12.94	1.35
Lower control limit (LCL)	12.14 − .58*1.35 = 11.36	0
Upper control limit (UCL)	12.14 + .58*1.35 = 12.92	2.12*1.35 = 2.86

14. For this table, we would construct a Pareto chart with the following information:

Reject Cause	Number
Contamination	15
Oxide defect	9
Misc	3
Corrosion	2
Metallization	2
Doping	1
Silicon defect	1

Focus on contamination and oxide defect. Tools to use here include:

- Cause-and-effect analysis.
- Checksheets.

15. Number of defects decreased from 33 to 19.
Significant decrease in oxide defects (from 9 → 1).
Significant decrease in contamination (from 15 → 8).
Increases in silicon defects.

Chapter 7

1. Inventory turnover rate: 7 times.
Inventory carrying cost: $150,000.

3. Item 1 = $607,500.
Item 2 = $540,000.
Item 3 = $81,900.
Item 4 = $333,000.
Item 5 = $9,900.
Total annual inventory carrying cost = $1,572,300.

6. a. EOQ = 1,789 cases.
Average inventory = 894.5 cases.
Inventory turnover = 223.6 times.
b. EOQ at $18 = 1,886 cases.
However, Foods Galore must order 10,000 cases to receive this price. Therefore, the calculated EOQ for the $18 price is not relevant.
TAC of ordering at the $20 price = $4,008,944.27.
TAC of ordering at the $18 price = $3,623,300.00.
Foods Galore should order 10,000 cases at a time because they would save $385,644.27.
c. Standard deviation of demand during lead time = 1,211.94 or 1,212 cases.
5% risk of stockout equals 1.65 deviations of safety stock = 2,000 cases.
Inventory carrying cost = $9,000.
1% risk of stockout = 2,824 cases.
Inventory carrying cost = $12,708.

8. Production order quantity 73.03 = 74 units.
Producing 74 units in a production run at a rate of 16 per day requires 74/16 = 4.625 days.

10. Standard deviation of demand during lead time = 204.27 = 205 units.
    SS = 339 units.
    EOQ = 707.11 = 708 units.
    TAC of ordering 708 units = $628,535.54.
    Average cycle stock = 354 units.
    Average inventory = 693 units.

Chapter 9

1. Unit fill rate = 95%.
   Line fill rate = 90%.
   Order fill rate = 80%.

3. 62.2%.

5. Unit fill rate = 96%.
   Line fill rate = 97.6%.
   Order fill rate = 96.6%.

Chapter 10

1. Supplier A's score is 2.7, Supplier B's is 3.15, Supplier C's 3.2. Judgment should be used to decide between Supplier B and Supplier C.
3. WebTex score is 3.25, CoolWeb is 2.6, Dazzling Designs is 4.05, and Major Marketing is 3.7. Dazzling Designs has the highest score and may be the best supplier to select.

Chapter 11

1. a. $99.66
   b. The 2-day shipment total cost = $109.86. The 2-day shipment is more expensive than the 5-day shipment. If the manager chose this option, the company would lose $10.20.

5. Air = $910.96
   Ground = $1,432.88
   Other considerations involved besides cost are the availability of these modes of transportation, customer desire for rapid delivery, and their dependability. If the customer wants the diamonds delivered as soon as possible and to ensure their safety, air is probably the best option. Although there are chances of delays, air transportation will probably deliver the diamonds more quickly with less handling and chances of damaging these expensive items.

8. Single shipments cost = $1,440.
   Consolidated shipment cost = $1,420.
   The consolidated shipment offer is the better choice. The company would save $20 by combining all 10 shipments into one.

10. X* = 47.647
    Y* = 32.647

Chapter 12

1. The weight put on one time period older than the most recent period is .24.
   Two periods older 0.096.

3. Forecast error = 3.
   F_{t+1} = 28.5, or 29 rounded up.

5. a.

Week	Demand	2-Week	Error	Absolute	4-week	Error	Absolute	6-week	Error	Absolute
1	232									
2	263									
3	271	247.5	23.5	23.5						
4	248	267	−19	19						
5	235	259.5	−24.5	24.5	253.5	−18.5	18.5			
6	261	241.5	19.5	19.5	254.3	6.8	6.8			
7	207	248	−41	41	253.8	−46.8	46.8	251.7	−44.7	44.7
8	243	234	9	9	237.8	5.3	5.3	247.5	−4.5	4.5
9	237	225	12	12	236.5	0.5	0.5	244.2	−7.2	7.2
10	293	240	53	53	237.0	56.0	56.0	238.5	54.5	54.5
11	243	265	−22	22	245.0	−2.0	2.0	246.0	−3.0	3.0
12	260	268	−8	8	254.0	6.0	6.0	247.3	12.7	12.7
13	253	251.5	1.5	1.5	258.3	−5.3	5.3	247.2	5.8	5.8
14	270	256.5	13.5	13.5	262.3	7.8	7.8	254.8	15.2	15.2
15	230	261.5	−31.5	31.5	256.5	−26.5	26.5	259.3	−29.3	29.3
16	253	250	3	3	253.3	−0.3	0.3	258.2	−5.2	5.2
17	238	241.5	−3.5	3.5	251.5	−13.5	13.5	251.5	−13.5	13.5
18	272	245.5	26.5	26.5	247.8	24.3	24.3	250.7	21.3	21.3
19	222	255	−33	33	248.3	−26.3	26.3	252.7	−30.7	30.7
20	243	247	−4	4	246.3	−3.3	3.3	247.5	−4.5	4.5
21	289	232.5	56.5	56.5	243.8	45.3	45.3	243.0	46.0	46.0
22	238	266	−28	28	256.5	−18.5	18.5	252.8	−14.8	14.8
23	262	263.5	−1.5	1.5	248.0	14.0	14.0	250.3	11.7	11.7
24	234	250	−16	16	258.0	−24.0	24.0	254.3	−20.3	20.3
			−14.0	20.5		−19.0	17.5		−10.5	19.2
			MFE	MAD		MFE	MAD		MFE	MAD

The four-week moving average has the lowest MAD. It also has the highest level of bias, in that the forecast tends to overestimate the demand. In this situation, it would be better to overforecast than to underforecast.

b. The alpha of 0.25 results in the lowest MFE value of 76.5. Although the MAD of 18 is not the lowest, it is very close to the lowest value. Thus, 0.25 is the best choice for the alpha value.

13. $FIT_7 = 69.3$.

15. $b = 7.8$, $a = 14.3$.

17. a. Sales (1000s) = 1.182 (PMI) + 71.99, $R^2 = 0.65$.
    b. Sales (1000s) = 1.73 (PMI) + 49.65, $R^2 = 0.91$.
    c. 133.

Chapter 13

1. Total level plan cost = \$271,400.
   Total chase plan cost (adjust workforce) = \$257,400.
   Total overtime plan cost = \$288,480.
   Total subcontract cost = \$260,640.
   Total hybrid cost = \$269,640.

3. Total cost = \$24,400,000.

5. a. 350 units per month.
   b. The maximum end-of-period inventory experienced would be 300 units.
      Total cost = \$539,000.
   c. Total cost = \$534,000.

7. Total level plan cost = \$29,610,000.
   Total case with overtime cost = \$30,500,000.
   Total Chase (Hiring/firing) Cost = \$28,960,000

Chapter 14

1. Es are components in Bs and Ds. Start with the Bs. 20 As × 2 Bs for each A = 40 Bs. 40 Bs × 4 Es for each B = 160 Es. Then determine the Es needed for the Ds. 20 As × 2 Ds for each A = 40 Ds. 40 Ds × 2 Es for each D = 80 Es. The total number of Es = 160 + 80 = 240.

   Cs are used directly to make As and also are used to make Ds. 20 As × 1 C for each A = 20 Cs. 20 As × 2 Ds for each A = 40 Ds. 40 Ds × 1 C for each D = 40 Cs. The total number of Cs = 20 + 40 = 60.

4. Fs are used in component Ds and component Cs. 15 As × 1 B for each A = 15 Bs. 15 Bs × 2 Ds for each B = 30 Ds. 30 Ds × 4 Fs for each D = 120 Fs. 15 As × 4 Cs for each A = 60 Cs. 60 Cs × 1 F for each C = 60 Fs. 60Cs × 3 Ds for each C = 180 Ds. 180 Ds × 4 Fs for each D = 720 Fs. Total Fs = 120 + 60 + 720 = 900 Fs.

   If part D is purchased, the number of levels in the BOM will be reduced from four levels to three levels. The components that are used to make Ds (E and F) will not be shown in the BOM.

   If D is purchased, C is the only parent of F in the BOM. 15 As × 4 Cs for each A = 60 Cs. 60 Cs × 1 F for each C = 60 Fs. Only 60 Fs will be needed. The other Fs will be purchased and used by the supplier who provides component D.

10.

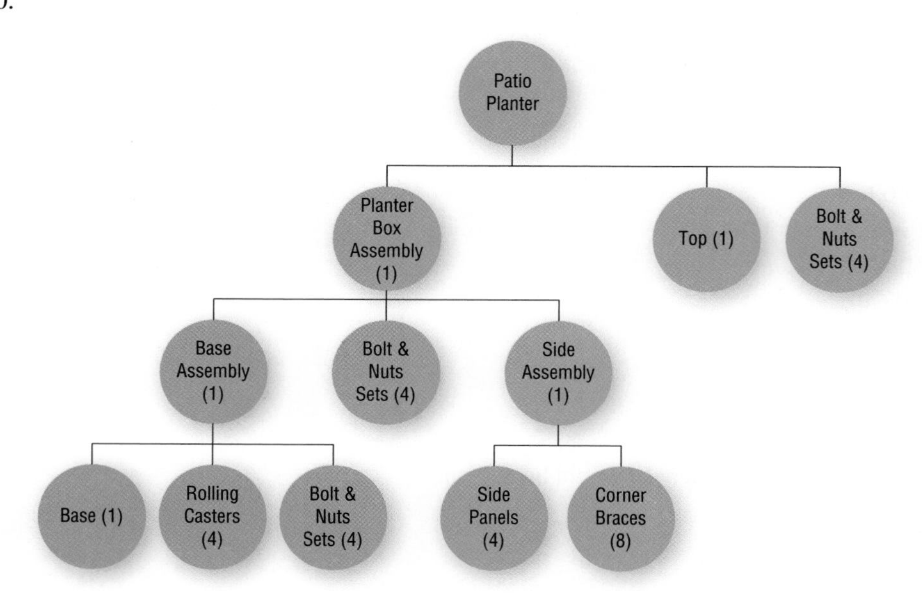

The total number of bolt and nuts sets = 32 + 32 + 32 = 96 sets.

11.

MRP Record Lead time = 2 weeks On hand = 0 Safety stock = 0 Order quantity: L4L	Week 1	Week 2	Week 3	Week 4	Week 5	Week 6	Week 7	Week 8
Part Name: Bicycle frame								
Gross requirements	70	50	80	80	70	60	80	80
Scheduled receipts	70	50						
Available inventory								
Net requirements			80	80	70	60	80	80
Planned order receipts			80	80	70	60	80	80
Planned order releases	80	80	70	60	80	80		

MRP Record Lead time = 2 weeks On hand = 0 Safety stock = 0 Order quantity: FOQ = 100	Part Name: Bicycle frame Week 1	Week 2	Week 3	Week 4	Week 5	Week 6	Week 7	Week 8
Gross requirements	70	50	80	80	70	60	80	80
Scheduled receipts	100	100						
Available inventory	30	80		20	50	90	10	30
Net requirements				80	50	10		70
Planned order receipts				100	100	100		100
Planned order releases		100	100	100		100		

Compared to the FOQ strategy, the L4L strategy orders more often (six times compared to four times) but has no inventory costs. The FOQ strategy has inventory costs. The L4L also provides a truer picture of actual demand to the supplier.

17.

Processing time = 9 minutes	Part Name: Computer keyboard Week 1	Week 2	Week 3	Week 4	Week 5	Week 6	Week 7	Week 8
Planned order releases	1,000	1,200	900	1,300	1,400	1,000	800	1,100
Processing load (hours)	150.0	180.0	135.0	195.0	210.0	150.0	120.0	165.0
Available capacity (hours)	200	200	200	200	200	200	200	200

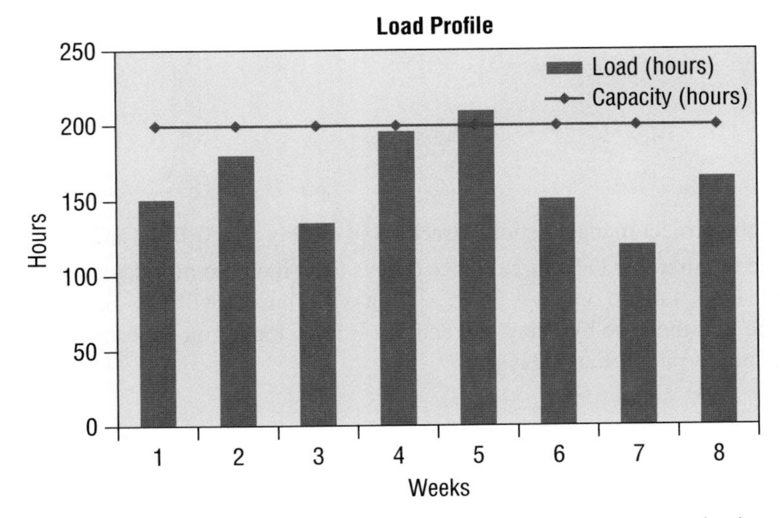

The load exceeds capacity in week 5, and there are significant levels of excess capacity in weeks 1, 3, 6, and 7. Perhaps product can be made in week 3 and held in inventory for week 5.

Chapter 15

6. a.

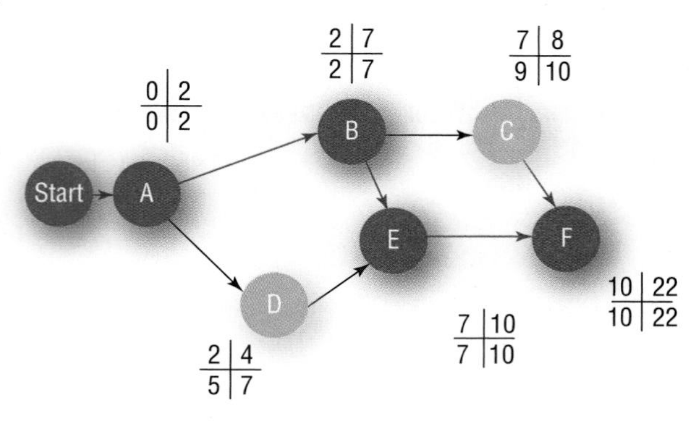

b. The critical path is A, B, E, F

Task	Immediate Predecessors	Earliest Start (ES)	Earliest Completion (EC) = ES + task duration
A	None	0	2
B	A	2	7
C	B	7	8
D	A	2	4
E	B, D	7	10
F	C, E	10	22

Task	Immediate Successors	Latest completion	Latest Start (LS) = LC − task duration	Slack = LS − ES
F	None	22	10	10−10 = 0
E	F	10	7	7−7 = 0
D	E	7	5	5−2 = 3
C	None	10	9	9−8 = 1
B	E	7	2	2−2 = 0
A	B, D	2	0	0−0 = 0

c. The activities that the project manager should track most closely are A, B, E, and F. They are on the critical path.

d. Increasing the time required for D from 2 days to 6 days is an increase of 4 days. Activity D currently has 3 days of slack [LC − EC (7 − 4 days) or LS − ES (5 − 2 days)]. Thus, D will now be on the critical path and the overall project time will increase by 1 day and activity B is no longer on the critical path. The ES and LS time for activity E becomes 8 rather than 7 days.

8. The critical path tasks are C, F, H, I, K.

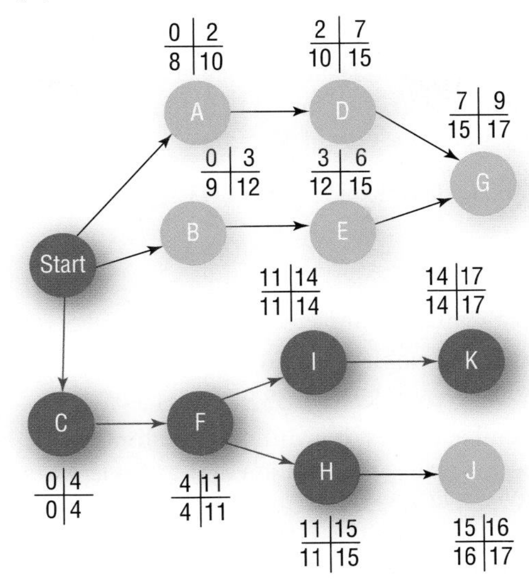

Task	Immediate Predecessors	Earliest Start (ES)	Earliest Completion (EC) = ES + task duration
A	None	0	2
B	None	0	3
C	None	0	4
D	A	2	7
E	B	3	6
F	C	4	11
G	D, E	7	9
H	F	11	15
I	F	11	14
J	H	15	16
K	I	14	17

Task	Immediate Successors	Latest Completion (LC)	Latest Start (LS) = LC − task duration	Slack = LS − ES
K	None	17	14	14−14 = 0
J	None	17	16	16−15 = 1
I	K	14	11	11−11 = 0
H	J	15	11	11−11 = 0
G	None	17	15	15−7 = 8
F	H, I	11	4	4−4 = 0
E	G	15	12	12−3 = 9
D	G	15	10	10−2 = 8
C	F	4	0	0−0 = 0
B	E	12	9	9−0 = 9
A	D	10	8	8−0 = 8

Chapter 15S

3. The project must be crashed by an additional two days. To do this, you must crash Prepare Documentation by 2 days at a cost of $400/day and Populate System Data by 1 day at a cost of $700. Thus, the total cost of crashing the project by 7 days is $4,600, which is more than the $4,000 bonus. The project could be shortened to 6 days by crashing Prepare Documentation by 1 day at a cost of $3,500.

5. The probability that the project will take less than 32 days is 53%, so the probability that the project will take more than 32 days is 47%.

7. a. 35 weeks.
   b. The likelihood that the critical path will be completed in 37 weeks is 75%.
   c. The likelihood that the project will be completed in 36 weeks is 63%.
   d. The likelihood that the project will be completed in 33 weeks is 37%.
   e. Because the two paths share several activities, it is difficult to estimate the likelihood that both paths will complete the project on time. However, because the duration of the "Code A" task is much shorter than the combined duration of tasks "Code B" and "Code C," we can be fairly sure that "Code A" will always be completed before both "Code B and "Code C" are completed. Using the expected durations, "Code A" has 6.66 days of slack. Therefore, we can be confident that the expected critical path will always dictate the actual length of the project, and we can be assured of the correctness of our estimates of project completion in parts a-d above that are based on the critical path alone.

Photo Credits

Chapter 1

Page 3: © Paul Faith/PA Wire URN: 8924566 (Press Association via AP Images).
Page 5: © AP Photo/Frank Franklin II.
Page 8: © Gary Conner/Getty Images.
Page 10: Roman Glass Factory (gouache on paper), Beraldi, Severino (b. 1930) / Private Collection / © Look and Learn/The Bridgeman Art Library International.
Page 14: © PhotoLink/Getty Images.

Chapter 2

Page 25: © AP Photo/Mel Evans.
Page 30: © Roberts Publishing Services.
Page 31: © Richard Hamilton Smith/Corbis.
Page 34: © Antoine Antonio/Bloomberg via Getty Images.
Page 35: © Shawn Thew/epa/Corbis.
Page 36: © Kyodo/Landov.

Chapter 3

Page 57: Photo courtesy of the authors.
Page 61: © AP Photo/Denver Post, Cyrus McCrimmon.
Page 63: © AP Photo/Barry Sweet.
Page 73 (left): © Buena Vista Pictures/Photofest.
Page 73 (right): © Jim Sugar/Corbis.
Page 76: © AP Photo/The Indianapolis Star, Matt Detrich.

Chapter 3 Supplement

Page 93: © SIU/Visuals Unlimited.

Chapter 4

Page 110: Photo courtesy of the authors.
Page 116: © PRNewsFoto/Crest Whitestrips.
Page 119: © Roberts Publishing Services.
Page 129: Exhibit created by RPS, © Roberts Publishing Services. Canon Cameras: © 2009 Canon U.S.A.
Page 132: © AP Photo/TSMC.
Page 133: © BMW of North America, LLC.

Chapter 5

Page 141: © Jose M. Osorio KRT/Newscom.
Page 146: © PRNewsFoto/Mars Direct Inc.
Page 150: © AP Photo/Steve Helber.
Page 151: © Ralph Orlowski/Getty Images.
Page 157 (top left): © AP Photo/Ted S. Warren.
Page 157 (top right): © AP Photo/Marcus R. Donner.
Page 157 (bottom right): © Iain Masterton/Alamy.

Chapter 6

Page 173: © AP Photo/Yonhap, Lee Sang-hyun.
Page 180: Image from Automation.com website. © www.
Page 190: © Stockbyte/Punchstock.
Page 191: © AP Photo/Jim Mone.

Chapter 7

Page 239: © Brand X Pictures/Punchstock.
Page 243: © Richard T Norwitz/Corbis.
Page 247: © AP Photo/Candice Towell.
Page 254: © AP Photo/Dusan Vranic.
Page 261: © AP Photo/Mark Lennihan.
Page 265: © AP Photo/Scott Sady.
Page 267: Courtesy of HowStuffWorks.com.
Page 268: © Scott Olson/Getty Images.
Page 271: © Stryker 1998-2010.

Chapter 8

Page 287: © David Joel/Stone/Getty Images.
Page 288 (top left): © Steven Chernin/Getty Images.
Page 288 (top right): © Koichi Kamoshida/ Getty Images.
Page 288 (bottom left): © Roslan Rahman/ AFP/Getty Images.
Page 288 (bottom right): © AP Photo/Joseph Kaczmarek.
Page 289: © Associated Press.
Page 299: Courtesy of The Hands-On Group, Inc. www.handsongroup.com.
Page 300: © Joshua Hodge Photography/Getty Images/RF.
Page 301 (top): Courtesy of PCM Electronics.
Page 301 (bottom): © 1993 to 2009 London Electronics Ltd.

Chapter 9

Page 313: © Tengku Bahar/AFP/Getty Images.
Page 315: © AP Photo/Jae C. Hong.
Page 324: © AP Photo/Al Behrman.
Page 325: © Zak Hoke/Addicted-To-Retail.com (ATR).
Page 327: © AP Photo/Ron Wurzer.
Page 328: © AP Photo/Danny Johnston.

Chapter 10

Page 337: © Ian Paterson/Alamy.
Page 340: © AP Photo/Stuart Ramson.
Page 341: © John A Rizzo/Getty Images.
Page 343: © Tim Boyle/Getty Images.
Page 349: © AP Photo/Bill Waugh.

Chapter 11

Page 365: © Philip Scalia/Alamy.
Page 374: © Slow Images/Getty Images.
Page 379: Copyright © John J. Bartholdi, III and Steven T. Hackman. All Rights Reserved.
Page 380: © 2012 Dots LLC. All Rights Reserved.
Page 382: © Nippon Filing Co., Ltd.
Page 387: © AP Photo/Ron Heflin.

Chapter 12

Page 399: © AP Photo/Kiichiro Sato.
Page 402: © AP Photo/Bryon Rollins.
Page 406: © STR/AFP/Getty Images.
Page 426: Courtesy of Rebecca C. Matthias, Destination Maternity Corporation.
Page 428: © Deepak G. Pawar/The India Today Group/Getty Images.

Chapter 13

Page 443: © Ed Young/Corbis.
Page 451: © Kimimasa Myama/Bloomberg via Getty Images.
Page 458: © Jupiterimages/Getty Images/RF.

Chapter 14

Page 471: © Taro Yamasaki/Time Life Pictures/Getty Images.
Page 474: © 2009 Specialty Living Inc. All Rights Reserved.
Page 475: © Dr. Barry Slavin/Visuals Unlimited.
Page 488: © ZUMA Press/Newscom.

Chapter 15

Page 507: © Eric Charbonneau/Le Studio/ Wireimage/Getty Images.
Page 510: © Associated Press.
Page 517: © Li wei - imaginechina/AP Photos.
Page 523: © Alberto Riva/Bloomberg via Getty Images.

Chapter 16

Page 554: © Art Directors & TRIP / Alamy.
Page 557: Copyright © State of Florida.
Page 558: © 2012 SolarCity. All rights reserved.
Page 562: © 2009 Herman Miller, Inc.
Page 569: © Rob Elliott/AFP/Getty Images.
Page 579: © 2009 General Motors.

Name Index

Note: Page numbers followed by n refer to notes.

H

I

J

K

L

M

N

O

P

R

Subject Index

Note: Page numbers followed by n refer to notes.

D

E

F

G

H

I

J

K

N

O

P

Q

R

S

T